Graphis Inc. is committed to celebrating exceptional work in Design, Advertising, Photography, & Art/Illustration internationally.

Published by **Graphis** | Publisher & Creative Director: **B. Martin Pedersen**

Chief Visionary Officer: **Patti Judd** | Design Director: **Hee Ra Kim** | Senior Designer: **Hie Won Sohn**

Associate Editor: **Colleen Boyd** | Publisher's Assistant/Designer: **Yuan Zhuang** | Account/Production: **Bianca Barnes**

Interns: **Maggie Herrera, Eli Hiscott, Samantha Mayer**

Graphis Poster Annual 2025

Published by:
Graphis Inc.
389 Fifth Avenue, Suite 1105
New York, NY 10016
Phone: 212-532-9387
www.graphis.com
help@graphis.com

ISBN 13: 978-1-954632-33-2

We extend our heartfelt thanks to
the international contributors
who have made it possible to publish
a wide spectrum of the best work
in Design, Advertising, Photography,
and Art/Illustration.
Anyone is welcome to submit
work at www.graphis.com.

Copyright © 2024 Graphis, Inc.
All rights reserved.
Jacket and book design copyright
© 2024 by Graphis, Inc.
No part of this book may be
reproduced, utilized, or transmitted
in any form without written
permission of the publisher.

Any Photography, Advertising,
Design, and Art/Illustration work
must be completely original. No
content owned by another copyright
holder can be used or submitted
unless the entrant has been granted
specific usage rights. Graphis is
not liable or responsible for any
copyright infringement on the part
of an entrant, and will not become
involved in copyright disputes.

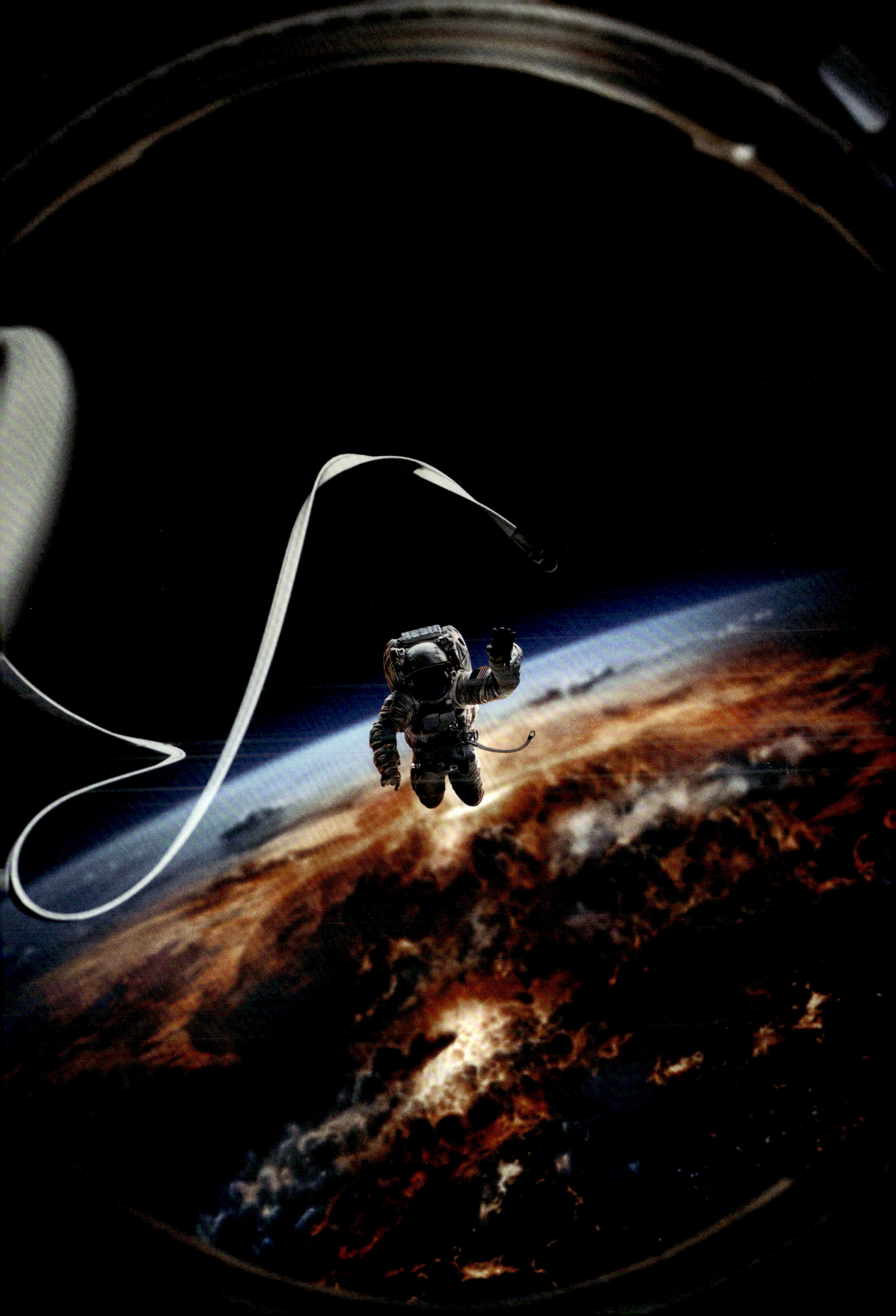

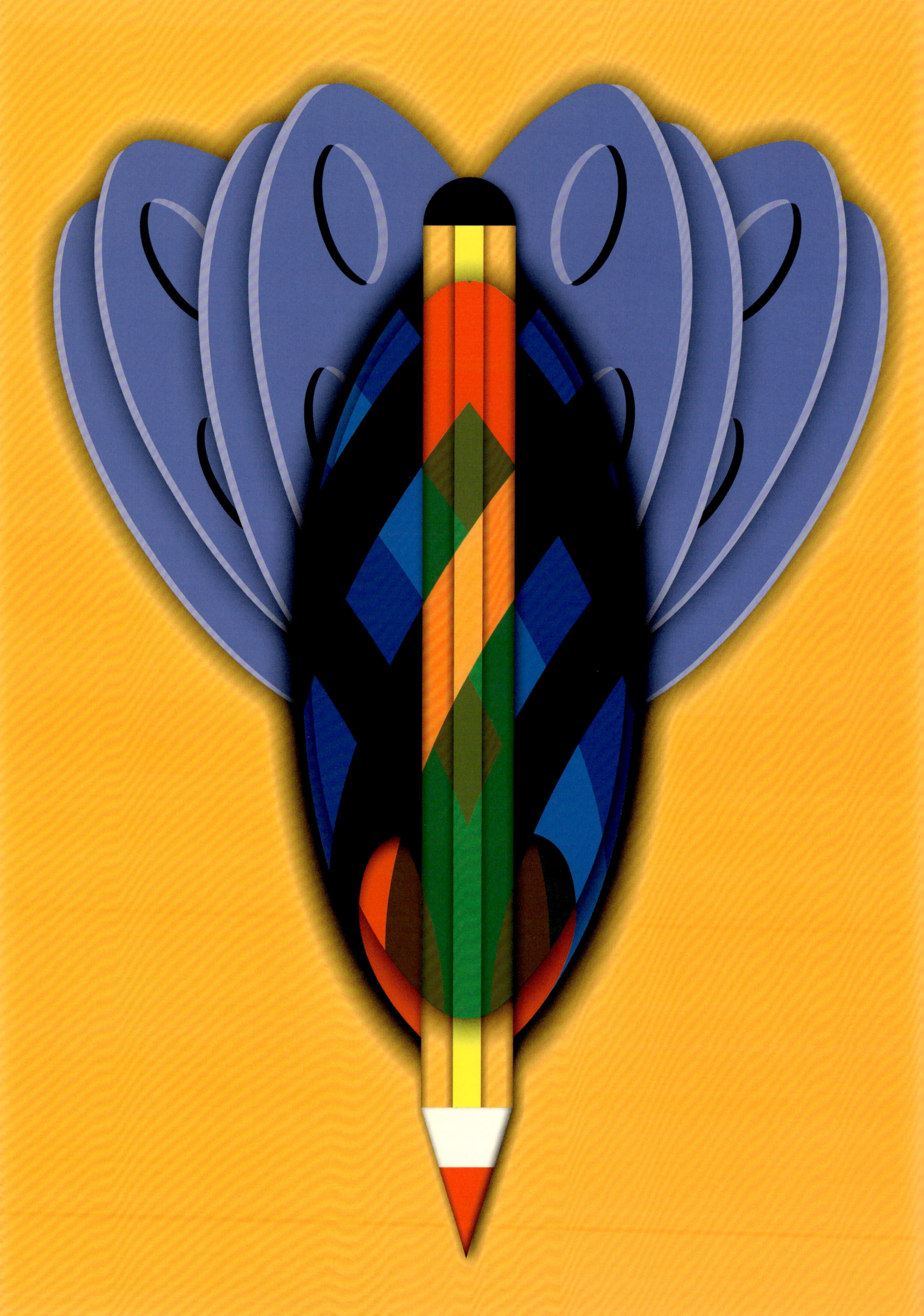

Contents

List of Poster Museums ... 6	Dance ... 43	Opera ... 104	**Silver Awards** ... 144
A Decade in Posters ... 8	Education ... 44	Promotion ... 109	**Honorable Mention** ... 223
Competition Judges ... 18	Entertainment ... 52	Public & Social Services ... 113	**Credits & Commentary** ... 230
Platinum Awards ... 26	Environment ... 66	Social & Political ... 117	Index ... 245
Platinum Winners' Bios & Headshots ... 27	Events ... 68	Sports ... 128	Winners Directory ... 249
Platinum Award-Winning Work ... 28	Exhibits ... 71	Television ... 129	Winners by Country ... 253
Gold Awards ... 40	Festivals ... 82	Theater ... 134	Graphis Titles ... 254
AI ... 41	Film ... 88	Tourism ... 140	
Commemorative ... 42	Museum ... 93	Typography ... 141	
	Music ... 96	Zoo ... 143	

Page 3: *"I.S.S. Payoff Poster,"* designed by MOCEAN
Page 4: *"Cinanima 24,"* designed by João Machado Design

6 LIST OF POSTER MUSEUMS

THE AMERICAS

Art Gallery of Ontario
www.ago.ca
317 Dundas St. W
Toronto, ON M5T 1G4
Canada
Tel +1 416 979 6648

Art Institute of Chicago
www.artic.edu
111 S. Michigan Ave.
Chicago, IL 60603
United States
Tel +1 312 443 3600

Canadian Museum of History
www.historymuseum.ca
100 Laurier S.
Gatineau, QC K1A 0M8
Canada
Tel +1 819 776 7000

Contemporary Arts Center
www.contemporaryartscenter.org
44 E. 6th St.
Cincinnati, OH 45202
United States
Tel +1 513 345 8400

**Cooper Hewitt,
Smithsonian Design Museum**
www.cooperhewitt.org
2 E. 91st St.
New York, NY 10128
United States
Tel +1 212 849 8400

El Museo del Barrio
www.elmuseo.org
1230 5th Ave. & 104th St.
New York, NY 10029
United States
Tel +1 212 831 7272

Letterform Archive
www.letterformarchive.org
2325 3rd St., Floor 4R
San Francisco, CA 94107
United States
Tel +1 415 802 7485

**Los Angeles County Museum
of Art**
www.lacma.org
5905 Wilshire Blvd.
Los Angeles, CA 90036
United States
Tel +1 323 857 6000

**Modern Art Museum of
Fort Worth**
www.themodern.org
3200 Darnell St.
Fort Worth, TX 76107
United States
Tel +1 817 738 9215

**Museo de Arte
Contemporaneo**
www.mac.uchile.cl
Av. Matucana, 464
Metropolitan Santiago
Chile
Tel +56 2 2977 1765

**Museo de Arte Contemporáneo
de Buenos Aires**
www.museomacba.org
Av. San Juan, 328
Buenos Aires C1147AAO
Argentina
Tel +54 11 5263 9988

Museo Nacional de Bellas Artes
www.bellasartes.gob.ar
Av. Del Libertador, 1473
Buenos Aires
Argentina
Tel +54 011 5288 9900

Museo Nacional del Cartel
www.munal.mx
Tacuba 8, Centro Histórico
Mexico City, 06010
Mexico
Tel +52 55 8647 5430

Museu de Arte de São Paulo
www.masp.org.br
Av. Paulista, 1578
São Paulo, 01310-200
Brazil
Tel +55 11 3149 5959

**Museu de Arte Moderna,
São Paulo**
www.mam.org.br
Pedro Álvares Cabral,
s/n° - Vila Mariana
São Paulo - SP, 04094-000
Brazil
Tel +55 11 5085 1300

**Museum of Contemporary Art,
Detroit**
www.mocadetroit.org
4454 Woodward Ave.
Detroit, MI 48201
United States
Tel +1 313 832 6622

**Museum of Contemporary Art,
San Diego**
www.mcasd.org
700 Prospect St.
La Jolla, CA 92037
United States
Tel +1 858 454 3541

Museum of Modern Art (MoMA)
www.moma.org
11 W. 53rd St.
New York, NY 10019
United States
Tel +1 212 708 9400

**National Gallery of Art,
Washington DC**
www.nga.gov
Constitution Ave. NW.
Washington, DC 20565
United States
Tel +1 202 737 4215

**National Museum of
American History**
www.americanhistory.si.edu
1300 Constitution Ave. NW
Washington, DC 20560
United States
Tel +1 202 633 1000

**National Museum of
Mexican Art**
www.nationalmuseumofmexicanart.org
1852 W. 19th St.
Chicago, IL 60608
United States
Tel +1 312 738 1503

Philadelphia Museum of Art
www.philamuseum.org
2600 Benjamin Franklin Parkway
Philadelphia, PA 19130
United States
Tel +1 215 763 8100

Poster House
www.posterhouse.org
119 W. 23rd St.
New York, NY 10011
United States
Tel +1 917 722 2439

**San Francisco Museum of
Modern Art**
www.sfmoma.org
151 3rd St.
San Francisco, CA 94103
United States
Tel +1 415 357 4000

Seattle Art Museum
www.seattleartmuseum.org
1300 1st Ave.
Seattle, WA 98101
United States
Tel +1 206 654 3100

The Art Institute of Chicago
www.artic.edu
111 S. Michigan Ave.
Chicago, IL 60603
United States
Tel +1 312 443 3600

The Guggenheim
www.guggenheim.org
1071 5th Ave.
New York, NY 10128
United States
Tel +1 212 423 3500

The Met
www.metmuseum.org
1000 5th Ave.
New York, NY 10028
United States
Tel +1 212 535 7710

The Mexican Museum
www.mexicanmuseum.org
2 Marina Blvd., Building D
San Francisco, CA 94123
United States
Tel +1 415 202 9700

**The Museum of
Contemporary Art**
www.moca.org
250 S. Grand Ave.
Los Angeles, CA 90012
United States
Tel +1 213 626 6222

EUROPE & AFRICA

Agentura Provas
www.agenturaprovas.com
Rybná 695
110 00 Staré Město
Czech Republic
Tel +420 224 819 359

**Amsterdam Museum
(Het Hart)**
www.amsterdammuseum.nl
Amstel 51
1018 EJ Amsterdam
The Netherlands
Tel +31 20 523 1822

Ateneum Art Museum
www.ateneum.fi/en/
Kaivokatu 2
Helsinki, 00100
Finland
Tel +358 294 500 401

**Bauhaus Archives
(Bauhaus-Archiv)**
www.bauhaus.de
Knesebeckstraße 1-2
10623 Berlin-Charlottenburg
Germany
Tel +49 30 2540020

Design Museum Denmark
www.designmuseum.dk
Bredgade 68
DK-1260 Copenhagen K
Denmark
Tel +45 33 18 56 56

Design Museum Hilinski
www.designmuseum.fi
Korkeavuorenkatu 23
00130 Helsinki
Finland
Tel +358 9 6220 540

Disseny Hub DHUB Barcelona
www.museudeldisseny.cat
Plaça de les Glòries Catalanes
37, 08018 Barcelona
Spain
Tel +34 932 56 68 00

Hungarian National Gallery
www.en.mng.hu
Szent György tér 2.
Budapest 1014
Hungary
Tel +36 1 201 9082

Irish Museum of Modern Art
www.imma.ie
Royal Hospital Kilmainham
Dublin 8, D08 FW31
Ireland
Tel +353 1 612 9900

Iziko South Africa Museum
www.iziko.org.za
25 Queen Victoria St.
Company's Gardens, Cape Town
South Africa
Tel +27 021 481 3800

7 LIST OF POSTER MUSEUMS

Musee des Arts Decoratifs
www.madparis.fr
107 Rue de Rivoli
Paris, 75058
France
Tel +33 1 44 55 57 50

**Museo Nacional Centro
de Arte Reina Sofía**
www.museoreinasofia.es
C. de Sta. Isabel, 52
Madrid 28012
Spain
Tel +34 917 74 10 00

**Museo Nacional
de Antropología**
www.culturaydeporte.gob.es
C. de Alfonso XII, 68
Madrid 28014
Spain
Tel +34 915 30 64 18

Museum für Gestaltung Zürich
www.museum-gestaltung.ch/en/
Exhibitionstrasse 60, 8005
Zurich
Switzerland
Tel +41 43 446 66 77

Museum für Kommunikation
www.mfk.ch
Helvetiastrasse 16
3000 Bern 6, Berlin
Germany
Tel +41 31 357 55 55

Museum für Kunst und Gewerbe
www.mkg-hamburg.de
Steintorplatz
Hamburg, 20099
Germany
Tel +49 40 428134 880

Museum of Arts and Crafts
www.muo.hr
Republic of Croatia Square 10
Zagreb
Croatia
Tel +385 1 4882 111

**Museum of Decorative Arts
in Prague**
www.upm.cz
17. listopadu 2
110 00 Josefov
Czech Republic
Tel +420 778 543 900

Museum of Fine Arts, Budapest
www.mfab.hu
1146 Dózsa György út 41.
Budapest
Hungary
Tel +36 1 469 7100

**National Museum of
Contemporary Art Athens
(EMST)**
www.emst.gr
Leof. Kallirróis kai Amvr. Frantzí
Athina 117 43
Greece
Tel +30 21 1101 9000

Paris Museum of Modern Art
www.mam.paris.fr
11 Av. du Président Wilson
Paris 75116
France
Tel +33 1 53 67 40 00

People's History Museum
www.phm.org.uk
Left Bank, Spinningfields
Manchester M3 3ER
United Kingdom
Tel +44 161 838 9190

Poster Museum, Wilanów
www.postermuseum.pl
Stanisława Kostki Potockiego
10/16 02-958 Warsaw
Poland
Tel +48 22 842 48 48

**Schule fur Gestaltung
Basel**
www.sfgbasel.ch
Freilager-Platz 6
CH-4142 Munchenstein
Switzerland
Tel +41 61 267 45 09

**Sofia Arsenal Museum
of Contemporary Art**
www.nationalgallery.bg
2, Cherni Vrah Blvd.
Sofia 1421
Bulgaria
Tel +359 879 834 030

Staatliche Museen zu Berlin
www.smb.museum/en/home/
Matthäikirchplatz 8
Berlin, 10785
Germany
Tel +49 30 266424242

Standpoint Gallery
www.standpointlondon.co.uk
45 Coronet St.
Hoxton
London N1 6HD
United Kingdom
Tel +44 20 7739 4921

**The Museu Nacional d'Art de
Catalunya**
www.museunacional.cat
National Palace, Montjuïc Park
Barcelona, Catalonia 08038
Spain
Tel +34 936 22 03 60

Victoria & Albert Museum
www.vam.ac.uk
Cromwell Road,
Kensington & Chelsea
London, SW7 2RL
United Kingdom
Tel +44 20 7942 2000

Wilanów Poster Museum
www.postermuseum.pl
St. Kostki Potockiego 10/16
Warsaw, 02-958
Poland
Tel +48 22 842 48 48

ASIA & OCEANIA

**Asia University Museum
of Modern Art**
www.asiamodern.asia.edu.tw
No. 500號, Liufeng Road,
Wufeng Dist.
Taichung City 41354
Taiwan
Tel +886 4 2339 9981

**Australian Centre for
Contemporary Art**
www.acca.melbourne
111 Sturt St.
Southbank, VIC 3006
Australia
Tel +61 3 9697 9999

**Bangkok Art and Culture
Centre (BACC)**
www.bacc.or.th
939 Rama 1 Road, Wangmai
Pathumwan District,
Bangkok 10330
Thailand
Tel +66 02 214 6630

**City Gallery Wellington |
Te Whare To**
www.citygallery.org.nz
Te Ngākau Civic Square
Wellington
New Zealand
Tel +64 4 913 9032

Fukuoka Art Museum
www.fukuoka-art-museum.jp
1-6 Ohorikoen, Chuo Ward
Fukuoka, 810-0051
Japan
Tel +81 92 714 6051

**Museum of Contemporary
Art Australia**
www.mca.com.au
140 George St.,
The Rocks Sydney, NSW 2000
Australia
Tel +61 2 9245 2400

**Museum of Contemporary Art
Shanghai**
www.mocashanghai.org
Gate 7, People's Park
231 W. Nanjing Rd., Shanghai
China
Tel +86 216 6327 9900

**Museum of Contemporary
Art Tokyo**
www.mot-art-museum.jp
4-1-1 Miyoshi, Koto-ku
Tokyo, 135-0022
Japan
Tel +81 50 5541 8600

National Gallery of Australia
www.nga.gov.au
Parkes Place
Parkes ACT 2600
Australia
Tel +61 2 6240 6411

National Gallery of Victoria
www.ngv.vic.gov.au
180 St. Kilda Road
Melbourne, VIC 8006
Australia
Tel +61 3 8620 2222

National Museum of Art, Osaka
www.nmao.go.jp
4-2-55 Nakanoshima, Kita-ku
Osaka, 530-0005
Japan
Tel +06 6447 4680

**National Museum of
Modern & Contemporary Art,
Korea (MMCA)**
www.mmca.go.kr
Gwacheon 313,
Gwangmyeong-ro
Seoul
South Korea
Tel +82 2 2188 6000

**National Museum of
Modern Art, Tokyo**
www.momat.go.jp
3-1 Kitanomaru Park, Chiyoda-ku
Tokyo, 102-8322
Japan
Tel +81 050 5541 8600

Seoul Museum of Art
www.seoulmuseum.org
201 Buam-dong, Jongno-gu
Seoul
South Korea
Tel +82 2 395 0100

**Shanghai Propaganda Poster
Art Center**
www.shanghaipropagandaart.com
Room K, 7F East Tower
Hua Min Han Zhen International
726 Yan An Xi Road, Shanghai
China

Taiwan Design Museum
www.songshanculturalpark.org
133號, Guangfu S. Road,
Xinyi District
Taipei City 110
Taiwan
Tel +886 2 27458199

**Tasmanian Museum and
Art Gallery**
www.tmag.tas.gov.au
Dunn Place
Hobart TAS 7000
Tasmania
Tel +61 03 6165 7000

Tokyo Metropolitan Art Museum
www.tobikan.jp
8-36 Ueno Park, Taito-ku
Tokyo, 110-0007
Japan
Tel +81 03 3823 6921

ADDITIONAL MUSEUMS:

If you are a museum that collects posters and are not listed above, please contact us for inclusion in our next annual at help@graphis.com.

Posters A Decade Past: Winners from 2015

Alt Group 🇳🇿 Pg.9

Fons Hickmann m23 🇩🇪 Pg.10

Geray Gencer 🇹🇷 Pg.11

Jan Sabach Design 🇺🇸 Pg.12

John Paul Mitchell Systems (In-house Creative Department) 🇺🇸 Pg.13

Scott Laserow Posters 🇺🇸 Pg.14

The Cultural Affairs Bureau of the Macao S.A.R. 🇲🇴 Pg.15

Tsushima Design 🇯🇵 Pg.16

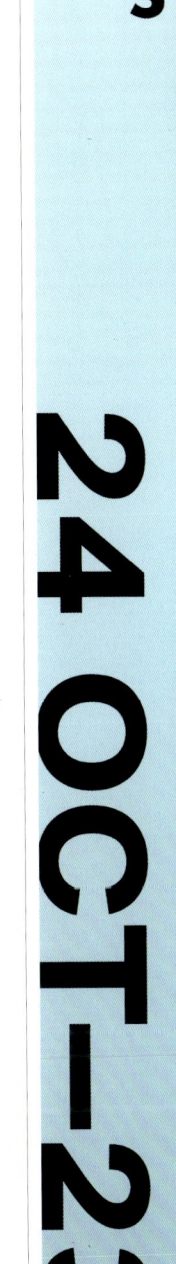

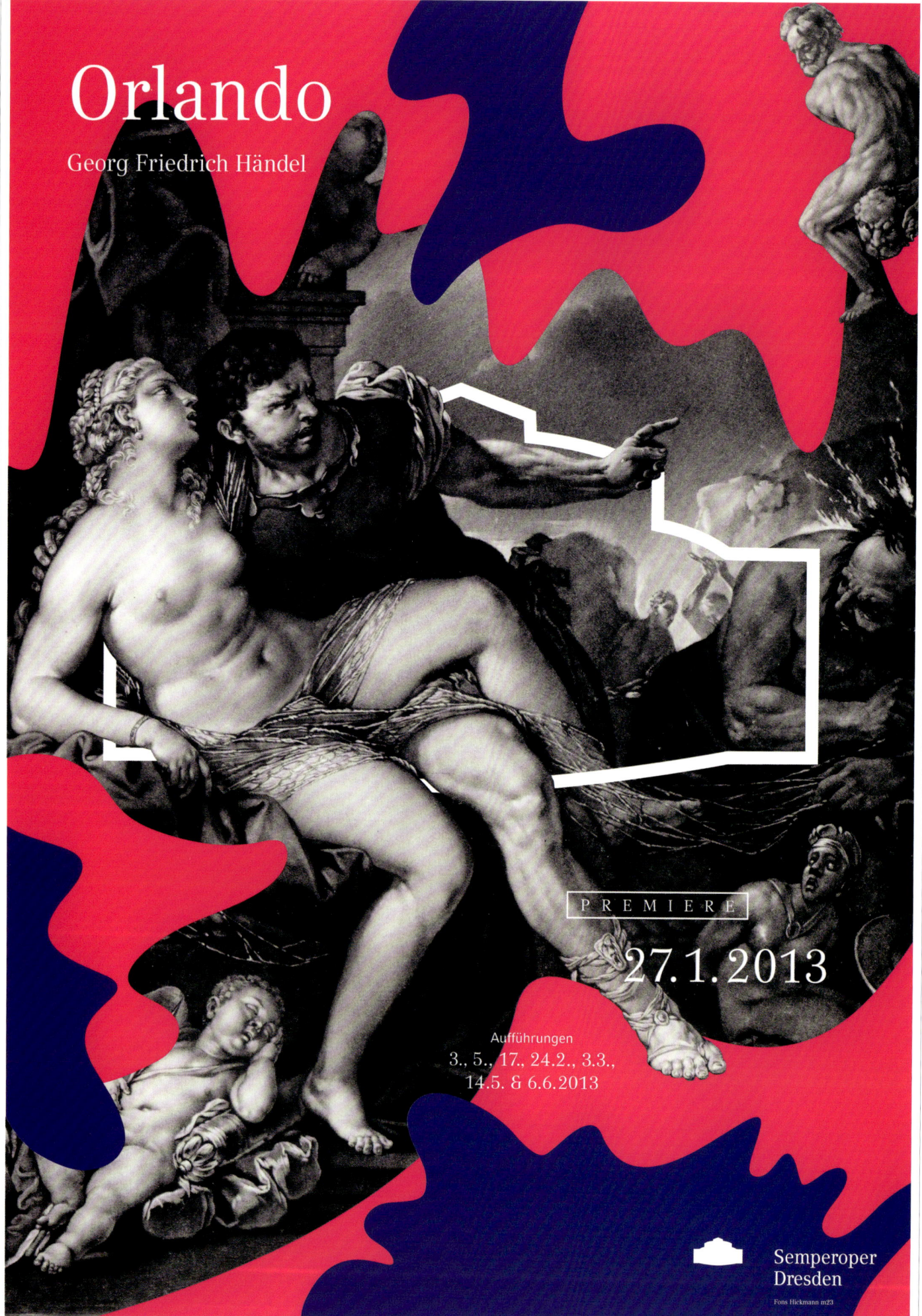

Title: Orlando | Client: Semper Opera | Design Firm: Fons Hickmann m23

11 GERAY GENCER **PLATINUM** POLITICAL

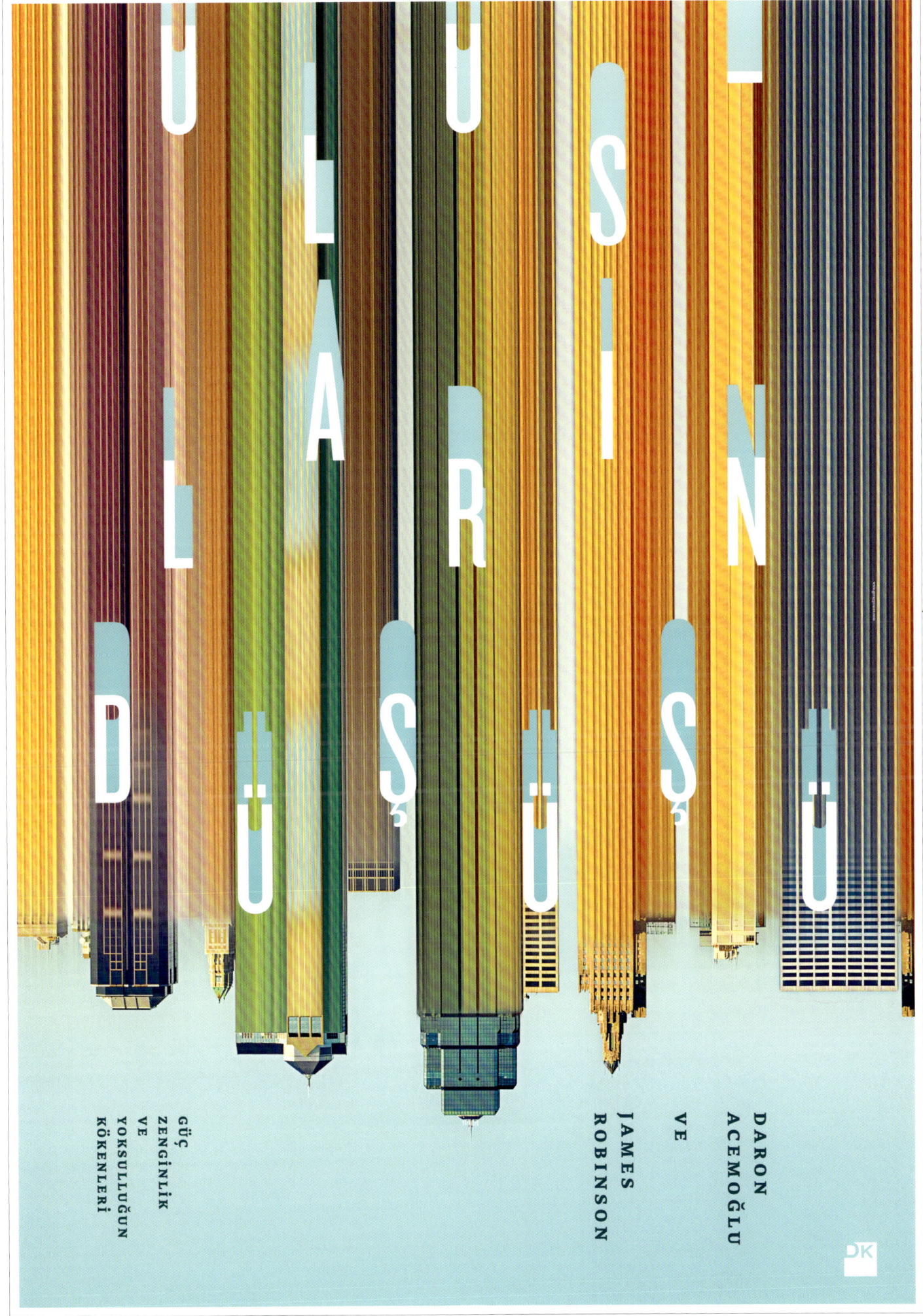

Title: Why Nations Fail | Client: Dogan Egmont Publishing, Istanbul | Design Firm: Geray Gencer

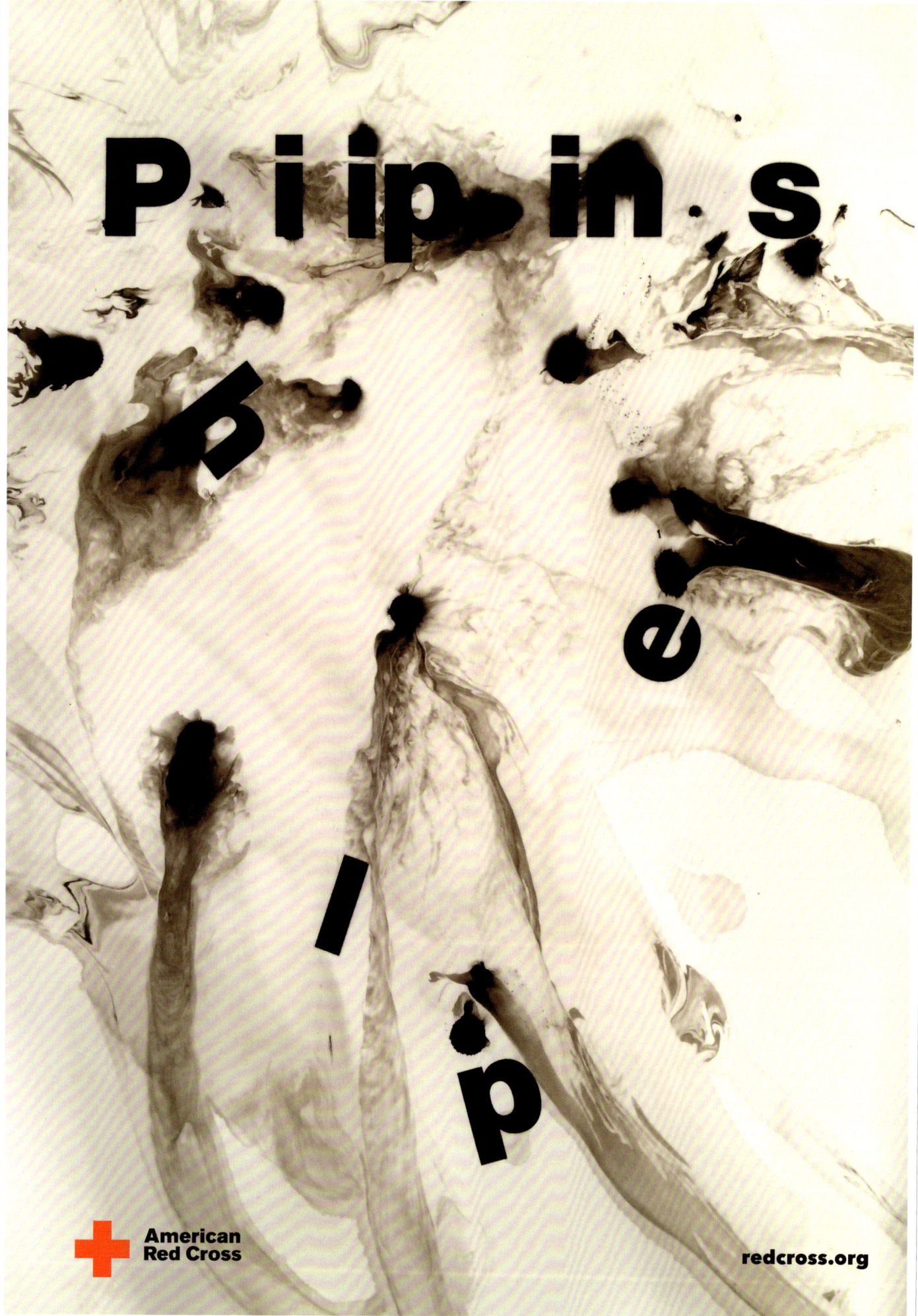

Title: Help Philippines | Clients: Self-initiated, American Red Cross | Design Firm: Jan Sabach Design

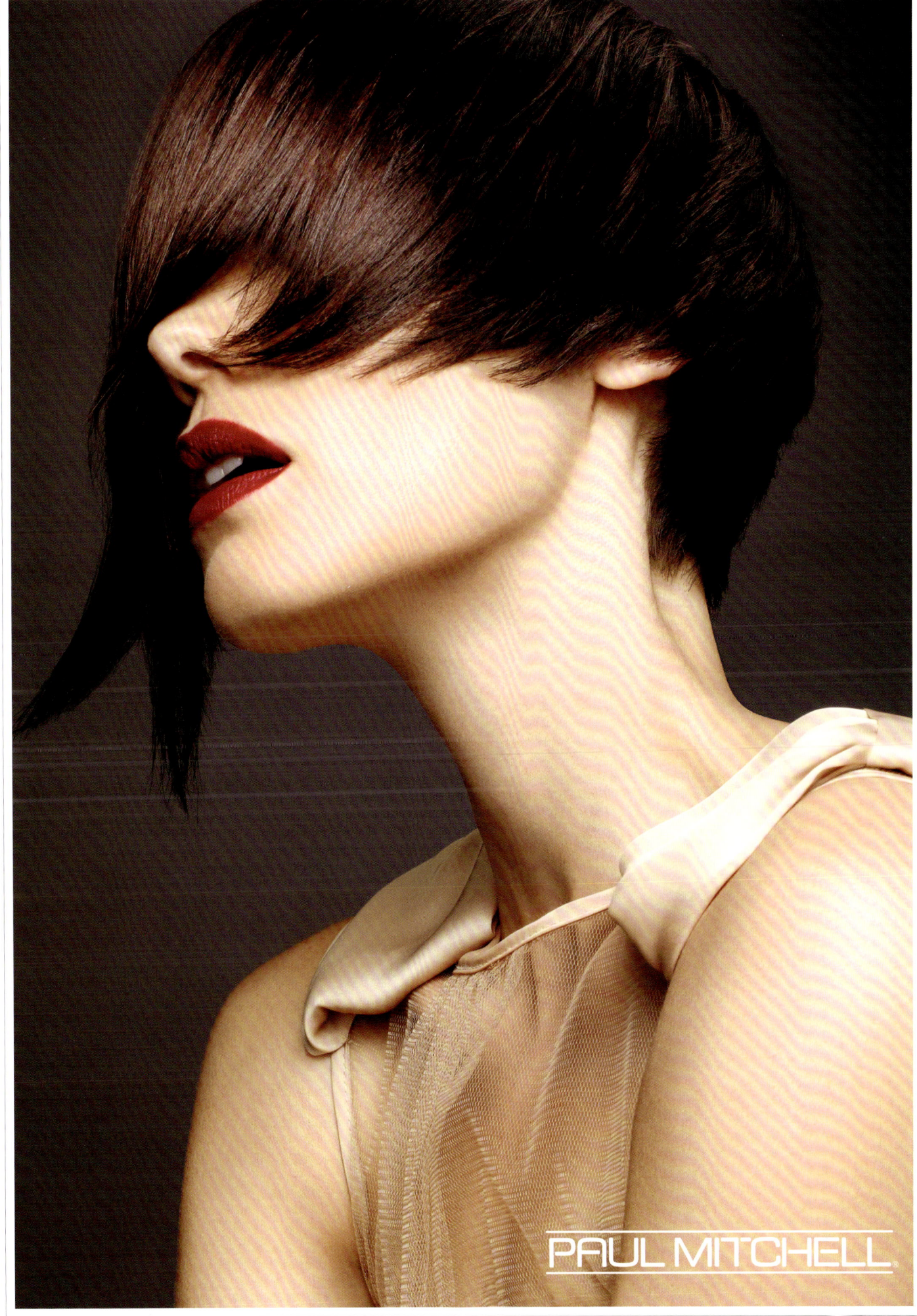

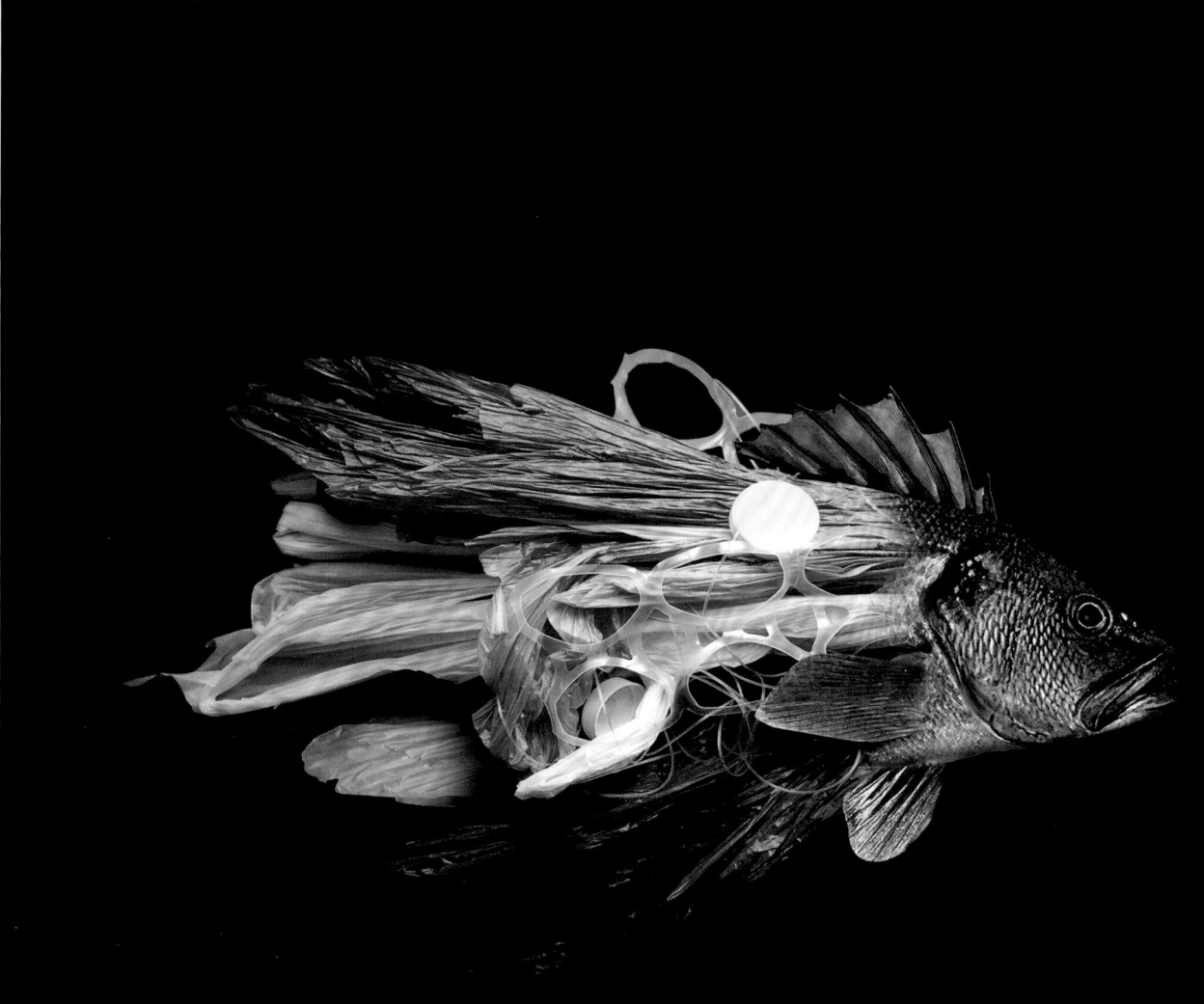

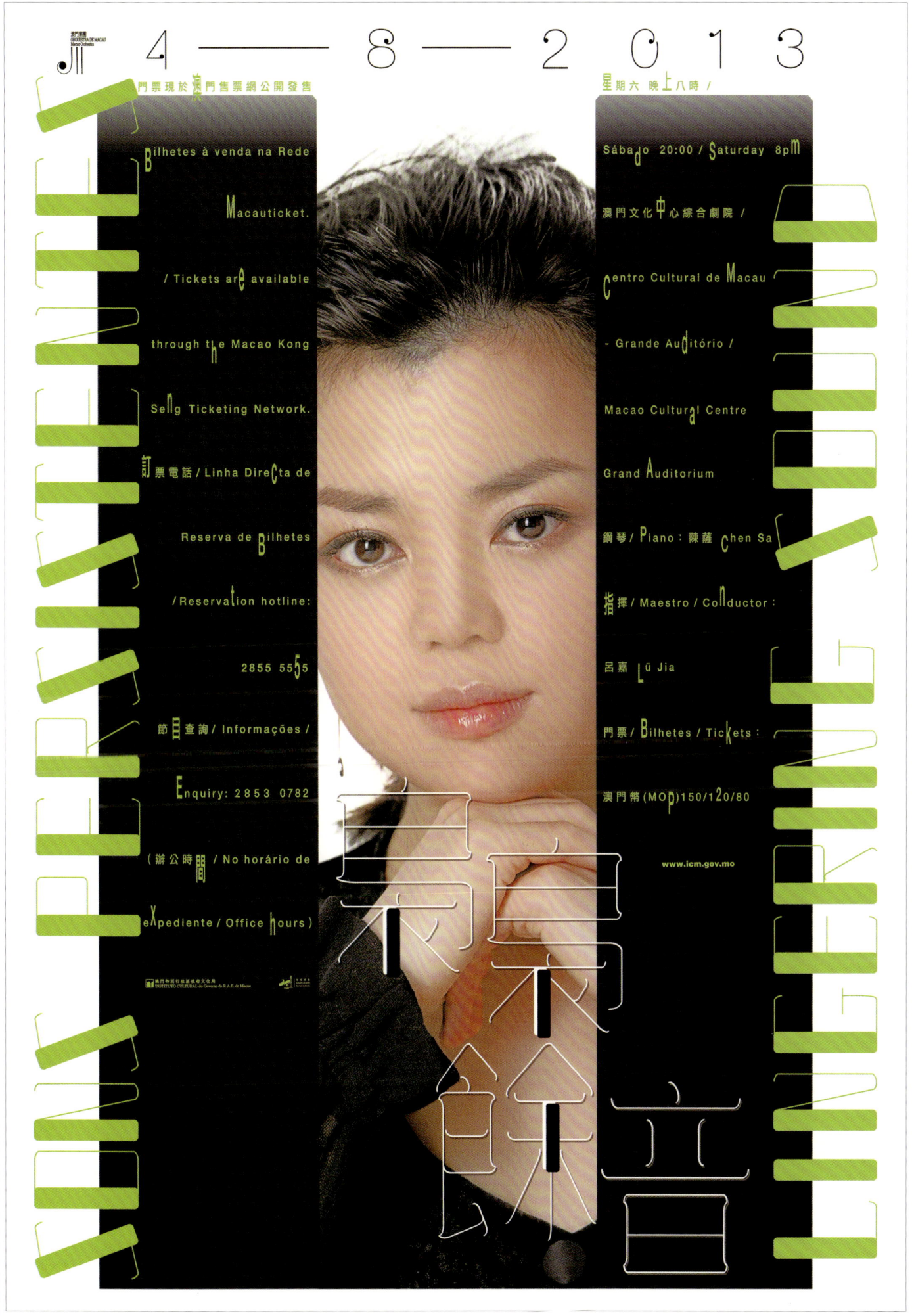

Title: Lingering Sound | **Client:** Macao Orchestra | **Design Firm:** The Cultural Affairs Bureau of the Macao S.A.R.

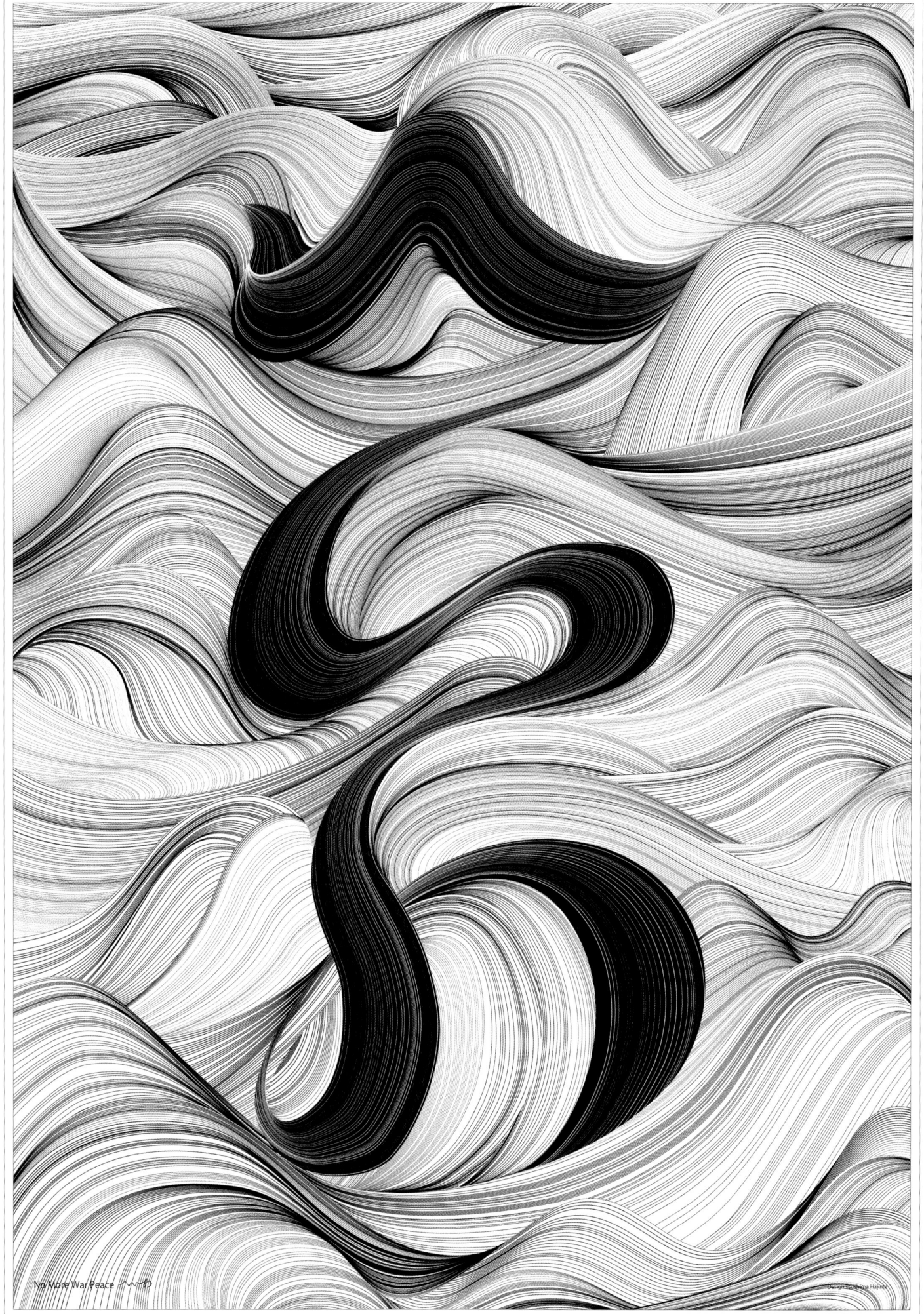

Title: Peace | **Client:** Japan Graphic Designers Association Hiroshima | **Design Firm:** Tsushima Design

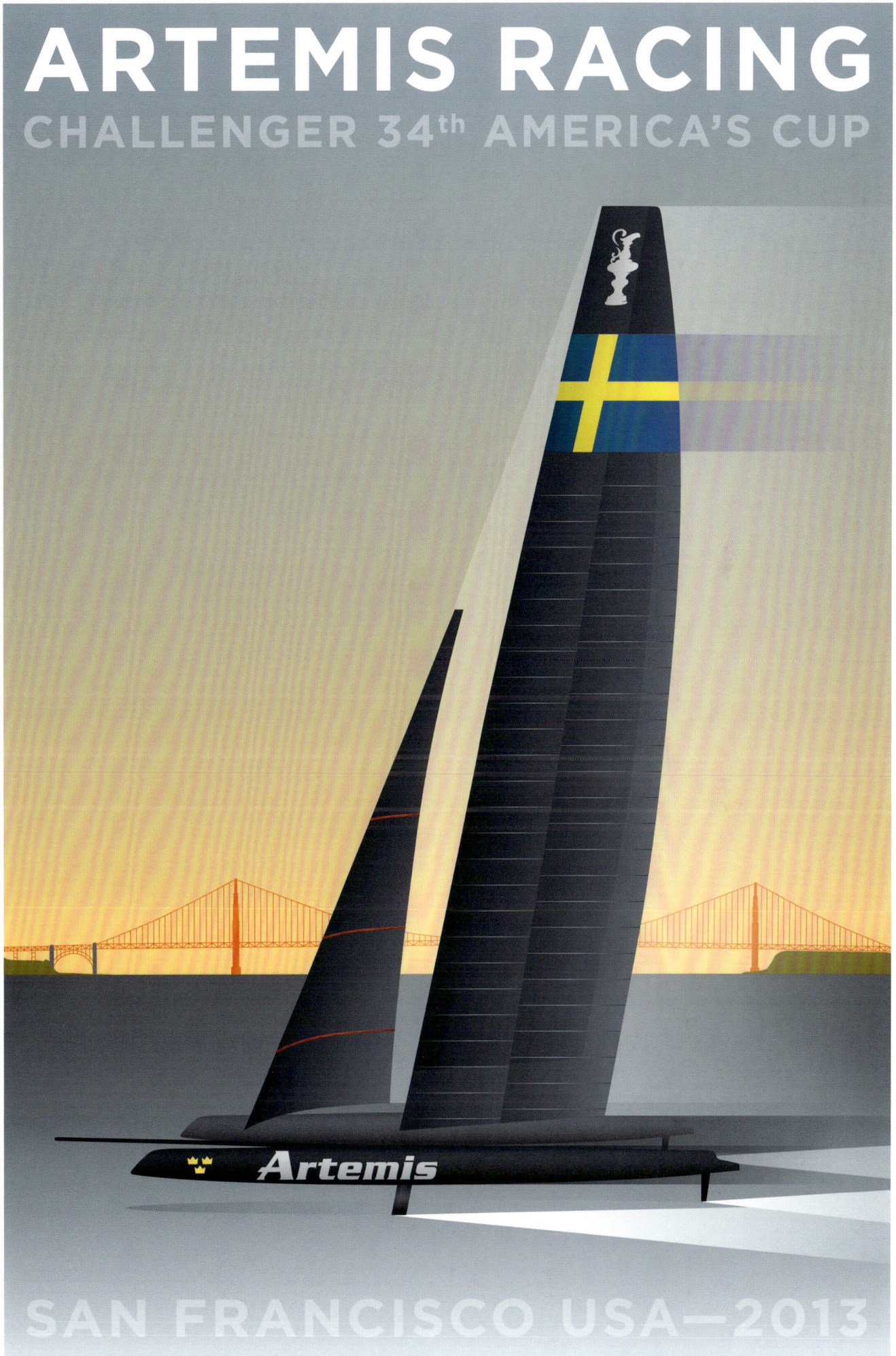

Title: Artemis Racing: Challenger 34th America's Cup | Client: Artemis Racing | Design Firm: Vanderbyl Design

GraphisJudges

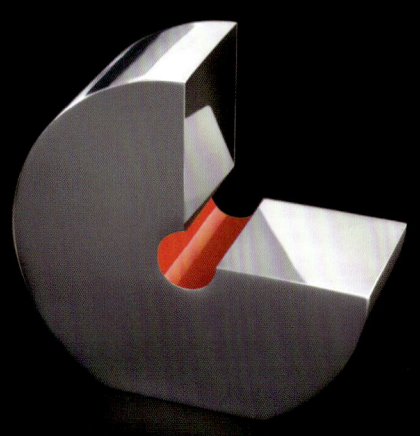

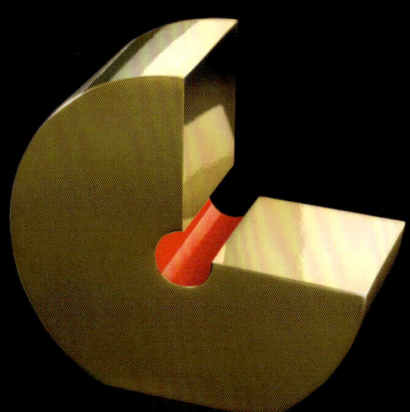

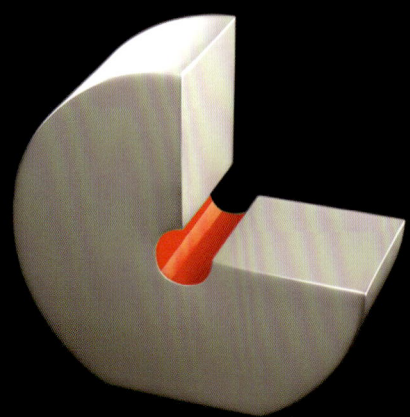

19 POSTER AWARDS 2025 COMPETITION JUDGES

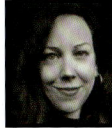

Liz English | MOCEAN | Senior Art Director
Biography: Liz English is a senior art director who lives in Los Angeles, California. Since 2003, she has worked in film and television advertising, collaborating on multiple award-winning campaigns for clients such as FX, HBO, Disney, A24, Lucasfilm, Warner Bros., and 20th Century Studios. Her work can be seen on billboards, bus shelters, and streaming services. The most valuable lesson she has learned from her two decades of experience is that fear is the enemy of creativity.
Commentary: As a lifelong admirer of Graphis, it was an honor and a pleasure to participate in judging the Graphis 2024 Poster Awards: the variety and immense creativity of the submissions made for an exciting and contemplative experience. The criteria for judging the breadth of work is based on the originality of concept, clarity of idea, composition, and execution. As a fellow artist, I believe AI is an intriguing category to judge. I look forward to the future of visual arts and how creatives will continue to utilize AI technology within their processes as we advance in our creative endeavors, both personally and commercially.

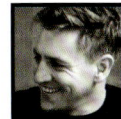

Paul Garbett | Studio Garbett | Co-founder & Designer
Biography: Paul Garbett is a co-founder of Studio Garbett, a design studio in Sydney, Australia, focused on brand, identity, and wayfinding design. His work has been featured in exhibitions, magazines, books, and textbooks and has even been the subject of high school examination questions. He has been an Alliance Graphique Internationale member since 2015.
Commentary: I feel honored to have been invited to judge this year's Graphis Poster Awards. Since my student days, Graphis has held a special place in my heart and on my bookshelf. This year's entries showcase a rich and diverse approach to poster design from all over the world. I was specifically looking for attention-grabbing entries with exciting typography and imagery that broke from traditional poster design and pushed the boundaries of the medium.

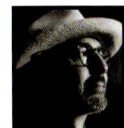

Brad Hochberg | The Refinery | Co-founder & Creative Director
Biography: Brad Hochberg is a founding partner and creative director at The Refinery, a multi-award-winning Los Angeles-based entertainment marketing agency. Brad has worked on major campaigns for studios and streamers for two decades, starting with Seiniger Advertising, Poetic Justice, Concept Arts, and Trailer Park before co-founding The Refinery in 2006. Brad deeply loves "the visual" and leads his team with a historical perspective and a modern lens. He believes the creative's job is simple: elicit a response, draw the eye to the message, and get an audience to connect.
Commentary: I have long admired the Graphis Poster Awards and their representation of such incredible work over the years, so having an opportunity to be part of this year's judging panel was truly an honor and pleasure. As expected, the entries didn't disappoint; from the stunning use of typography to the impeccable imagery, they truly were a symphony of visuals to behold. I applaud all those who took such care, talent, and craftsmanship in their work; every one of you deserves the praise and acknowledgment contained within the pages of this annual. Bravo to you all.

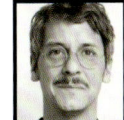

Sven Lindhorst-Emme | Studio Lindhorst-Emme+Hinrichs | Founder & Designer
Biography: Sven Lindhorst-Emme was born in 1978 in Bielefeld, Germany. He first trained as a lithographer and worked as such for ten years. He later studied graphic and communication design and moved to Berlin in 2011, where he founded his studio the same year. Since 2022, he has run Studio Lindhorst-Emme+Hinrichs together with Lea Hinrichs. In addition to hosting lectures and workshops nationally and internationally, he teaches book design and communication design at the Lette-Verein Berlin (School for Photography) and lectures at different colleges and universities. He is the editor or co-editor of several books on poster design and other creative subjects. Works from the studio have won numerous international competitions and been featured in exhibitions worldwide. Sven is a member of the Type Directors Club New York and the 100 Beste Plakate.
Commentary: What I find particularly striking about the Graphis Poster Competition is the excellent variety of posters and themes: there are posters for everything, from movies and advertising to free-author posters. As typography and its handling play a significant role in design for me, my focus was mainly on posters with a balanced typeface, posters that used type in an outstanding way, or posters that experimentally used typography and thus brought excitement to the design. My credo: only use as little design as necessary; everything else becomes decoration. Less is often more.

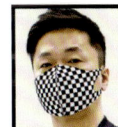

DaeKi Shim | DAEKI & JUN | Co-founder & Designer
Biography: DaeKi Shim earned a bachelor's degree in graphic design from the University of the Arts London (UAL) and a master's degree in digital anthropology from University College London (UCL) in London, UK. DaeKi later obtained a doctorate in design from Seoul National University (SNU) in Seoul, South Korea. Since establishing the design studio DAEKI and JUN in 2013, he has provided consultation, advice, and various design projects for the government-affiliated institutions Dongdaemun Design Plaza (DDP) and the Gangwon Institute of Design Promotion (GIDP). He is also an adjunct professor at Sejong University and the Seoul National University of Science and Technology.
Commentary: Many excellent works were submitted this year. I want to mention two of them. The first is Melchior Imboden's "Zeitzeugen, Schweizer Plakate im Weltformat, Swiss Poster Exhibition, Posters from 1940 till Today." I think it's great because it shows that it's possible to design a complete poster using only typography, grids, and color. I also liked "The Farthest Prime Time Asian Sitcom," created by Osborne Shiwan. It features multi-font lettering inspired by the Bauhaus aesthetic and the Memphis movement. I am captivated by how the poster perfectly and beautifully expresses the theme it embodies, combined with conceptually stylized typography and photography.

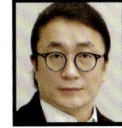

HyoJun Shim | DAEKI & JUN | Co-founder & Designer
Biography: HyoJun Shim earned a bachelor's degree in graphic design from the University of the Arts London (UAL). This was followed by a master's degree at Goldsmiths, University of London. He then pursued another master's degree in material and visual culture at University College London (UCL) in London, UK. In 2013, upon returning to Seoul, he co-founded the design studio DAEKI and JUN with his brother, DaeKi Shim. His design projects at DAEKI and JUN have received outstanding recognition, with over 40 accolades from prestigious international design organizations such as Graphis, the Type Directors Club, and the Red Dot Awards. Additionally, he teaches students as a professor at Dongduk Women's University.
Commentary: Among the many great posters, I would like to mention two posters. "The Lyceum Competition Call for Entries," designed by Nancy Skolos and Thomas Wedell, embodies sheer brilliance. Employing the metaphor of plexiglass dowel rods, it elegantly encapsulates the essence of the theme, "regenerative." Through meticulous typography and captivating graphics, the poster communicates the message and captivates the viewer with its visual finesse. "Tin Toy Times," designed by Steve Collier, adeptly employs illustrations alone to encapsulate the essence of tin toys, utilizing a densely arranged layout to achieve visual richness. This underscores the potent capability of illustration in conveying emotion and depth.

For judges who were also entrants and winners, special care was taken to insure that they did not judge their own work.

20 POSTER AWARDS 2025 JUDGE LIZ ENGLISH   TELEVISION

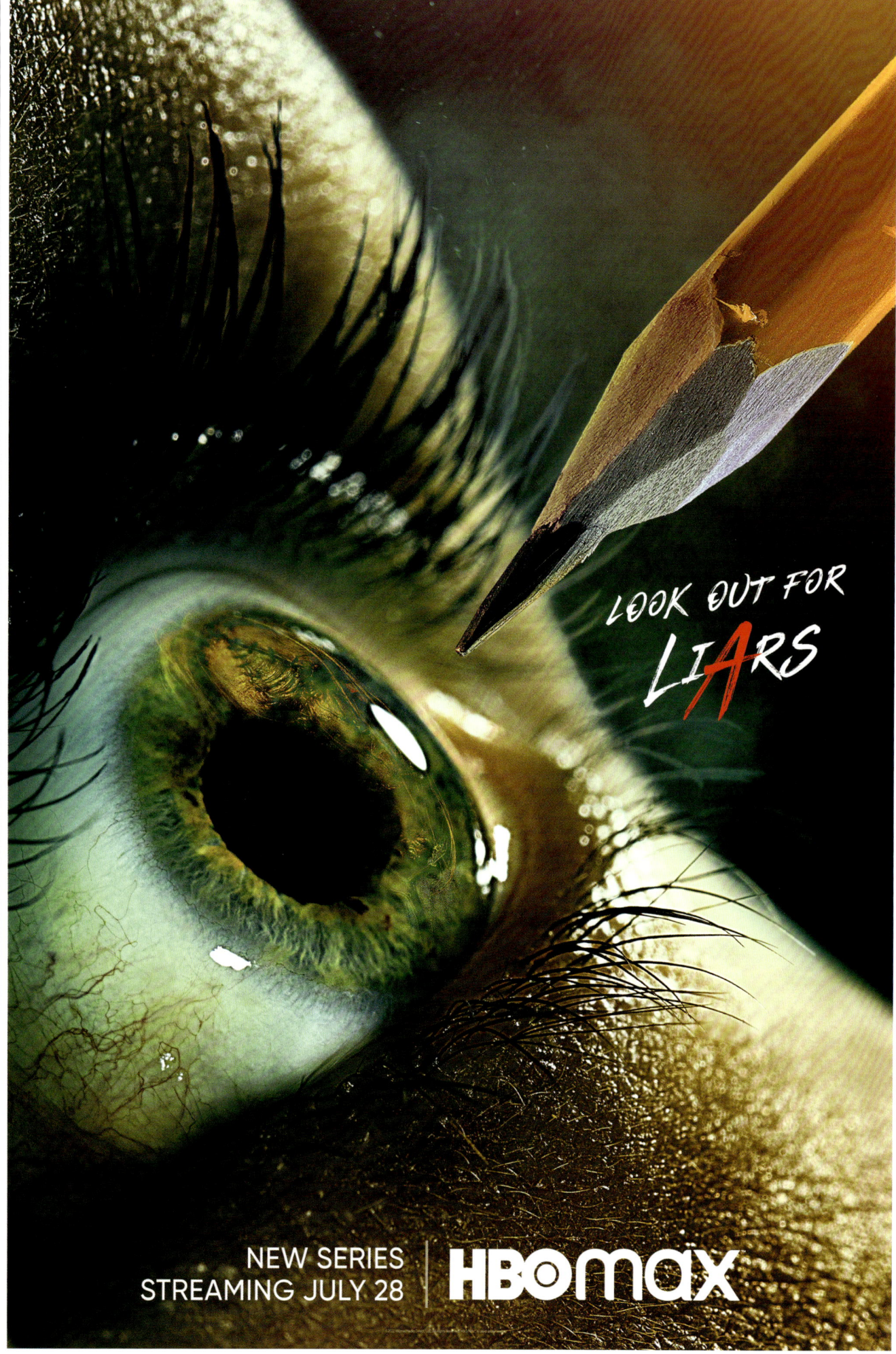

Title: Pretty Little Liars: Original Sin Teaser Campaign | Client: HBO Max | Design Firm: MOCEAN

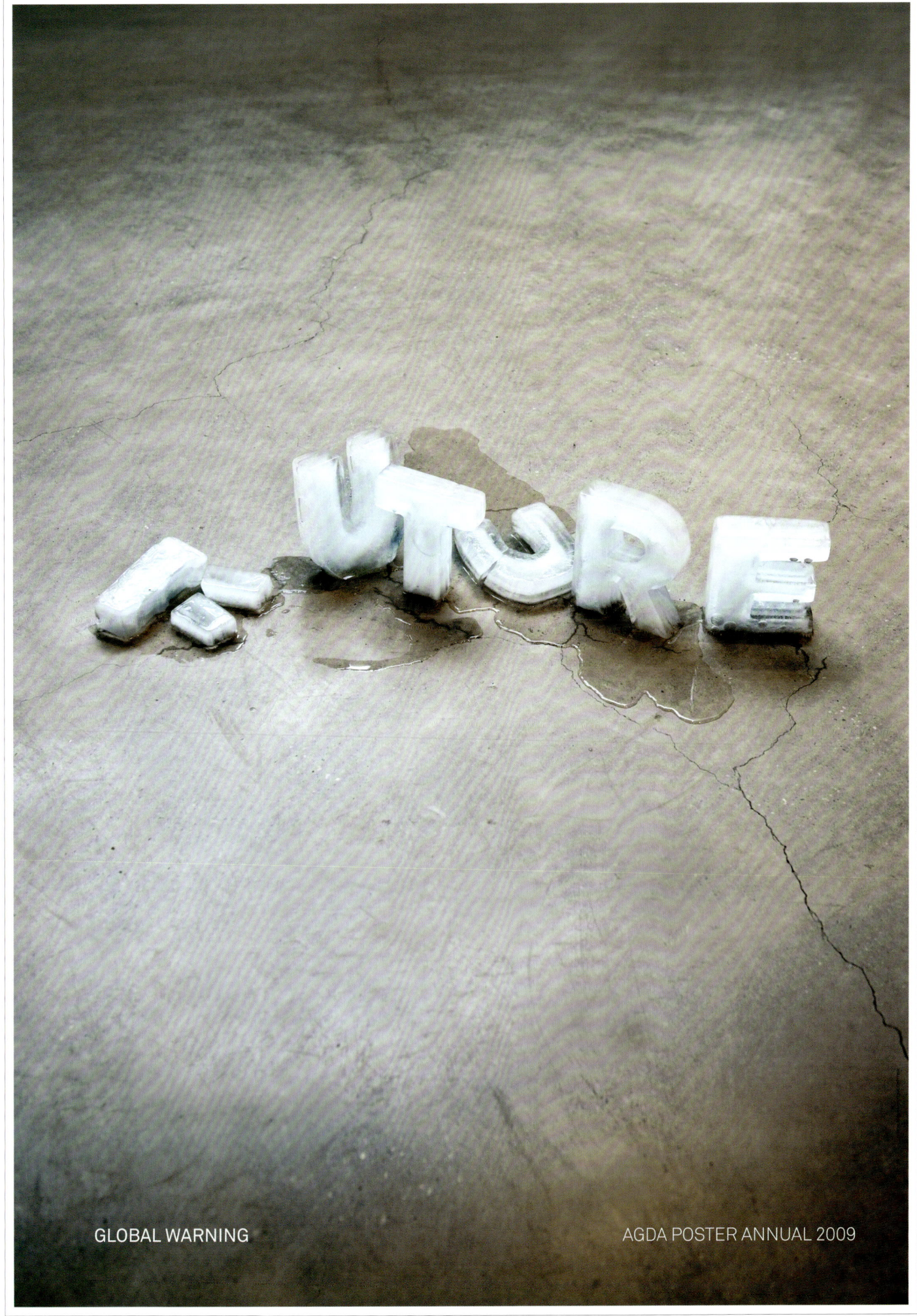

22 POSTER AWARDS 2025 JUDGE BRAD HOCHBERG FILM & TV

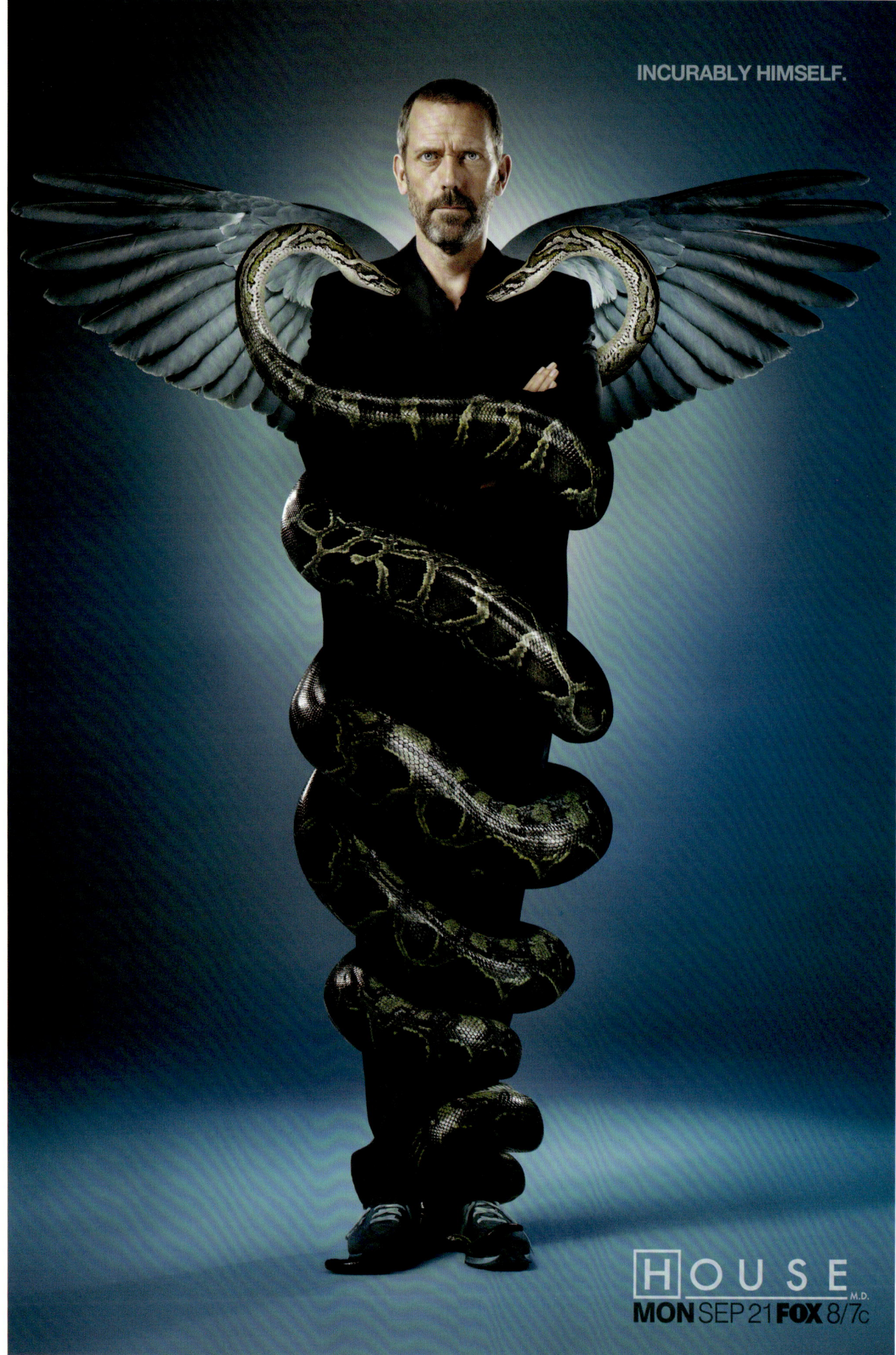

Title: House Season 6 | **Client:** FOX Broadcasting Company | **Design Firm:** The Refinery

Title: Free Wifi, Free Coffee, Free Work | **Client:** Raum für Drastische Maßnahmen | **Design Firm:** Studio Lindhorst-Emme+Hinrichs

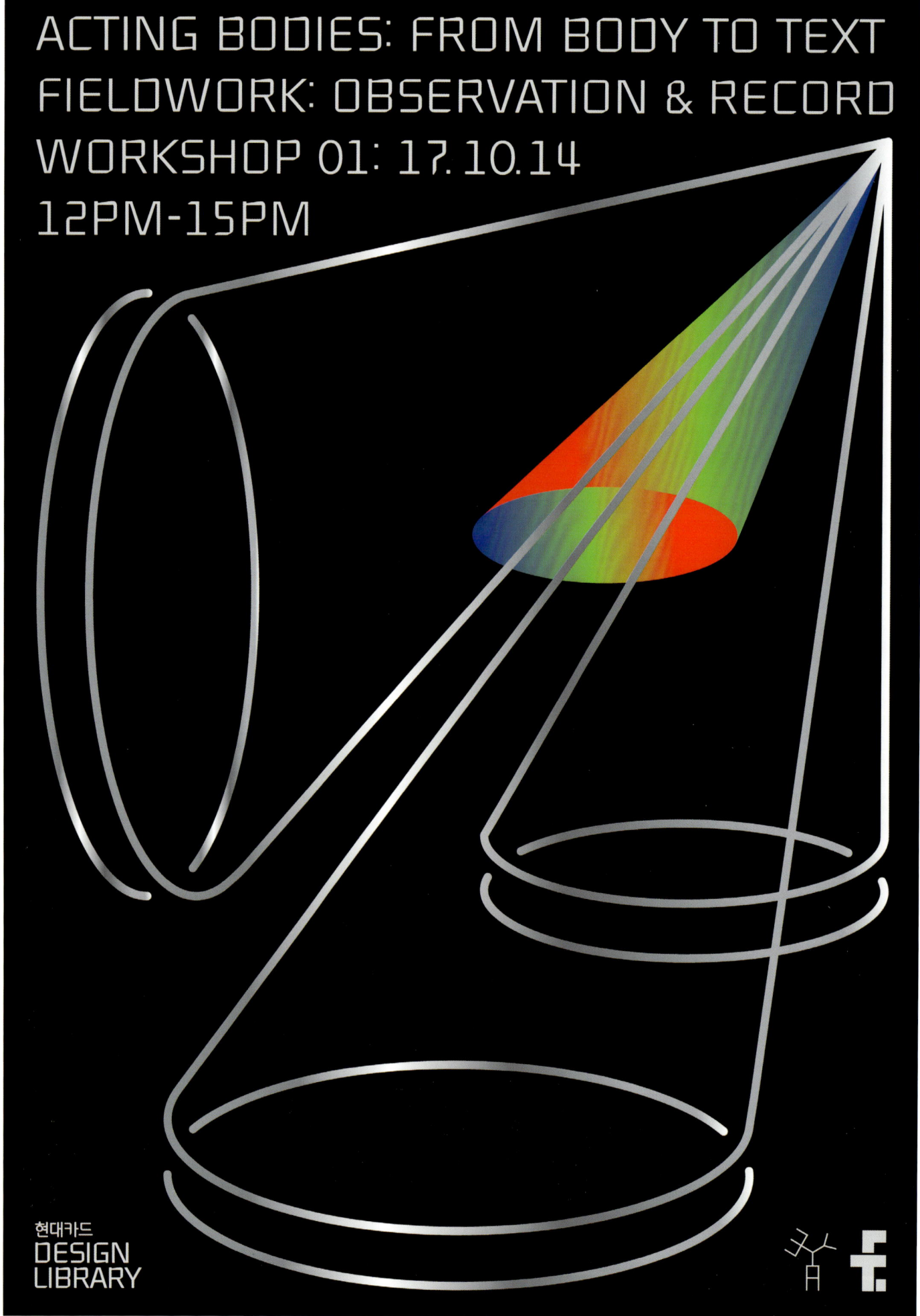

25 POSTER AWARDS 2025 JUDGES DAEKI SHIM, HYOJUN SHIM EXHIBITS

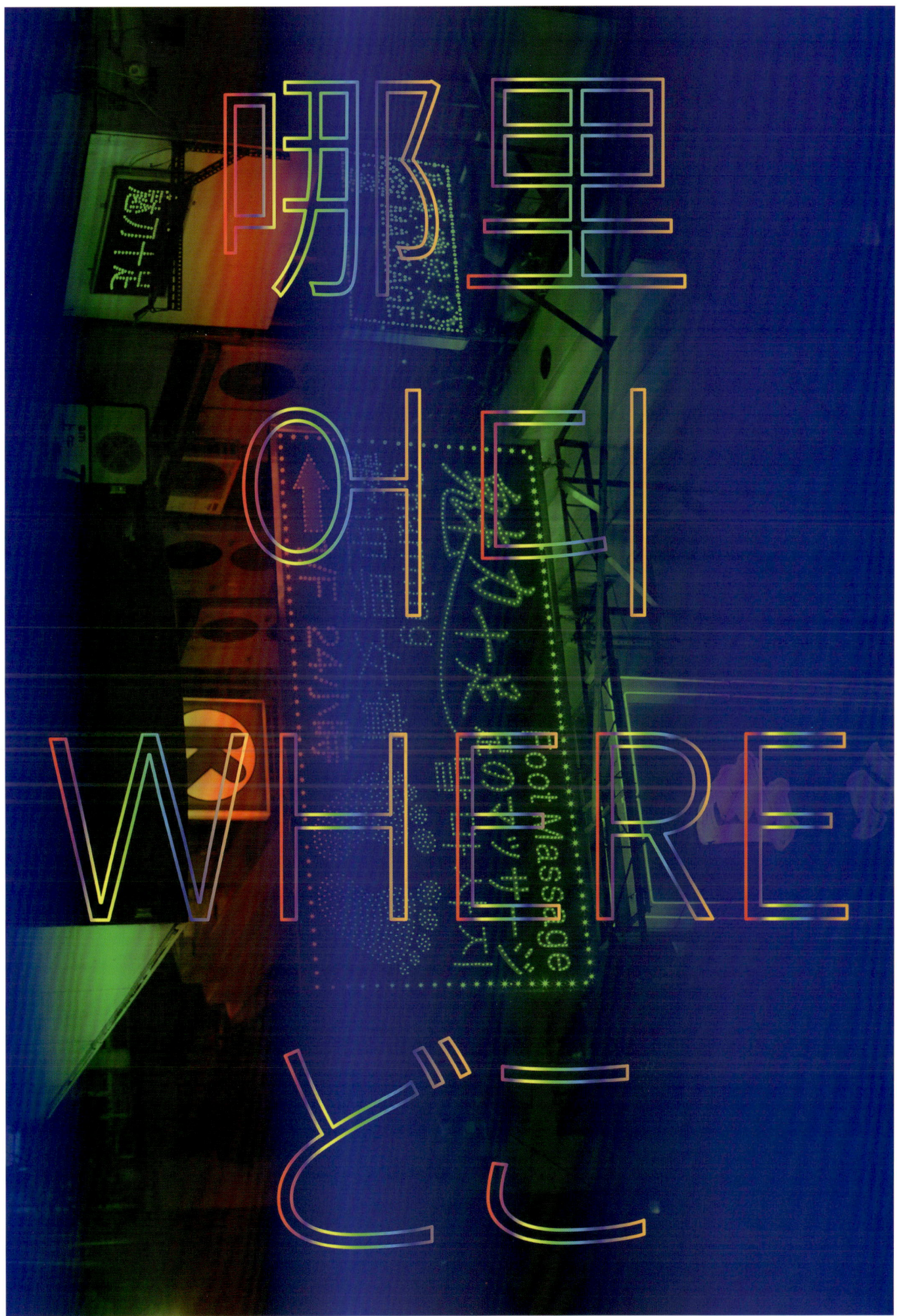

Title: Where 01: Multilingual | Clients: International Poster Invitation Exhibition, Beijing Design Week 2015 | Design Firm: DAEKI & JUN

Graphis Platinum Awards

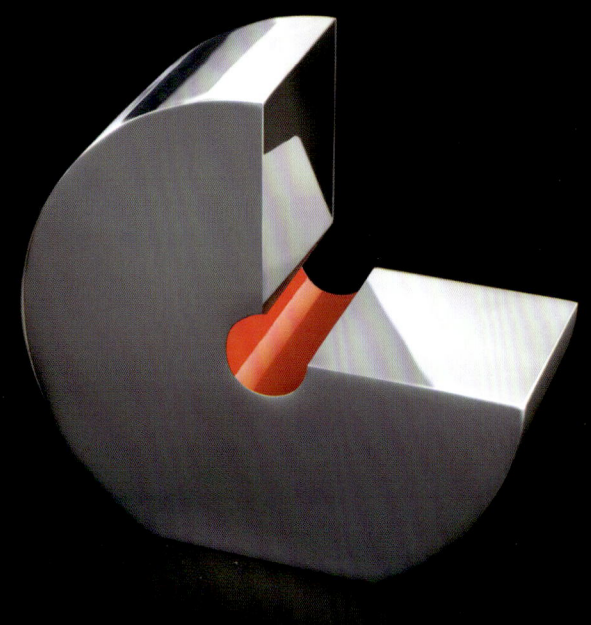

27 PLATINUM WINNERS

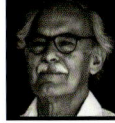

João Machado | João Machado Design | Designer | Page: 28 | www.joaomachado.com
Biography: João Machado studied sculpture at ESBAP-Portugal but is internationally recognized for his work in graphic design. He opened his studio in 1981, and has been exhibiting his work since 1983. He has won several awards, including the Icograda Excellence Award, the title of 'Design Master' from Graphis, and was nominated as a member of AGI. His passion for poster design is palpable, though he also excels in editorial design, with talents such as illustration and philately.

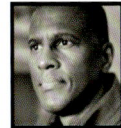

Steve James | The Union Design Company | Designer, Artist, & Illustrator | Page: 29 | www.uniondesigncompany.com
Biography: The Union Design Company is the studio of Steve James, an award-winning designer, artist, and illustrator. Steve has worked in visual communications for 30 years, and his commercial work spans many industries, from healthcare to retail. His artistic endeavors include printmaking, watercolor, and collage, which are shown at art exhibitions throughout the United States. He is an army veteran who also works as a lecturer at the University of Texas at Arlington and Texas A&M University-Commerce.

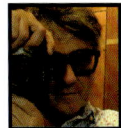

Melchior Imboden | Melchior Imboden | Graphic Designer, Artist, & Photographer | Page: 30 | www.melchiorimboden.ch
Biography: Born in Stans, Switzerland, in 1956, Melchior Imboden is a renowned artist, graphic designer, and photographer living in Buochs. He transitioned to graphic design at Lucerne, where he had originally studied interior design. His extensive travels to South America and the Mediterranean have inspired widely exhibited and collected photographic works. His art is held in prestigious collections such as the Fotomuseum Winterthur and Musée de l'Elysée.

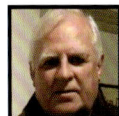

David Gwaltney | dGwaltneyArt | Art & Creative Director | Page: 31 | www.dgwaltneyart.com
Biography: An award-winning advertising art and creative director, David earned a BFA in communication art and design from Virginia Commonwealth University. He began his career as a graphic designer in the Atlanta design and illustration studios, GraphicsGroup and Whistl'n Dixie. A devoted Mac fan, David works on the Apple iPad Pro using the Procreate app for hand-drawn original signed and numbered limited edition canvas paintings.

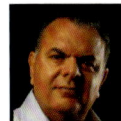

Ariel Freaner | Freaner Creative & Design | Principal & Founder | Page: 32 | www.freaner.com
Biography: Ariel Freaner is the principal and founder of Freaner Creative & Design. He has over 35 years of experience in creative development, Illustration, and design. His firm, founded in 1985 in San Diego, is an award-winning full-service, consultative creative, digital, and graphic design firm. Ariel Freaner has worked with clients in North America, Latin America, and abroad, earning him multiple Graphis awards and numerous international and industry awards.

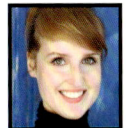

Katarzyna Zapart | Katarzyna Zapart | Freelance Graphic Designer | Page: 33 | www.behance.net/kazapart
Biography: Katarzyna Zapart is a Polish graphic and poster designer. She graduated from the Academy of Fine Arts in Kraków and has participated in many poster exhibitions and publications from Japan to the Americas. She has won three Graphis Platinum Awards and two Graphis Gold Awards. While Katarzyna creates logos, books, and other designs daily as a self-employed designer, her preferred creative media remains posters, especially focusing on cultural subject matter.

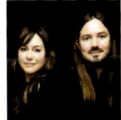

Sean Freeman & Eve Steben | THERE IS STUDIO | Co-founders | Page: 34 | www.thereis.co.uk
Biography: The creative vision of Sean Freeman and Eve Steben comes to life as a multidisciplinary studio specializing in art direction, typography, illustration, CGI, and photography. Driven by boundless curiosity and a passion for image-making, Sean and Eve seamlessly blend design, textures, craft, and art experimentations to produce work that is both singular and compelling, always tailoring their approach to the message.

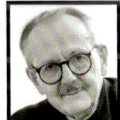

Stephan Bundi | Atelier Bundi AG | Designer & Art Director | Page: 35 | www.atelierbundi.ch
Biography: Stephan Bundi founded his studio after completing his graphic design studies at the Bern University of the Arts in Switzerland and the State Academy of Fine Arts in Stuttgart, Germany. As a designer and art director, he works for film producers, publishers, and corporate and institutional branding. He combines unconventional ideas with traditional and practical Swiss design. He views successful design as a process where thinking, designing, and rethinking continuously alternate until the final version is achieved. He has received several awards at international design biennales.

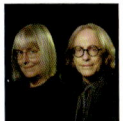

Nancy Skolos & Thomas Wedell | Skolos-Wedell | Co-founders | Page: 36 | www.skolos-wedell.com
Biography: Nancy Skolos and Thomas Wedell work to diminish the boundaries between graphic design and photography by creating collaged three-dimensional posters. Nancy and Thomas are well-known in the US and abroad through international exhibitions, publications, and awards. Their posters are included in graphic design collections of the Museum of Modern Art, the Metropolitan Museum of Art, and many others. Nancy and Thomas were awarded the AIGA Medal in 2017.

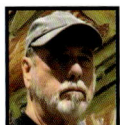

Steve Collier | CollierGraphica | Founder & Designer | Page: 37 | www.colliergraphica.com
Biography: Steve Collier began his graphic design career in Dallas, Texas, developing packaging and brand identities. He later worked at two design firms in Houston before founding Collier Studio (now CollierGraphica) in Seattle, Washington. This full-service design/marketing studio provides solutions for corporate identity, brochures, posters, packaging, and more. CollierGraphica serves advertising agencies, design firms, and direct clients. In 2004, Steve joined GalleryPlayer as a senior designer.

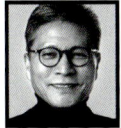

Byoung-il Sun | Gallery BI | Designer & Professor | Page: 38 | www.gallerybi.com
Biography: Born in Korea in 1958, Byoung-il Sun has been a visual information design professor at Namseoul University since 1995, where he now serves as professor emeritus and supervises graduate students. He has won numerous international design awards and founded the BIPB Poster Art Biennale in South Korea. His jury service includes prestigious competitions such as the Golden Bee and Graphis. Additionally, he has delivered special lectures globally, including at Purdue University and Nottingham Trent University.

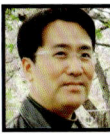

Hoon-Dong Chung | Dankook University | Designer & Professor | Page: 39 |
Biography: Hoon-Dong Chung is a professor at Dankook University in South Korea. He has received over 200 design awards, including the Graphis Annual Award, German Design Award, Red Dot Design Award, and the iF Design Award. He also received a commendation from the president of South Korea. Furthermore, his art is held in prestigious collections such as the Design Museum Munich, Museum für Kunst und Gewerbe, Hamburg, Museum für Gestaltung, Musée de la Publicité, Dansk Plakat Museum, and more.

Visit our Credits & Commentary section in the back of the book to read the full assignments, approaches, and results from this year's Platinum Winners.

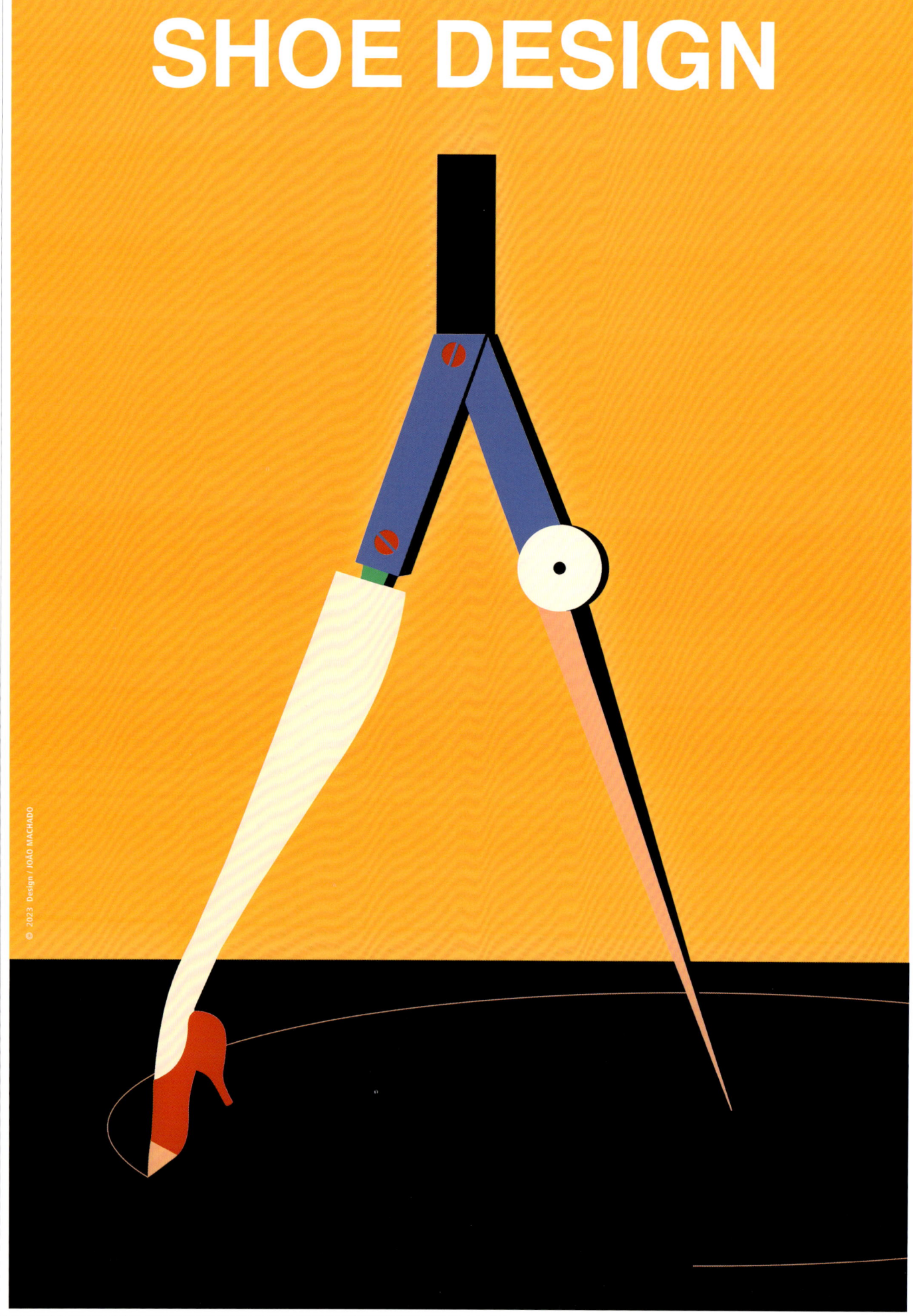

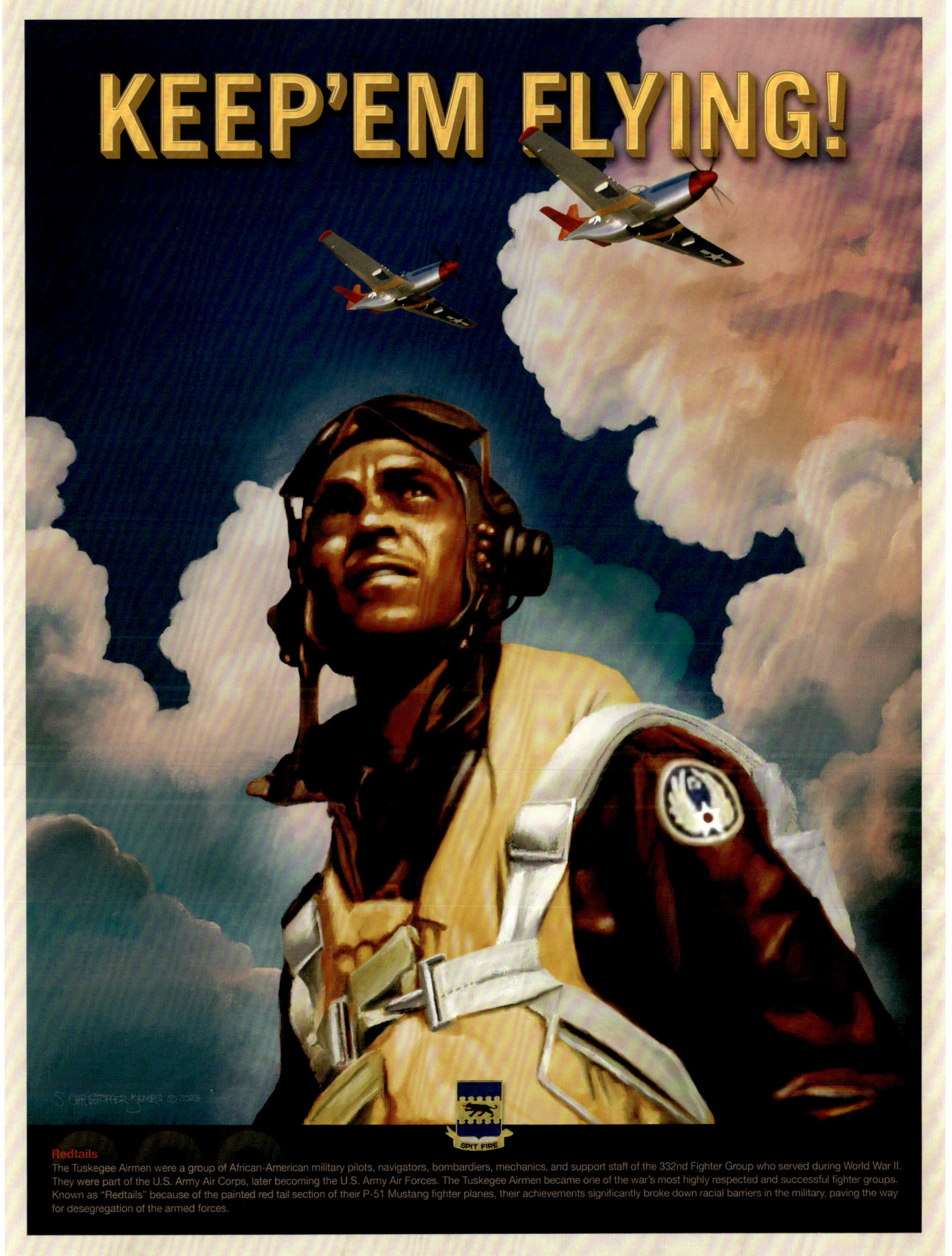

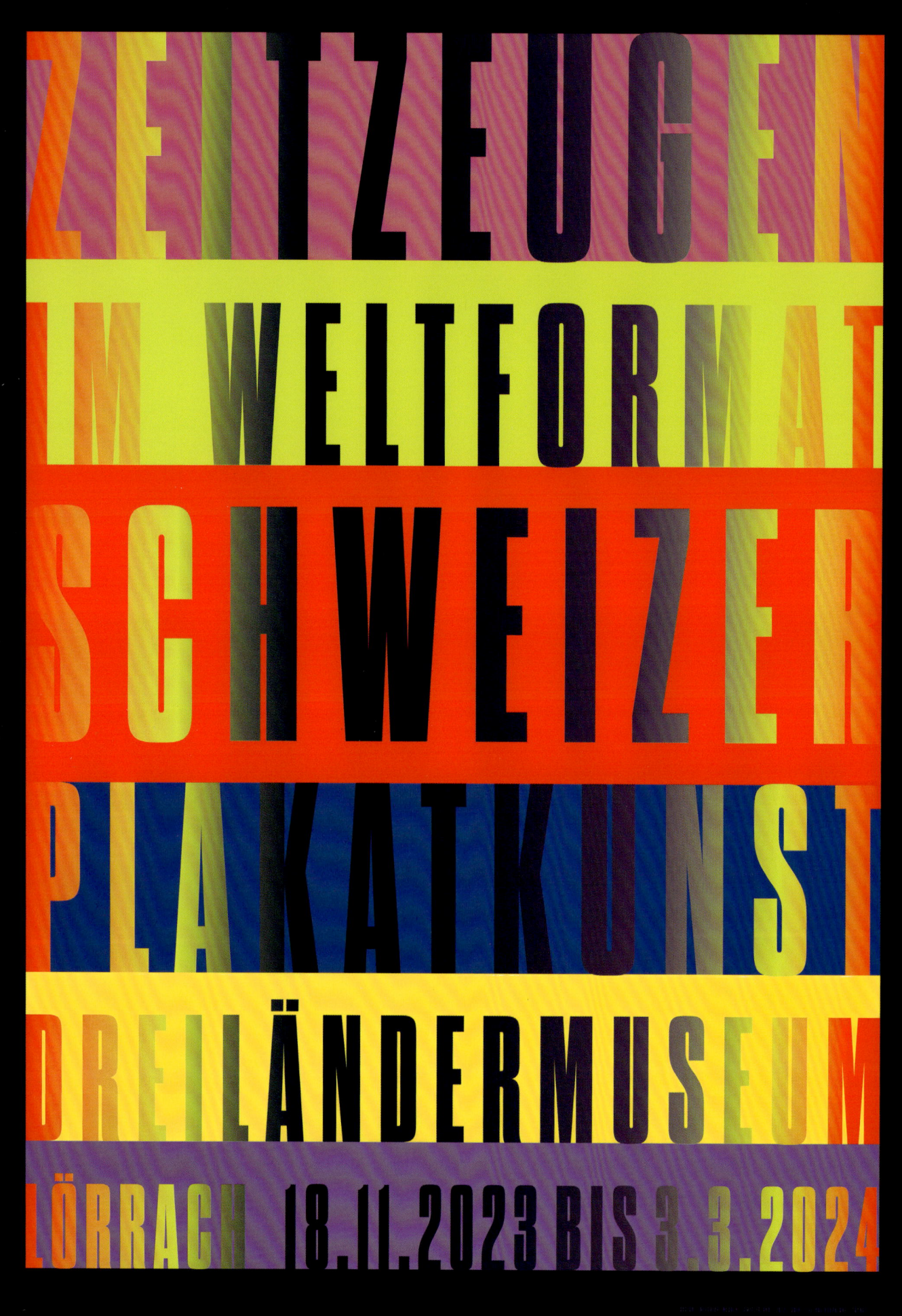

Title: Zeitzeugen, Schweizer Plakate im Weltformat, Swiss Poster Exhibition, Posters from 1940 till Today
Client: Dreiländer Museum Lörrach, Germany | **Design Firm:** Melchior Imboden | **P231:** Credit & Commentary

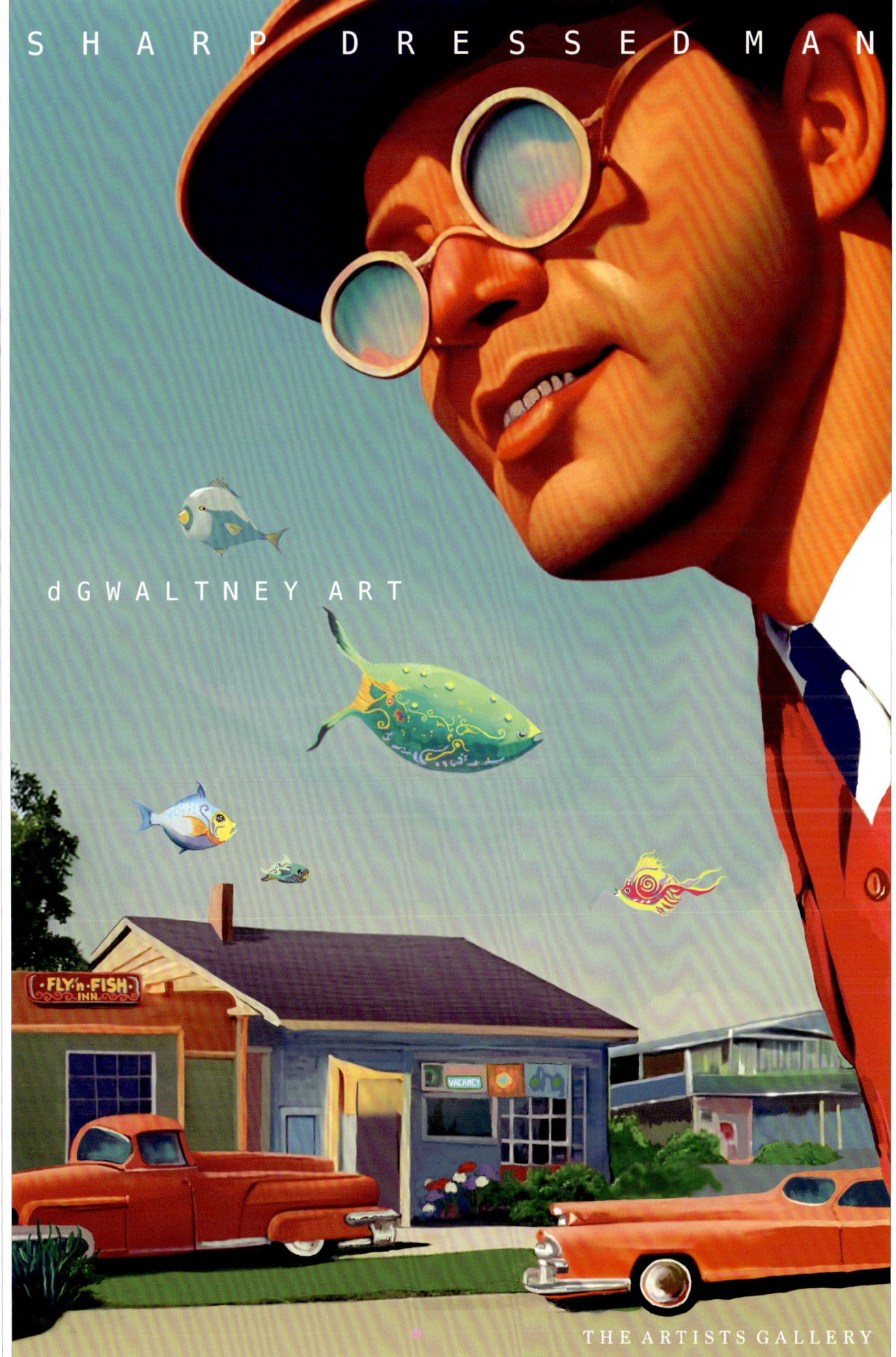

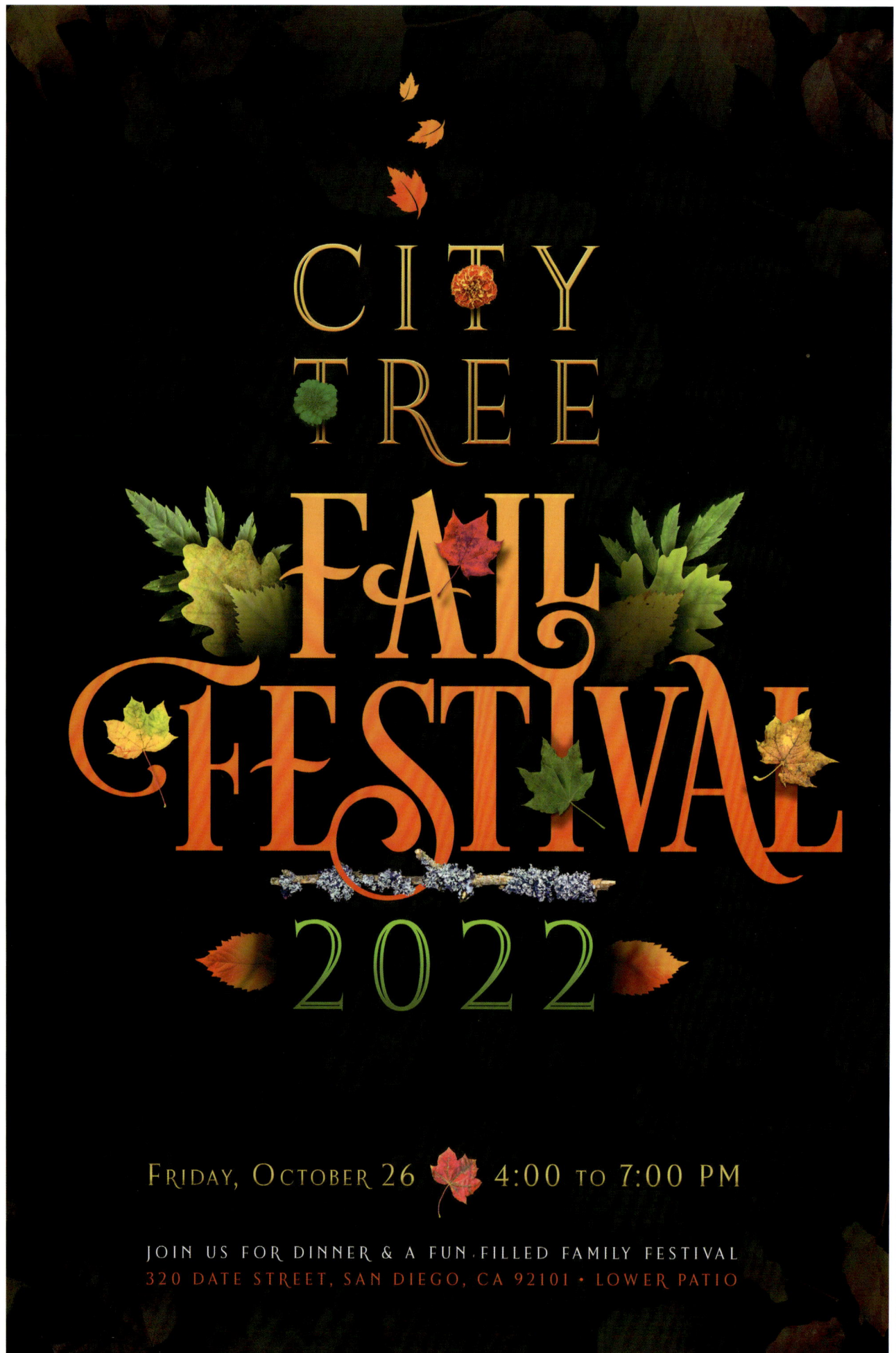

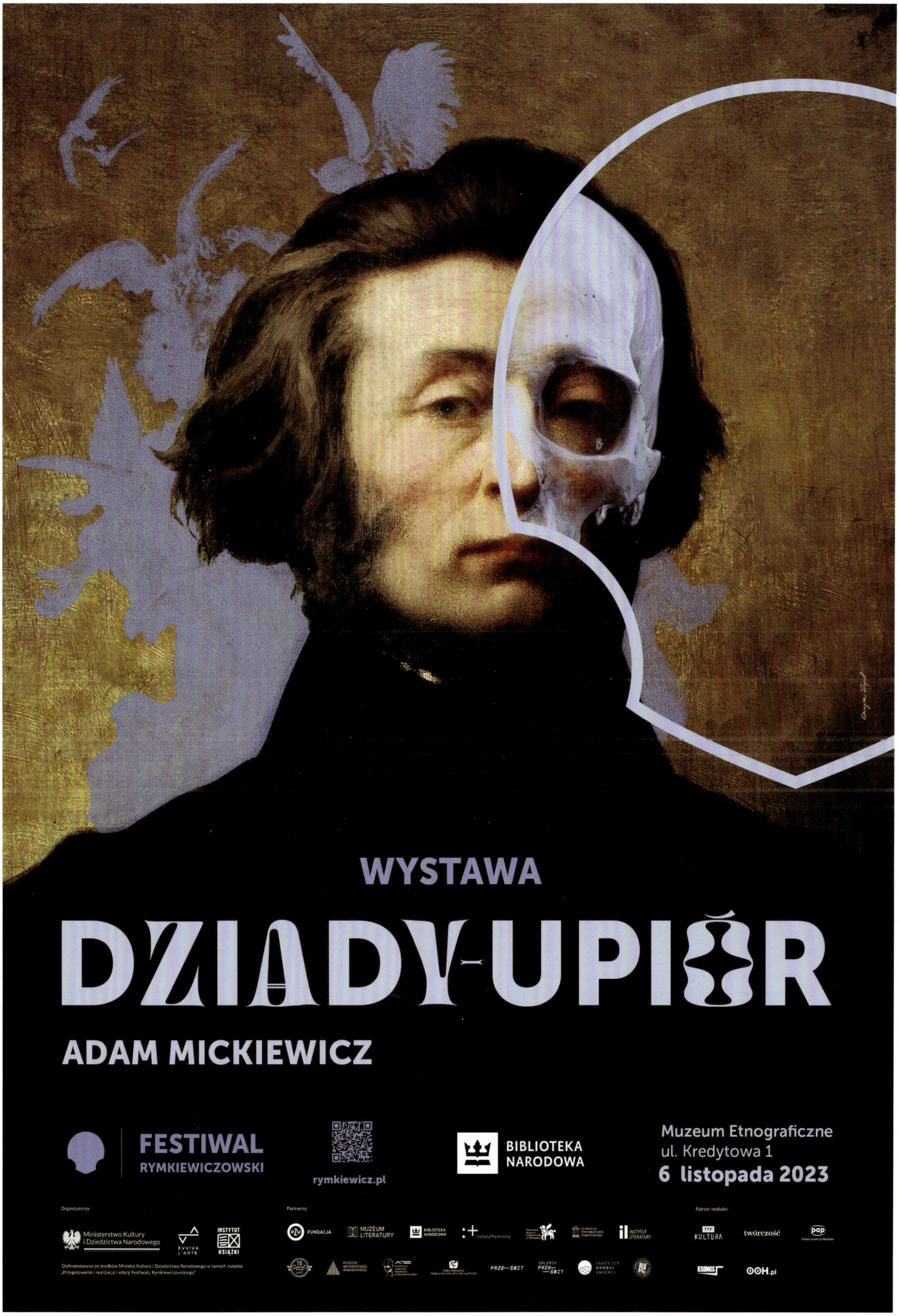

Title: Series of Event Posters for the Rymkiewicz Festival | **Client:** Fundacja Evviva L'arte
Design Firm: Katarzyna Zapart | **P231:** Credit & Commentary | Image 1 of 7

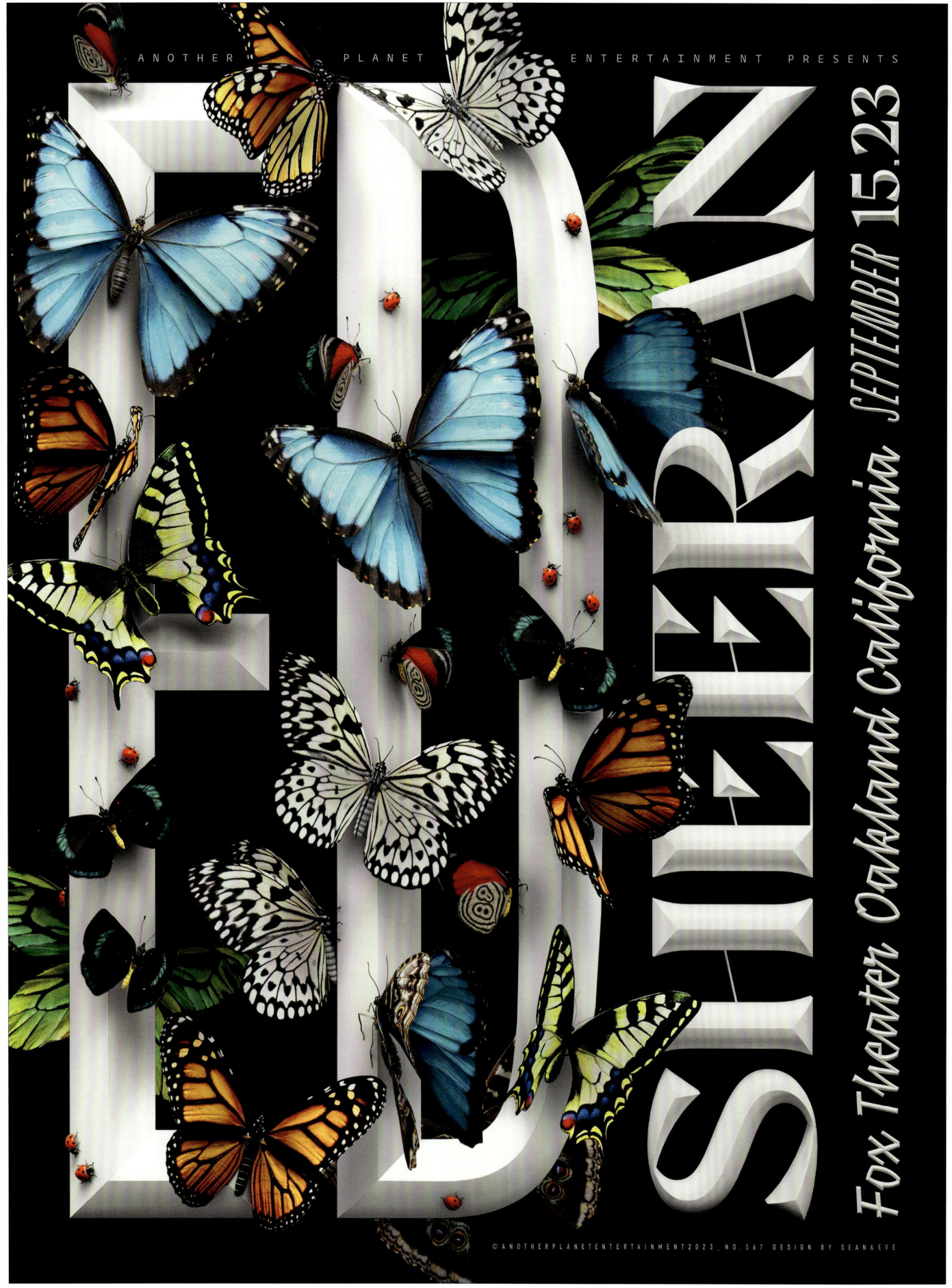

P231: Credit & Commentary Title: ED SHEERAN | Client: Another Planet Entertainment | Design Firm: THERE IS STUDIO

georges bizet
carmen
premiere 2. august 2024
sommeroper selzach.ch

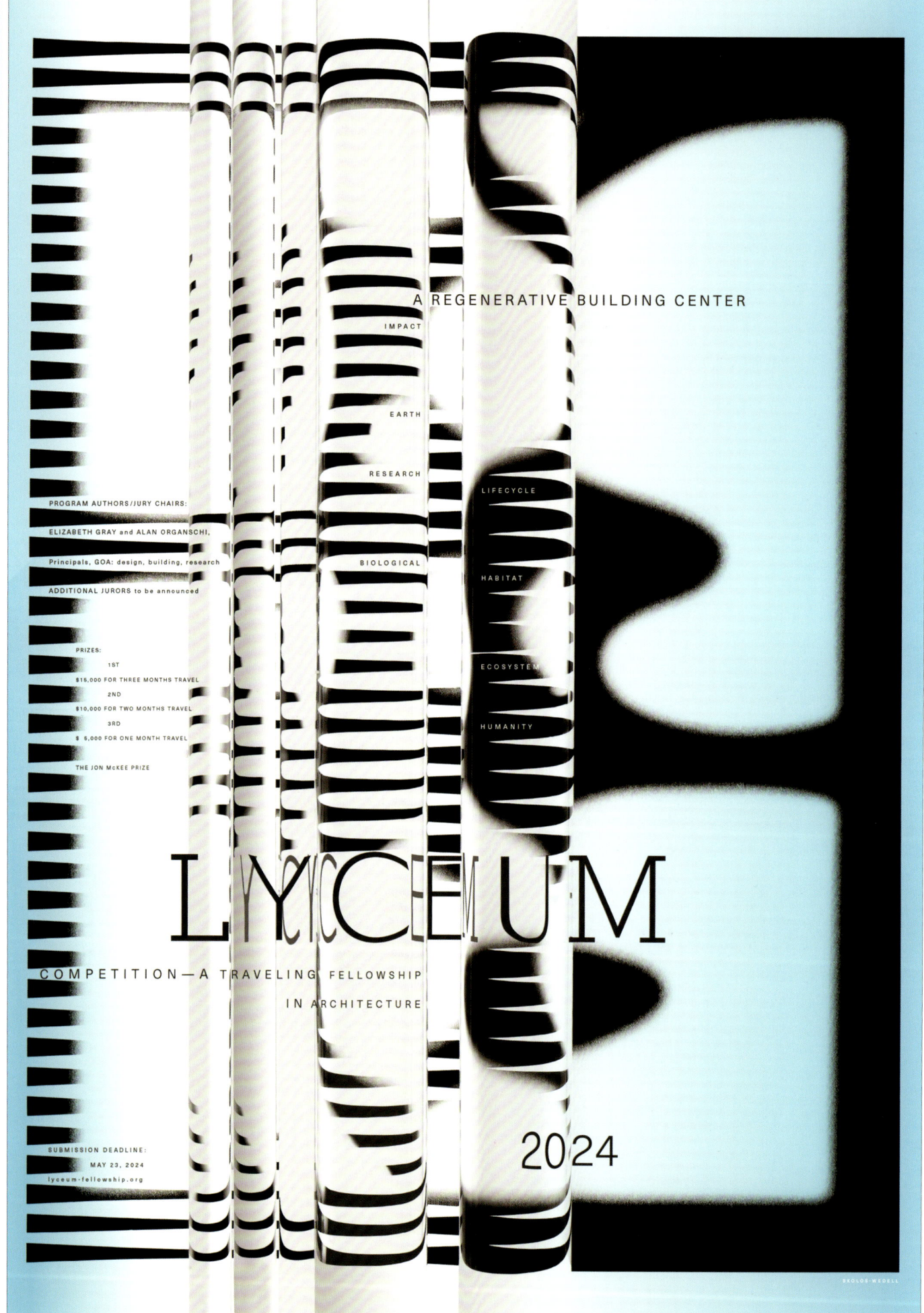

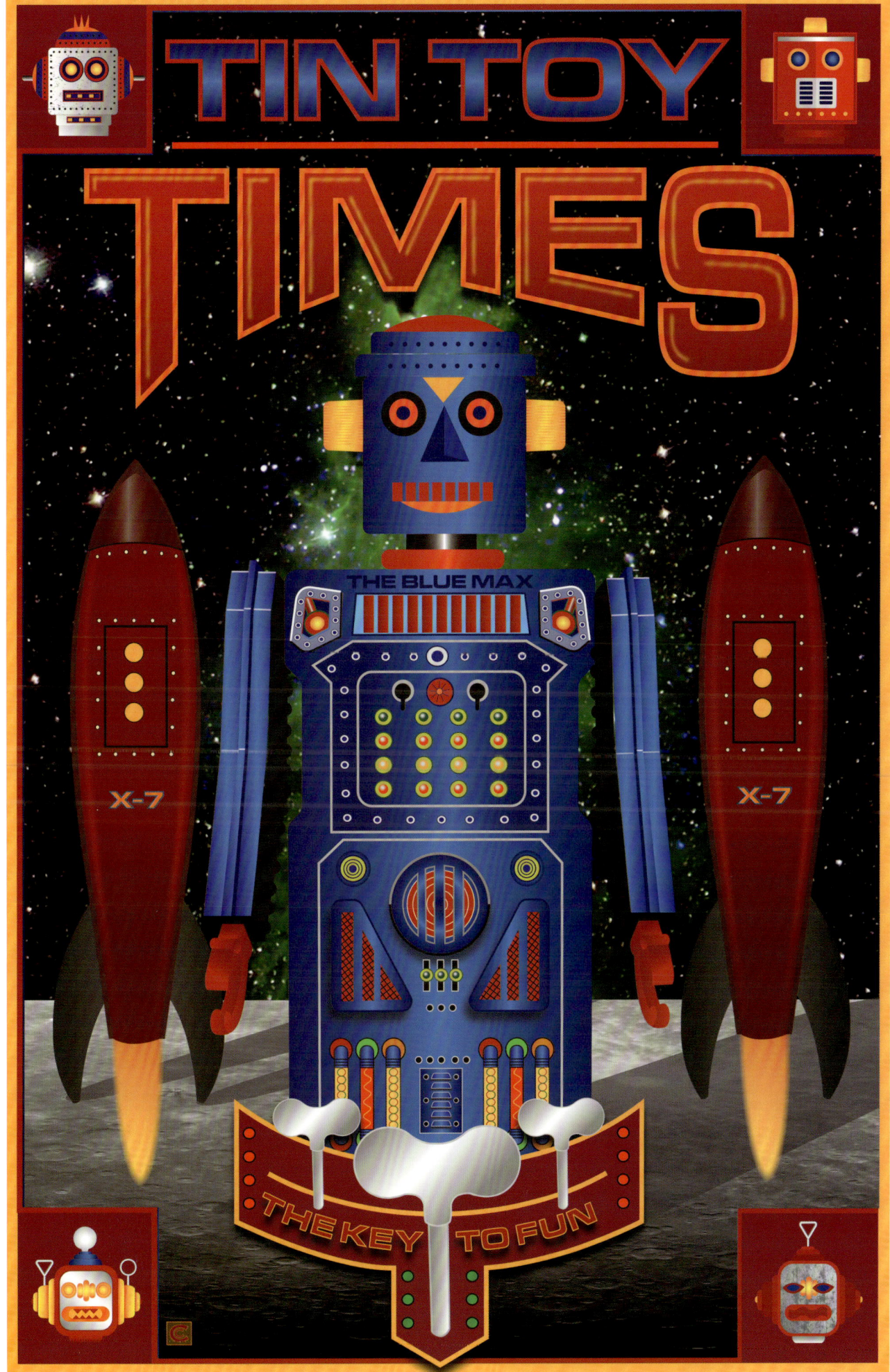

38 BYOUNG-IL SUN PLATINUM — SOCIAL & POLITICAL

Rights Now
www.rightsnow.com

WOMEN. LIFE
FREEDOM

Human rights are a basic set of freedoms and protections that all people should be entitled to regardless of their nationality, ethnicity, and gender. Around the world, women continue to face discrimination in many areas of their lives, including in access to education, employment, health care, and political participation. In some countries, women still have little control over their own lives and must quickly seek a life of freedom.

Title: Women. Life. Freedom. | **Client:** National Human Rights Commission of the Republic of Korea
Design Firm: Gallery BI | **P231:** Credit & Commentary

39 HOON-DONG CHUNG PLATINUM — SOCIAL & POLITICAL

The Ending Point of Conflict

The Starting Point of Tolerance

P231: Credit & Commentary   **Title:** Tolerance | **Client:** Self-initiated | **Design Firm:** Dankook University

Graphis Gold Awards

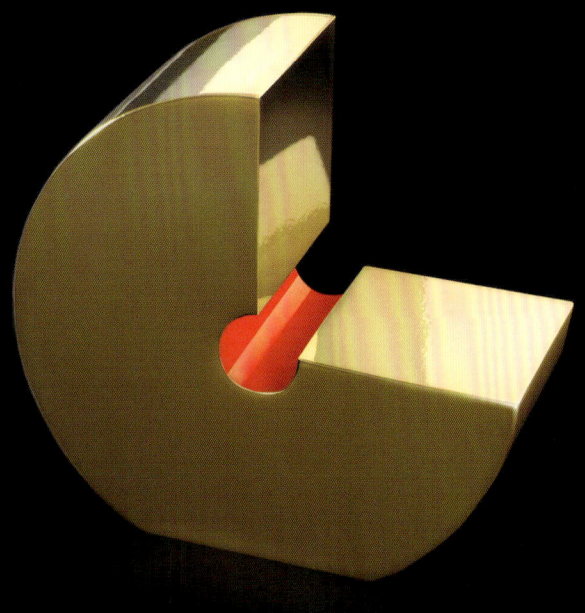

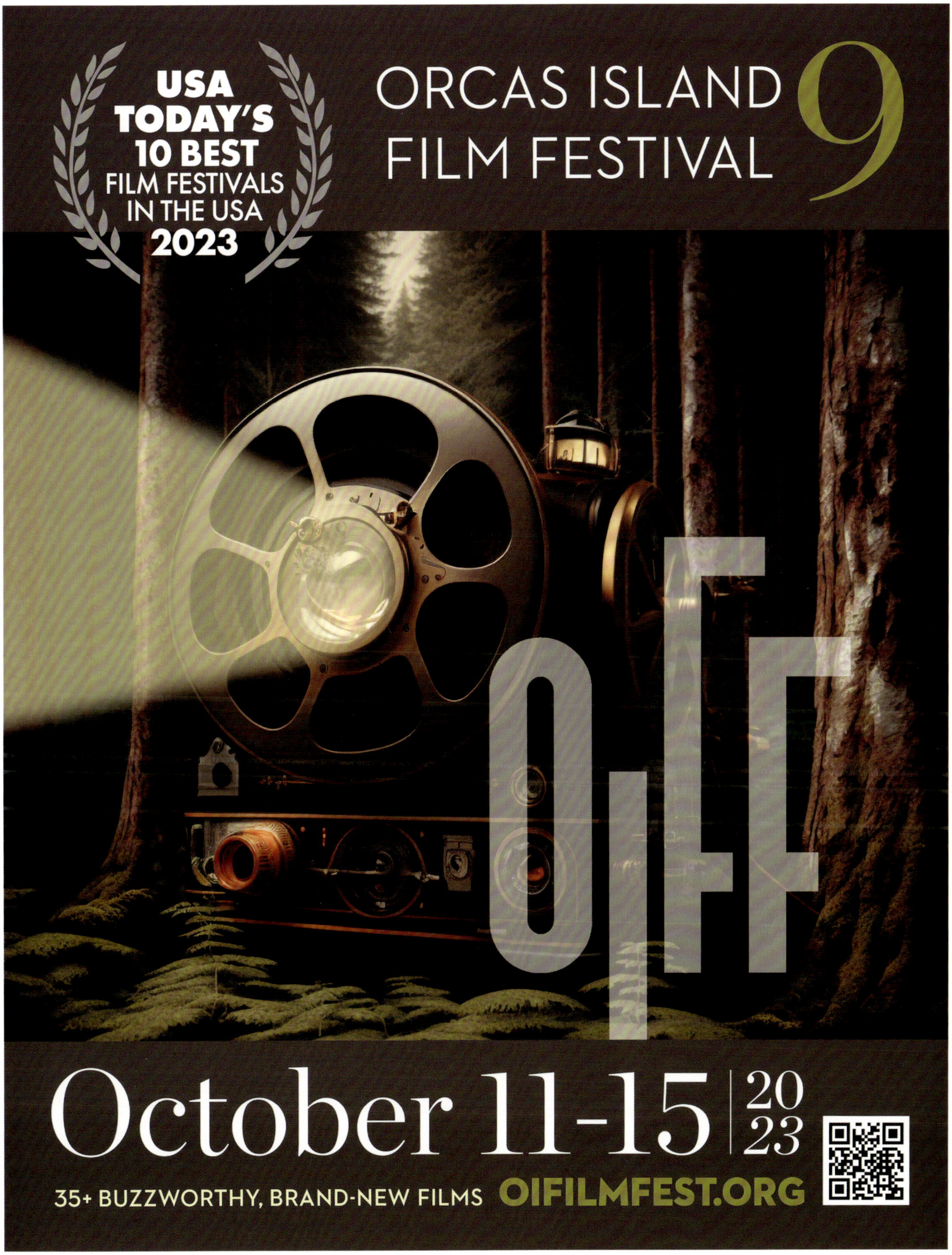

Title: Orcas Island Film Festival 2023 Poster | Client: Orcas Island Film Festival
Design Firm: Huber Design Werks | P231: Credit & Commentary

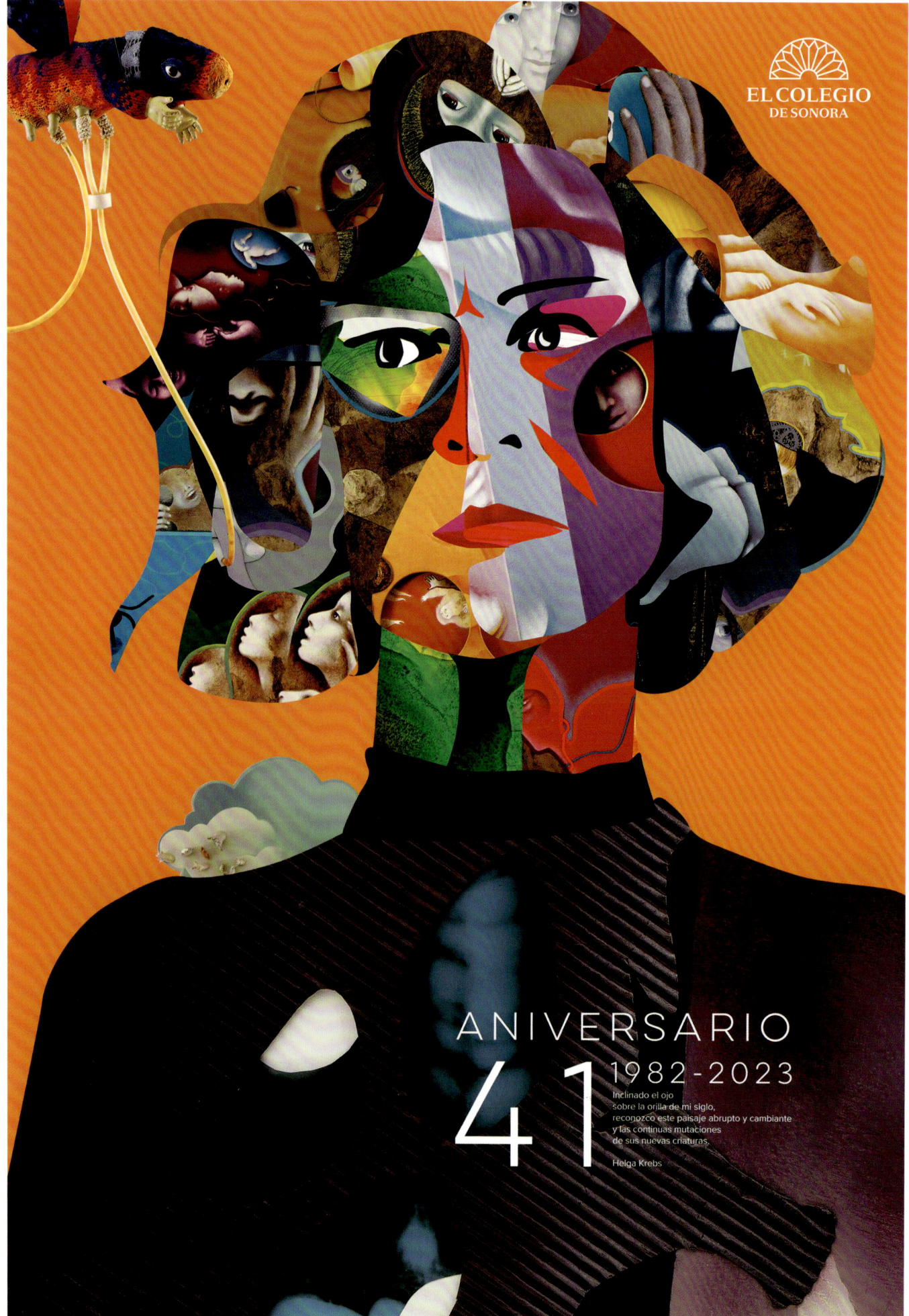

Title: 41st Anniversary of the Colegio de Sonora: Tribute to the Painter Helga Krebs | Client: Colson
Design Firm: Ivette Valenzuela Design | P231: Credit & Commentary

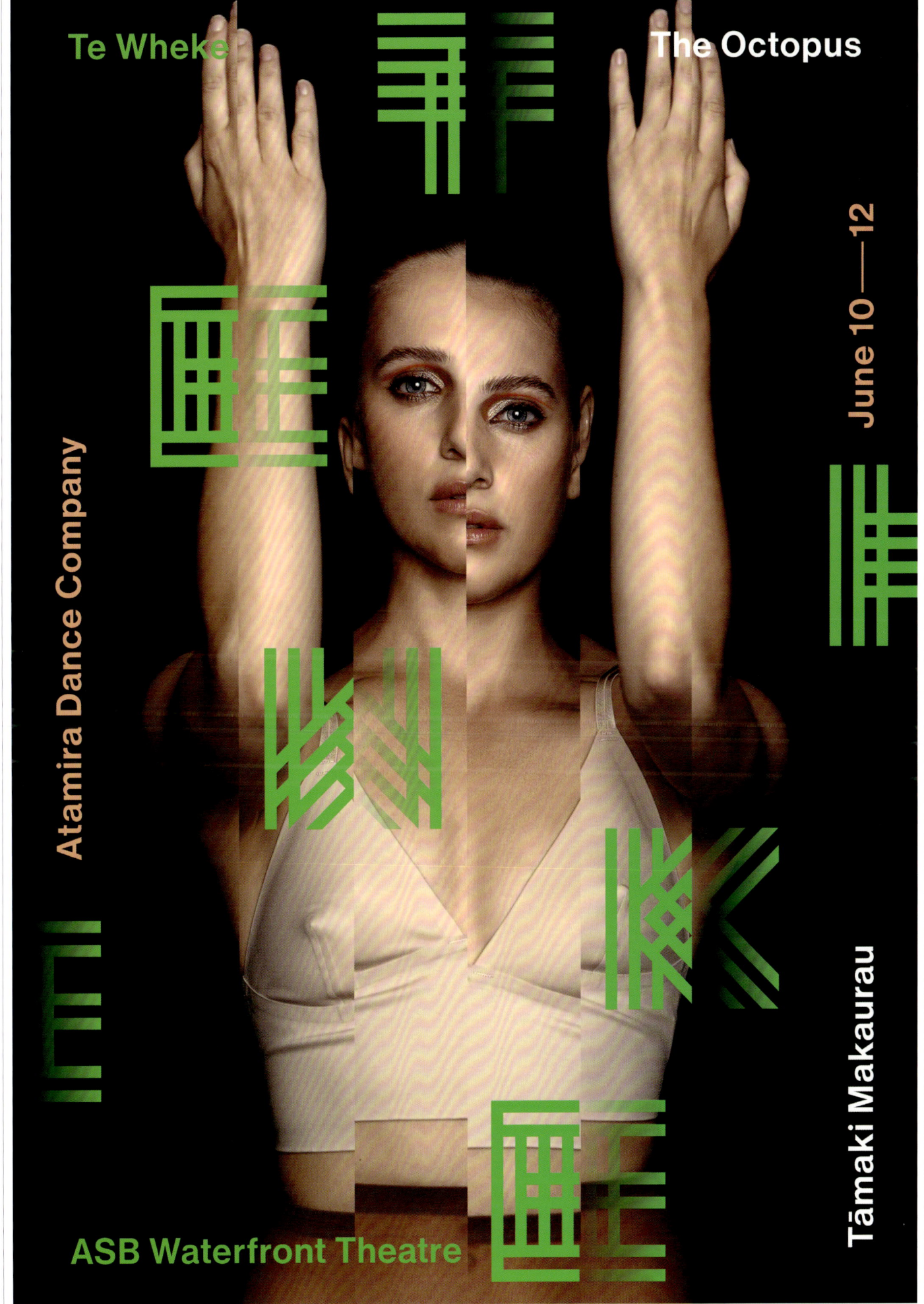

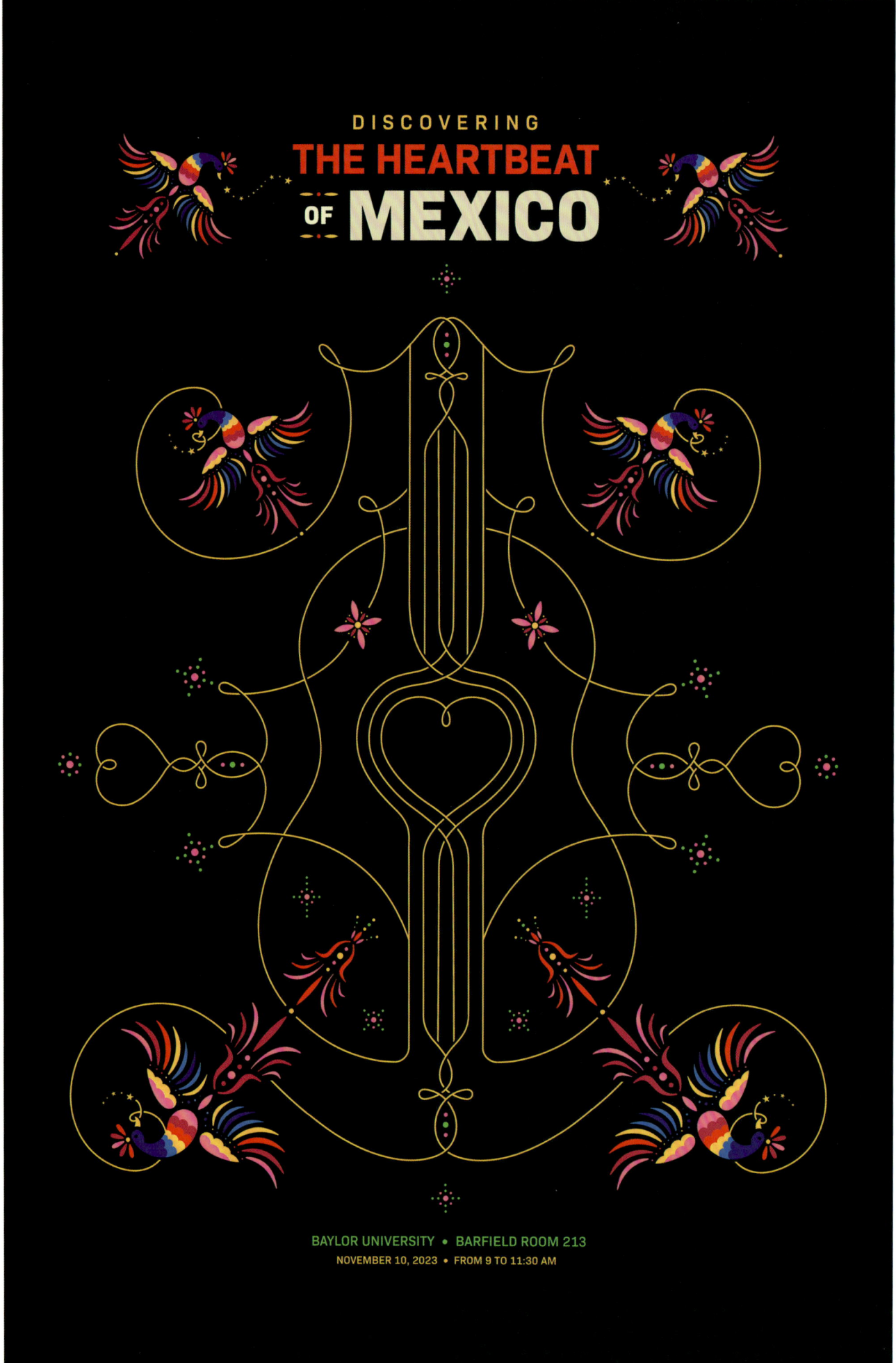

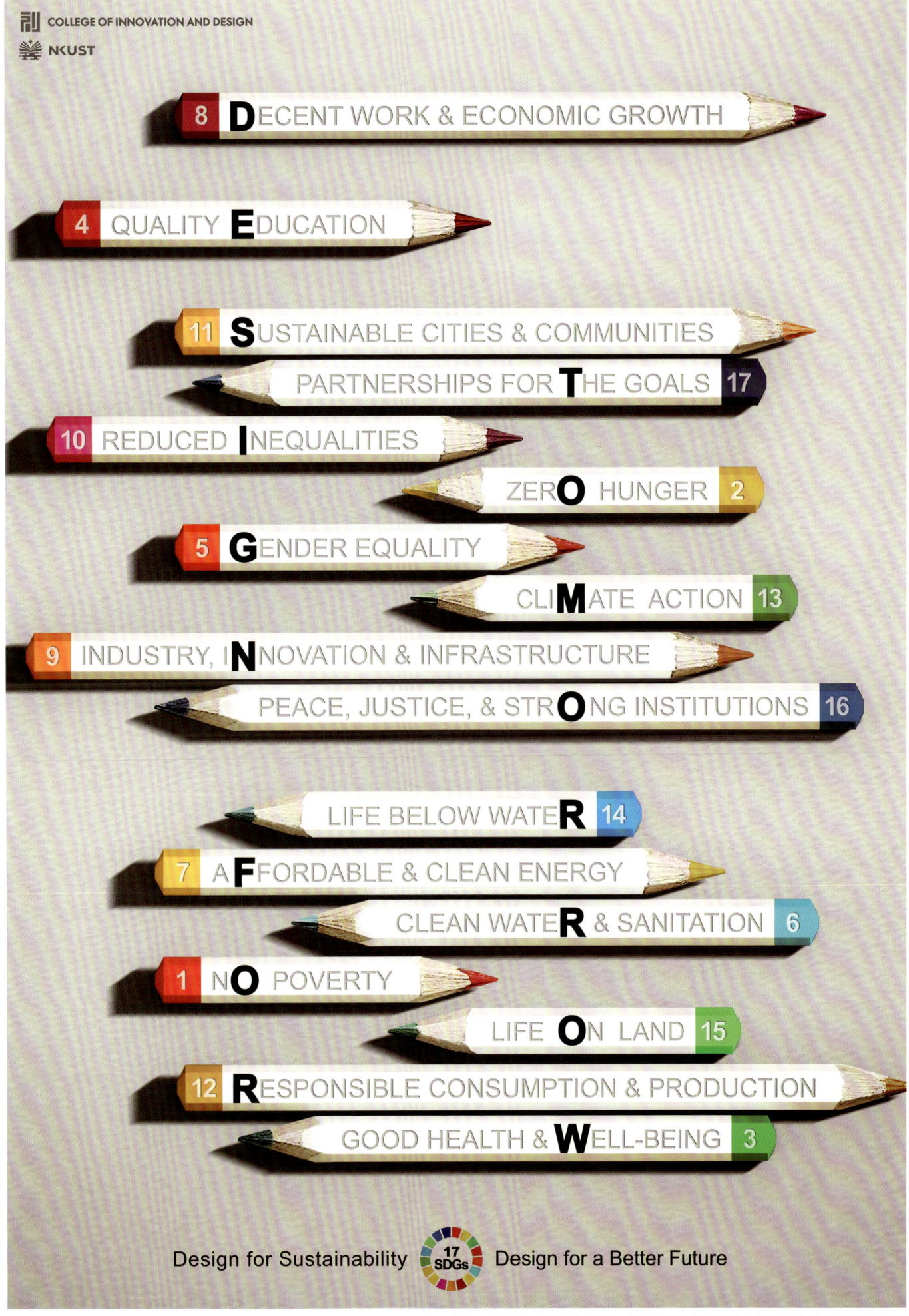

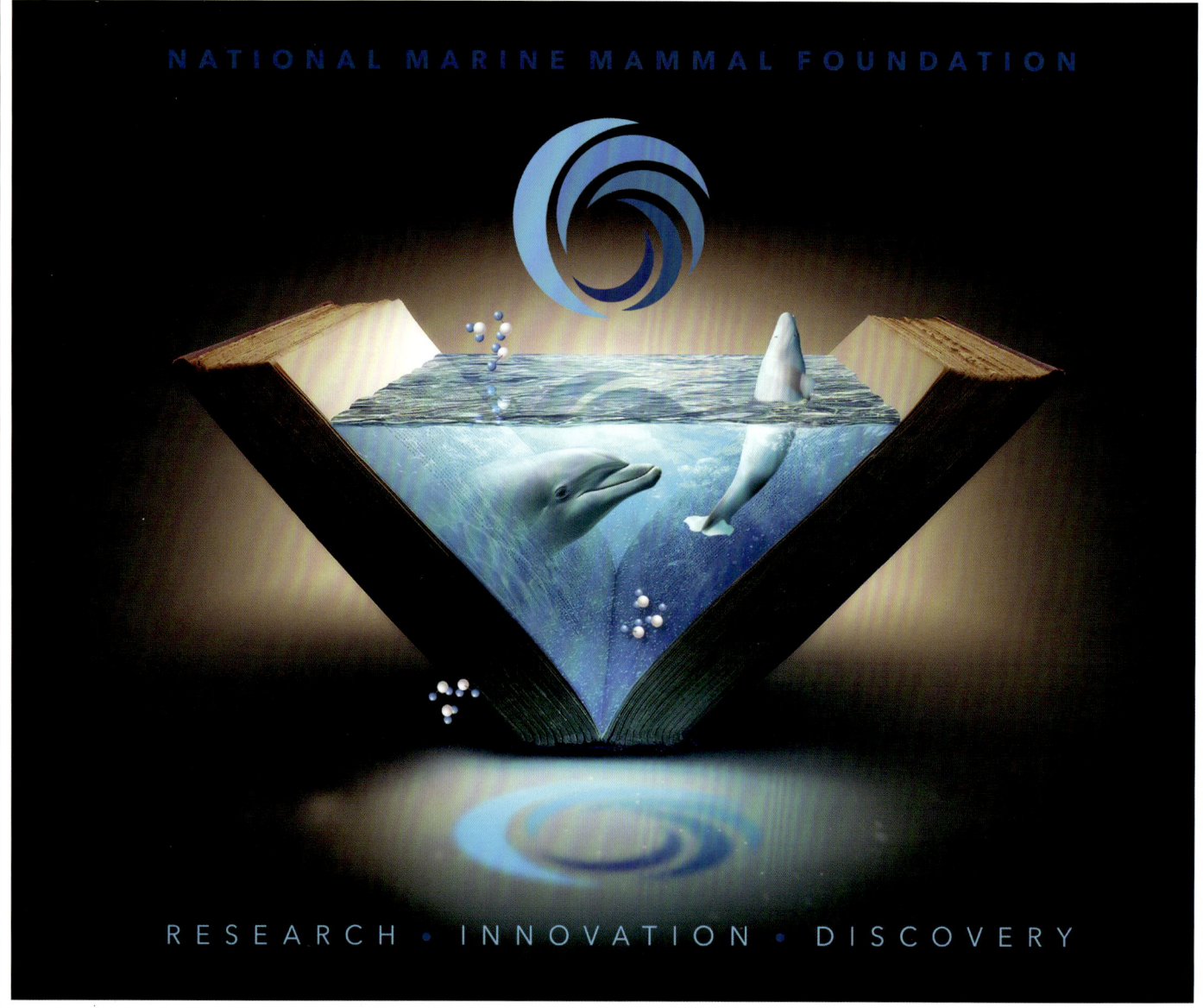

Title: National Marine Mammal Foundation: Research. Innovation. Discovery. | **Client:** National Marine Mammal Foundation
Design Firm: Freaner Creative & Design | **P232:** Credit & Commentary

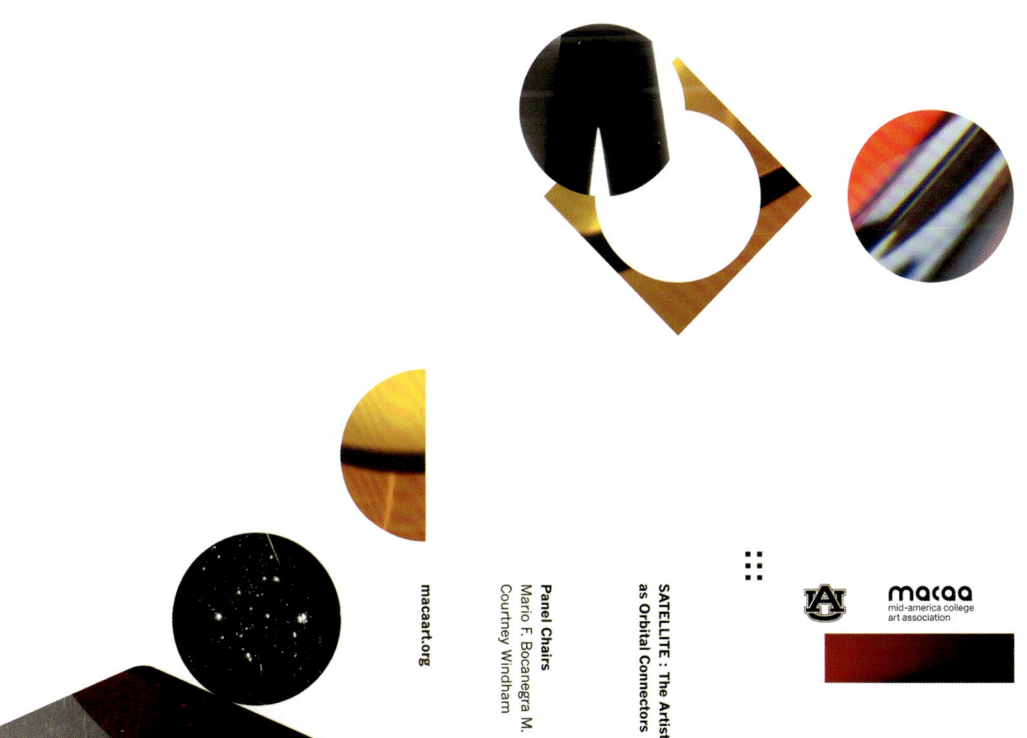

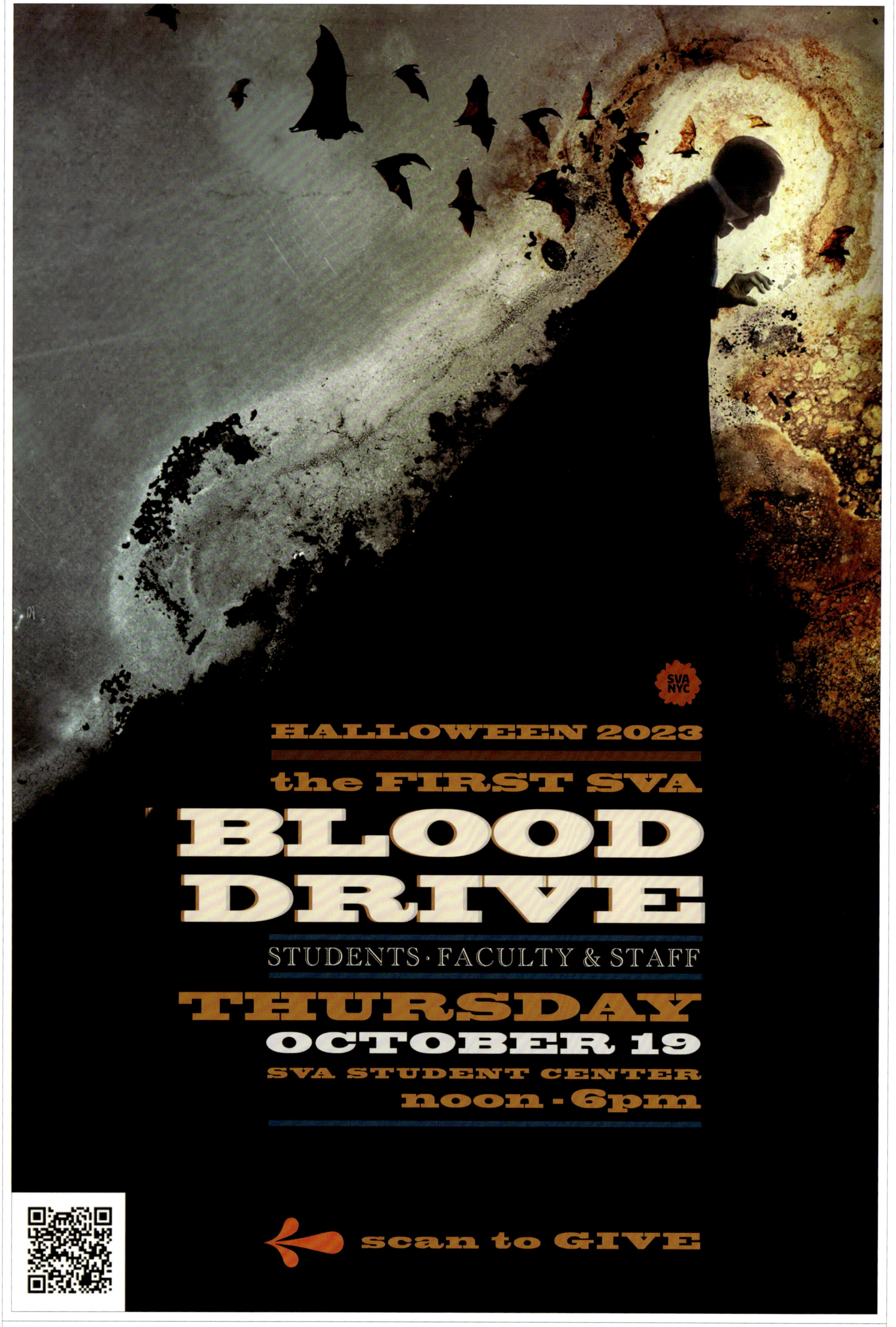

48 VIKTOR KOEN GOLD EDUCATION

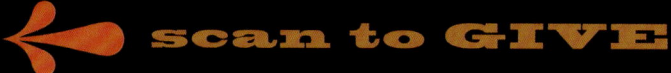

HALLOWEEN 2023
the FIRST SVA
BLOOD DRIVE
STUDENTS · FACULTY & STAFF
THURSDAY
OCTOBER 19
SVA STUDENT CENTER
noon - 6pm

scan to GIVE

P232: Credit & Commentary | Title: SVA Blood Drive | Client: School of Visual Arts | Design Firm: Viktor Koen

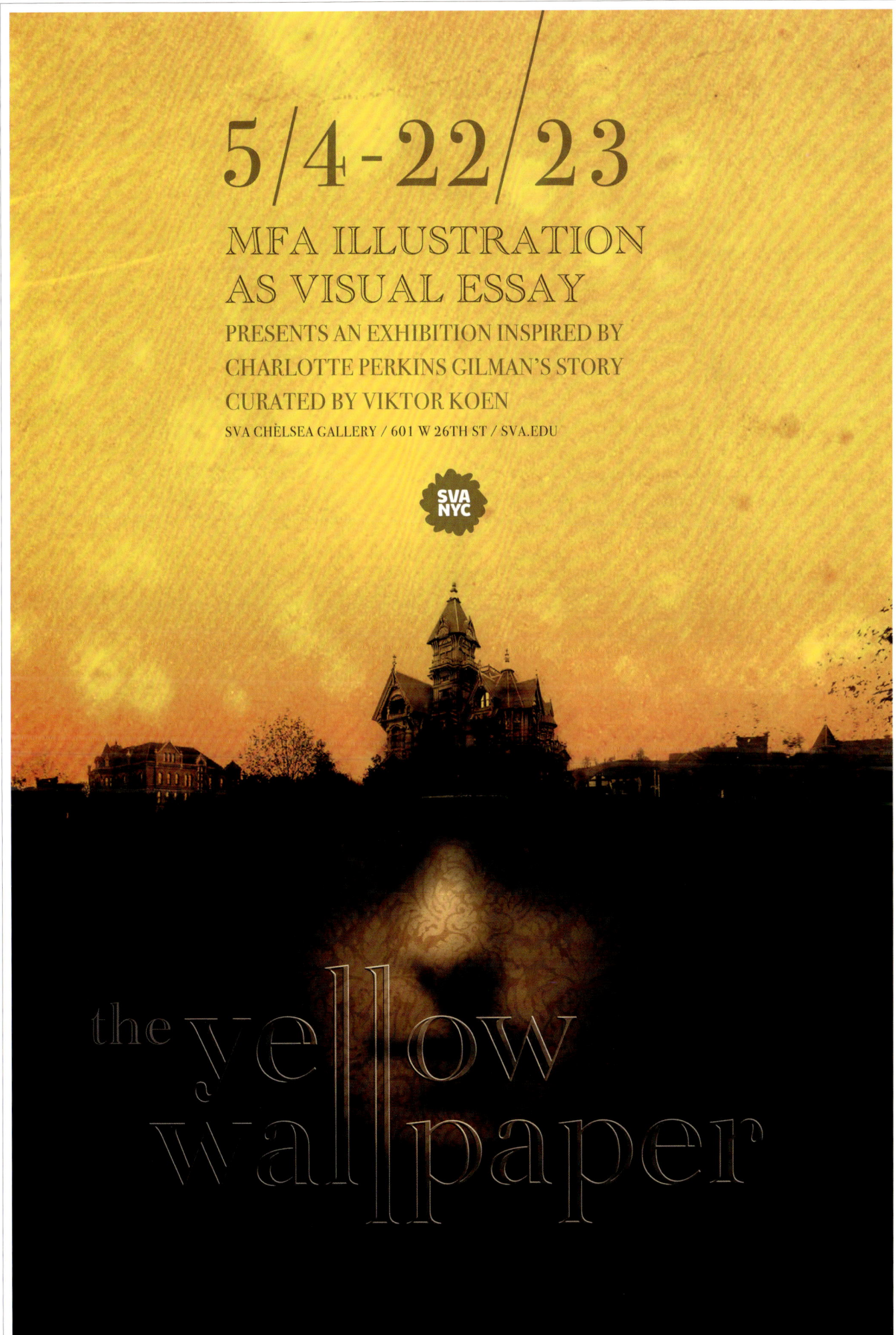

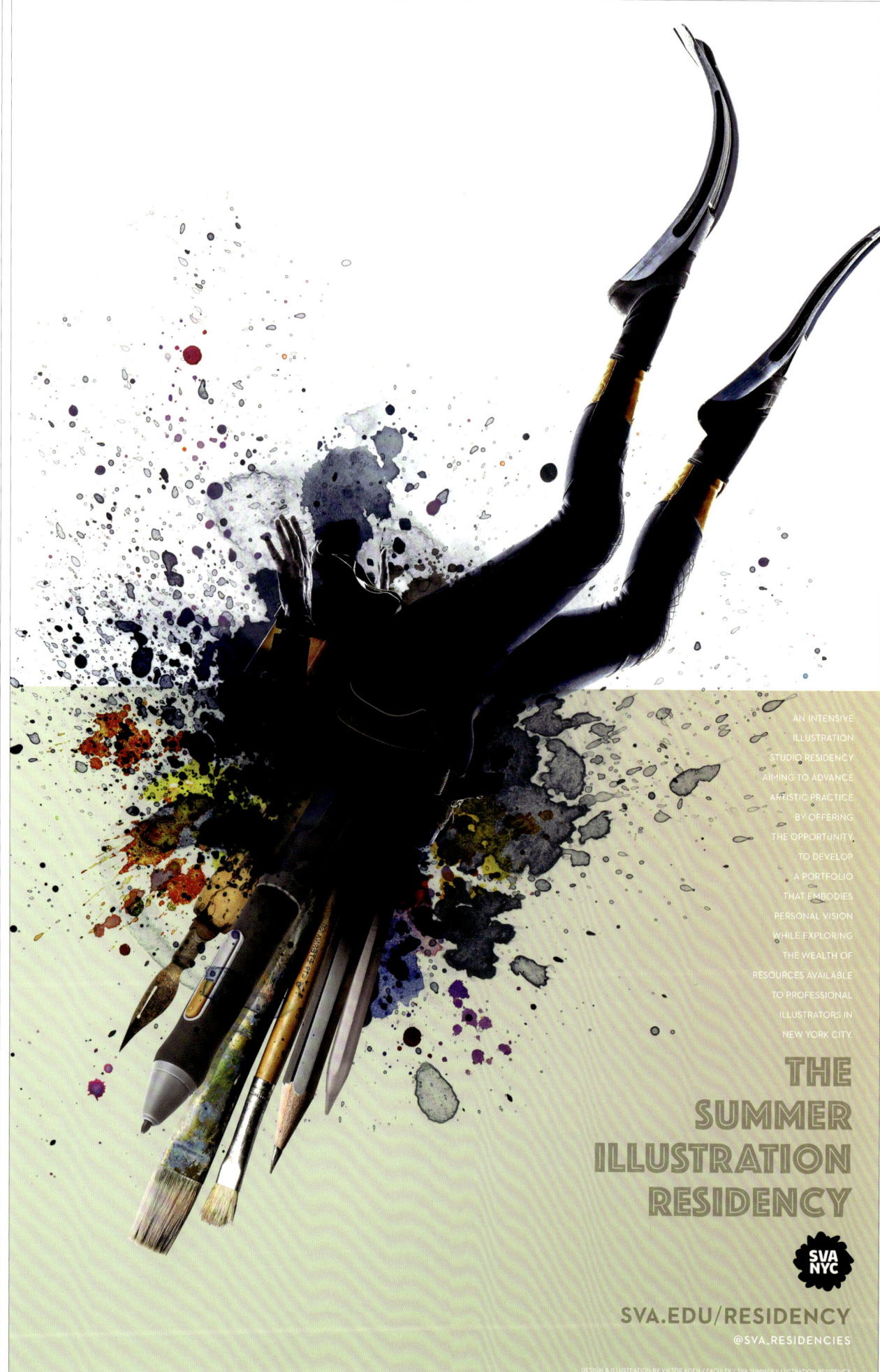

Title: SVA Summer Illustration Residency | **Client:** School of Visual Arts
Design Firm: Viktor Koen | **P232:** Credit & Commentary

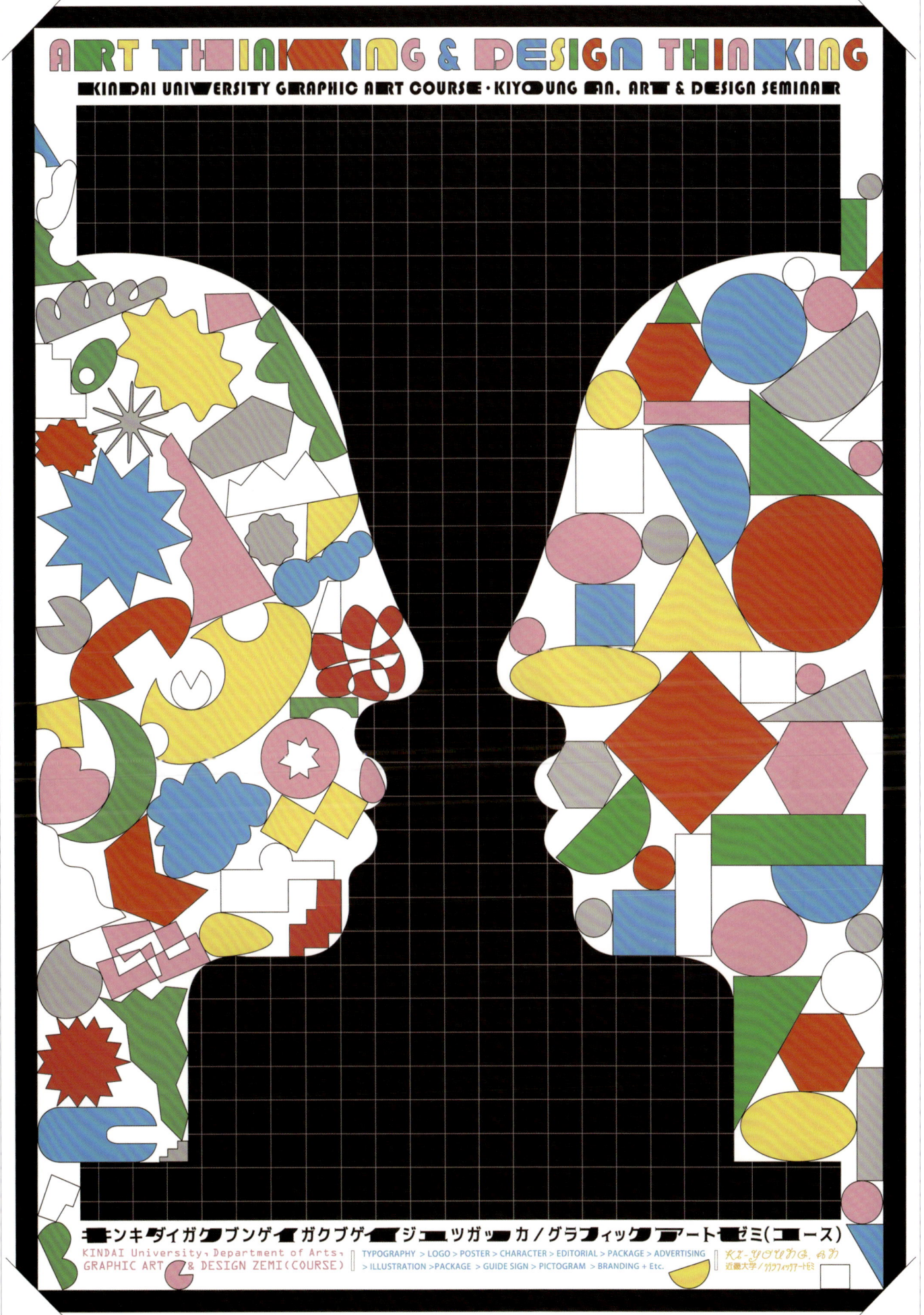

Title: "Art Thinking & Design Thinking" in the Graphic Art Course | **Client:** KINDAI University Department of Arts
Design Firm: Kiyoung An Graphic Art Course Laboratory | **P232:** Credit & Commentary

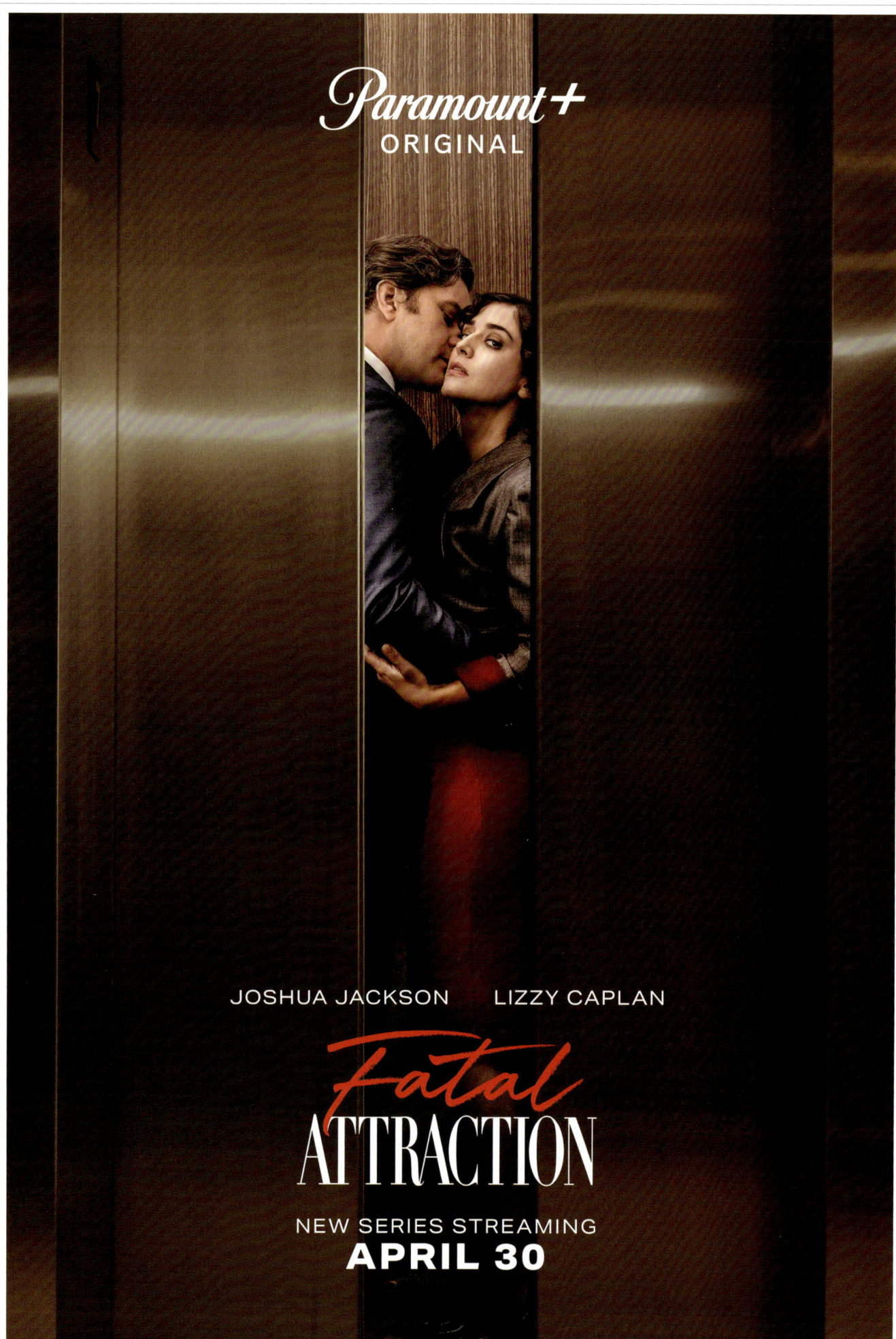

53 THE REFINERY **GOLD** ENTERTAINMENT

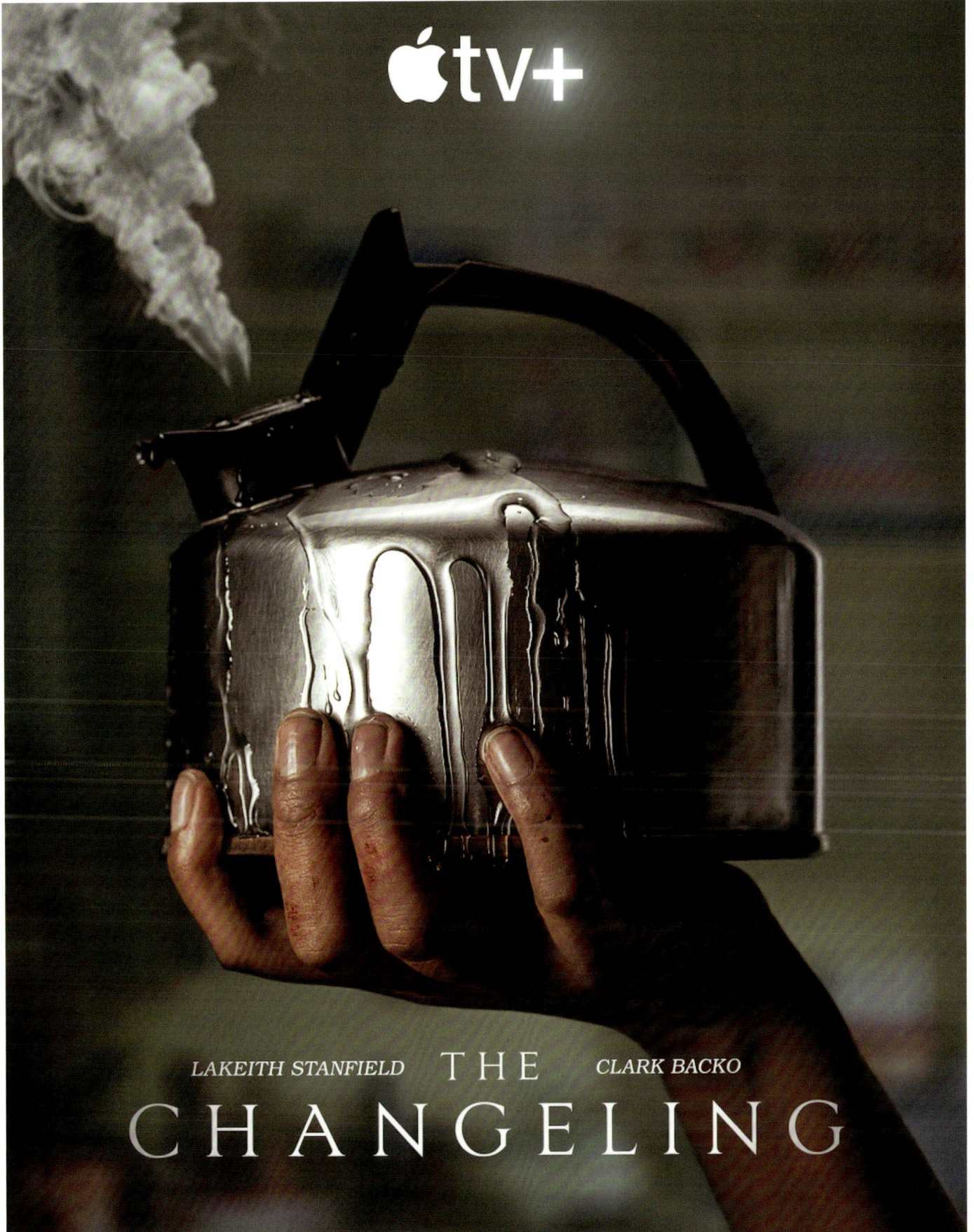

Title: The Changeling, Key Art | Client: Apple TV+ | Design Firm: The Refinery

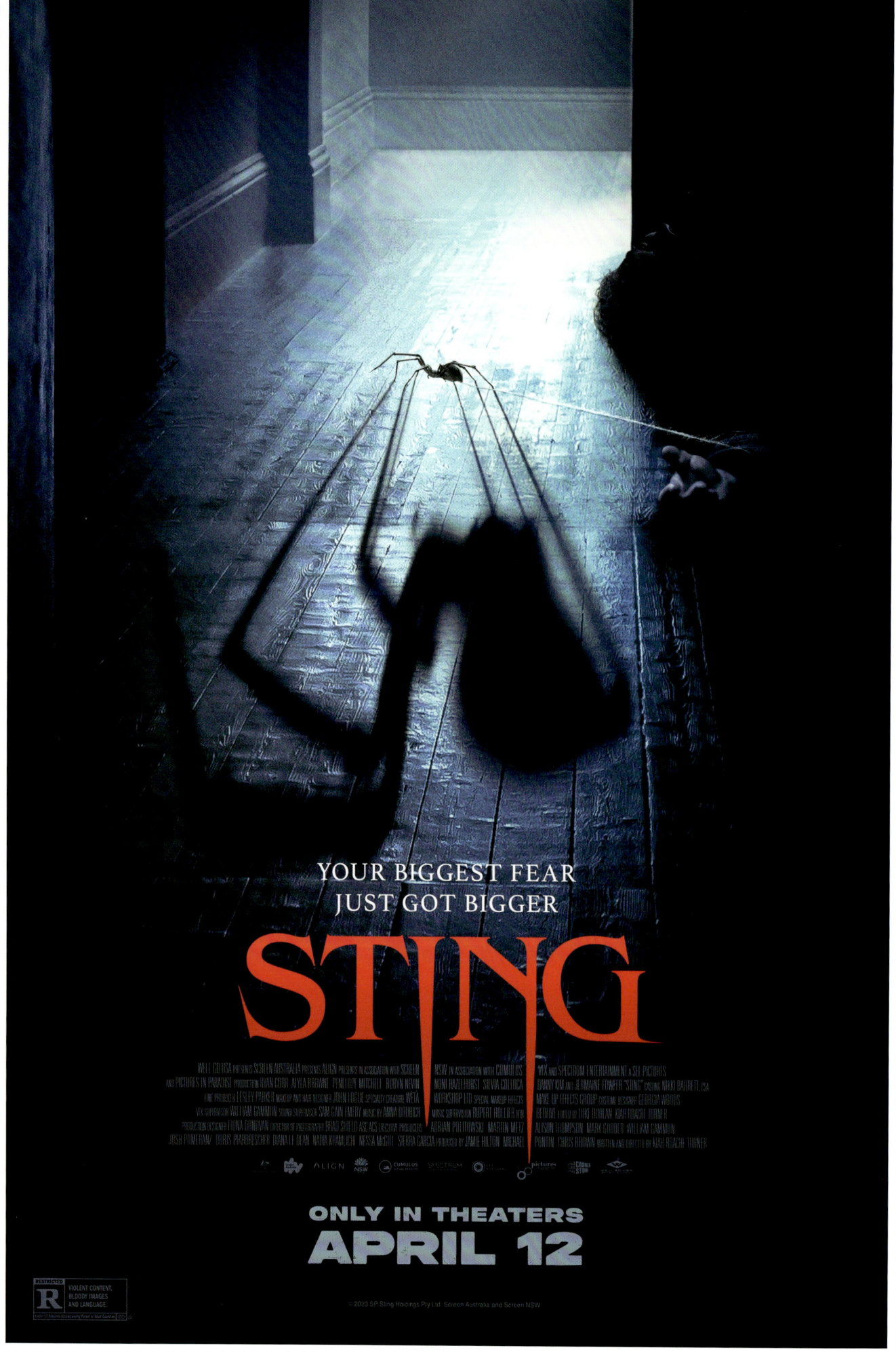

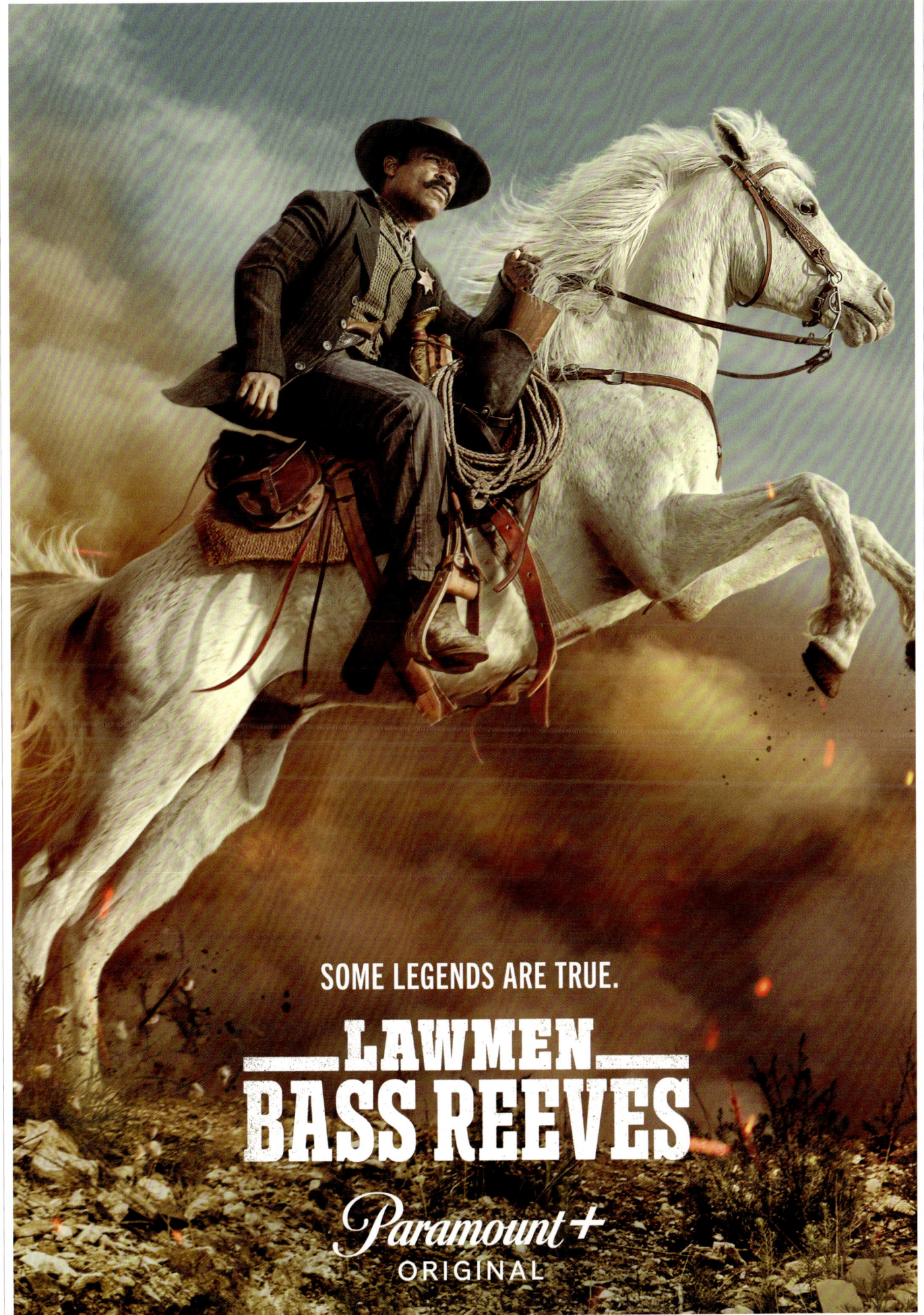

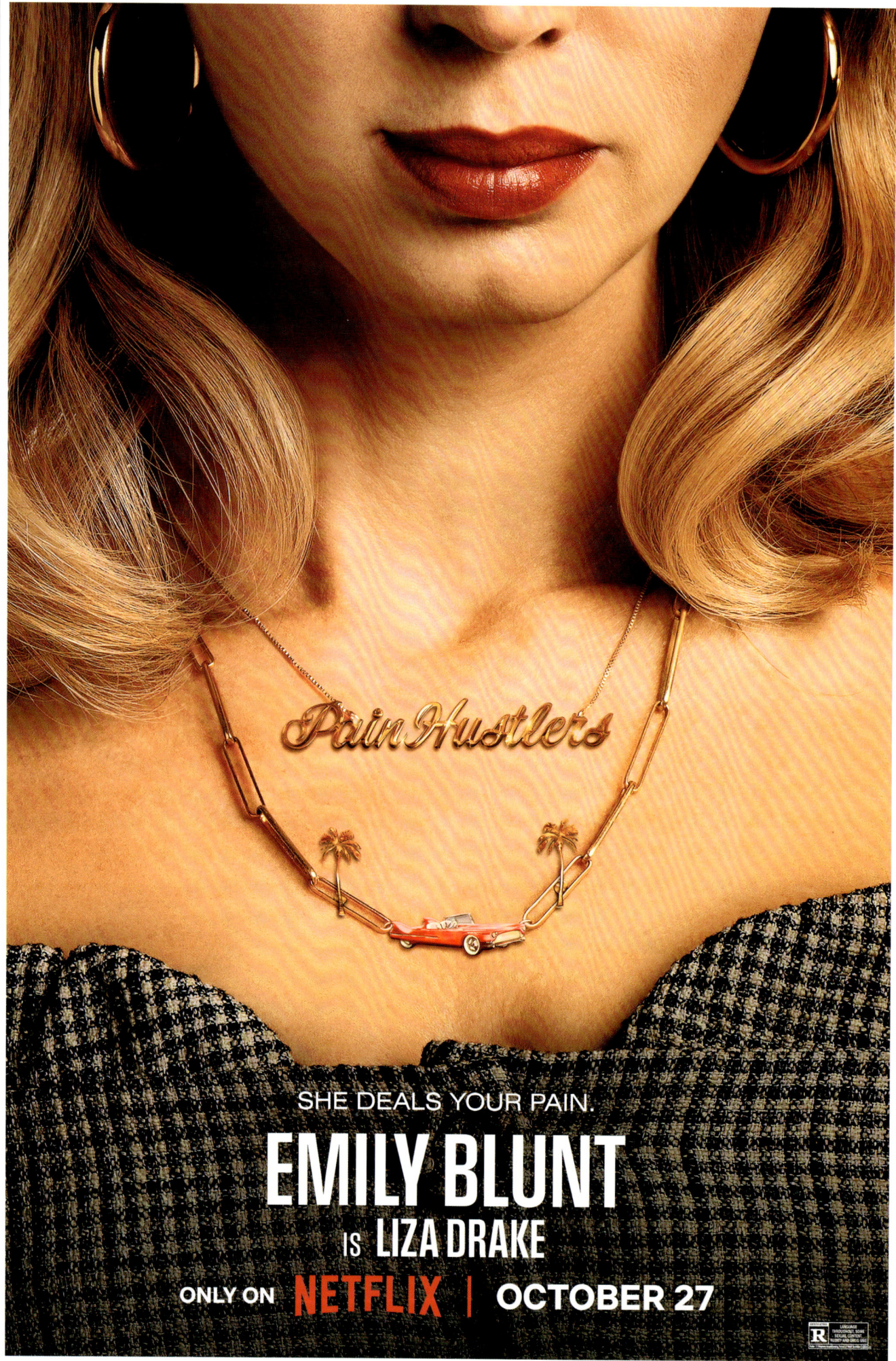

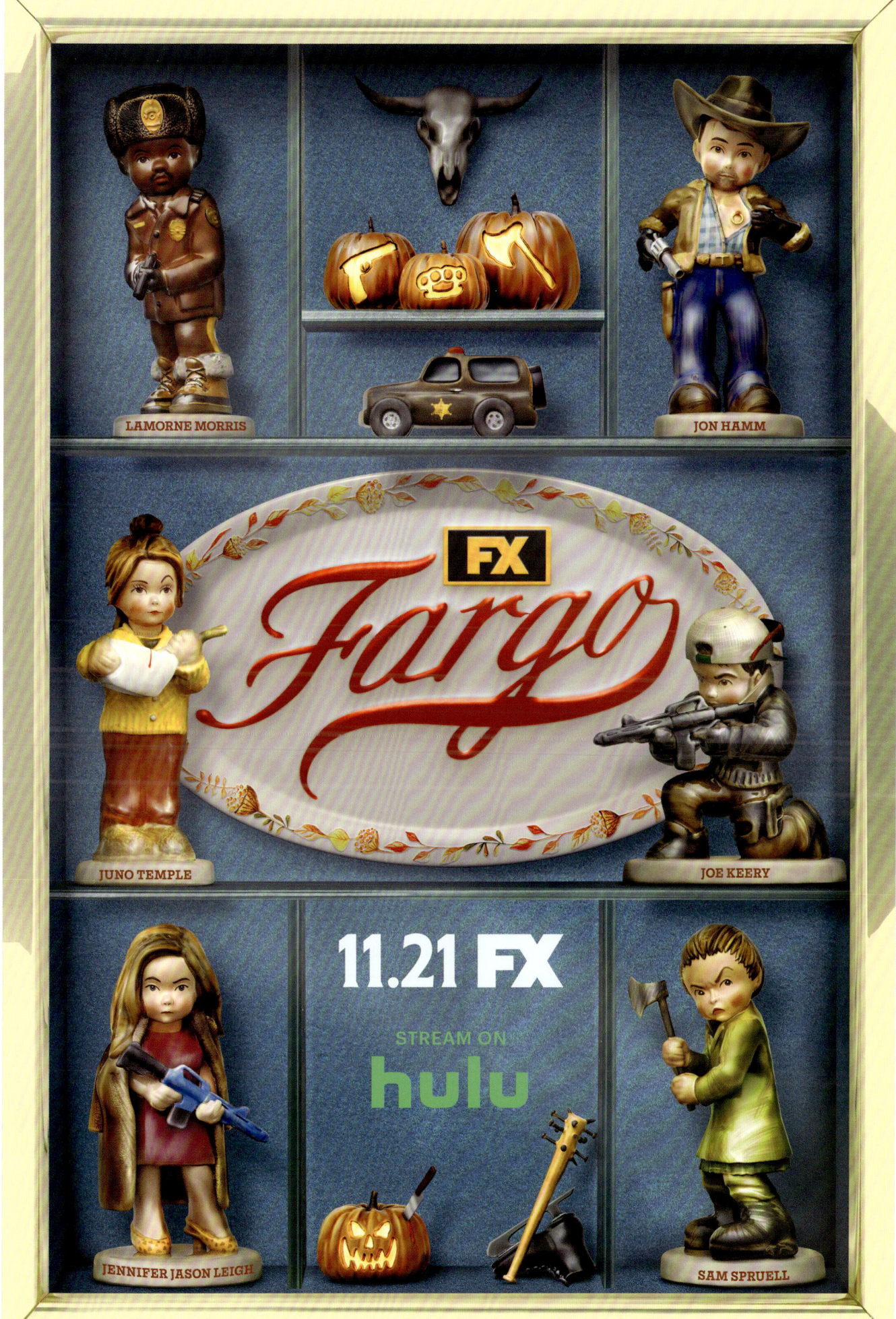

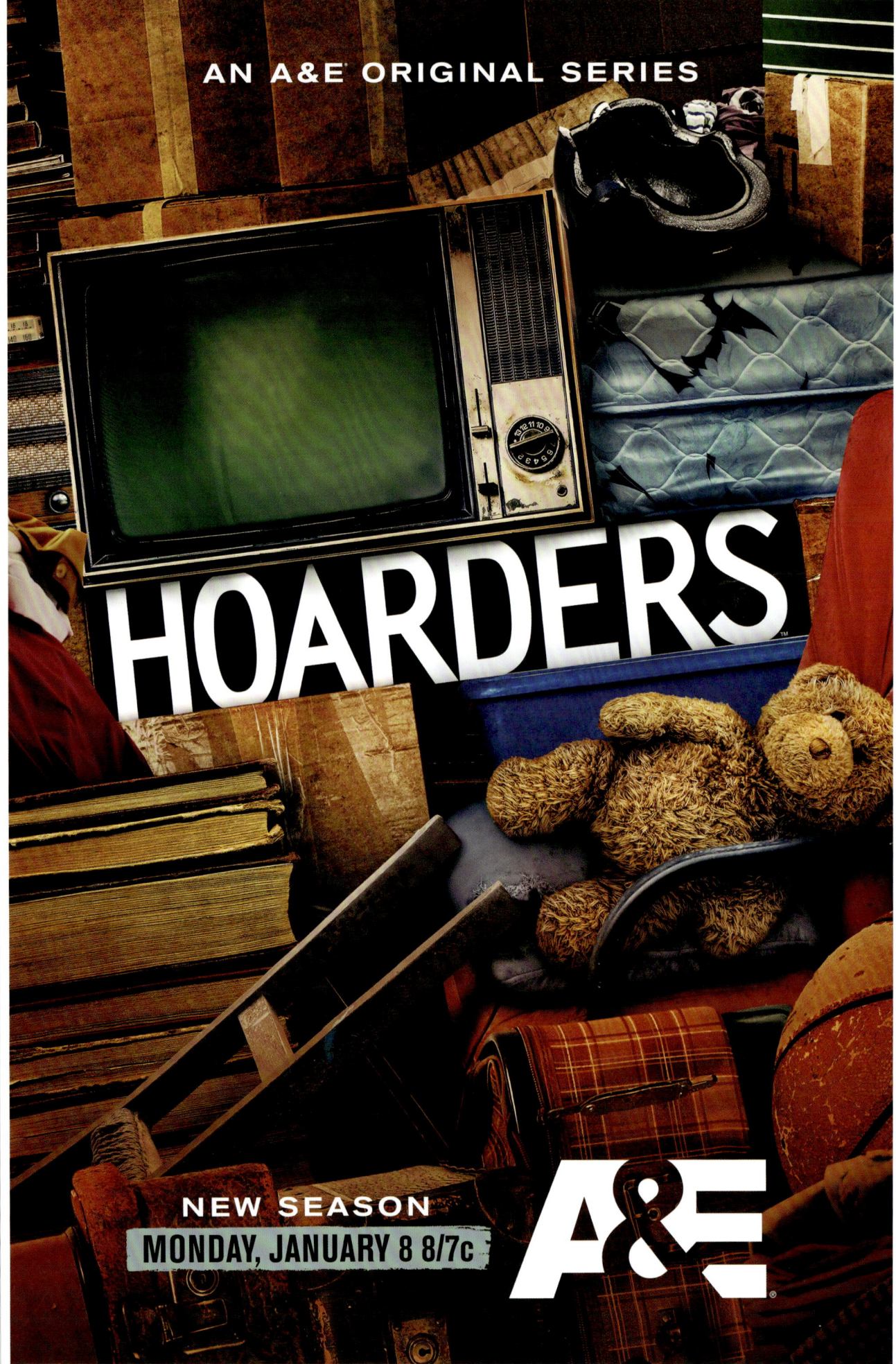

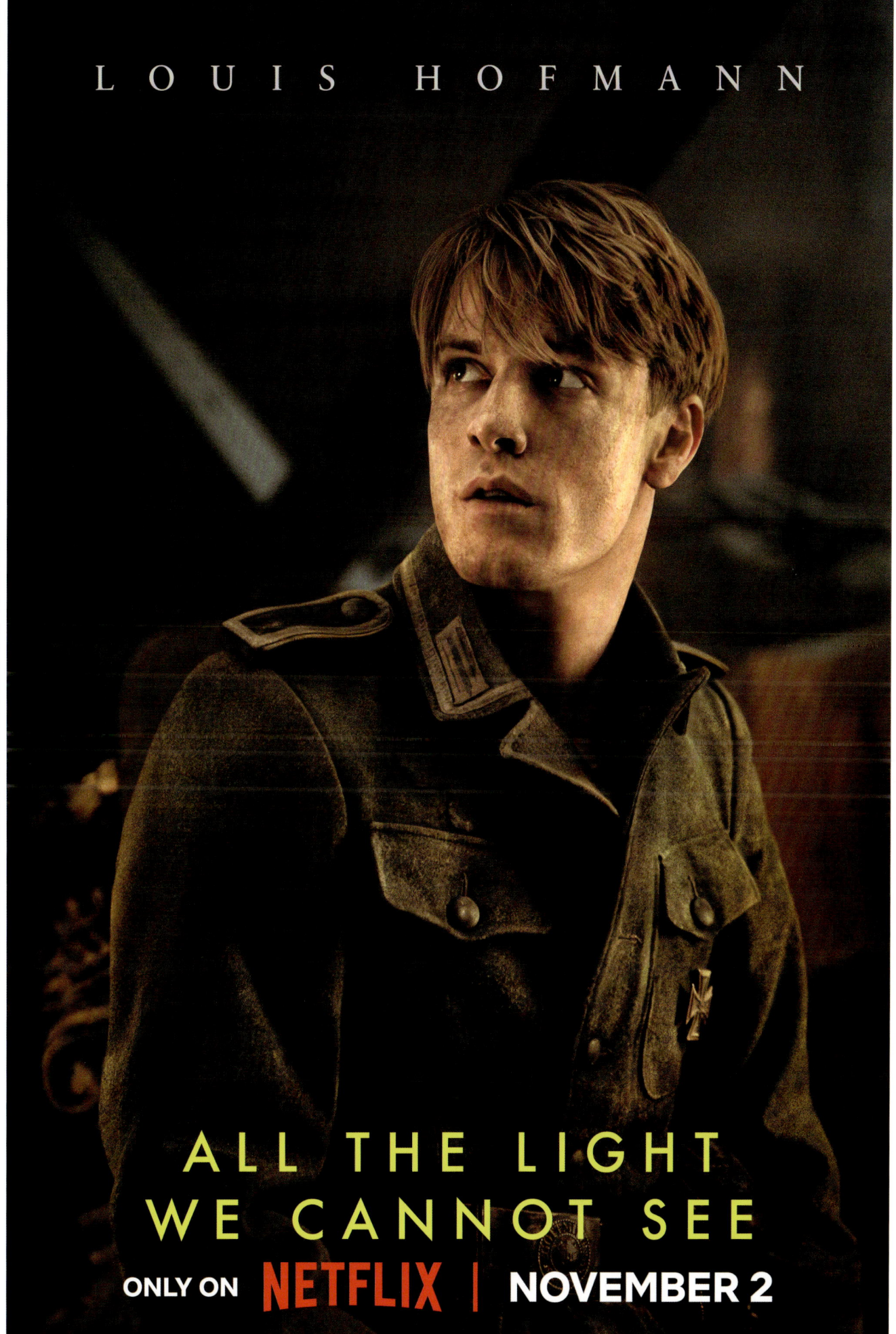

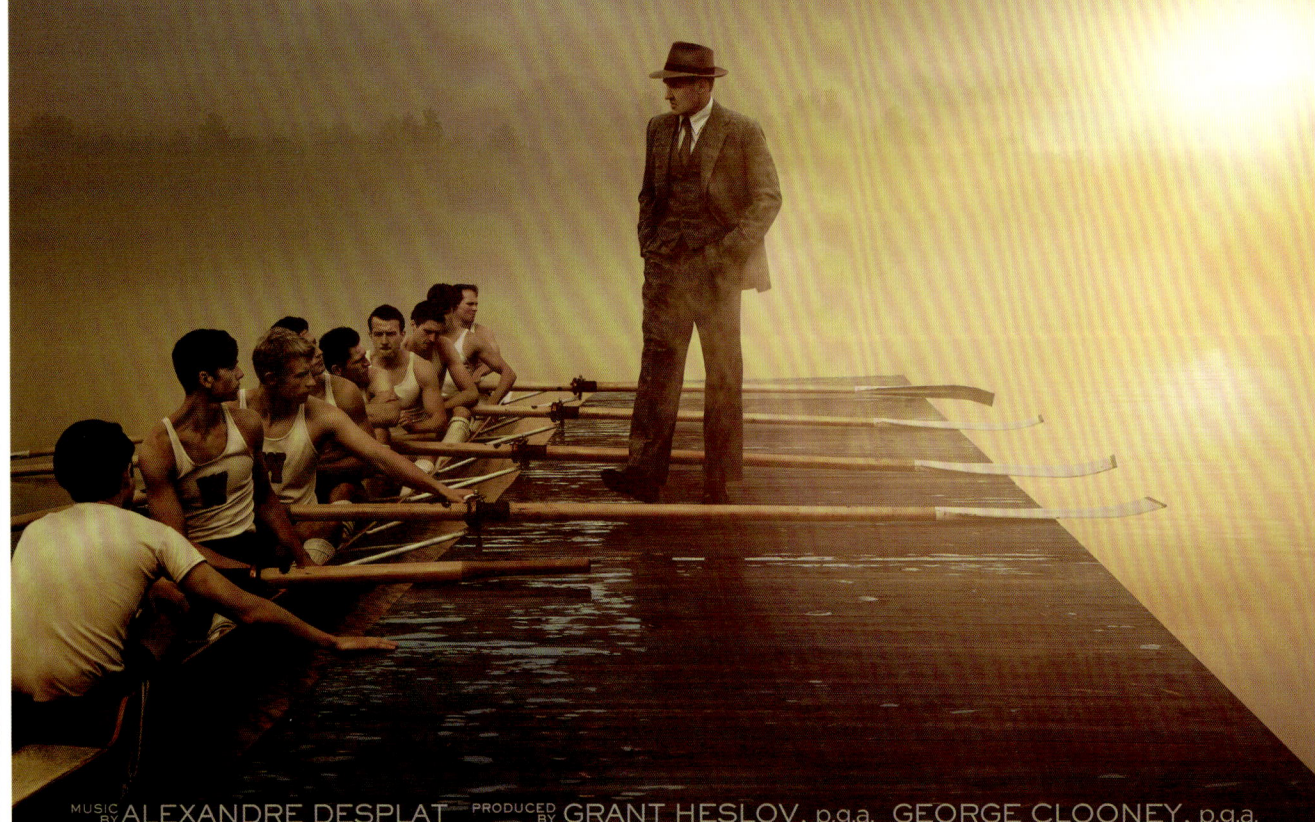

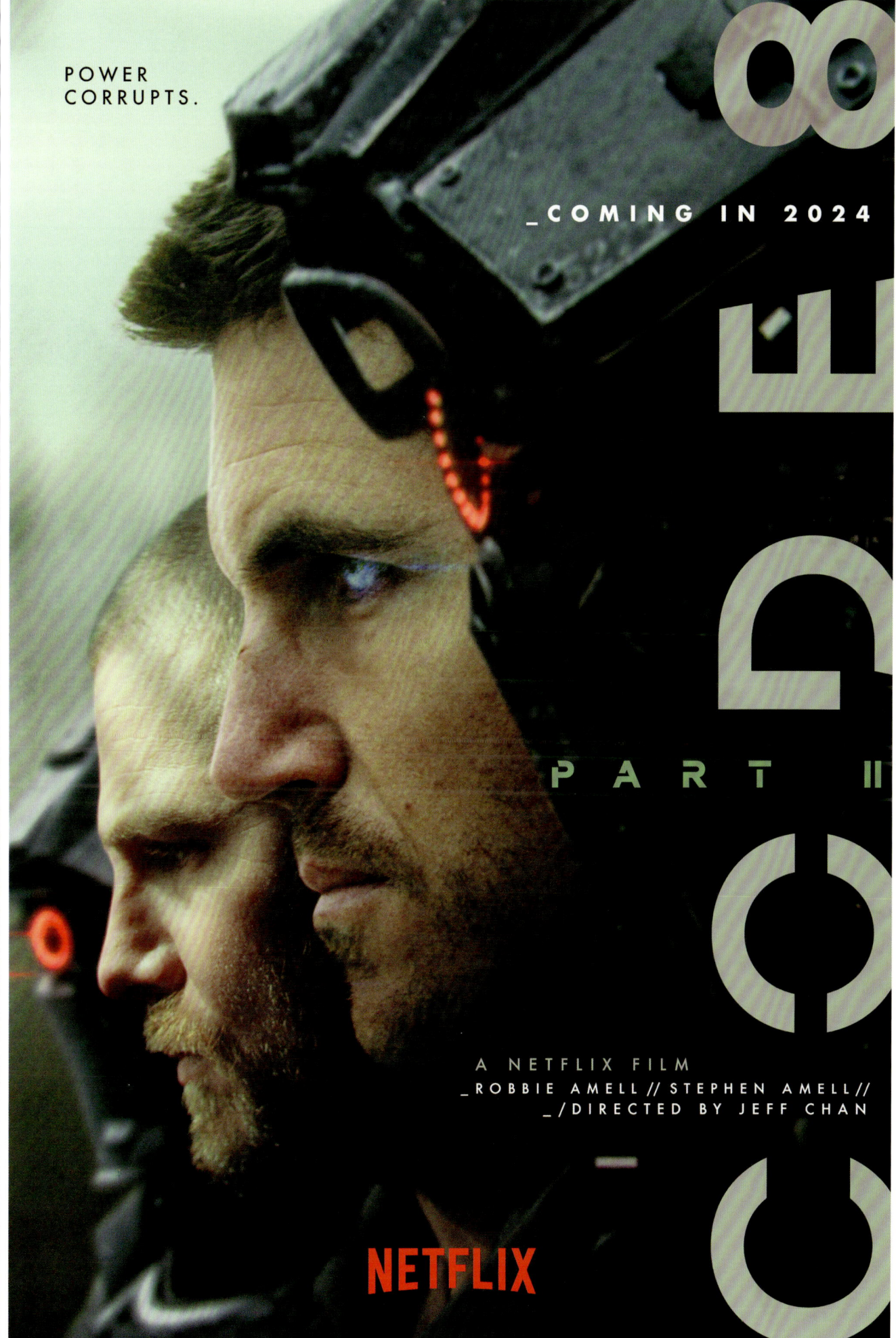

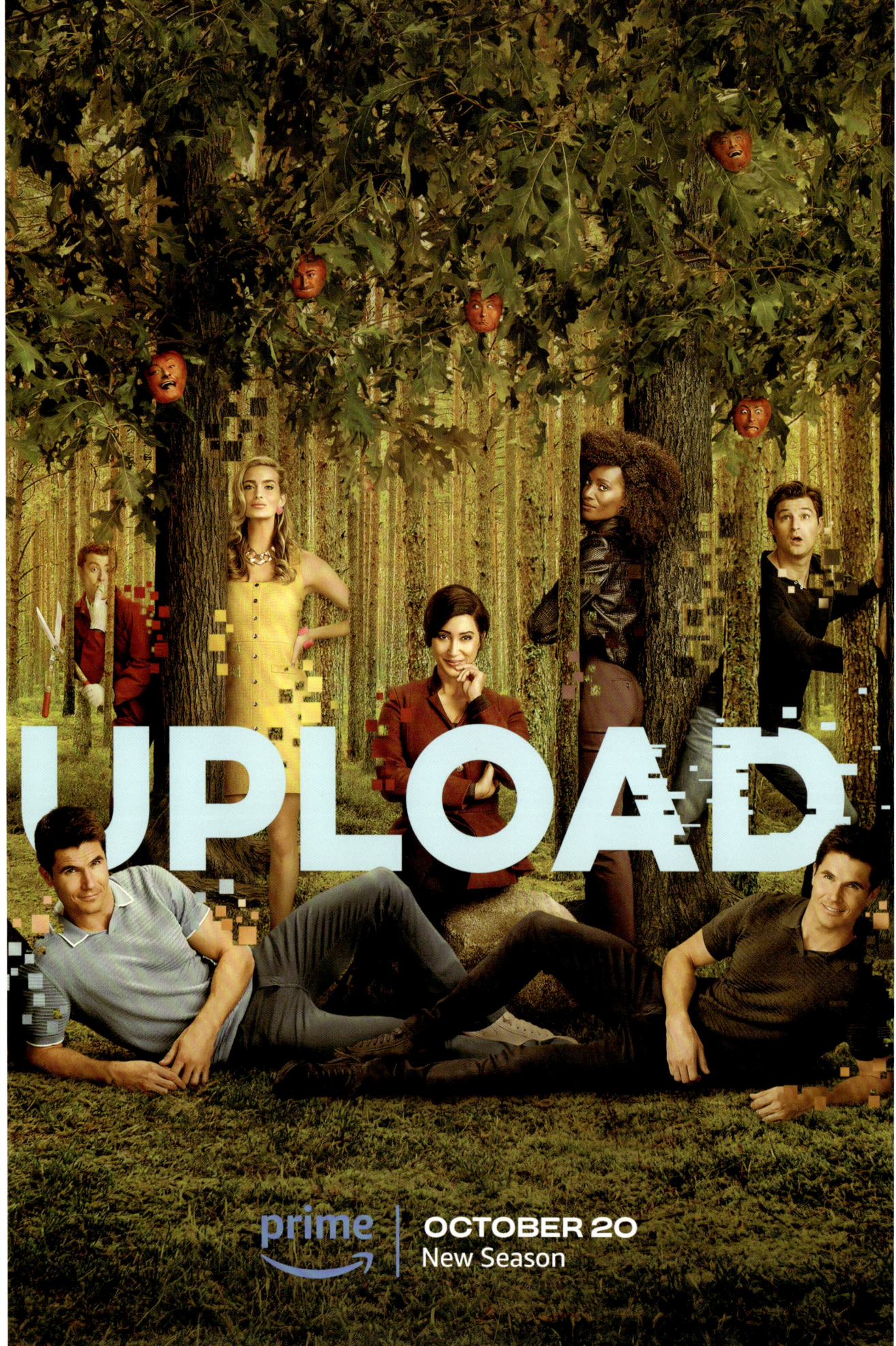

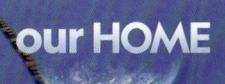

Title: Secrets of the Octopus | Clients: National Geographic, Chris Spencer, Brian Everett, Mariano Barreiro, Leah Wojda
Design Firm: SJI Associates | P233: Credit & Commentary

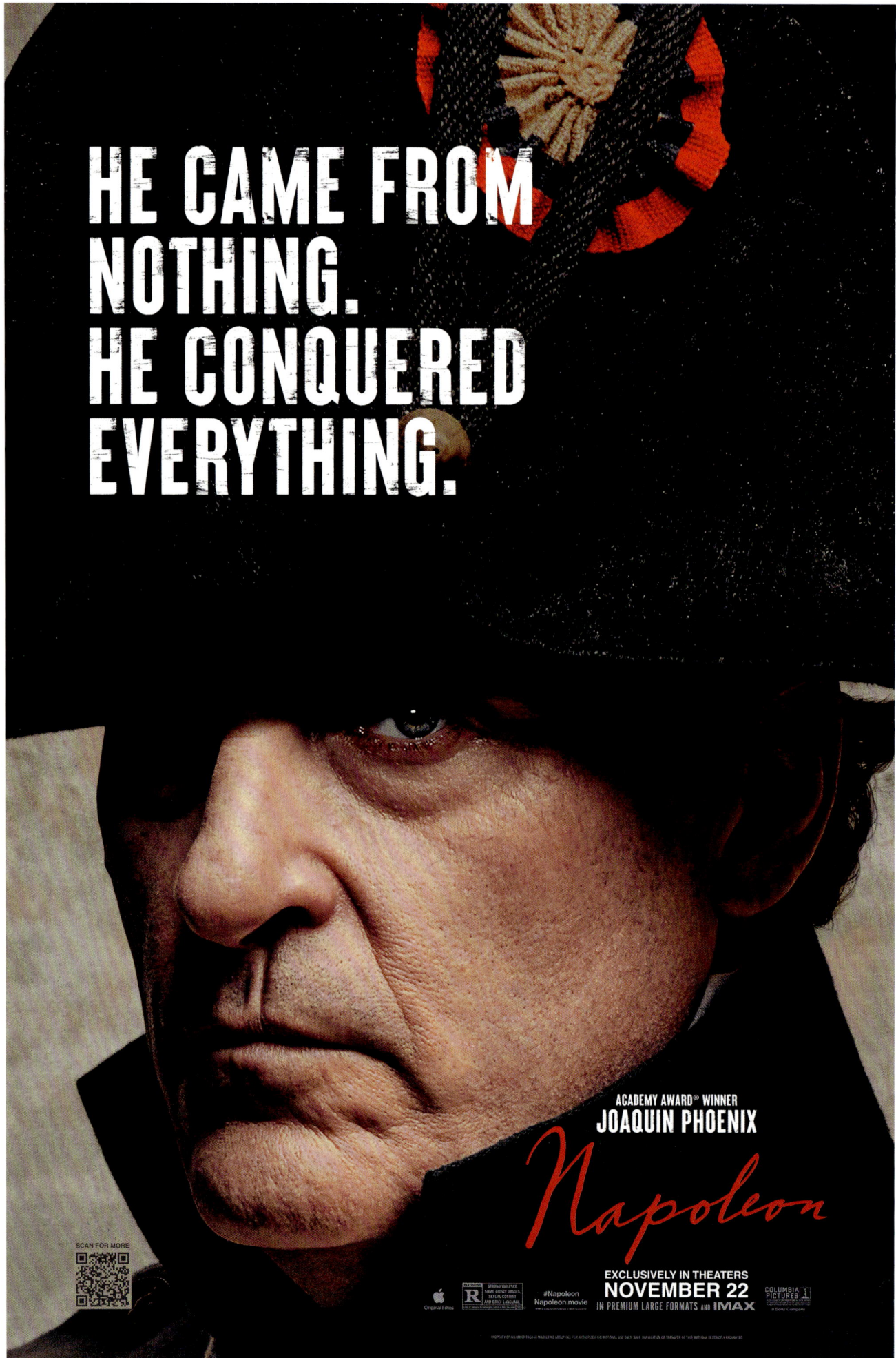

Title: Napoleon | Clients: Apple TV+, Sony Pictures Entertainment
Design Firm: The Refinery | P233: Credit & Commentary

Title: Napoleon | **Clients:** Apple TV+, Sony Pictures Entertainment
Design Firm: The Refinery | P233: Credit & Commentary

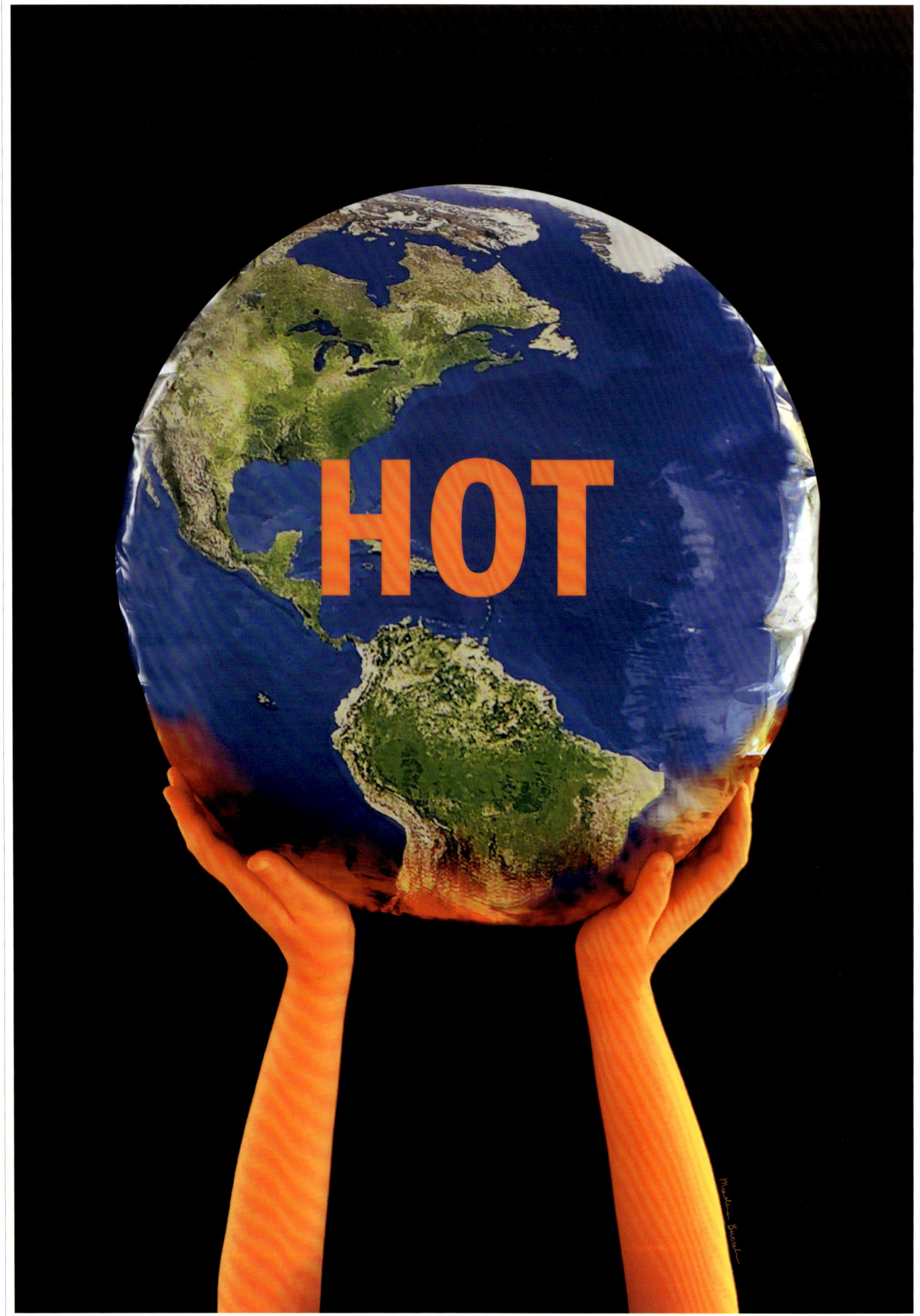

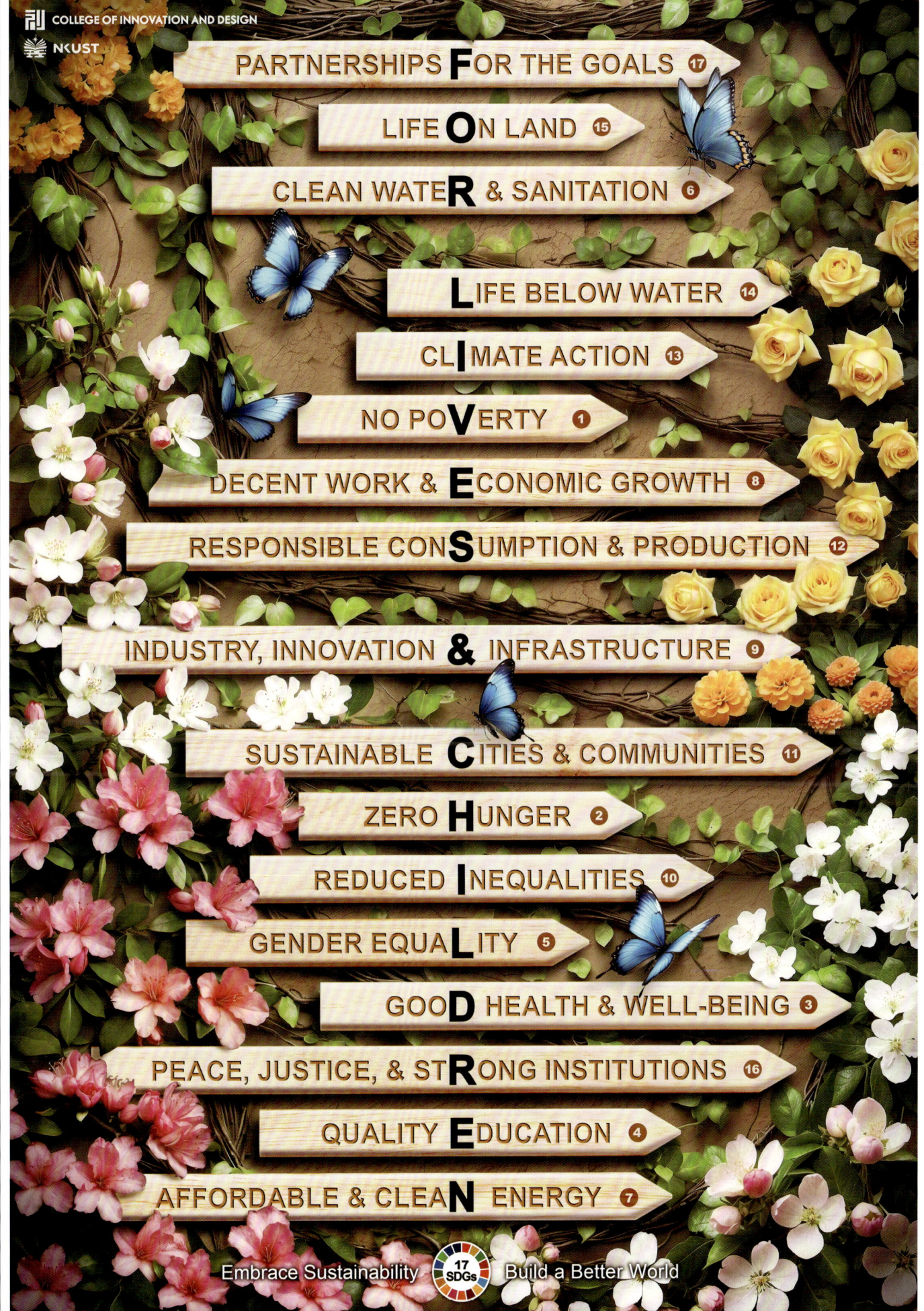

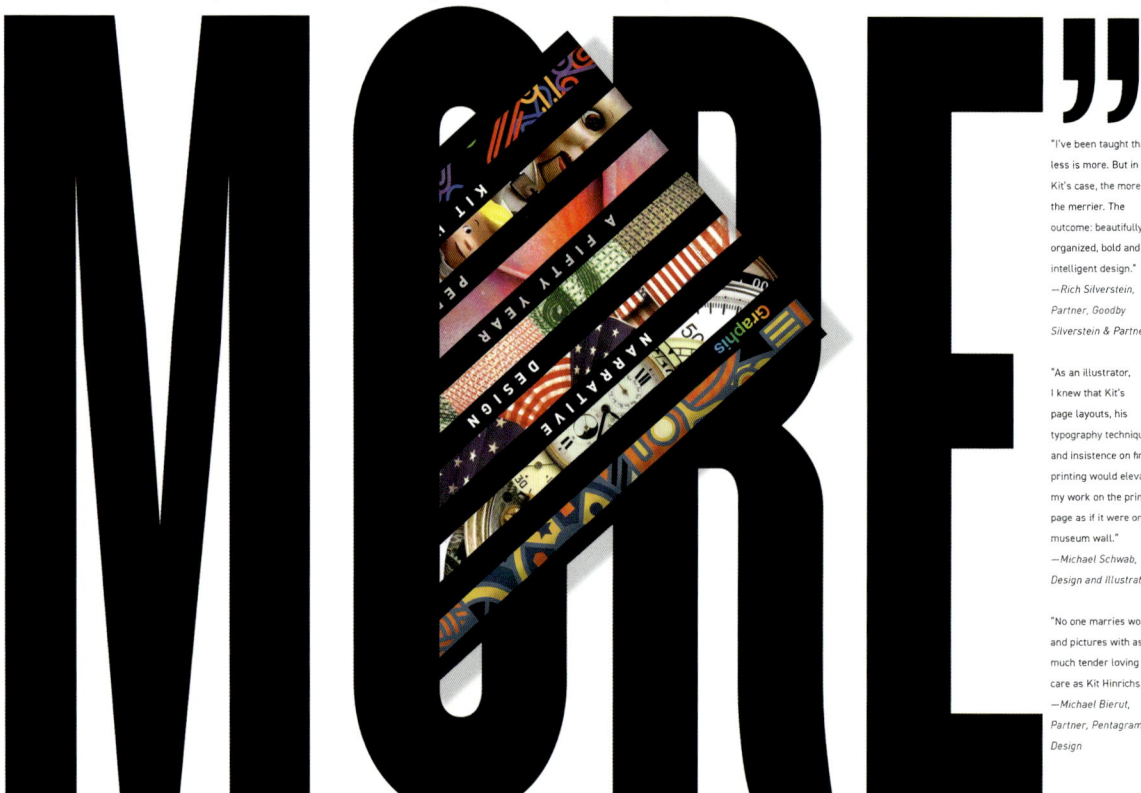

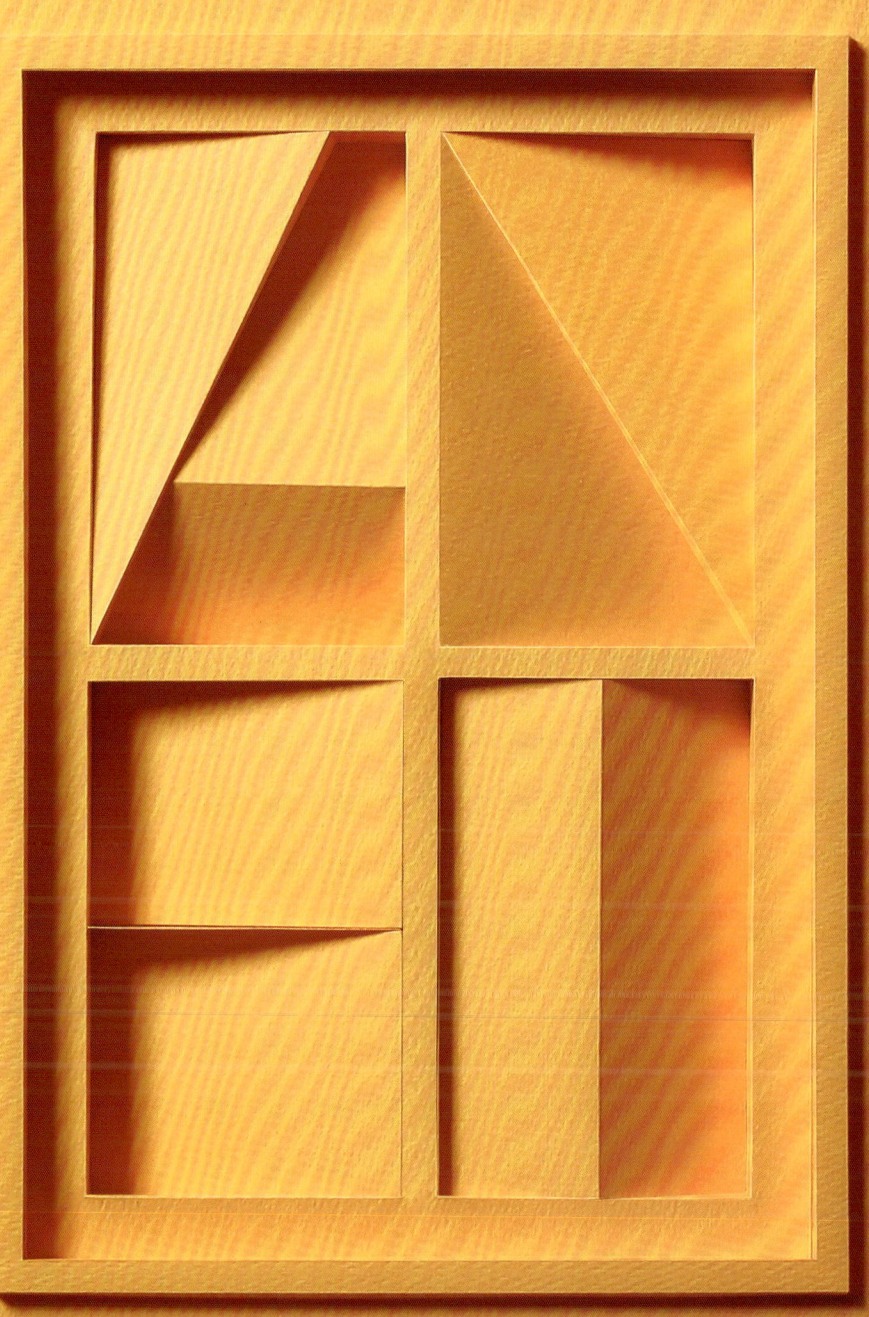

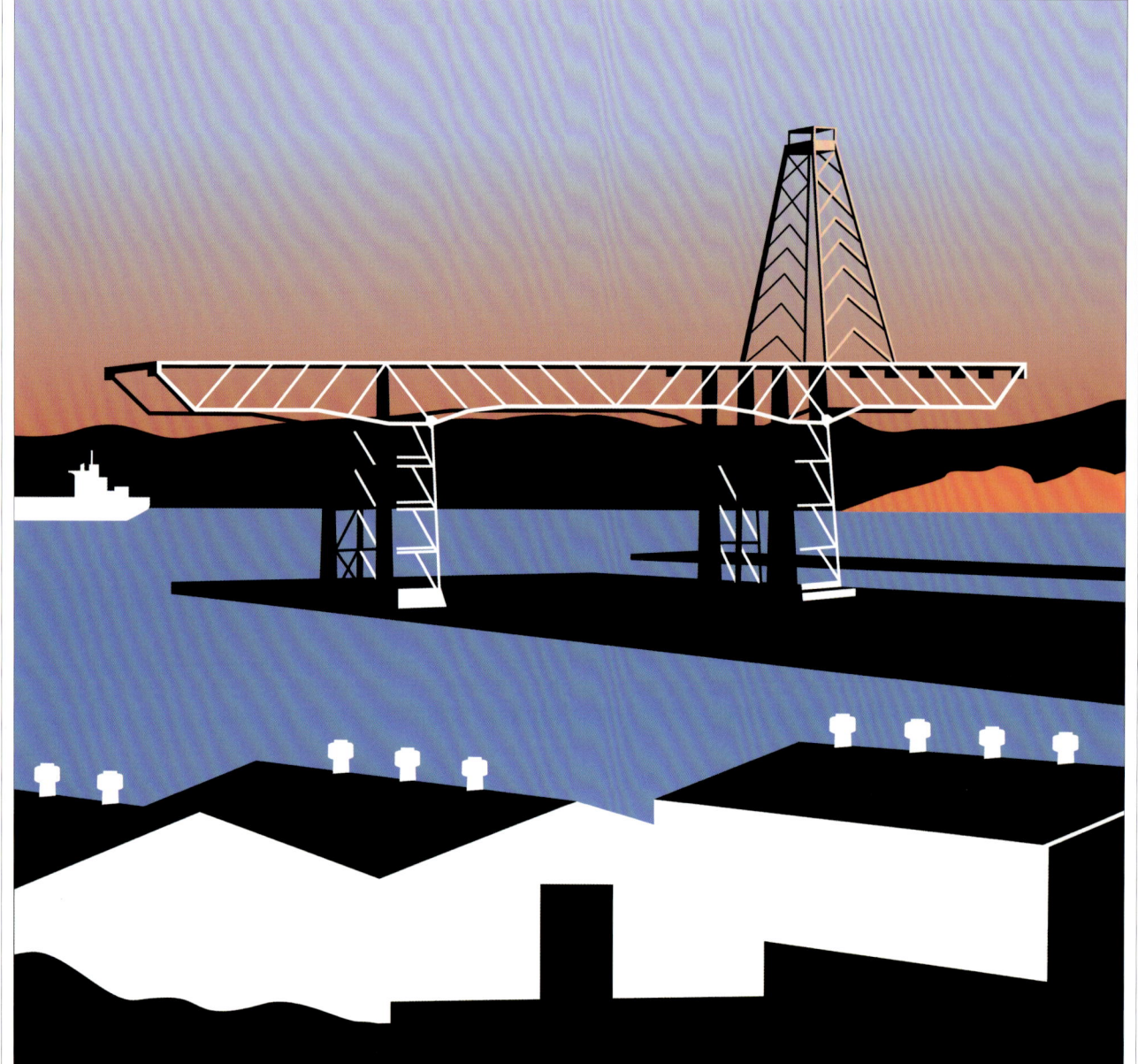

Title: Shipyard Open Studios Spring 2024 | Clients: Shipyard Trust for the Arts, Barbara Ockel
Design Firm: Craig-Teerlink Design | P233: Credit & Commentary

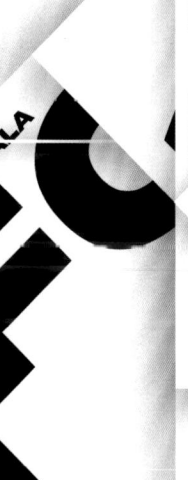

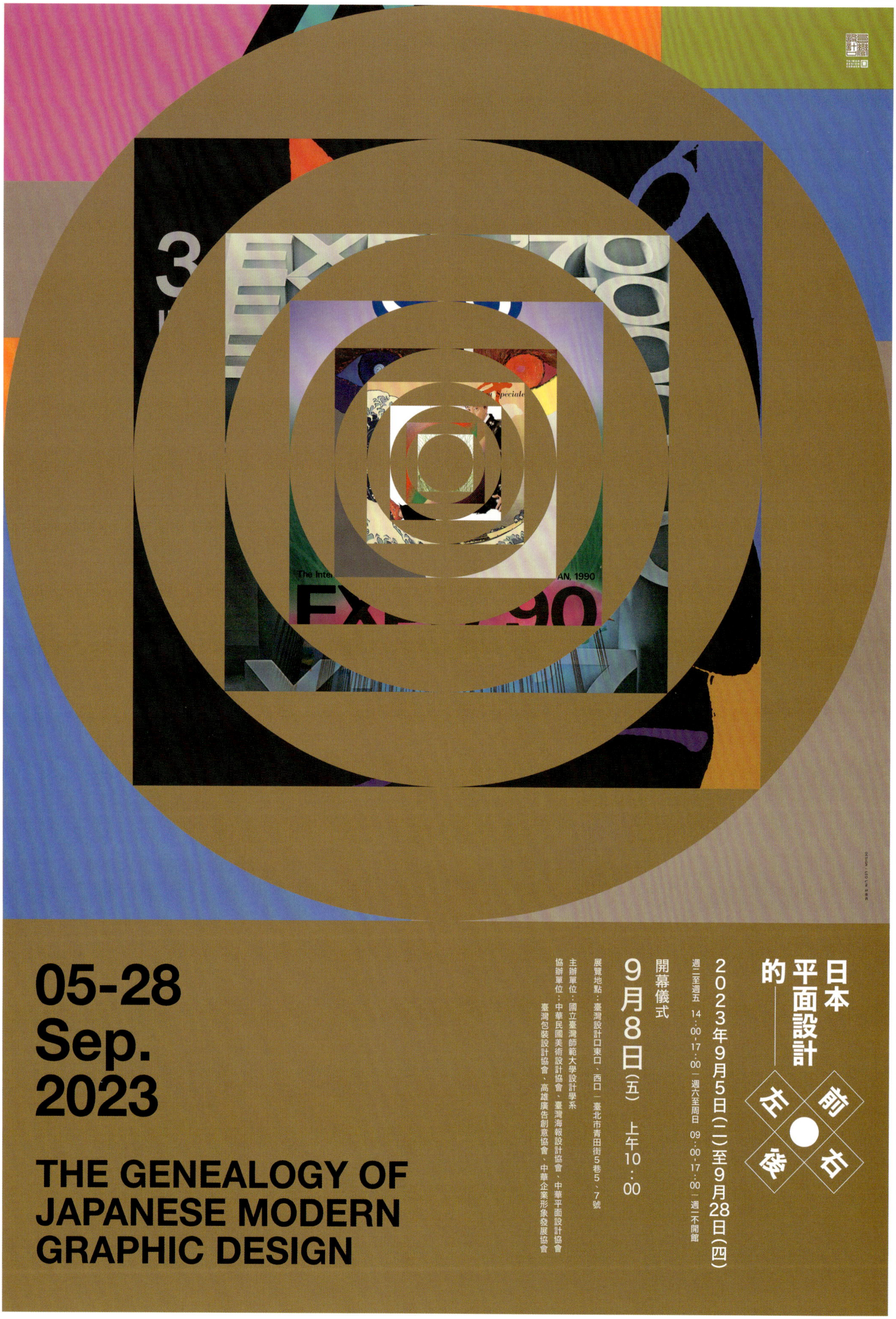

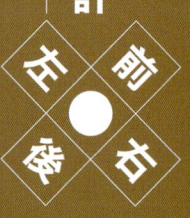

Title: The Genealogy of Japanese Graphic Design | Client: National Taiwan Normal University Department of Design
Design Firm: Leo Lin Design | P234: Credit & Commentary

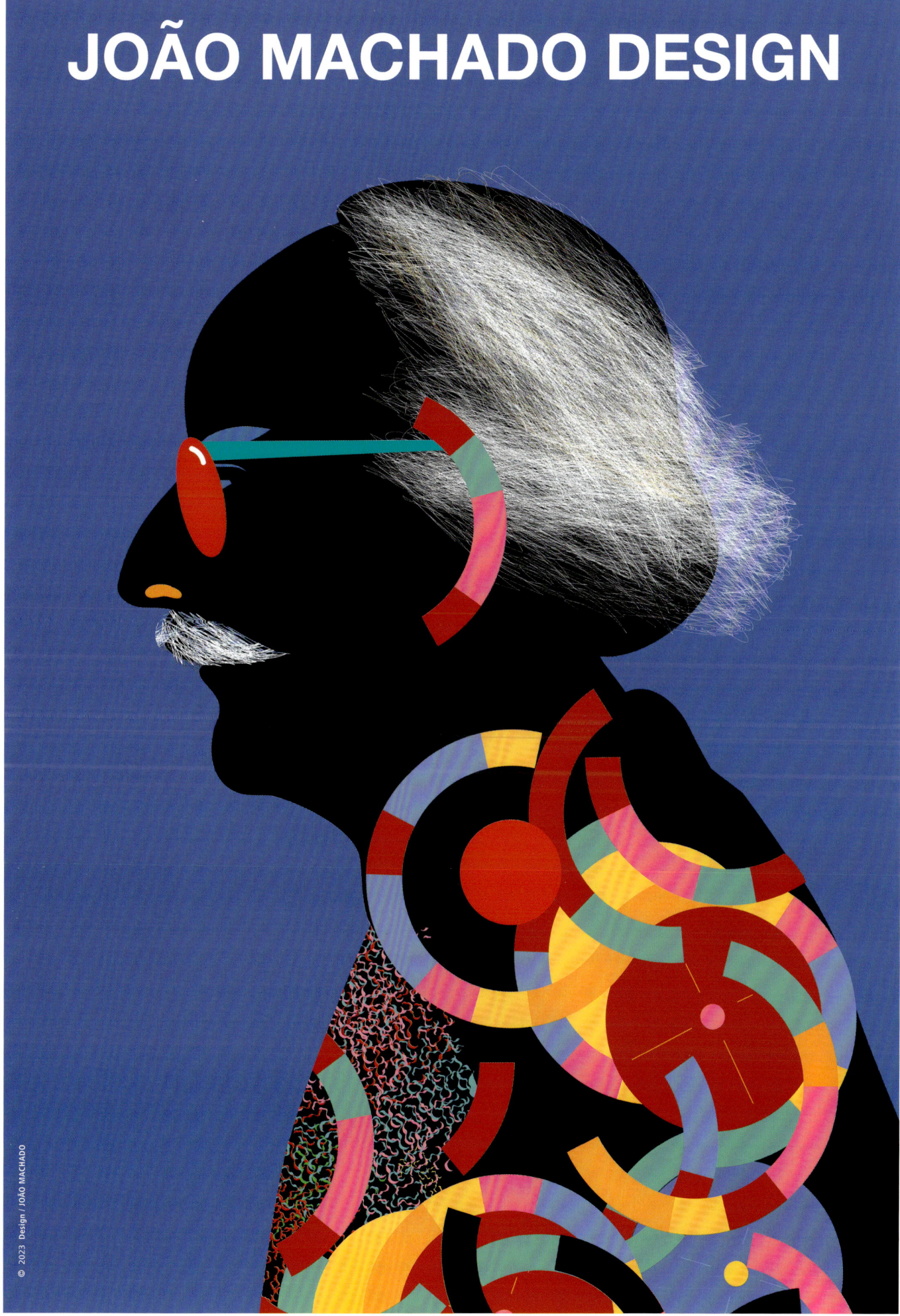

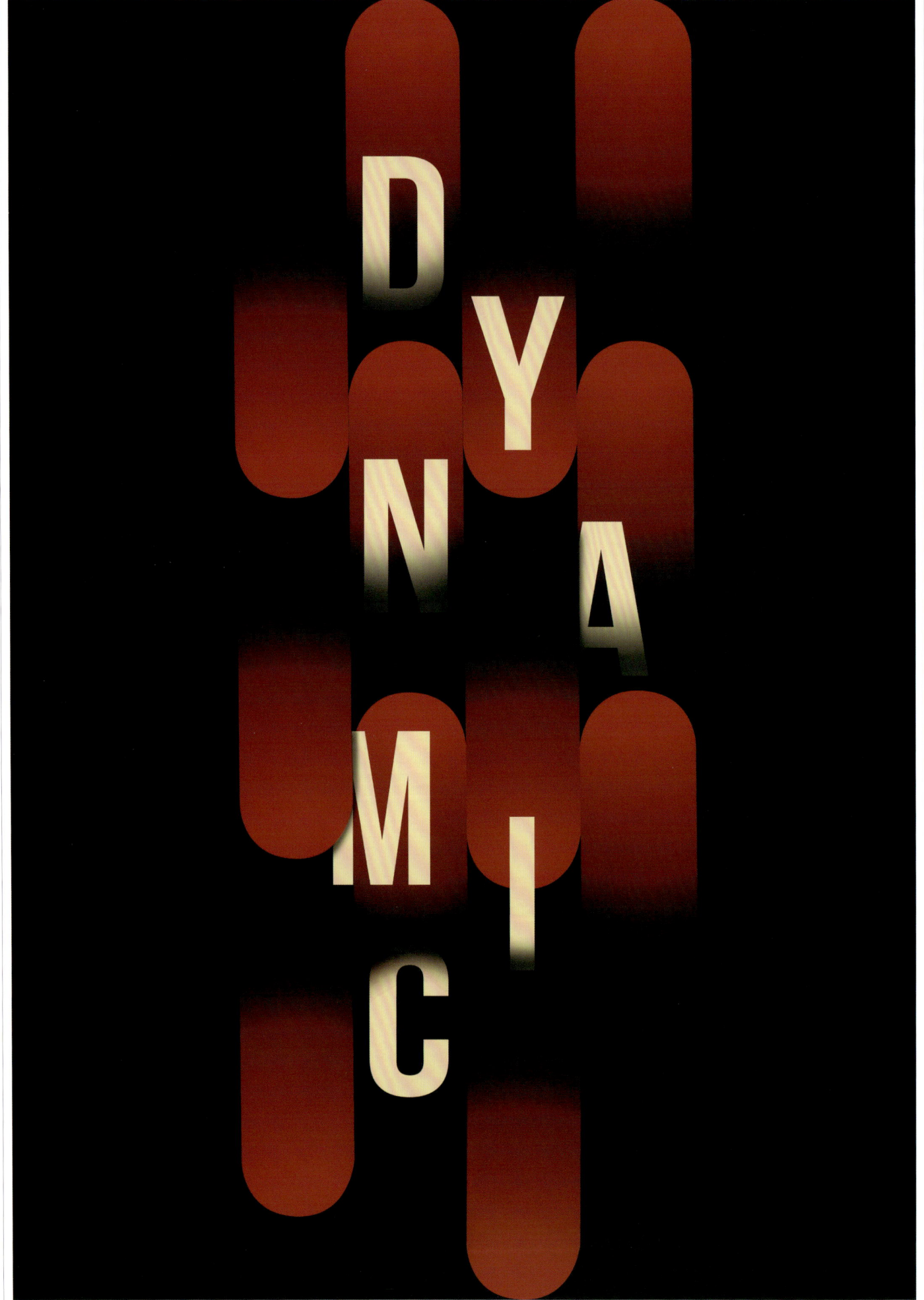

Title: Dynamic | Client: CEIDA (Chinese Europe International Design Culture Association)
Design Firm: Carmit Design Studio | P234: Credit & Commentary

75 HAJIME TSUSHIMA GOLD   EXHIBITS

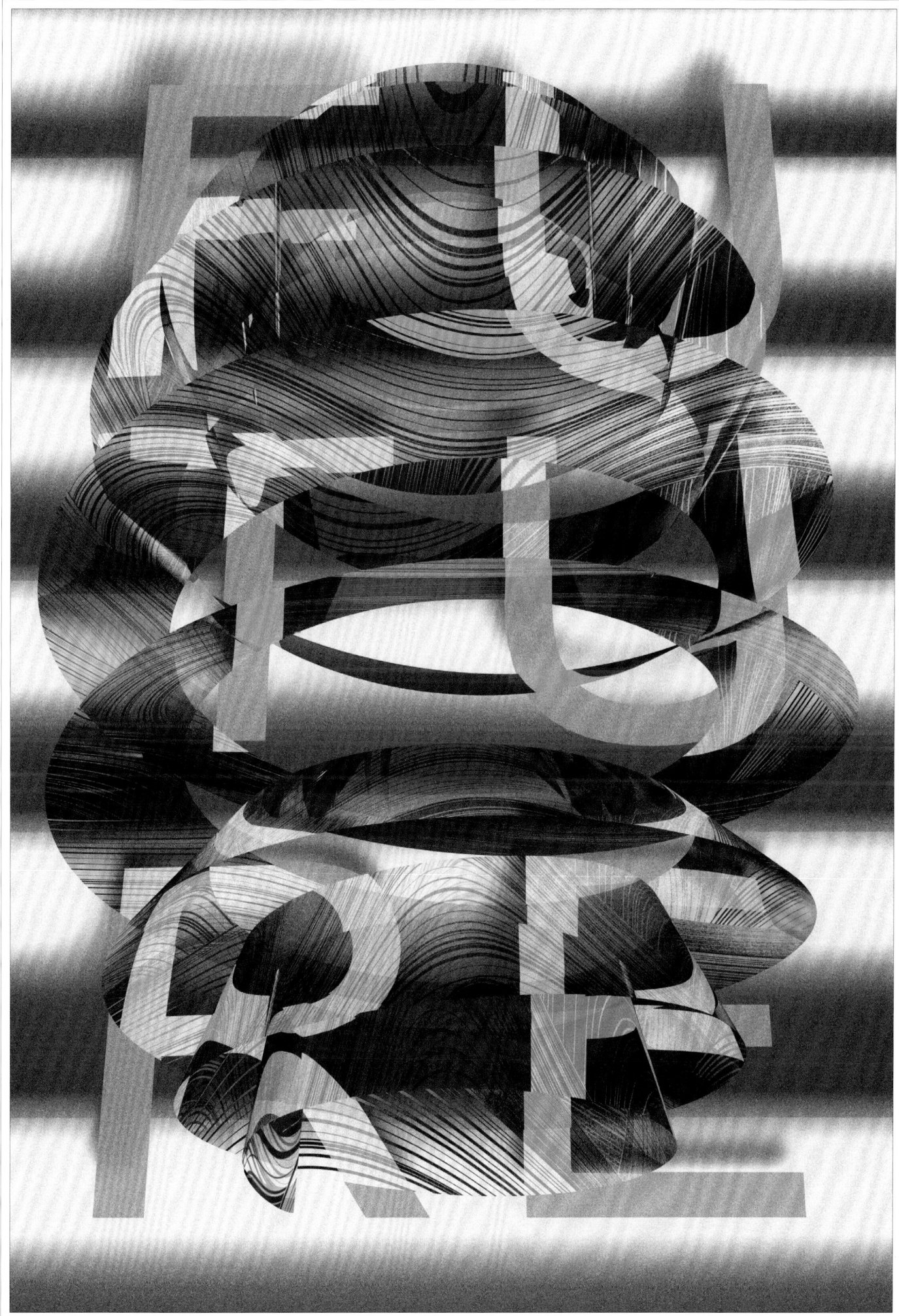

Title: FUTURE | **Client:** Osaka Poster Fest | **Design Firm:** Tsushima Design

76 JOÃO MACHADO GOLD EXHIBITS

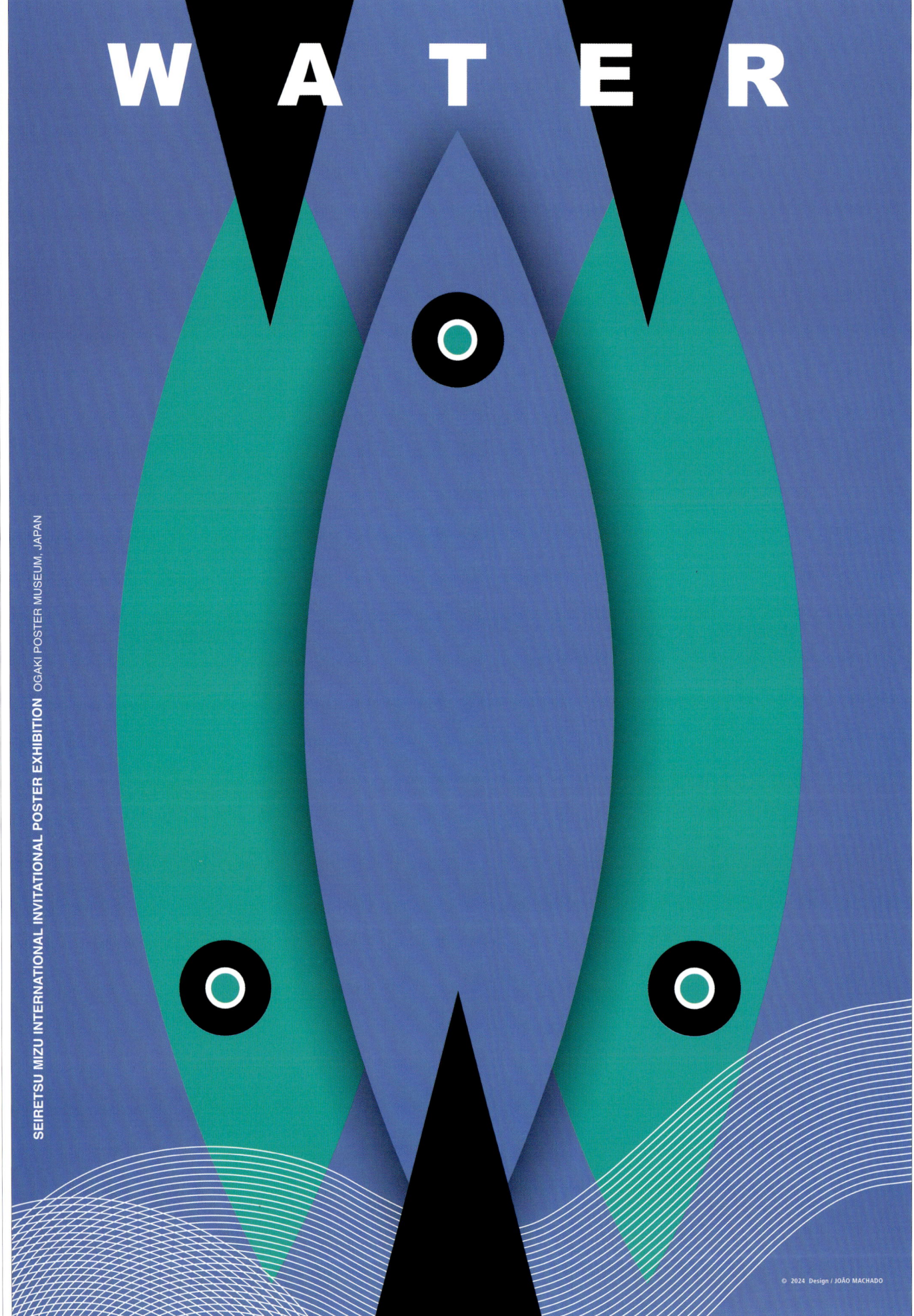

P234: Credit & Commentary **Title:** Water | **Client:** Ogaki Poster Museum | **Design Firm:** João Machado Design

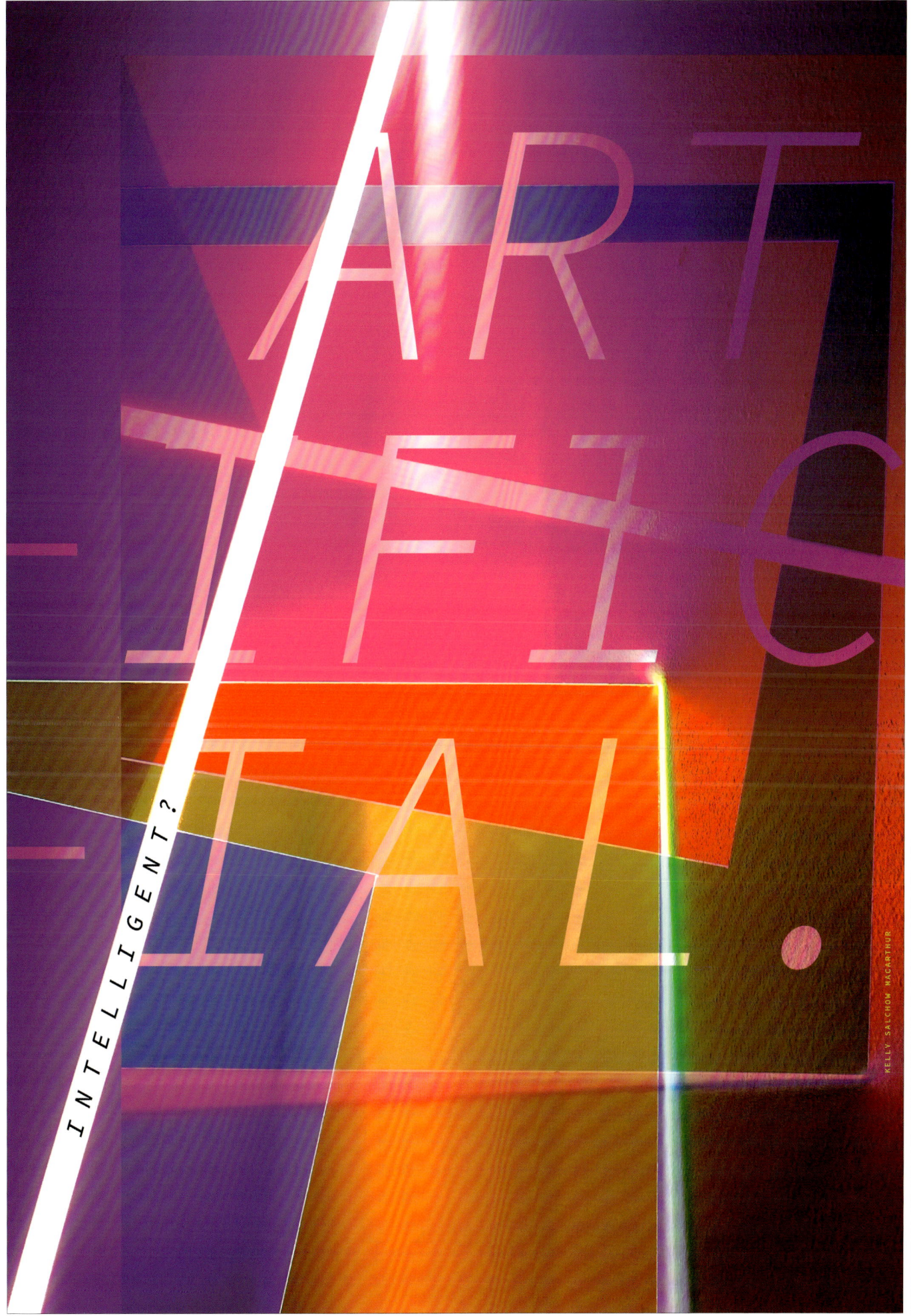

Title: Artificial. Intelligent? | **Client:** 27th BDAK International Exhibition
Design Firm: Elevate Design | **P234:** Credit & Commentary

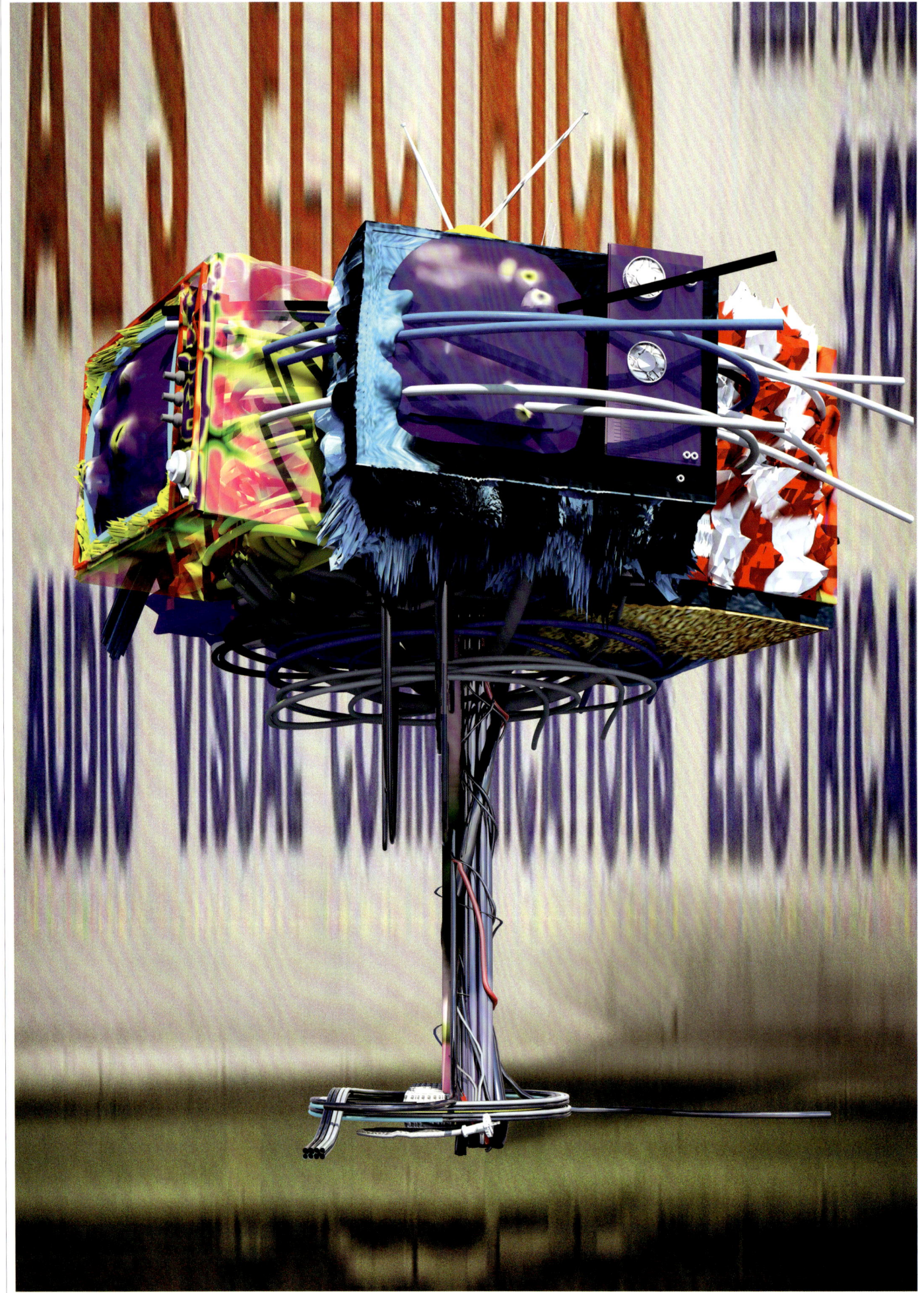

Title: Things You and I Met | Client: Self-initiated | Design Firm: TopLeft LLC

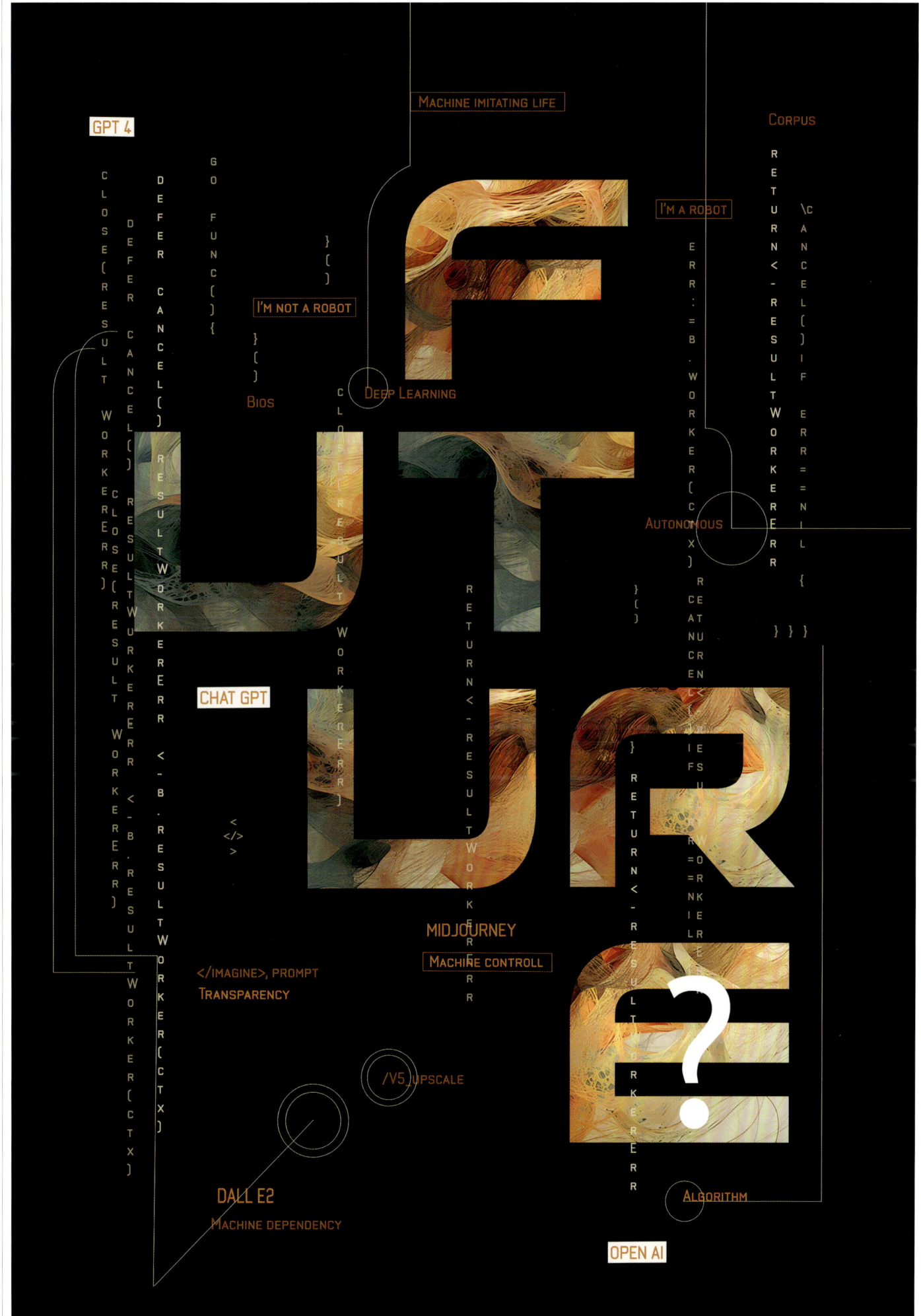

Title: Future? | Client: Osaka Poster Fest | Design Firm: Carmit Design Studio

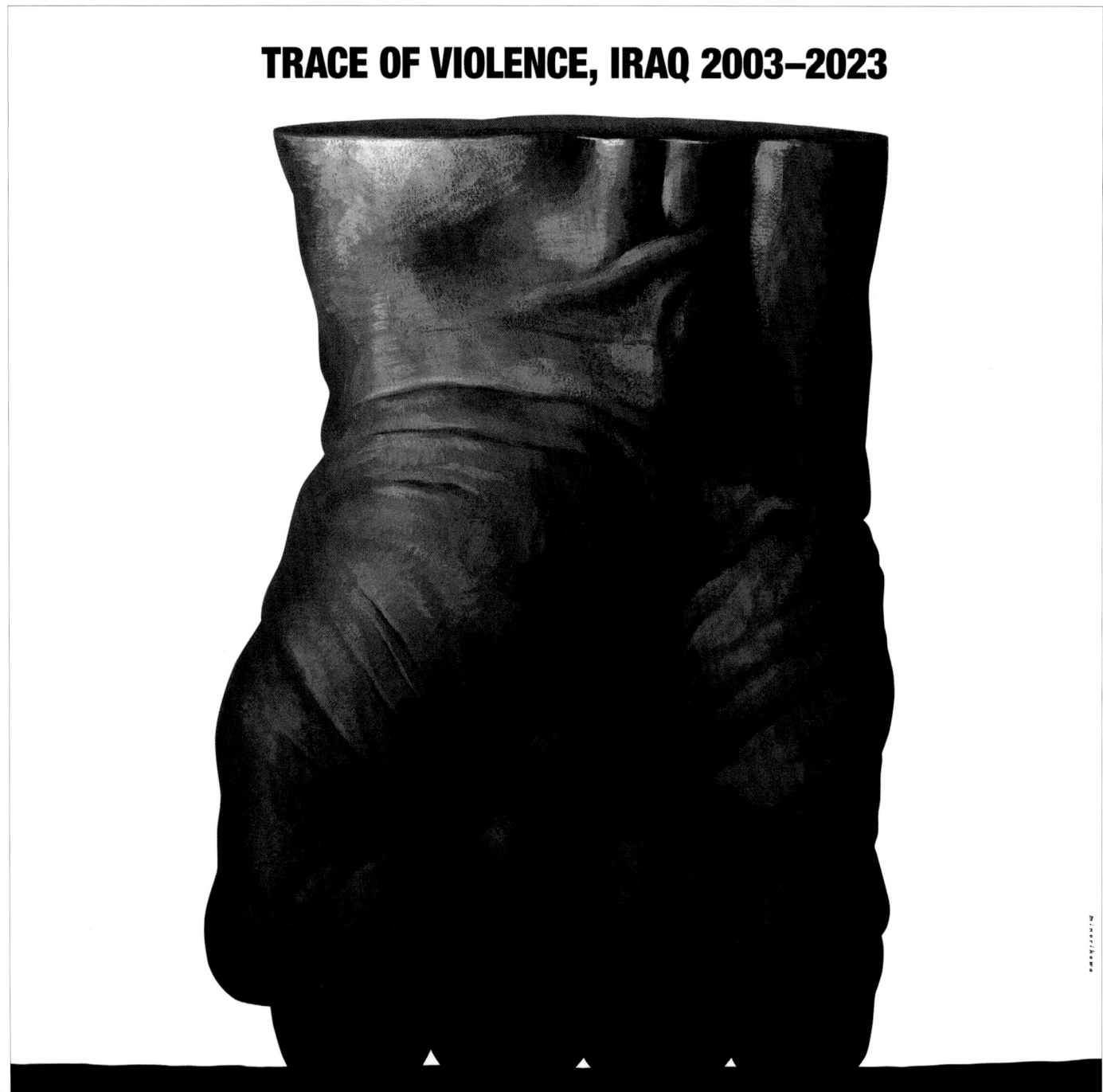

81 LEA HINRICHS, SVEN LINDHORST-EMME, ERKIN KARAMEMET, SOPHIA RICHTER GOLD   EXHIBITS 🇩🇪

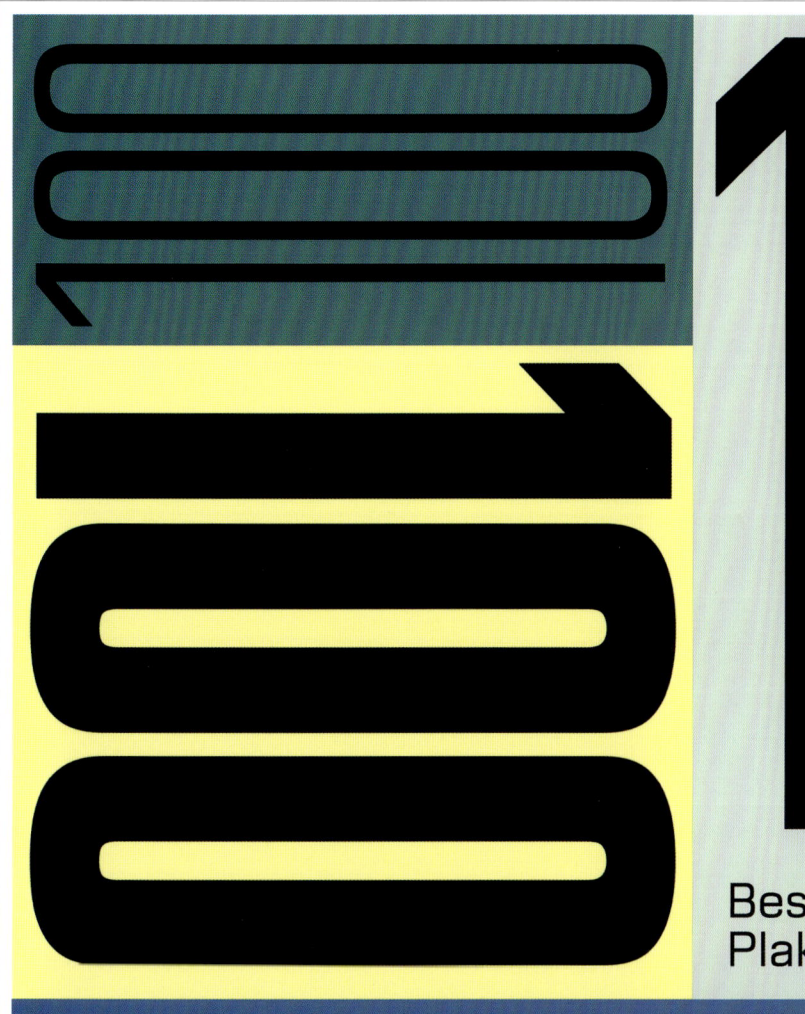

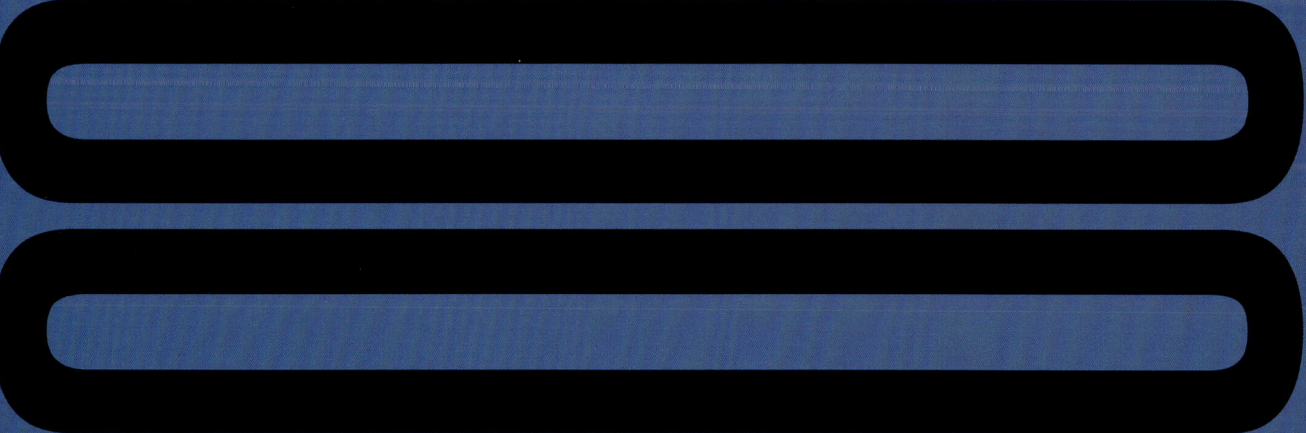
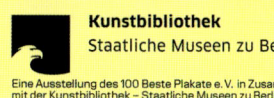
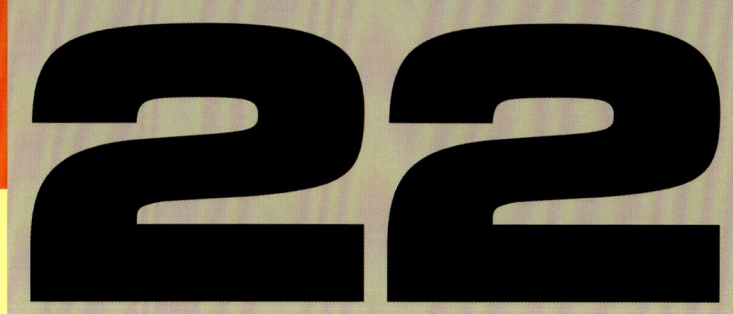

Title: 100 Best Poster 22 (Main Exhibition 2023) | **Client:** 100 Beste Plakate Verein
Design Firm: Studio Lindhorst-Emme+Hinrichs | **P234:** Credit & Commentary

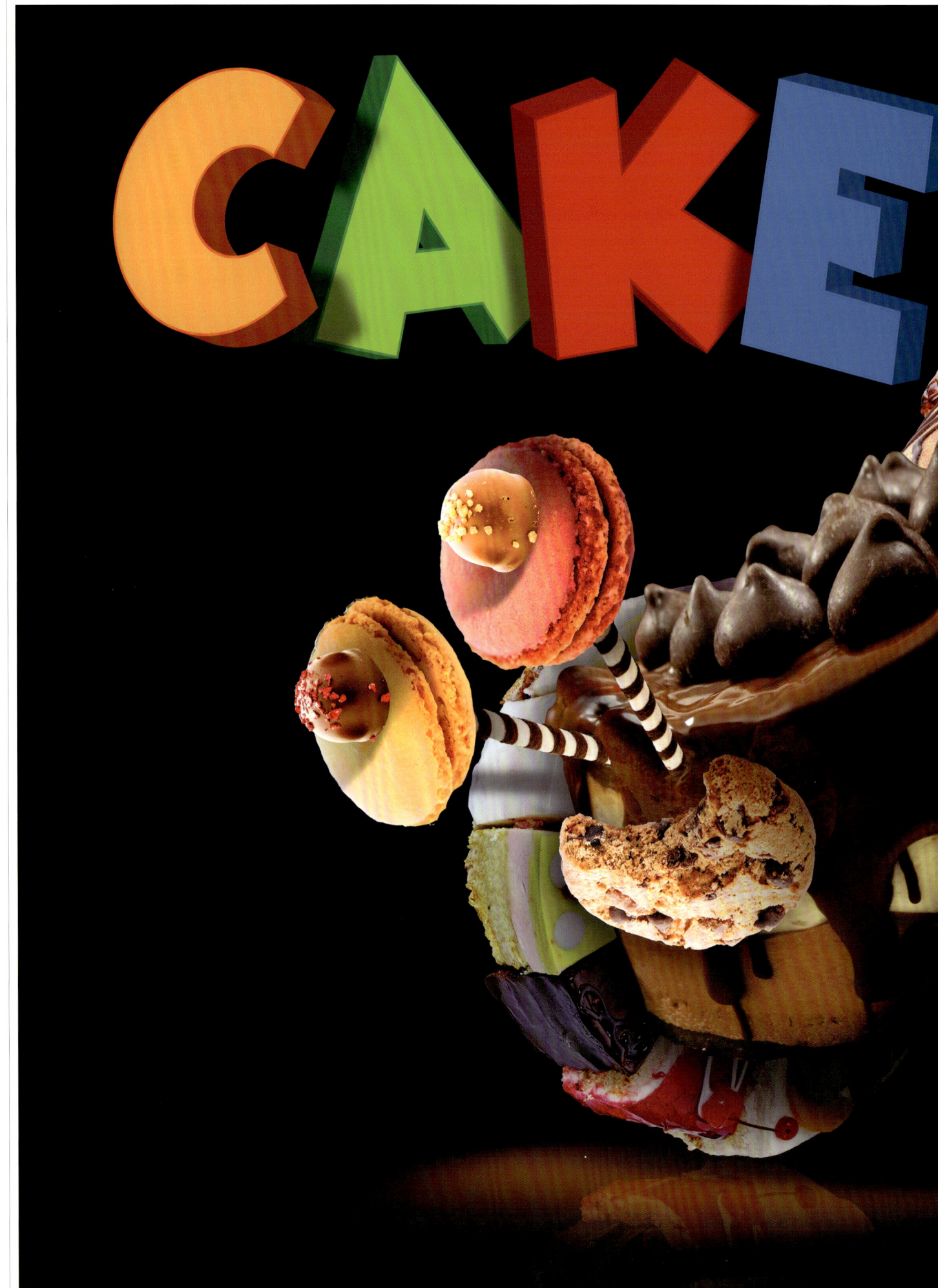

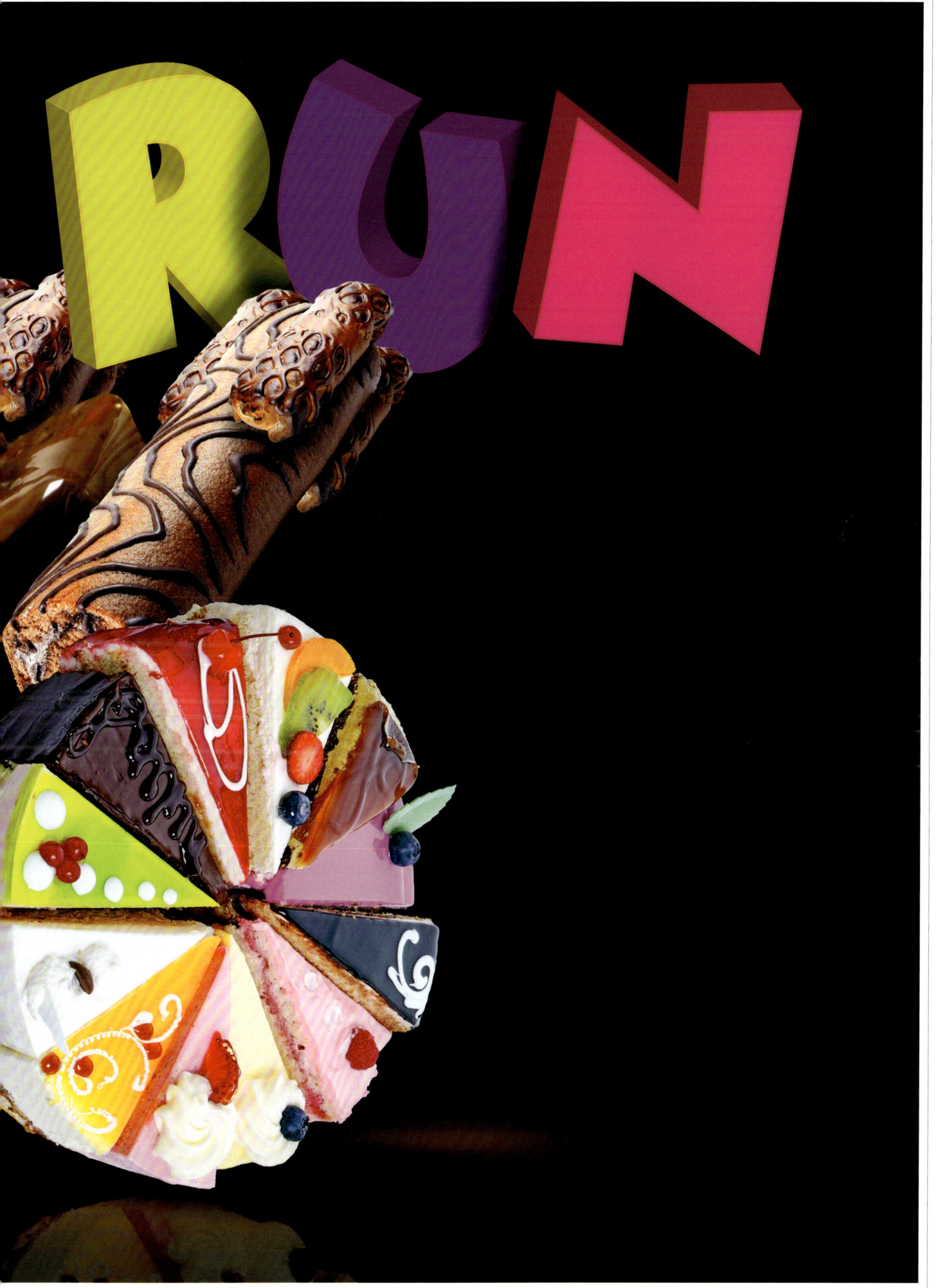

Title: City Tree Annual Festival Cake Run Poster | **Client:** City Tree Christina Schools | **Design Firm:** Freaner Creative & Design

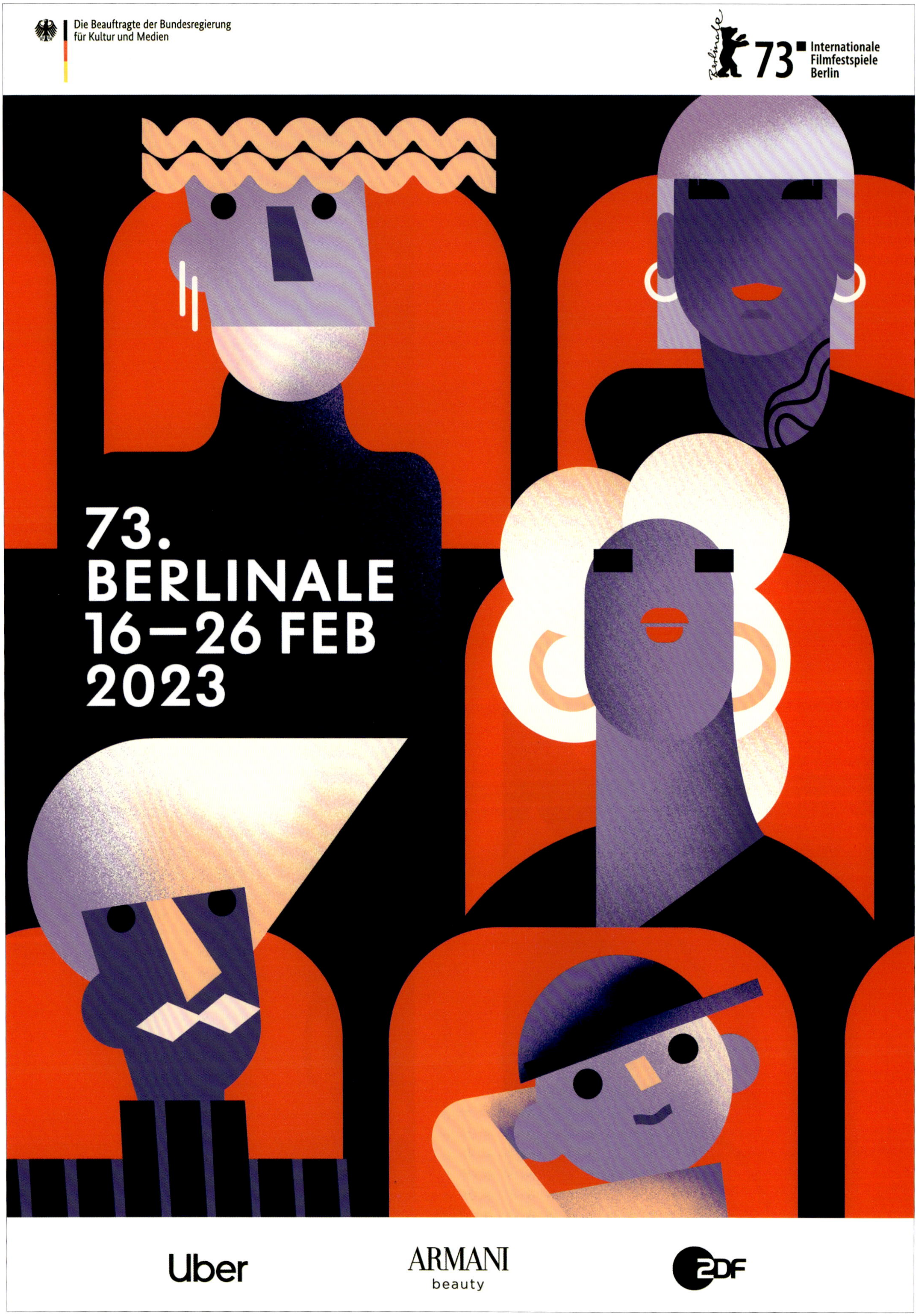

84 CLAUDIA SCHRAMKE GOLD FESTIVALS

Title: 73. BERLINALE – Key Visual and Posters | **Client:** International Film Festival Berlin – Berlinale
Design Firm: Claudia Schramke | **P234:** Credit & Commentary | Image 1 of 7

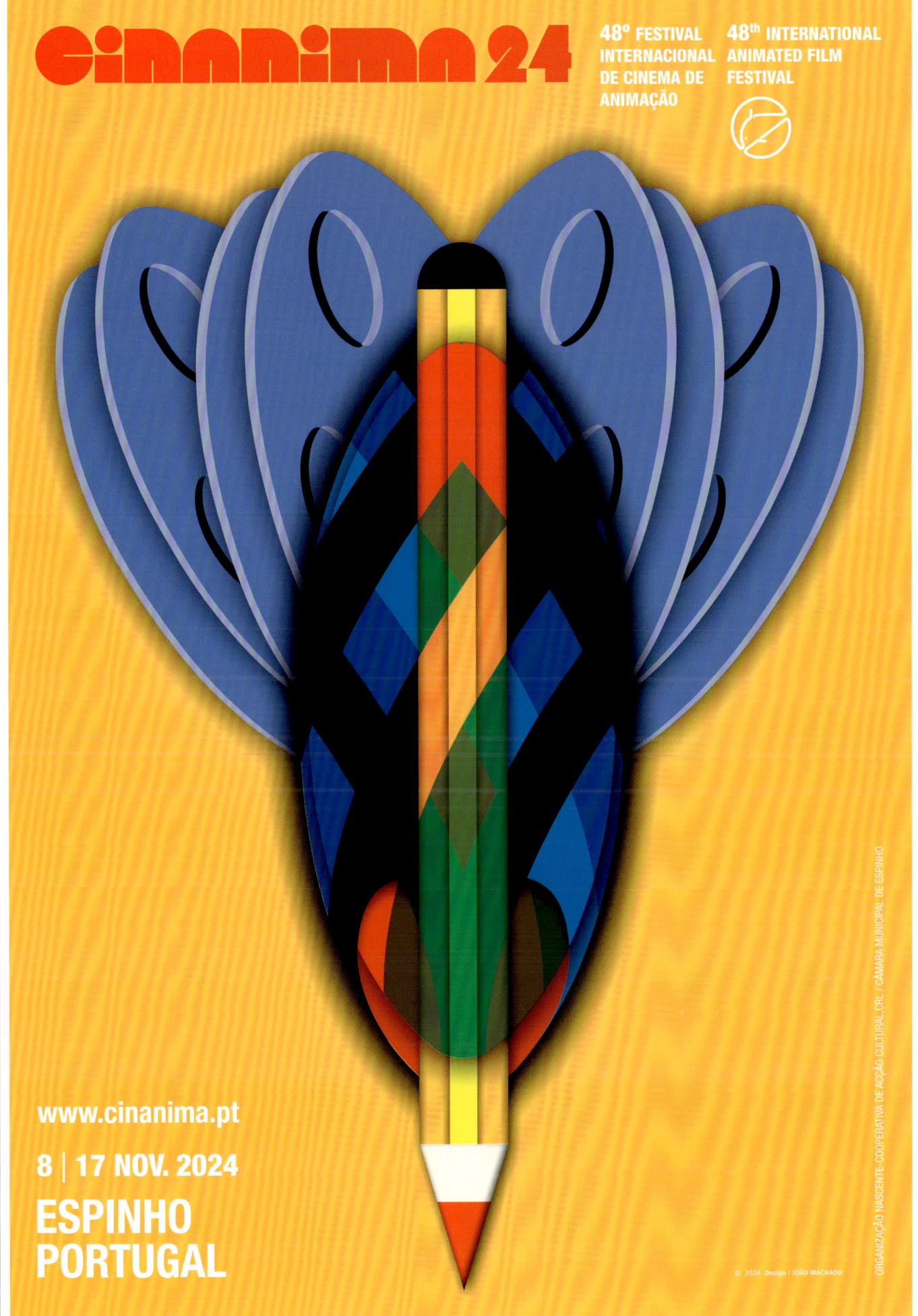

Title: Cinanima 24 | Clients: Organização Nascente - Cooperativa de Acção Cultural - CRL, Câmara Municipal de Espinho
Design Firm: João Machado Design | P234: Credit & Commentary

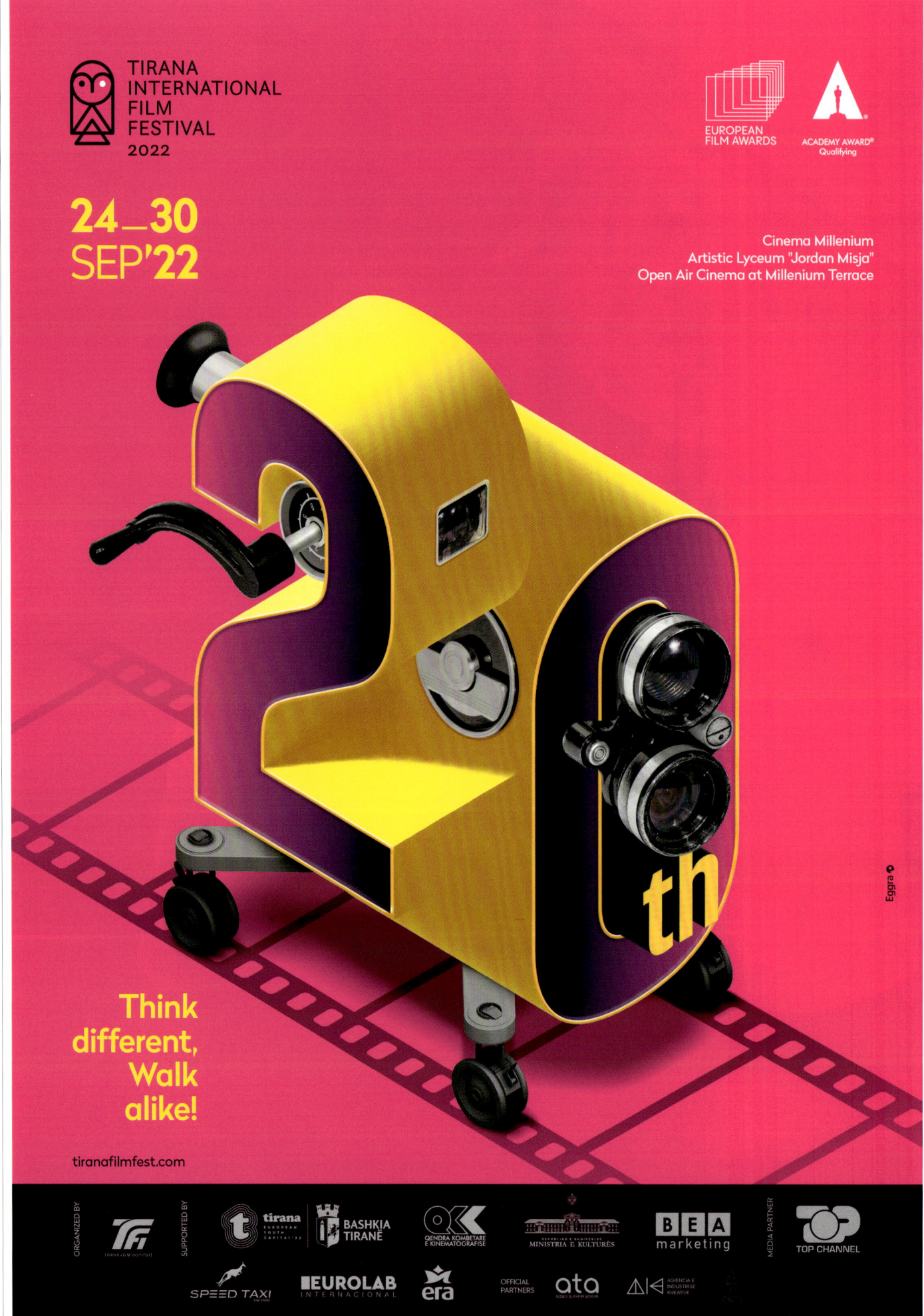

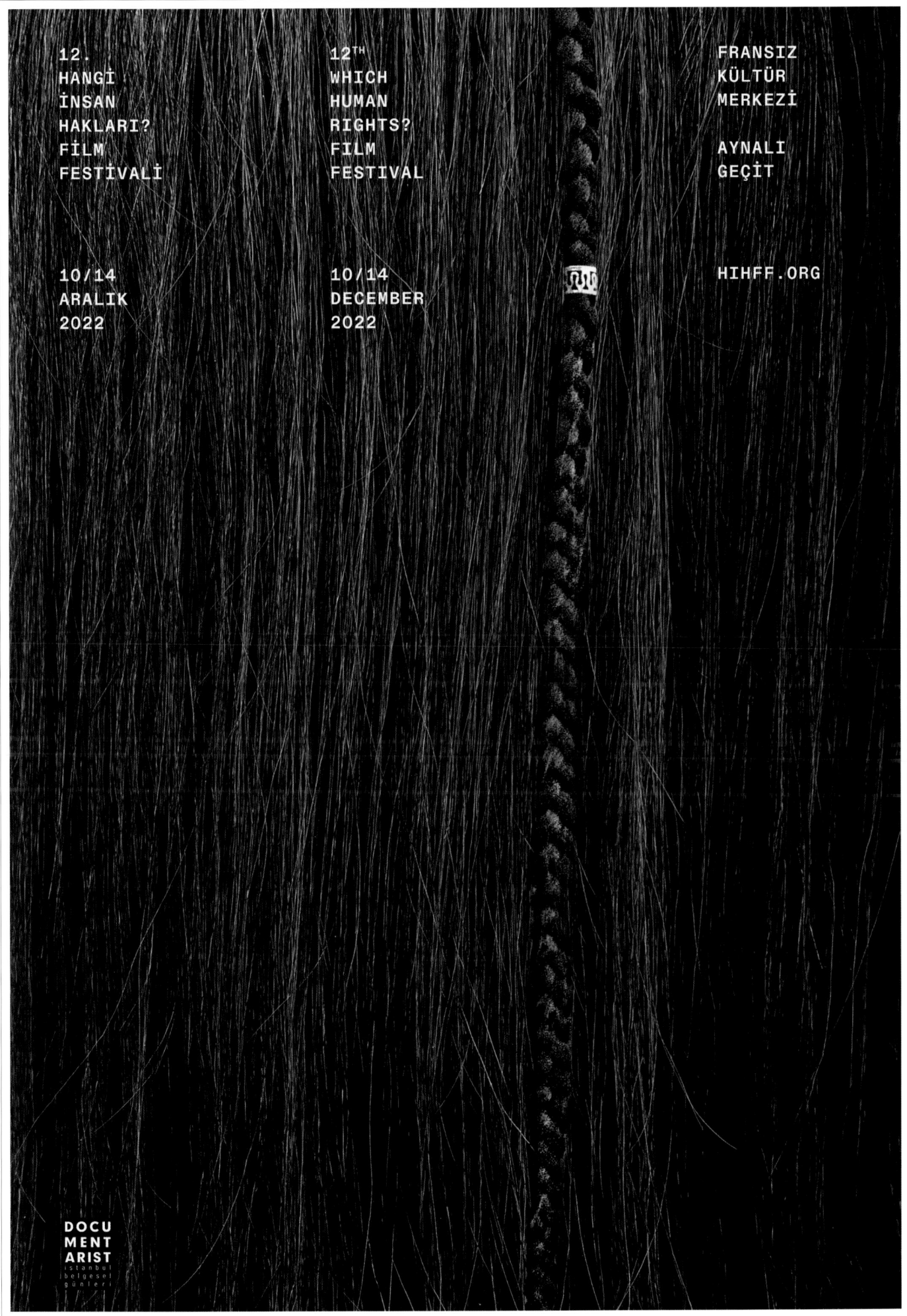

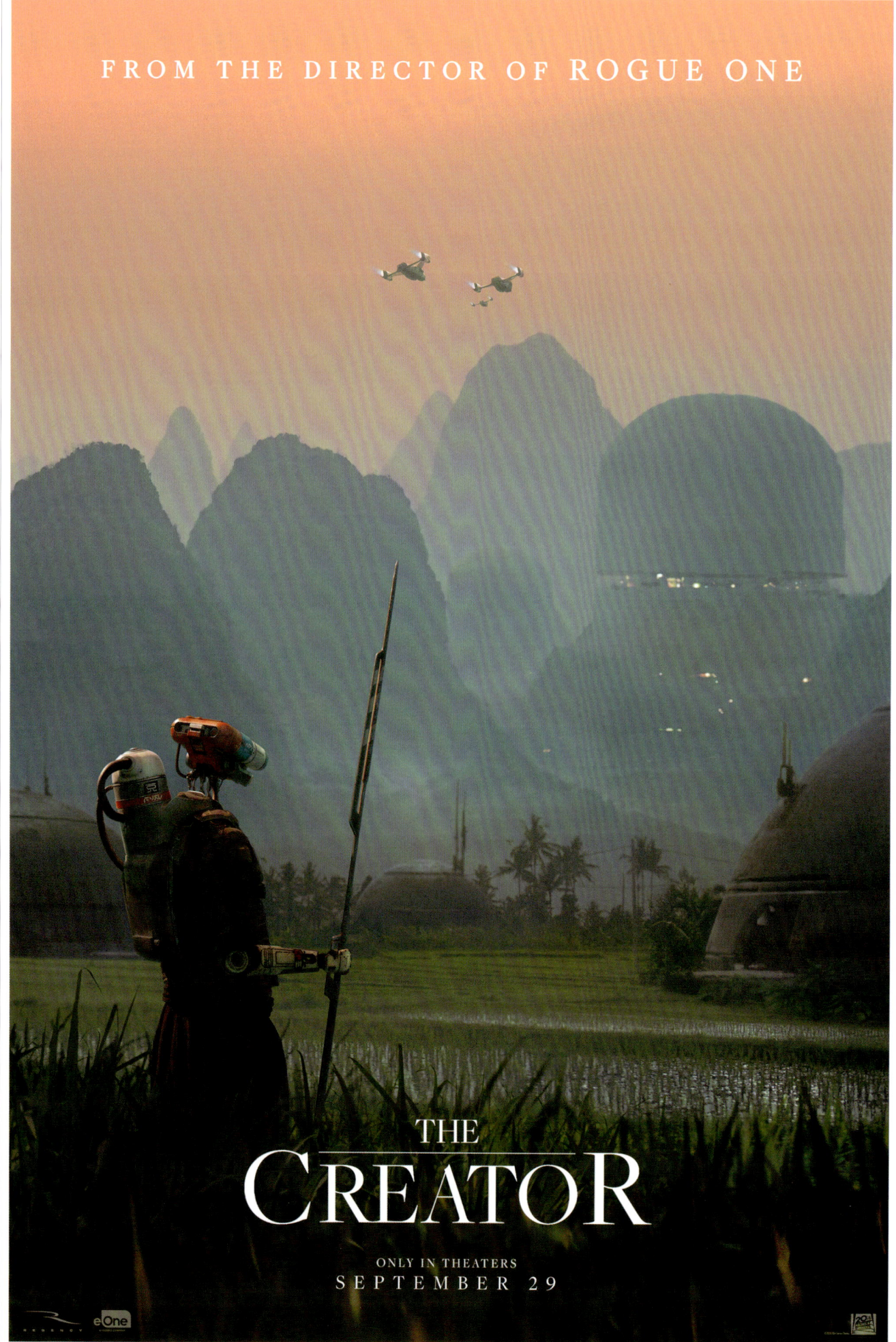

Title: The Creator - Teaser Poster | Clients: 20th Century Studios, Jordan Stallings, Arnaldo D'Alfonso, Joe Tamusaitis
Design Firm: AV Print | P235: Credit & Commentary

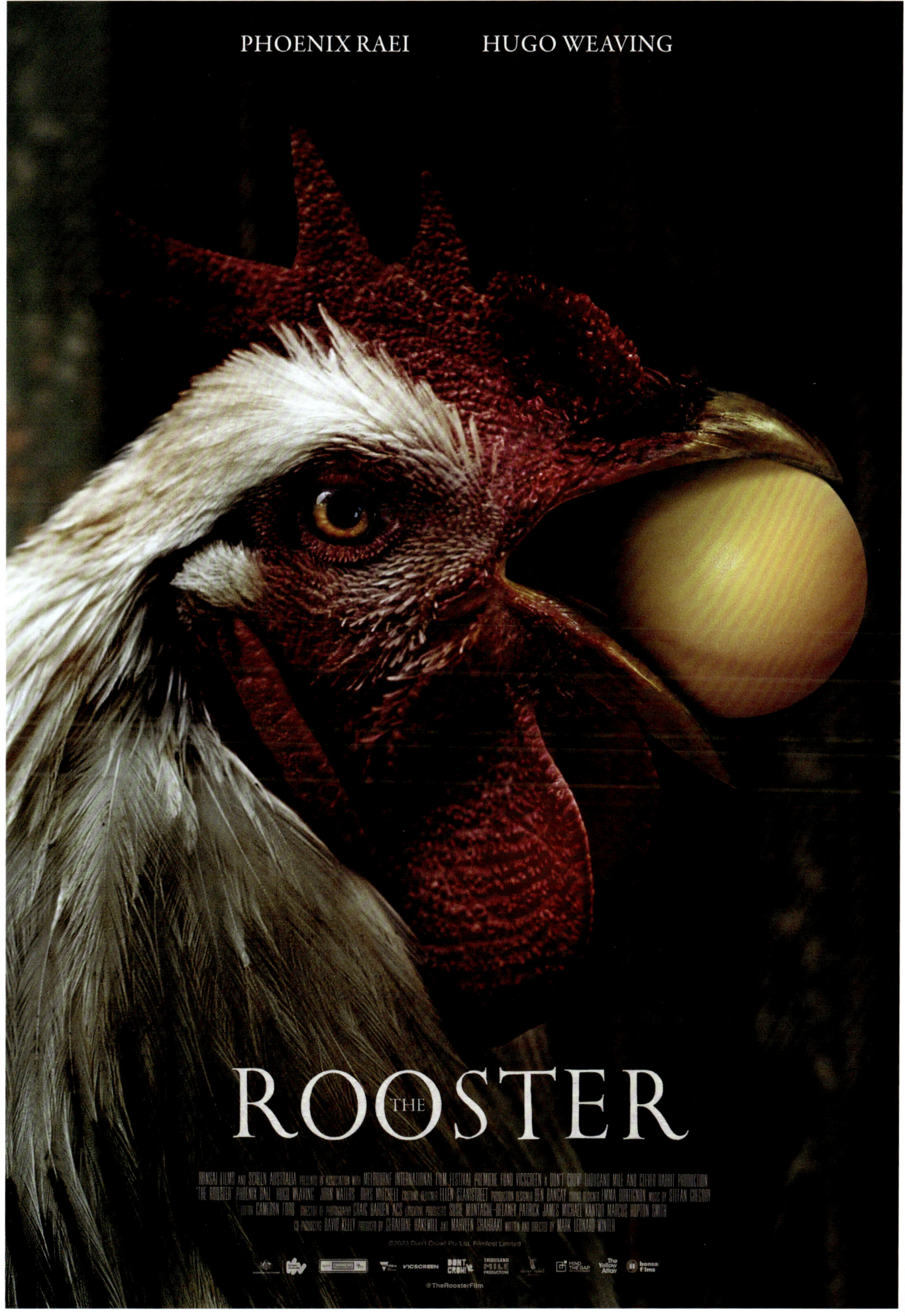

Title: The Rooster Teaser Key Art | Client: Thousand Mile Productions
Design Firm: Barlow.Agency | P235: Credit & Commentary

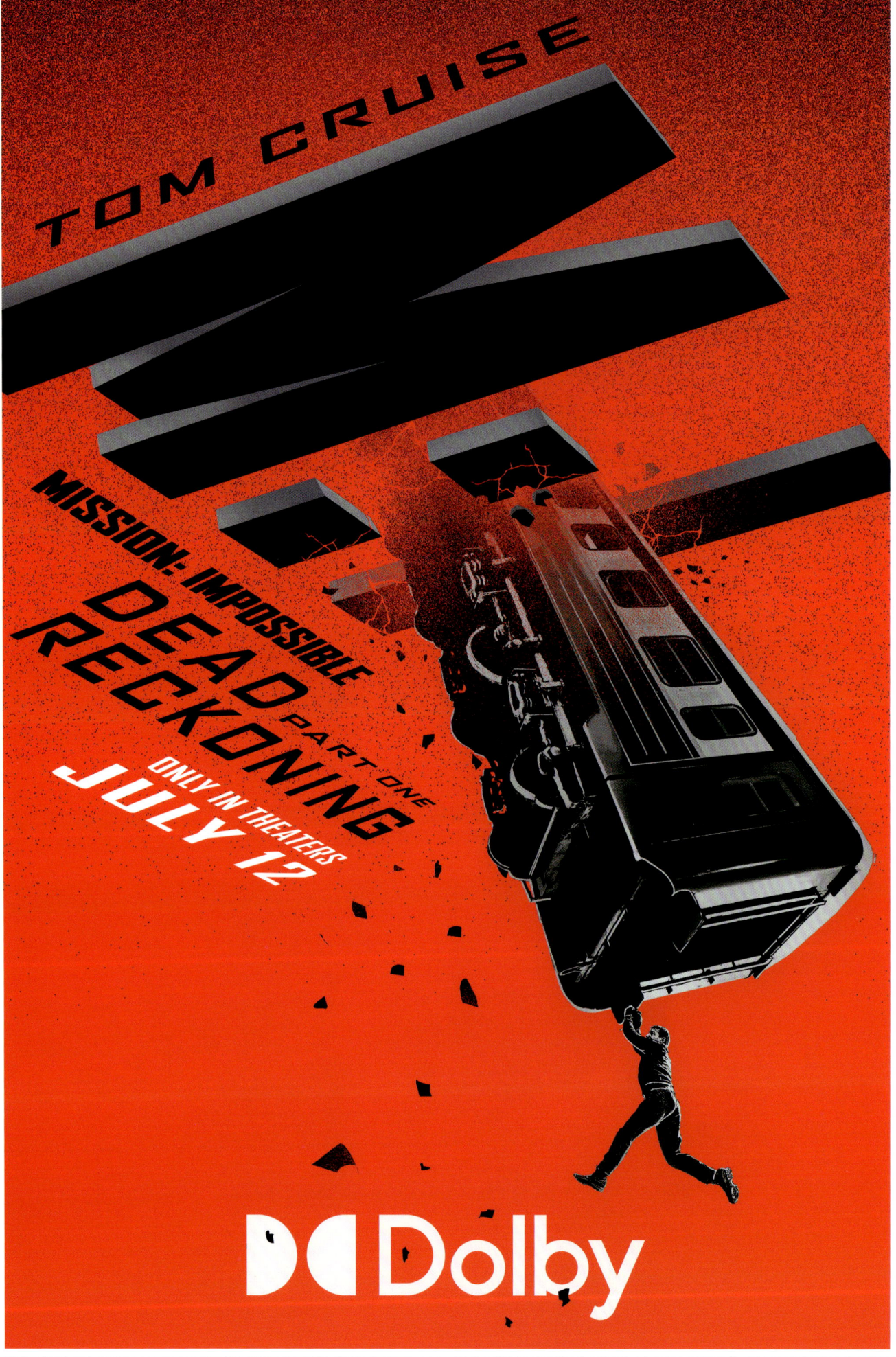

Title: Mission: Impossible - Dead Reckoning Part 1, Dolby Exclusive Poster | Clients: Paramount Pictures, Brian Pianko, Charlie Ward
Design Firm: AV Print | P235: Credit & Commentary

91 AV PRINT GOLD FILM

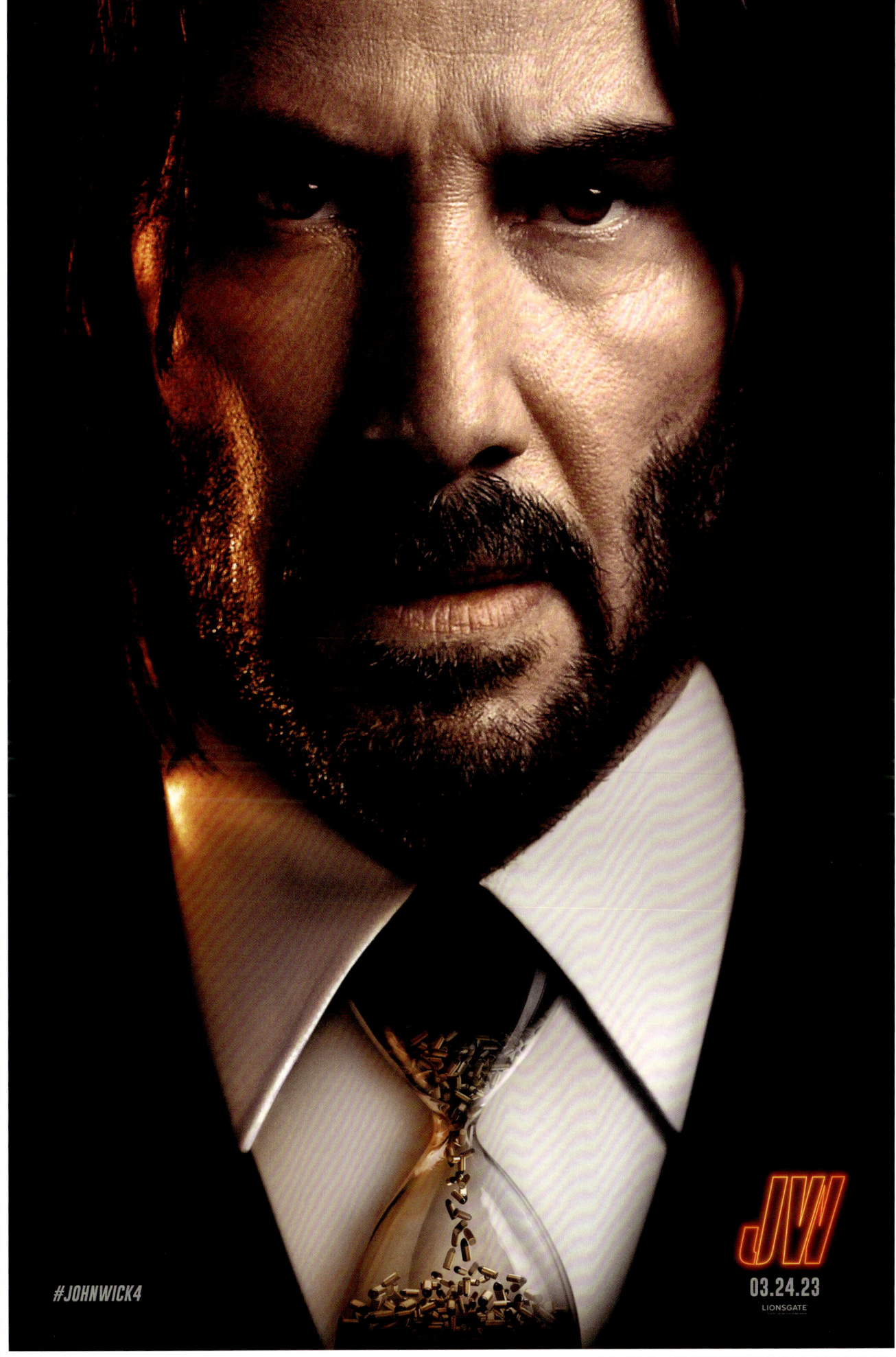

Title: John Wick: Chapter 4 - Theatrical Campaign | **Clients:** Lionsgate, Keri Moore, Jack Teed, John Cunha
Design Firm: AV Print | P235: Credit & Commentary | Image 1 of 7

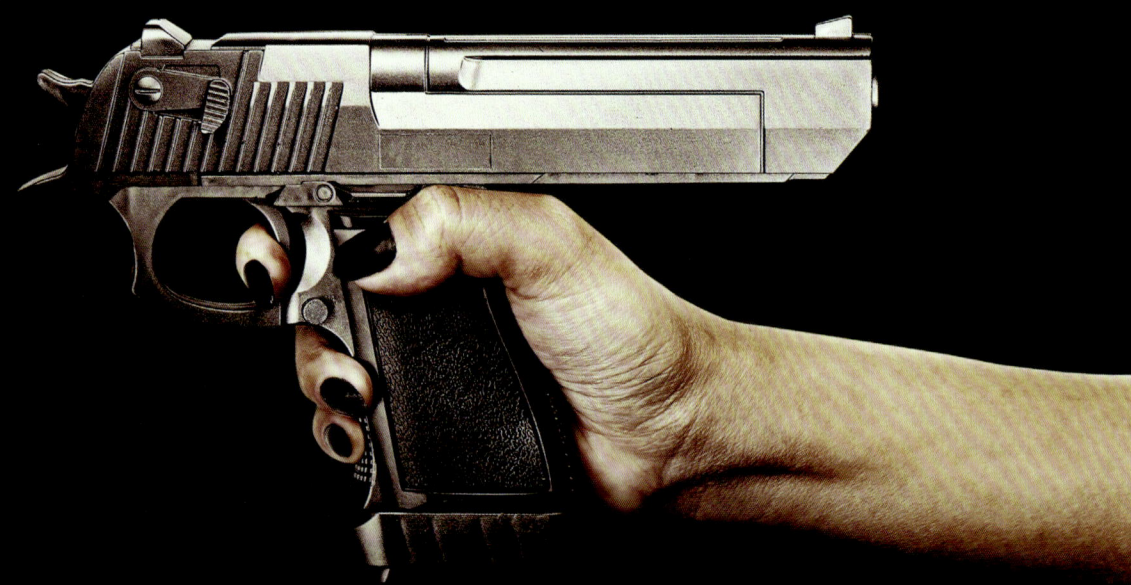

Title: Disarmed Short Film Key Art | **Client:** Last One Standing Productions
Design Firm: Barlow.Agency | **P235:** Credit & Commentary

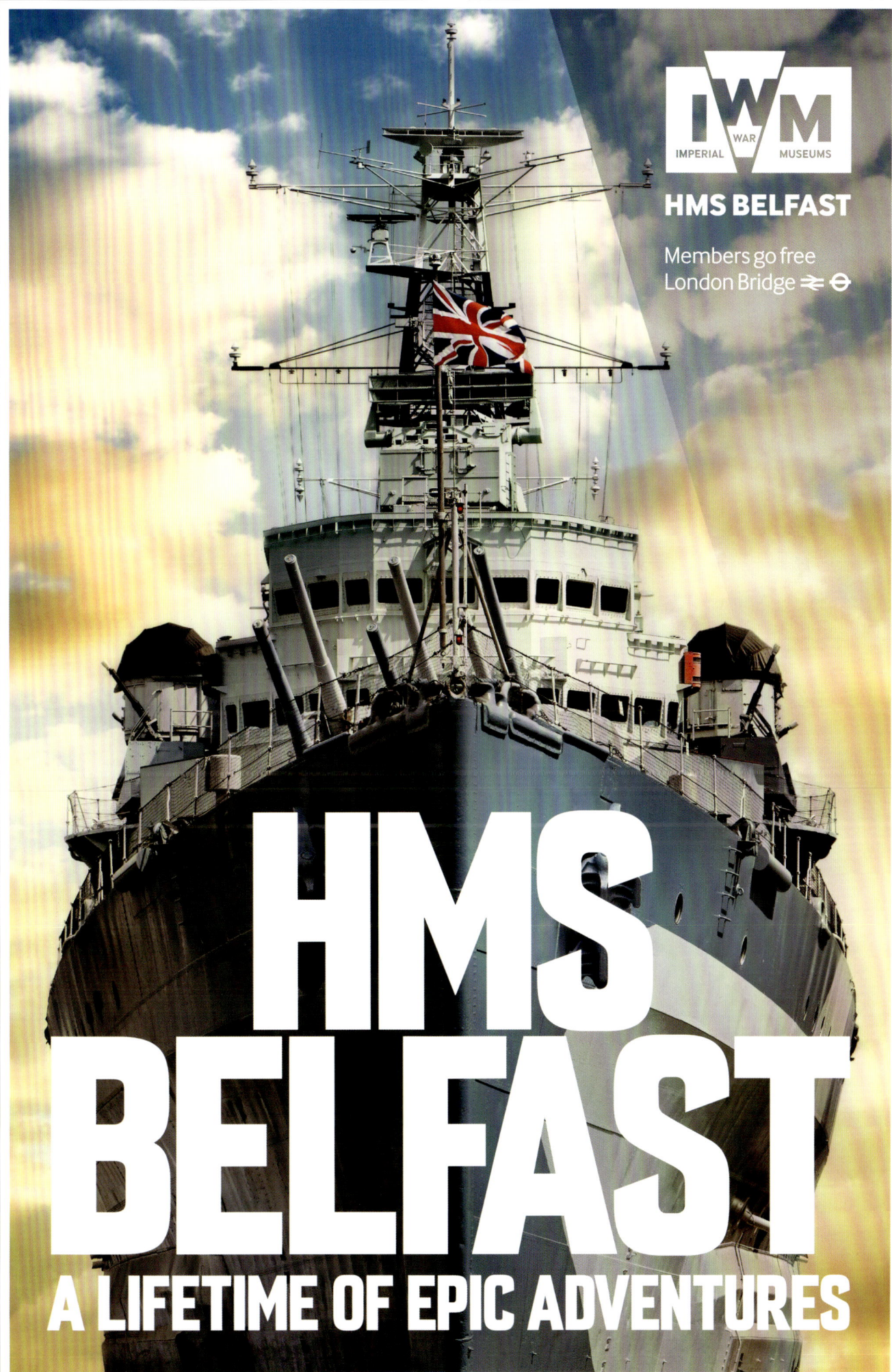

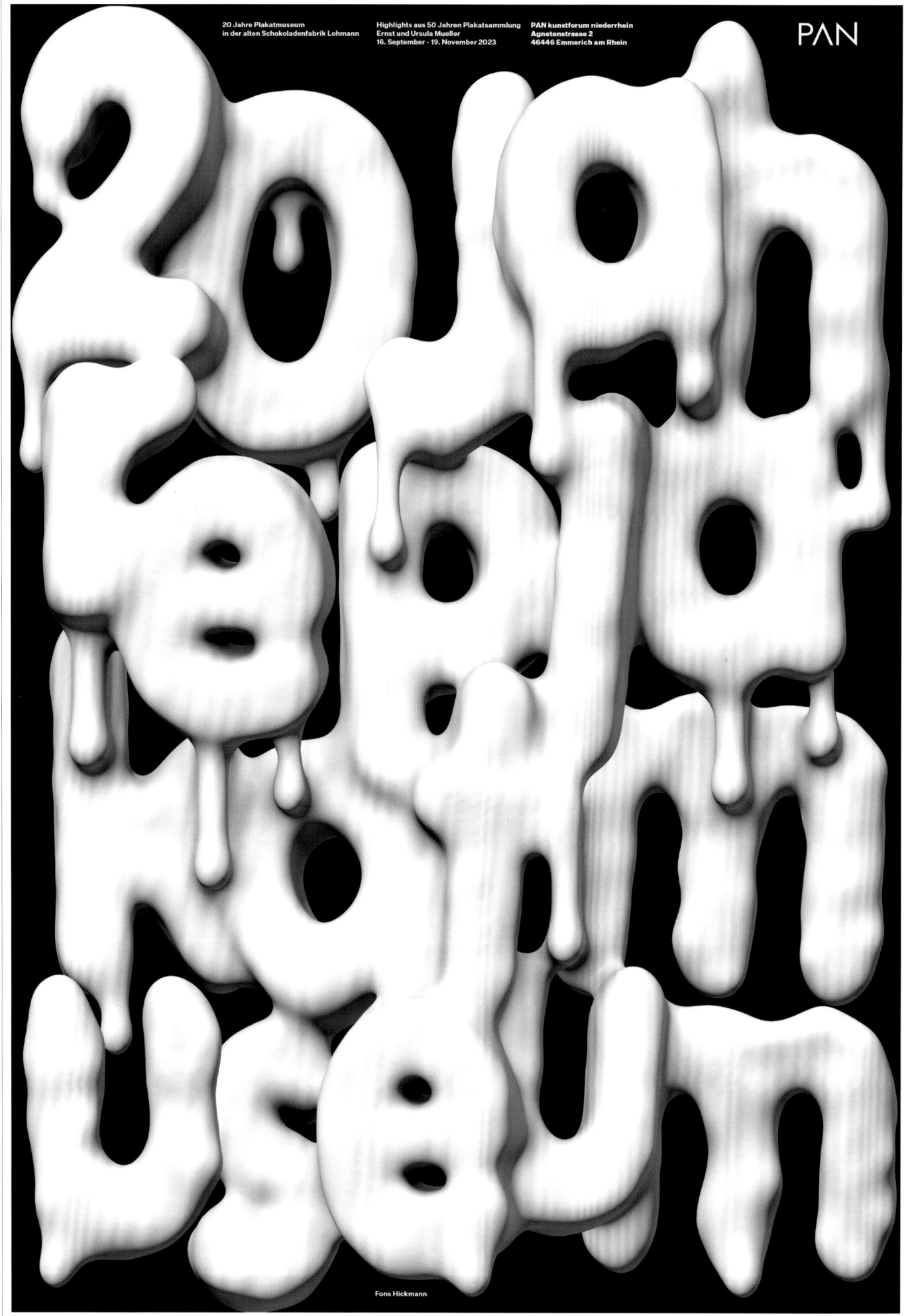

Title: 20 Years Poster Museum | **Client:** Plakatmuseum Emmerich
Design Firm: Fons Hickmann m23 | **P235:** Credit & Commentary

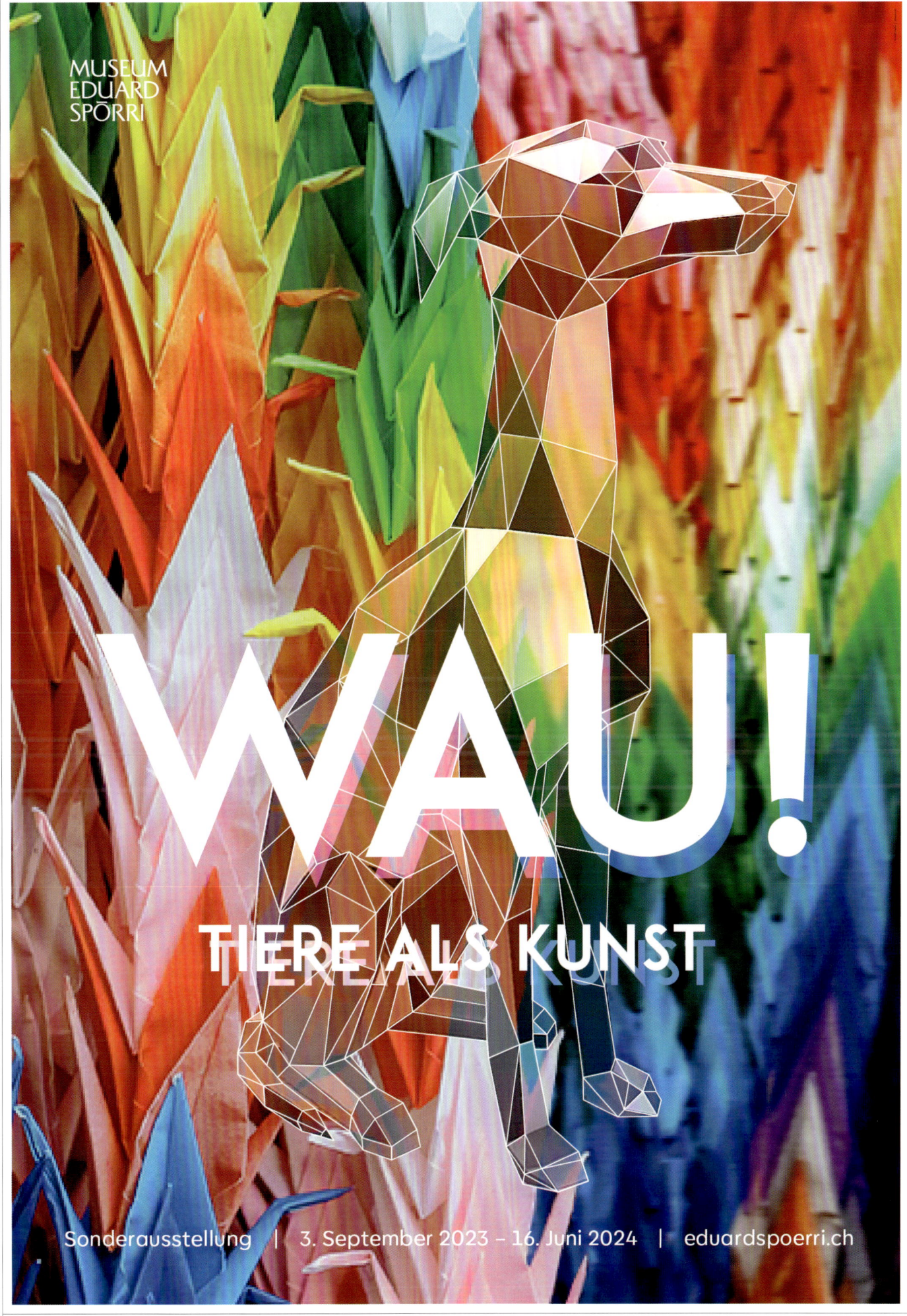

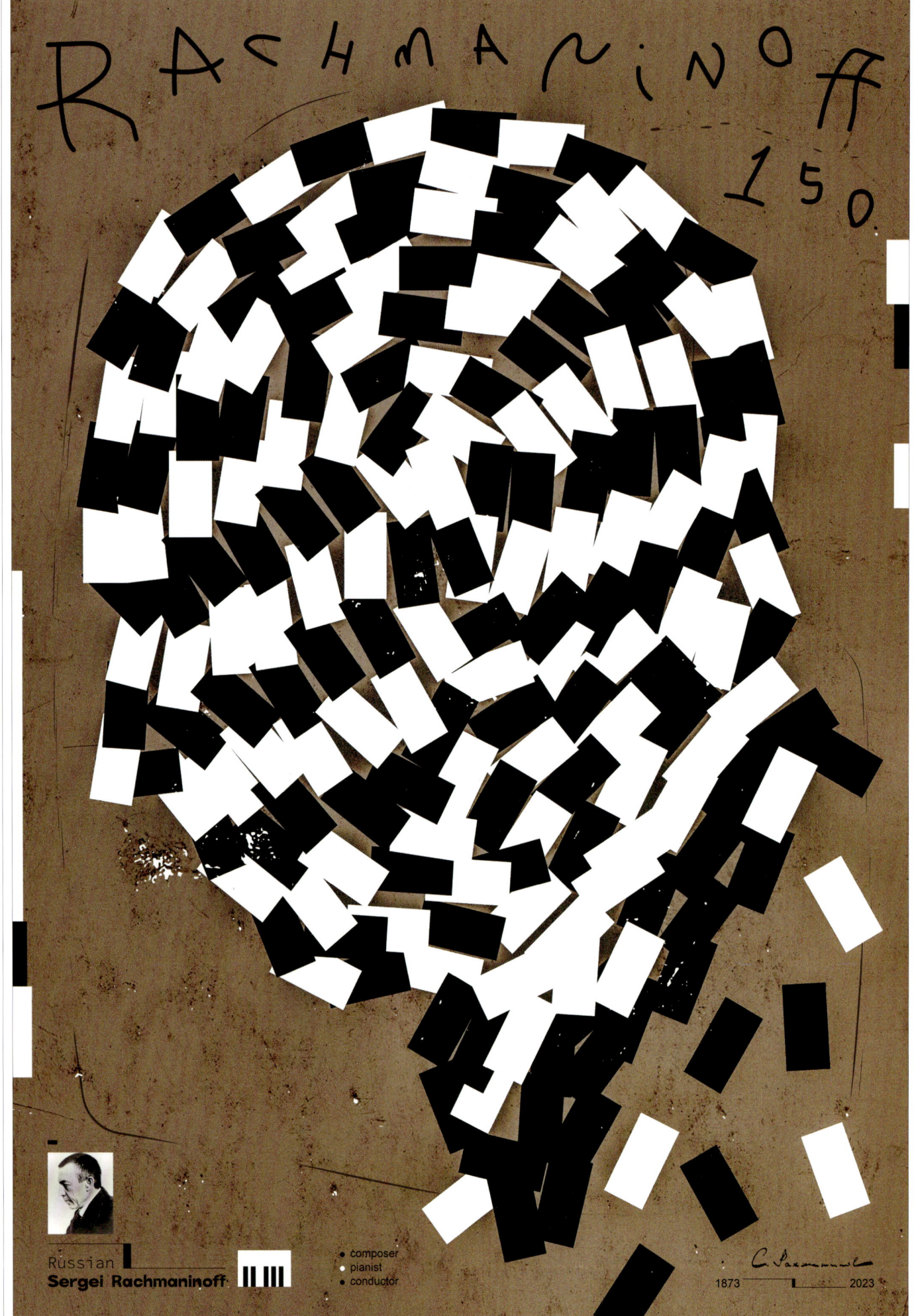

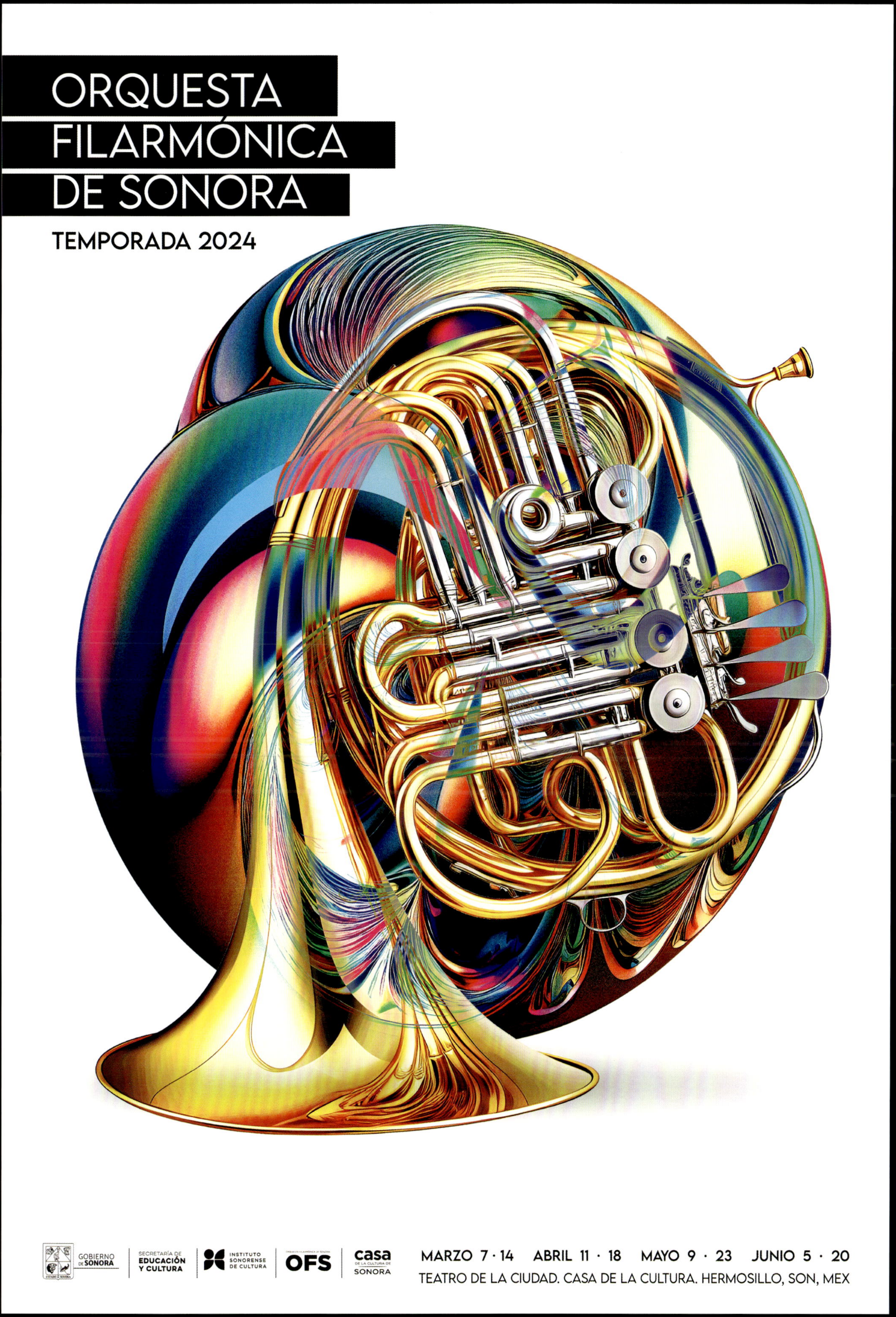

ORQUESTA FILARMÓNICA DE SONORA
TEMPORADA 2024

MARZO 7 · 14   ABRIL 11 · 18   MAYO 9 · 23   JUNIO 5 · 20
TEATRO DE LA CIUDAD. CASA DE LA CULTURA. HERMOSILLO, SON, MEX

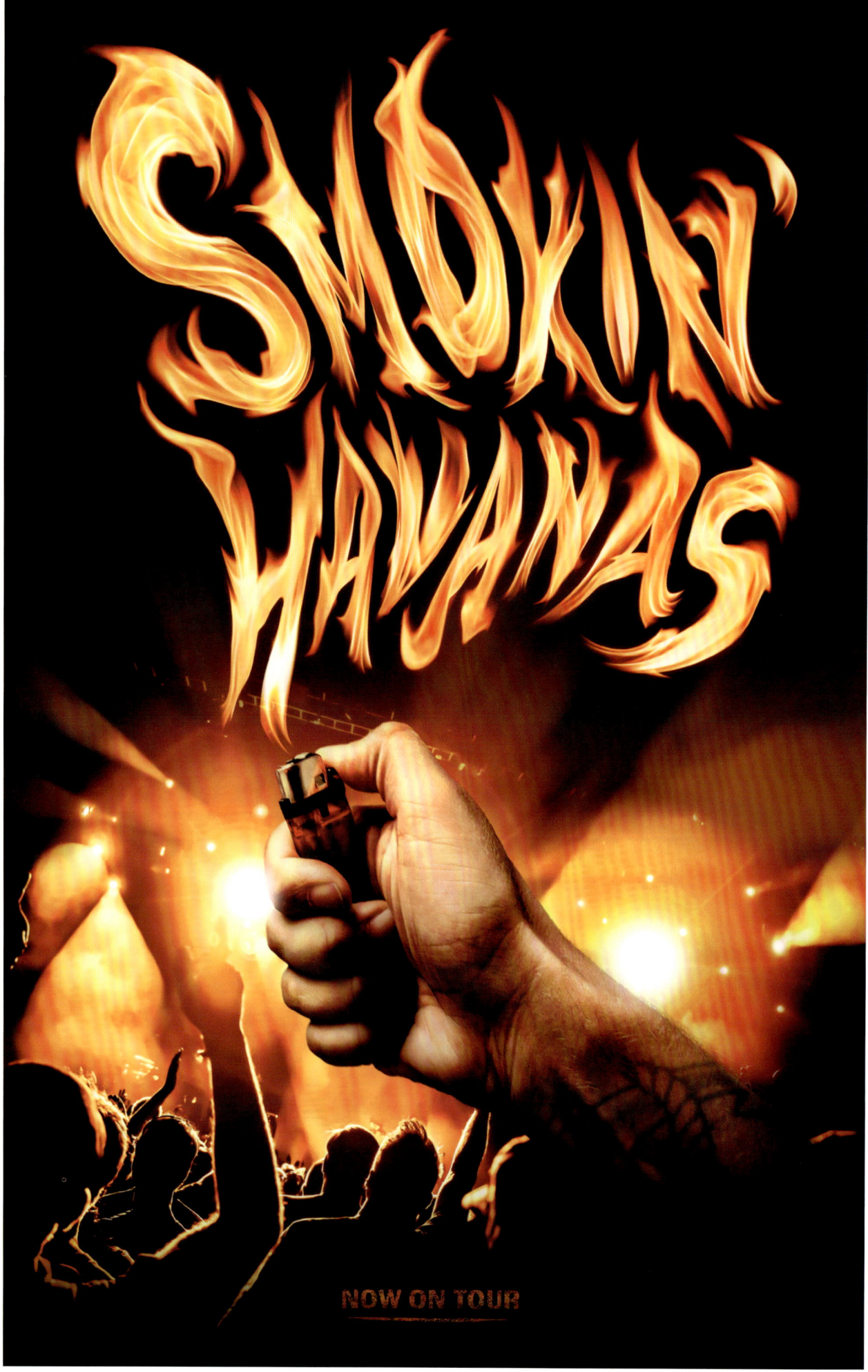

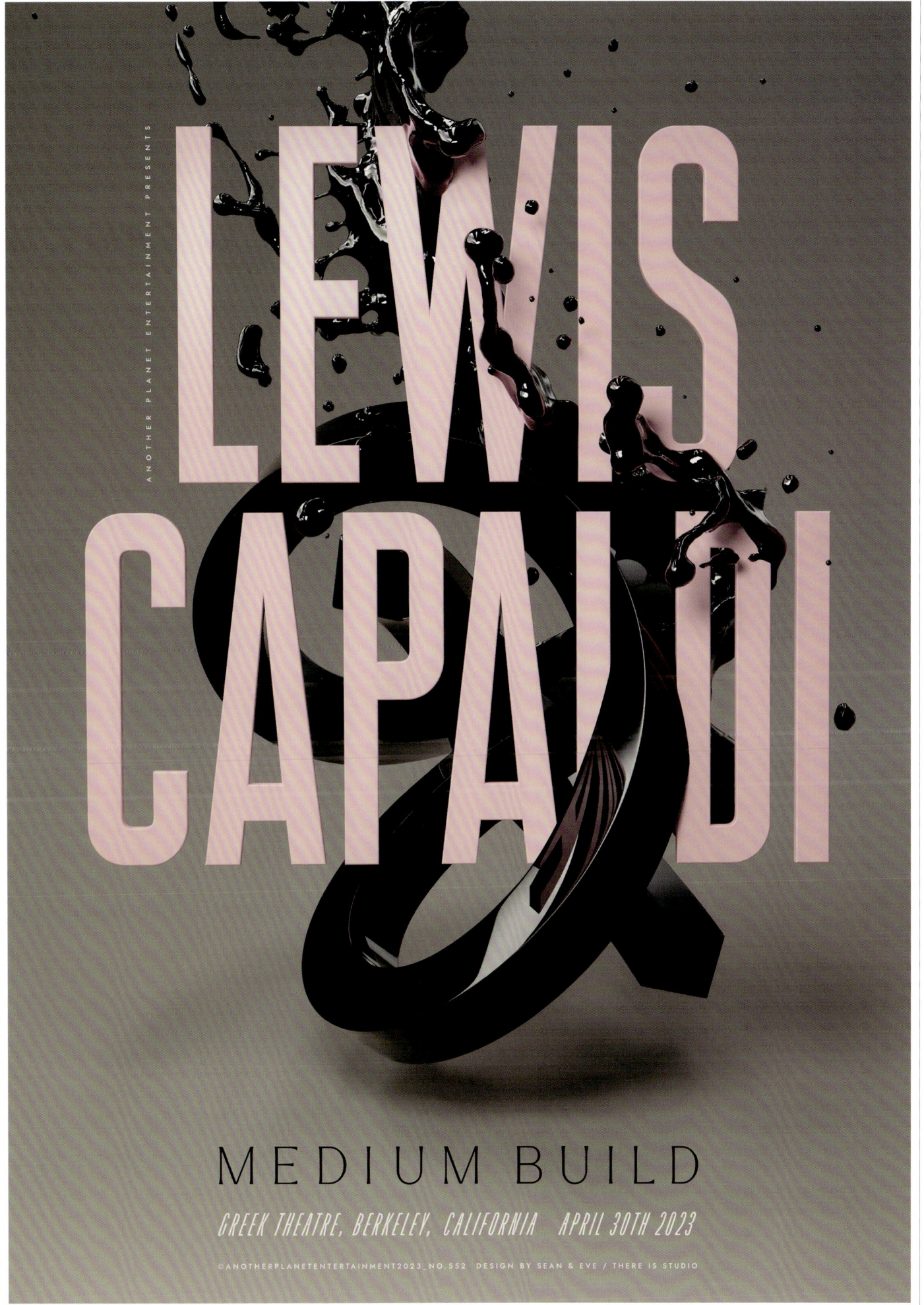

Title: LEWIS CAPALDI | Client: Another Planet Entertainment
Design Firm: THERE IS STUDIO | P236: Credit & Commentary

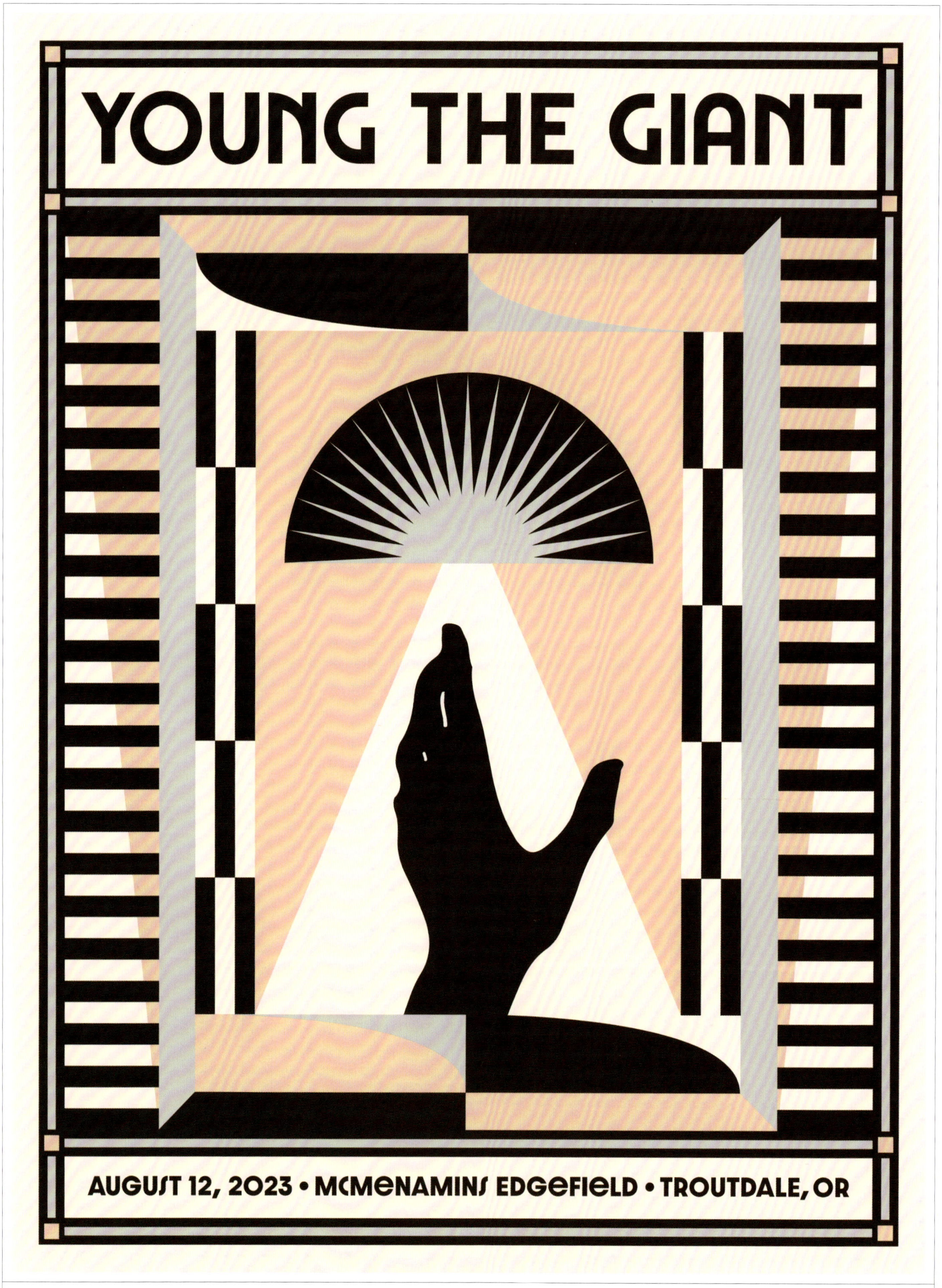

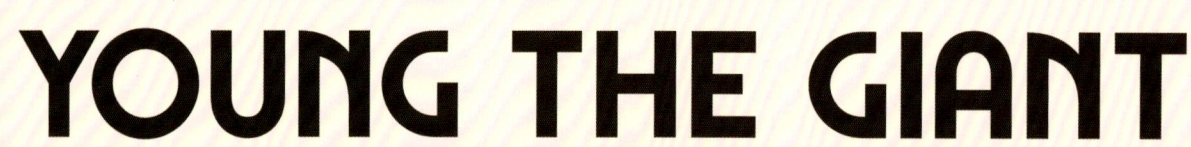

Title: Young the Giant — Live in Oregon | Client: Young the Giant
Design Firm: The Studio of Mikey Lavi | P236: Credit & Commentary

101 **MIKEY LAVI** GOLD   MUSIC

MONTREAL, QC   OSHEAGA   AUGUST 5TH, 2023
                          MUSIC & ARTS FESTIVAL

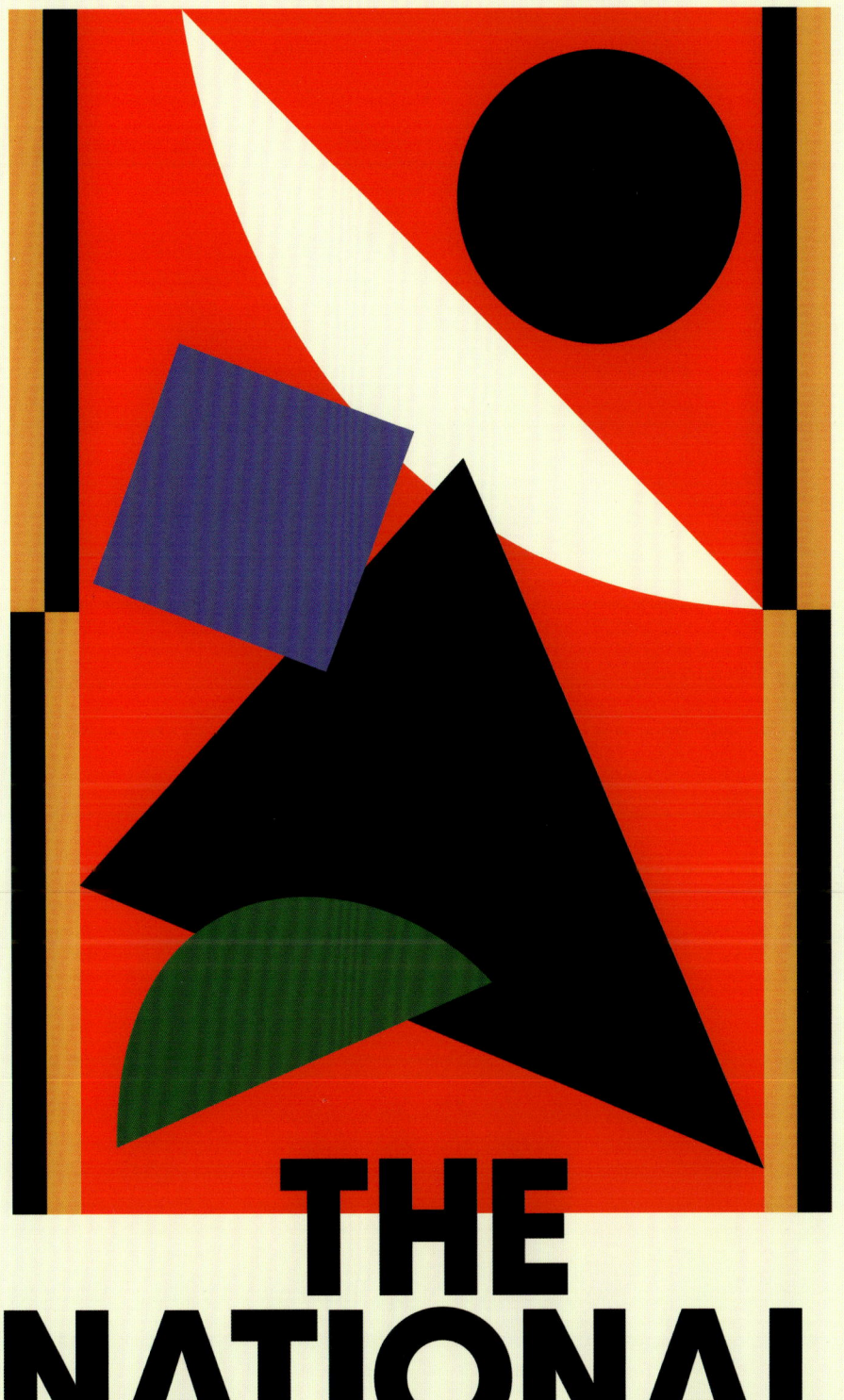

Title: The National — Live at Osheaga | **Client:** The National
Design Firm: The Studio of Mikey Lavi | **P236:** Credit & Commentary

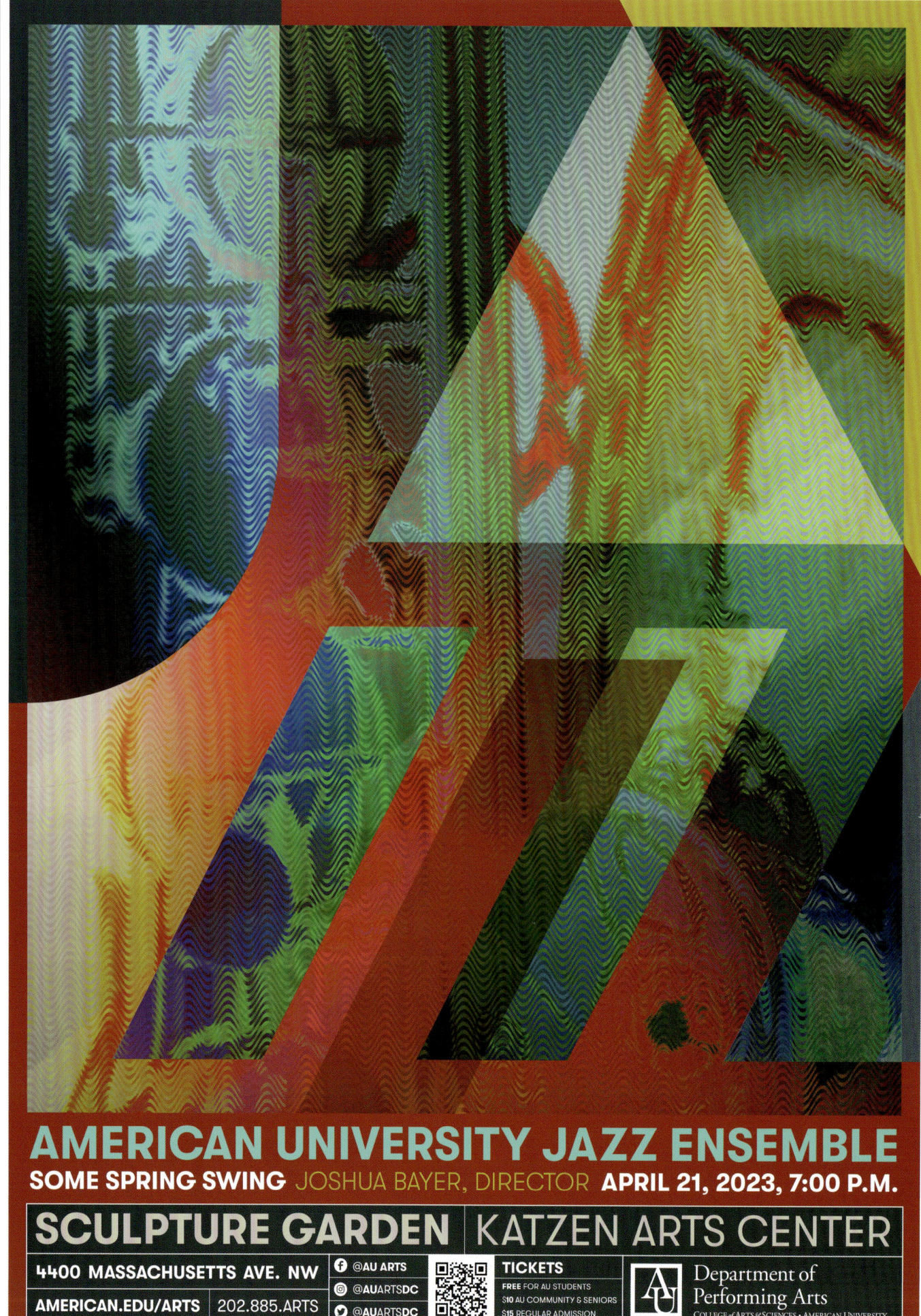

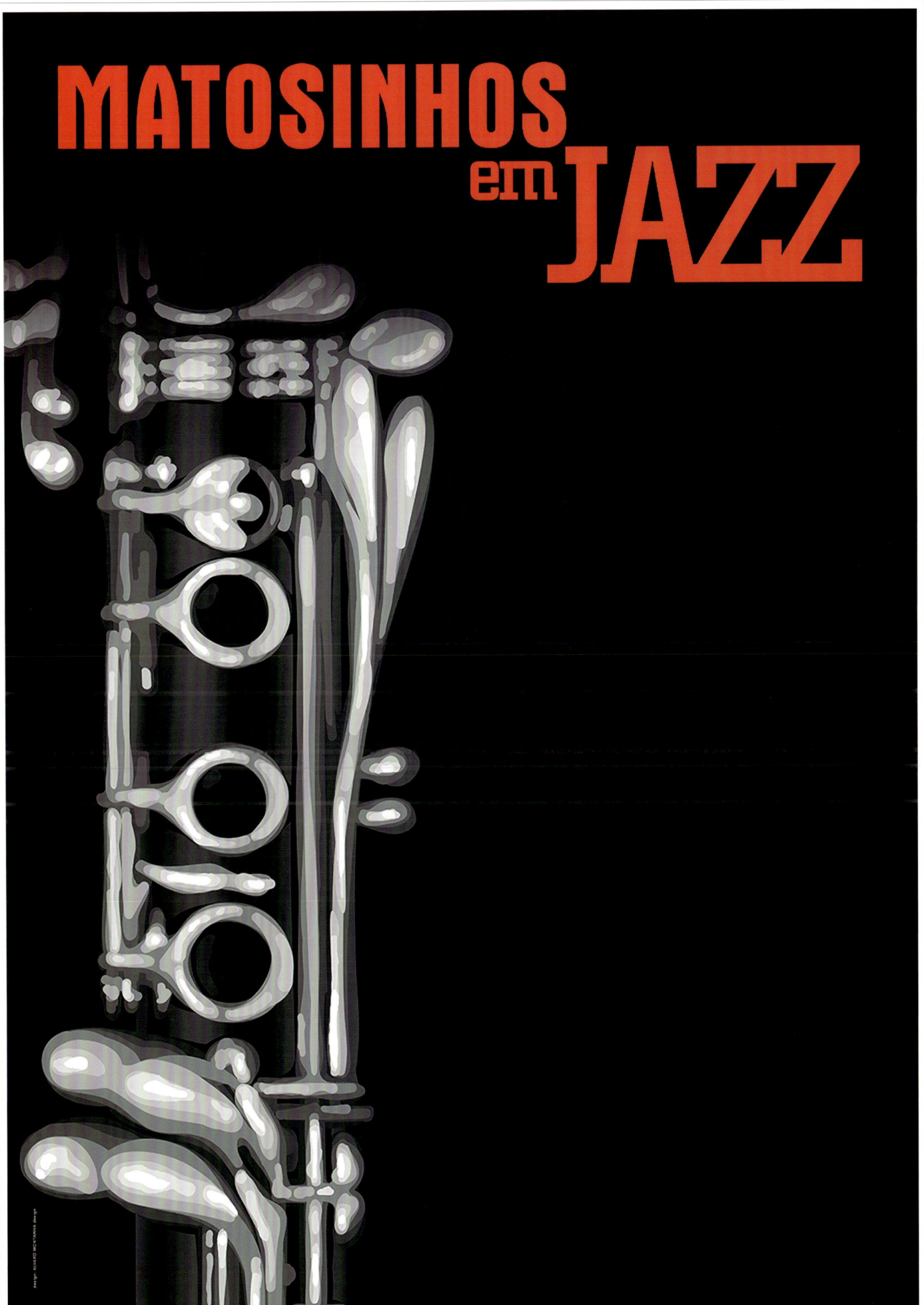

Title: Jazz & Clarinet | Client: Matosinhos City Councel
Design Firm: ALVARO MONTANHA Design | P236: Credit & Commentary

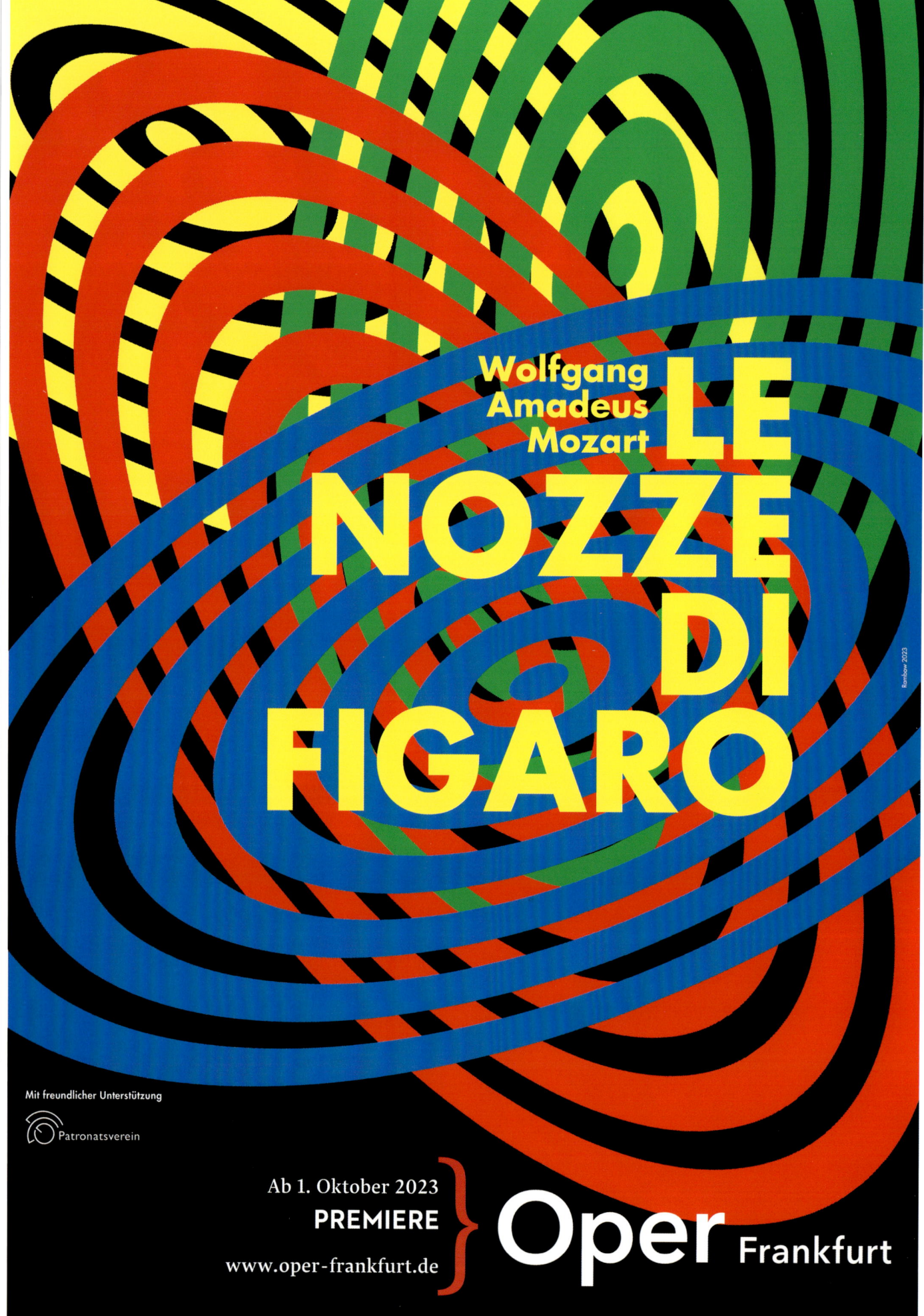

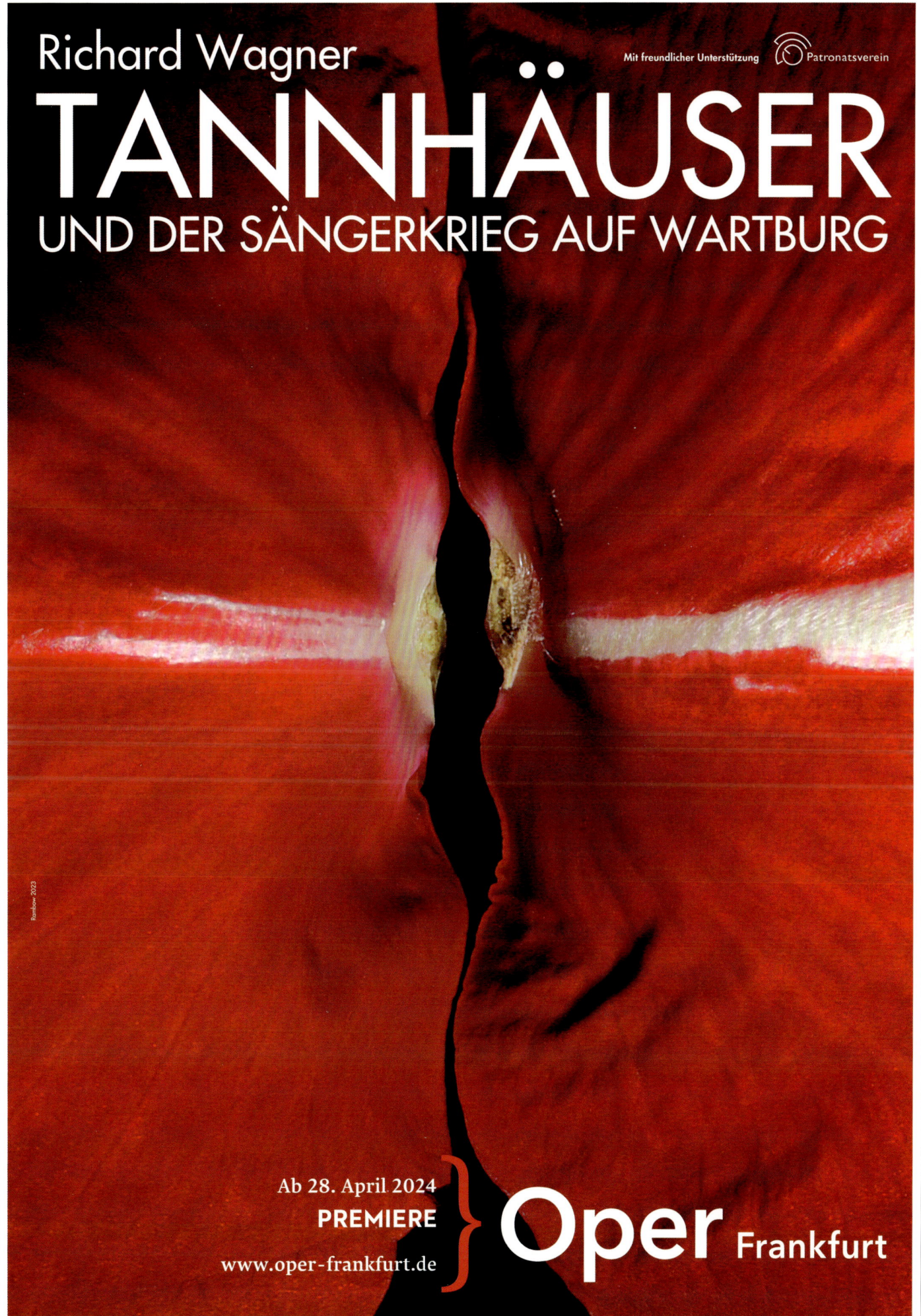

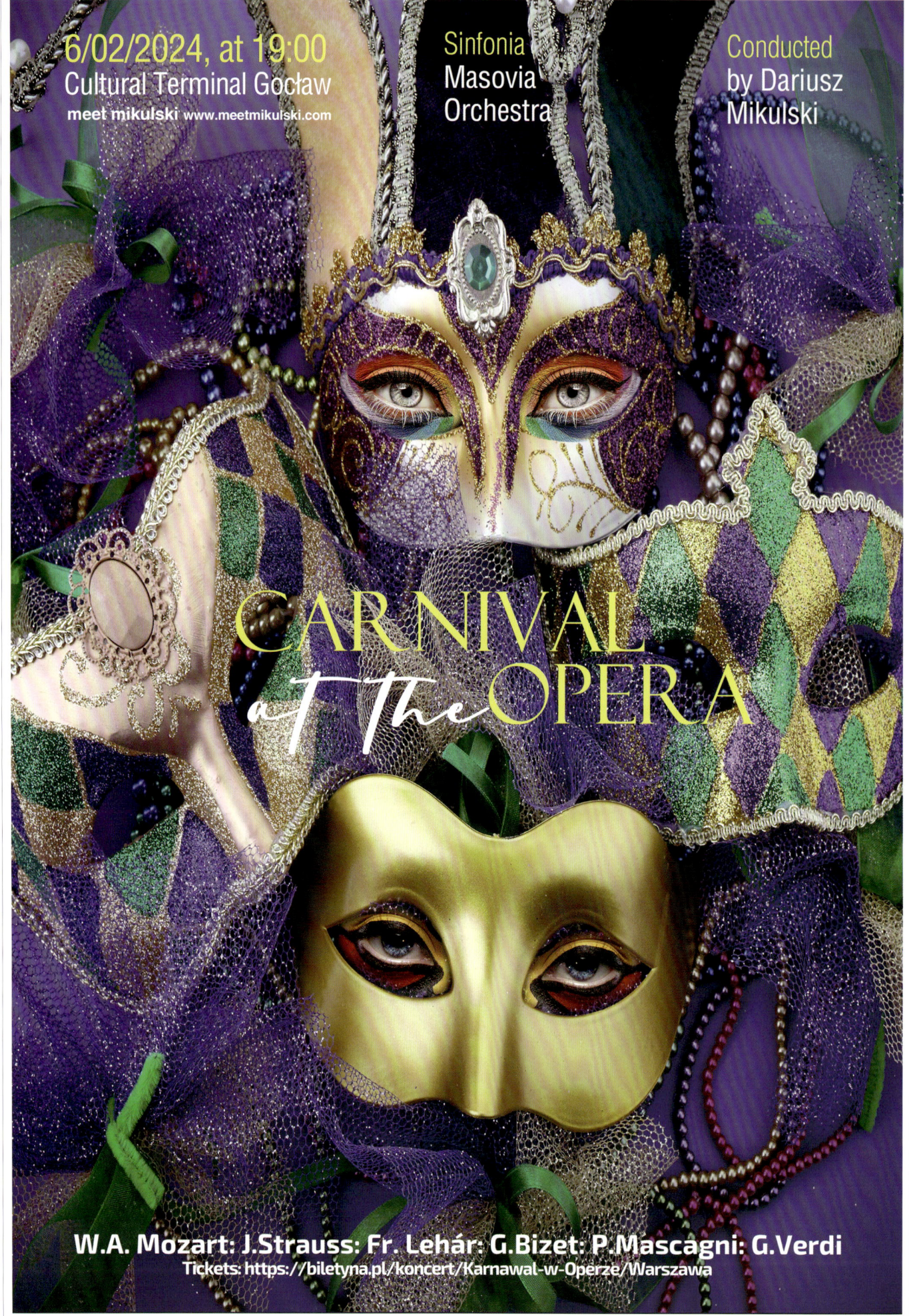

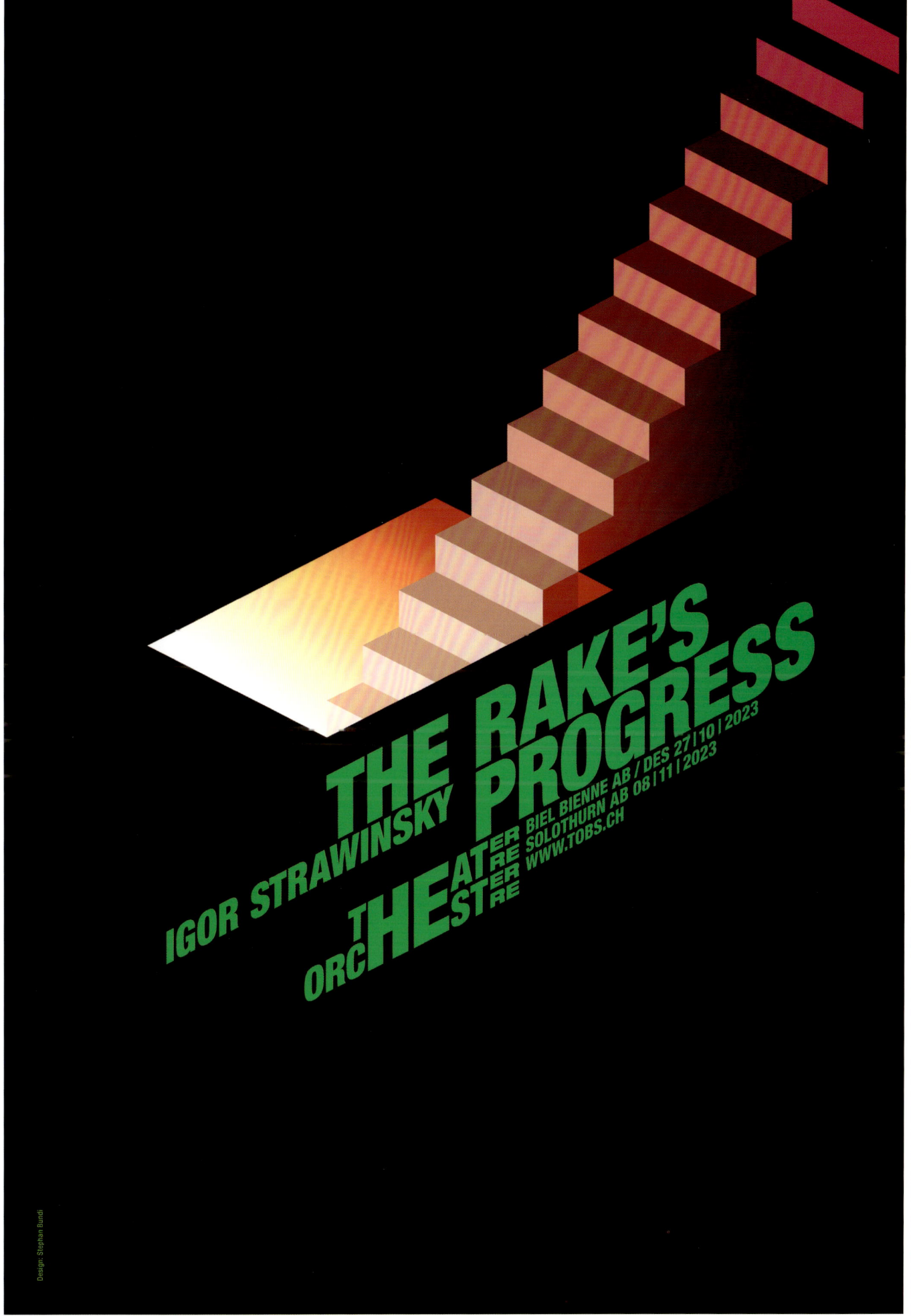

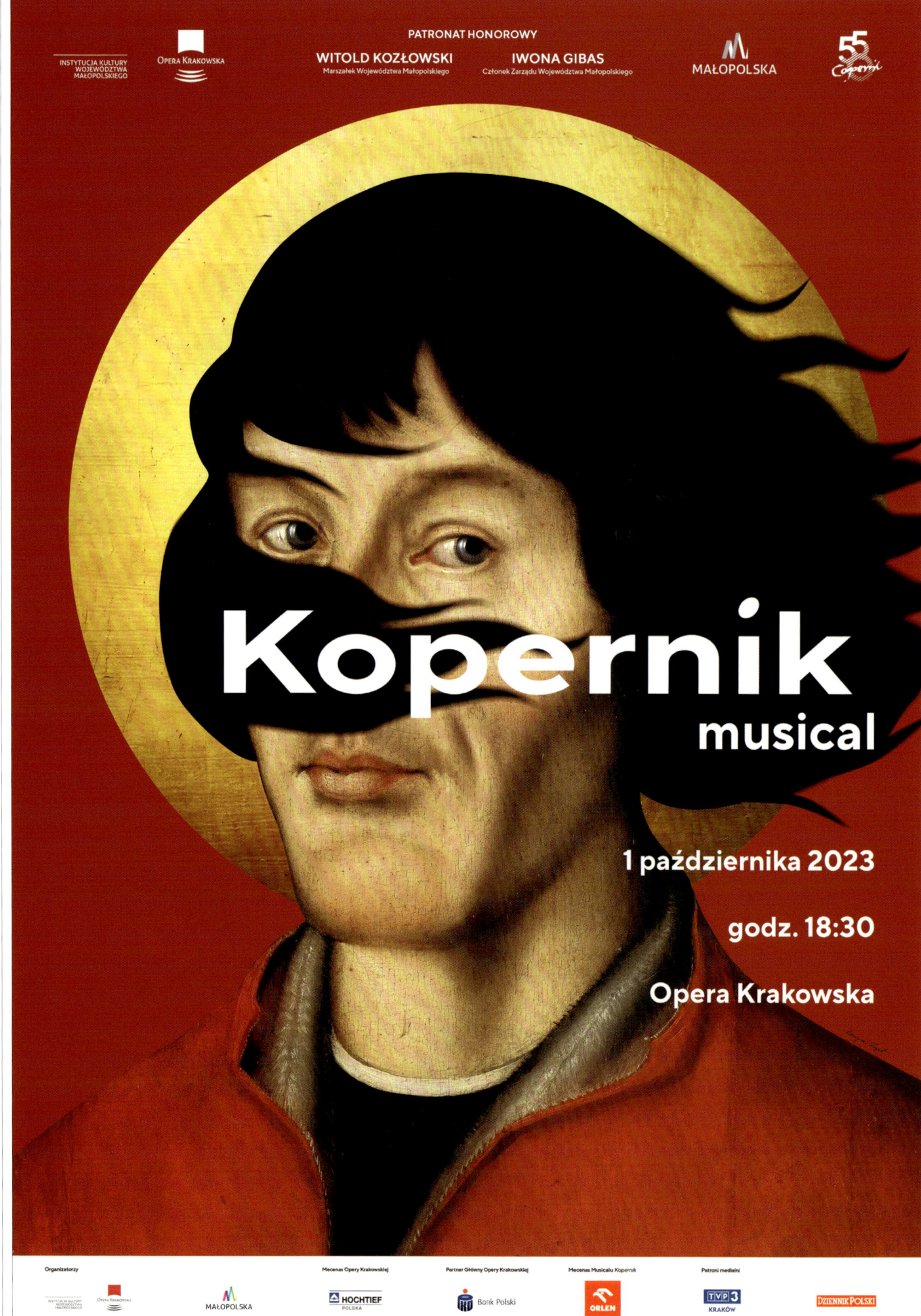

Title: Musical Kopernik (Copernicus) | Client: Opera Krakowska
Design Firm: Katarzyna Zapart | P236: Credit & Commentary

109 ALVARO MONTANHA DESIGN GOLD   PROMOTION

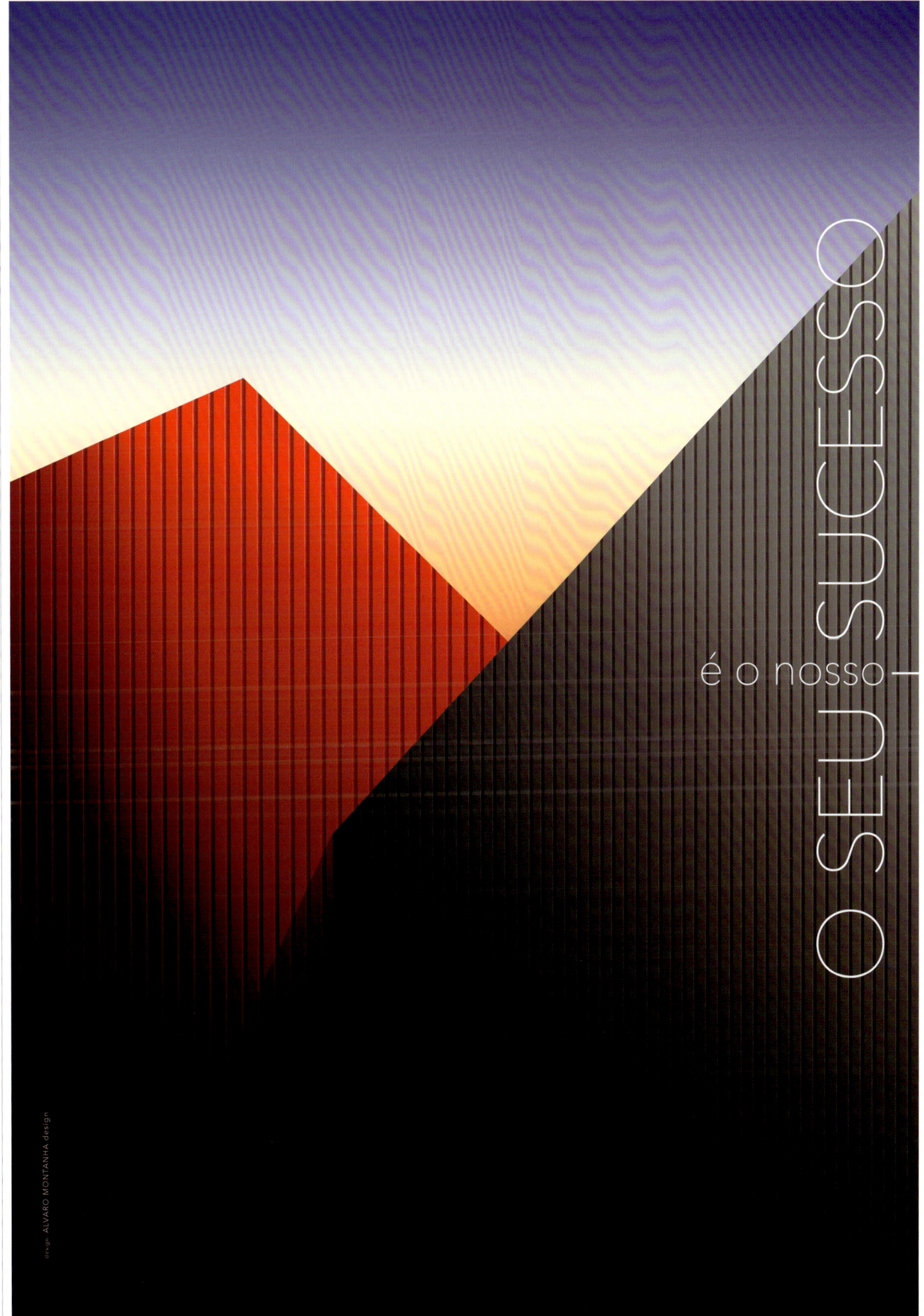

P236: Credit & Commentary   Title: Success | Client: Self-initiated | Design Firm: ALVARO MONTANHA Design

110 BOB AUFULDISH GOLD

TODD HIDO THE END SENDS ADVA

PRINTED ON THE OCCASION OF PARIS PHOTO, NOVEMBER 9–12, 2023
PUBLISHED BY NAZRAELI PRESS

WARNING #11851-3642

Title: Todd Hido: The End Sends Advance Warning | Client: Nazraeli Press | Design Firm: Aufuldish & Warinner

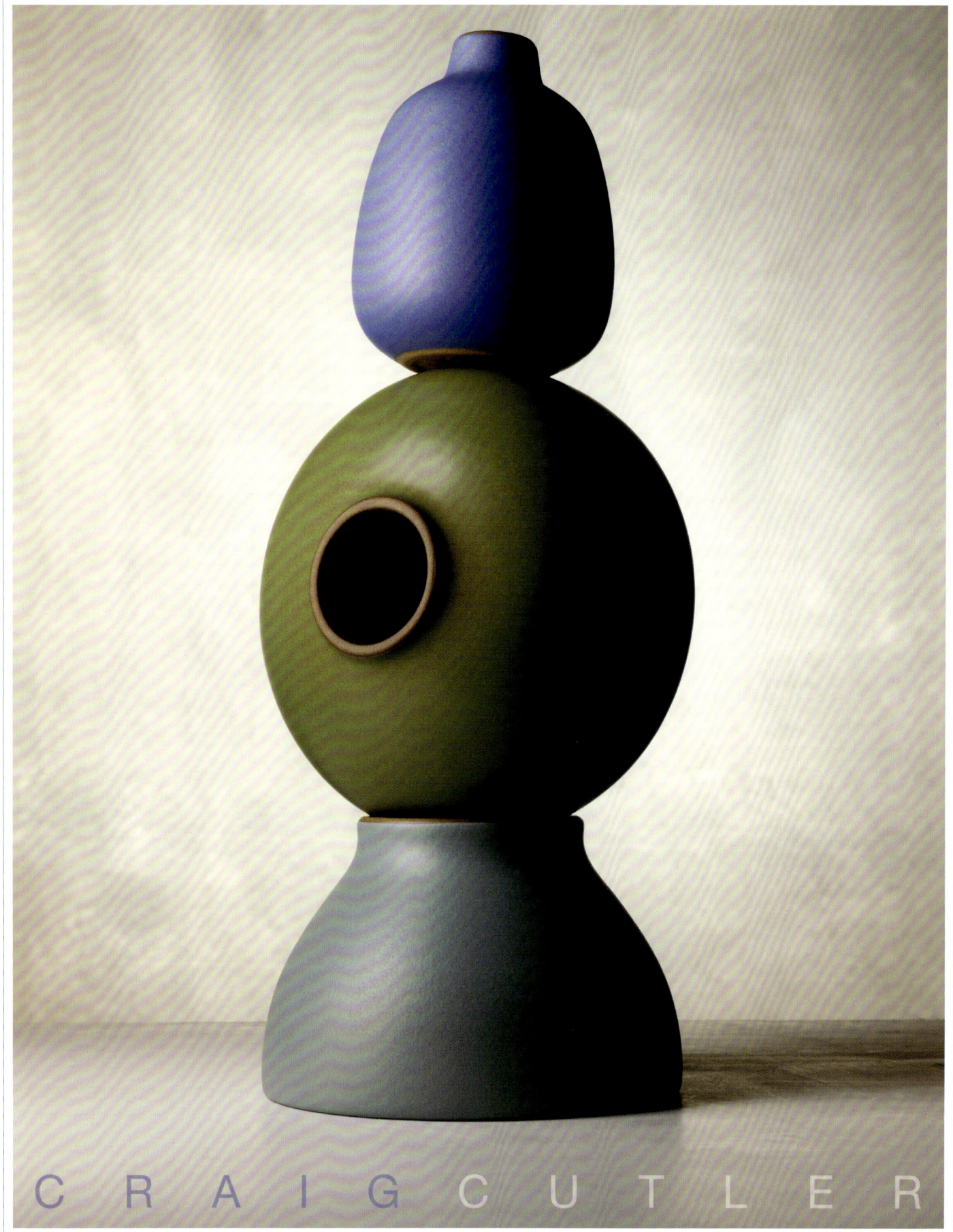

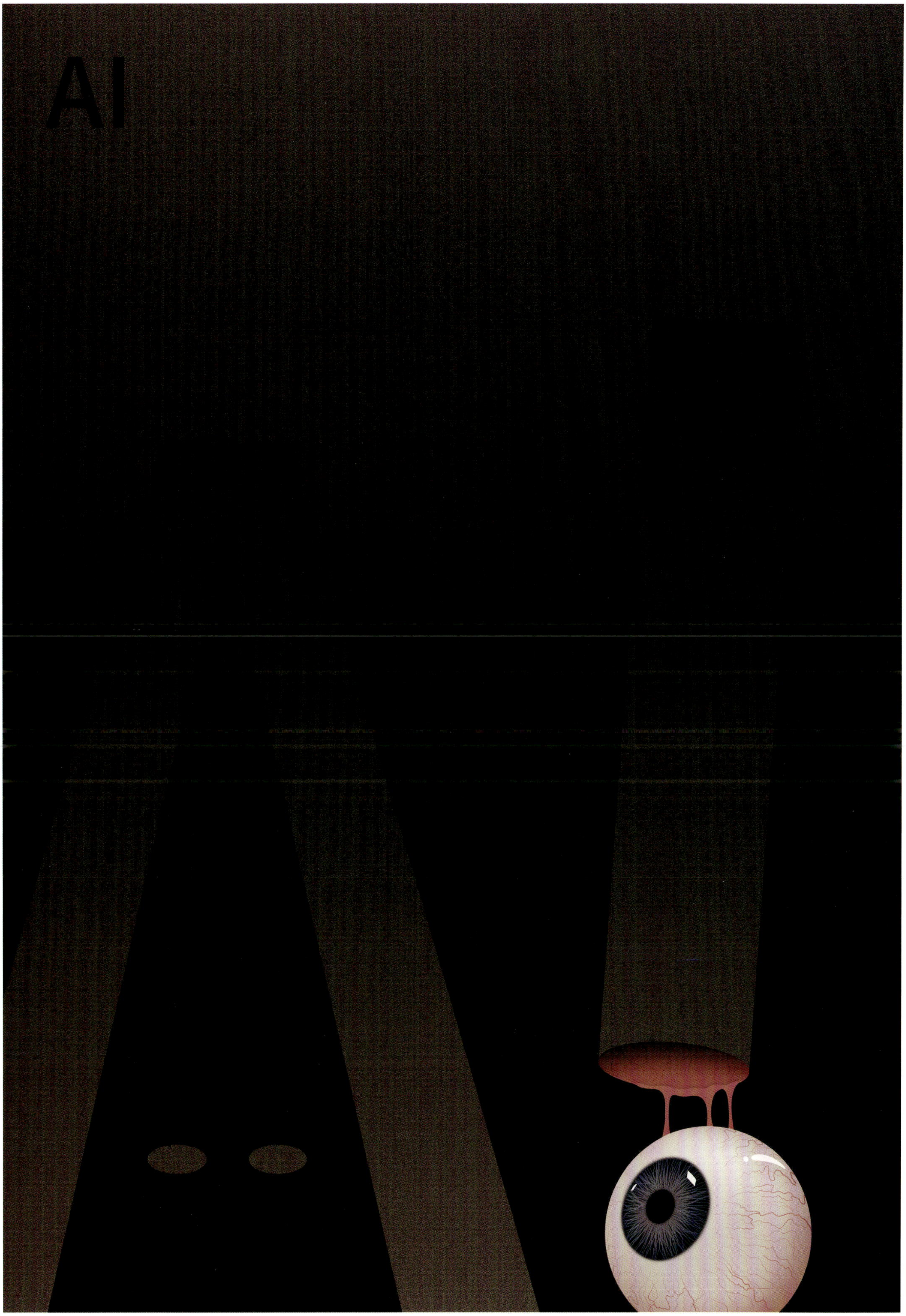

113 ZHONGJUN YIN GOLDPUBLIC & SOCIAL SERVICES

P236: Credit & CommentaryTitle: Awakening of AI | Client: Self-initiated | Design Firm: Dalian RYCX Design

After

20

Incredible Years

of performing in the circus, they were going to give Leon something special for his retirement.

Stop the abuse of big cats.

Learn more at BigCatRescue.org

PUBLIC & SOCIAL SERVICES

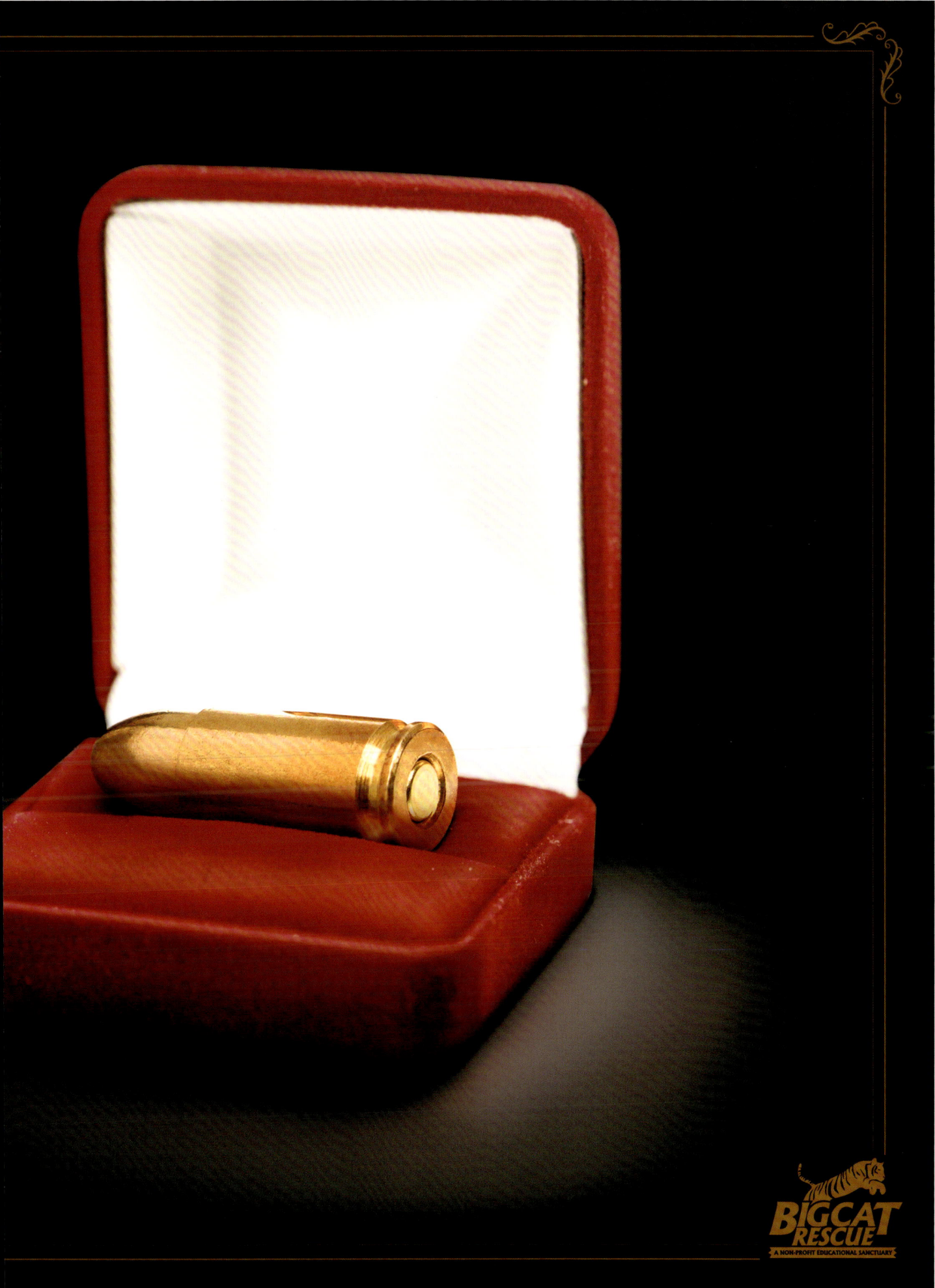

Title: Special Retirement Gift | Client: Big Cat Rescue | Design Firm: PPK

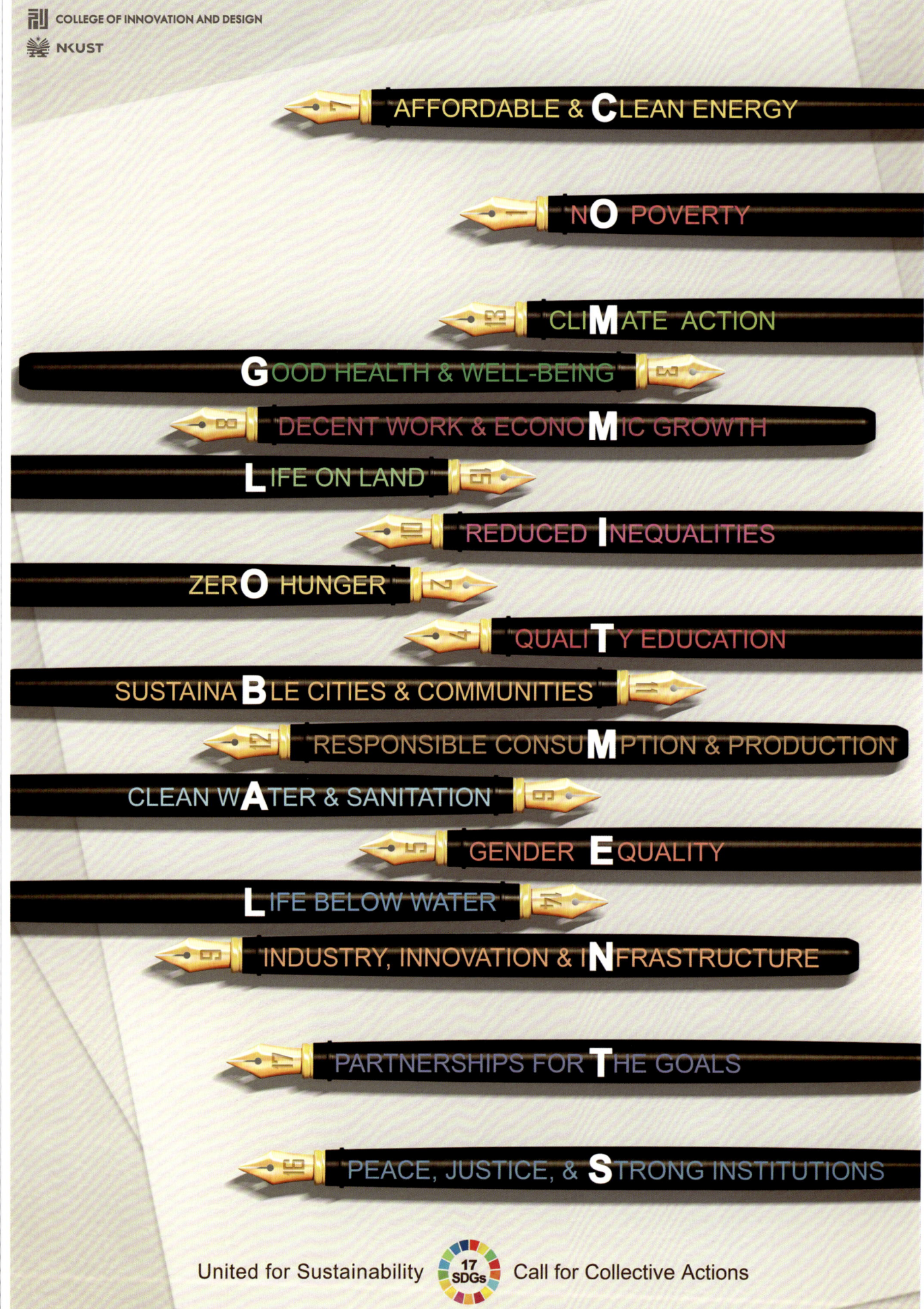

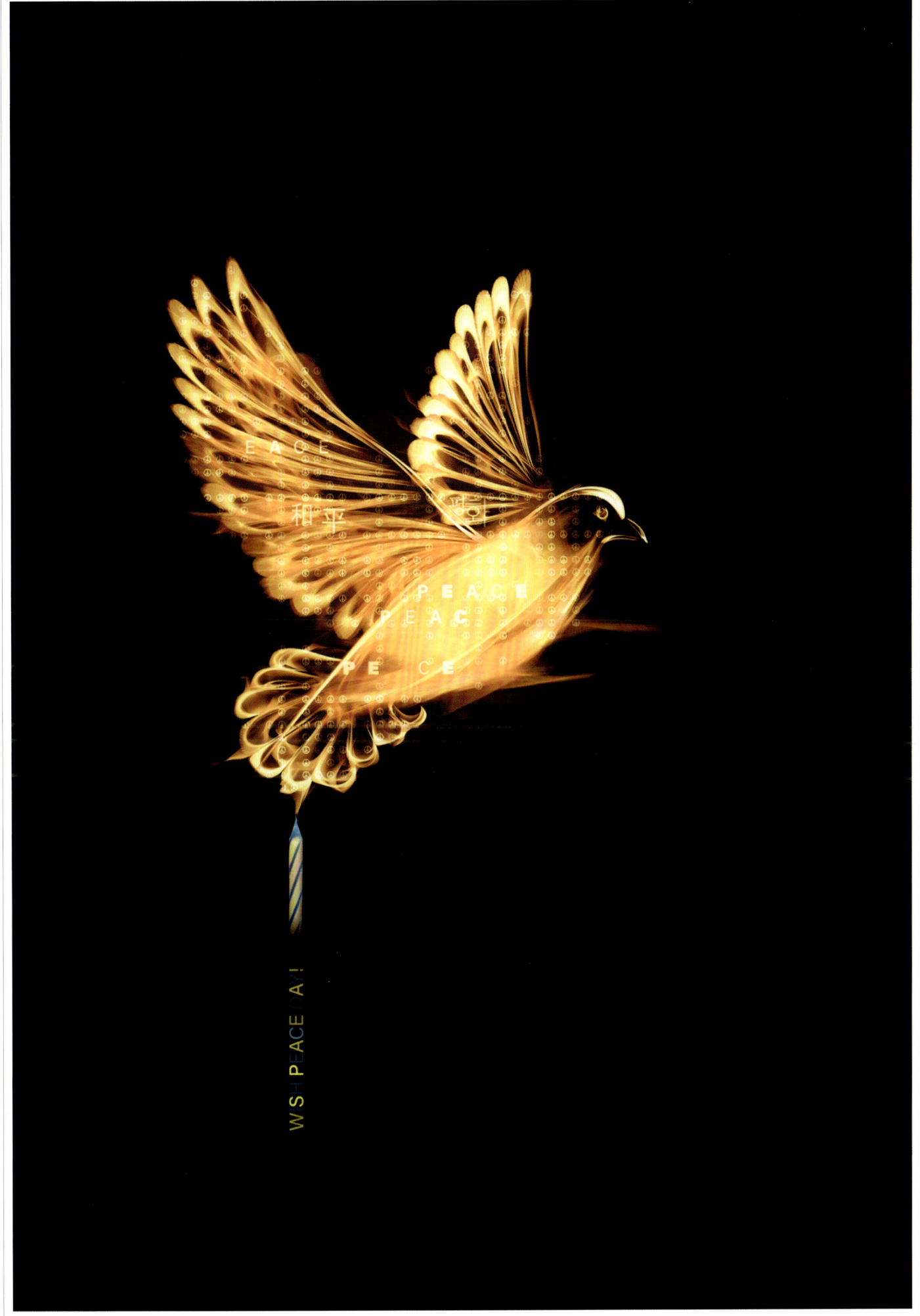

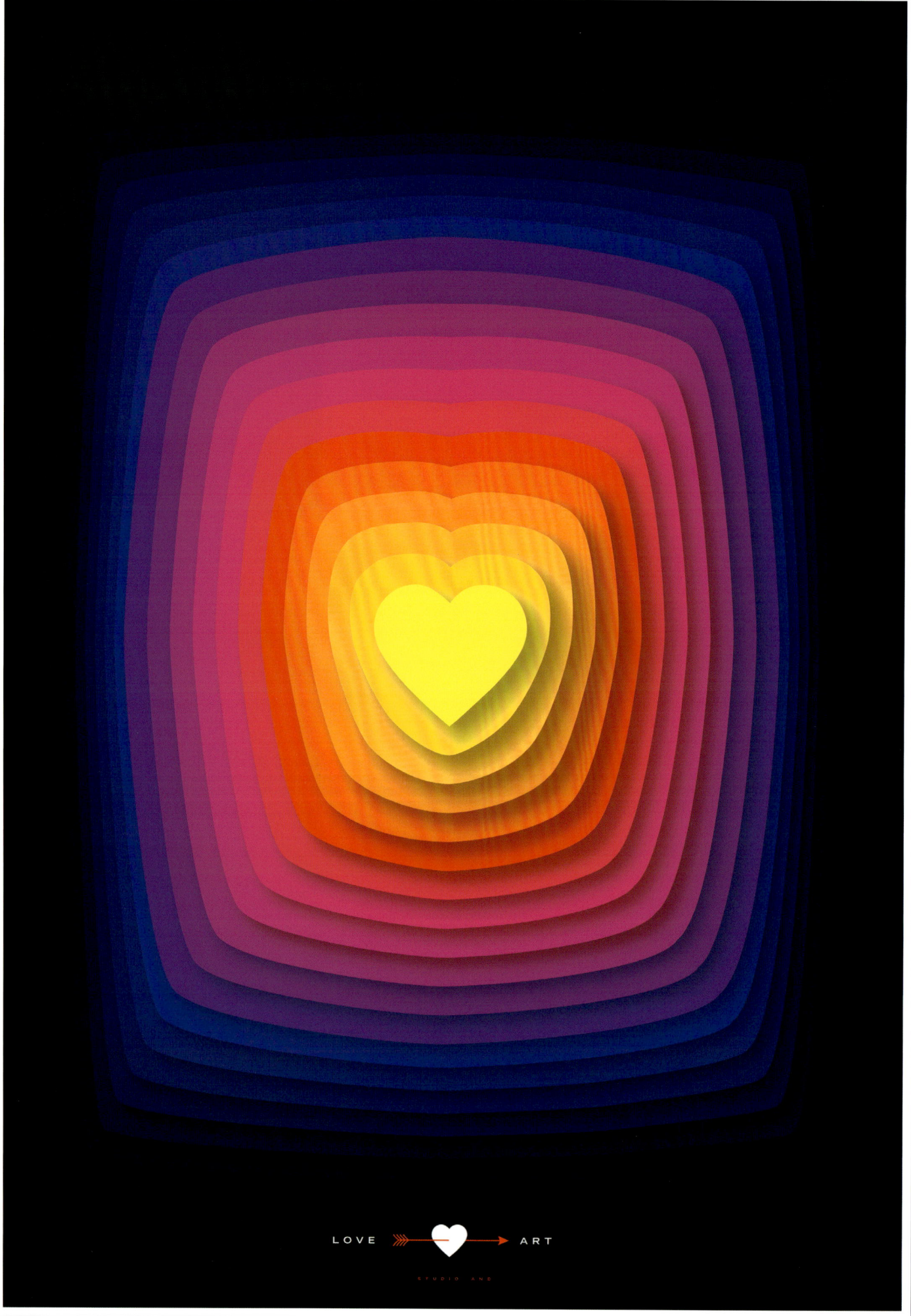

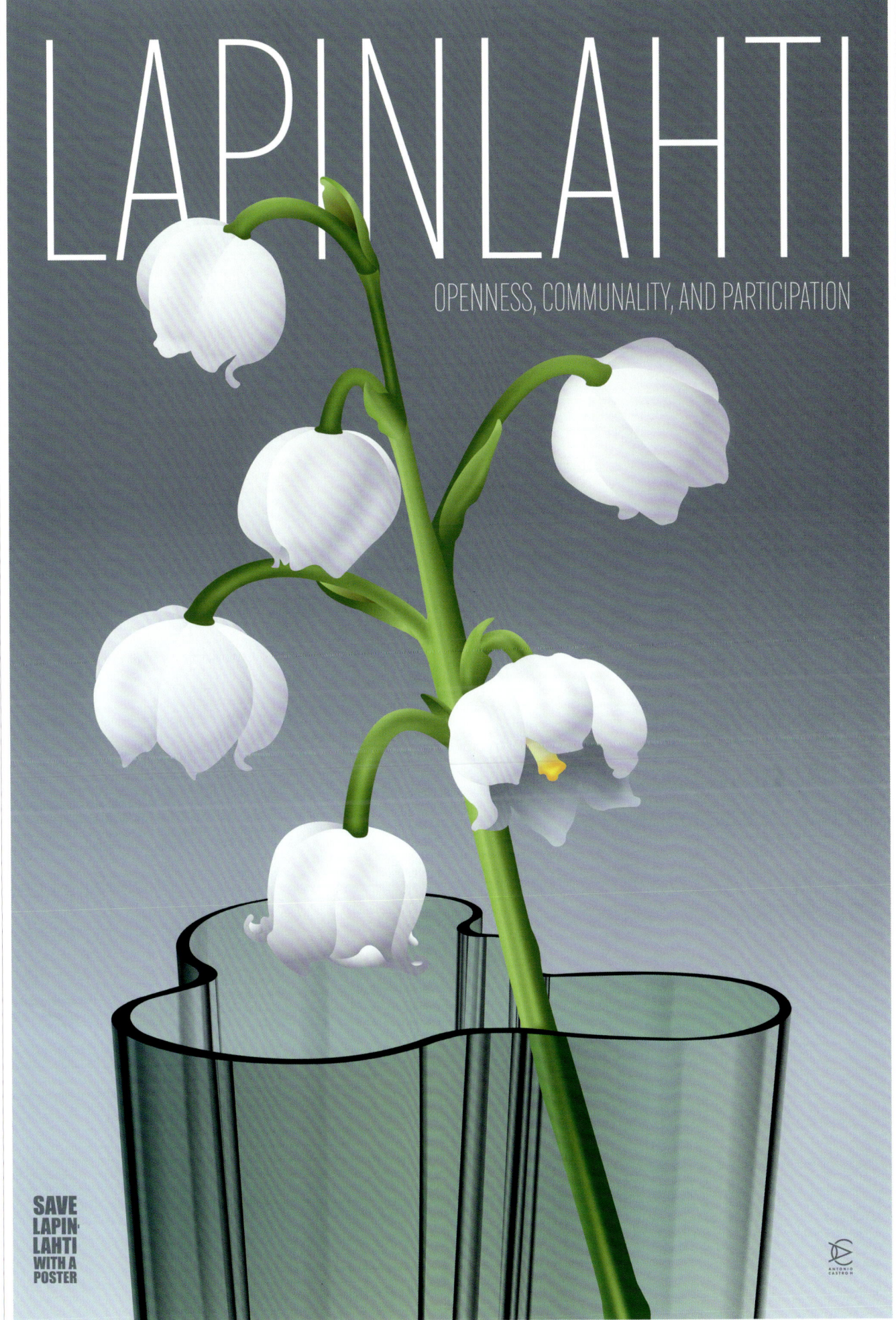

Title: Lapinlahti, Openness, Communality, and Participation | Client: Save Lapinlahti with a Poster
Design Firm: Antonio Castro Design | P237: Credit & Commentary

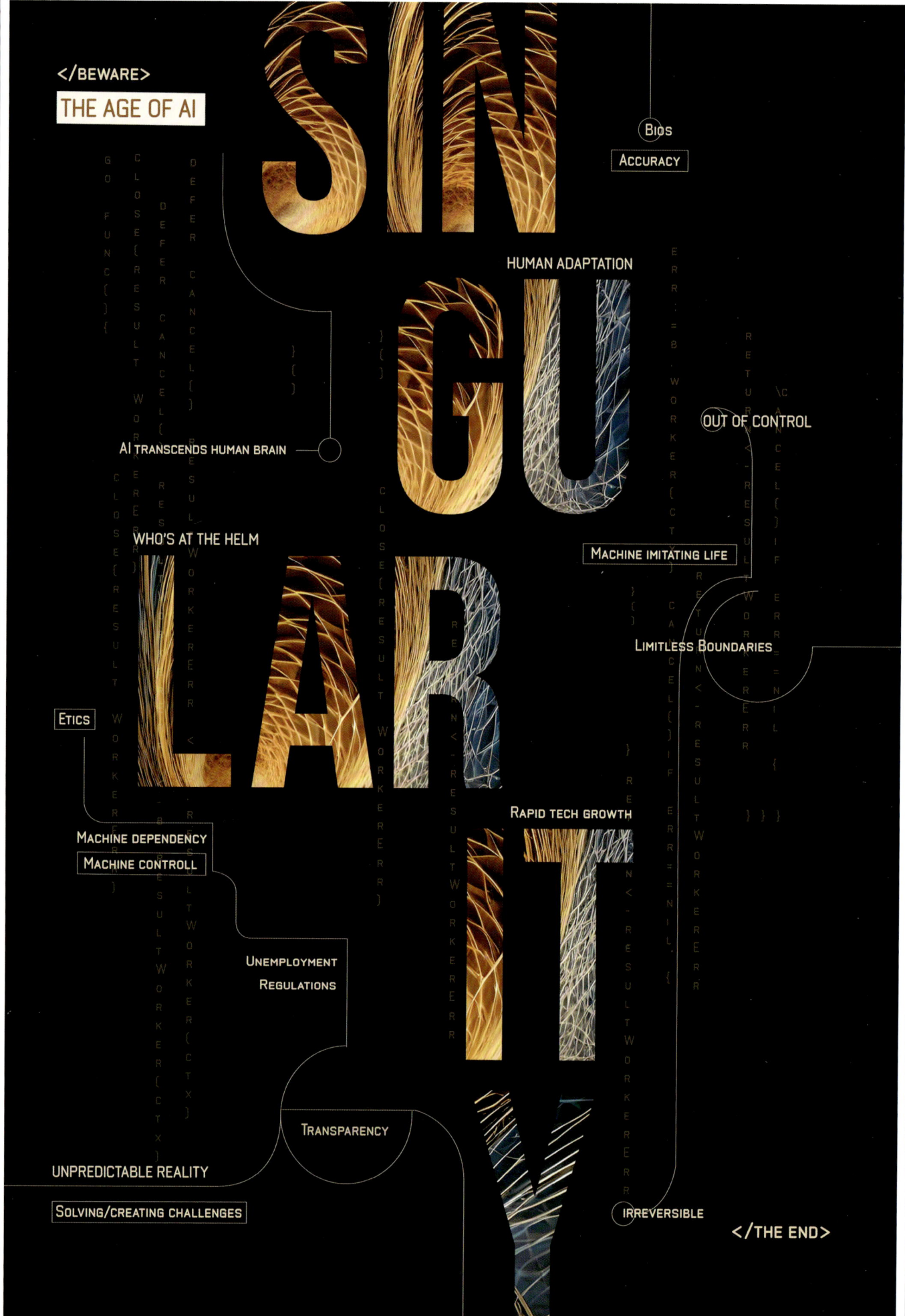

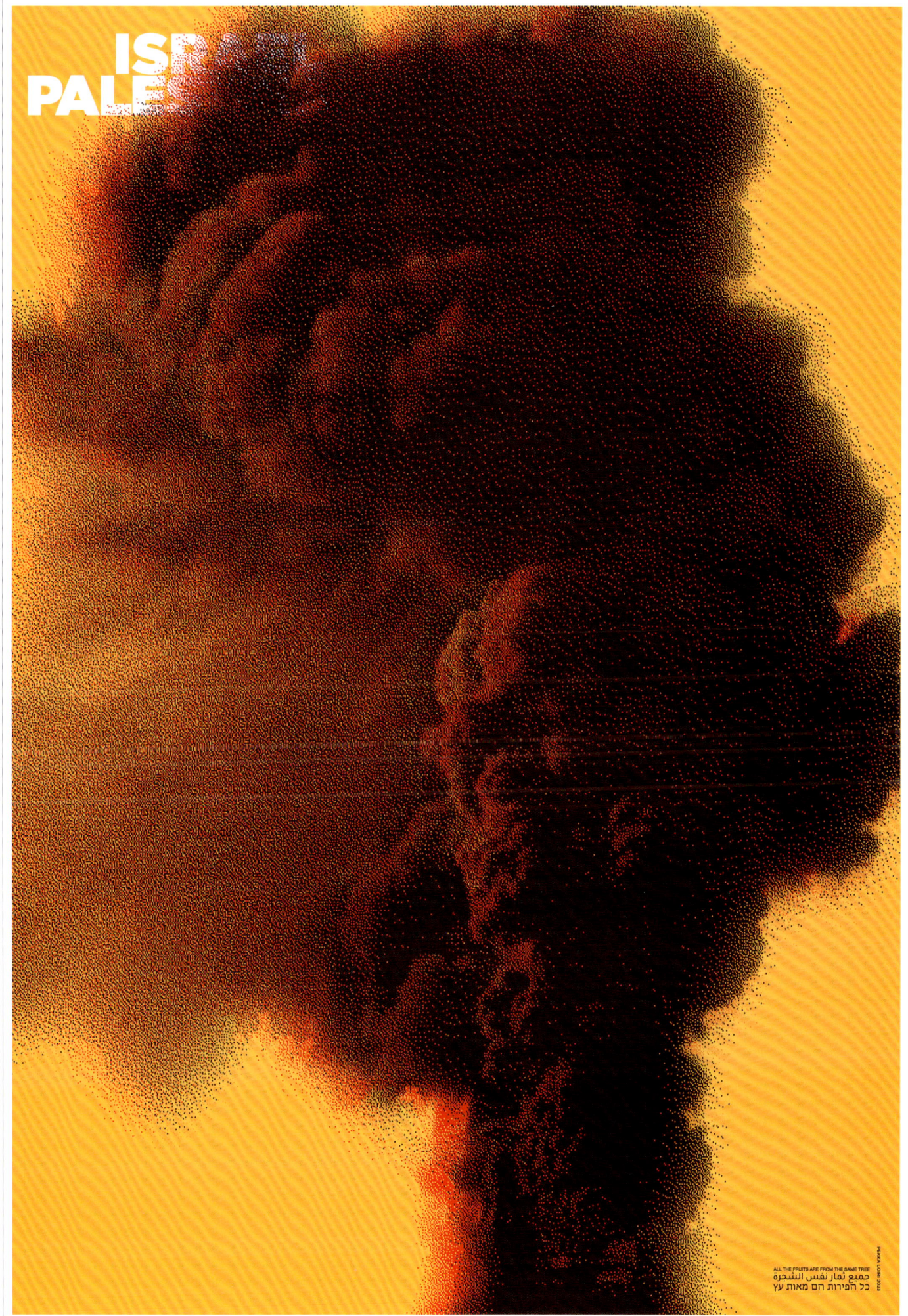

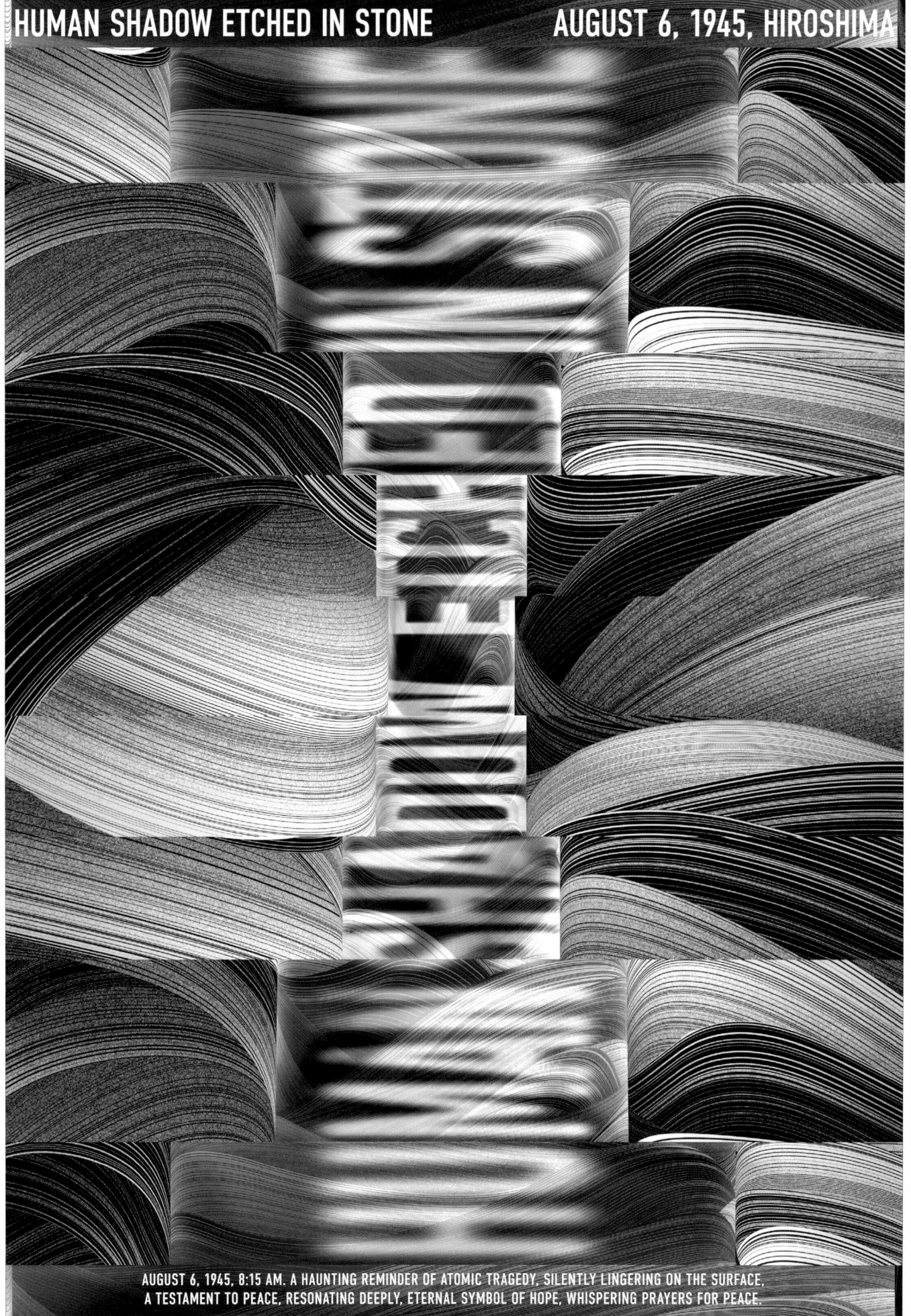

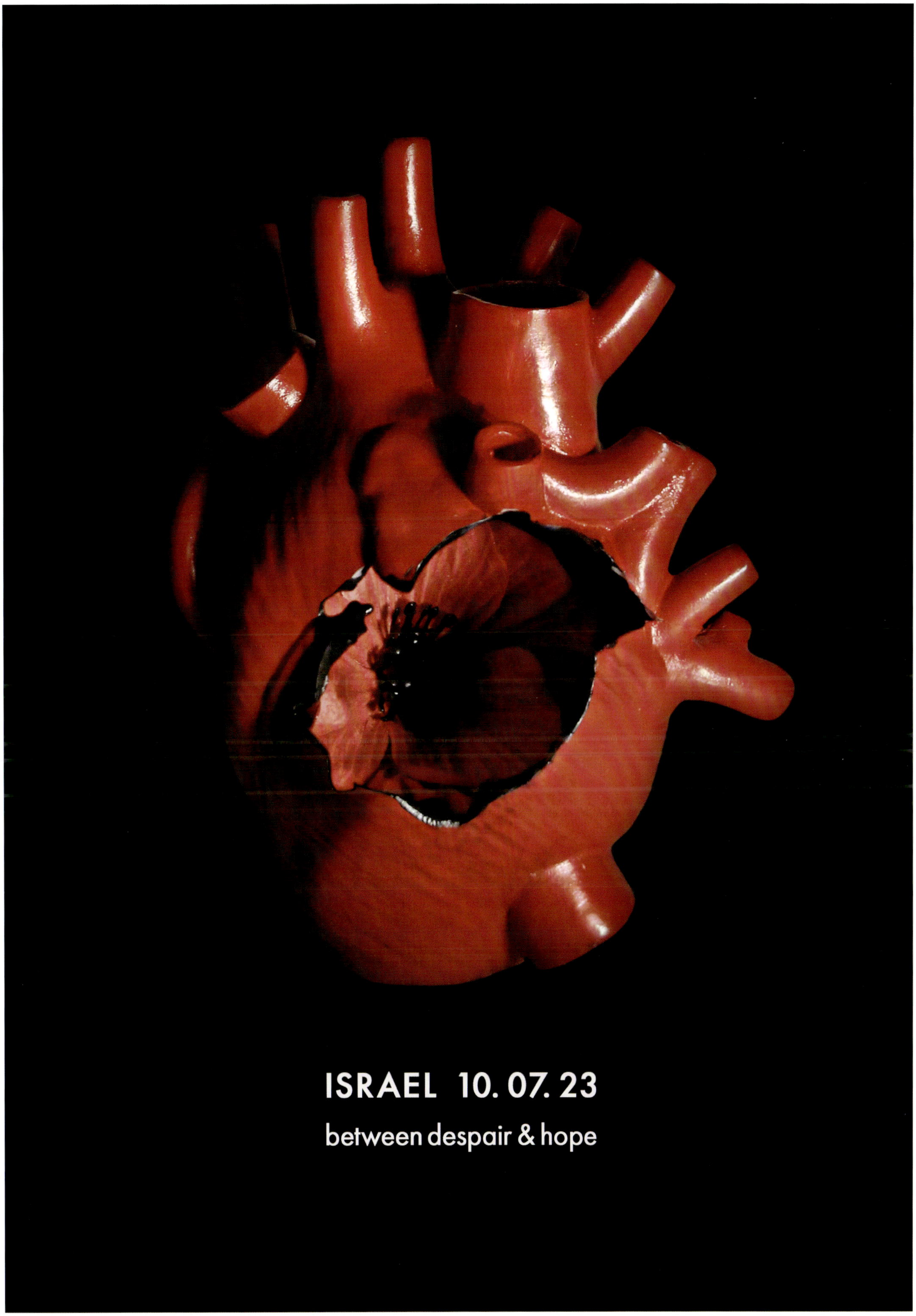

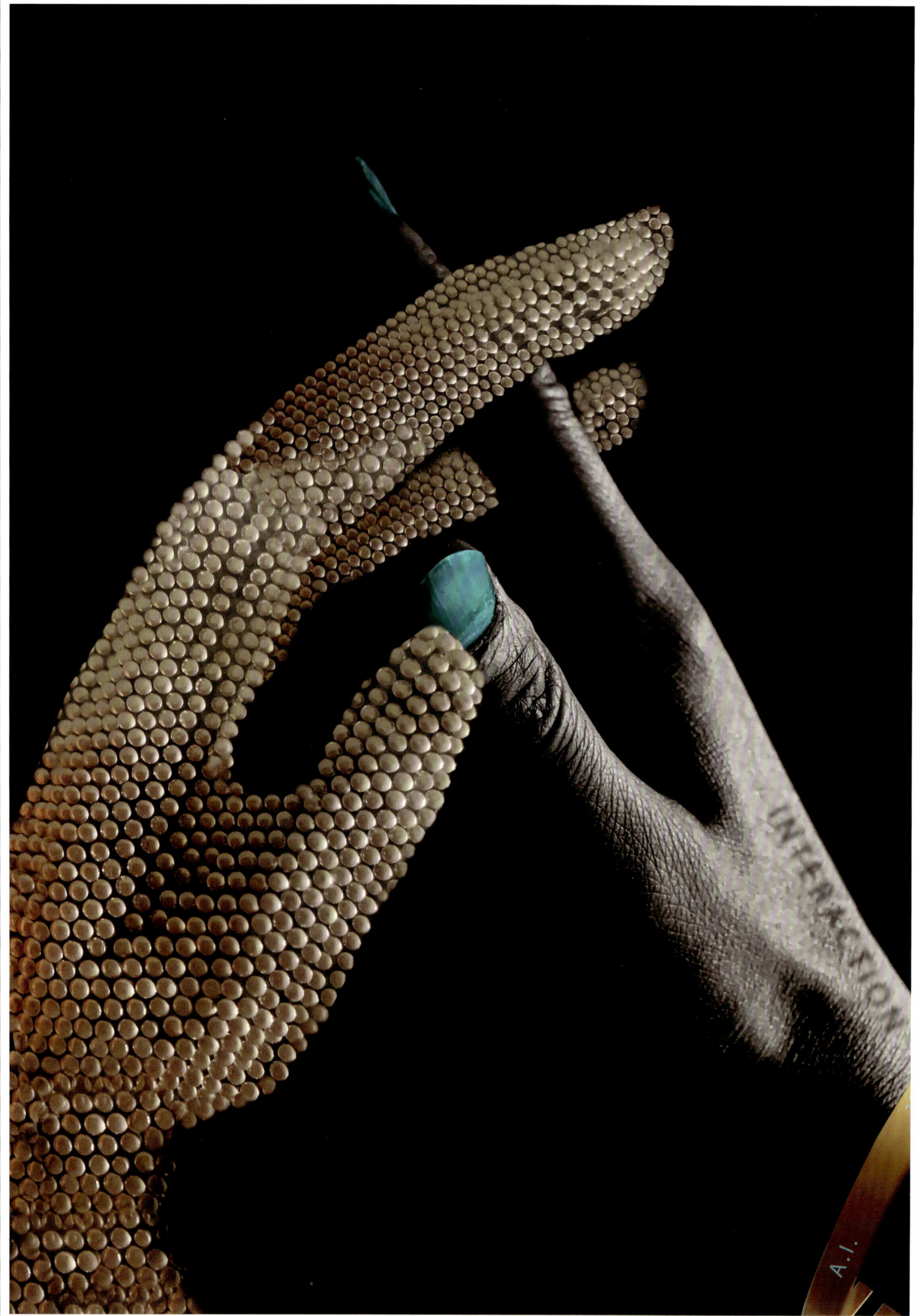

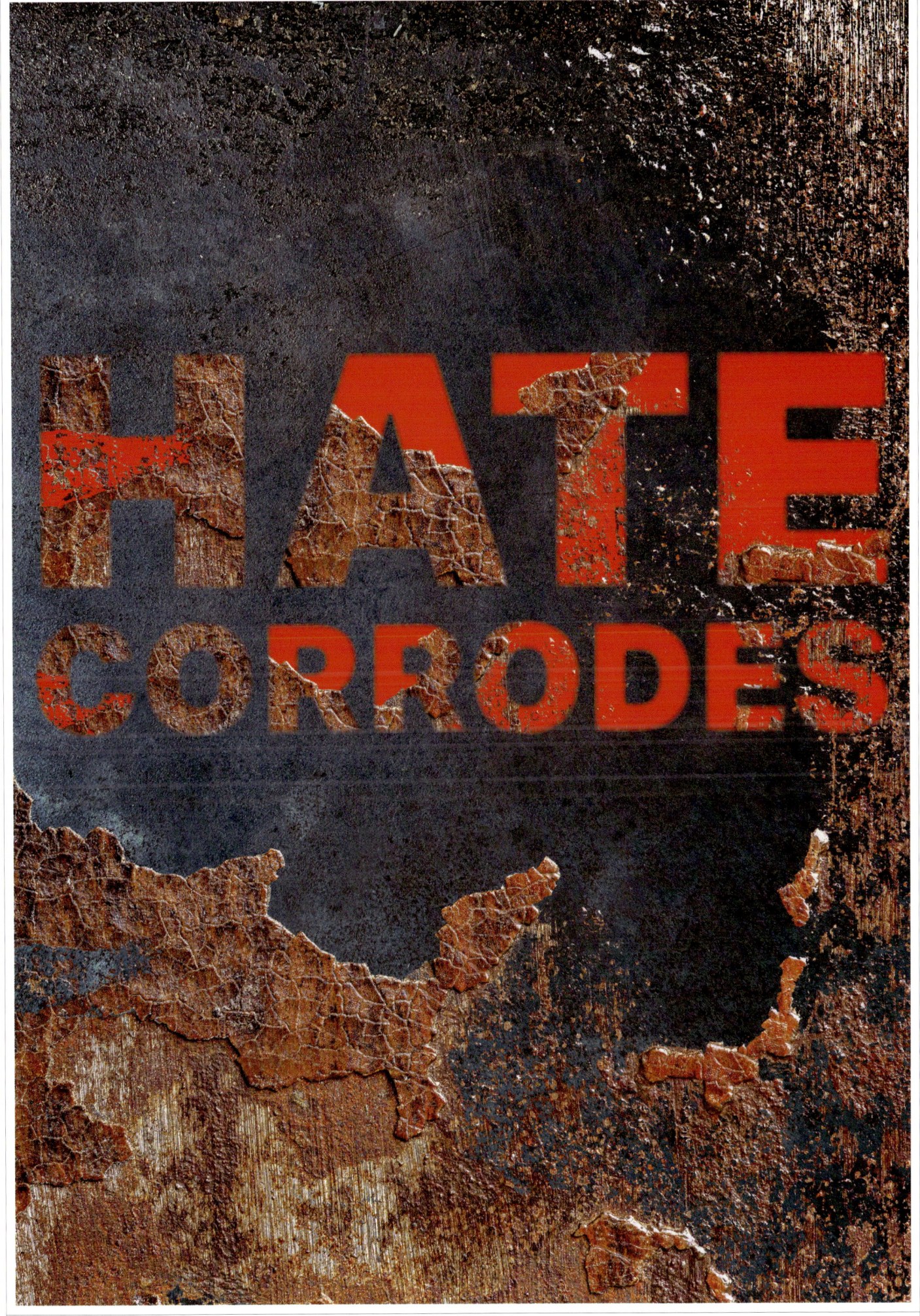

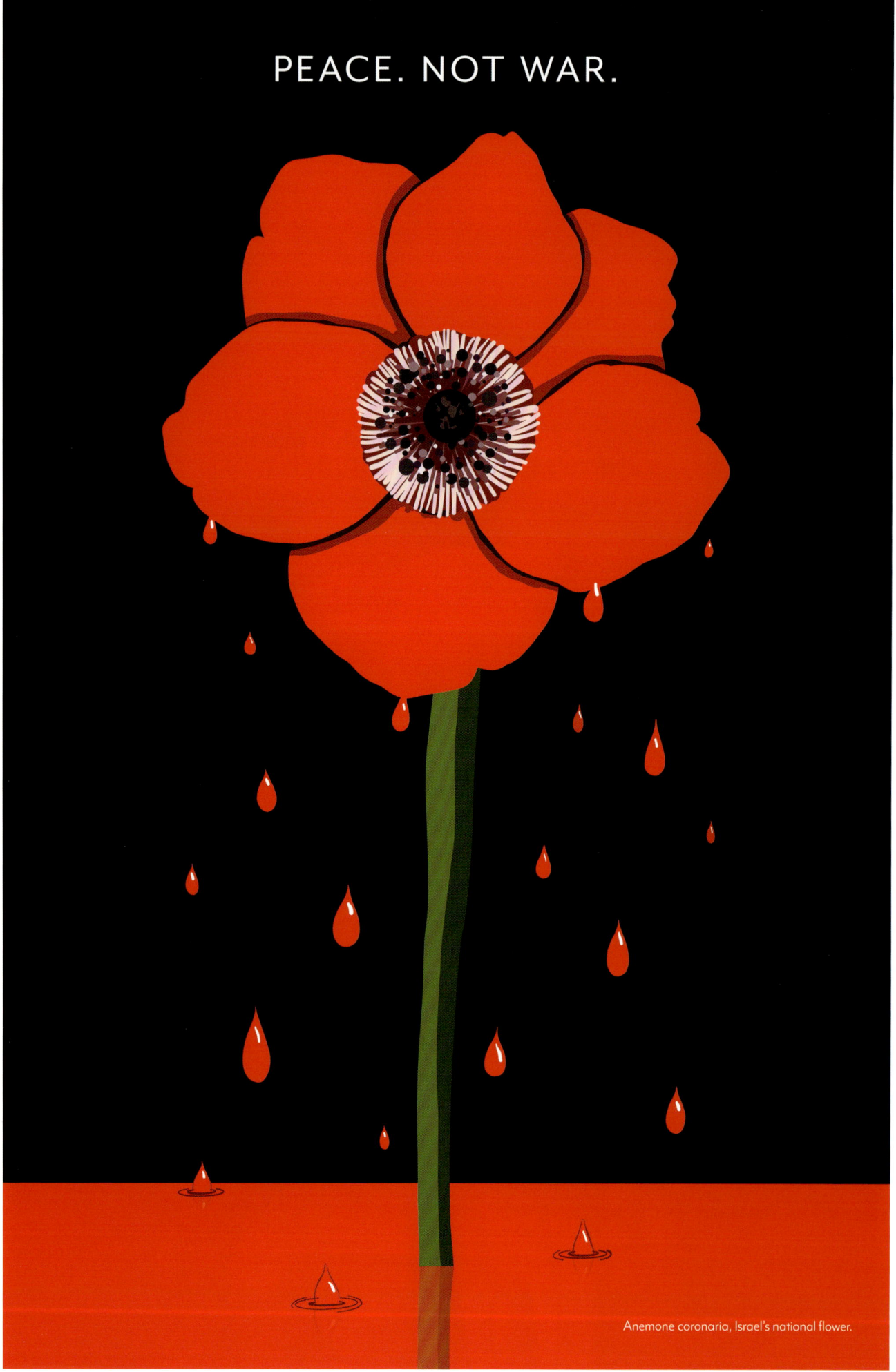

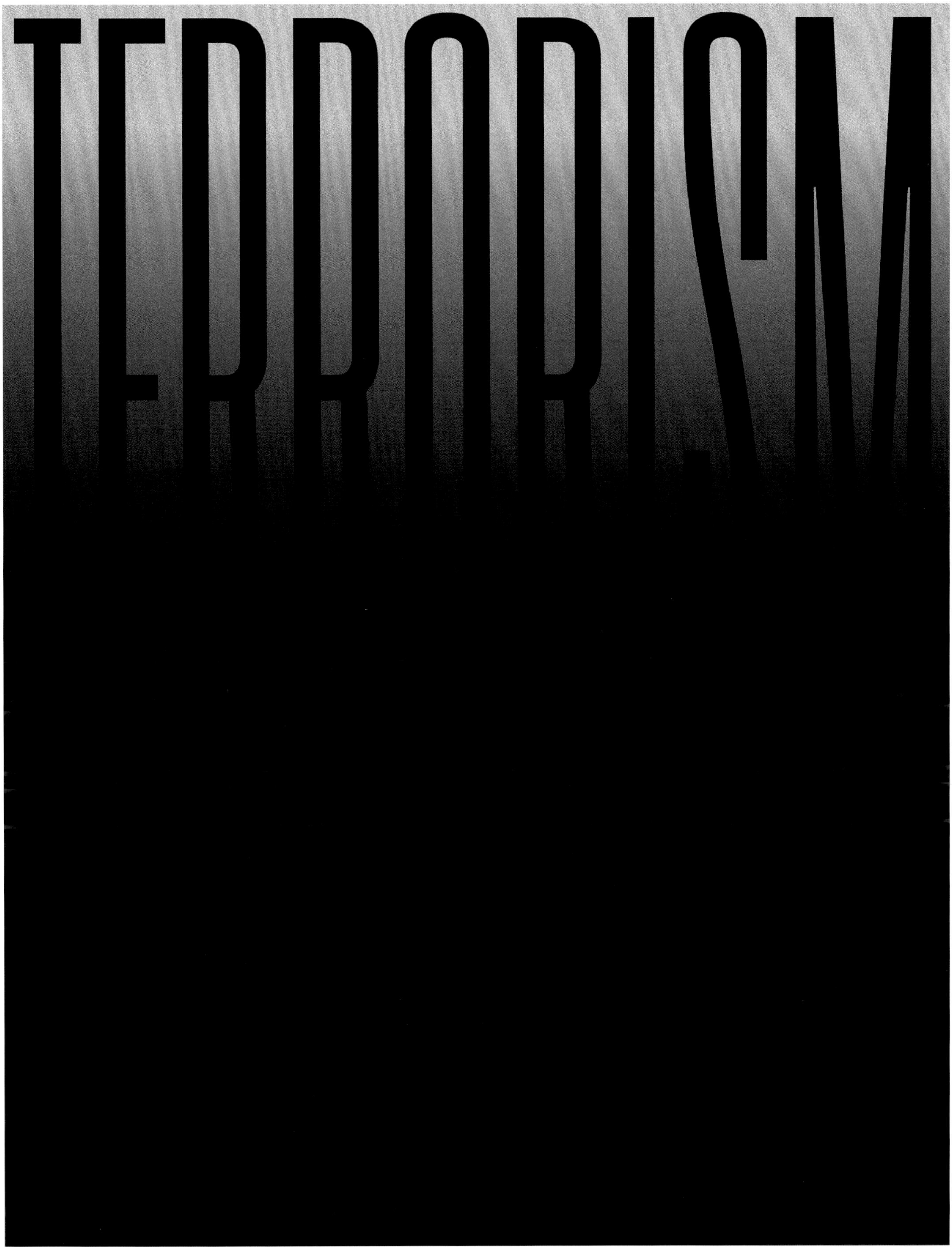

127 DERWYN GOODALL GOLD SOCIAL & POLITICAL

TERRORISM

P237: Credit & Commentary   **Title:** Terrorism | **Client:** Self-initiated | **Design Firm:** Goodall Integrated Design

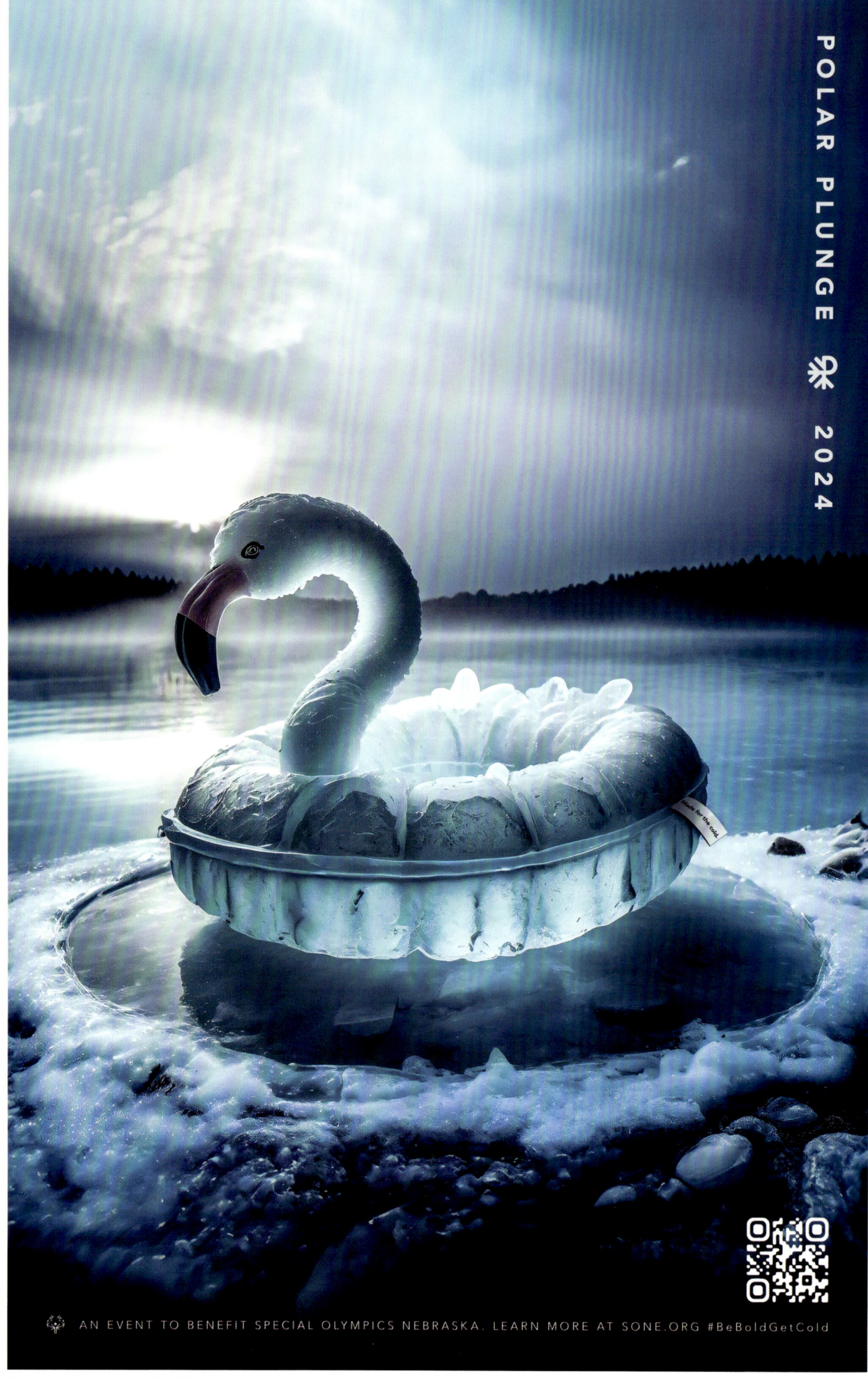

Title: Made for the Cold | **Client:** Special Olympics Nebraska
Design Firm: Bailey Lauerman | **P237: Credit & Commentary**

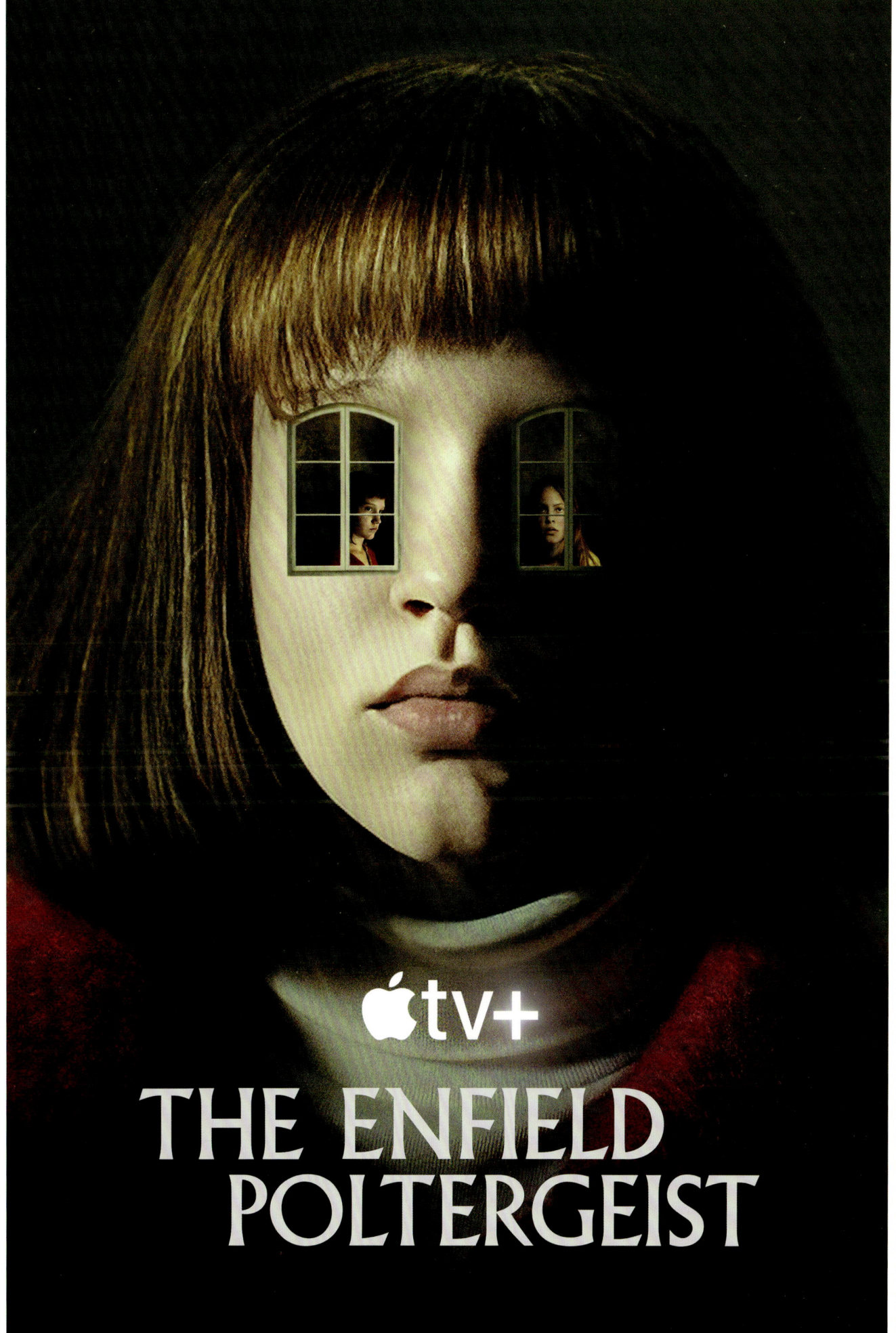

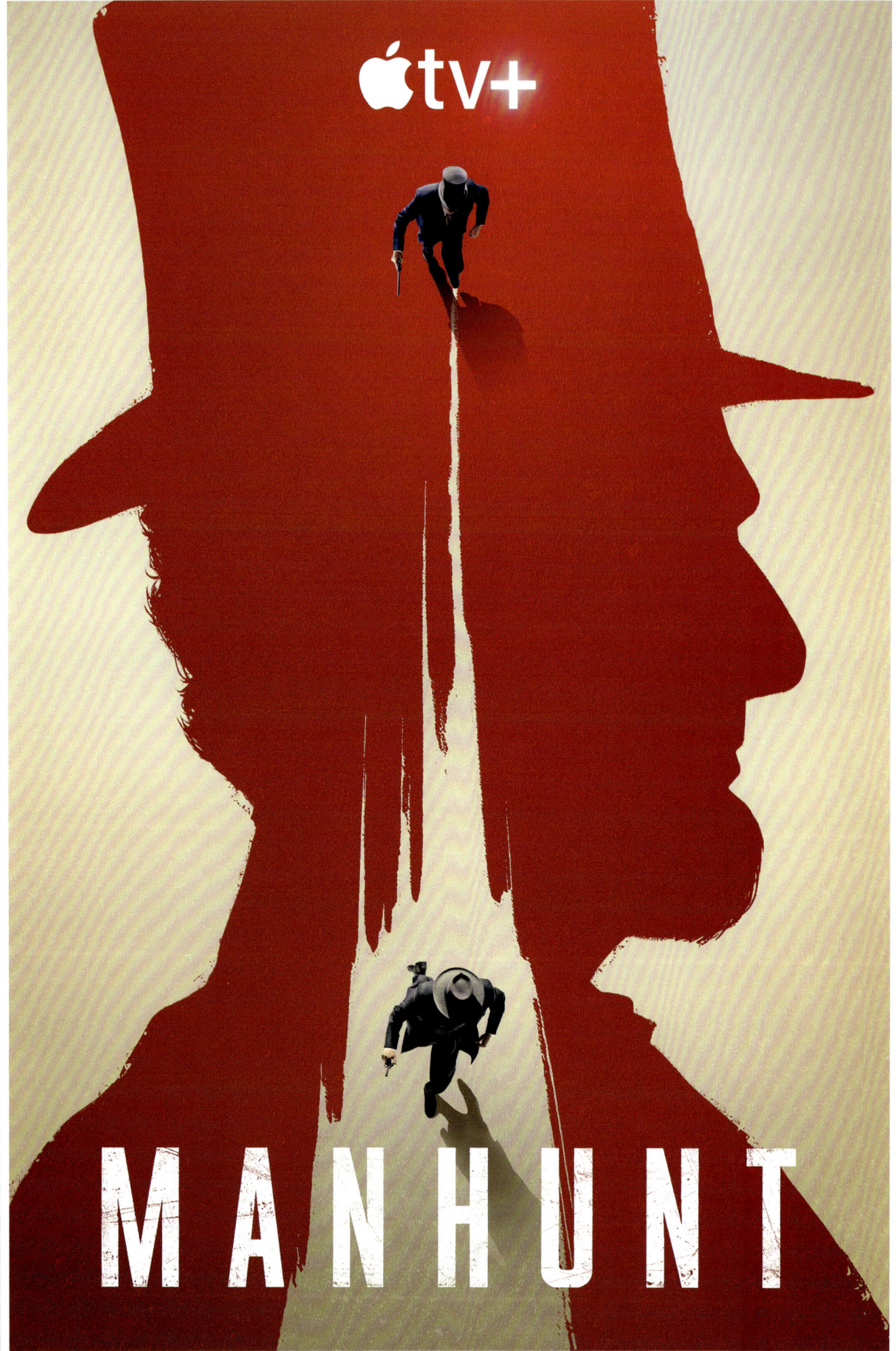

131 CÉLIE CADIEUX GOLD   TELEVISION

BETTER ANGELS
THE GOSPEL ACCORDING TO TAMMY FAYE

FROM DIRECTOR DANA ADAM SHAPIRO AND EXECUTIVE PRODUCERS ELTON JOHN & DAVID FURNISH

Title: Better Angels: The Gospel According to Tammy Faye | **Client:** Vice Studios
Design Firm: Célie Cadieux | **P237:** Credit & Commentary

132 LEROY & ROSE GOLD

TELEVISION

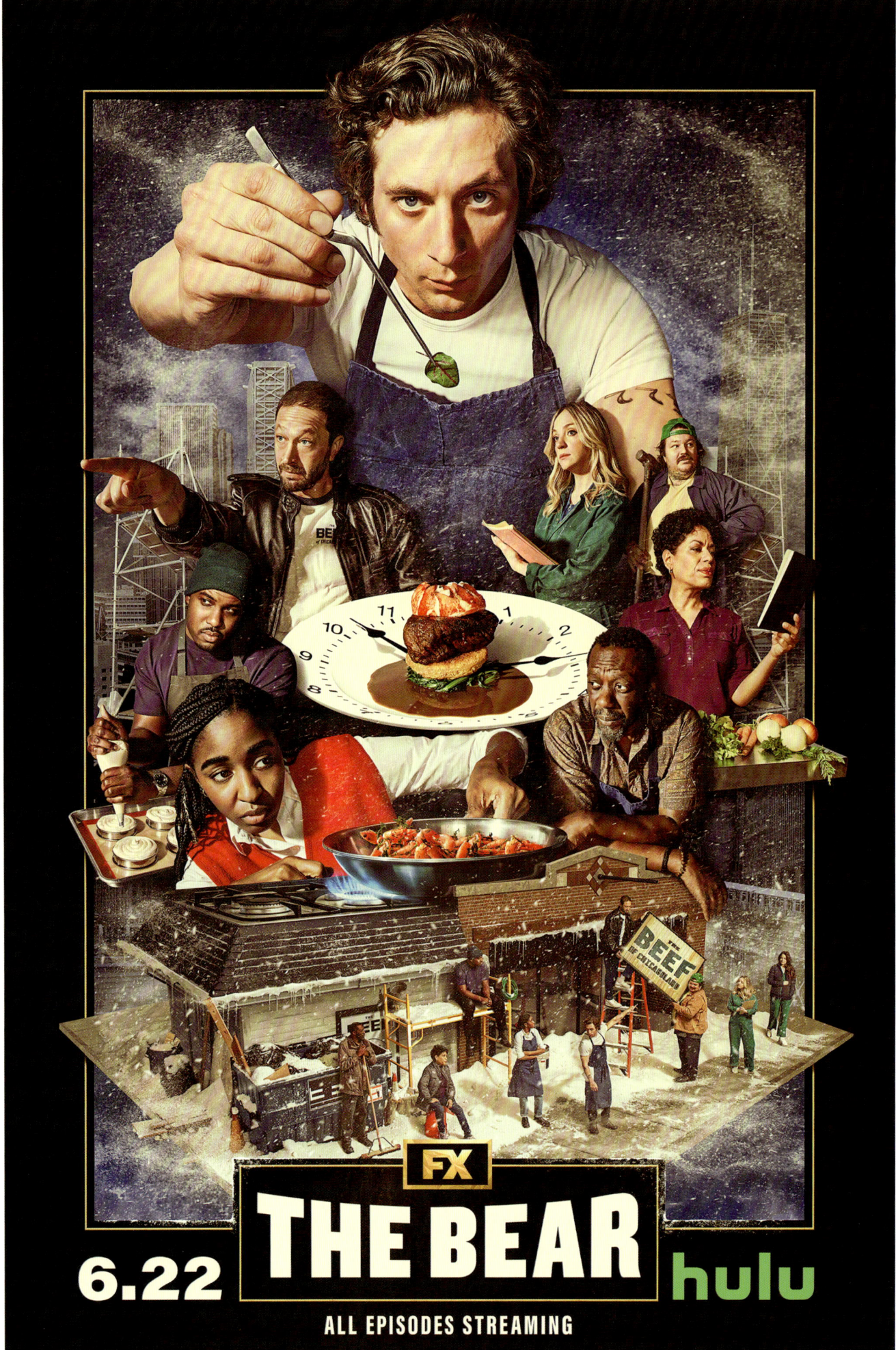

P237: Credit & Commentary Title: The Bear: Season 2 | Client: FX | Design Firm: Leroy & Rose

133 KISHAN MUTHUCUMARU GOLD TELEVISION

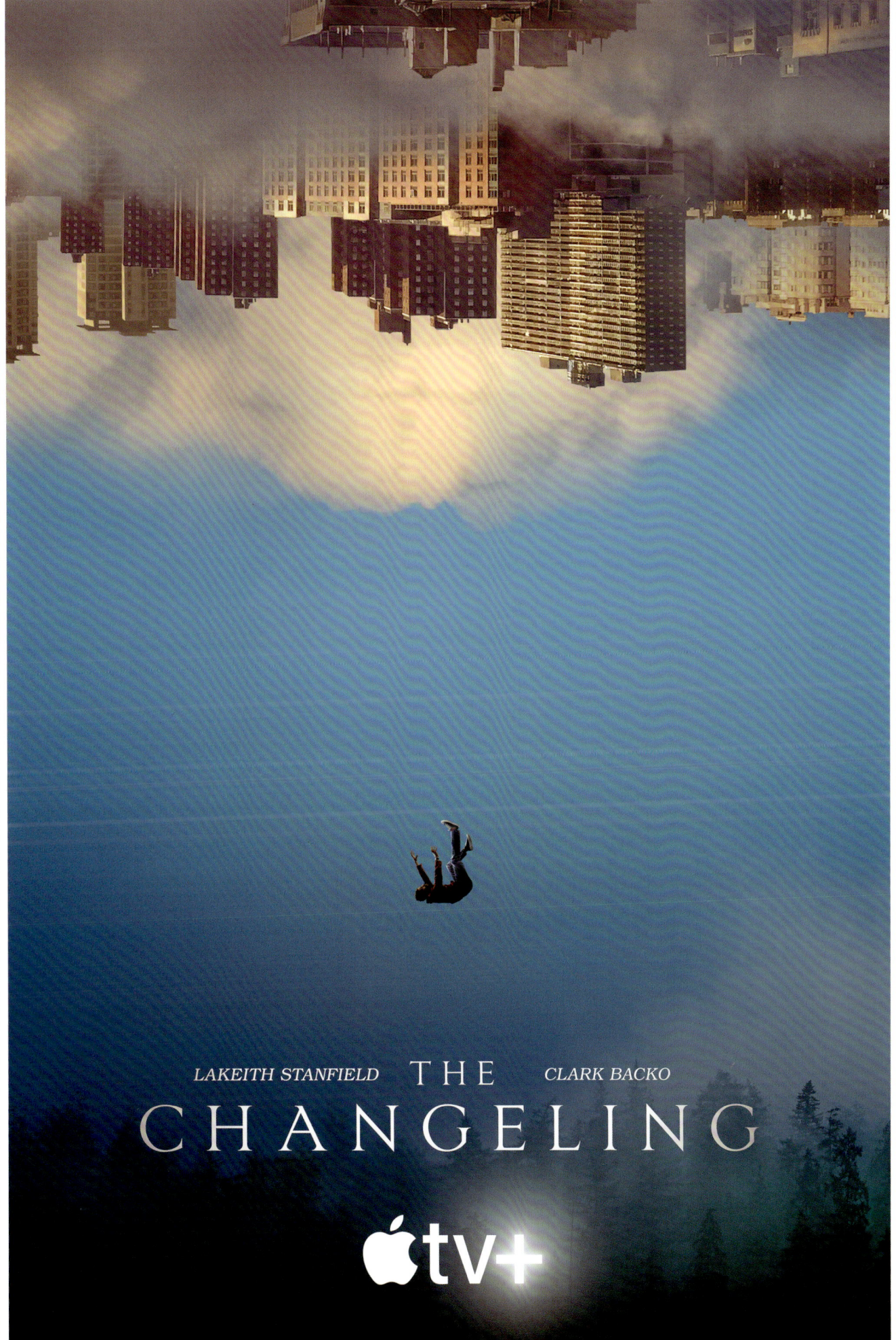

P238: Credit & Commentary   **Title:** The Changeling Teaser Key Art | **Client:** Apple TV+ | **Design Firm:** MOCEAN

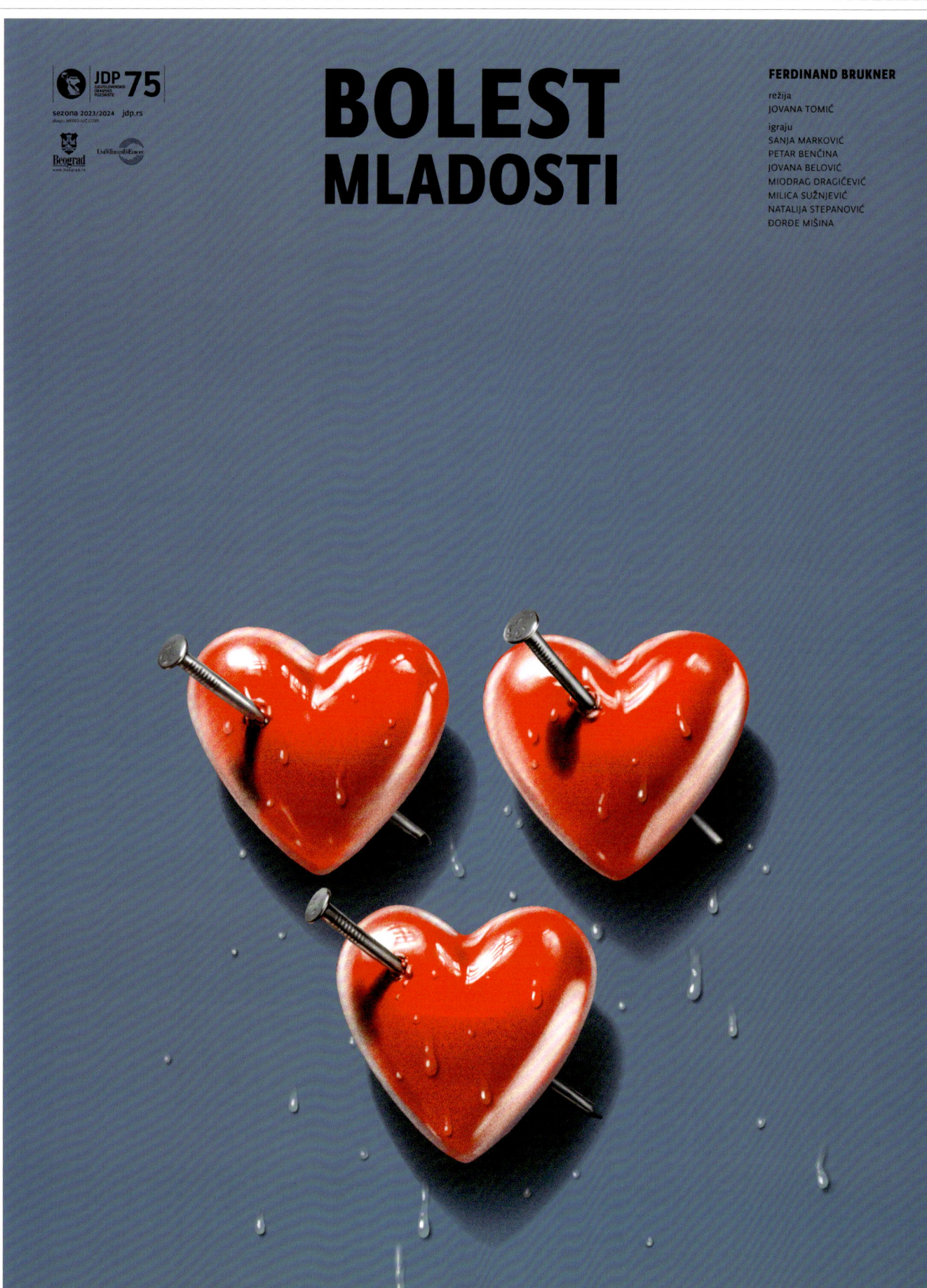

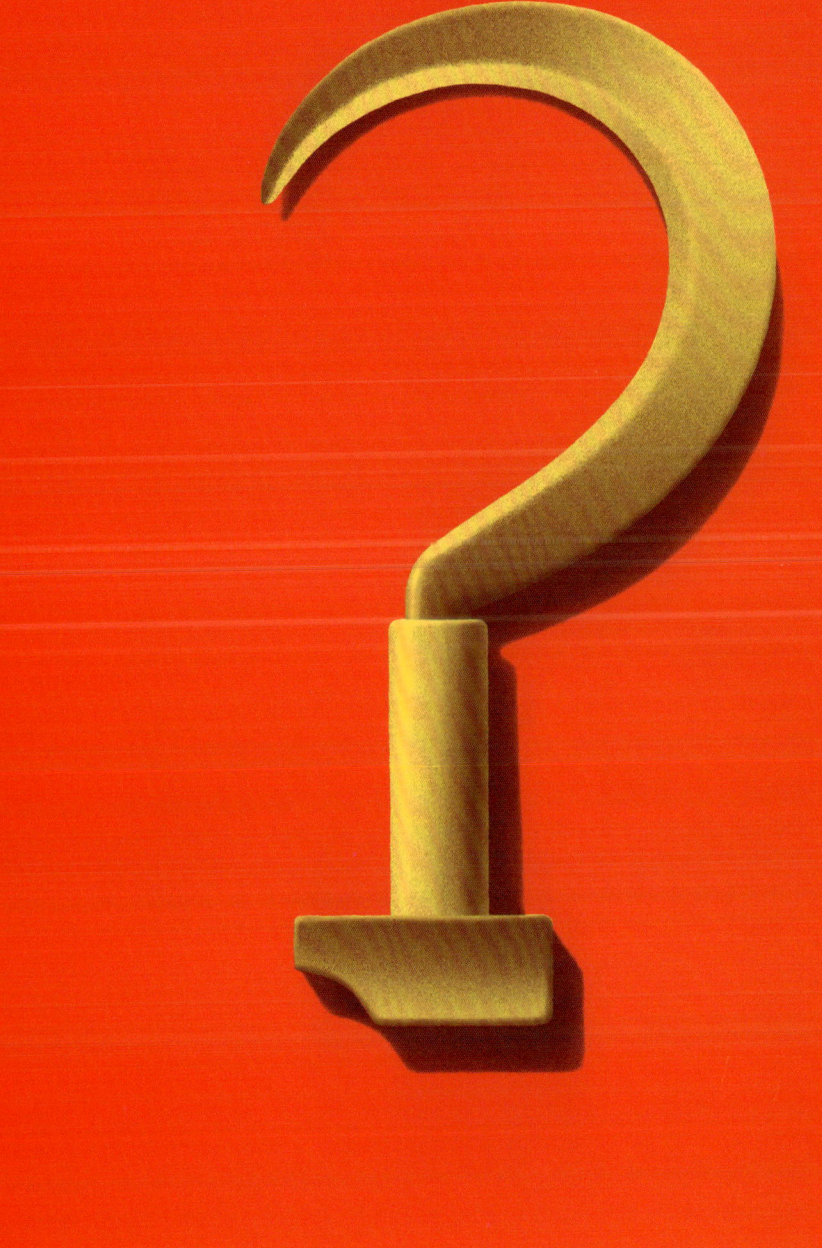

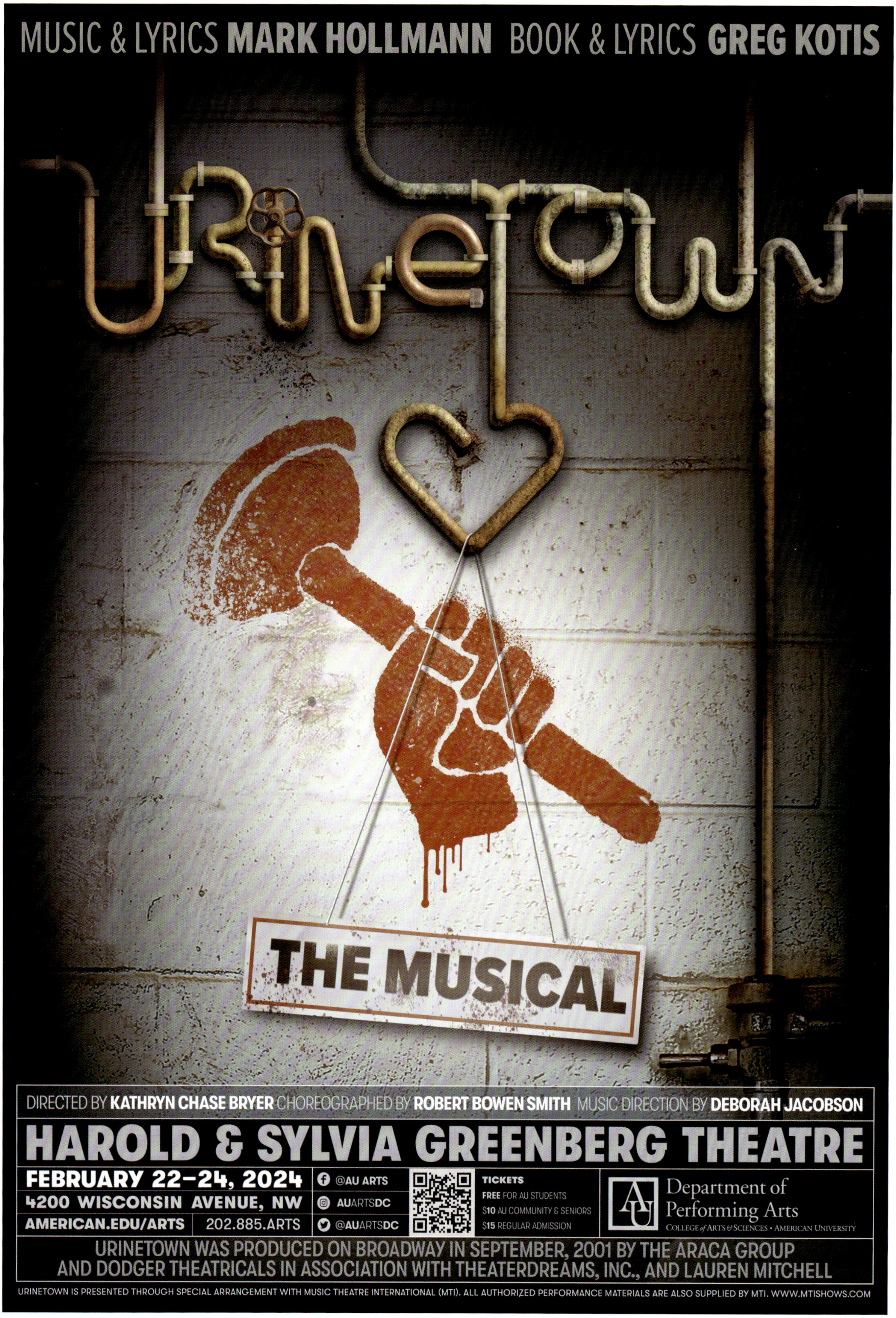

Title: Urinetown: The Musical | **Client:** American University Department of Performing Arts
Design Firm: Chemi Montes Design | **P238:** Credit & Commentary

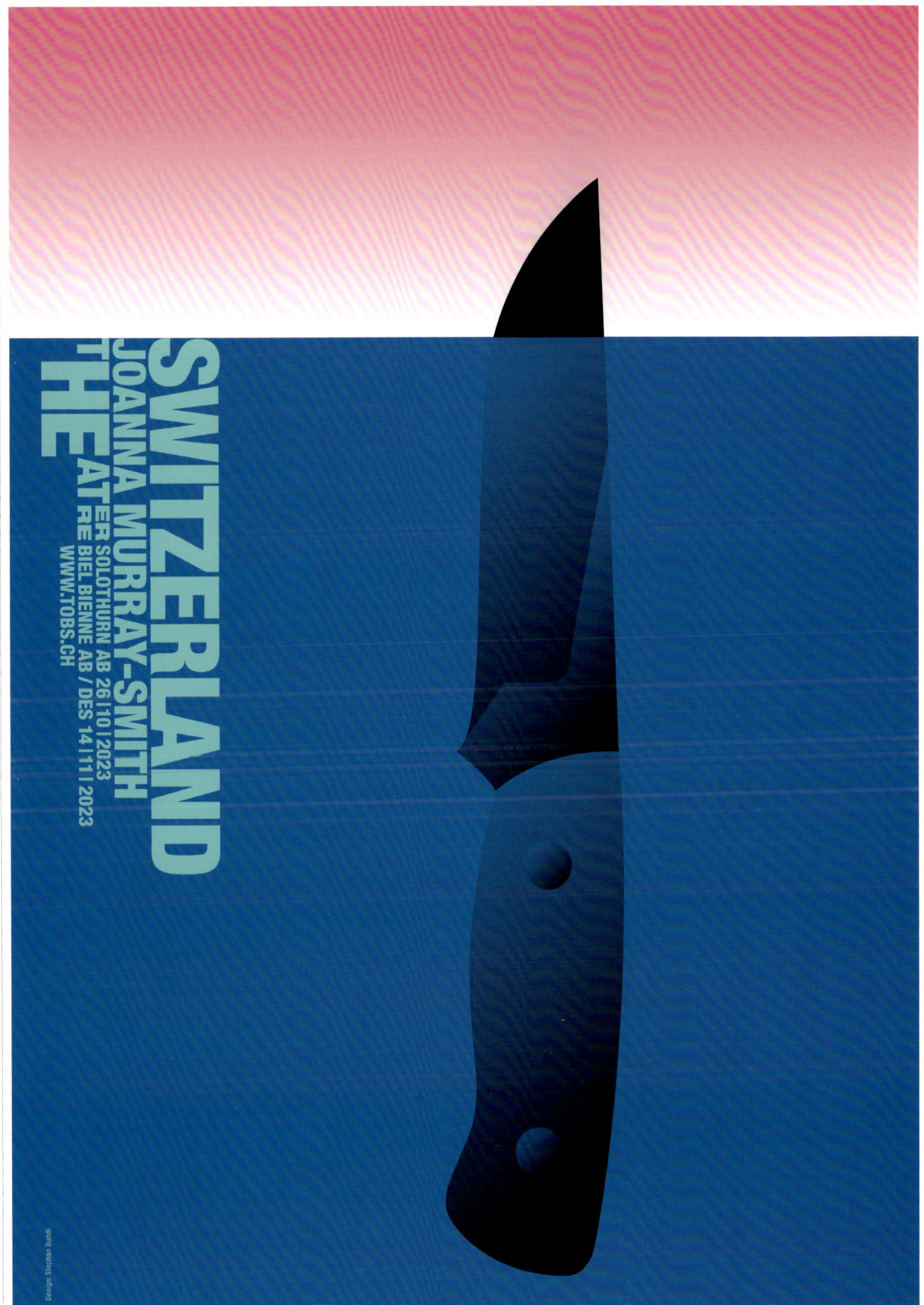

Title: Das kurze Leben der Fakten (The Lifespan of a Fact) | **Client:** Theater Orchester Biel Solothurn
Design Firm: Atelier Bundi AG | **P238:** Credit & Commentary

139 STEPHAN BUNDI GOLD | THEATER

Title: Cyrano | **Client:** Theater Orchester Biel Solothurn
Design Firm: Atelier Bundi AG | **P238:** Credit & Commentary

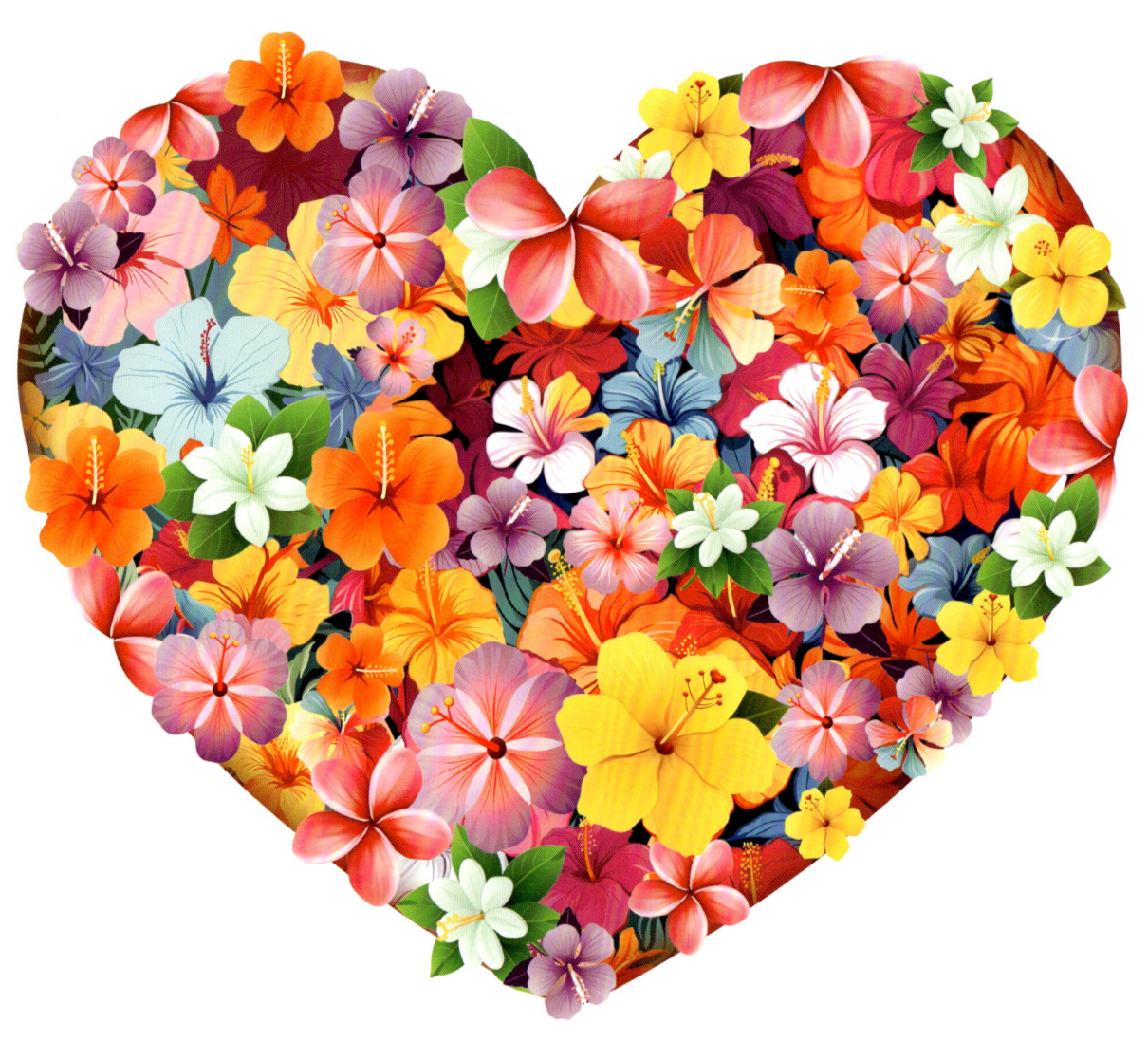

LĀHAINĀ MAUI HAWAI'I

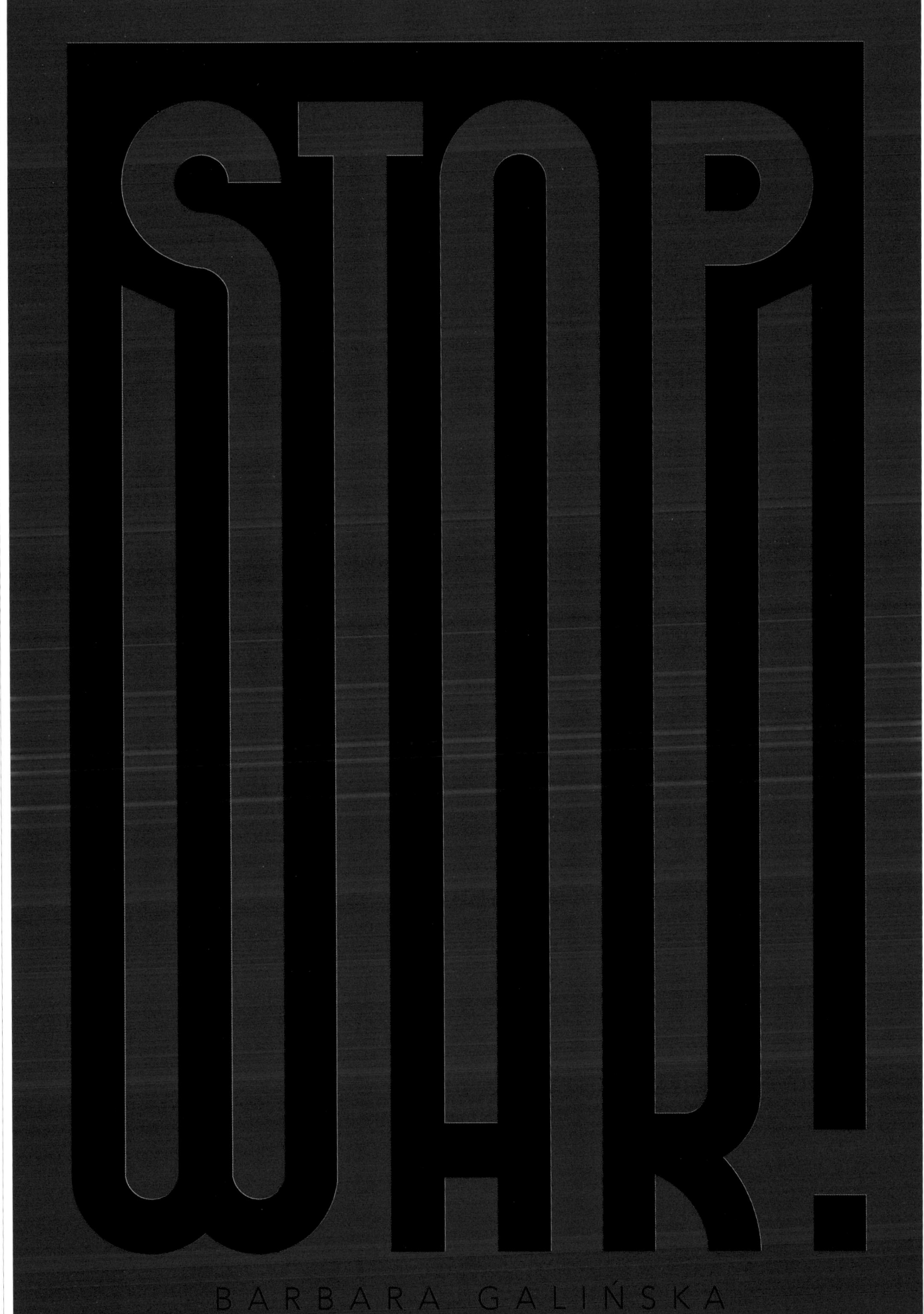

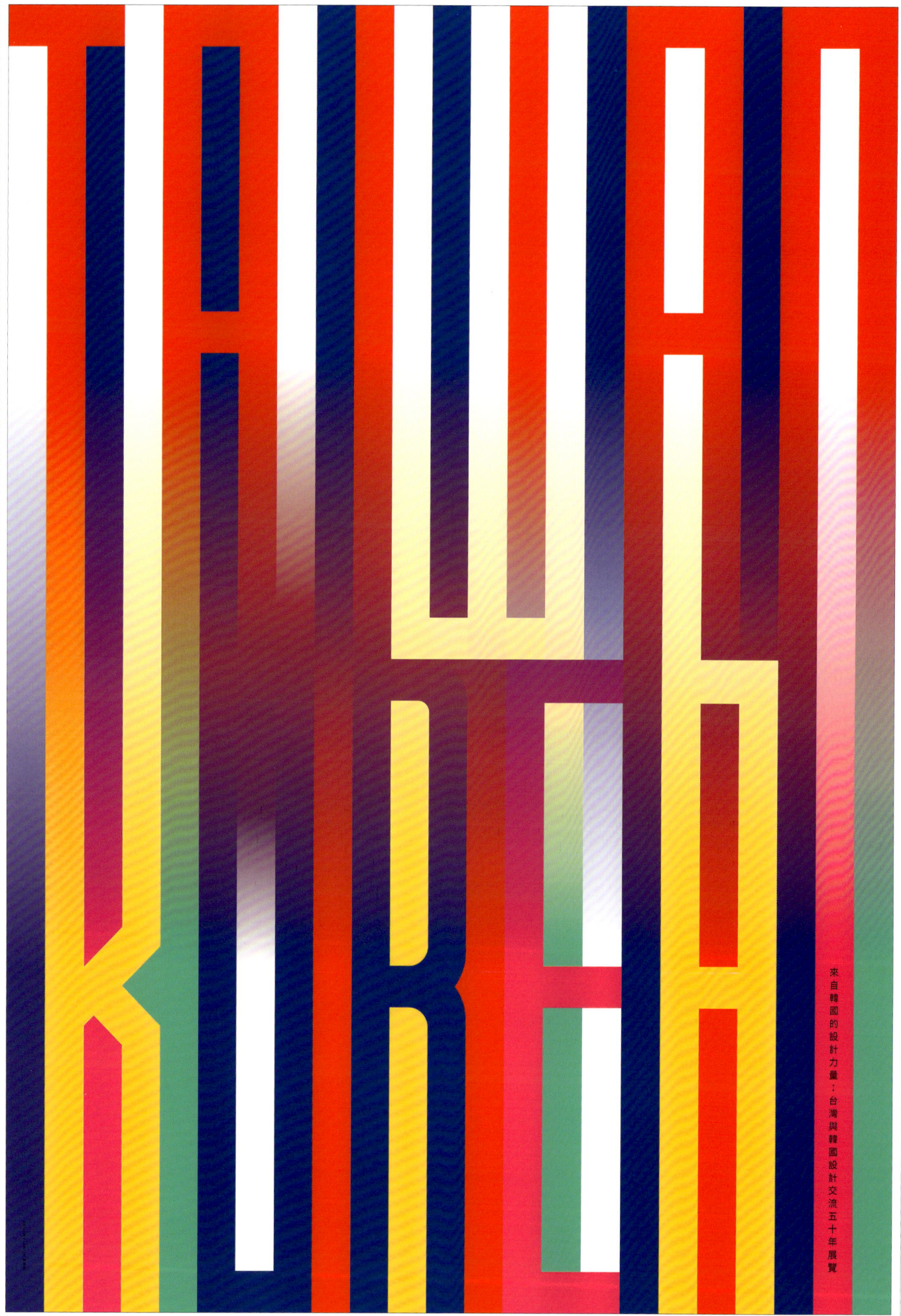

Title: Poster of Exhibition on Fifty Years of Design Exchange Between Taiwan and South Korea
Client: National Taiwan Normal University Department of Design | **Design Firm:** Leo Lin Design | **P238:** Credit & Commentary

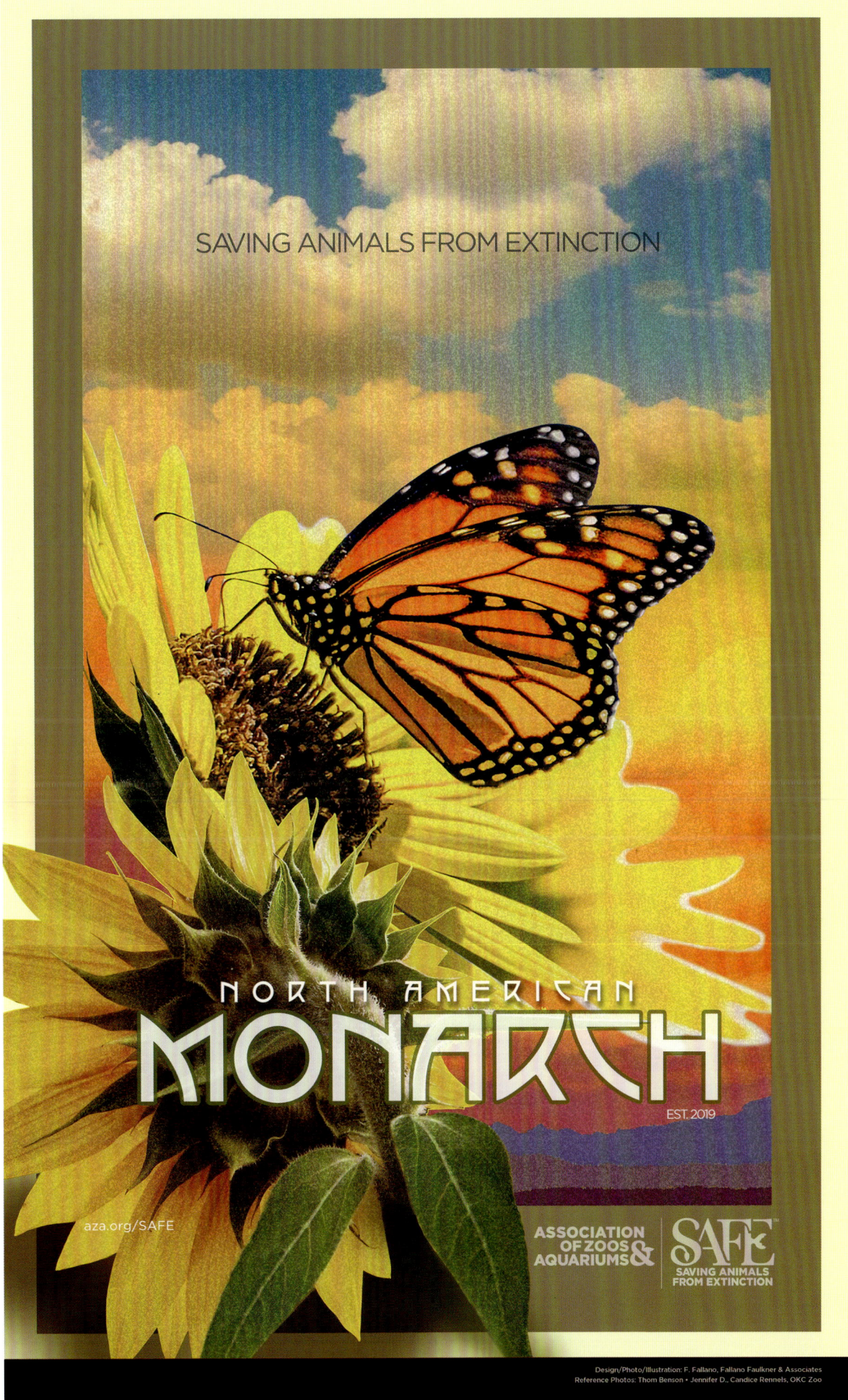

Graphis Silver Awards

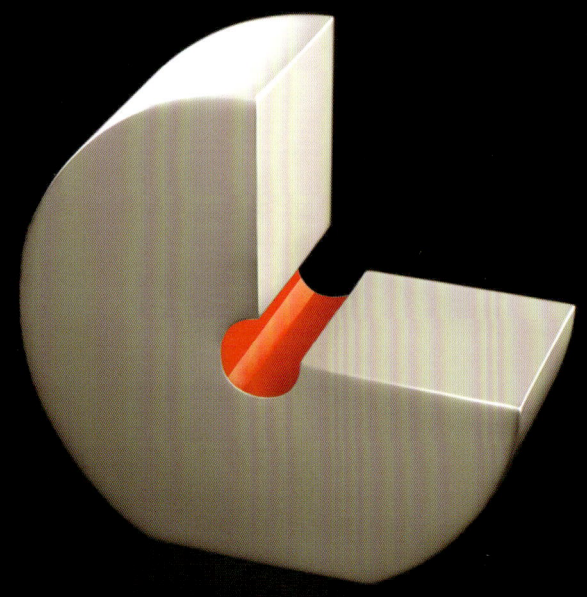

145 SILVER ARCHITECTURE, AUTOMOTIVE

STUDIO CRAIG BYERS

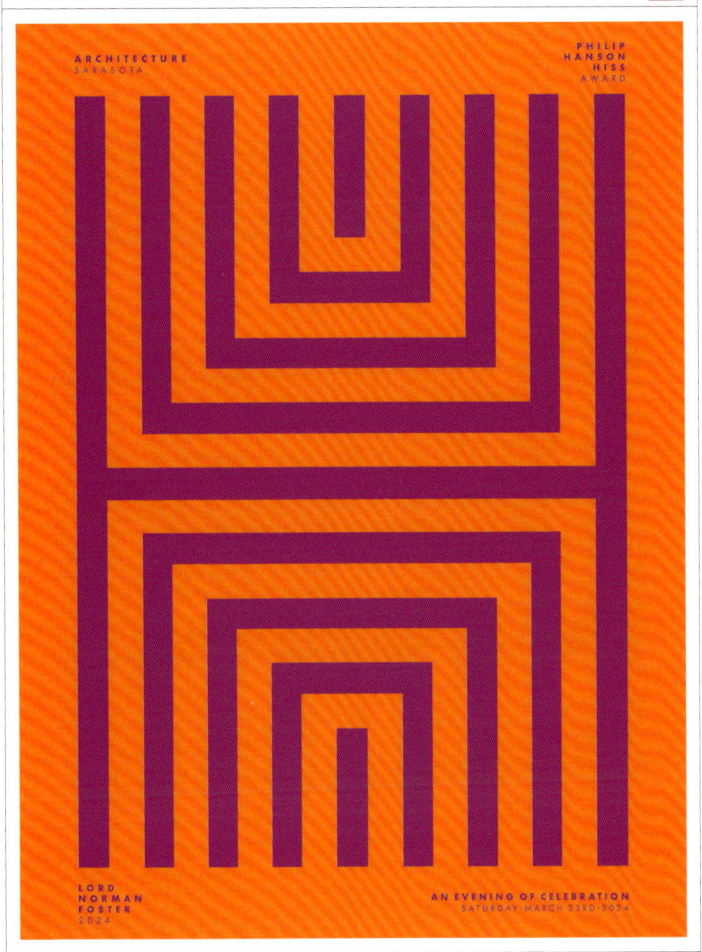

Title: Philip Hanson Hiss Award Celebration Poster
Client: Architecture Sarasota | **Design Firm:** Studio Craig Byers

STUDIO CRAIG BYERS

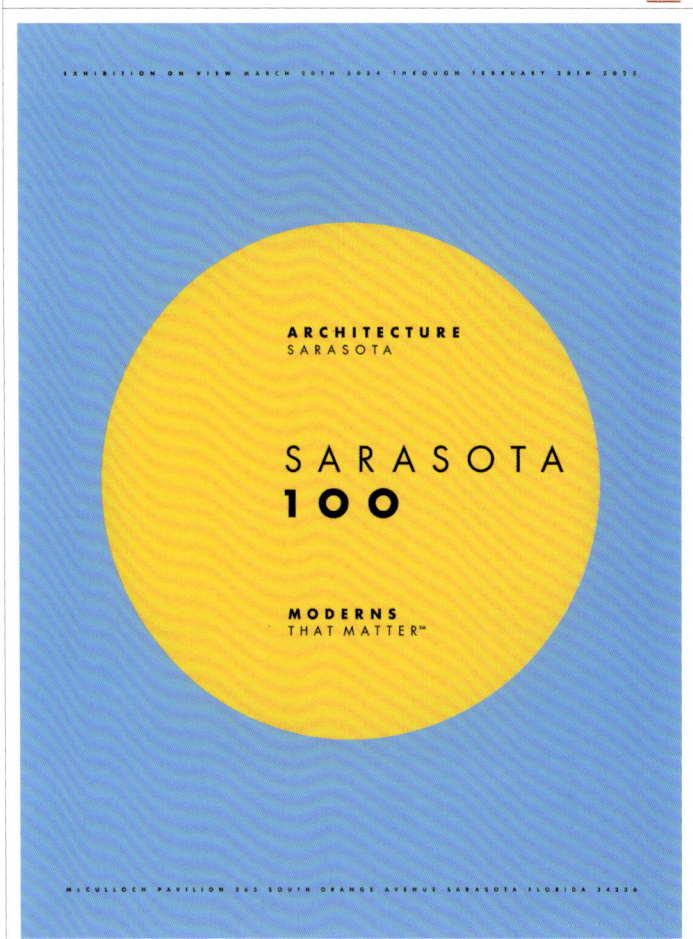

Title: Architecture Sarasota Moderns That Matter: Sarasota 100 Exhibition Poster | **Client:** Architecture Sarasota | **Design Firm:** Studio Craig Byers

MIKE BASSE

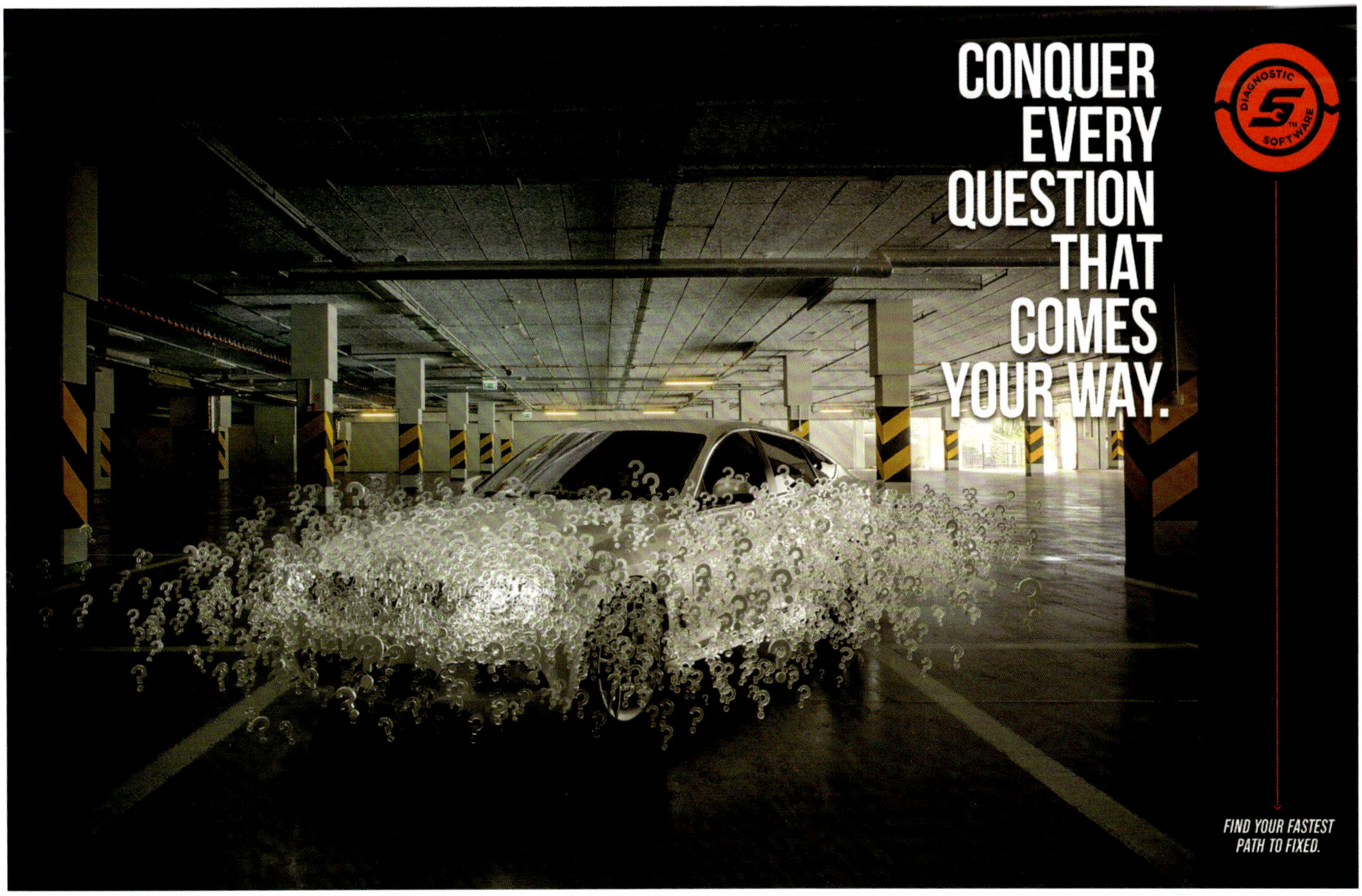

Title: Questions Conquered | **Client:** Snap-on Diagnostics | **Design Firm:** Traction Factory

146 SILVER   BEAUTY & FASHION, COMMEMORATIVE

MINA KIM 🇺🇸

Title: Stila, the Perfect Line | **Client:** Self-initiated
Design Firm: Stila (In-House)

ANDREA RUGGIERO 🇺🇸

Title: Sixty Years of Design in Crystal | **Client:** Arnolfo di Cambio
Design Firm: Andrea Ruggiero Design

ALAN RELLAFORD 🇺🇸

Title: St. Francis of The Mountains | **Client:** Episcopal Diocese of Northern California | **Design Firm:** Alan Rellaford Design

MICHAEL BRALEY 🇺🇸

Title: Rachmaninoff 150
Clients: Golden Bee Biennale, Self-initiated | **Design Firm:** Braley Design

147 SILVER COMMEMORATIVE

MICHAEL BRALEY 🇺🇸

Title: Rachmaninoff 150
Clients: Golden Bee Biennale, Self-initiated
Design Firm: Braley Design

BOJANA FAJMUT 🇸🇮

Title: 60 Years of ARS Program - RTV National Public Broadcaster Slovenia
Clients: RTV Slovenija, Radio Slovenia Third Channel - ARS Program
Design Firm: Bojana Fajmut

SCOTT RAY 🇺🇸

Title: Homage to PELE Poster | **Client:** Self-initiated
Design Firm: Ray Visual Communications

COCO CERRELLA 🇦🇷

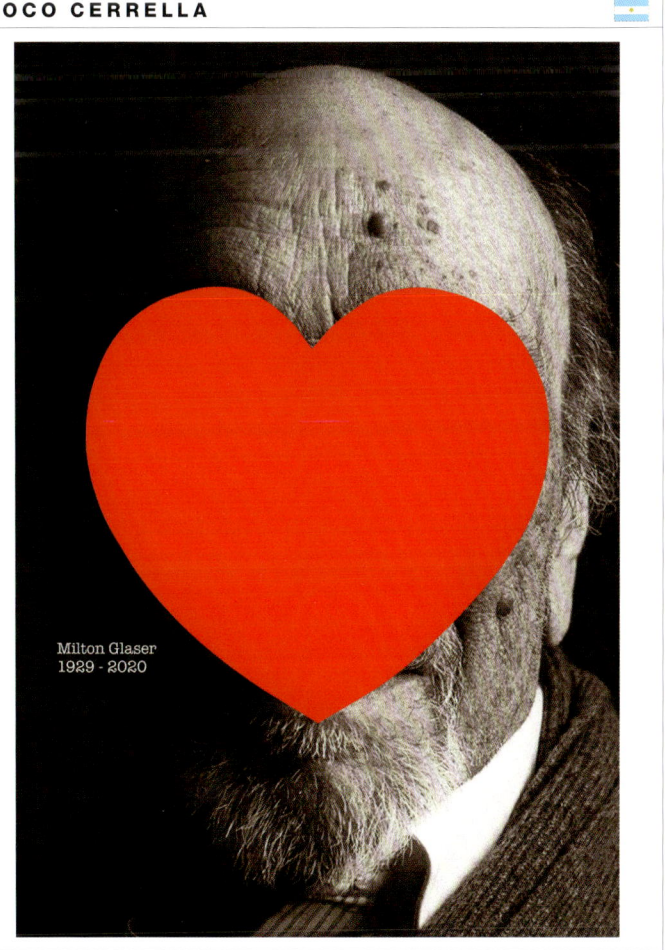

Title: Milton Love | **Client:** Designers for Milton Glaser
Design Firm: Coco Cerrella

148 SILVER   COMMEMORATIVE, CORPORATE

JOHN GRAVDAHL 🇺🇸

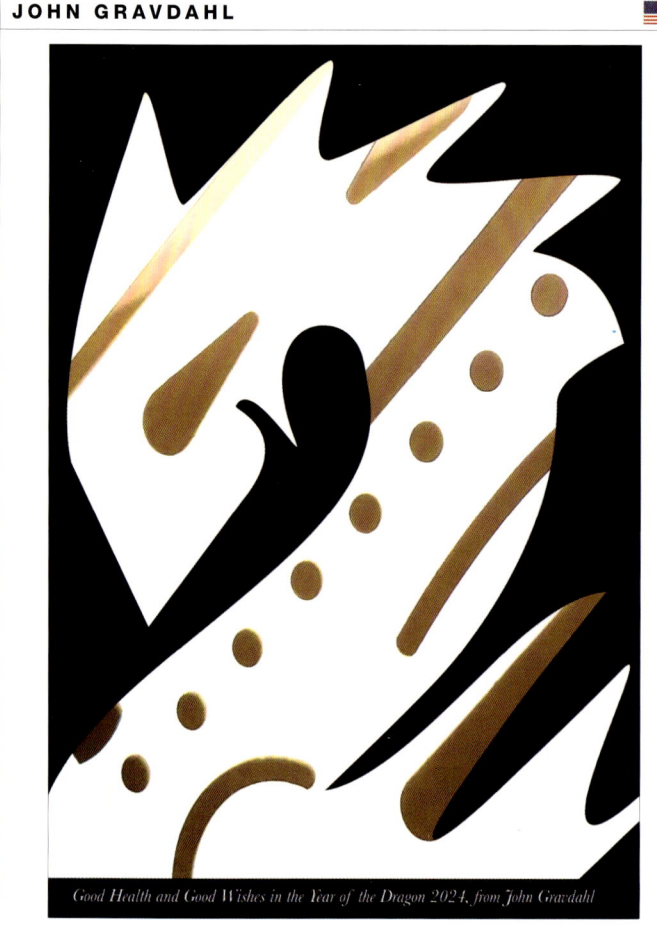

Good Health and Good Wishes in the Year of the Dragon 2024, from John Gravdahl

Title: Year of the Dragon
Client: Self-initiated
Design Firm: Gravdahl Design

ARIEL FREANER 🇺🇸

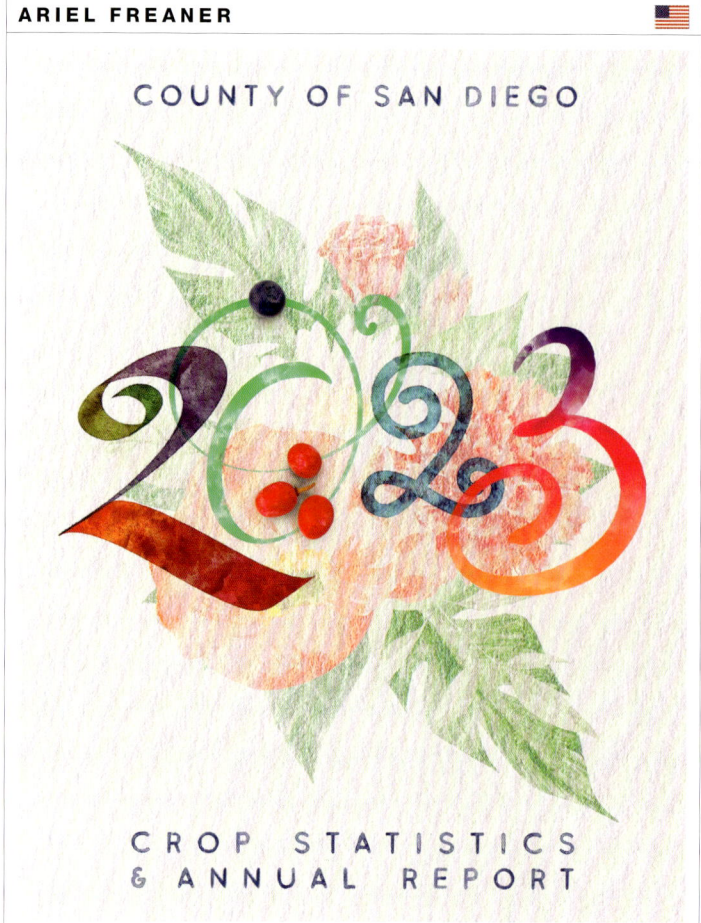

COUNTY OF SAN DIEGO
2023
CROP STATISTICS & ANNUAL REPORT

Title: County of San Diego Crop Statistics & Annual Report
Client: County of San Diego Agriculture, Weights and Measures
Design Firm: Freaner Creative & Design

NIKKEISHA, INC. 🇯🇵

Title: Make This Year the Greatest. | **Client:** Self-initiated | **Design Firm:** Nikkeisha, Inc.

ARIEL FREANER

Title: LUEG Budget Exhibit Posters
Clients: County of San Diego Land Use & Environment, Donna Durckel
Design Firm: Freaner Creative & Design

ARIEL FREANER

Title: Red Cross Corporate Poster Series
Clients: Red Cross of Tijuana, Jorge Astiazaran
Design Firm: Freaner Creative & Design

ARIEL FREANER

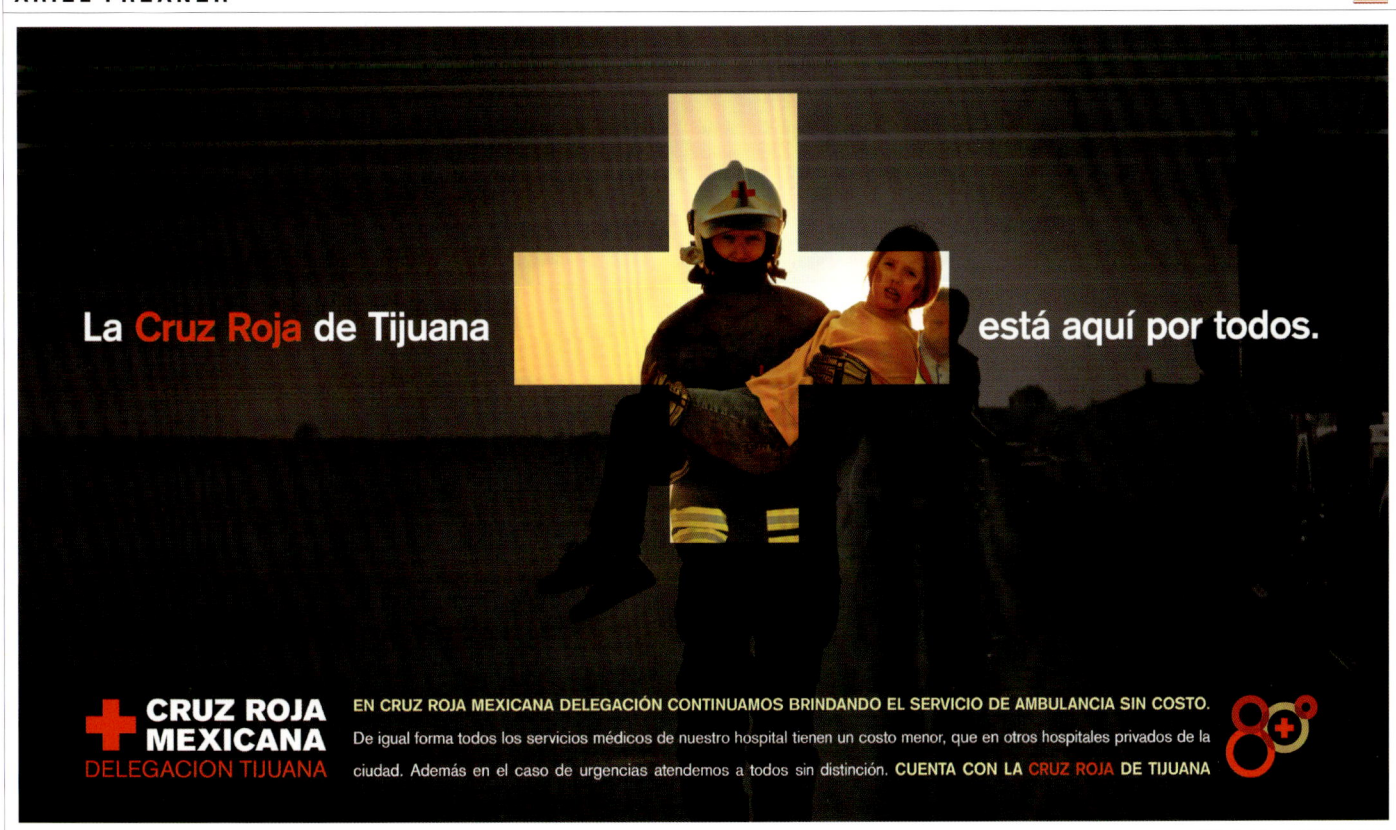

Title: Red Cross Always Here For You Posters Campaign | **Clients:** Red Cross of Tijuana, Jorge Astiazaran | **Design Firm:** Freaner Creative & Design

HYUNGJOO A. KIM

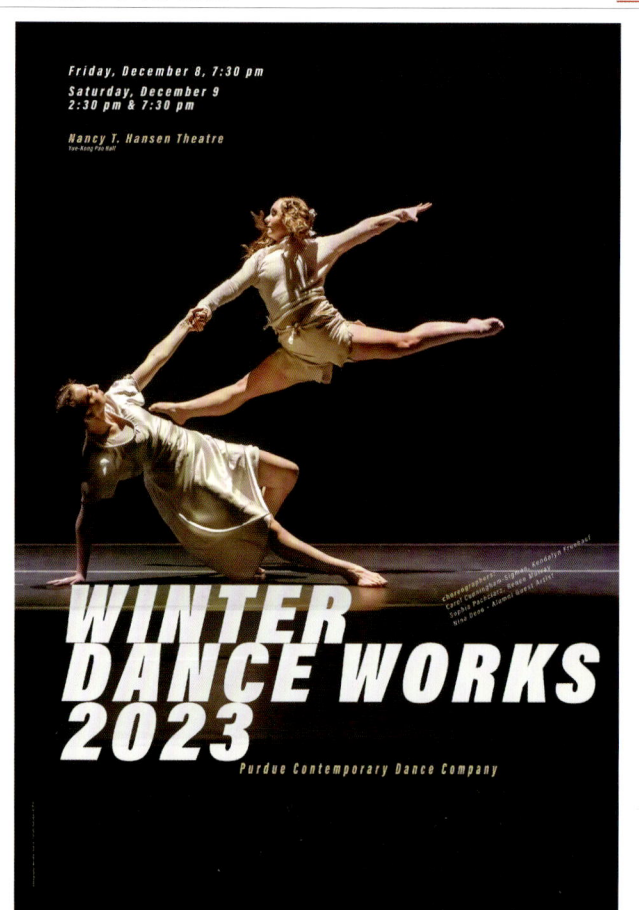

Title: Winter Dance Works 2023 | **Client:** Purdue Contemporary Dance Company | **Design Firm:** Hyungjookim Designlab

HYUNGJOO A. KIM

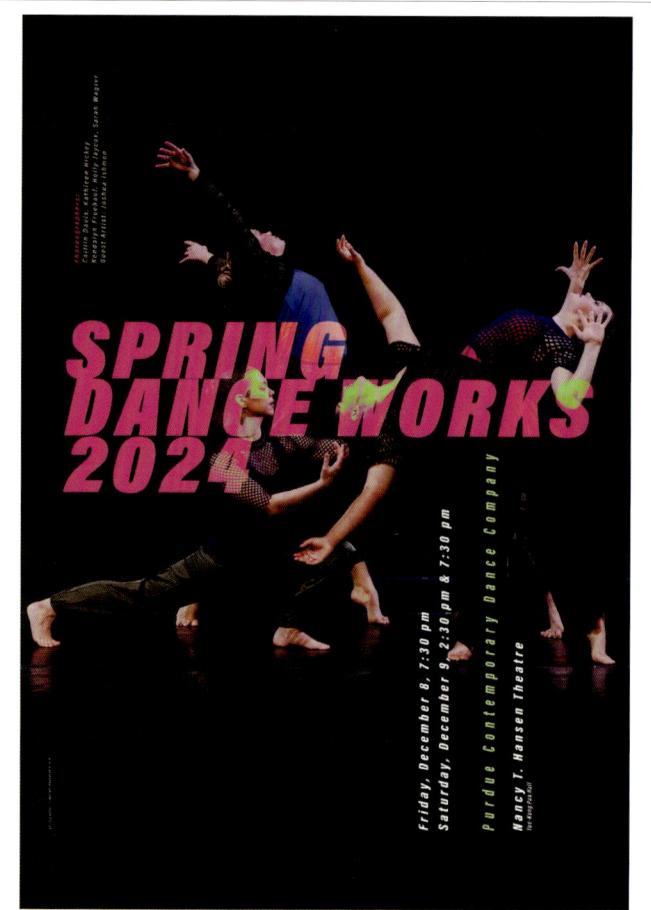

Title: Spring Dance Works 2024 | **Client:** Purdue Contemporary Dance Company | **Design Firm:** Hyungjookim Designlab

ALEX-MARIE ABLAN

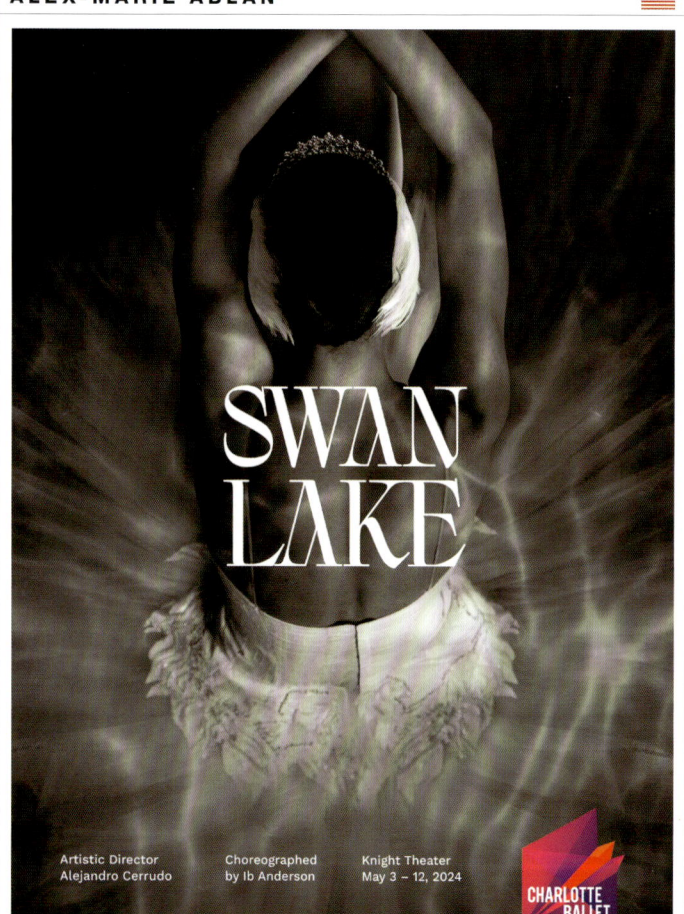

Title: Swan Lake – 2023/2024 Season Performance
Client: Charlotte Ballet | **Design Firm:** Mythic

YIJUN JIANG

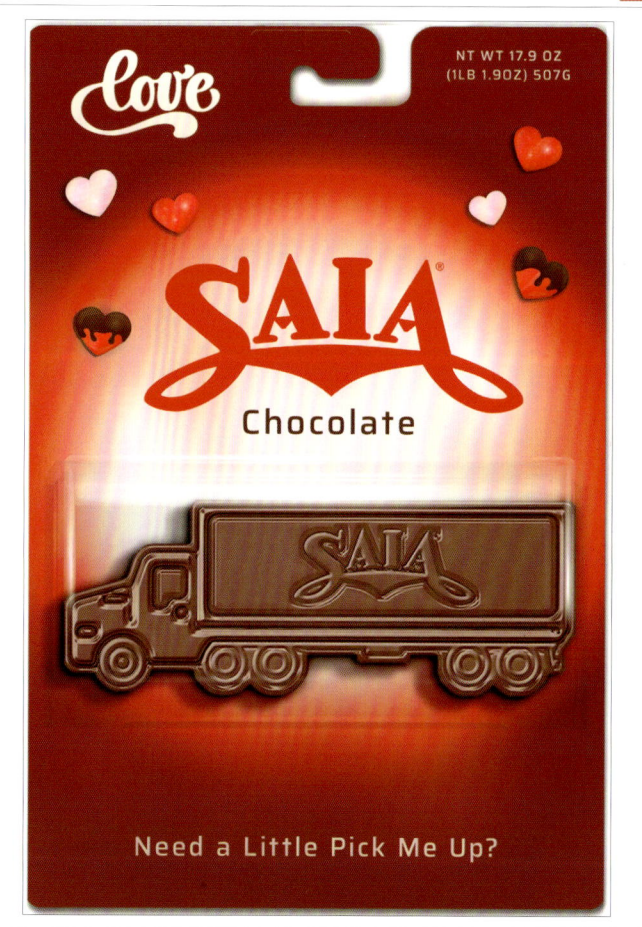

Title: Need a Little Pick Me Up?
Client: Saia LTL Freight | **Design Firm:** DEFINITION 6 (Bridgenext)

151 SILVER — EDUCATION

BOB AUFULDISH 🇺🇸

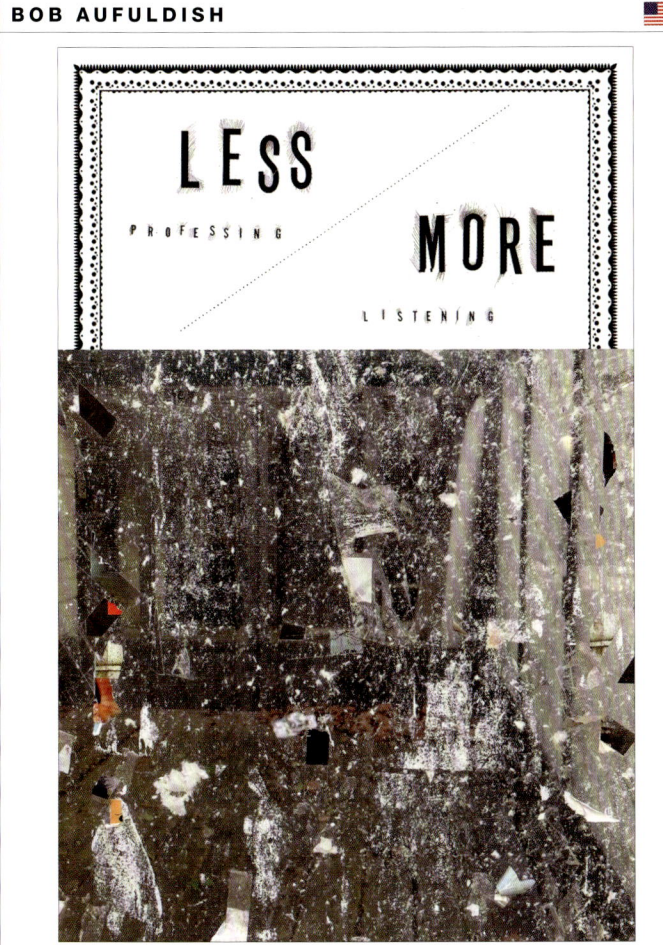

Title: Profess Less / Listen More | **Client:** I Profess: The Graphic Design Manifesto 20th Anniversary Exhibition | **Design Firm:** Aufuldish & Warinner

MICHAEL BRALEY 🇺🇸

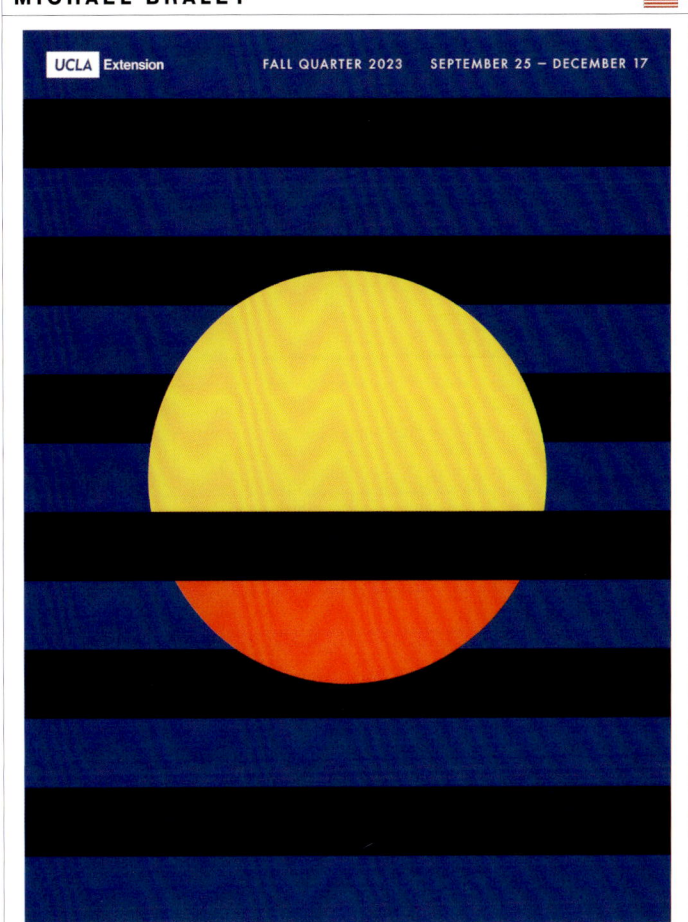

Title: UCLA Extension Fall_Quarter 2023 | **Client:** UCLA Extension
Design Firm: Braley Design

KIYOUNG AN 🇯🇵

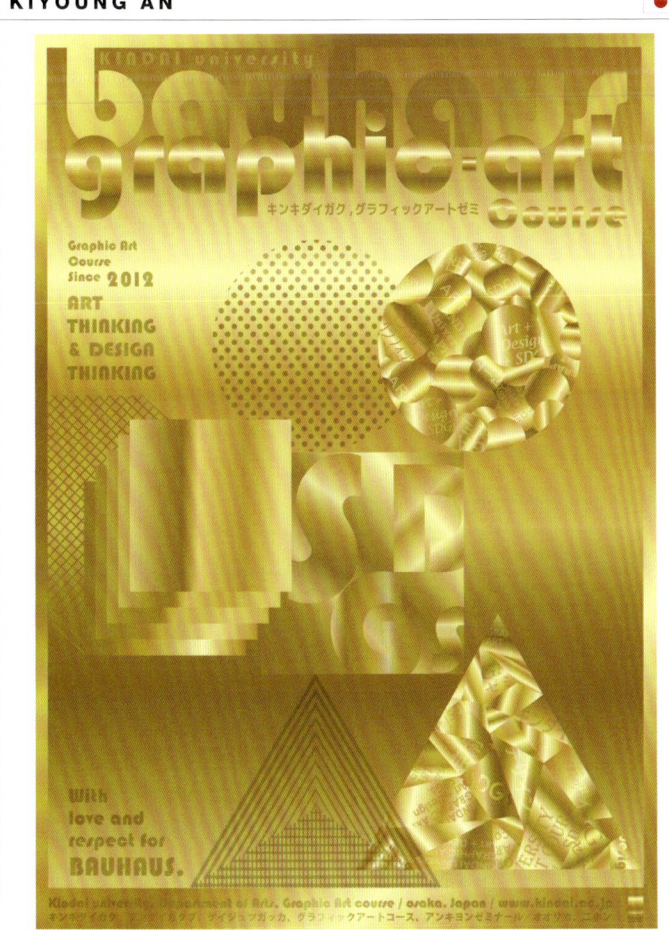

Title: Bauhaus & KINDAI Graphic Art Course | **Client:** KINDAI University Department of Arts | **Design Firm:** Kiyoung An Graphic Art Course Laboratory

CHIA-HUI LIEN 🇹🇼

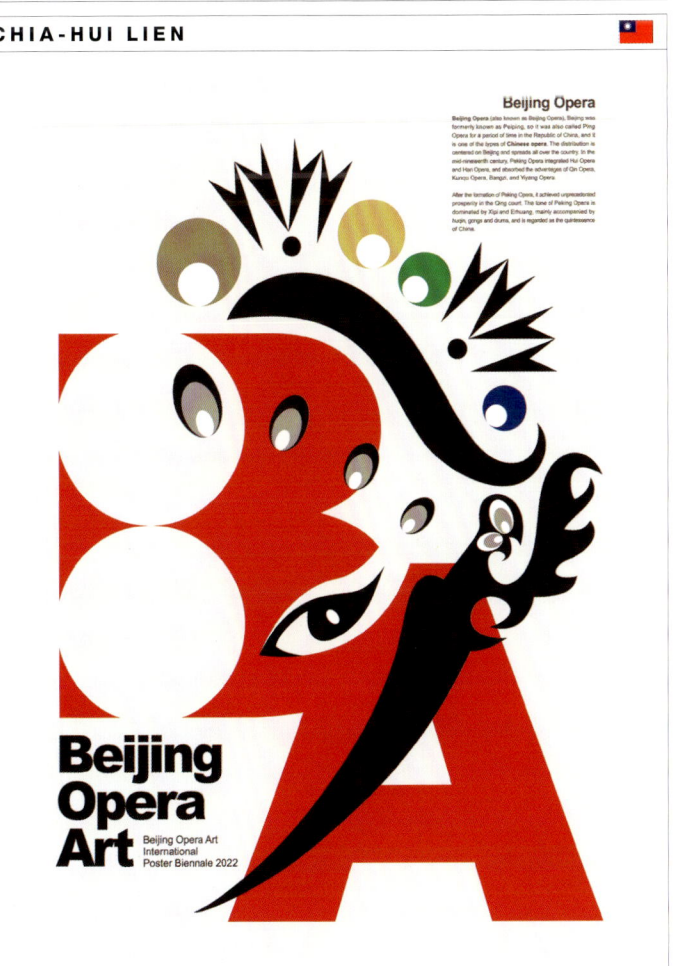

Title: Beijing Opera Culture | **Client:** Self-initated
Design Firm: Tainan University of Technology

DONNA MANAHAN

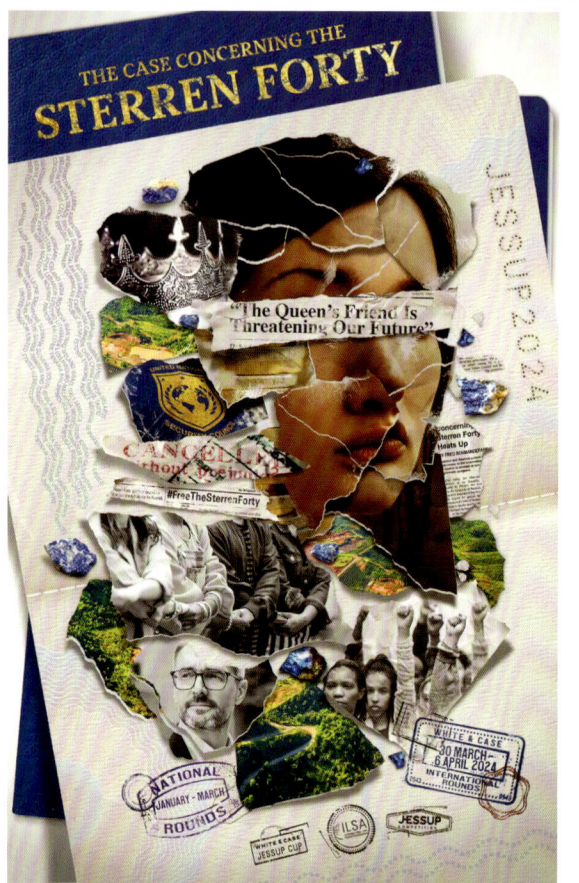

Title: Jessup 2024: The Case Concerning the Sterren Forty
Client: International Law Students Association
Design Firm: White & Case LLP

MICHAEL BRALEY

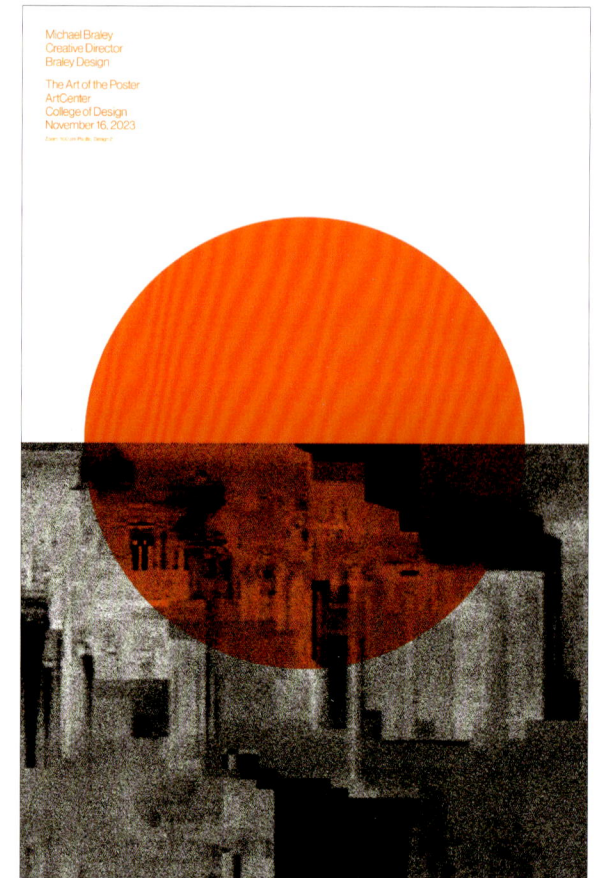

Title: The Art of the Poster: ArtCenter Lecture
Clients: Self-initiated, ArtCenter College of Design
Design Firm: Braley Design

CARLOS CASIMIRO COSTA, JACINTA COSTA [COSTAS]

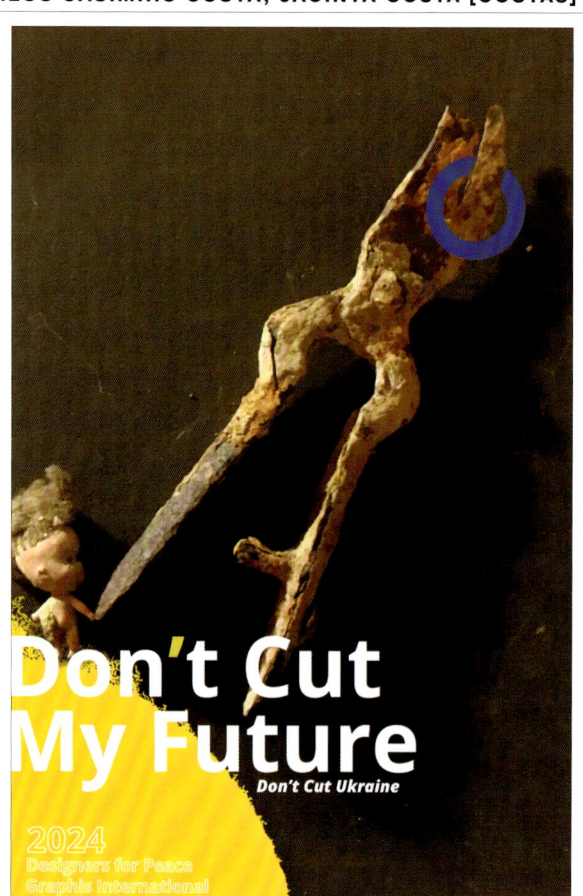

Title: Don't Cut My Future
Client: IPB Community
Design Firm: CCC + JC. Jacinta & Carlos

PRATT INSTITUTE CREATIVE SERVICES

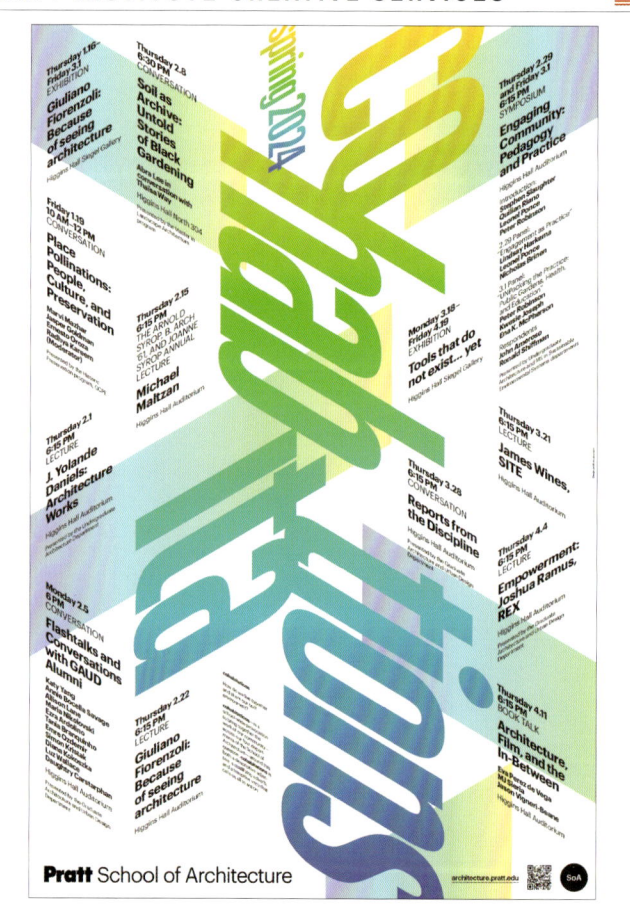

Title: Cohabitations: Fall/Spring 2023-2024 Event Series
Client: Pratt Institute School of Architecture
Design Firm: Pratt Institute Communications & Marketing

153 SILVER — EDUCATION

MICHAEL BRALEY 🇺🇸

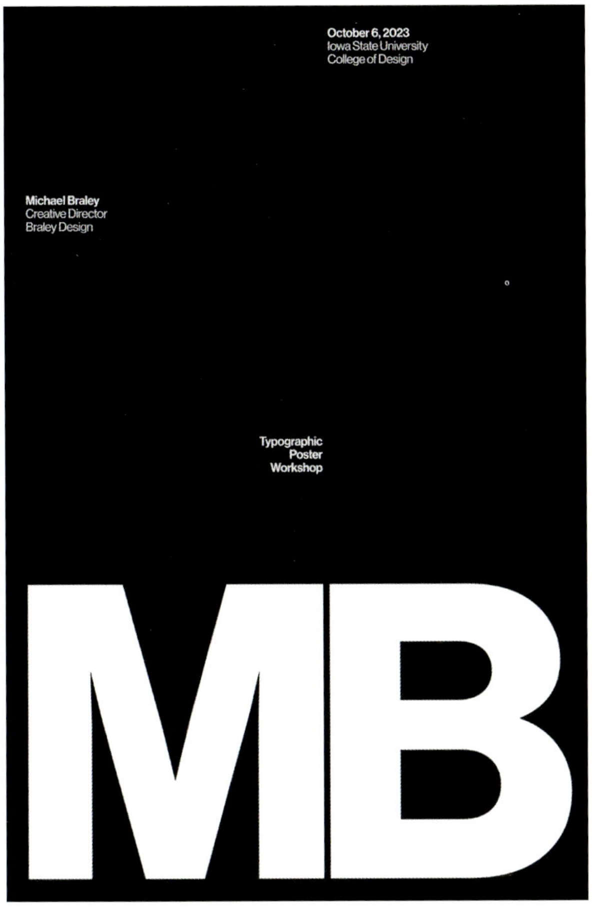

Title: MB: Typographic Poster Workshop | **Clients:** Self-initiated, Iowa State University | **Design Firm:** Braley Design

DERWYN GOODALL 🇨🇦

Title: No Now | **Client:** Self-initiated
Design Firm: Goodall Integrated Design

ROBERT SHAW WEST 🇺🇸

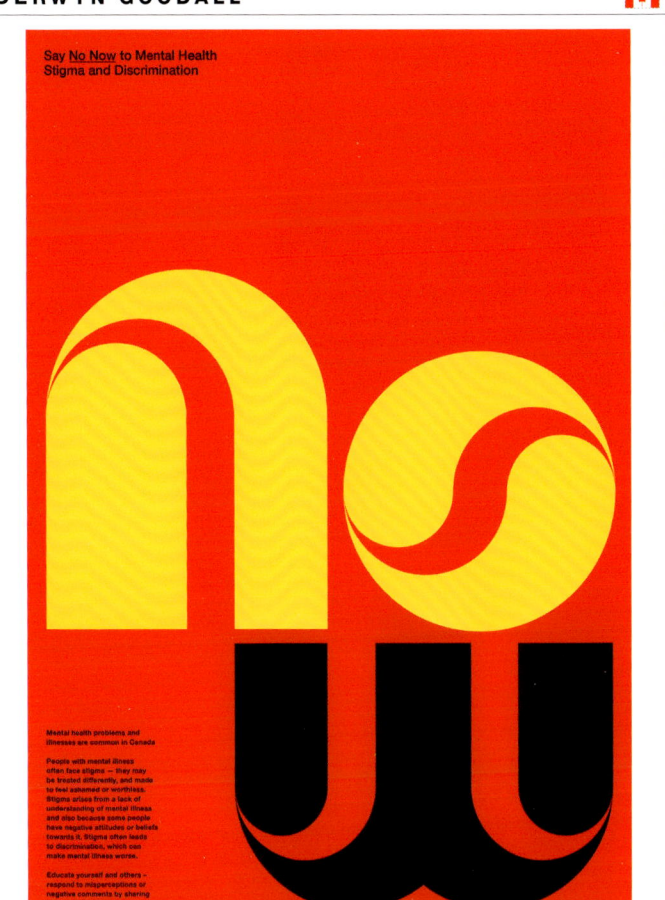

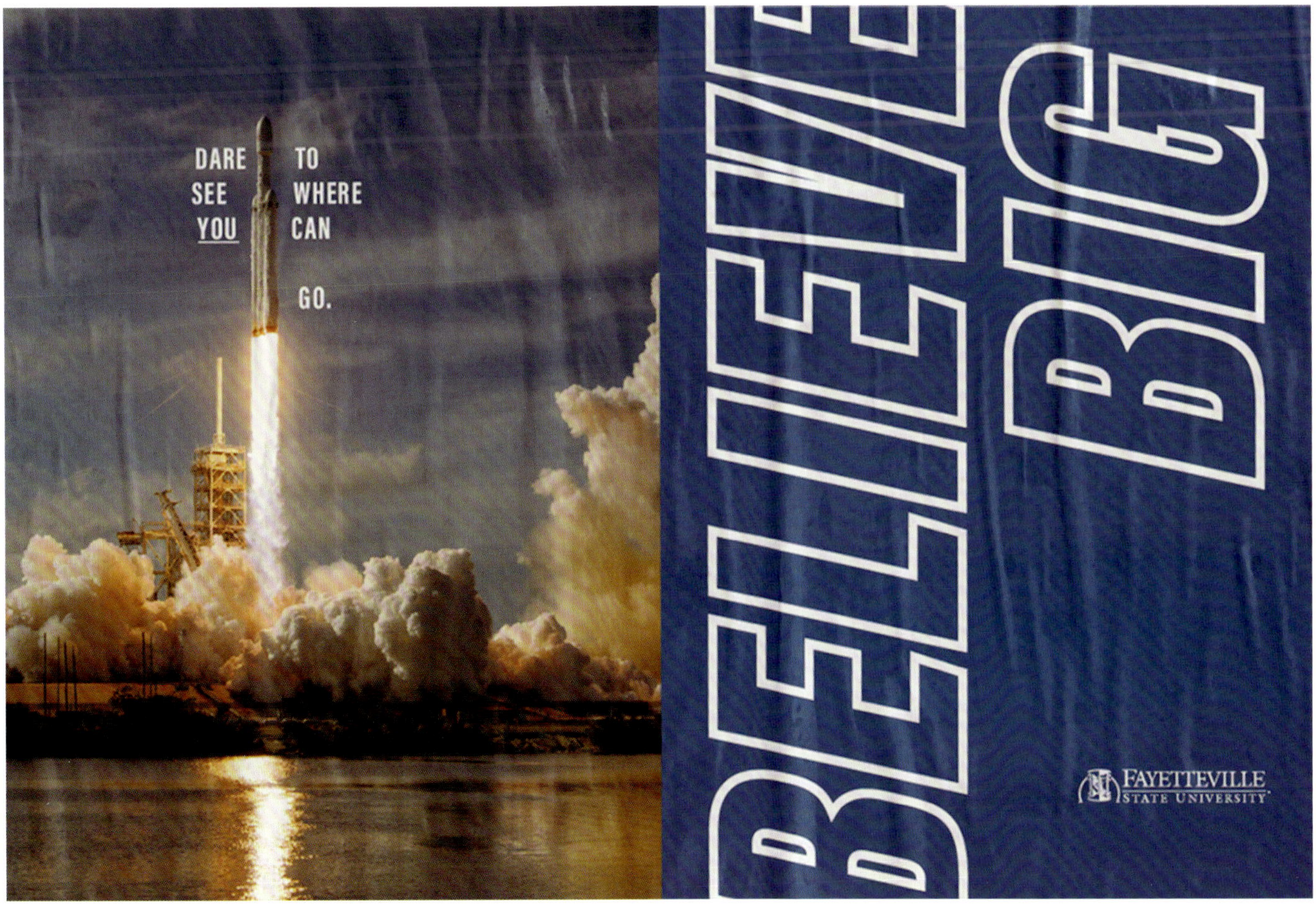

Title: Fayetteville State University-Poster Campaign | **Client:** Fayetteville State University | **Design Firm:** The Republik

JOHN GRAVDAHL

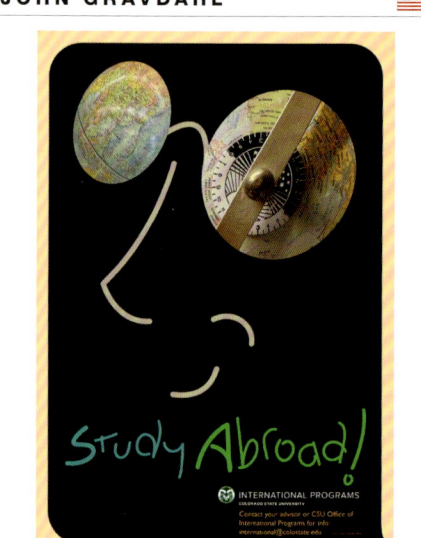

Title: Study Abroad with CSU!
Client: Colorado State University International Programs | **Design Firm:** Gravdahl Design

JACK HARRIS

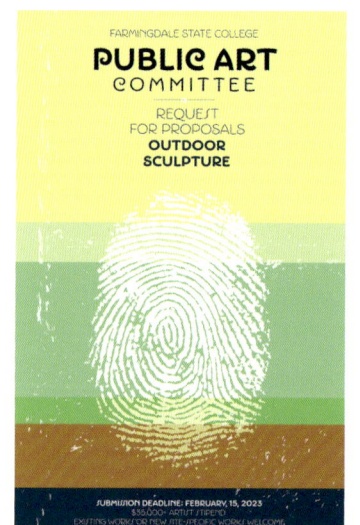

Title: Public Art, Call for Proposals
Client: Farmingdale State College
Design Firm: Jack Harris

GARY MUELLER (+4)

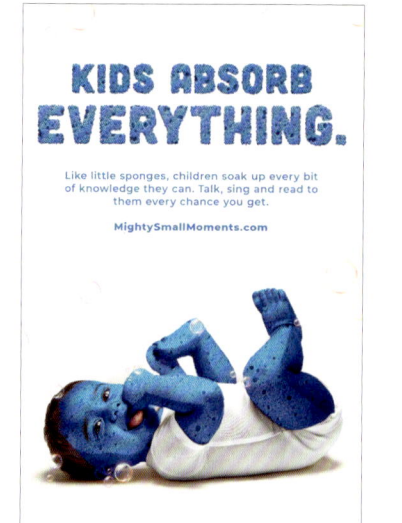

Title: Kids Are Sponges
Client: Office of Early Childhood Initiative
Design Firm: Serve Marketing

RANDY CLARK

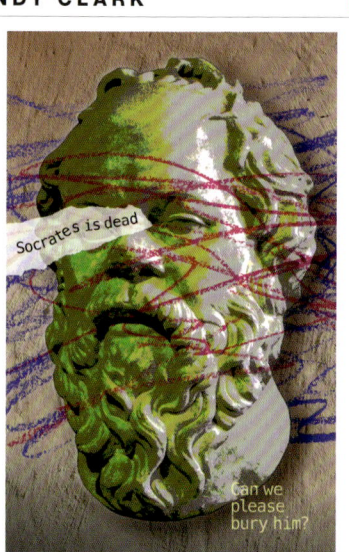

Title: Socrates
Client: Self-initiated
Design Firm: Randy Clark

TERRITORY STUDIO

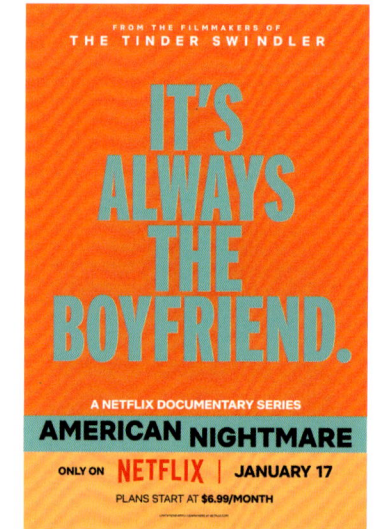

Title: American Nightmare
Client: Netflix
Design Firm: Territory Studio

SJI ASSOCIATES

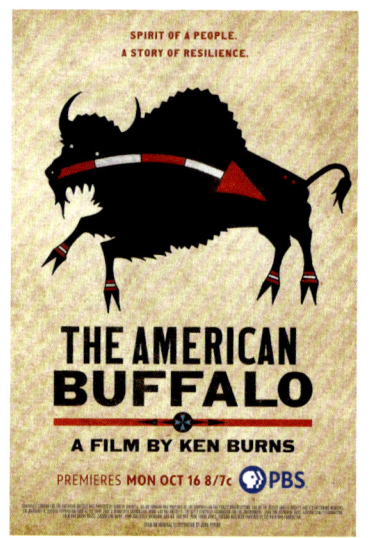

Title: The American Buffalo
Client: PBS Creative Services
Design Firm: SJI Associates

MINKWAN KIM

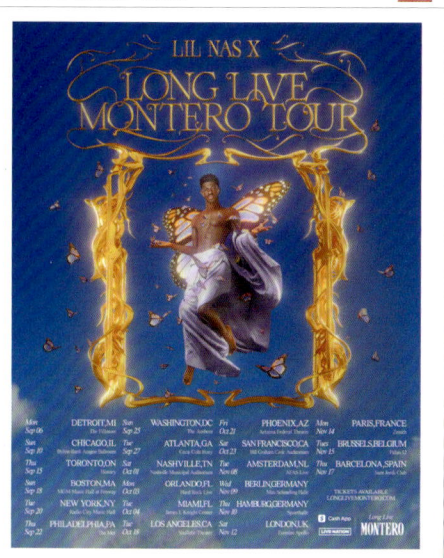

Title: Lil Nas X - Long Live Montero Tour Poster
Client: Lil Nas X
Design Firm: Saad Moosajee

ANNA FARKAS

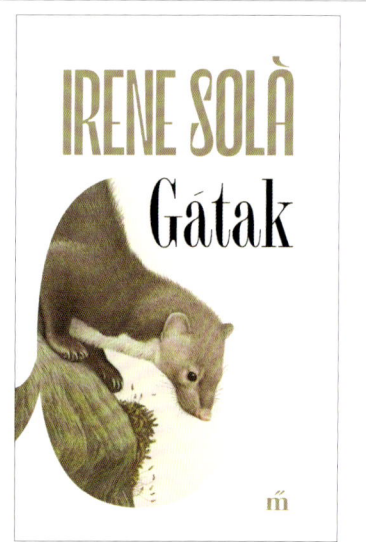

Title: Irene Solà
Client: Magvető
Design Firm: Anagraphic

SJI ASSOCIATES

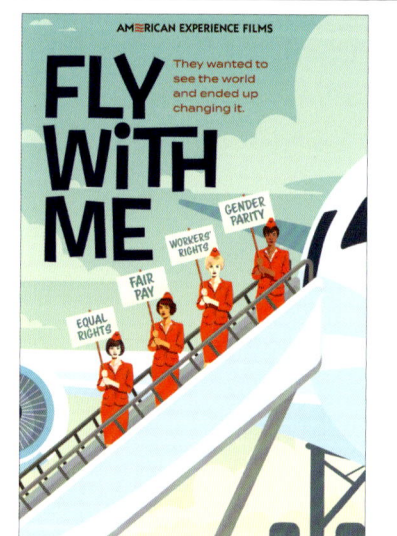

Title: Fly With Me | **Clients:** Chika Offurum, American Experience Films
Design Firm: SJI Associates

155 SILVER | ENTERTAINMENT

SJI ASSOCIATES

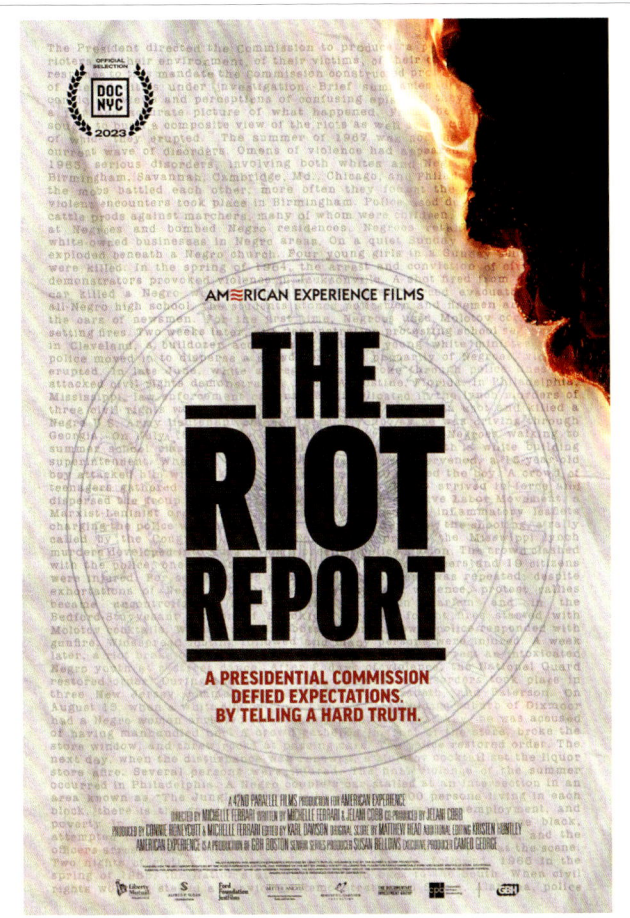

Title: The Riot Report | **Clients:** Chika Offurum, American Experience Films | **Design Firm:** SJI Associates

SJI ASSOCIATES

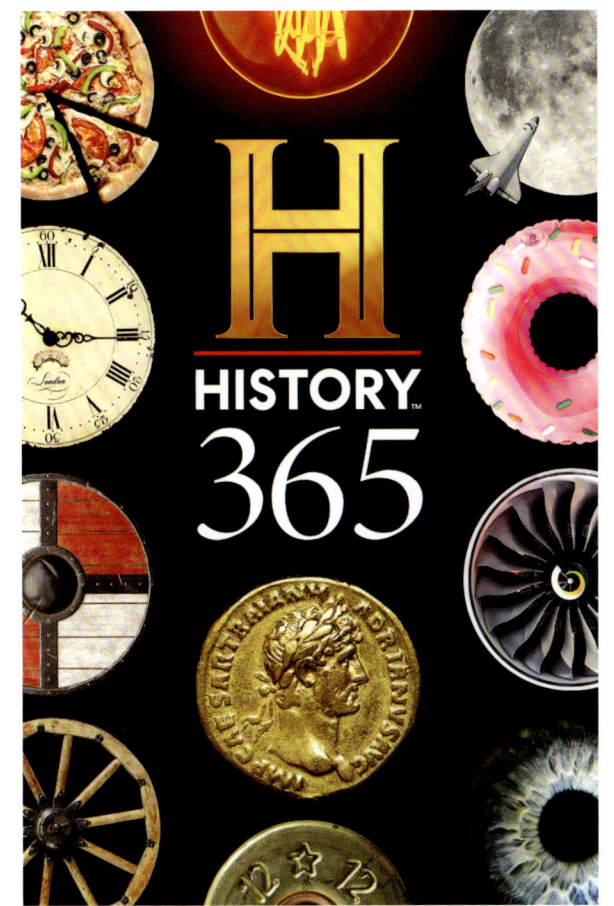

Title: History 365 (Fast Channel Brand Identity) | **Client:** A+E Networks
Design Firm: SJI Associates

THE REFINERY

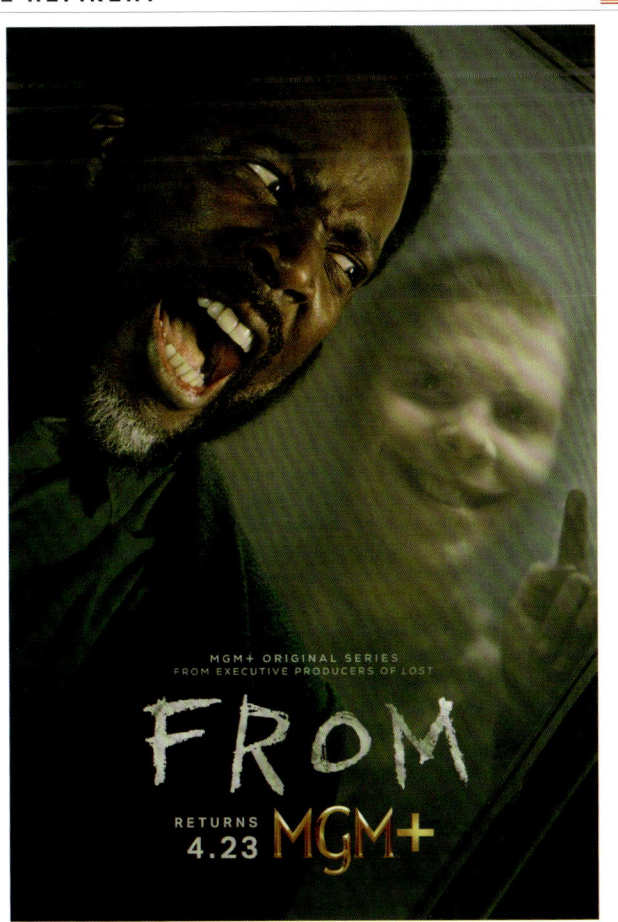

Title: From S2, Key Art | **Client:** MGM+
Design Firm: The Refinery

THE REFINERY

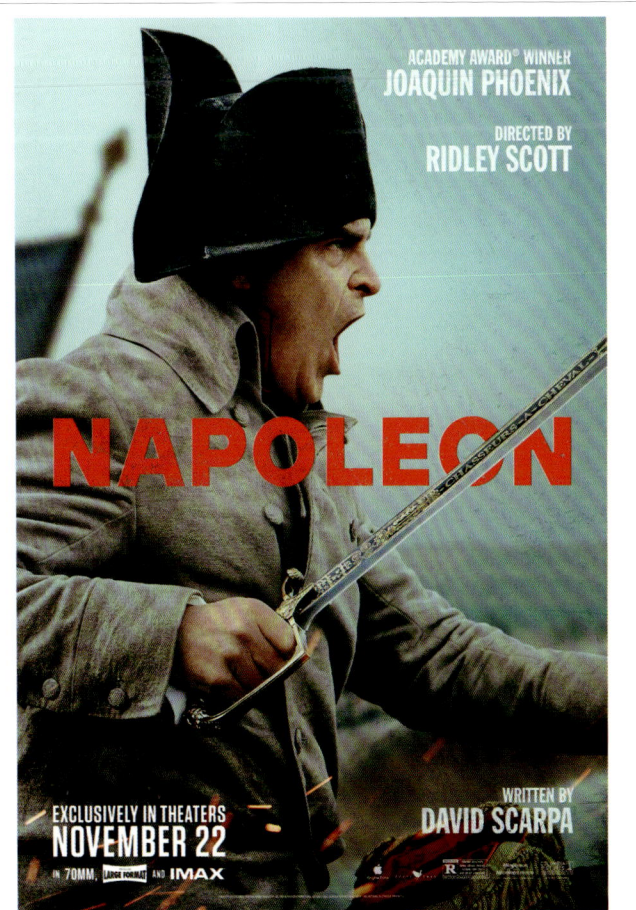

Title: Napoleon, Key Art | **Clients:** Apple TV+, Sony Pictures Entertainment | **Design Firm:** The Refinery

156 SILVER   ENTERTAINMENT

RHUBARB

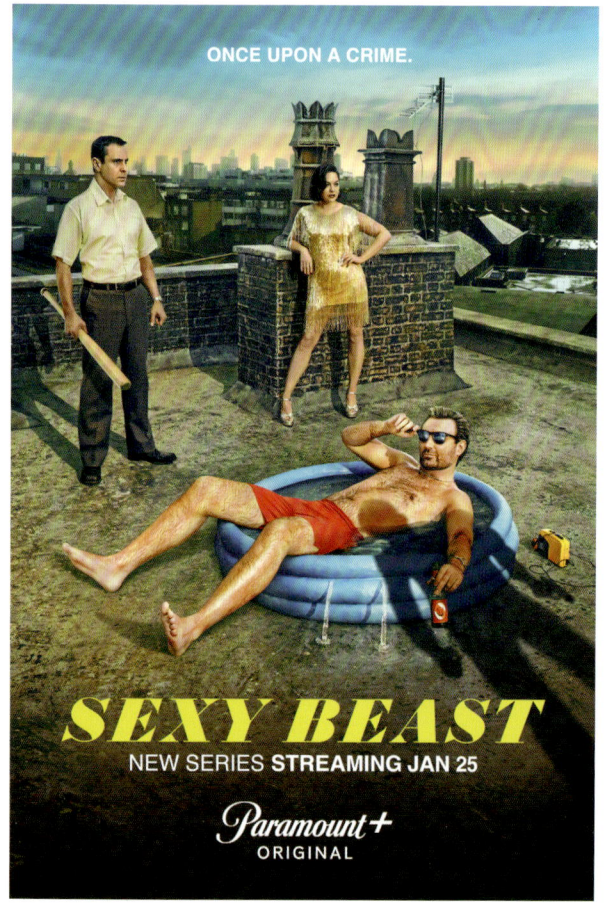

Title: Sexy Beast Campaign Art | Client: Paramount+
Design Firm: Rhubarb

ARSONAL, FX NETWORKS

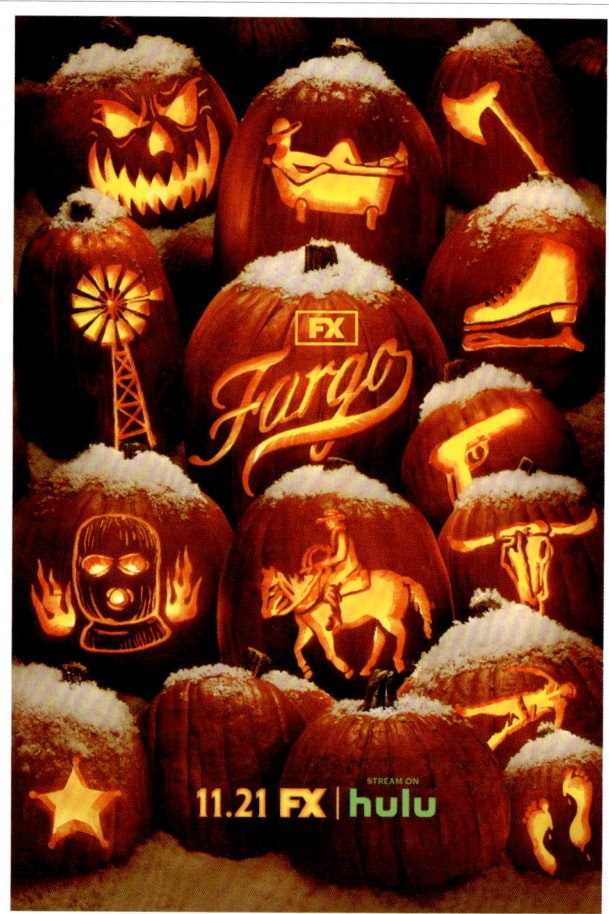

Title: Fargo | Client: FX Networks
Design Firm: ARSONAL

THE REFINERY

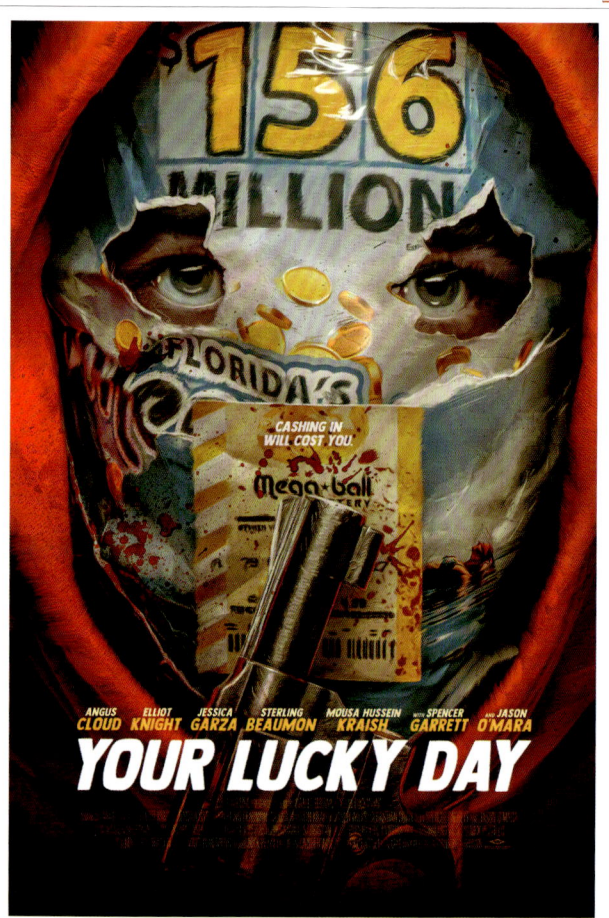

Title: Your Lucky Day | Client: Well Go USA Entertainment
Design Firm: The Refinery

THE REFINERY

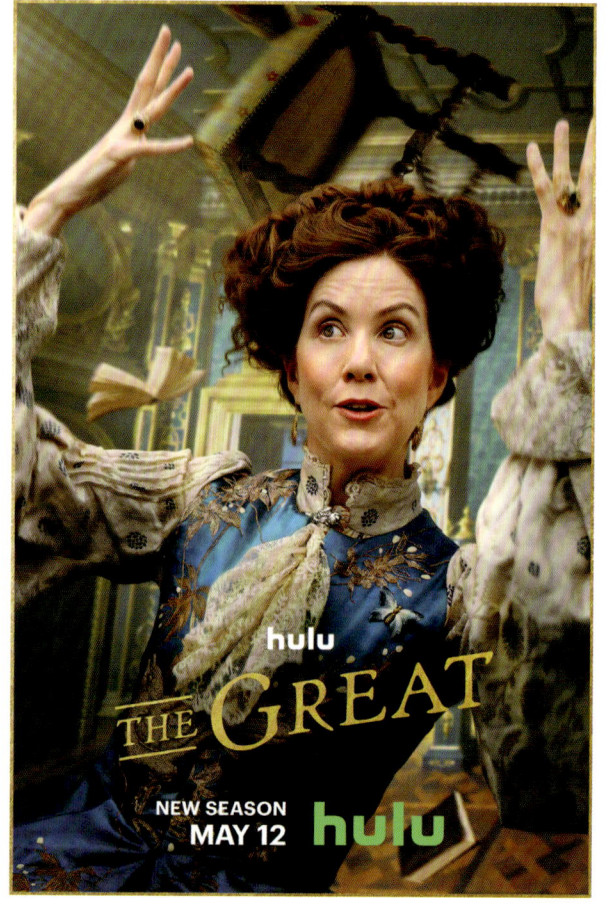

Title: The Great S3 | Client: Hulu
Design Firm: The Refinery

THE REFINERY

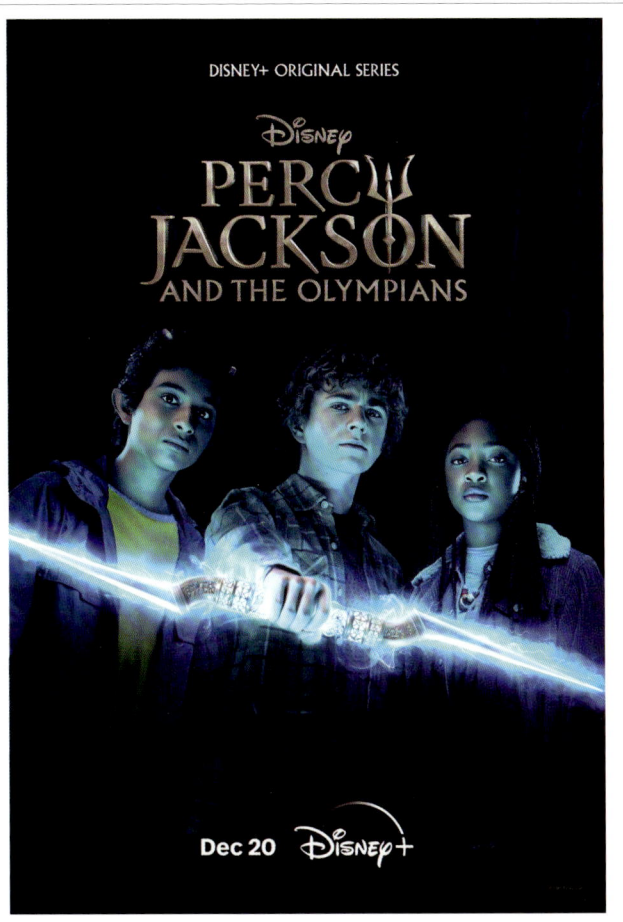

Title: Percy Jackson and the Olympians
Client: Disney Entertainment Television | **Design Firm:** The Refinery

SJI ASSOCIATES

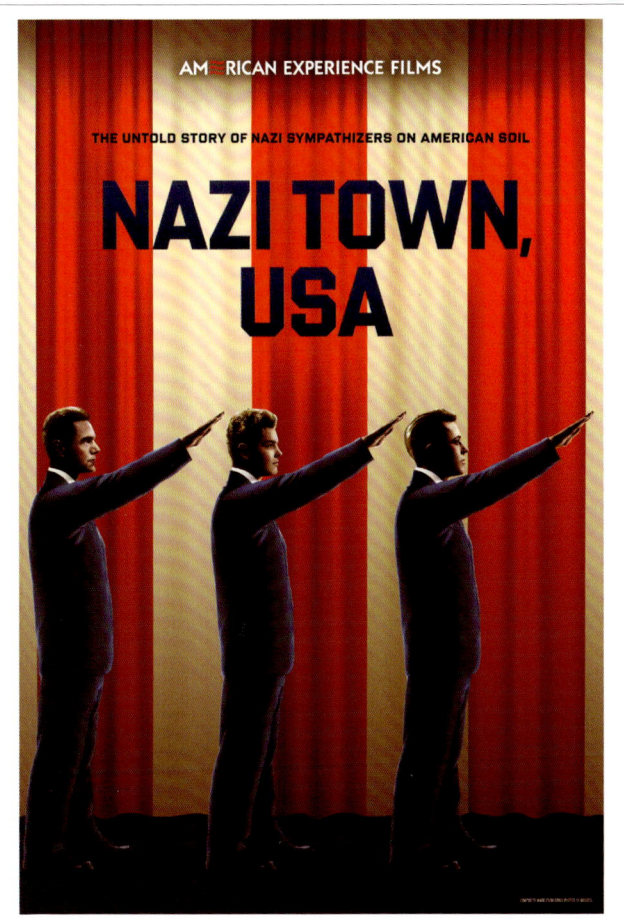

Title: Nazi Town, USA | **Clients:** Chika Offurum, American Experience Films | **Design Firm:** SJI Associates

SJI ASSOCIATES

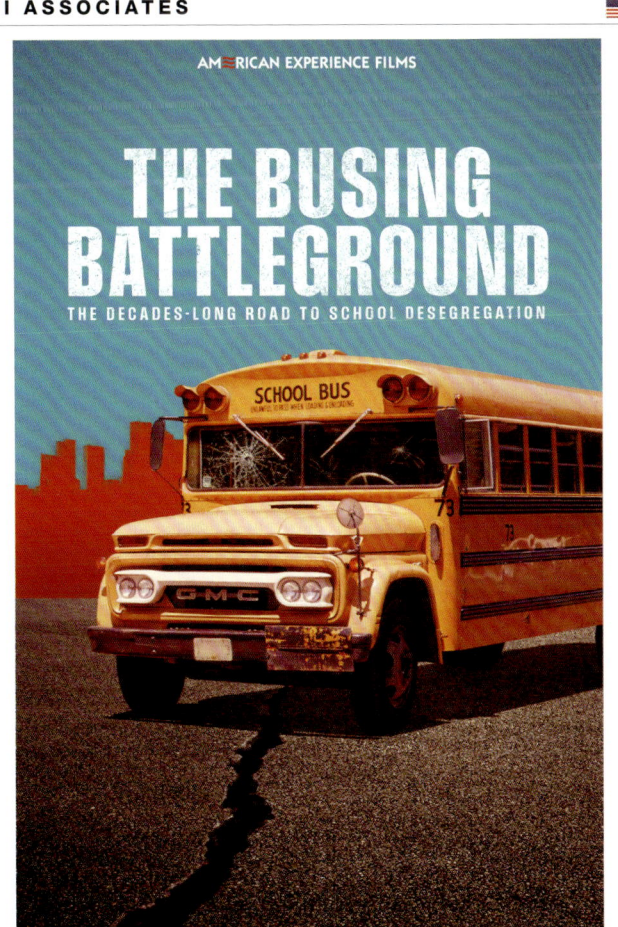

Title: The Busing Battleground | **Clients:** Chika Offurum, American Experience Films | **Design Firm:** SJI Associates

THE REFINERY

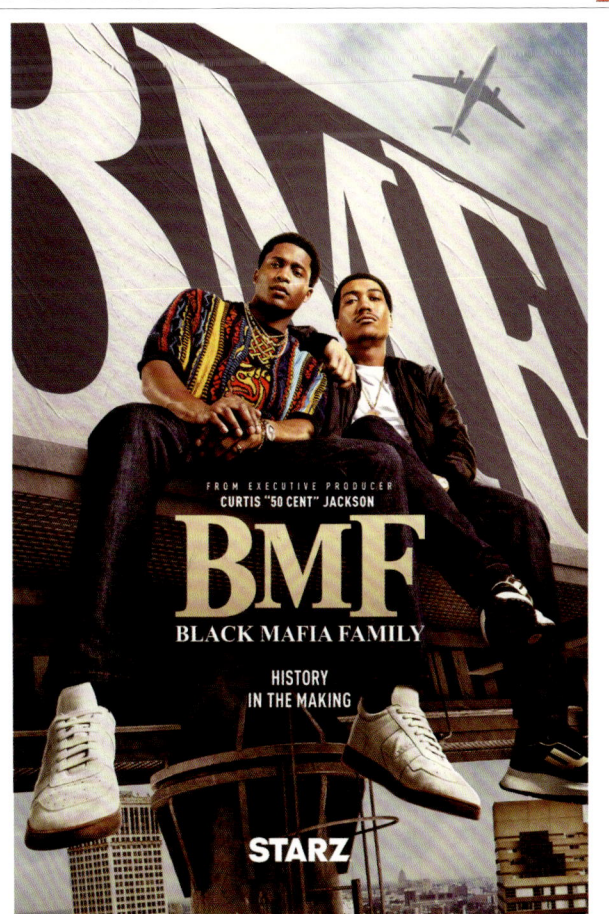

Title: Black Mafia Family S3, Key Art | **Client:** STARZ
Design Firm: The Refinery

THE REFINERY

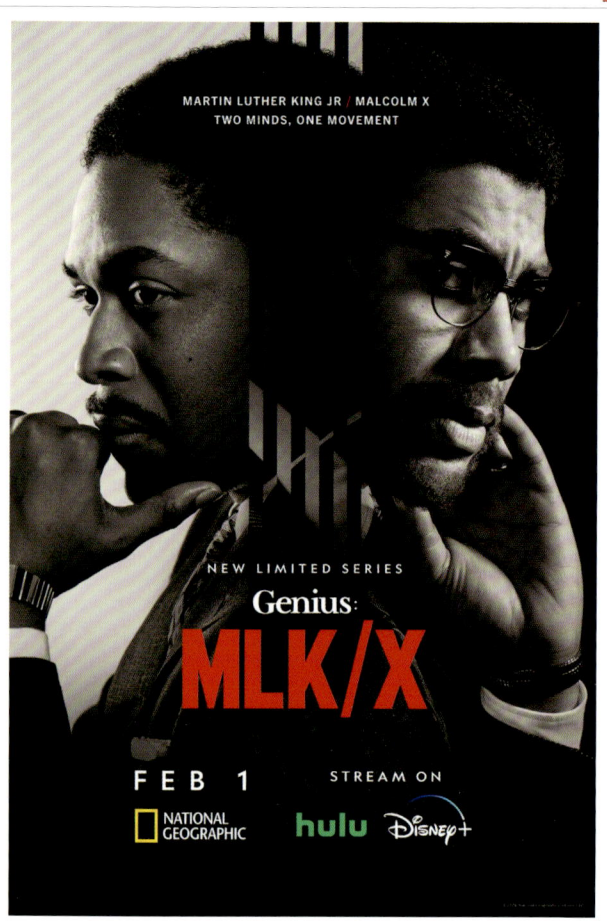

Title: Genius: MLKX, Key Art | **Client:** National Geographic
Design Firm: The Refinery

THE REFINERY

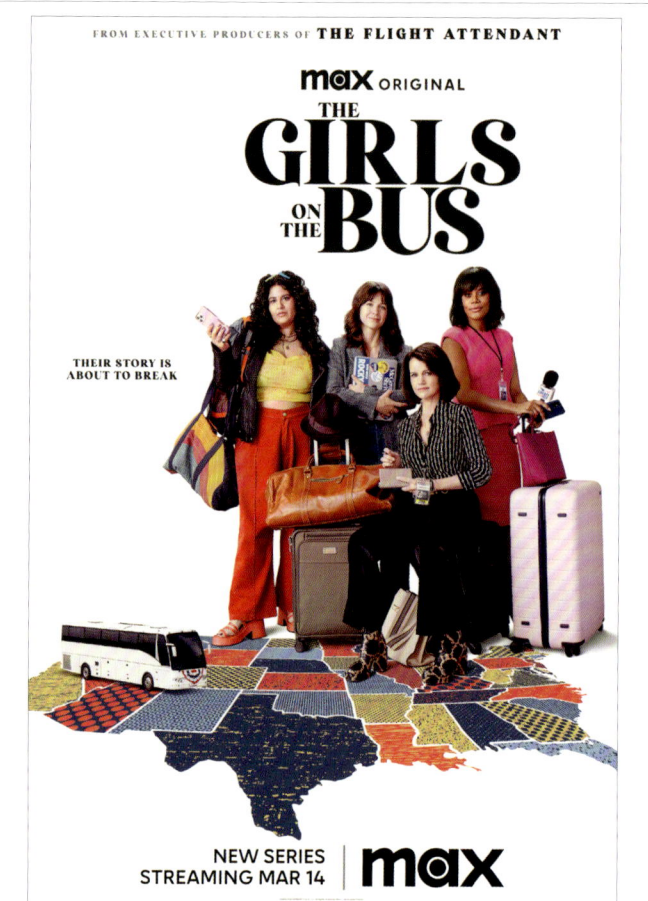

Title: The Girls on the Bus | **Client:** Max
Design Firm: The Refinery

SJI ASSOCIATES

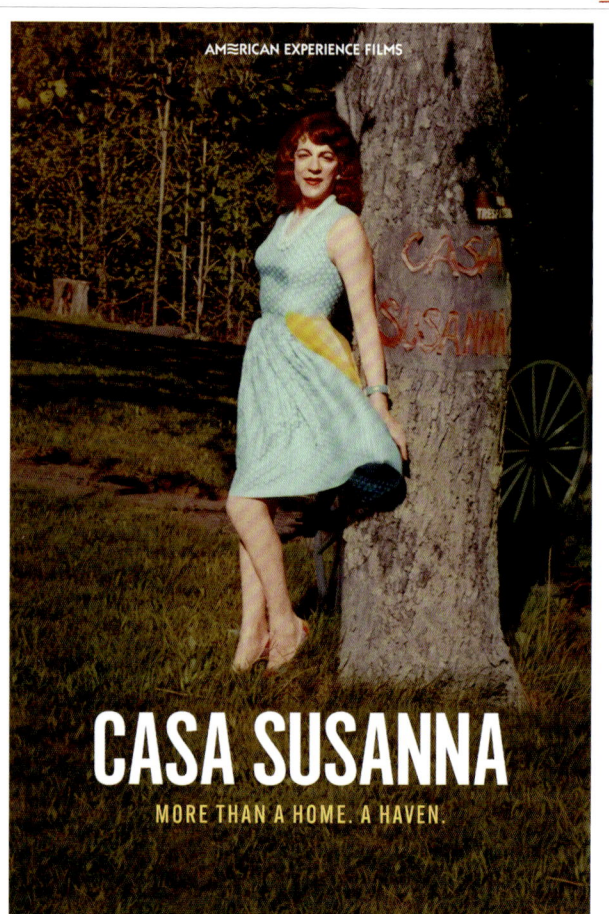

Title: Casa Susanna | **Clients:** Chika Offurum, American Experience Films | **Design Firm:** SJI Associates

SJI ASSOCIATES

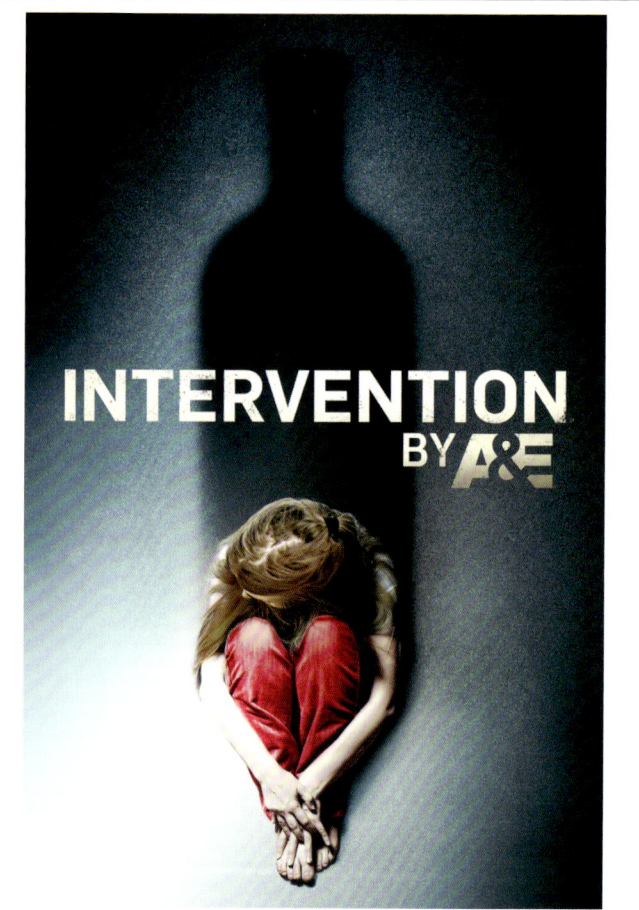

Title: Intervention (Fast Channel Brand Identity) | **Client:** A+E Networks
Design Firm: SJI Associates

159 **SILVER** ENTERTAINMENT

RHUBARB

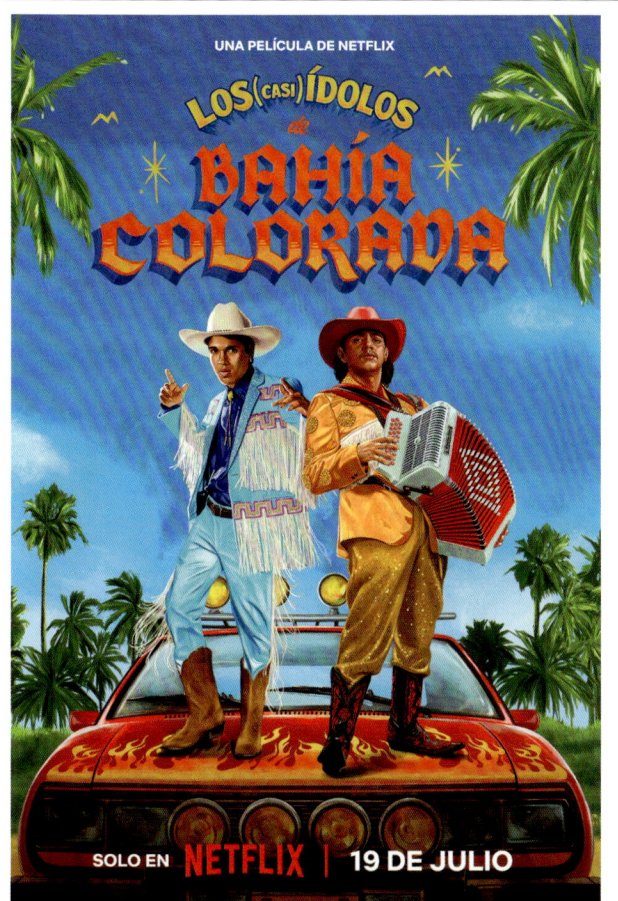

Title: Los (Casí) Ídolos de Bahía Colorada Key Art | **Client:** Netflix
Design Firm: Rhubarb

THE REFINERY

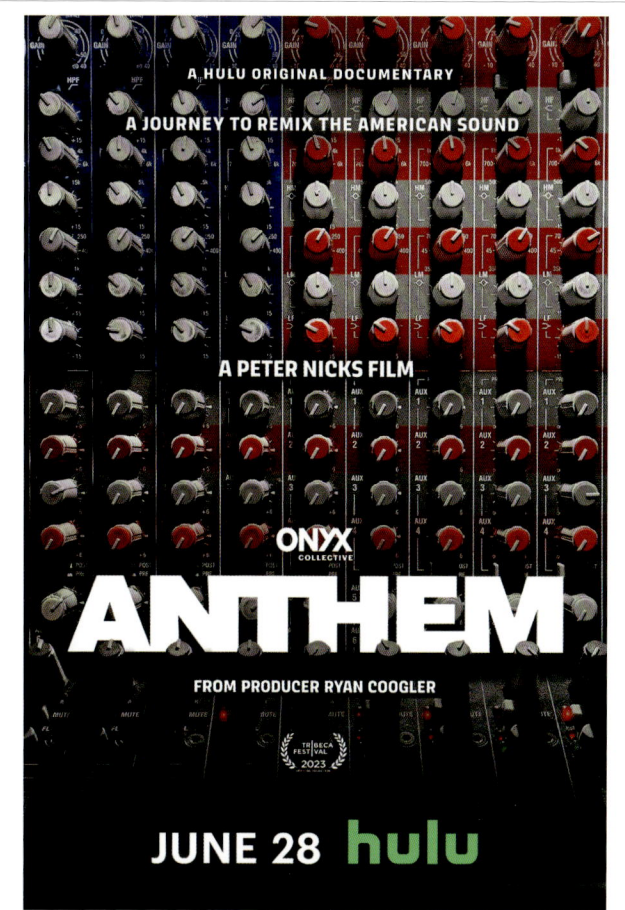

Title: Anthem | **Client:** Hulu
Design Firm: The Refinery

ARSONAL

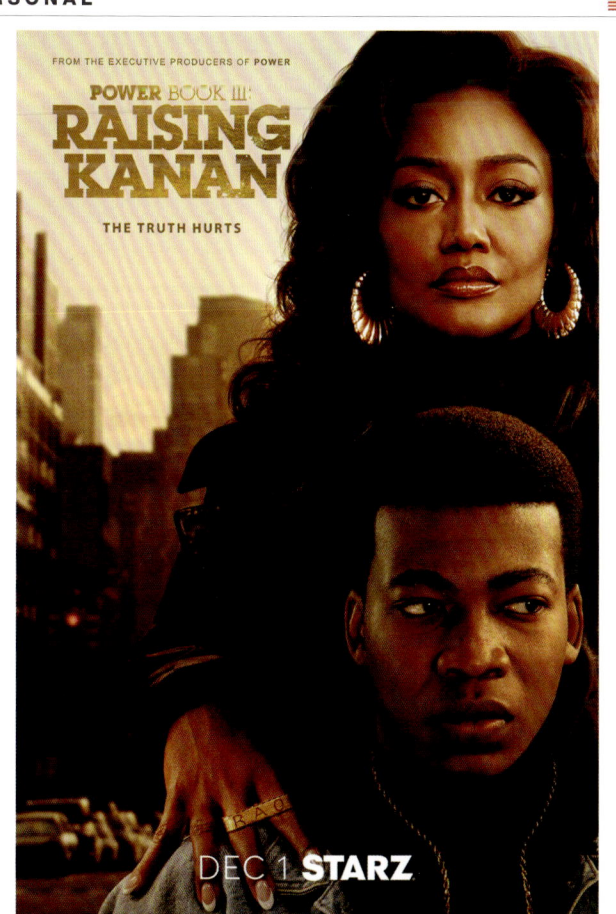

Title: RAISING KANAN | **Client:** STARZ
Design Firm: ARSONAL

THE REFINERY

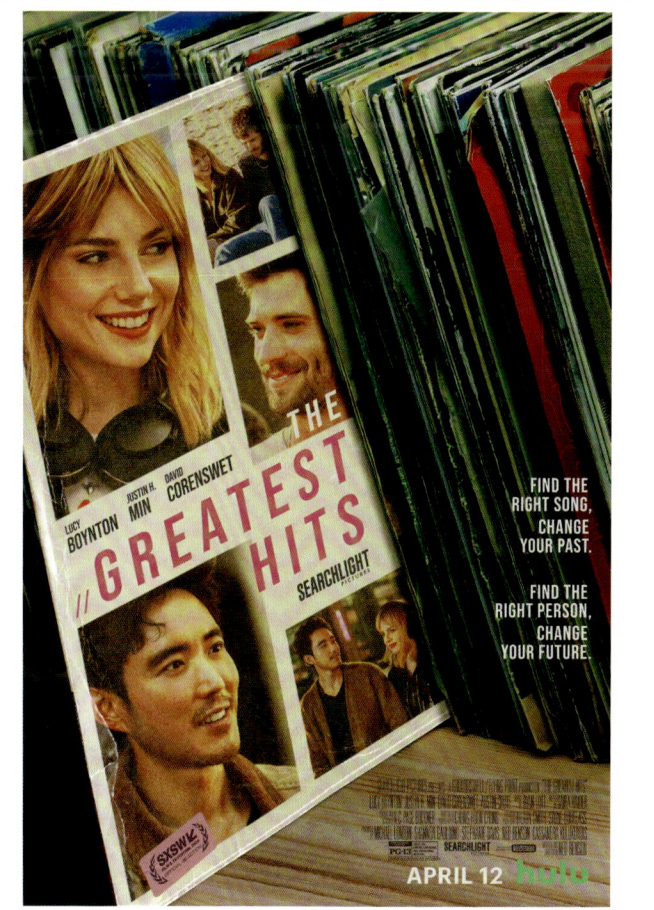

Title: The Greatest Hits | **Client:** Searchlight Pictures
Design Firm: The Refinery

160 **SILVER**　　　　　　　　　　　　　　　　　　　　　　　　　　　　　　　　　　　　　　ENTERTAINMENT

SJI ASSOCIATES 🇺🇸

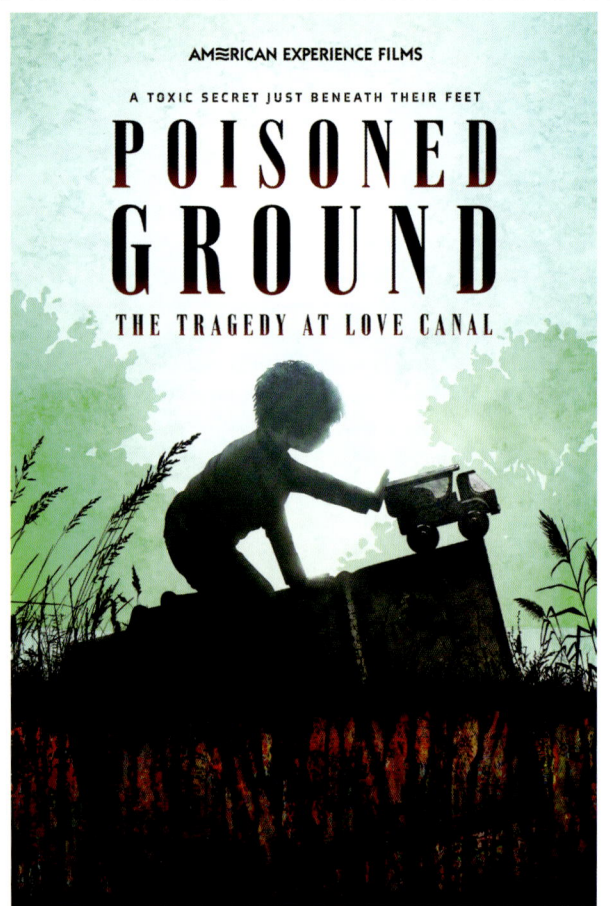

Title: Poisoned Ground: The Tragedy at Love Canal | **Clients:** Chika Offurum, American Experience Films | **Design Firm:** SJI Associates

RHUBARB 🇺🇸

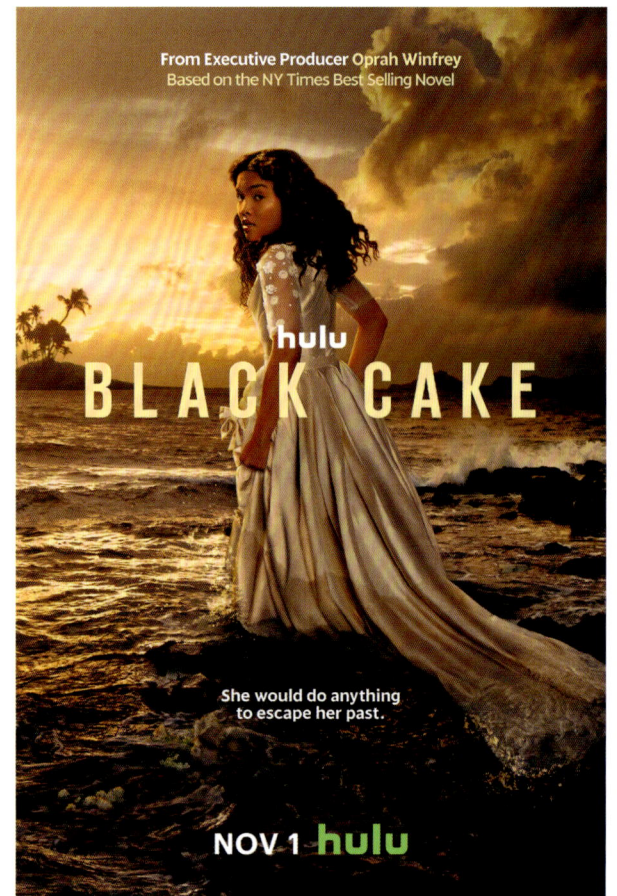

Title: Black Cake Key Art | **Client:** Hulu
Design Firm: Rhubarb

THE REFINERY 🇺🇸

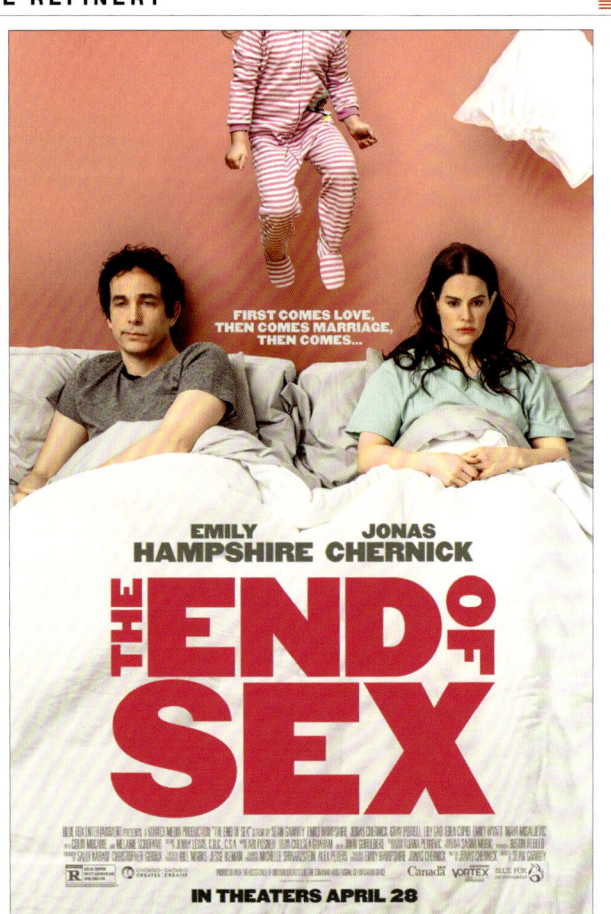

Title: The End of Sex | **Client:** Blue Fox Entertainment
Design Firm: The Refinery

THE REFINERY 🇺🇸

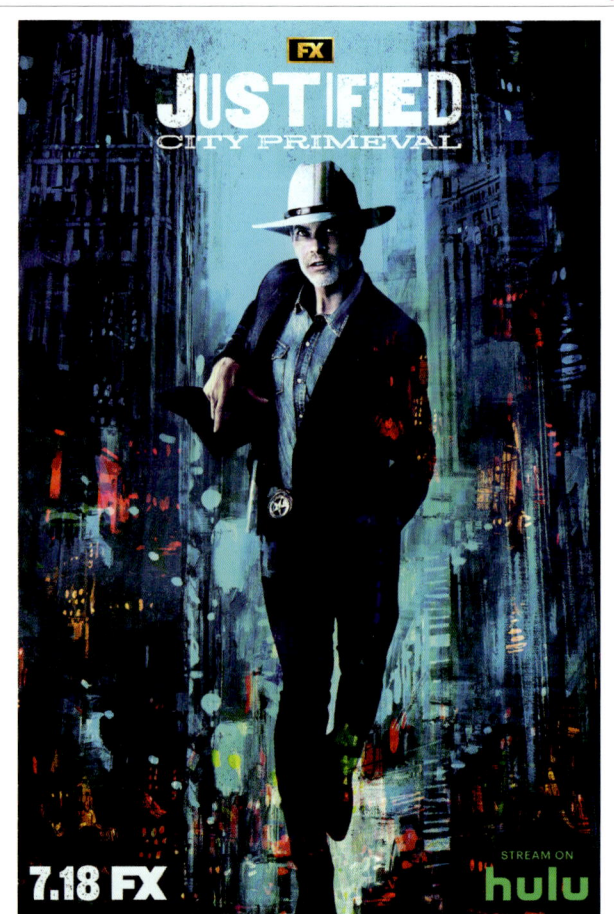

Title: Justified: City Primeval, Key Art | **Client:** FX Networks
Design Firm: The Refinery

161 SILVER   ENTERTAINMENT

THE REFINERY

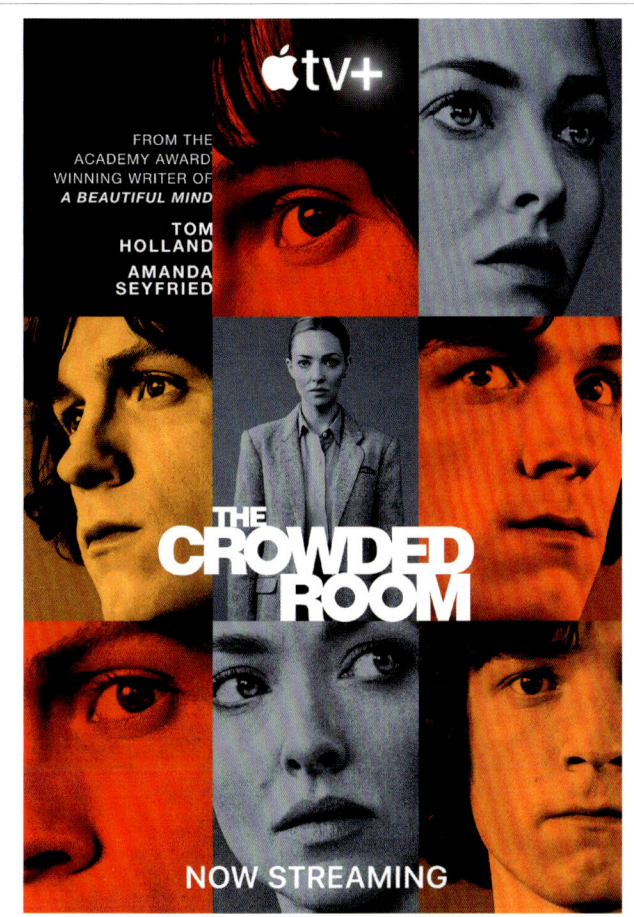

Title: The Crowded Room, Key Art | **Client:** Apple TV+
Design Firm: The Refinery

THE REFINERY

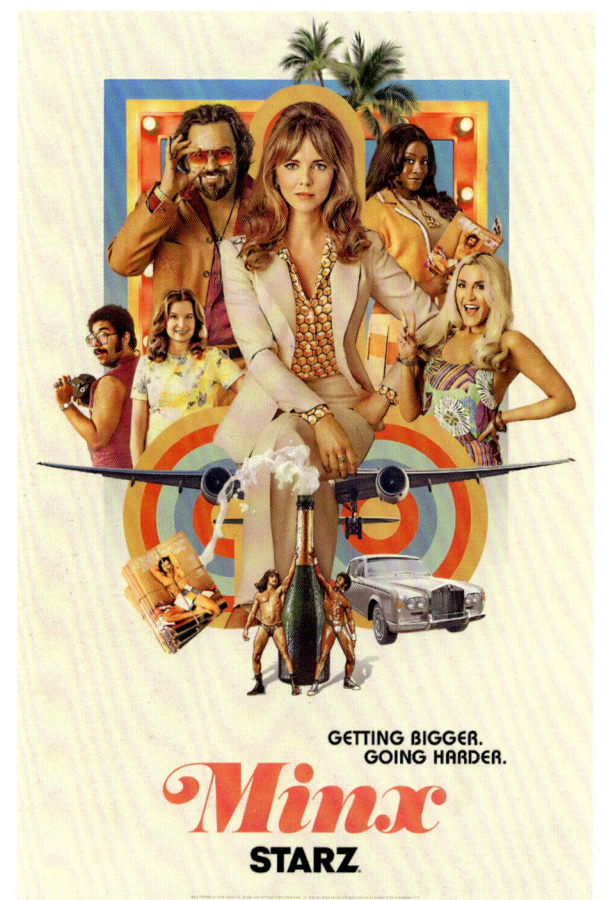

Title: Minx S2, Key Art | **Client:** STARZ
Design Firm: The Refinery

RHUBARB

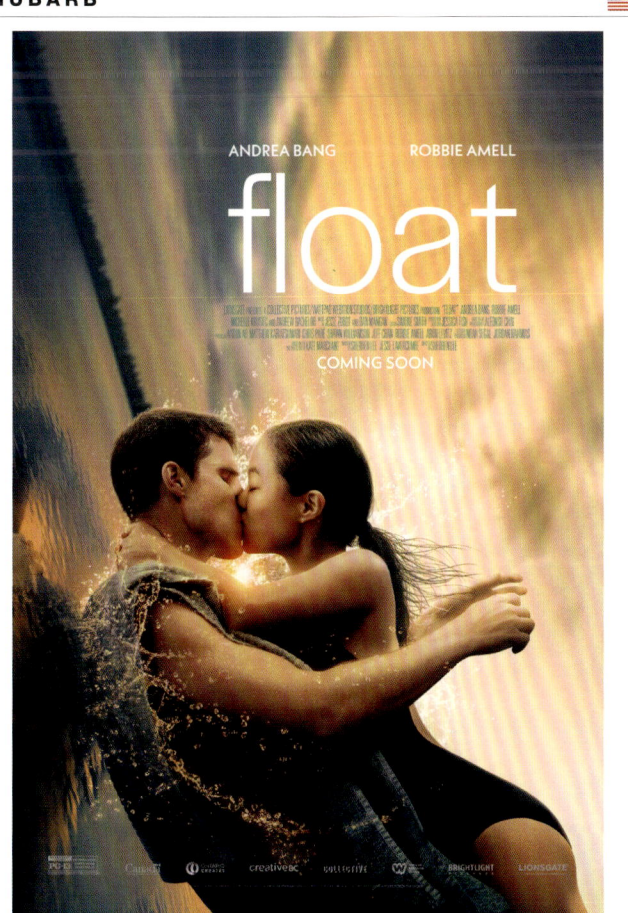

Title: Float Key Art | **Client:** Lionsgate
Design Firm: Rhubarb

THE REFINERY

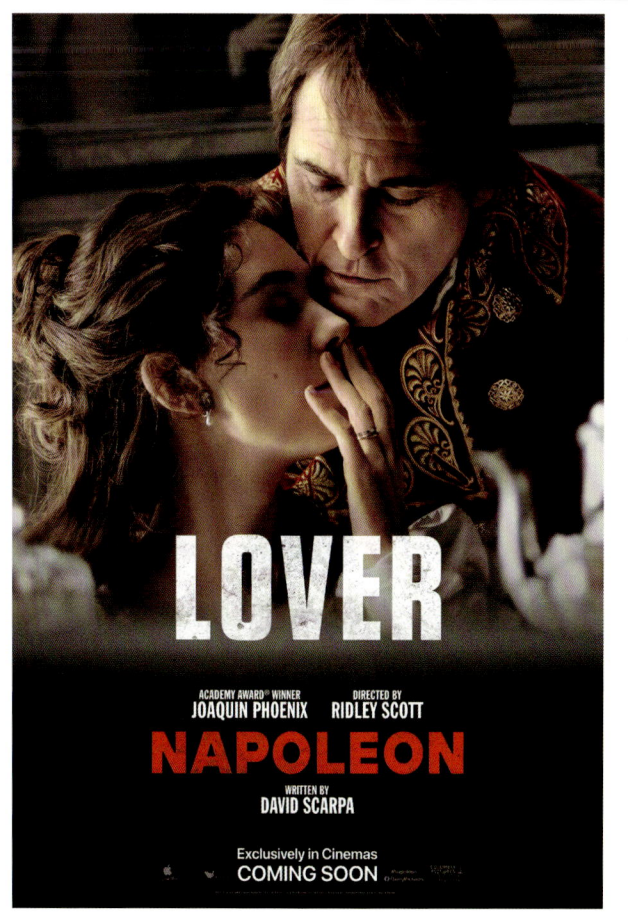

Title: Napoleon, International Wildposts | **Clients:** Apple TV+, Sony Pictures Entertainment | **Design Firm:** The Refinery

162 SILVER

ENVIRONMENT

CHIA-HUI LIEN

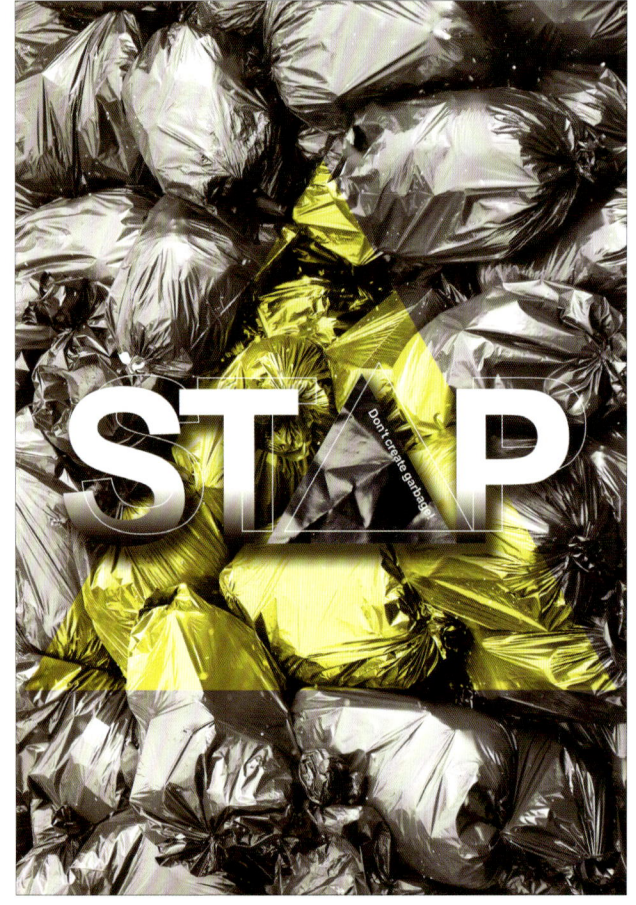

Title: Don't Create Garbage | **Client:** Self-initiated
Design Firm: Tainan University of Technology

LEE WALTERS

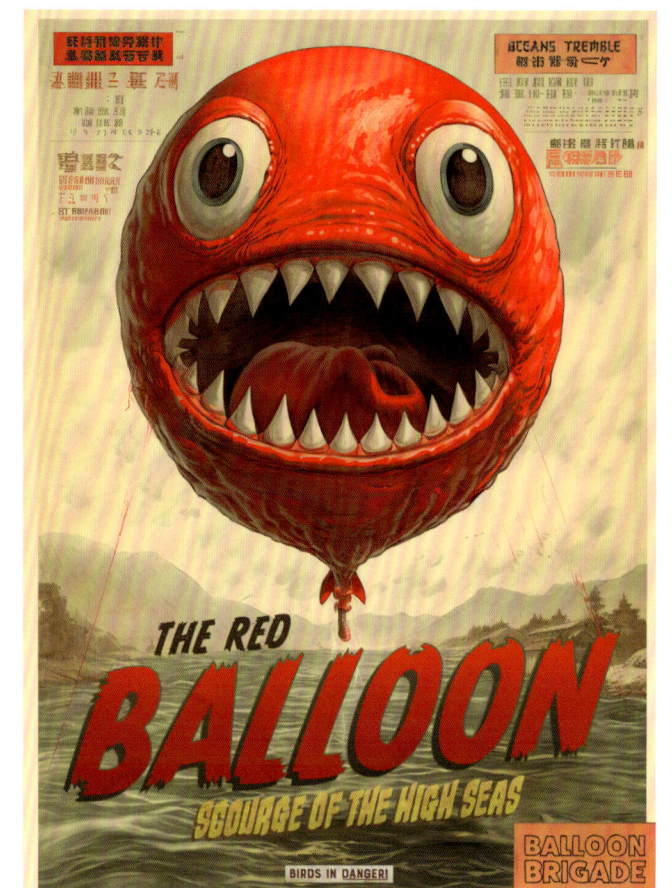

Title: Balloons are Monsters | **Client:** Balloon Brigade
Design Firm: Arcana Academy

MI-JUNG LEE

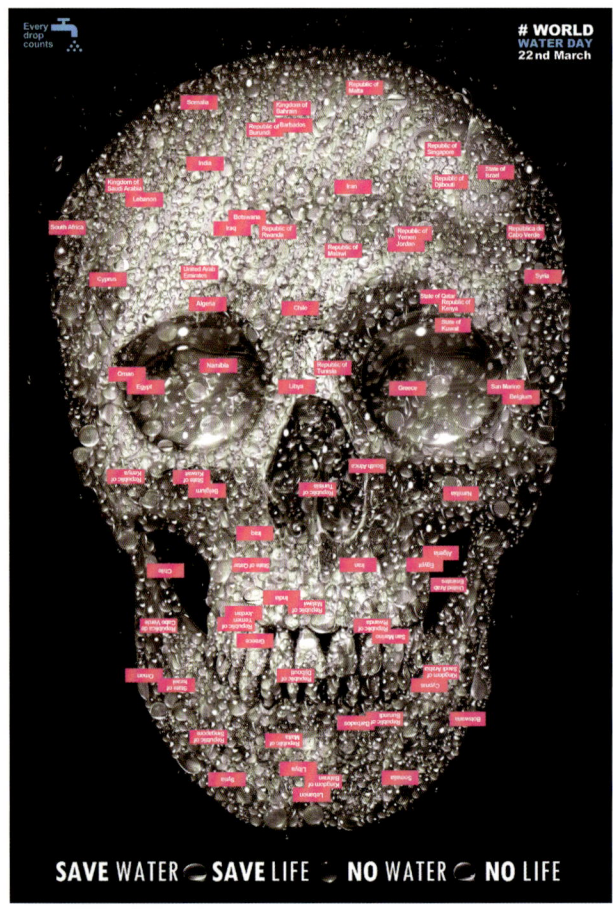

Title: SAVE WATER, SAVE LIFE, NO WATER, NO LIFE
Client: Ministry of Environment | **Design Firm:** Namseoul University

DERWYN GOODALL

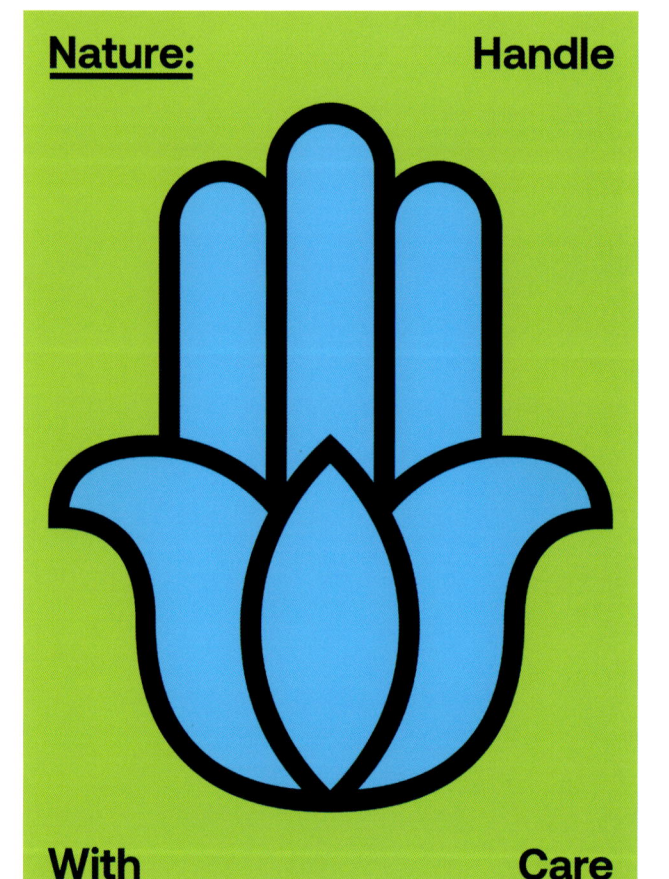

Title: Nature: Handle with Care | **Clients:** 2nd Yangmingshan Art Festival, 22th Tianmu Waterway Festival | **Design Firm:** Goodall Integrated Design

163 SILVER ENVIRONMENT

HAJIME TSUSHIMA

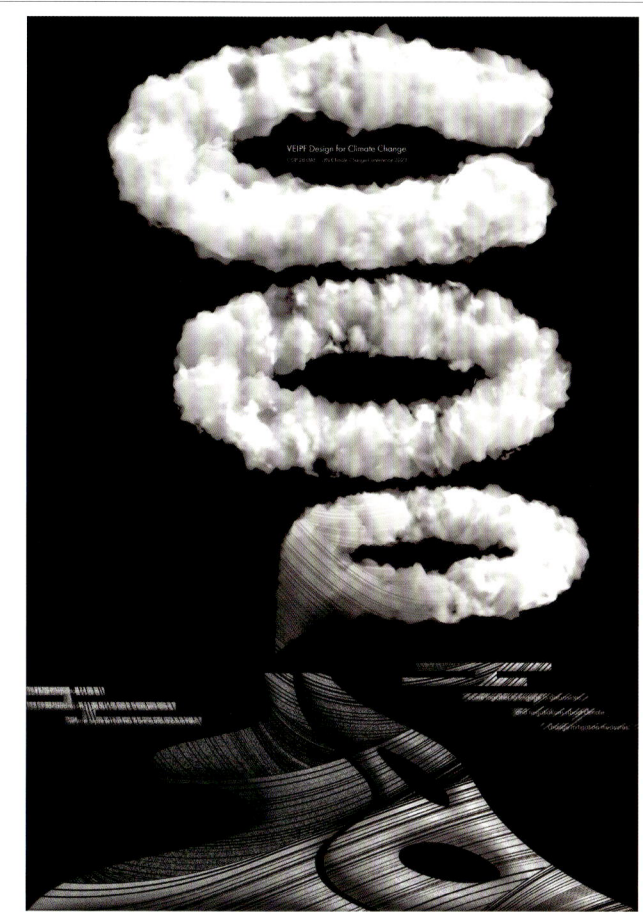

Title: COP28 | **Client:** Emirates International Poster Festival
Design Firm: Tsushima Design

JOÃO MACHADO

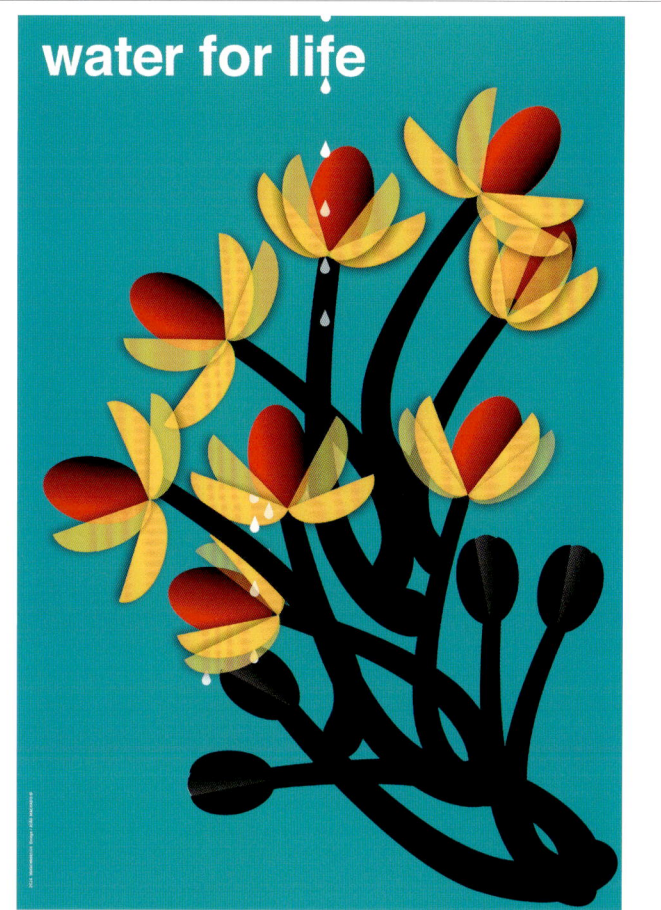

Title: Water for Life | **Client:** UnknownDesign
Design Firm: João Machado Design

ANNE M. GIANGIULIO

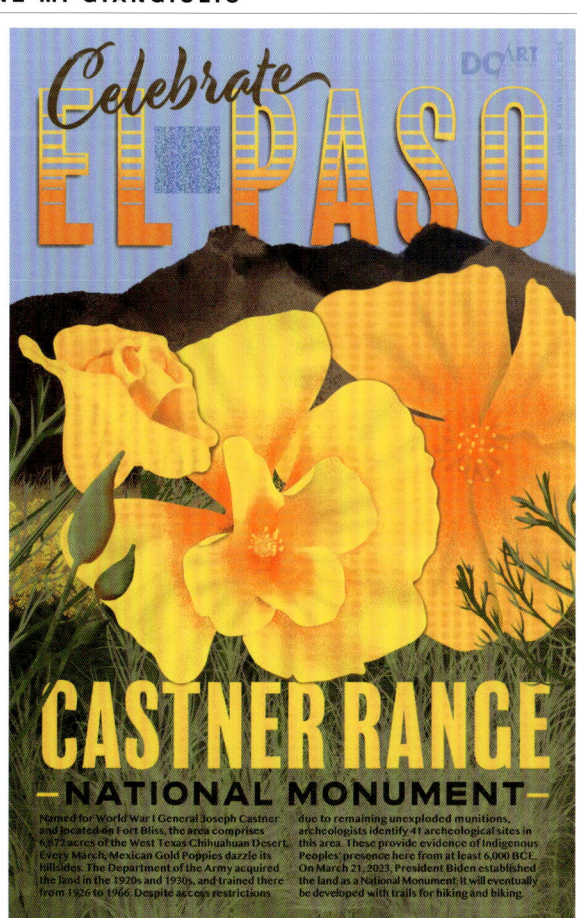

Title: Celebrate El Paso: Castner Range National Monument
Client: Self-initiated | **Design Firm:** Anne M. Giangiulio

DOUGLAS MAY

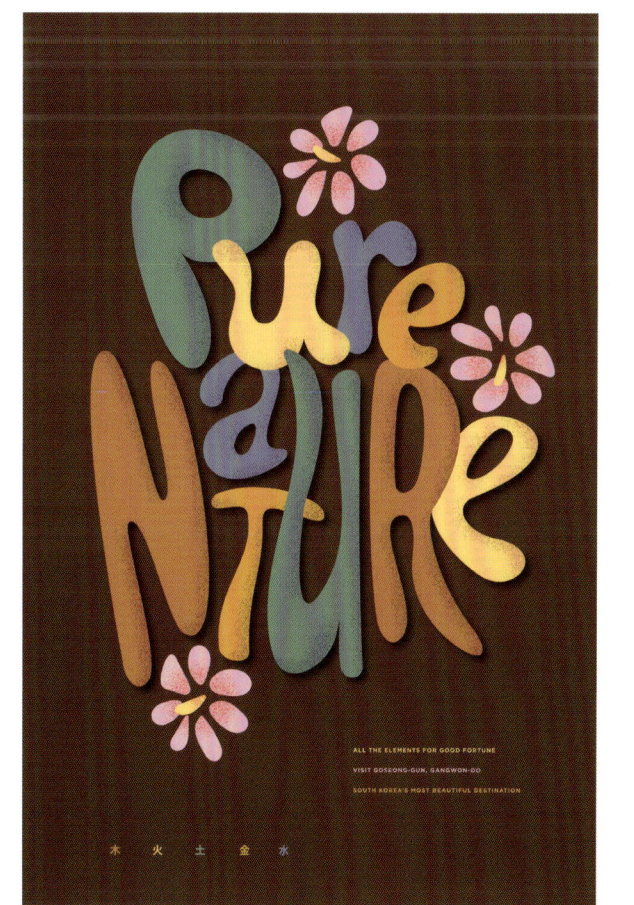

Title: Pure Nature | **Client:** 2023 CDAK International Special Exhibition
Design Firm: May & Co.

164 SILVER ENVIRONMENT

MICHAEL BRALEY 🇺🇸

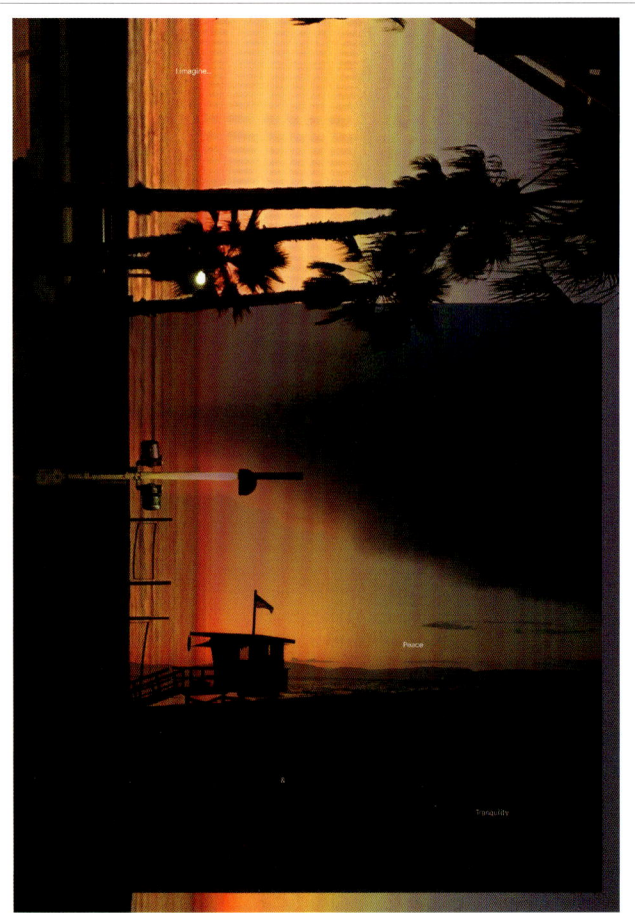

Title: I Imagine... Peace and Tranquility | **Client:** Self-initiated
Design Firm: Braley Design

JOÃO MACHADO 🇵🇹

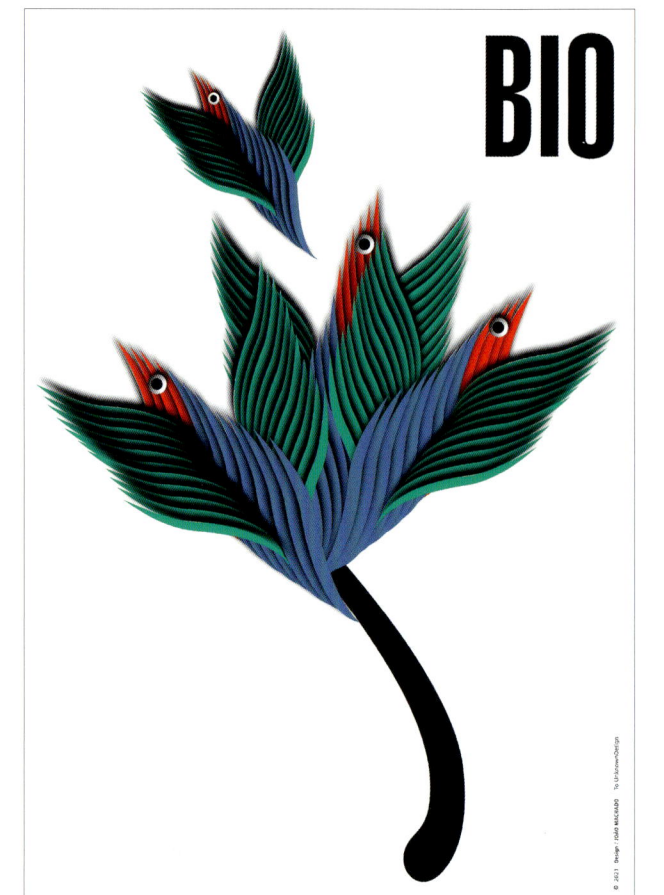

Title: BIO | **Client:** UnknownDesign
Design Firm: João Machado Design

HYUNGJOO A. KIM 🇺🇸

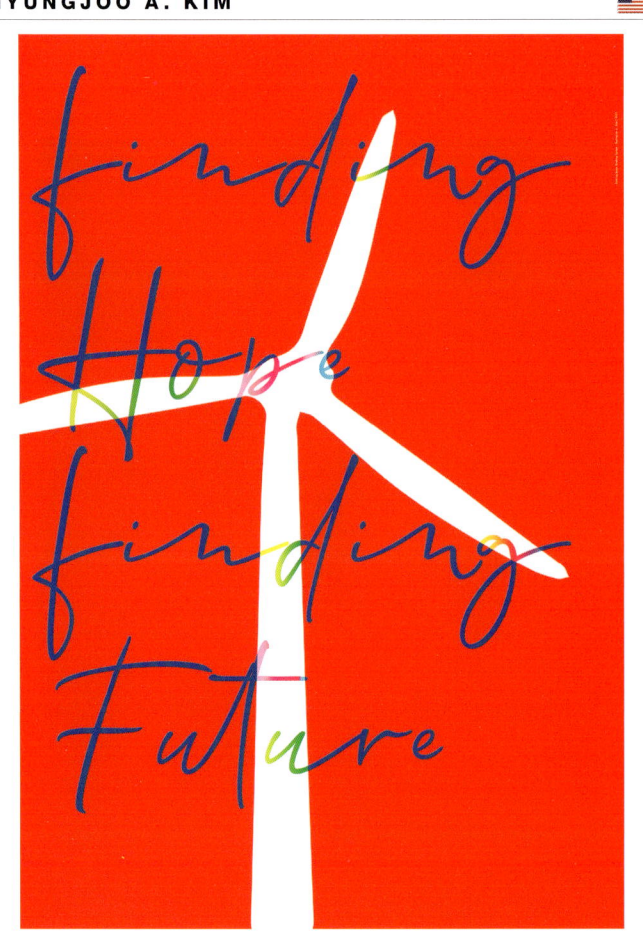

Title: Finding Hope, Finding Future | **Client:** Emirates International Poster Festival | **Design Firm:** Hyungjookim Designlab

JG DEBRAY 🇺🇸

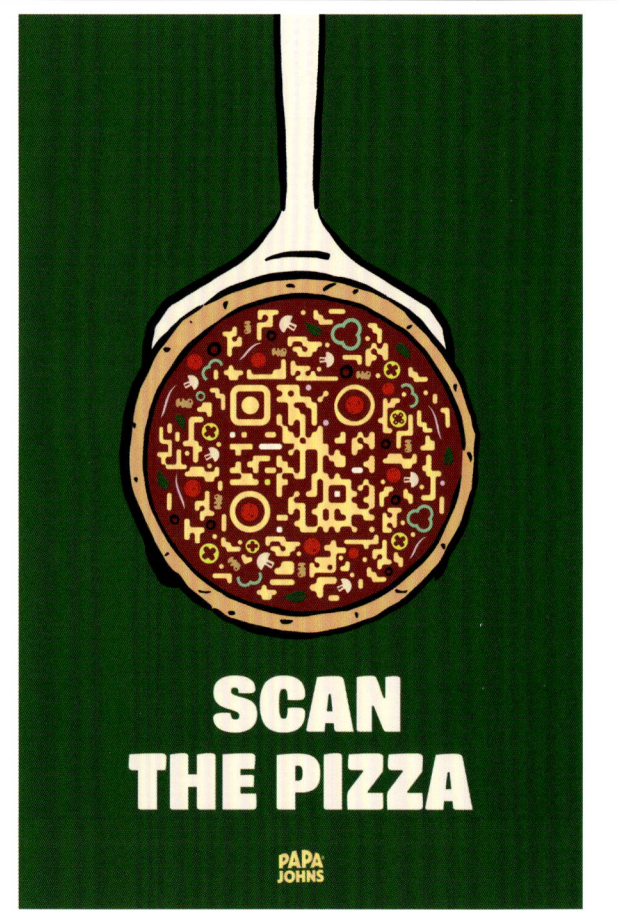

Title: Papa Johns Posters | **Client:** Papa Johns
Design Firm: Addison

165 SILVER ENVIRONMENT

WESAM MAZHAR HADDAD 🇺🇸

Title: Orange Forest | **Client:** Self-initiated
Design Firm: Wesam Mazhar Haddad

JOÃO MACHADO 🇵🇹

Title: Save Me | **Client:** UnknownDesign
Design Firm: João Machado Design

TOYOTSUGU ITOH 🇯🇵

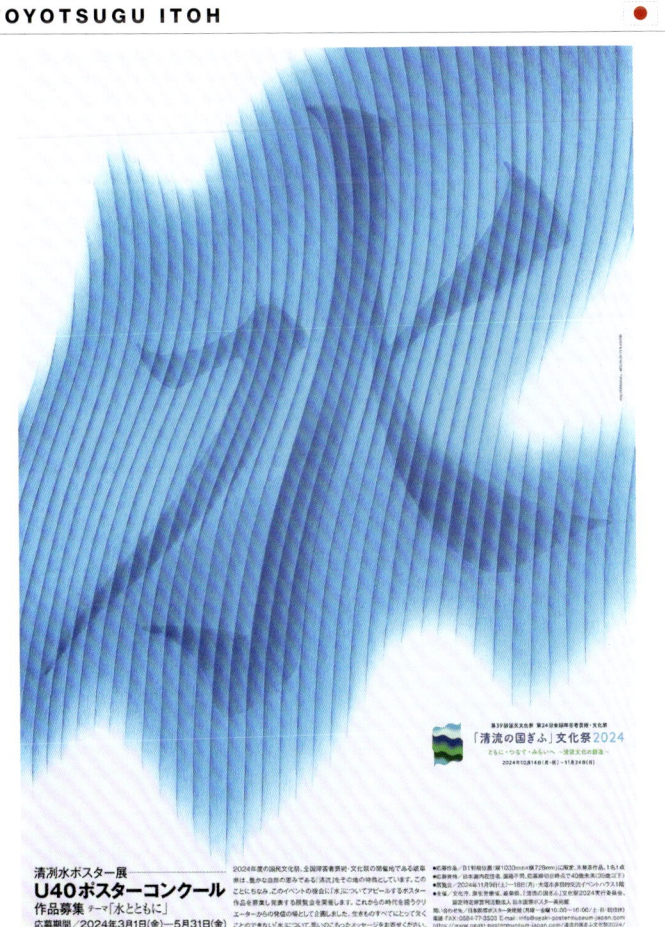

Title: "Clean Water" U40 Poster Design Competition
Client: Ogaki Poster Museum | **Design Firm:** Toyotsugu Itoh Design Office

CHONG-WEN CHEN 🇹🇼

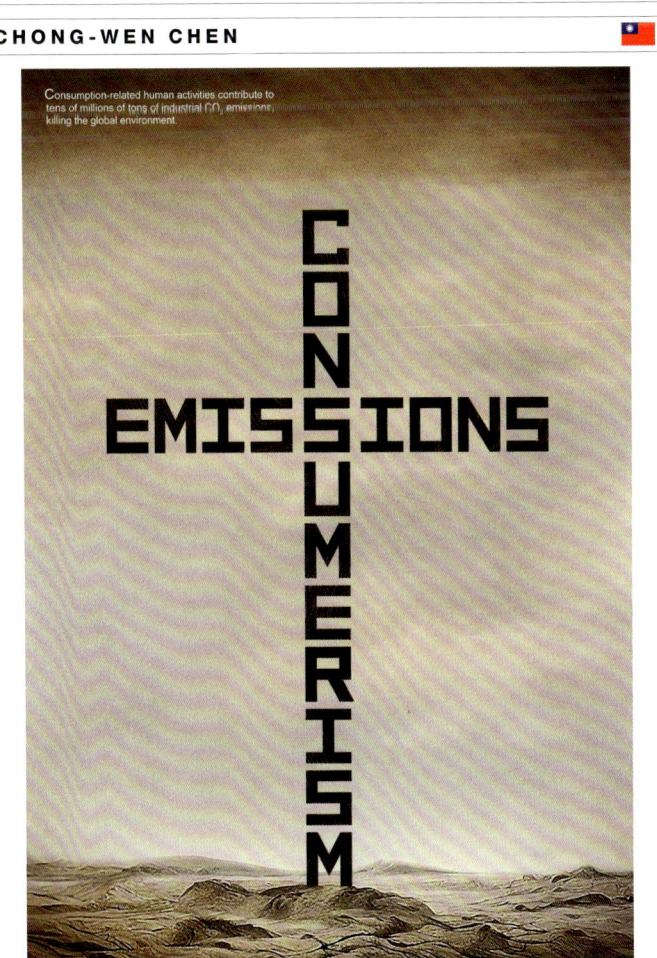

Title: Final Footprint | **Client:** Self-initiated | **Design Firm:** National Kaohsiung University of Science & Technology (NKUST)

MICHAEL BRALEY

Title: Herbert Bayer Homage | **Client:** United States International Poster Biennial (USIPB) | **Design Firm:** Braley Design

LEE GILTAE

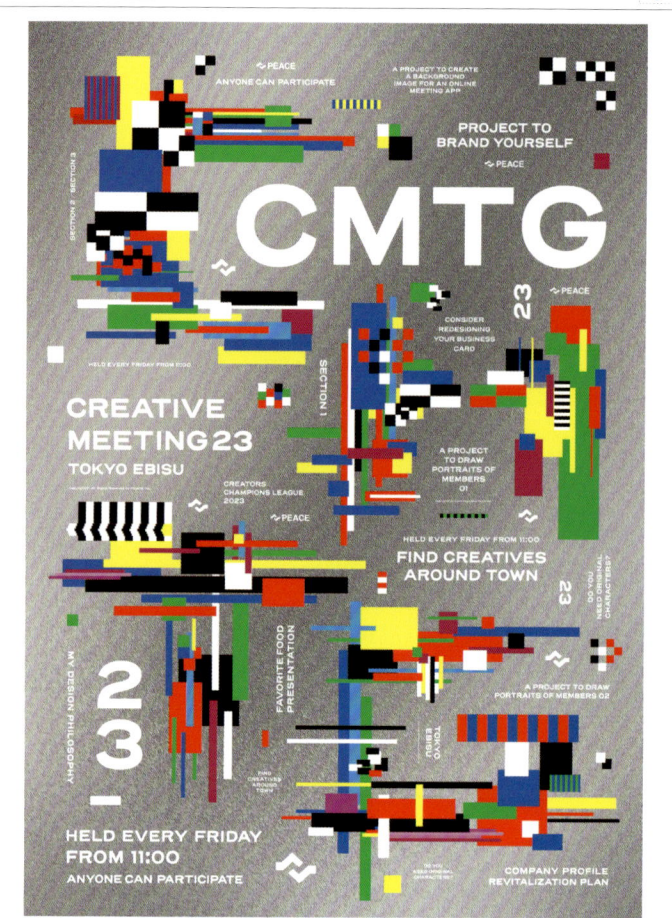

Title: CMTG 2023 | **Client:** Self-initiated
Design Firm: PEACE Inc.

JOSHUA LOWE

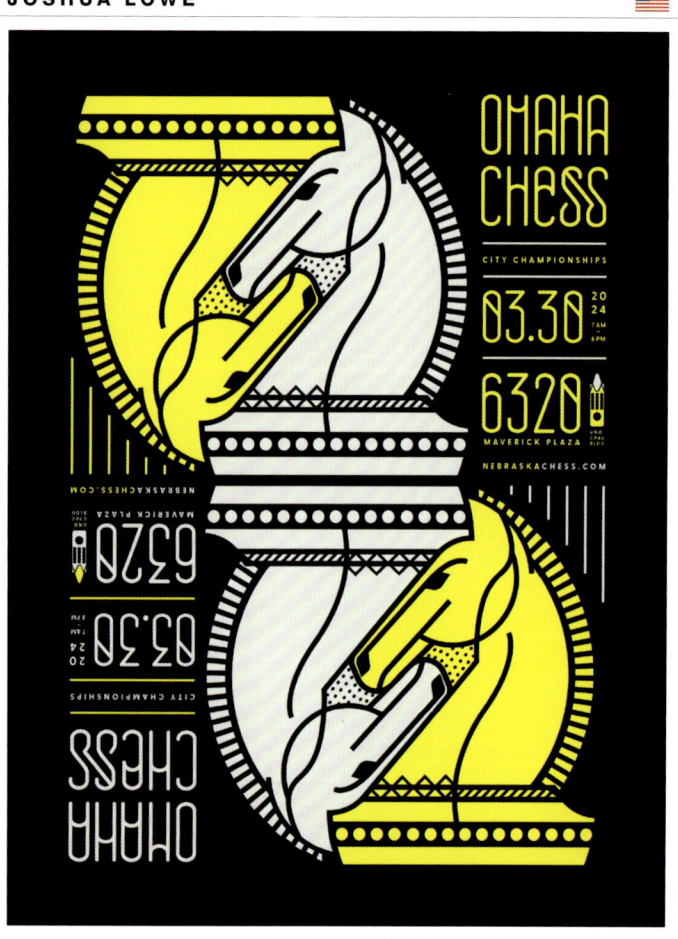

Title: Omaha Chess City Championships | **Client:** Nebraska State Chess Association | **Design Firm:** University of Nebraska

DAVID HABBEN

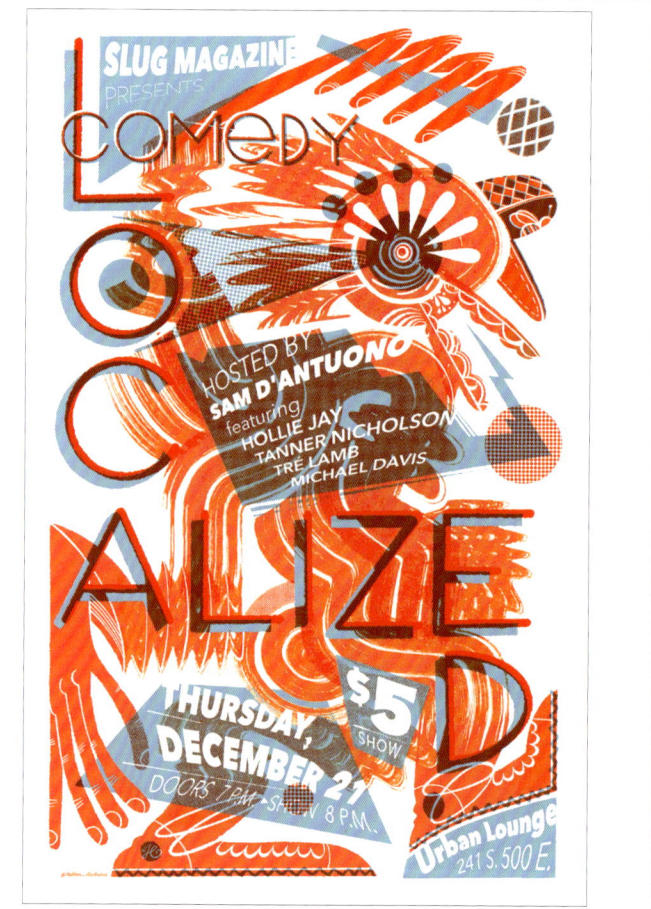

Title: Comedy Localized Poster | **Client:** SLUG Magazine
Design Firm: David Habben Illustration

167 SILVER EVENTS

MICHAEL BRALEY 🇺🇸

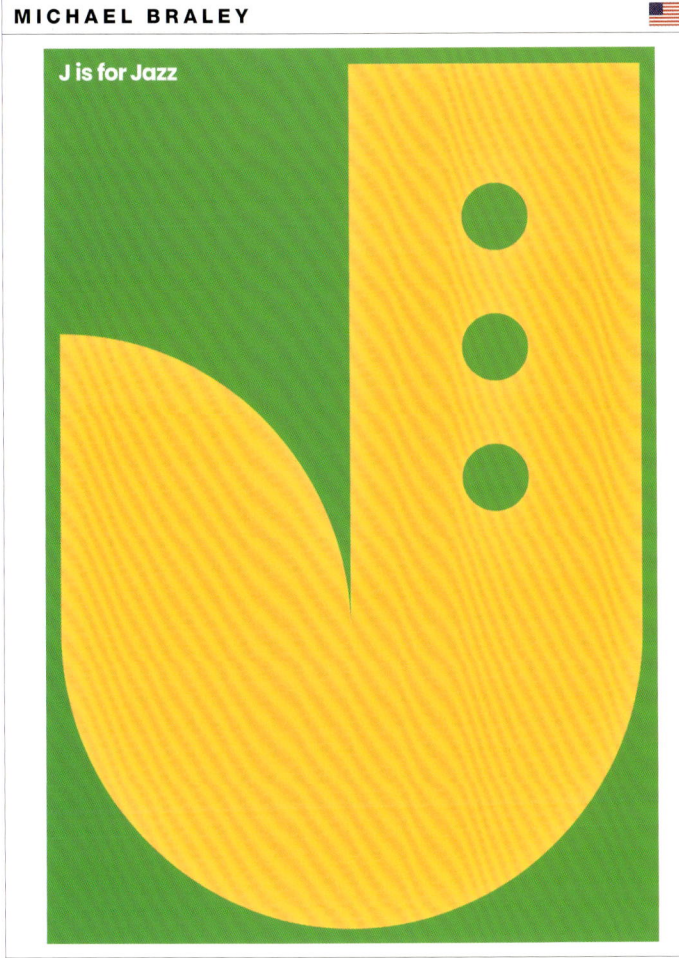

Title: J is for Jazz | **Client:** We Want Jazz 2023
Design Firm: Braley Design

CHIKAKO OGUMA 🇯🇵

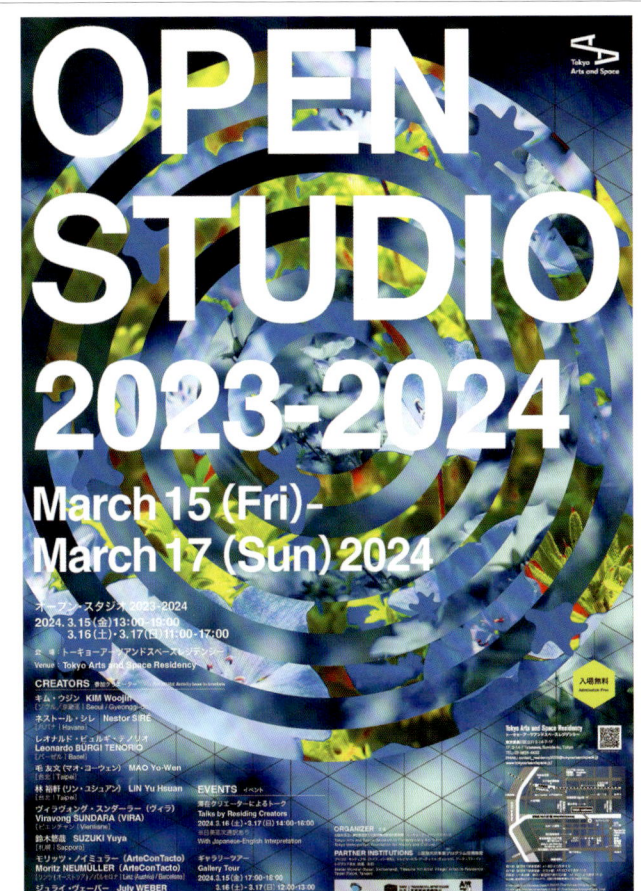

Title: TOKAS OPEN STUDIO | **Client:** TOKAS (Tokyo Arts and Space)
Design Firm: Chikako Oguma

AYA KAWABATA 🇯🇵

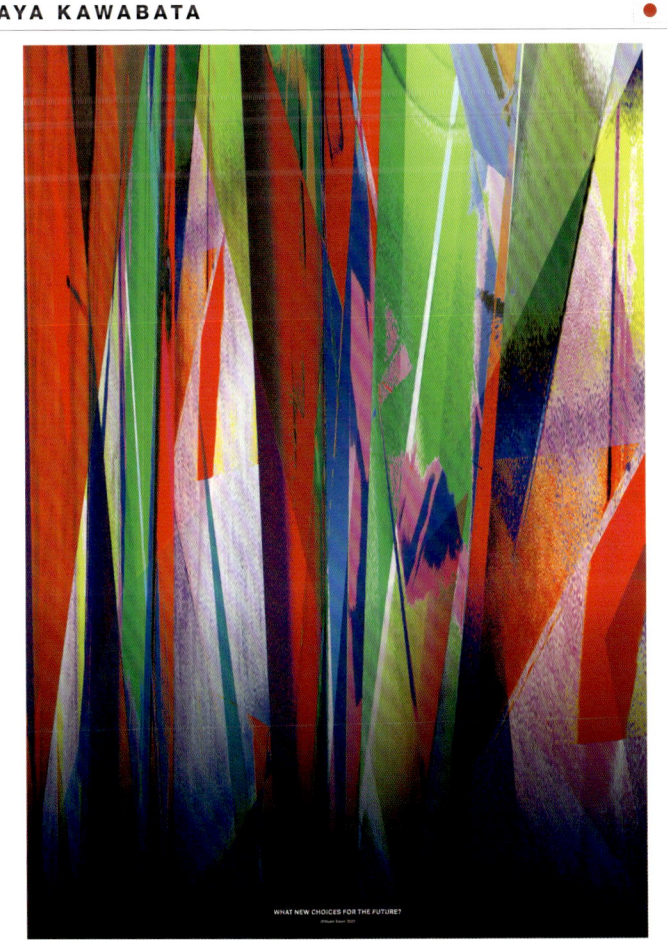

Title: WHAT NEW CHOICES FOR THE FUTURE?
Client: Design Event Shibuya 2023 | **Design Firm:** AYA KAWABATA DESIGN

FONS HICKMANN 🇩🇪

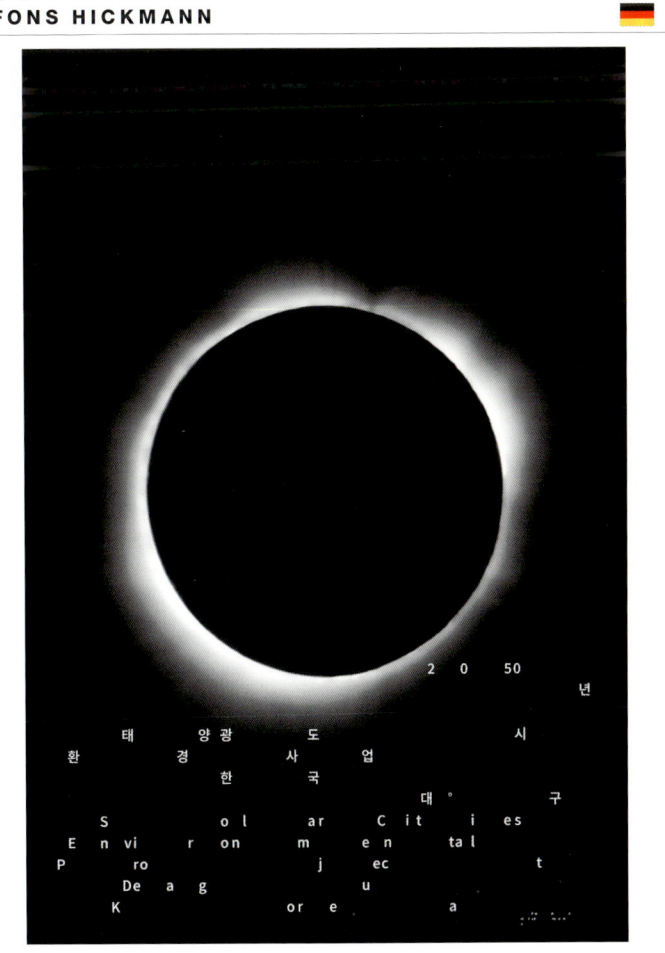

Title: Solar Cities | **Client:** Daegu Korea
Design Firm: Fons Hickmann m23

168 SILVER   EVENTS

MICHAEL BRALEY

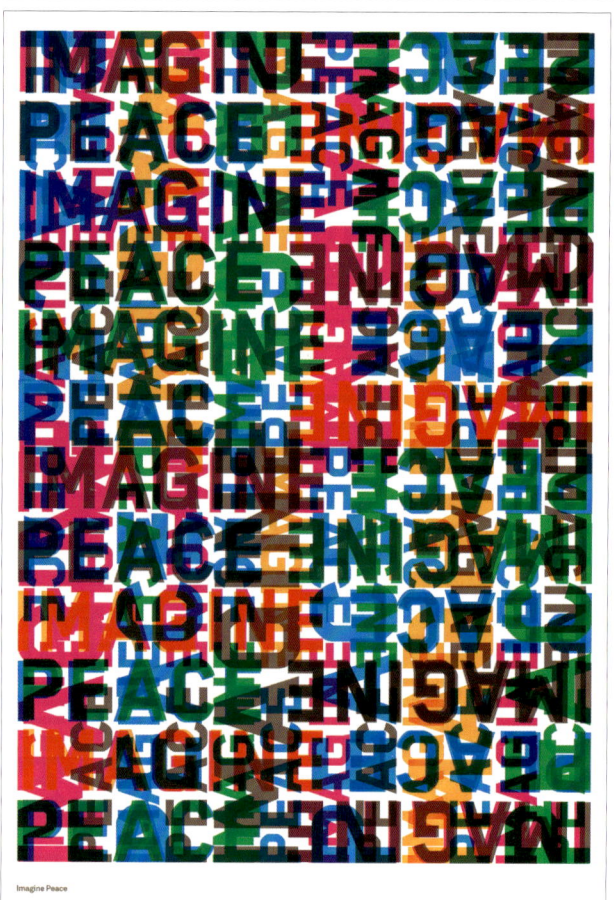

Title: Imagine Peace | **Client:** Nanjing International Biennial of Poster for Peace 2023 | **Design Firm:** Braley Design

MICHAEL BRALEY

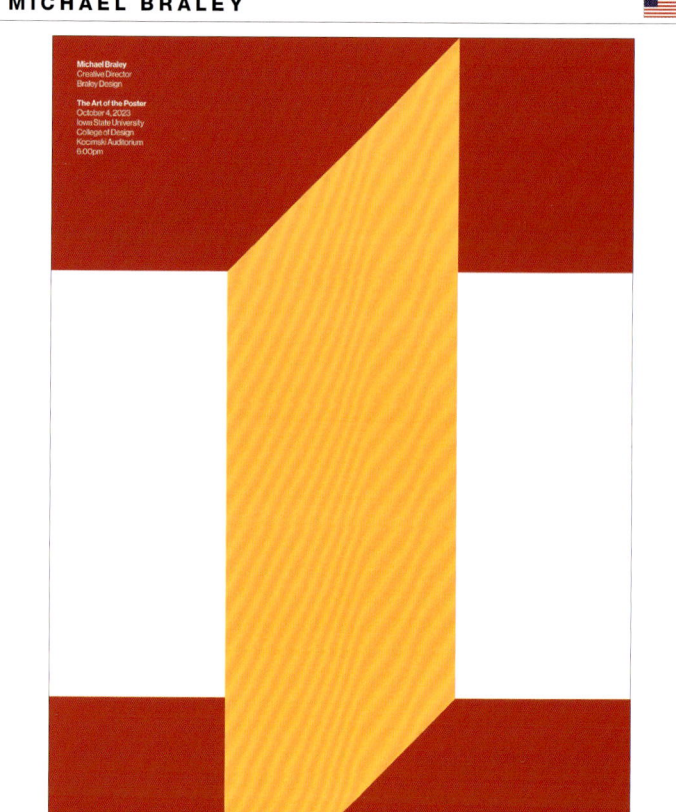

Title: Iowa State University Lecture Poster | **Clients:** Self-initiated, Iowa State University | **Design Firm:** Braley Design

OVIDIU HRIN

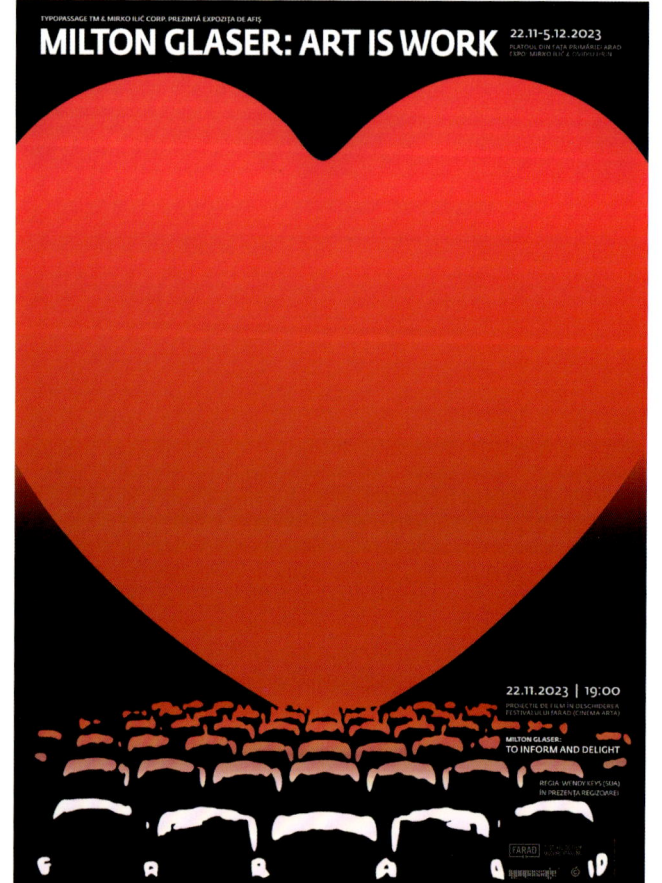

Title: MILTON GLASER | **Client:** Typopassage TM Poster Museum
Design Firm: Synopsismedia

MICHAEL BRALEY

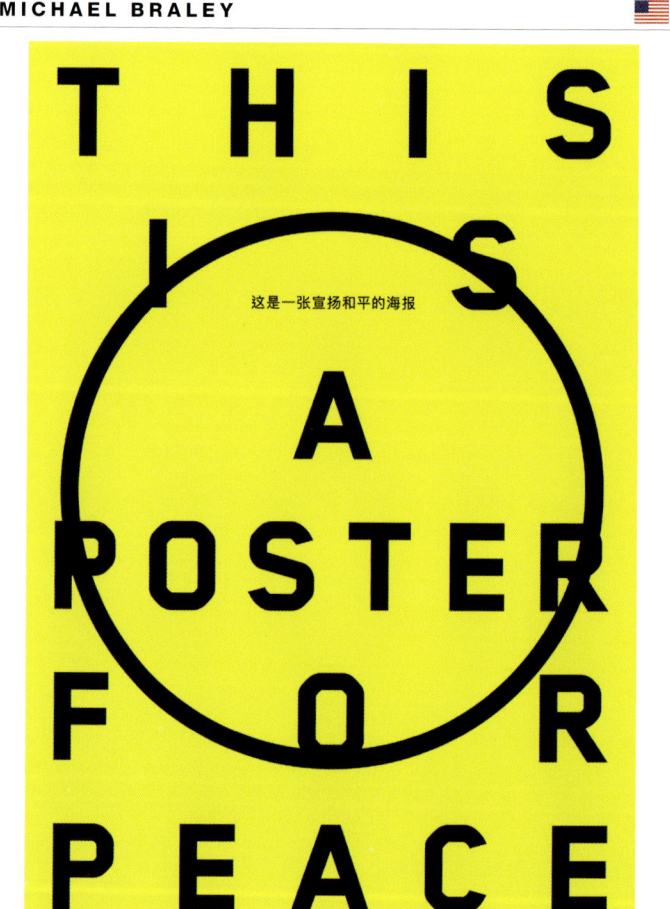

Title: This is a Poster for Peace | **Client:** Nanjing International Biennial of Poster for Peace 2023 | **Design Firm:** Braley Design

169 SILVER — EVENTS

KIT HINRICHS 🇺🇸

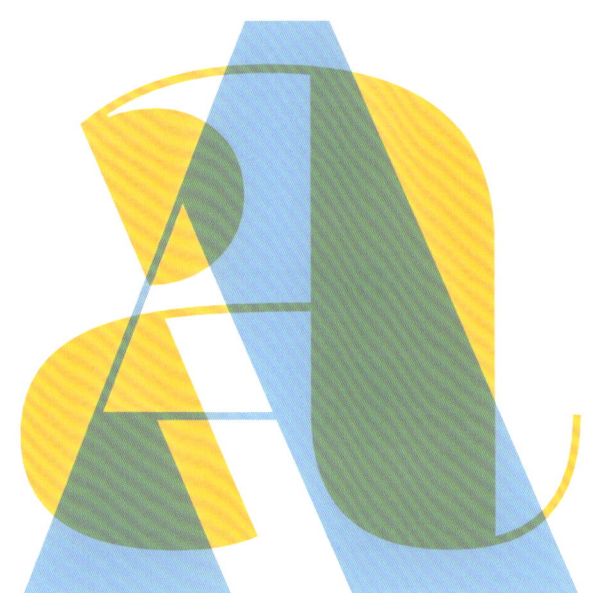

Title: San Francisco Antiquarian Book & Paper Fair | **Client:** Nancy Johnson Events Management | **Design Firm:** Studio Hinrichs

MICHAEL BRALEY 🇺🇸

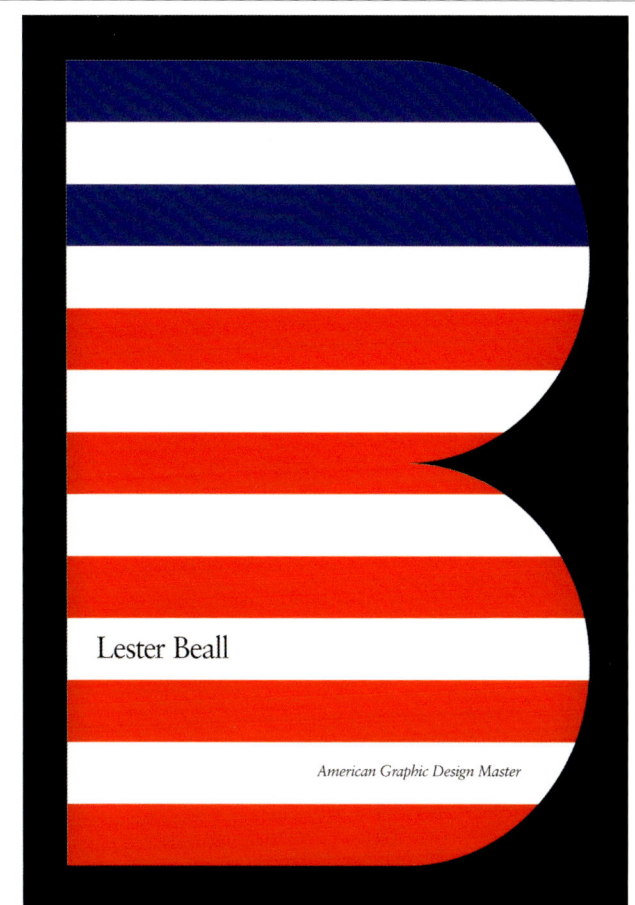

Title: Lester Beall Homage | **Client:** United States International Poster Biennial (USIPB) | **Design Firm:** Braley Design

ALEXANDRIA CANCHOLA 🇺🇸

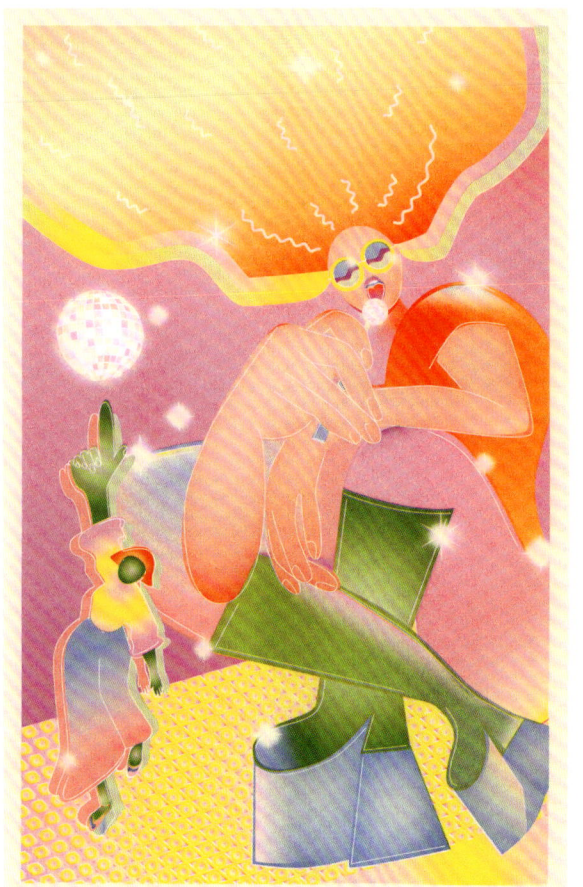

Title: Wigout at the Disco | **Client:** K Space Contemporary
Design Firm: Everything Looks Good

R.P. BISSLAND 🇺🇸

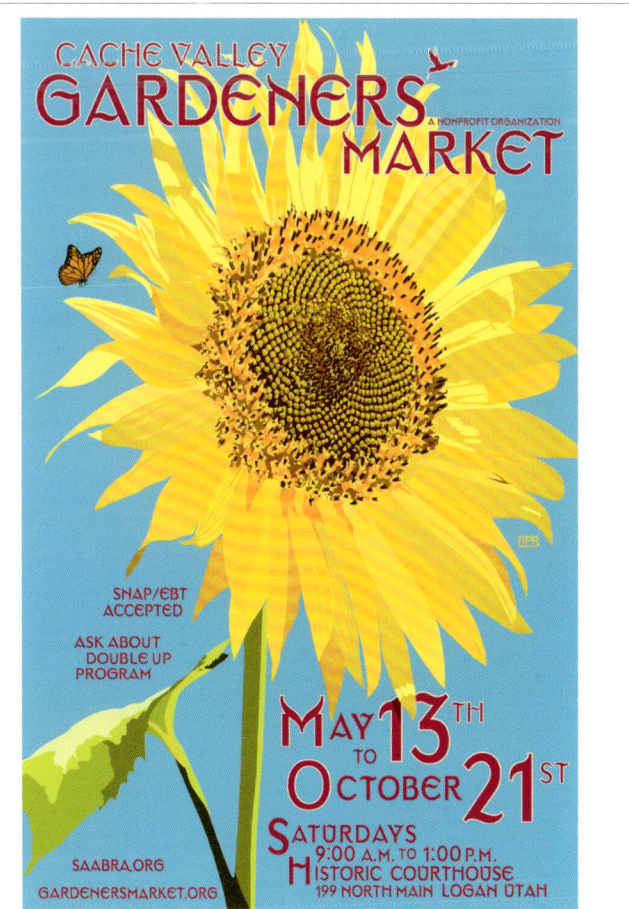

Title: 2023 Gardeners' Market Poster | **Client:** Cache Valley Gardeners' Market Association | **Design Firm:** Design SubTerra

EVENTS, EXHIBITS

SHANTANU SUMAN
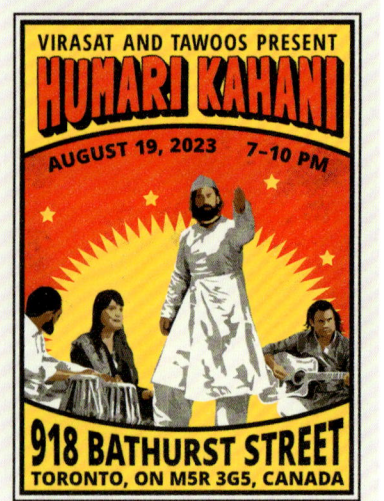
Title: Humari Kahani Posters
Clients: Tawoos Initiative, Virasat
Design Firm: Shantanu Suman

AUTOMOTIVE EVENTS
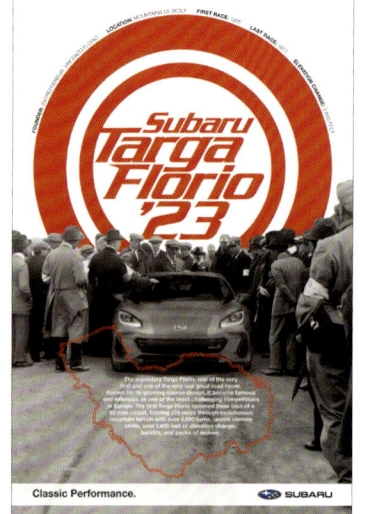
Title: Subaru Targa Florio Poster
Clients: Dominick Infante, Subaru of America
Design Firm: Automotive Events

CARMIT MAKLER HALLER
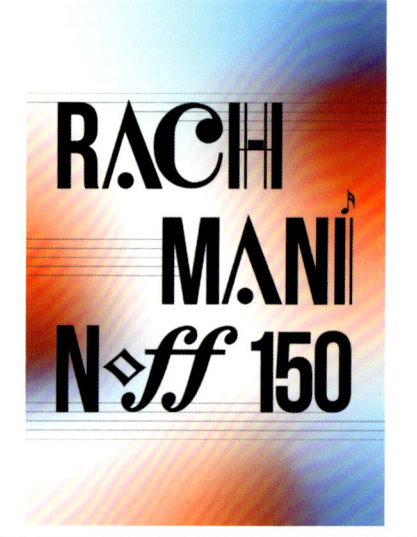
Title: Rachmaninoff
Client: Golden Bee Biennale
Design Firm: Carmit Design Studio

KIT HINRICHS
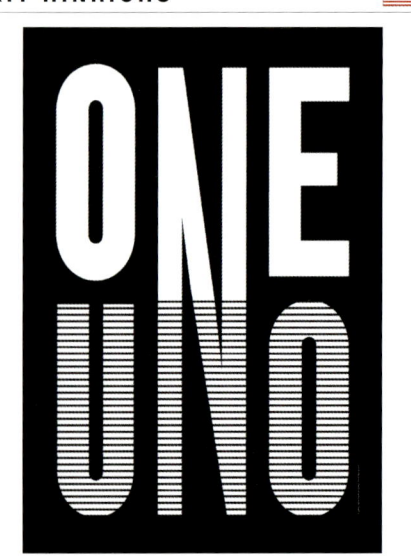
Title: AGI Special Project 2023: One/Uno
Client: Alliance Graphique Internationale (AGI)
Design Firm: Studio Hinrichs

ARI SANTIAGO
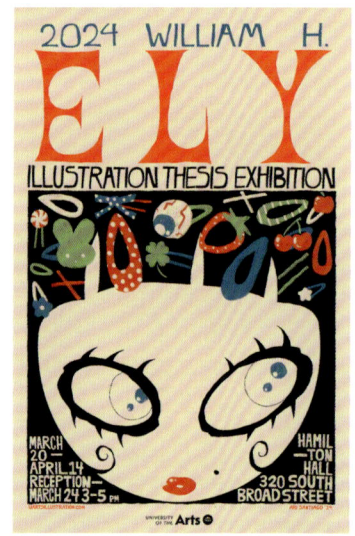
Title: 2024 William H. Ely Illustration Thesis Exhibition | **Client:** Self-initiated
Design Firm: University of the Arts

MICHAEL BRALEY
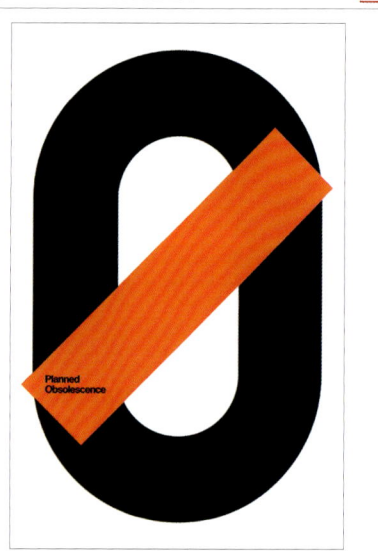
Title: Planned Obsolescence
Client: SIPSM: Salón Internacional del Póster San Mateo | **Design Firm:** Braley Design

MARTIN FRENCH
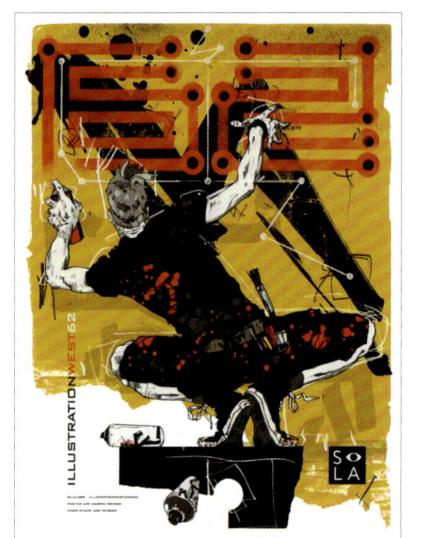
Title: Illustration West 62
Client: Society of Illustrators Los Angeles
Design Firm: Martin French Studio

FEIXUE MEI
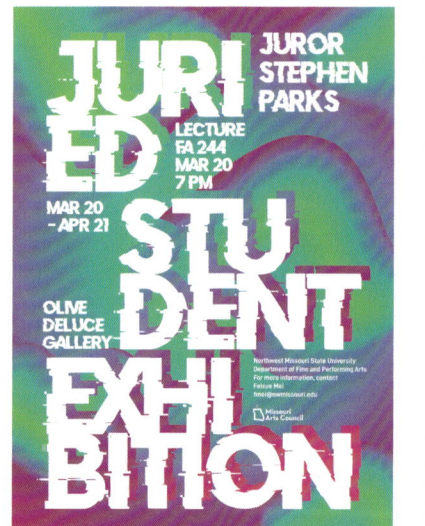
Title: Juried Student Exhibition Poster (Northwest Missouri State University) | **Client:** Northwest Missouri State University | **Design Firm:** Feixue Mei

SIYU MAO
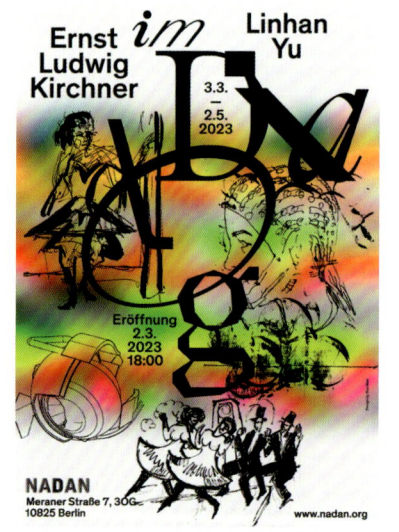
Title: In Dialogue — Ernst Ludwig Kirchner and Linhan Yu | **Client:** Gallery Nadan
Design Firm: Team Mao

171 SILVER | EXHIBITS

YUTA TOMOKUSA

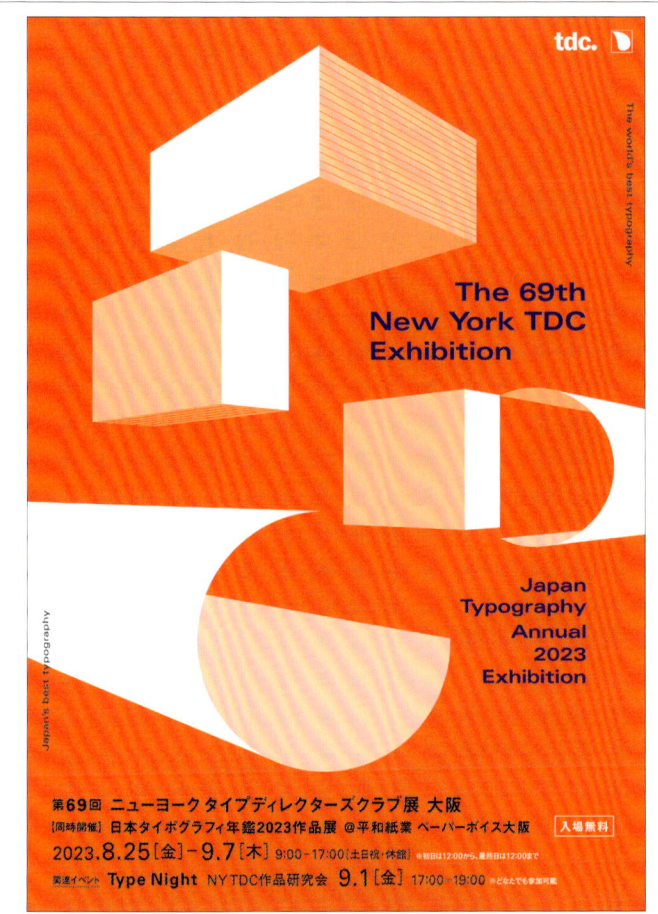

Title: The 69th New York TDC Exhibition at Osaka
Client: Japan Typography Association | **Design Firm:** TOMOKUSA DESIGN

BRAD TZOU

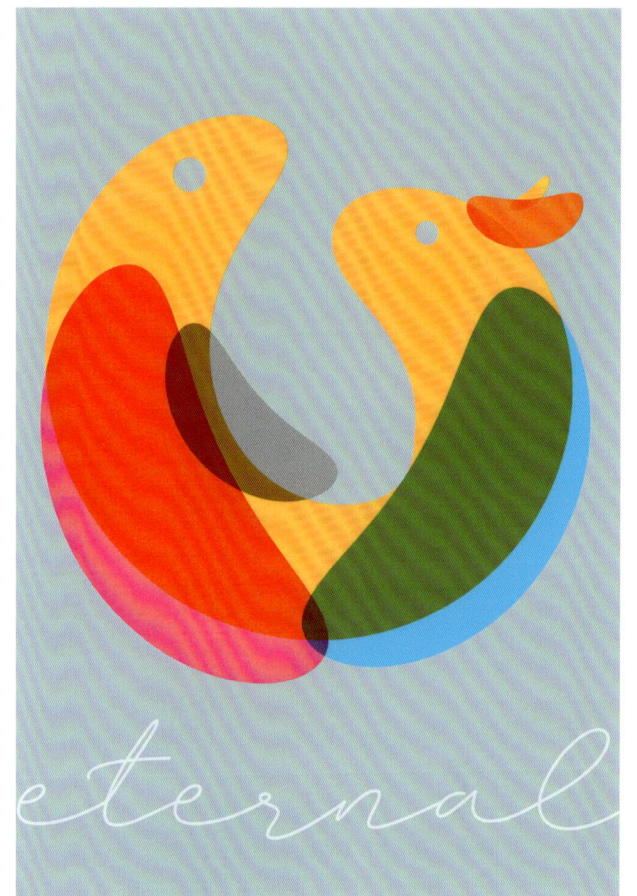

Title: Eternal | **Client:** Self-initiated
Design Firm: Human Paradise Studio

ANDREA SZABÓ

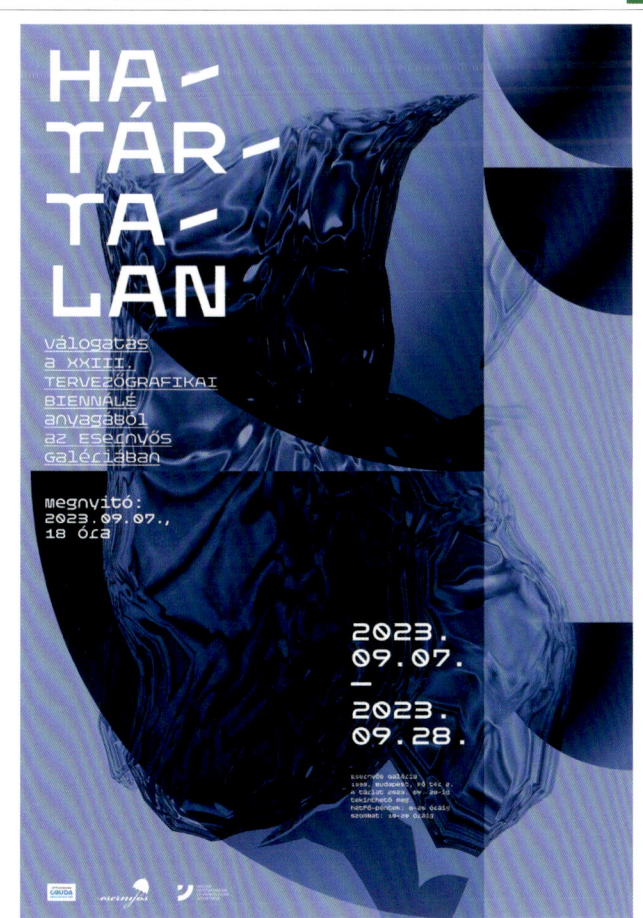

Title: Borderless | **Client:** Association of Hungarian Fine and Applied Artists | **Design Firm:** Andrea Szabó

RES EICHENBERGER DESIGN

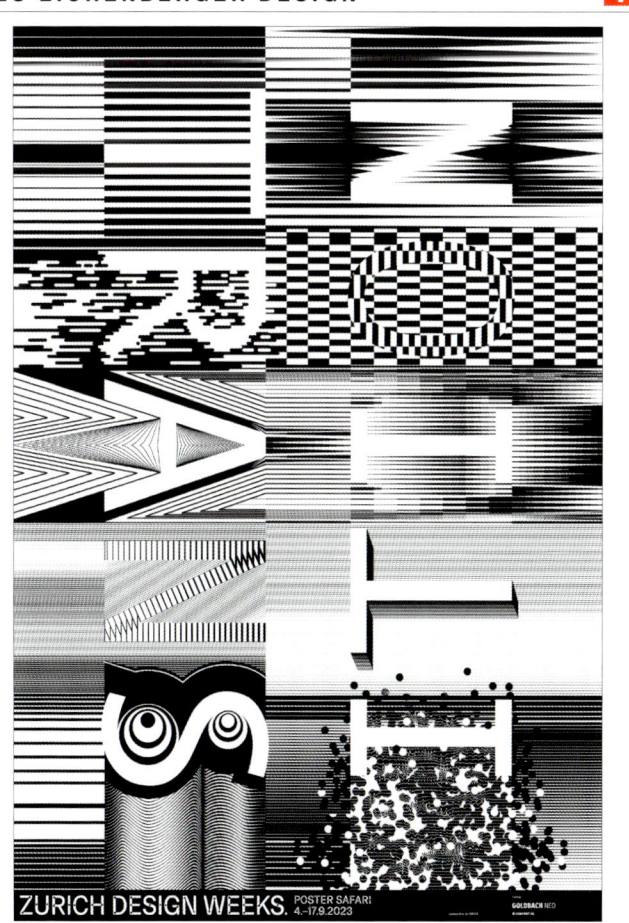

Title: Transition. Zurich Design Weeks 2023
Client: Zurich Design Weeks | **Design Firm:** Res Eichenberger Design

EXHIBITS

CHLOE ZHANG 🇺🇸

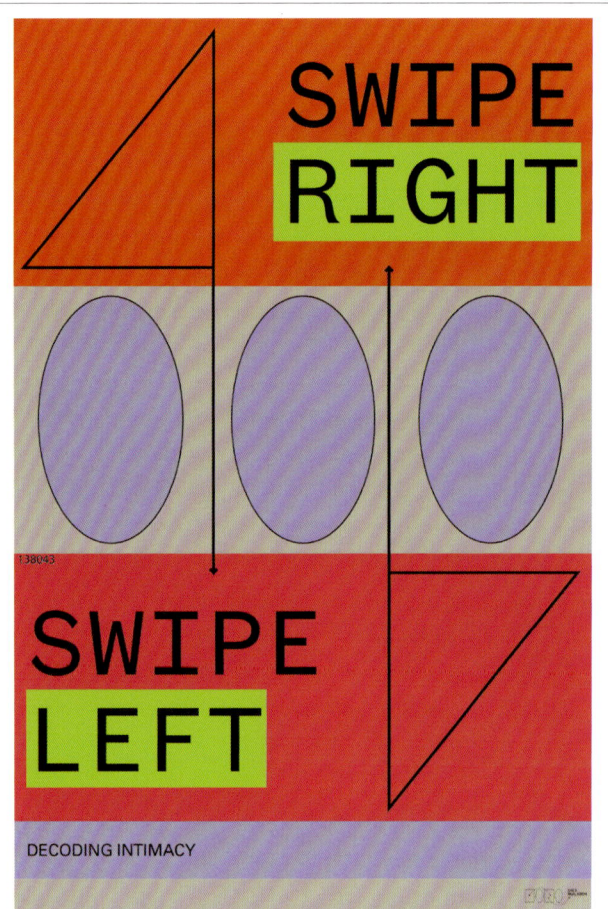

Title: Sensorial System- Decoding Intimacy Through Multi-sensory Information Design | **Client:** Self-initiated | **Design Firm:** Chloe Zhang

SASCHA FRONCZEK 🇩🇪

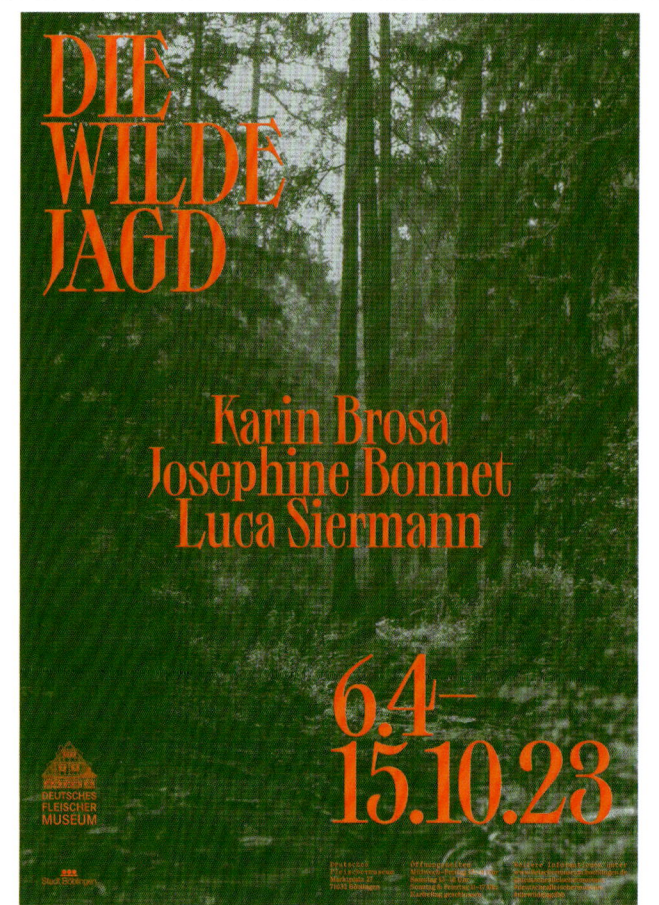

Title: Die Wilde Jagd [The Wild Hunt]
Client: Deutsches Fleischermuseum | **Design Firm:** Studio +Fronczek

MICHAEL BRALEY 🇺🇸

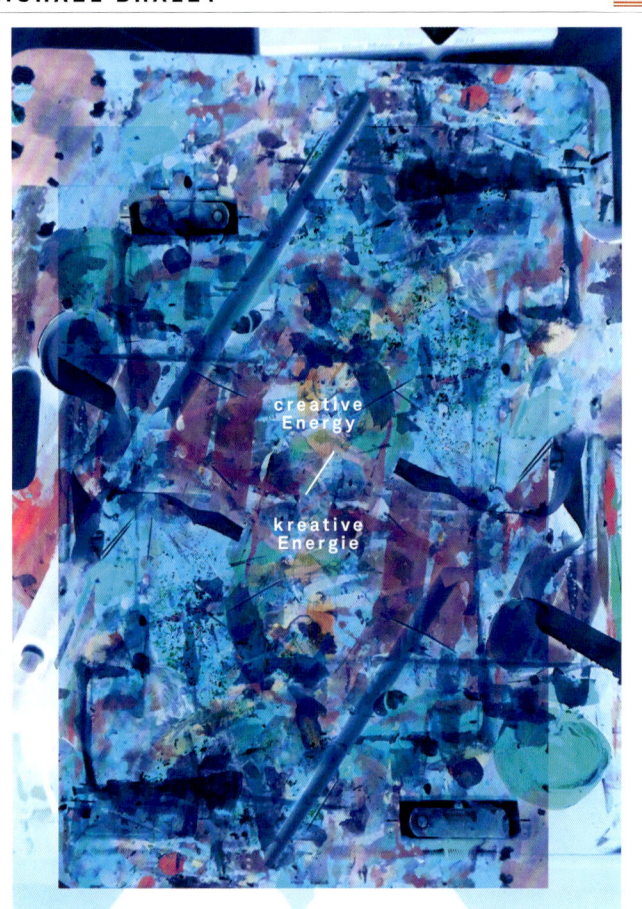

Title: Creative Energy / Kreative Energie | **Client:** Anfachen Awards VI
Design Firm: Braley Design

UNDERLINE STUDIO 🇨🇦

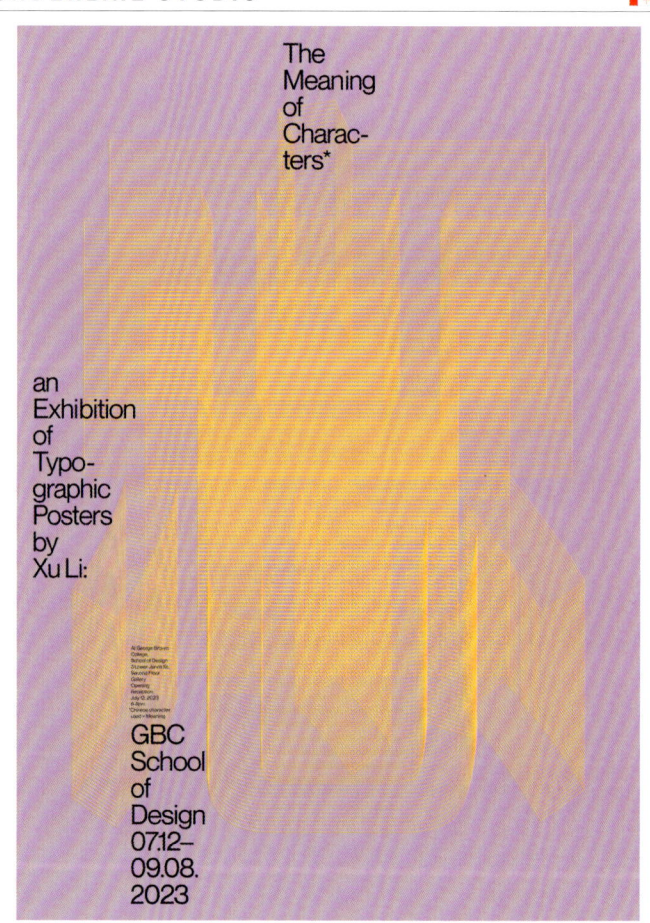

Title: Xu Li School of Design Exhibition Posters | **Client:** George Brown College School of Design | **Design Firm:** Underline Studio

173 SILVER — EXHIBITS

LISA WINSTANLEY

Title: Flight of Good Fortune | **Client:** KWVD International Invitational Design Exhibition | **Design Firm:** Lisa Winstanley Design

MIYOKO KAWAMURA

Title: STARTING from ZERO | **Client:** New Art ZERO Association
Design Firm: Design Studio FLORALIEN Inc.

MICHAEL BRALEY

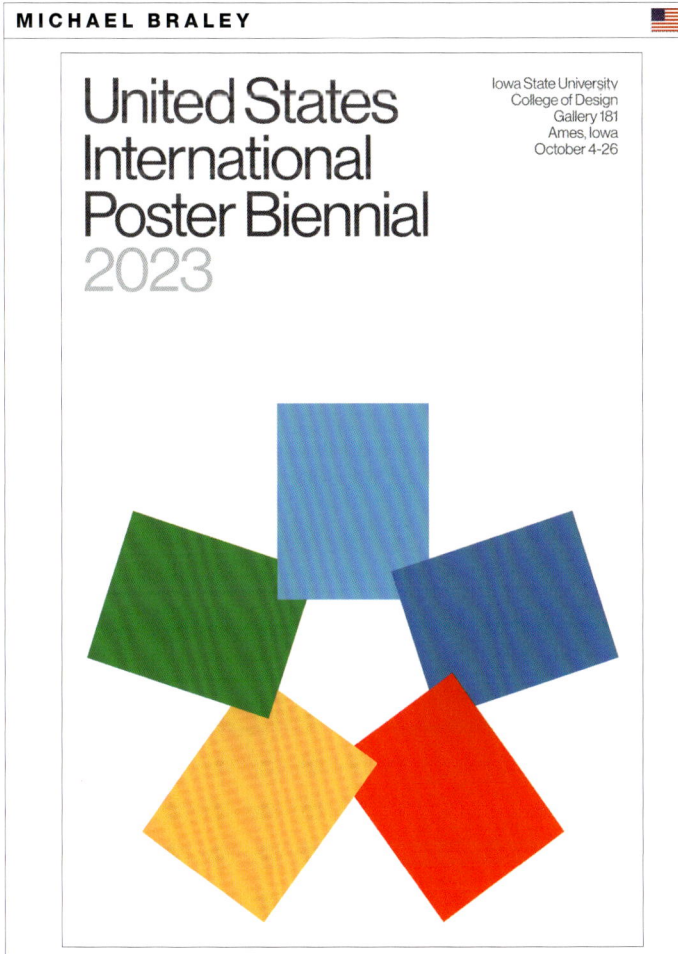

Title: United States International Poster Biennial 2023 | **Client:** United States International Poster Biennial (USIPB) | **Design Firm:** Braley Design

CHOE GON

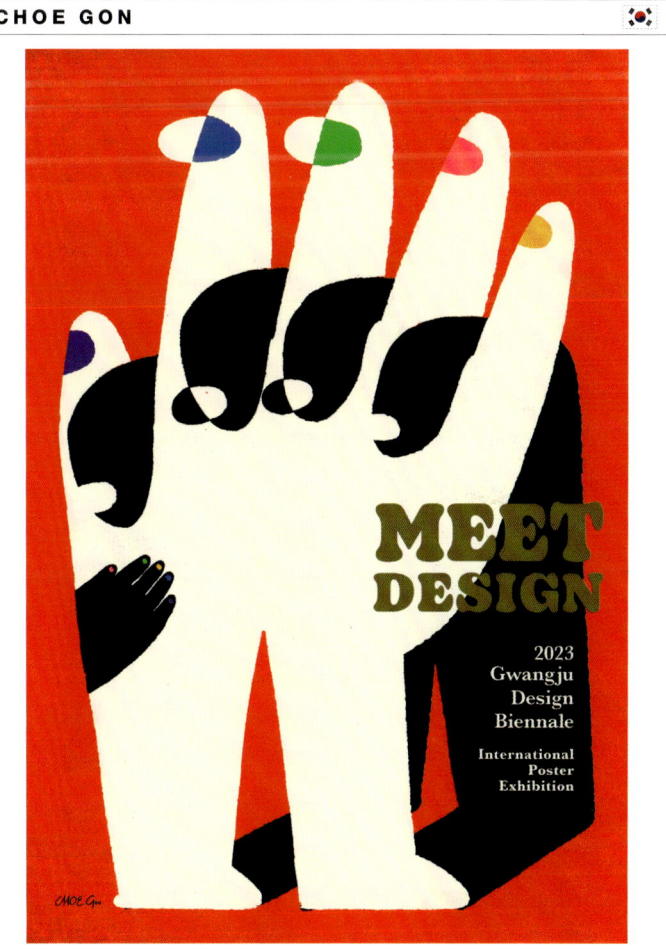

Title: Meet Design | **Client:** Gwangju Design Biennale 2023
Design Firm: Gon.C Studio

KATELYN HARRIS

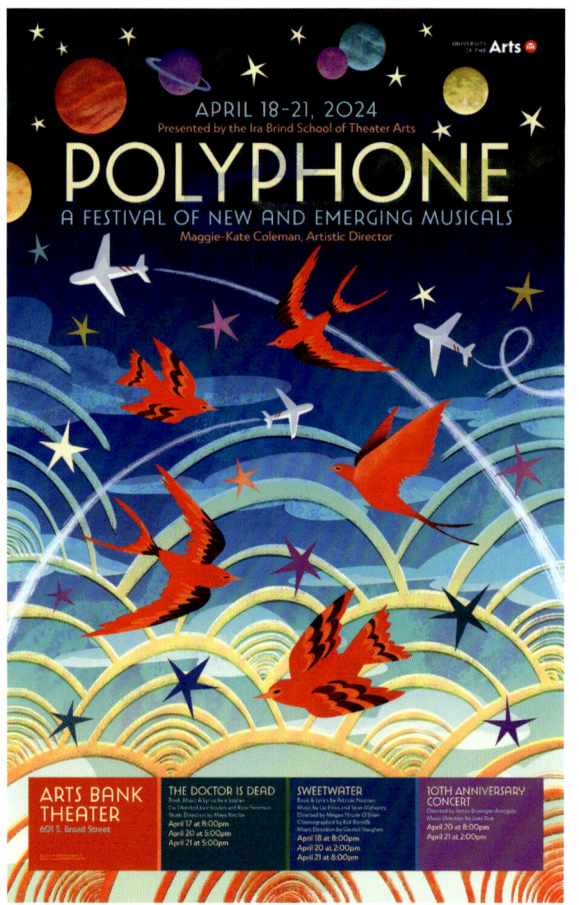

Title: 2024 Polyphone Festival: A Festival of New and Emerging Musicals | Client: Self-initiated | Design Firm: University of the Arts

EDUARD CEHOVIN

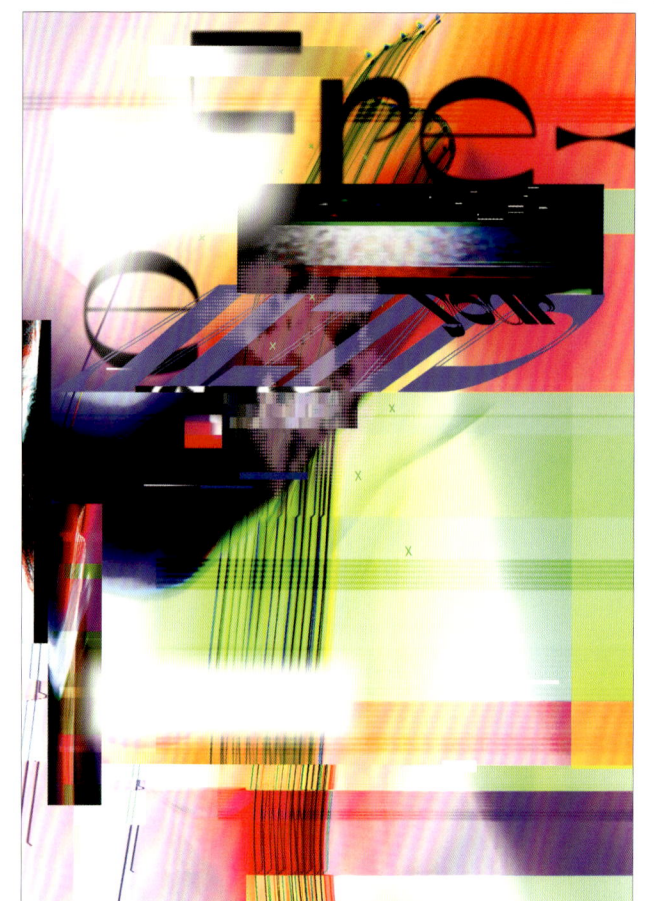

Title: … Free Your Mind | Client: 2023 First Contemporary Local Youth Art Festival, China | Design Firm: Studio Eduard Cehovin

WEPLAYDESIGN

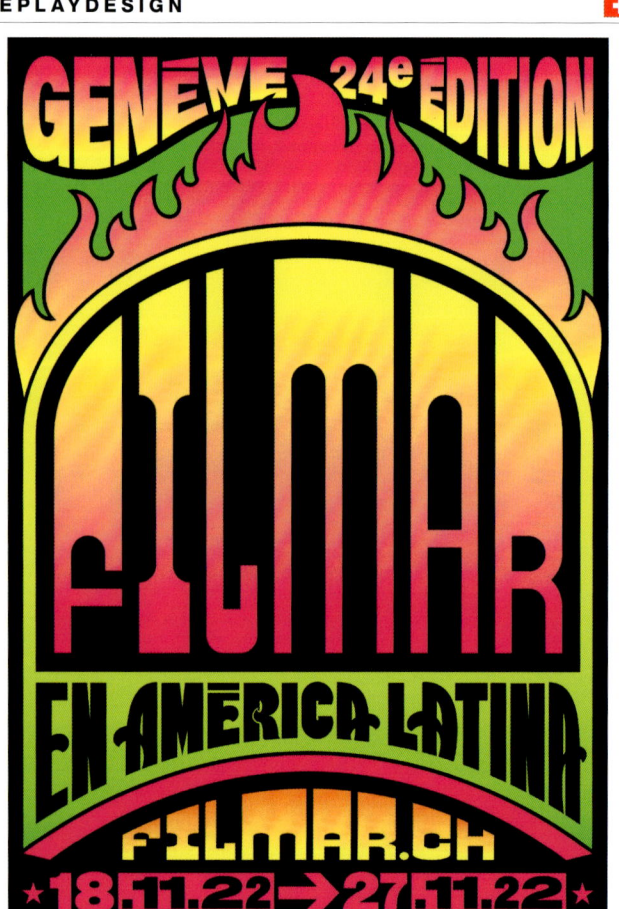

Title: Festival Filmar en América Latina 22 | Client: Filmar en América Latina | Design Firm: WePlayDesign

SCOTT RAY

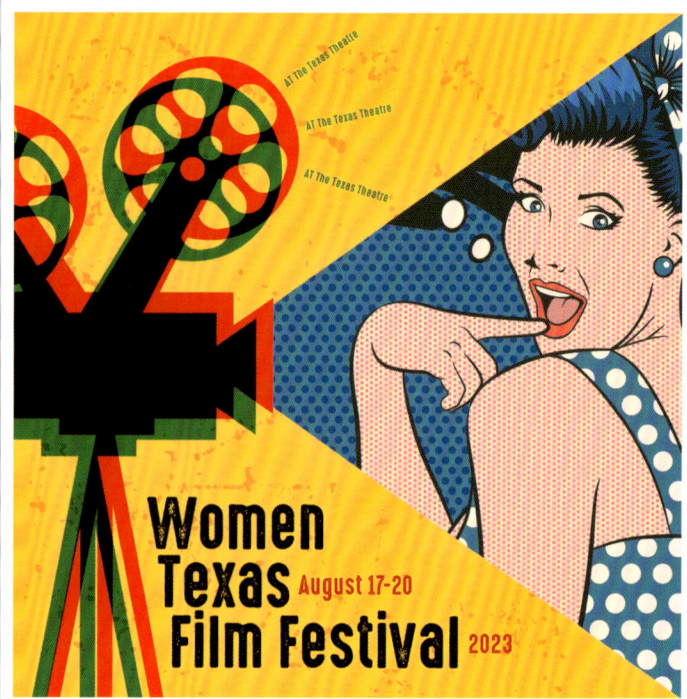

Title: Women Texas Film Festival Poster 2023 | Client: Women Texas Film Festival | Design Firm: Ray Visual Communications

175 SILVER   FESTIVALS

MICHAEL BRALEY 🇺🇸

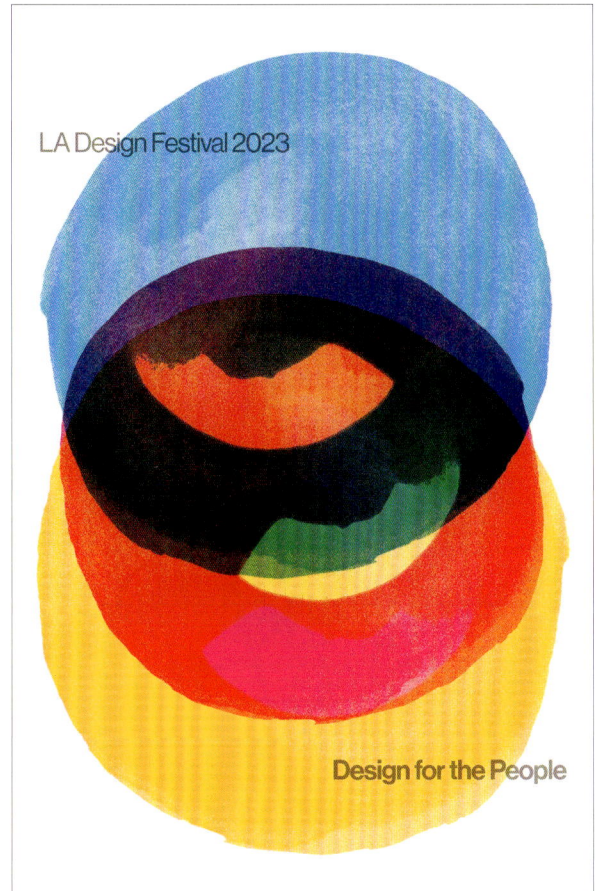

Title: LA Design Festival 2023: Design for the People
Client: LA Design Festival 2023 | **Design Firm:** Braley Design

WEPLAYDESIGN 🇨🇭

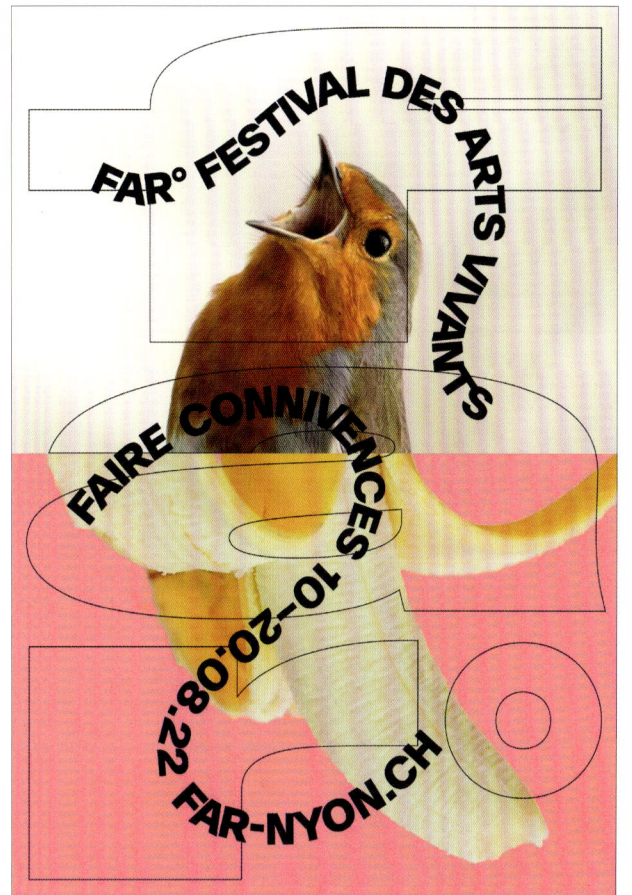

Title: Far^ – Festival des Arts Vivants
Client: Far° | **Design Firm:** WePlayDesign

SIYU MAO 🇩🇪

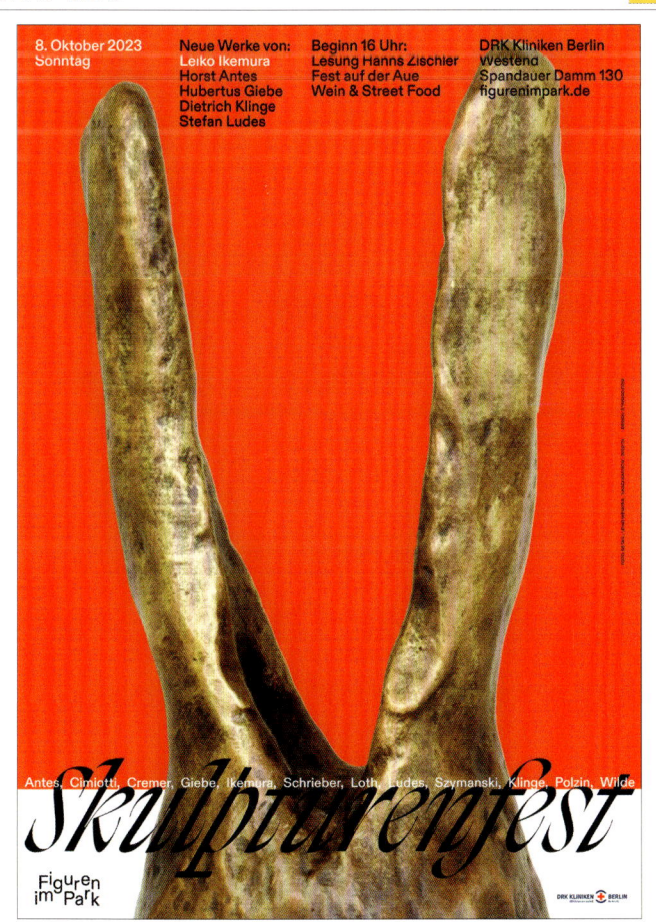

Title: Sculpture Festival | **Client:** DRK Kliniken Berlin Westend
Design Firm: Team Mao

YVONNE CAO 🇺🇸

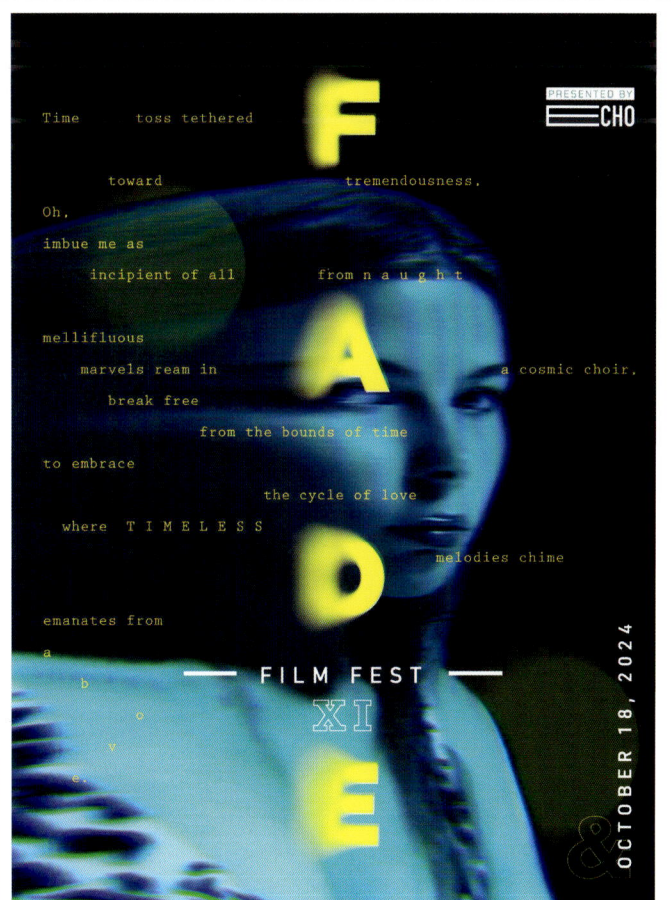

Title: FADE Poster by Echo Film Festival | **Client:** ECHO Film Festival
Design Firm: CAO Design

AV PRINT

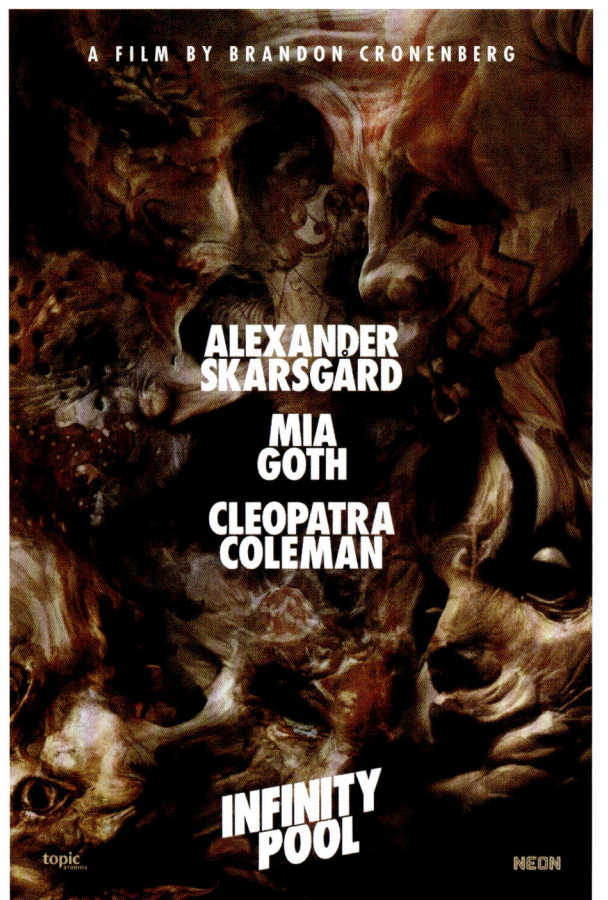

Title: Infinity Pool - Masks Teaser Poster | **Client:** NEON
Design Firm: AV Print

FONG 'CAPTAIN' HUANG

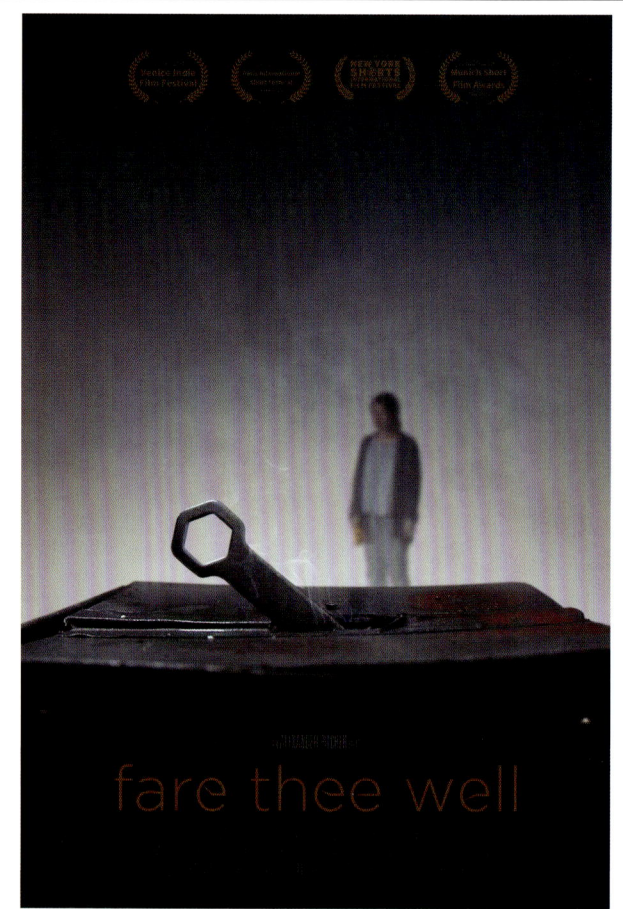

Title: Untitled | **Client:** Alexander Pitcher
Design Firm: VIEW - Visual Impact East West

JEFF WADLEY

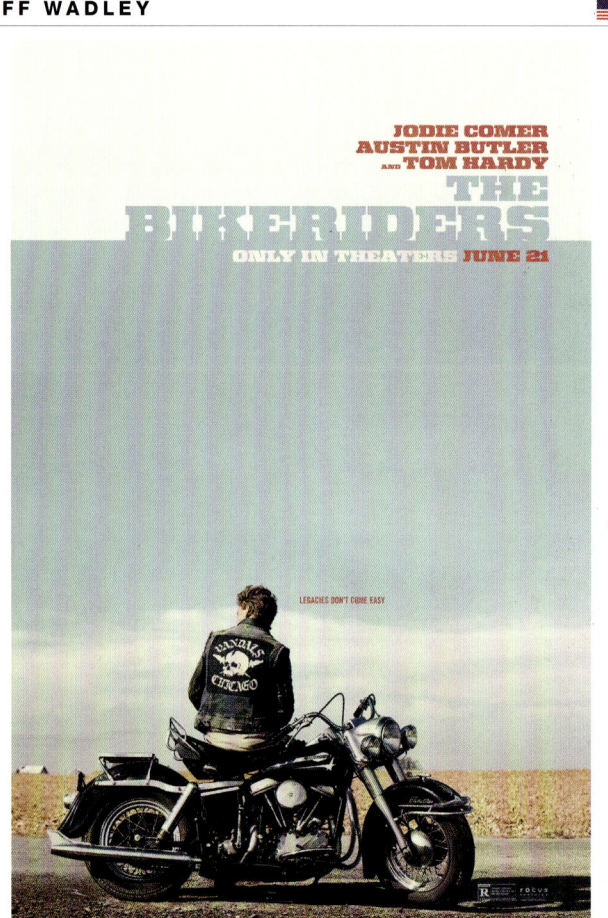

Title: The Bikeriders Teaser Poster
Clients: 20th Century Fox, Focus Features | **Design Firm:** MOCEAN

CÉLIE CADIEUX

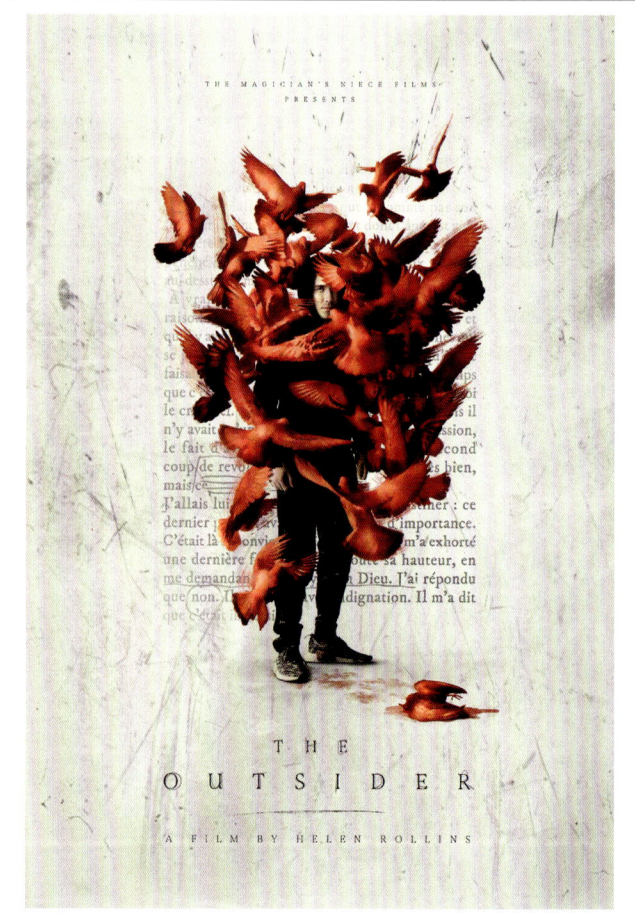

Title: The Outsider
Client: The Magician's Niece | **Design Firm:** Célie Cadieux

177 SILVER — FILM

AV PRINT 🇺🇸

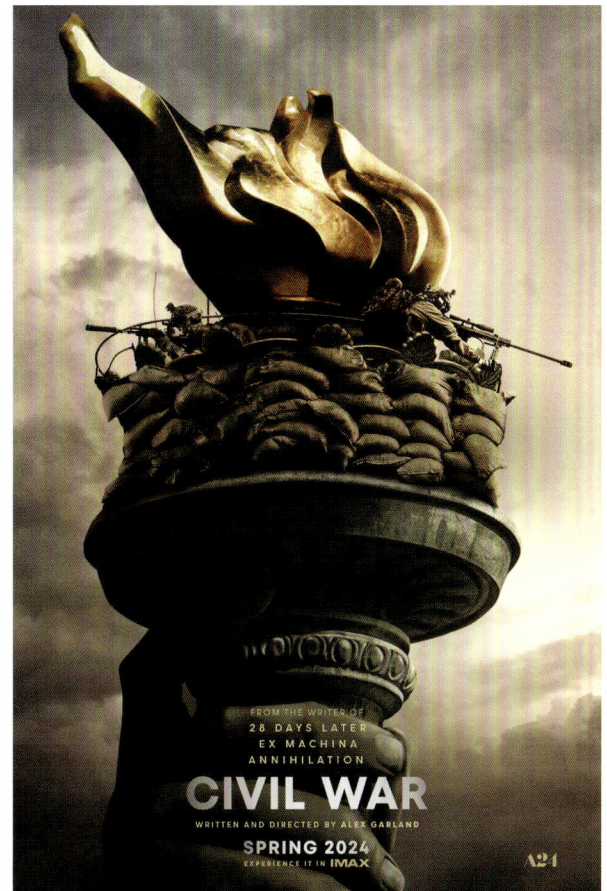

Title: Civil War - Liberty Teaser Poster | **Client:** A24
Design Firm: AV Print

JEFF WADLEY, ROBERT DUNBAR 🇺🇸

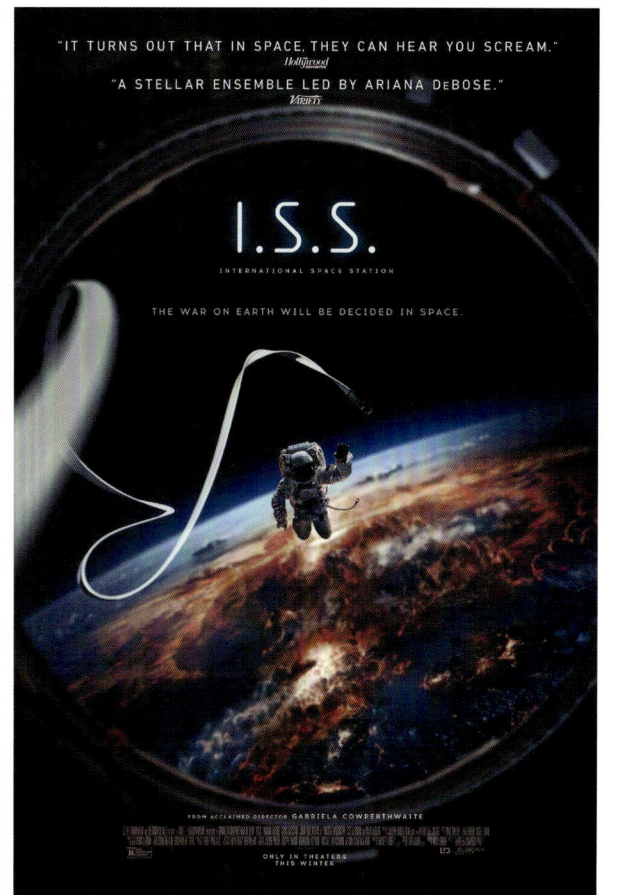

Title: I.S.S. Payoff Poster | **Client:** Bleecker Street Media
Design Firm: MOCEAN

LEROY & ROSE 🇺🇸

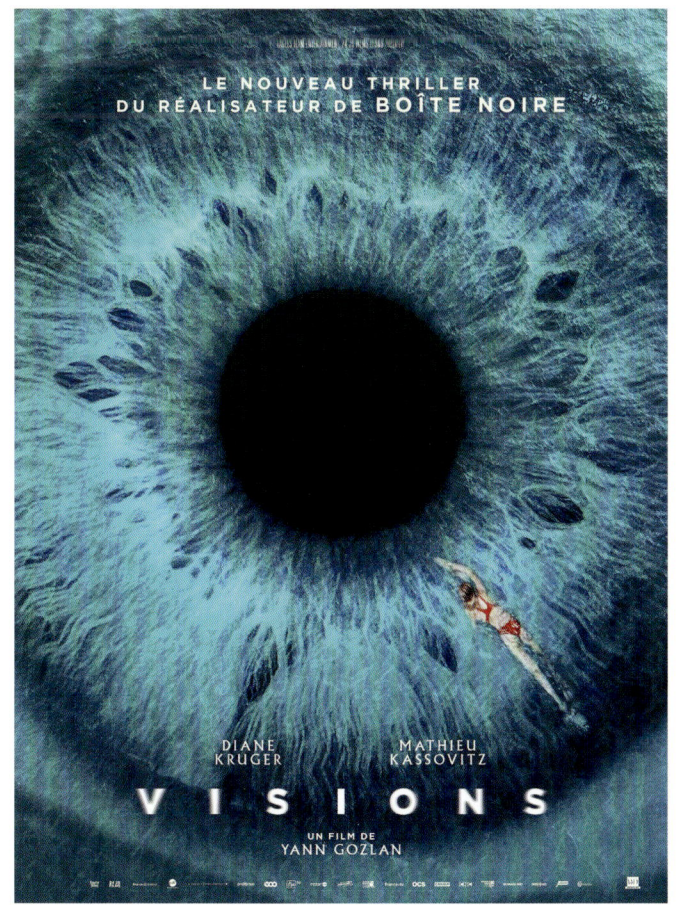

Title: Visions | **Client:** SND
Design Firm: Leroy & Rose

BOB DELGADO 🇺🇸

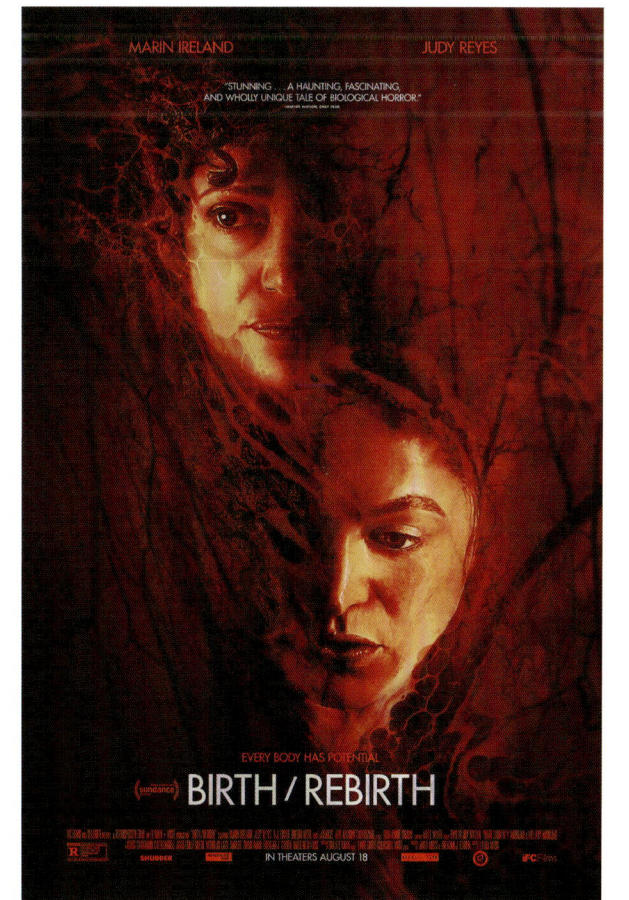

Title: Birth/Rebirth Payoff Poster | **Client:** IFC Films
Design Firm: MOCEAN

178 SILVER   **FILM**

ROBERT DUNBAR, KISHAN MUTHUCUMARU, BOB DELGADO 🇺🇸

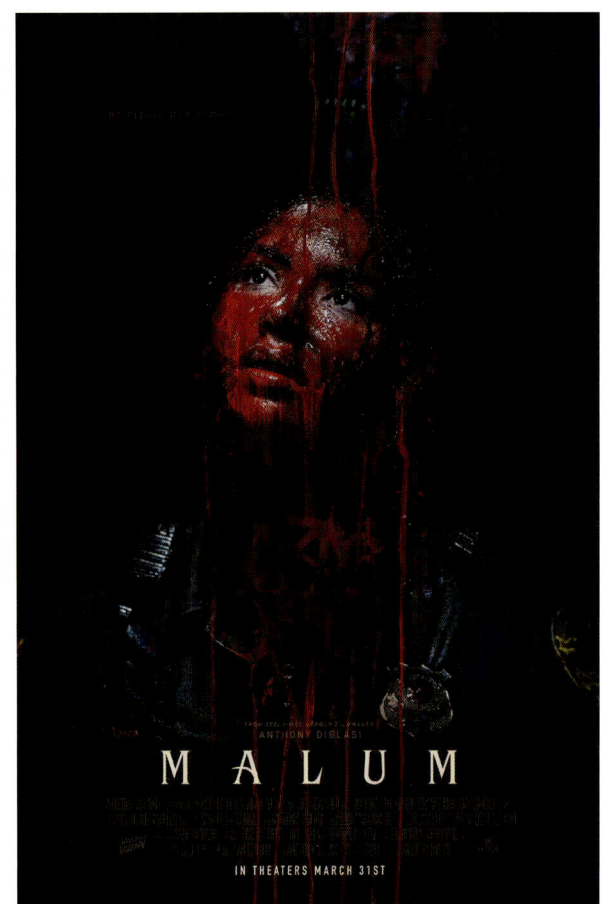

Title: Malum Teaser and Digital Posters
Client: Welcome Villain | **Design Firm:** MOCEAN

FONG 'CAPTAIN' HUANG 🇺🇸

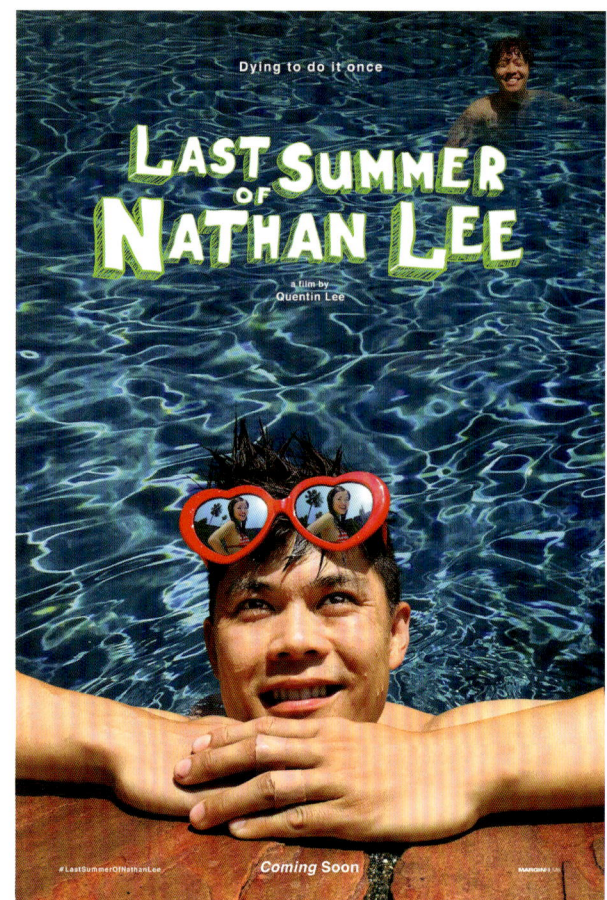

Title: Last Summer of Nathan Lee
Client: Quentin Lee | **Design Firm:** VIEW - Visual Impact East West

LEROY & ROSE 🇺🇸

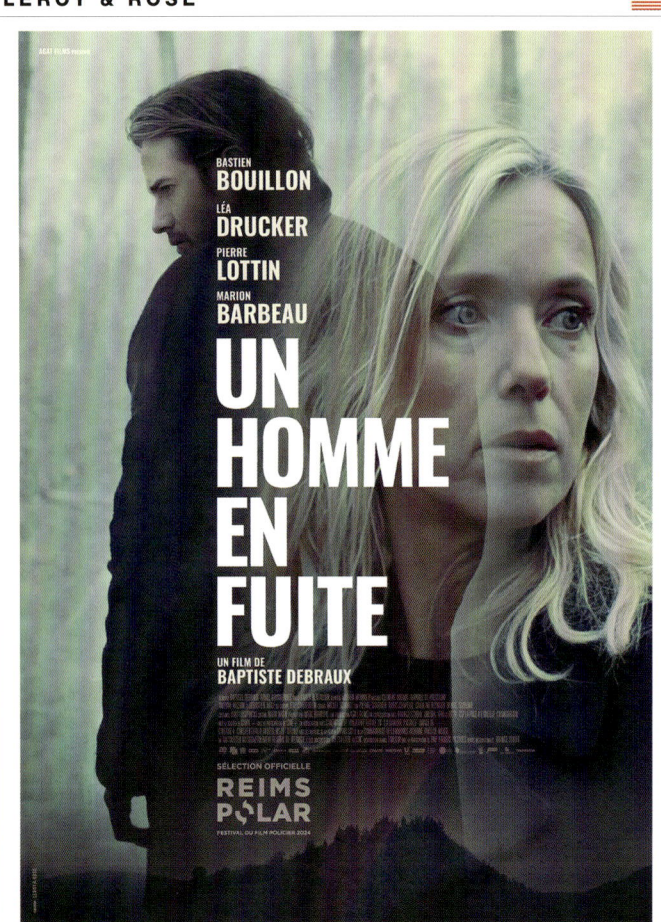

Title: Un Homme En Fuite | **Client:** Tandem Films
Design Firm: Leroy & Rose

CRISTIANA RODRIGUES 🇵🇹

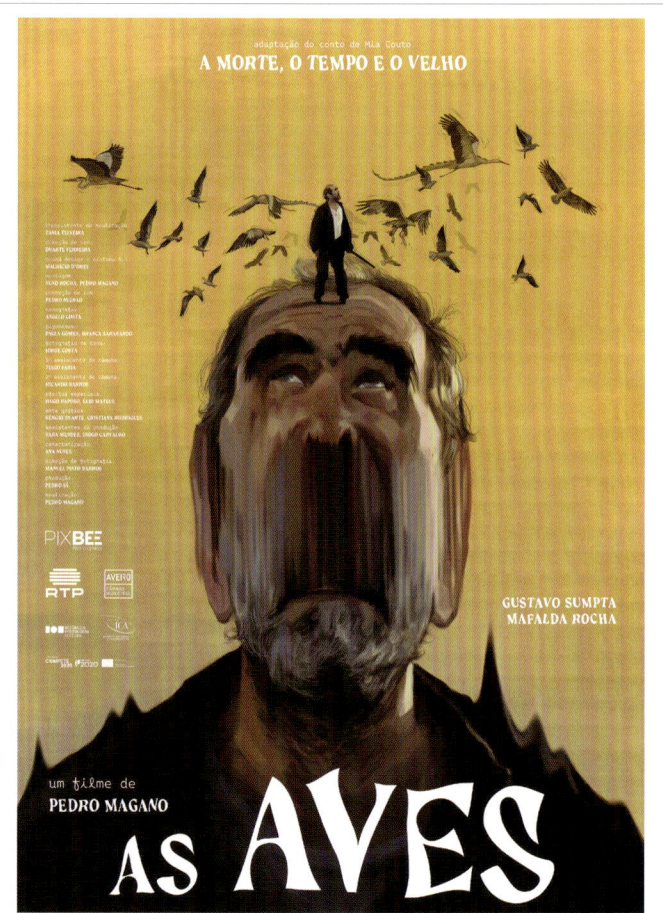

Title: As Aves | **Client:** Pixbee
Design Firm: Duas Faces Design

CHARLIE LE 🇺🇸

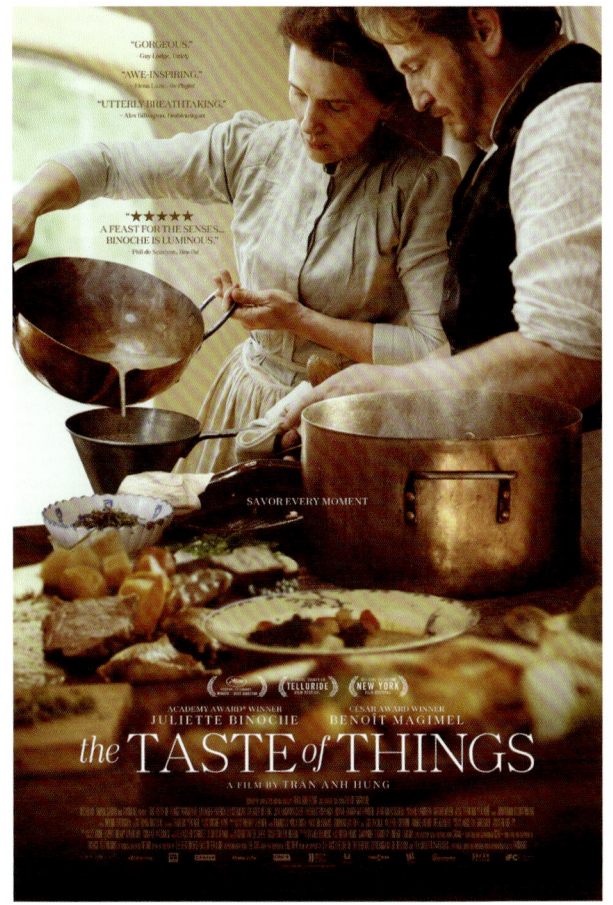

Title: The Taste of Things Payoff Poster | **Client:** IFC Films
Design Firm: MOCEAN

ERIC VAN DEN BRULLE 🇺🇸

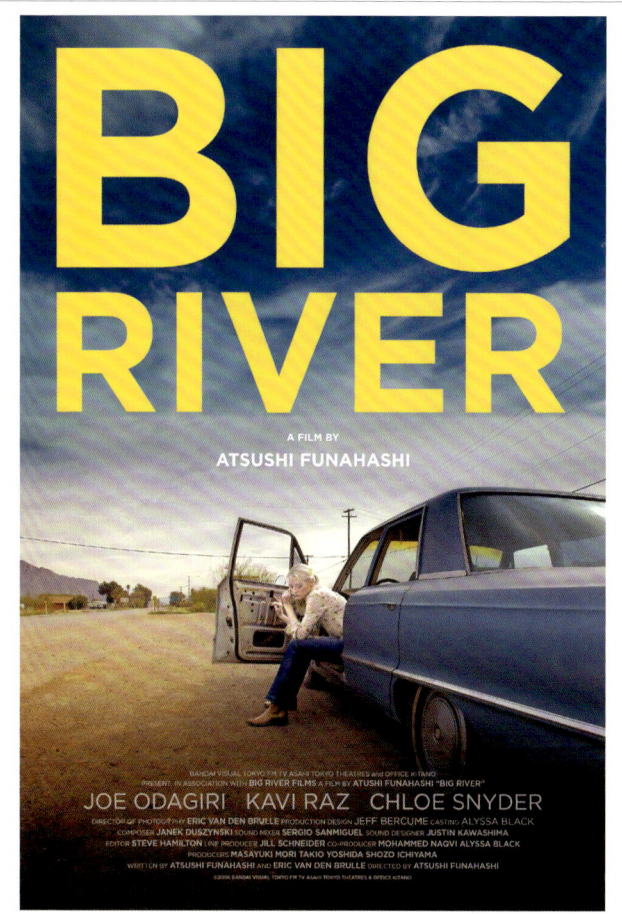

Title: Big River | **Client:** Atsushi Funahashi
Design Firm: Evb Creative, Inc.

JEFF WADLEY 🇺🇸

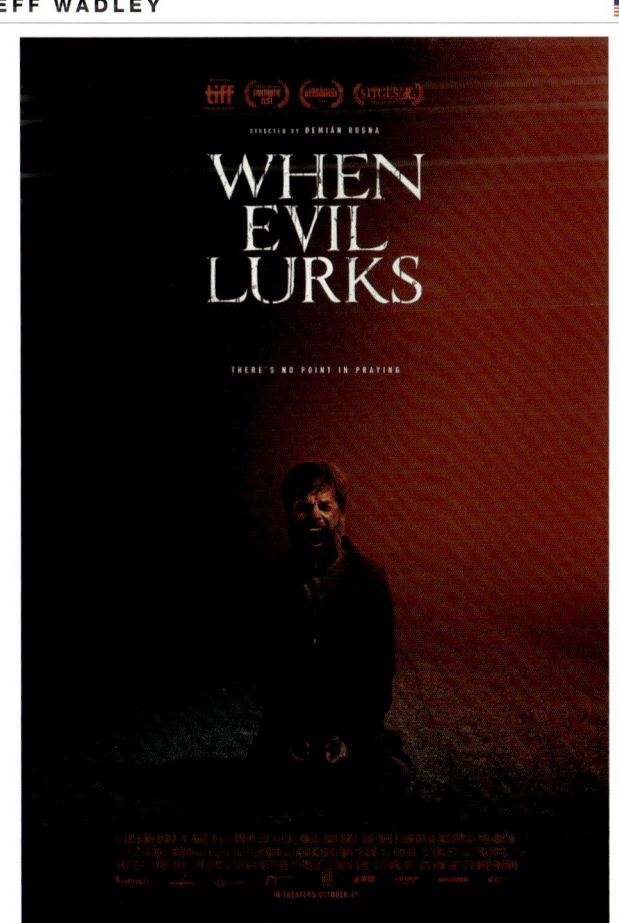

Title: When Evil Lurks Payoff and Digital Poster | **Client:** IFC Films
Design Firm: MOCEAN

LEROY & ROSE 🇺🇸

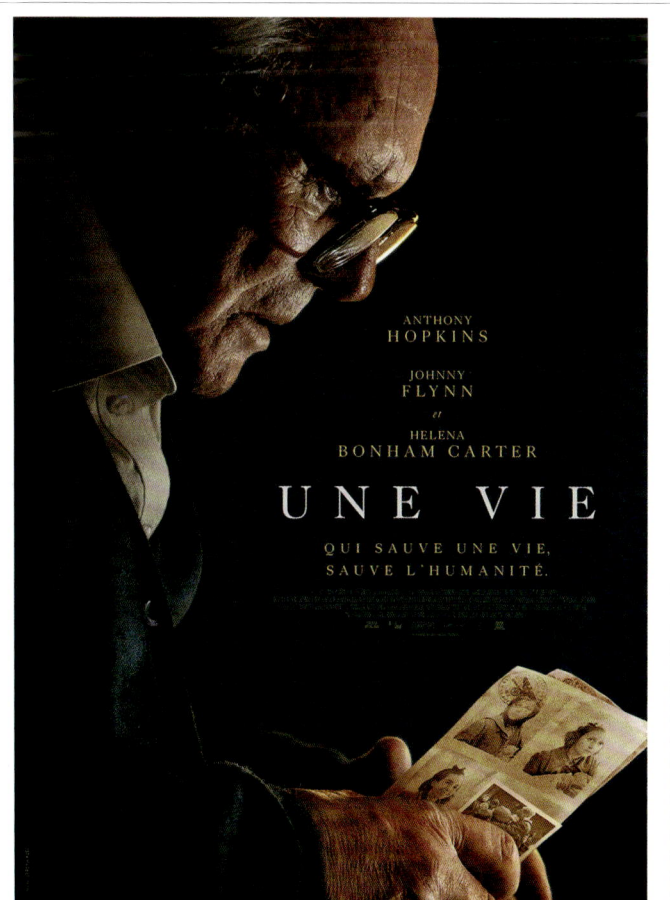

Title: Une Vie | **Client:** SND
Design Firm: Leroy & Rose

180 SILVER — FILM

OWEN GILDERSLEEVE 🇬🇧
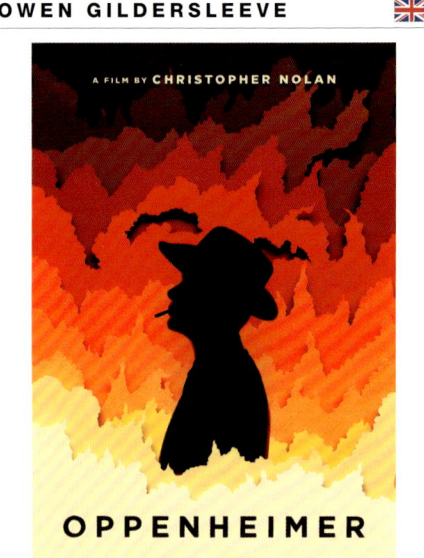
Title: Oppenheimer
Client: Self-initiated
Design Firm: Owen Gildersleeve Ltd.

AV PRINT 🇺🇸
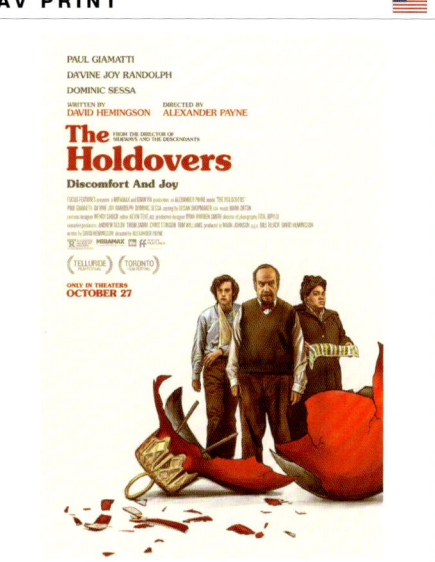
Title: The Holdovers - Payoff Poster
Client: Focus Features
Design Firm: AV Print

AV PRINT 🇺🇸
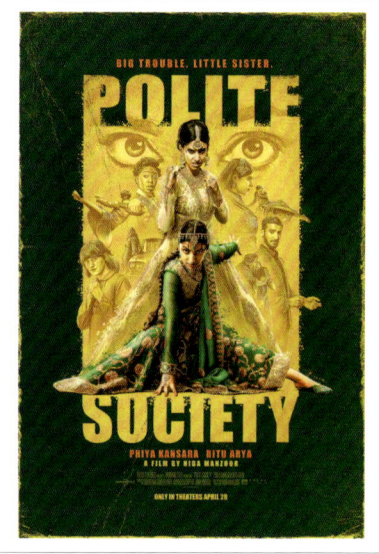
Title: Polite Society - Payoff Poster
Client: Focus Features
Design Firm: AV Print

AV PRINT 🇺🇸
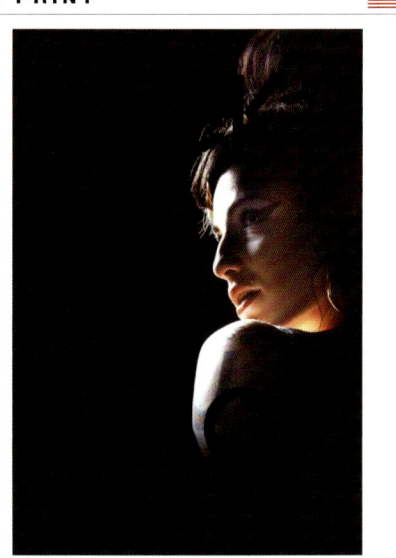
Title: Back to Black - Black Teaser
Client: Focus Features
Design Firm: AV Print

STEPHANIE SCOTT 🇨🇦
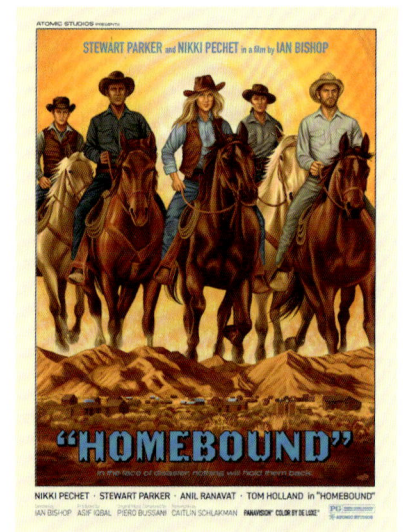
Title: Atomic Studios Presents
Client: Atomic
Design Firm: Stephanie Scott Designs

EDIN BESLIC 🇧🇦
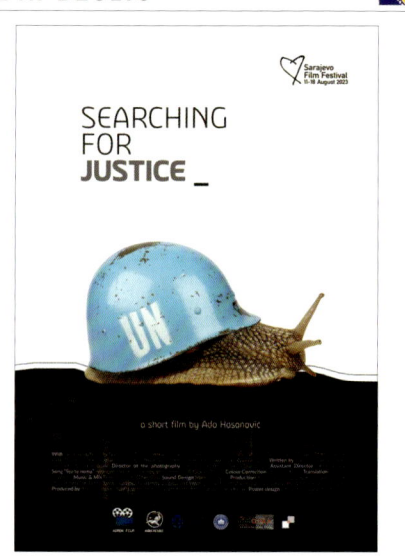
Title: Searching for Justice
Client: Admon Film
Design Firm: Articoolisan

ADAM MAIDA 🇨🇦
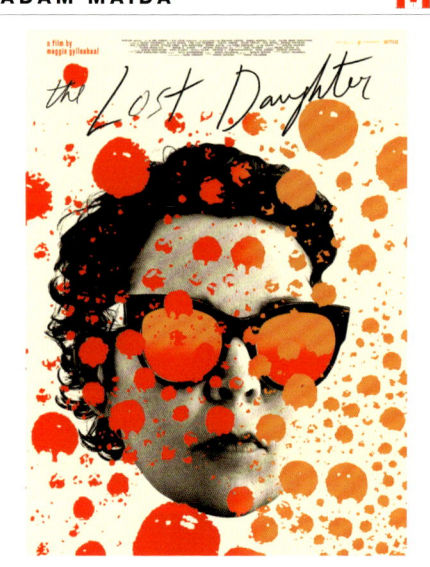
Title: The Lost Daughter Film Poster Series
Clients: Netflix, Mondo
Design Firm: Maida Studio

OBERT DUNBAR 🇺🇸
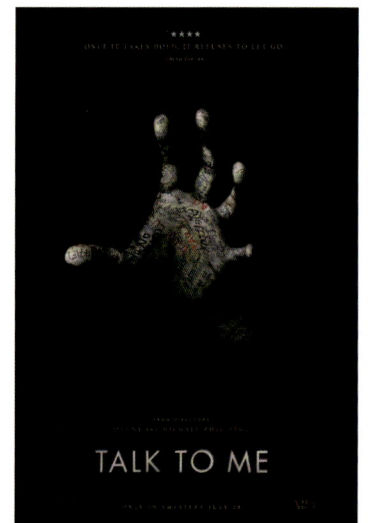
Title: Talk To Me Teaser Poster
Client: A24
Design Firm: MOCEAN

AFI CONSERVATORY 🇮🇹
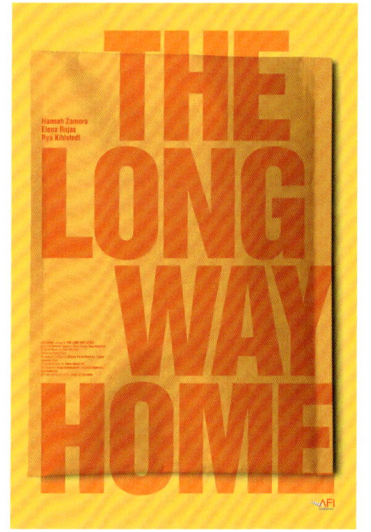
Title: Posters for the Short Film "The Long Way Home" | **Client:** Chloë De Carvalho
Design Firm: Tangram Strategic Design

181 SILVER FILM

CÉLIE CADIEUX

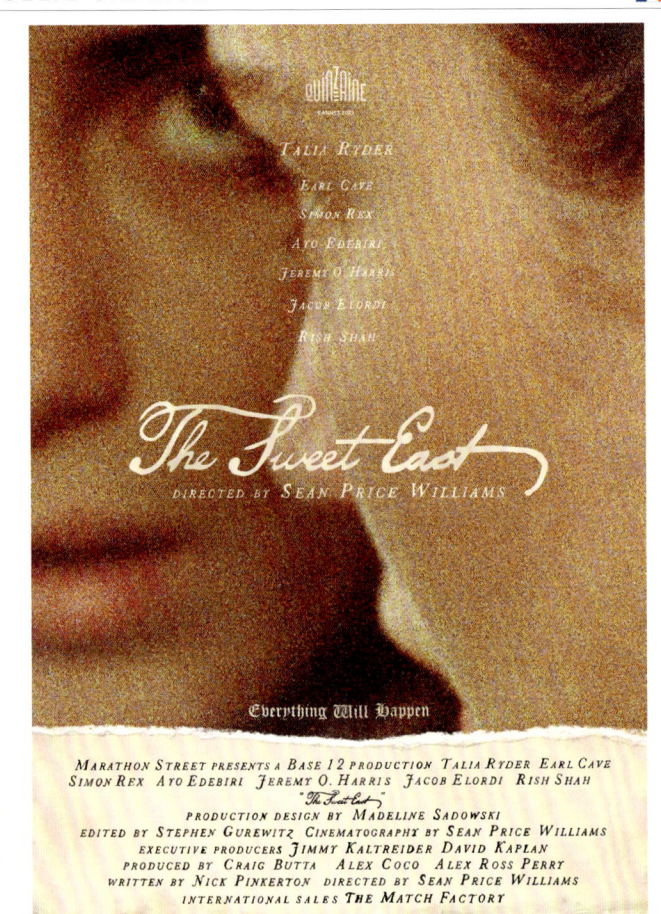

Title: The Sweet East | **Client:** The Match Factory
Design Firm: Célie Cadieux

SCOTTI EVERHART, NATHANIEL WHEELER

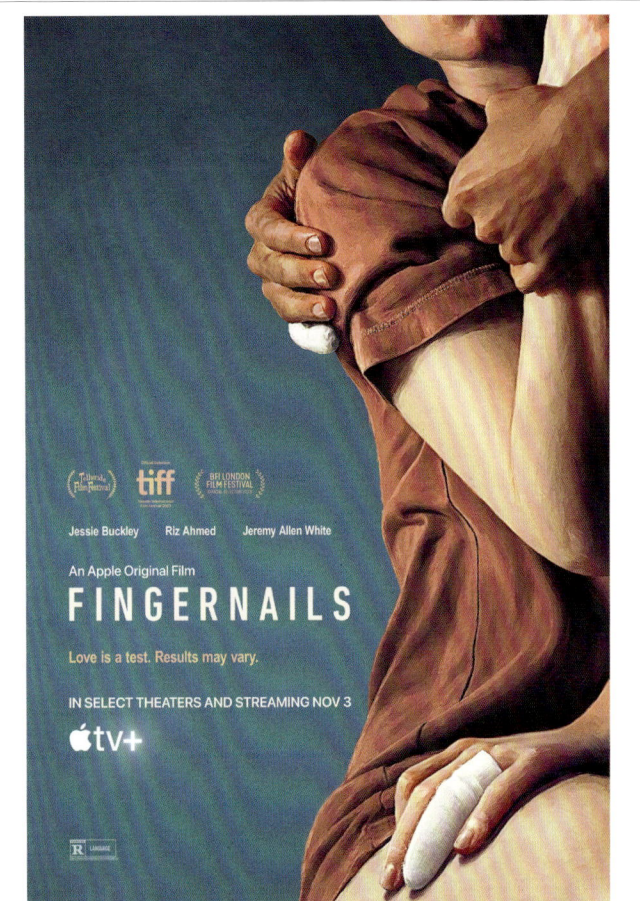

Title: Fingernails Teaser and Payoff Posters | **Client:** Apple TV+
Design Firm: MOCEAN

BARLOW.AGENCY

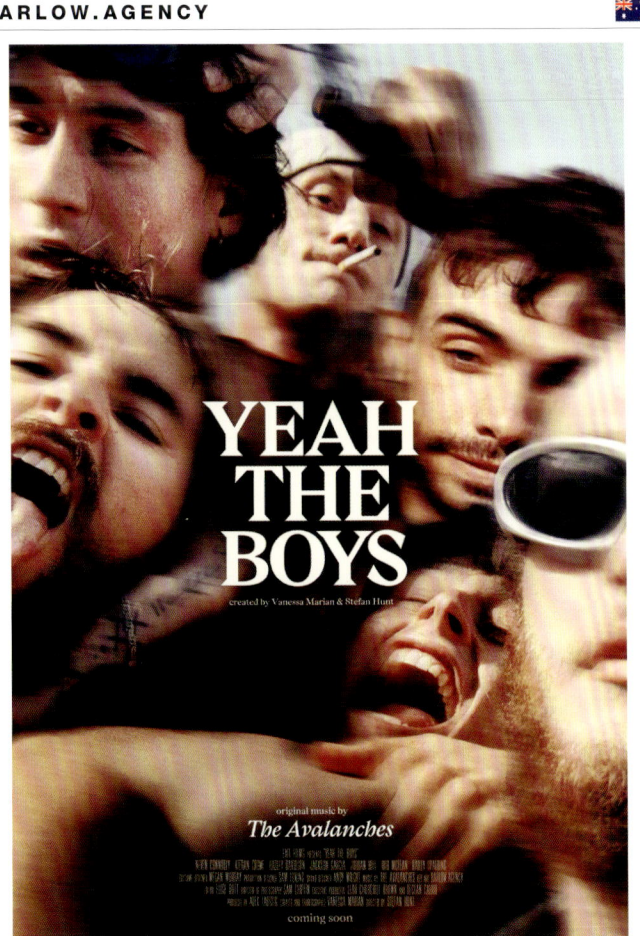

Title: Key The Boys Short Film Key Art | **Client:** Stefan Hunt Films
Design Firm: Barlow.Agency

LEROY & ROSE

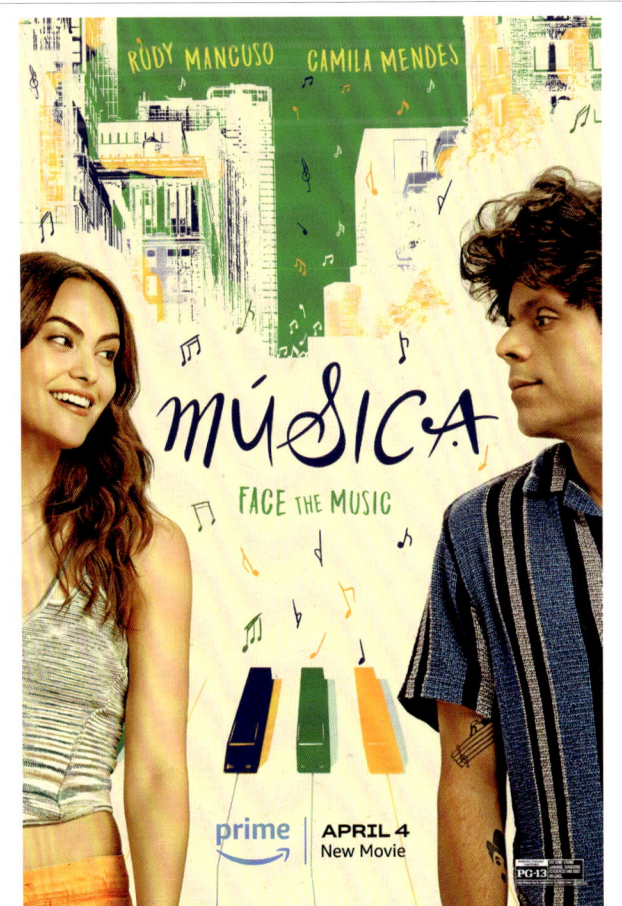

Title: Musica ("City") | **Client:** Amazon
Design Firm: Leroy & Rose

182 SILVER FOOD & BEVERAGE

ROBERT SHAW WEST

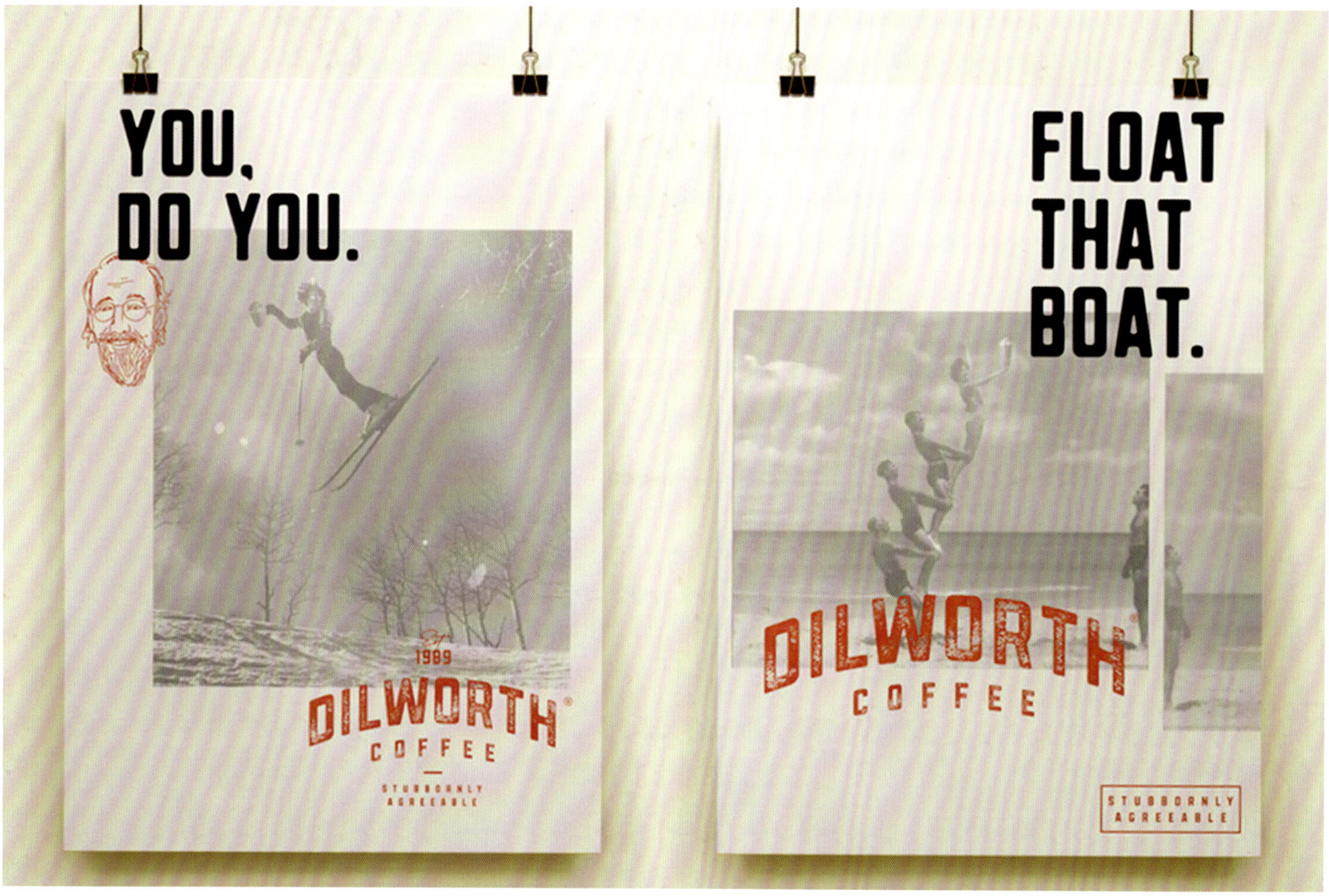

Title: Dilworth Coffee Poster Campaign | **Client:** Dilworth Coffee | **Design Firm:** The Republik

LEGIS DESIGN

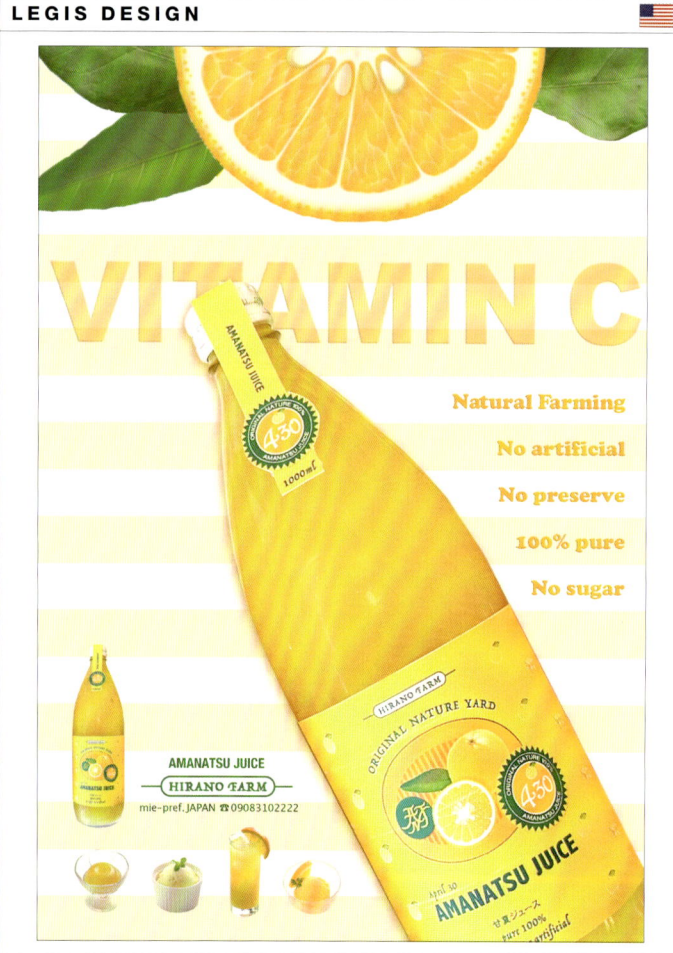

Title: Amanatsu Juice Campaign Poster | **Client:** Hirano Farm
Design Firm: Legis Design

MICHAEL SCHILLIG, GABBY COTILLA

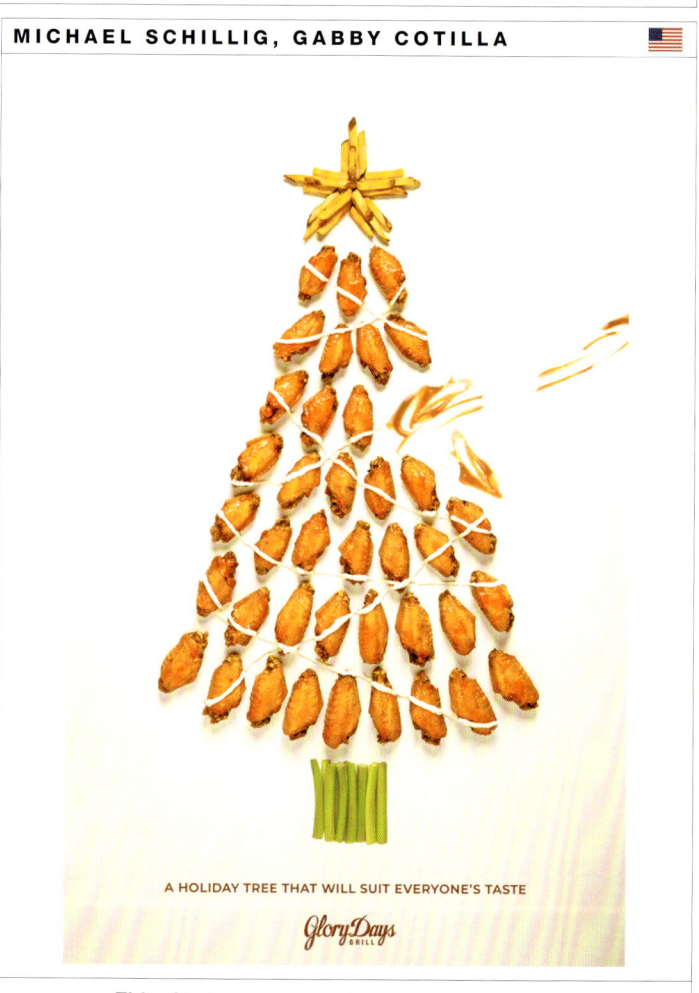

Title: Glorious Wing Tree | **Client:** Glory Days Grill
Design Firm: PPK

CRAIG FRAZIER

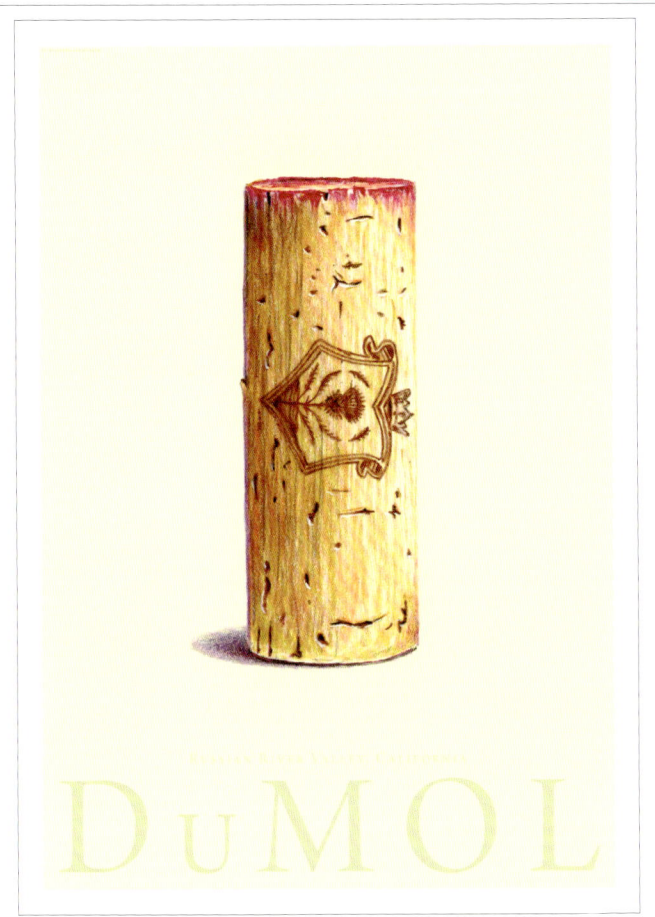

Title: DuMOL 2023 Collector's Poster | **Client:** DuMOL Winery
Design Firm: Craig Frazier Studio

CRAIG CUTLER

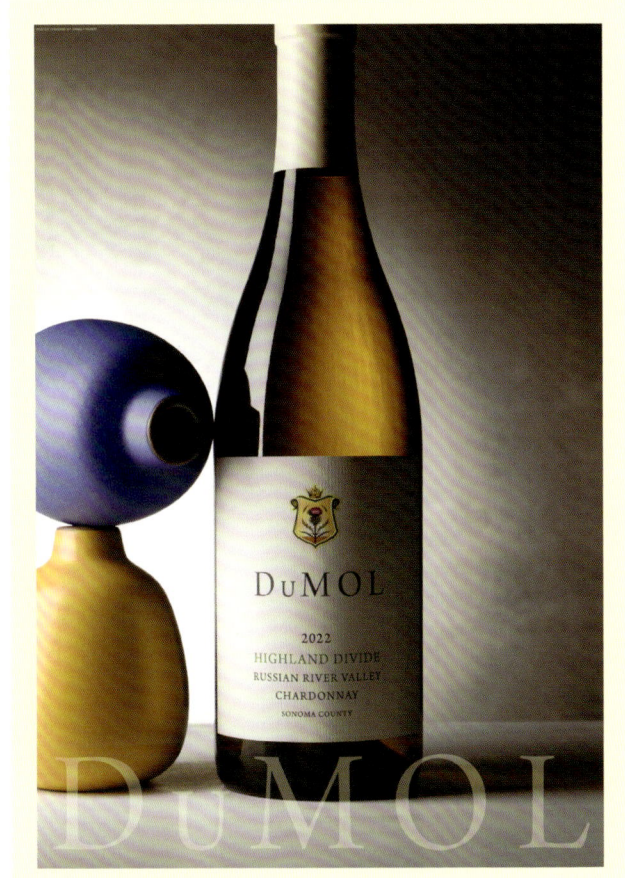

Title: DuMol Posters | **Client:** DuMOL Winery
Design Firm: Craig Frazier Studio

ROB FIOCCA

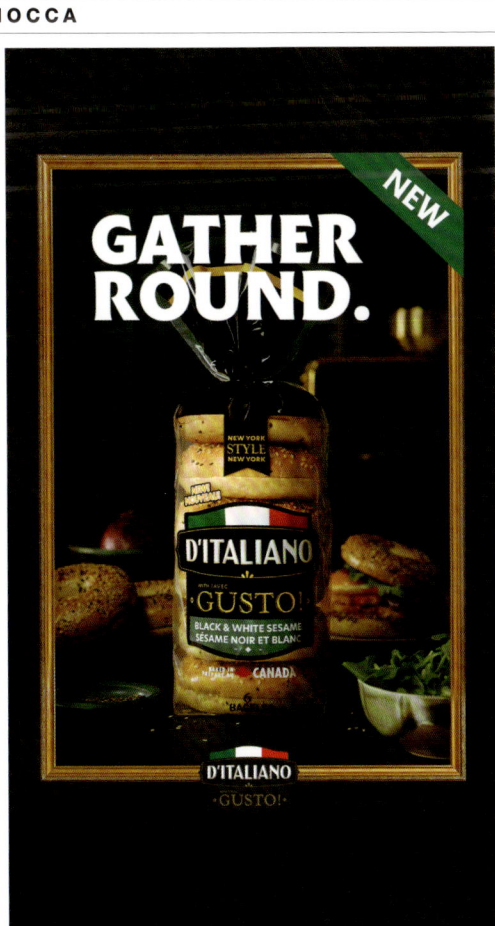

Title: Soak It All In | **Client:** D'Italiano
Design Firm: Rob Fiocca

SHELL ROYSTER

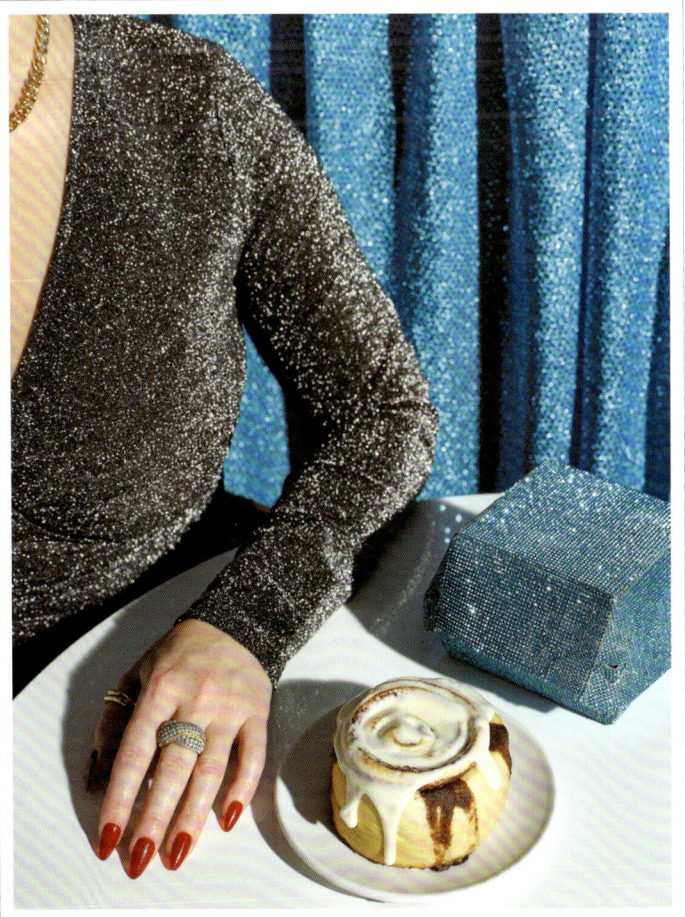

Title: Glam Bon | **Client:** Cinnabon
Design Firm: Shell Royster

ACTIVISION, PETROL ADVERTISING 🇺🇸

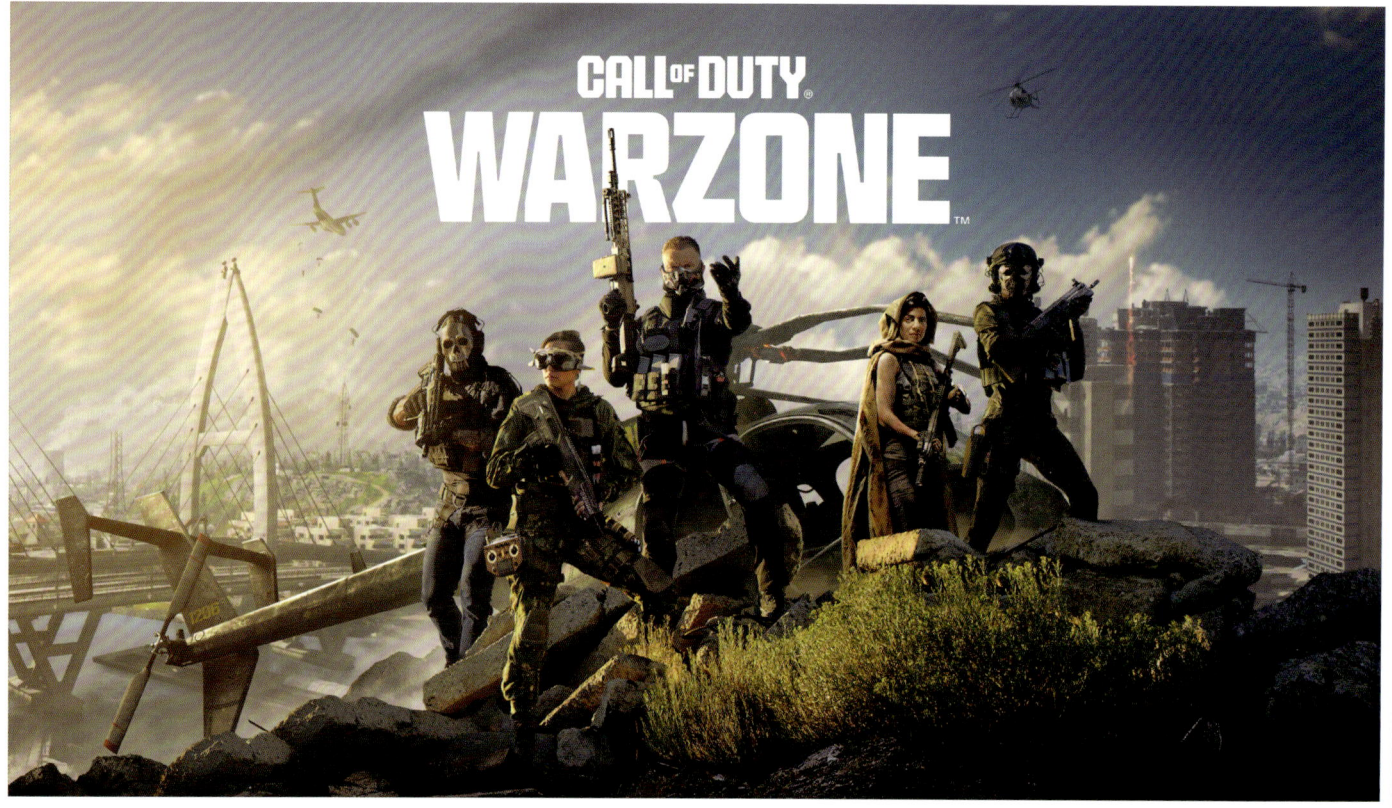

Title: Call of Duty: Modern Warfare III x Warzone - Key Art Poster Series
Clients: Activision, Infinity Ward, Raven Software | **Design Firm:** PETROL Advertising

BLIZZARD ENTERTAINMENT, PETROL ADVERTISING 🇺🇸

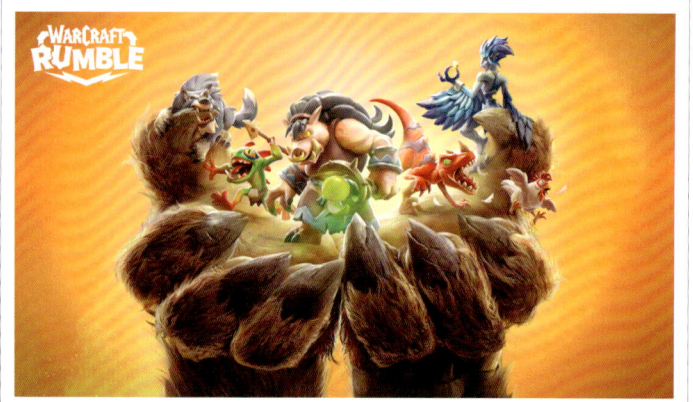

Title: Warcraft Rumble - Campaign Key Art Posters
Client: Blizzard Entertainment | **Design Firm:** PETROL Advertising

NEOWIZ, PETROL ADVERTISING 🇺🇸

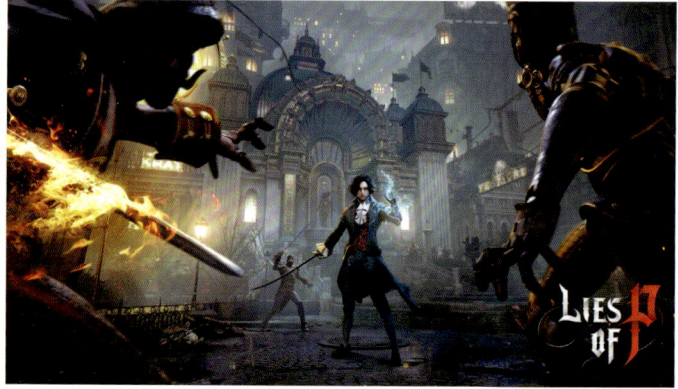

Title: Lies of P - Campaign Key Art Poster Series
Client: Neowiz | **Design Firm:** PETROL Advertising

CI GAMES, PETROL ADVERTISING 🇺🇸

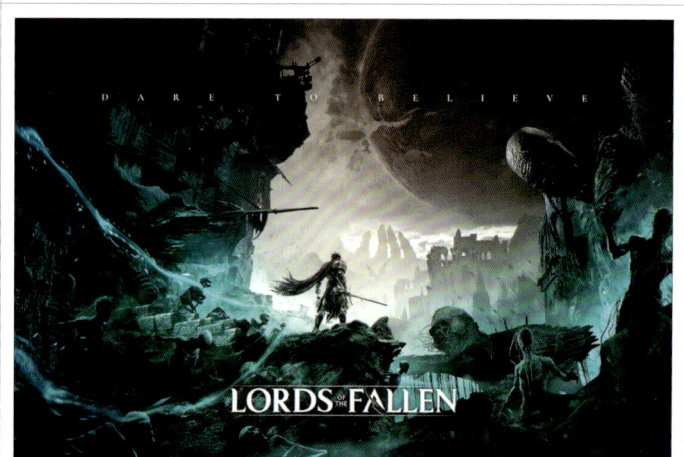

Title: Lords of the Fallen - Wide World Art
Client: CI Games | **Design Firm:** PETROL Advertising

CI GAMES, PETROL ADVERTISING 🇺🇸

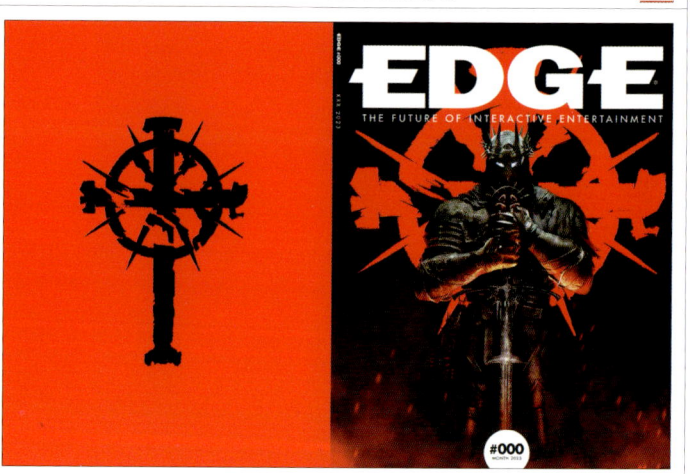

Title: Lords of the Fallen - Edge Cover
Clients: CI Games, Hexworks | **Design Firm:** PETROL Advertising

185 SILVER — GAMES

UBISOFT, PETROL ADVERTISING

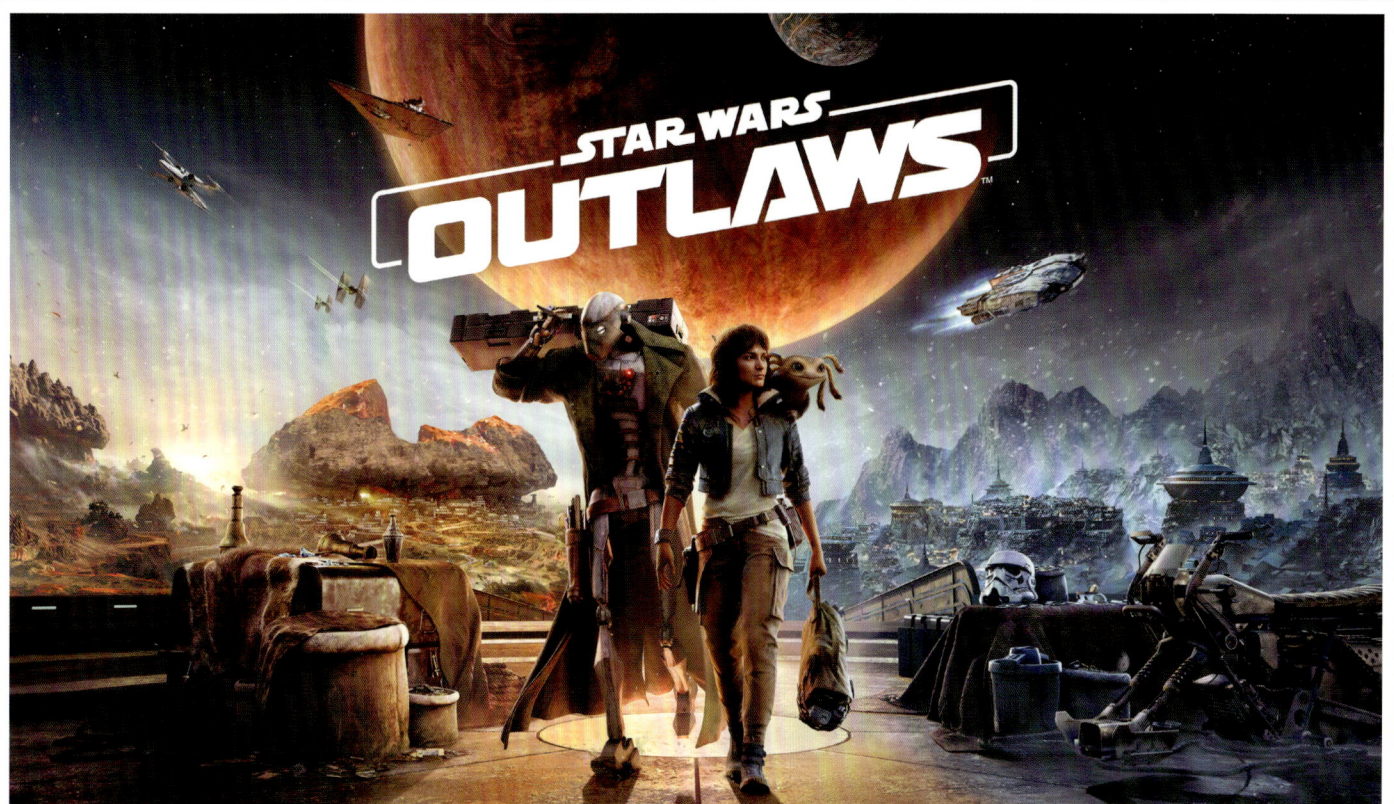

Title: Star Wars Outlaws - Primary Key Art Poster | Clients: Ubisoft, Massive Entertainment | Design Firm: PETROL Advertising

JBL QUANTUM, PETROL ADVERTISING

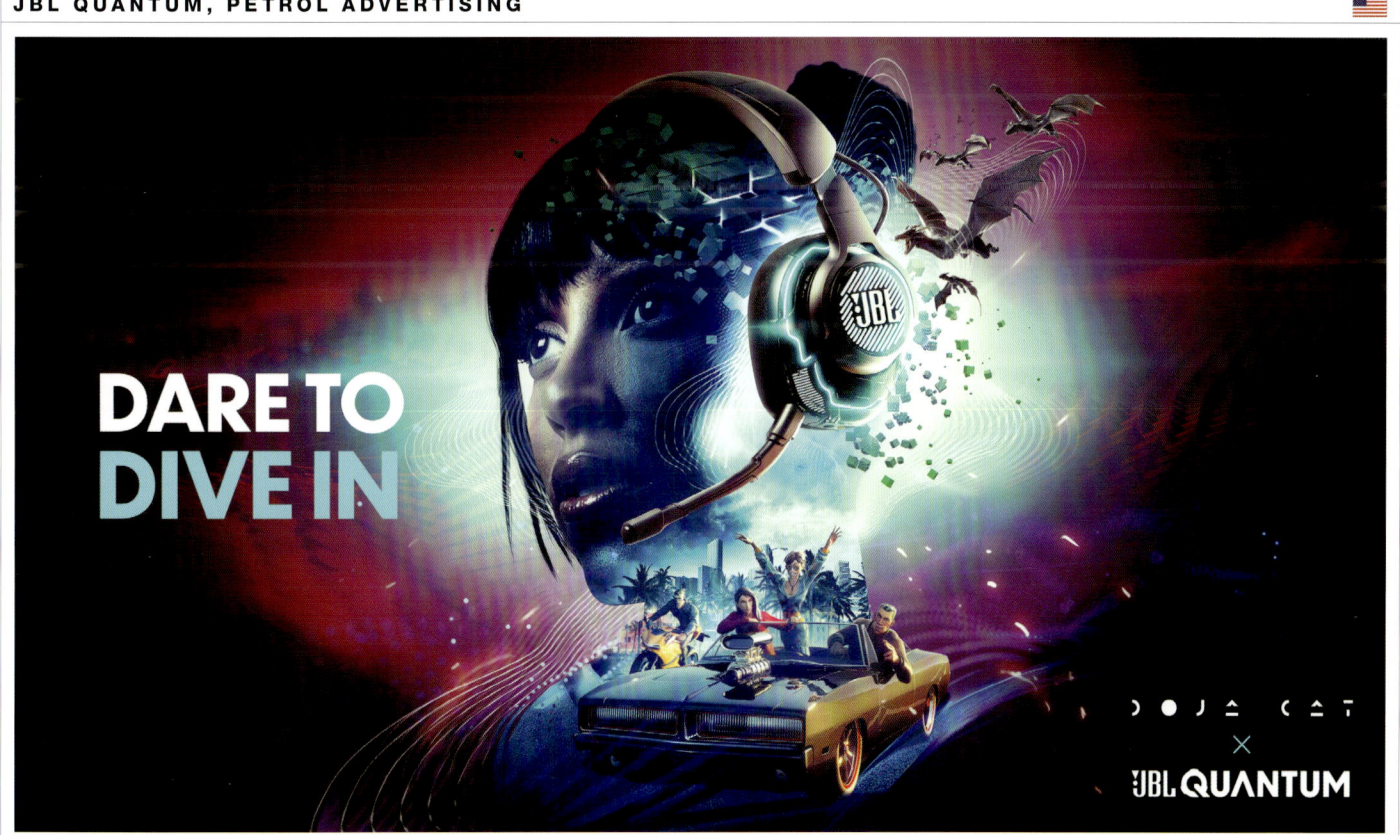

Title: JBL - Dare to Dive In Campaign Poster Series | Client: JBL Quantum | Design Firm: PETROL Advertising

ACTIVISION, PETROL ADVERTISING

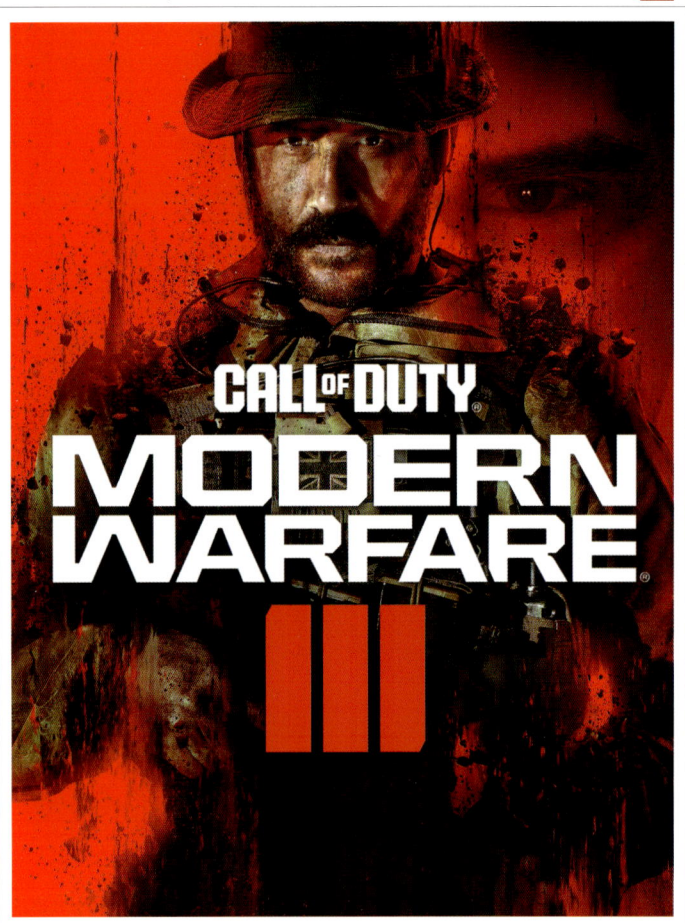

Title: Call of Duty: Modern Warfare III - Key Art Poster Series
Clients: Activision, Infinity Ward | **Design Firm:** PETROL Advertising

JUSTIN KUNZ

Title: Hideaway Island Poster
Client: Quest Posse | **Design Firm:** Justin Kunz Illustration

BEATRIZ ANTUNES

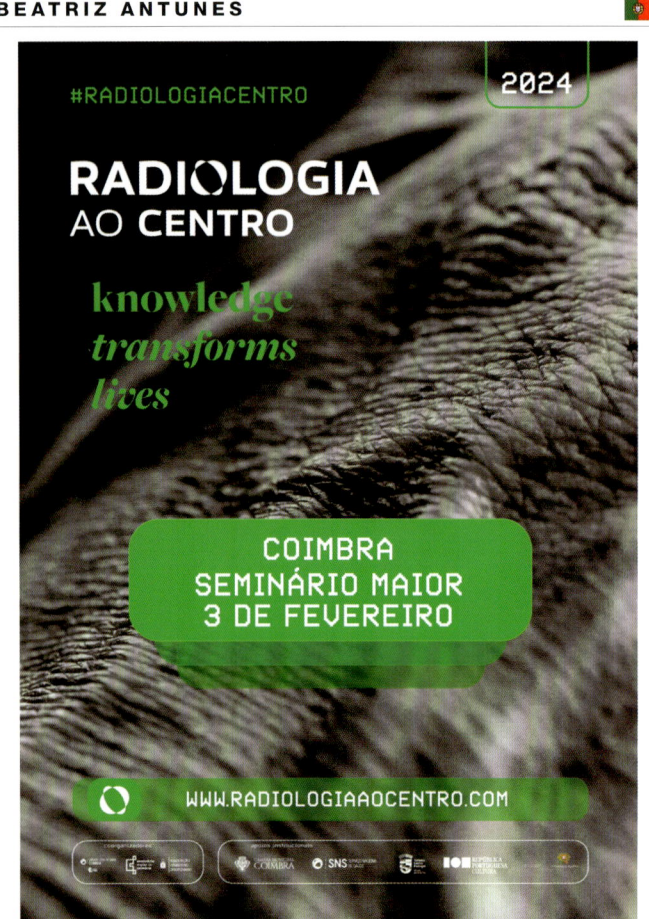

Title: Radiologia ao Centro | **Client:** Associação Hemisfério Disciplinado
Design Firm: Duas Faces Design

SIYU MAO

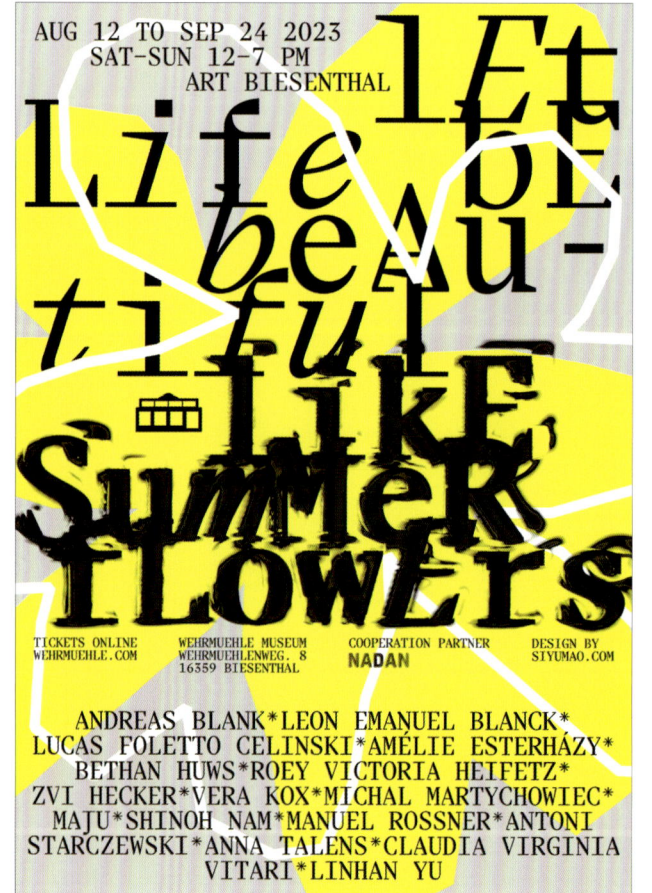

Title: Like Summer Flowers | **Client:** Museum Wehrmuehle
Design Firm: Team Mao

187 SILVER — MUSEUM, MUSIC

ANNA FARKAS 🇭🇺

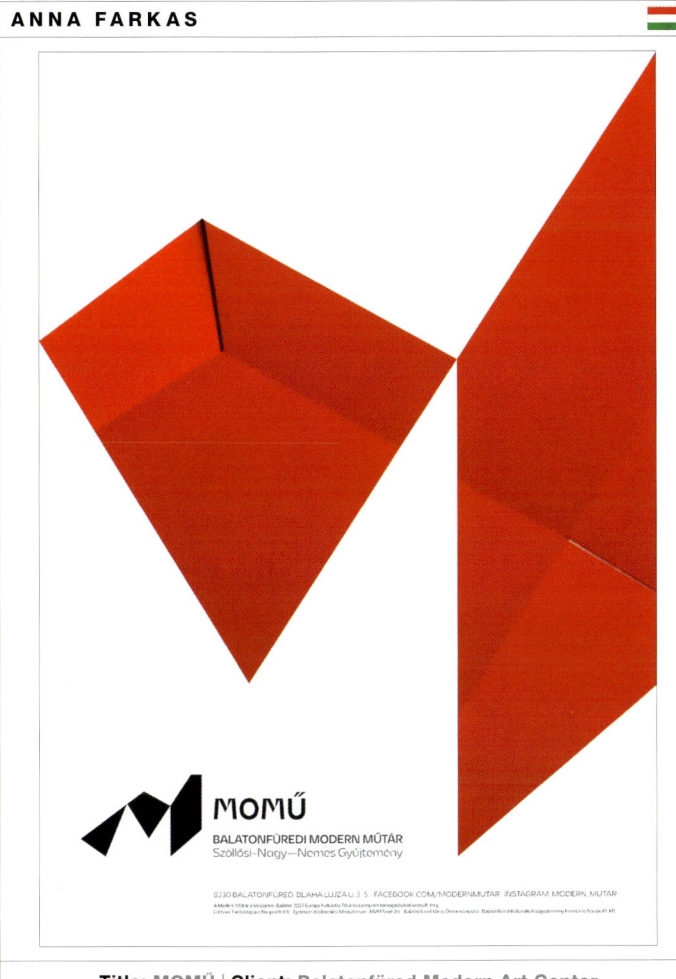

Title: MOMŰ | **Client:** Balatonfüred Modern Art Center
Design Firm: Anagraphic

MARC PHILIP SEIDEL 🇨🇭

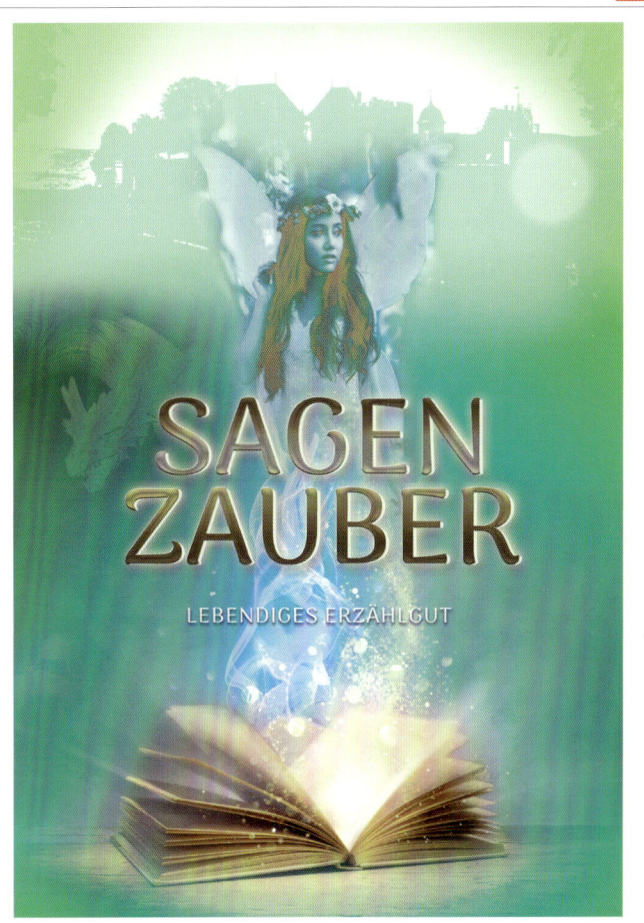

Title: SAGENZAUBER | **Client:** Museum Burghalde Lenzburg
Design Firm: Dreamis GmbH

FONS HICKMANN 🇩🇪

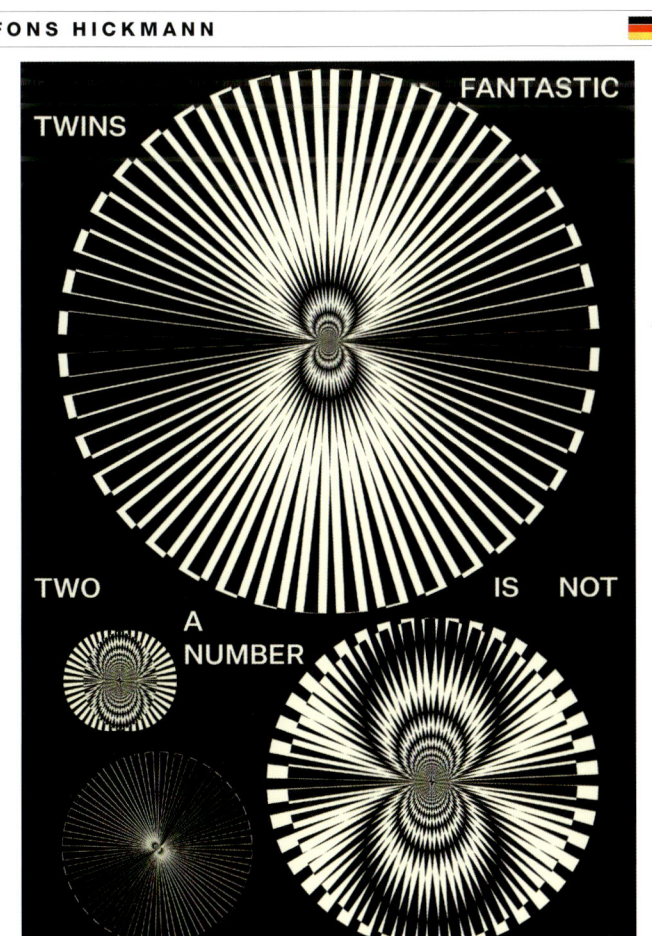

Title: Two is Not a Number | **Client:** Fantastic Twins
Design Firm: Fons Hickmann m23

JAN ŠABACH 🇺🇸

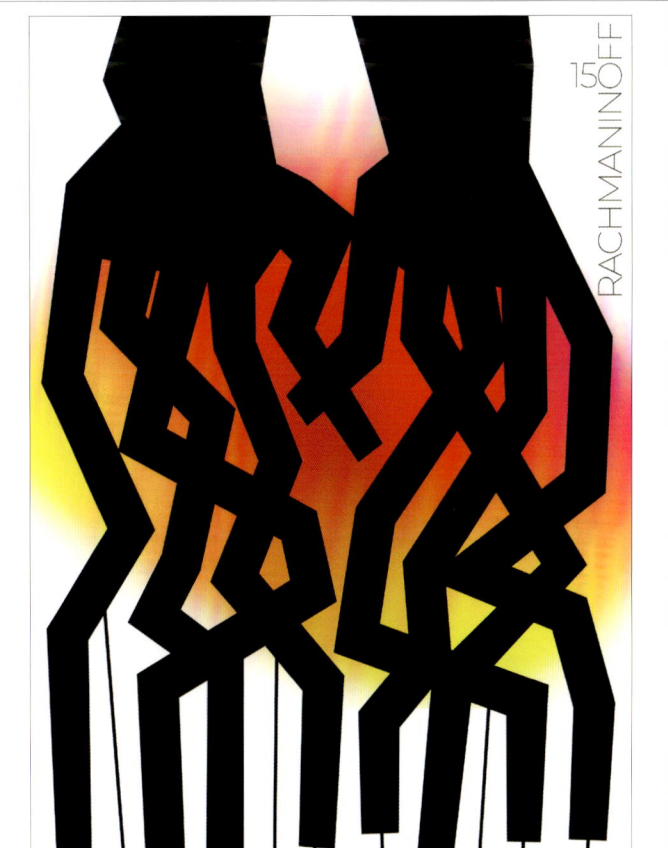

Title: Rachmaninoff 150 | **Client:** Golden Bee Biennale
Design Firm: Code Switch

188 SILVER — MUSIC

CARLO FIORE 🇮🇹

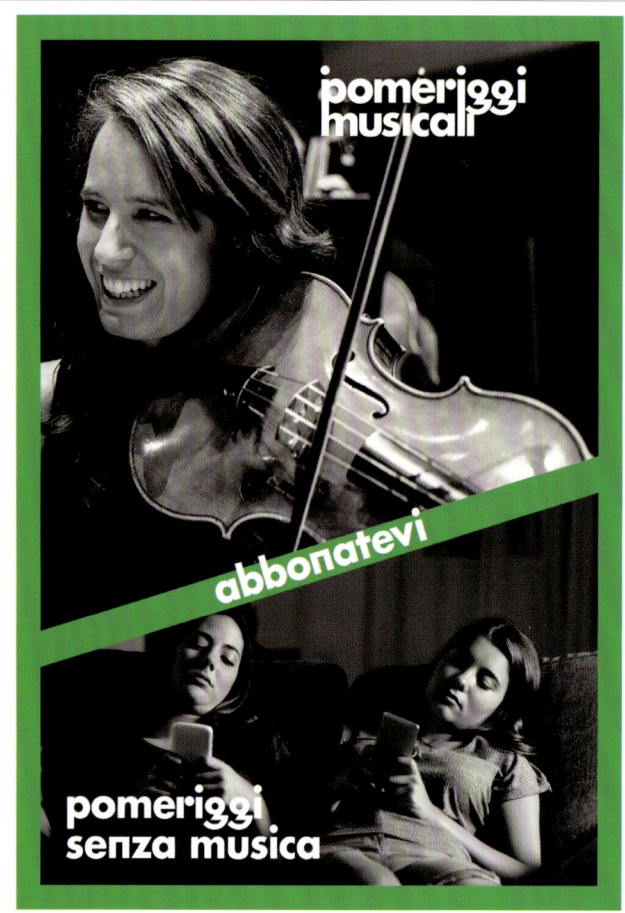

Title: Pomeriggi Musicali 2023-2024 | **Client:** Fondazione I Pomeriggi Musicali - Milano | **Design Firm:** Venti Caratteruzzi

RON TAFT 🇺🇸

Title: Unfinished Symphony | **Client:** Orchestra Moderne NYC
Design Firm: Ron Taft Brand Innovation & Media Arts

R.P. BISSLAND 🇺🇸

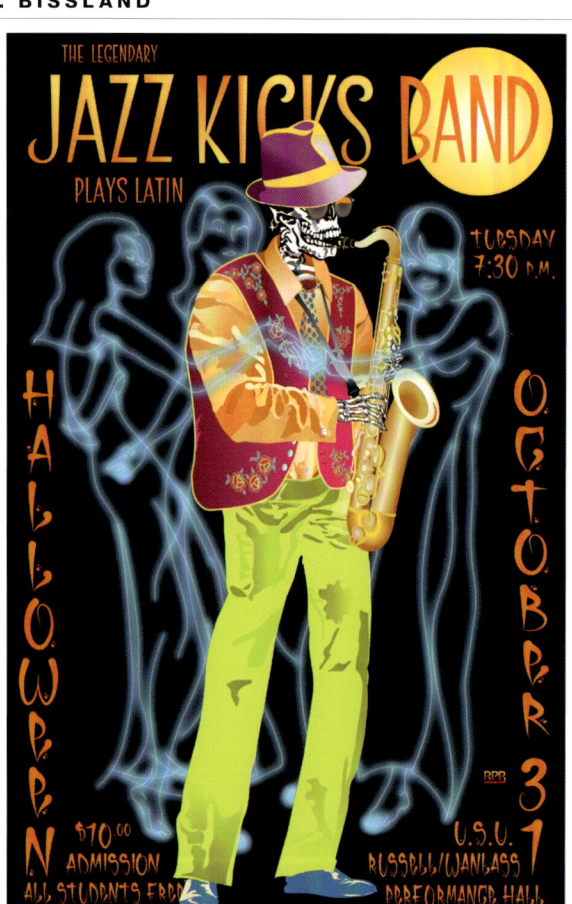

Title: Jazz Kicks Band Halloween Concert
Client: Jazz Kicks Band | **Design Firm:** Design SubTerra

ERIK SPANGLER, WENDEL PATRICK 🇺🇸

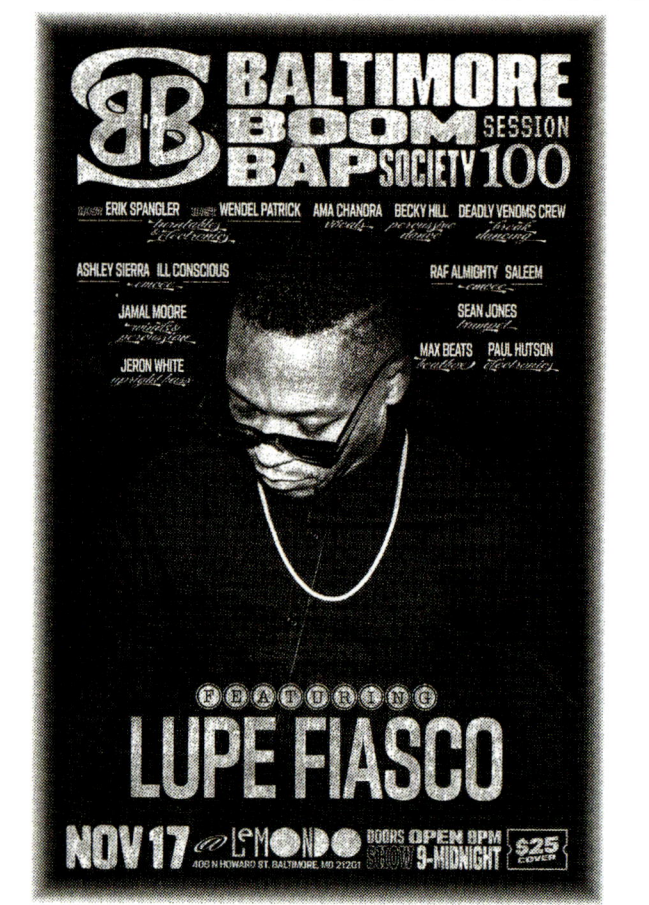

Title: Baltimore Boom Bap Society Performance Poster Series
Client: Baltimore Boom Bap Society | **Design Firm:** Isaac Jung

MICHAEL BRALEY

Title: Ambrosius: Album Release Concert Poster
Client: Ambrosius | Design Firm: Braley Design

IVAN KASHLAKOV

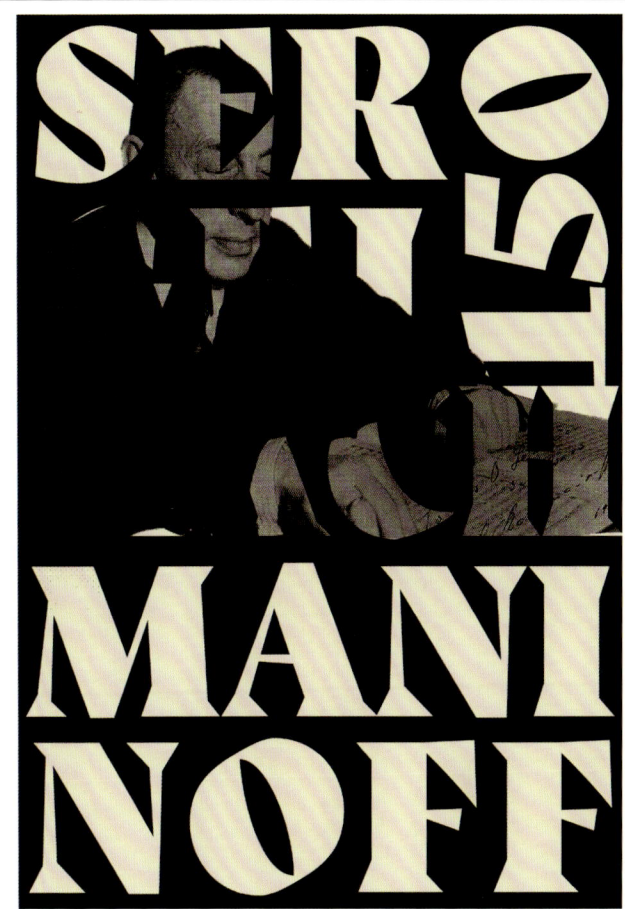

Title: Rachmaninoff 150
Client: Golden Bee Biennale | Design Firm: Ivan Kashlakov

MARTIN FRENCH

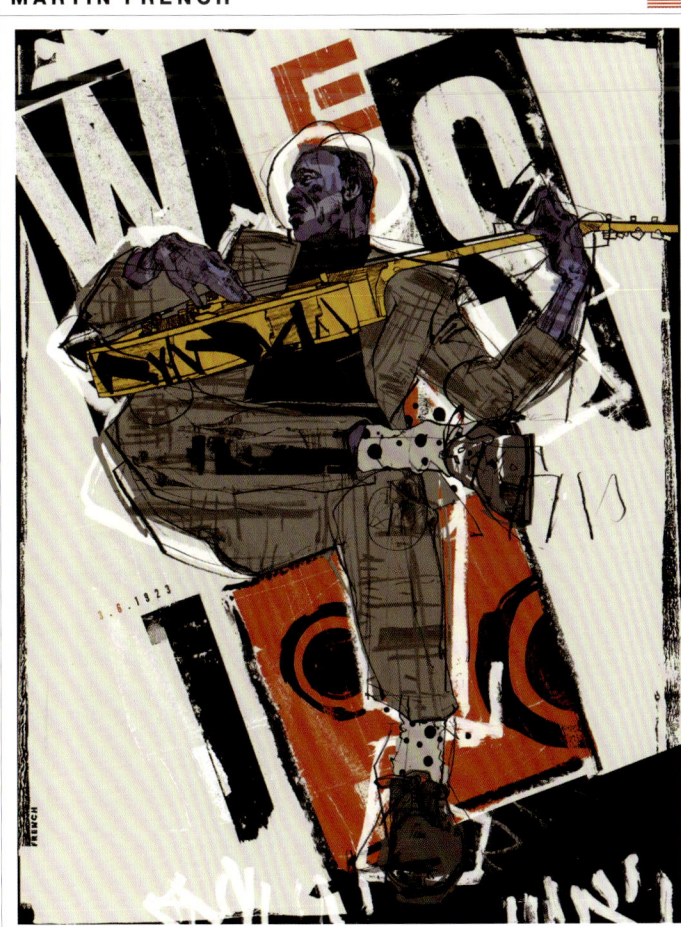

Title: Wes 100 | Client: 33Third
Design Firm: Martin French Studio

PRIMOZ ZORKO

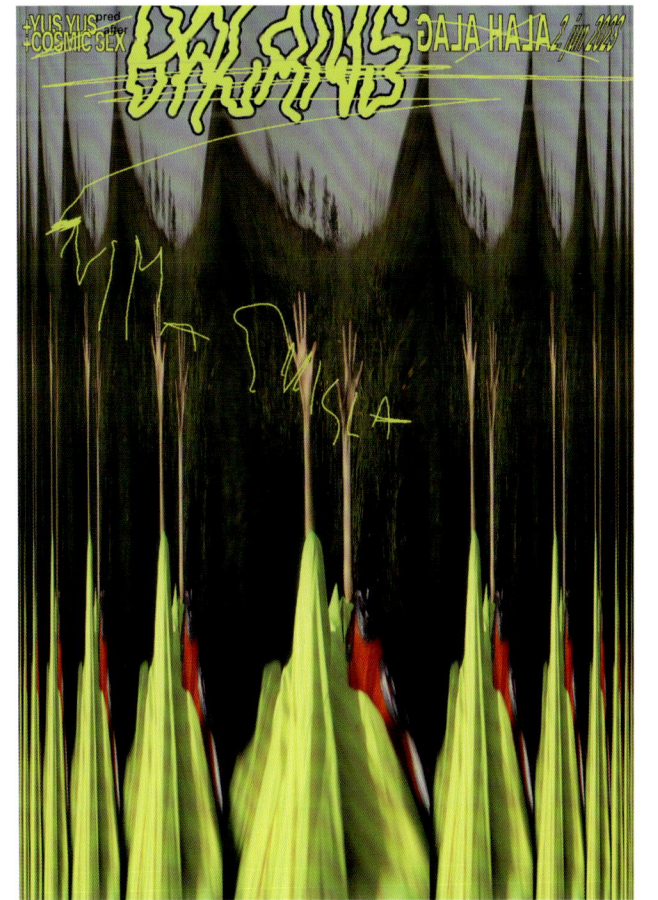

Title: Mima Smisla - Balans (Poster) | Client: Balans
Design Firm: Primoz Zorko

GUNTER RAMBOW 🇩🇪

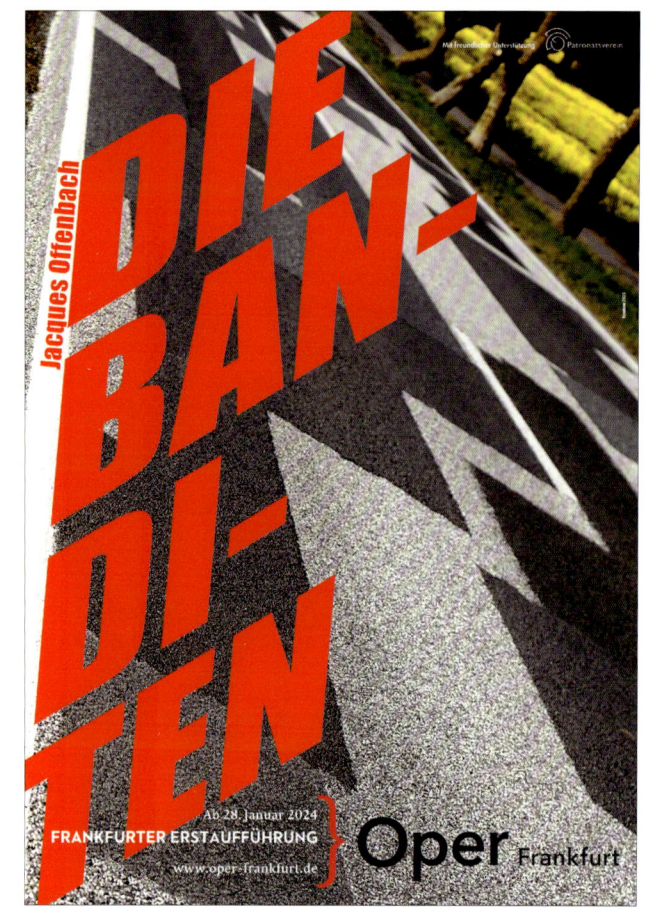

Title: Die Banditen - The Bandits | **Client:** Oper Frankfurt
Design Firm: Institut für Visuelle Kommunikation

GUNTER RAMBOW 🇩🇪

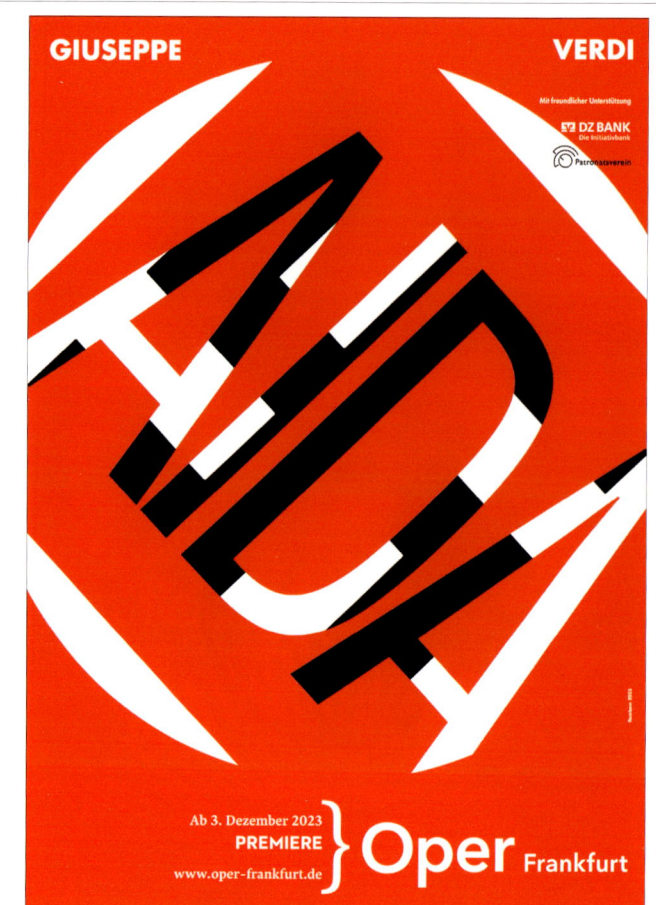

Title: AIDA | **Client:** Oper Frankfurt
Design Firm: Institut für Visuelle Kommunikation

CARLO FIORE 🇮🇹

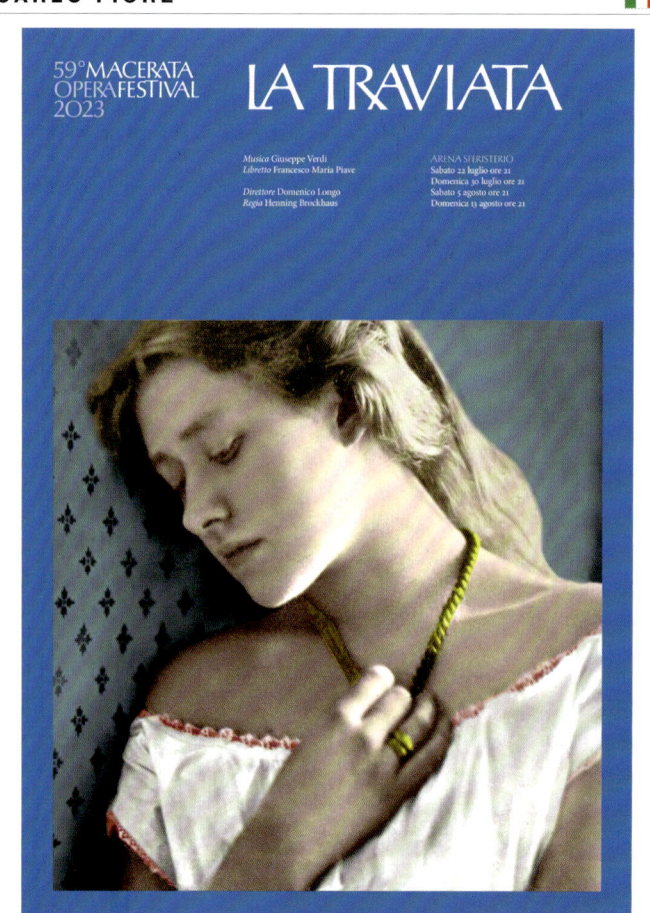

Title: Macerata Opera Festival 2023
Client: Associazione Arena Sferisterio | **Design Firm:** Venti Caratteruzzi

SARAH NORTHCUTT 🇺🇸

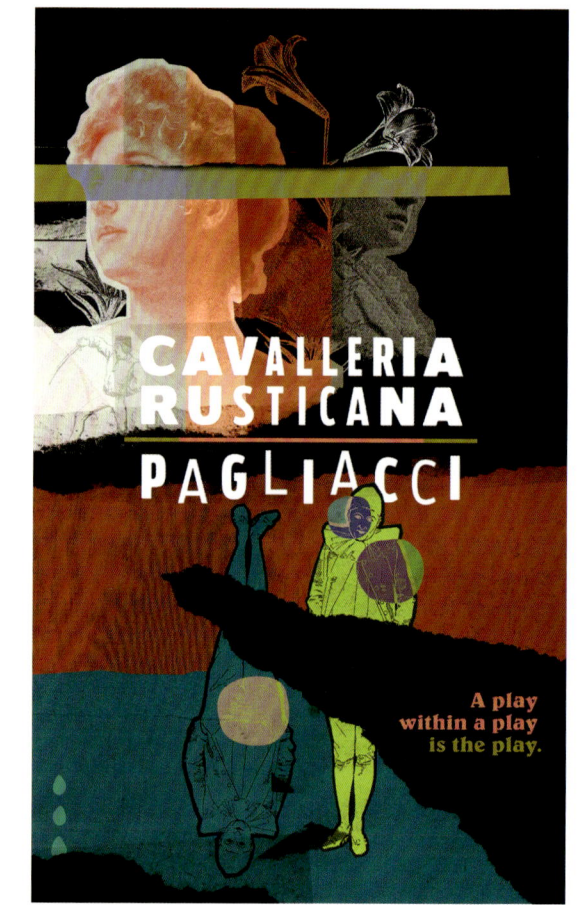

Title: LOKC Season Posters 2023
Client: Lyric Opera of Kansas City | **Design Firm:** Bailey Lauerman

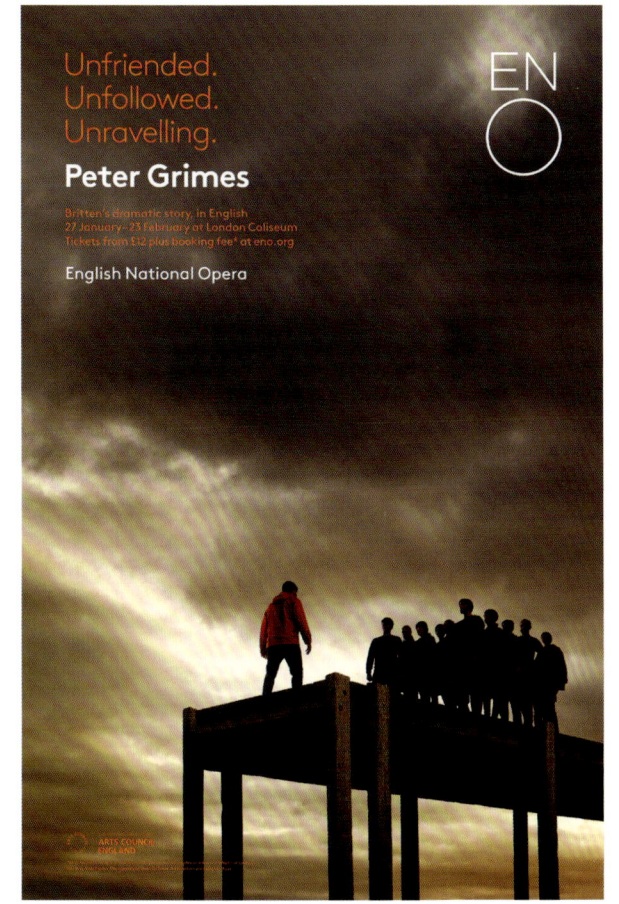

Title: Peter Grimes | **Client:** English National Opera
Design Firm: Rose

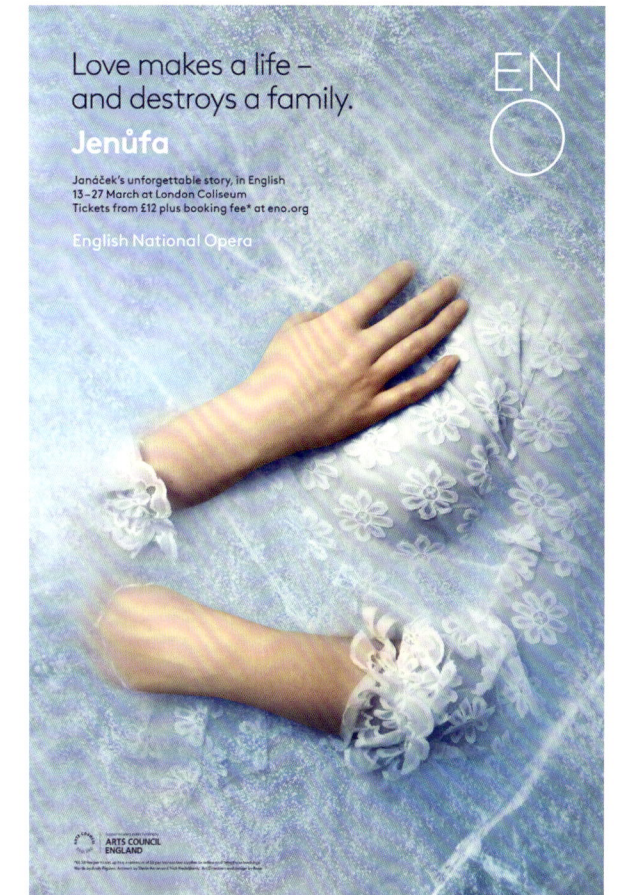

Title: Jenůfa | **Client:** English National Opera
Design Firm: Rose

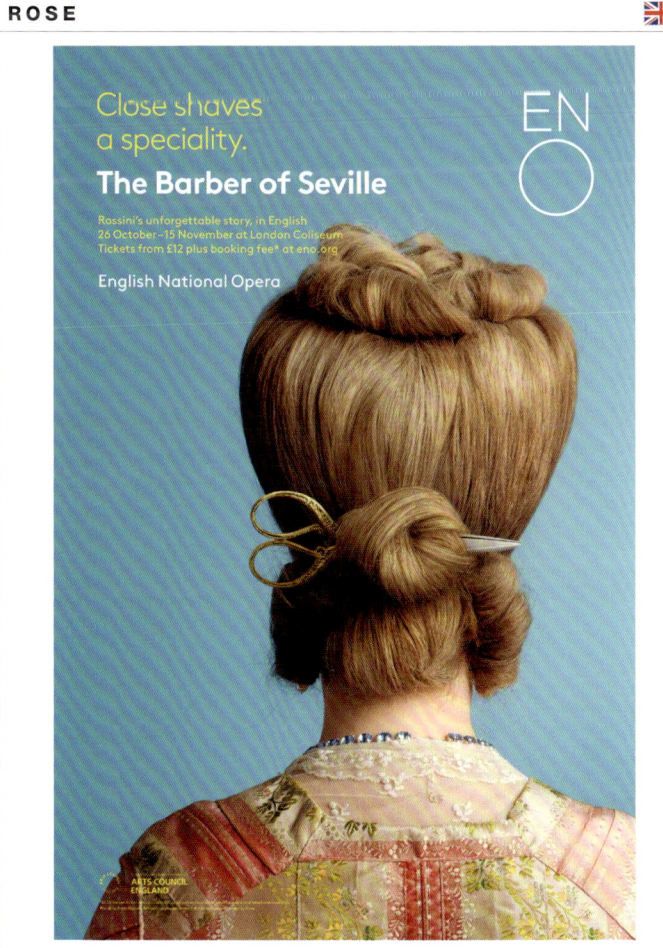

Title: The Barber of Seville | **Client:** English National Opera
Design Firm: Rose

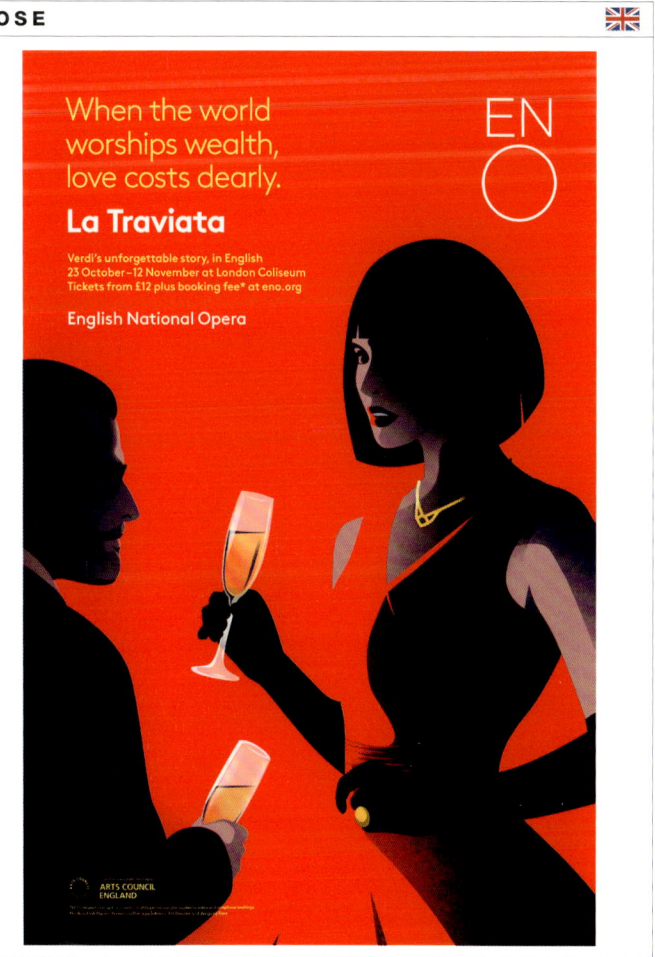

Title: La Traviata | **Client:** English National Opera
Design Firm: Rose

KANTA ABE

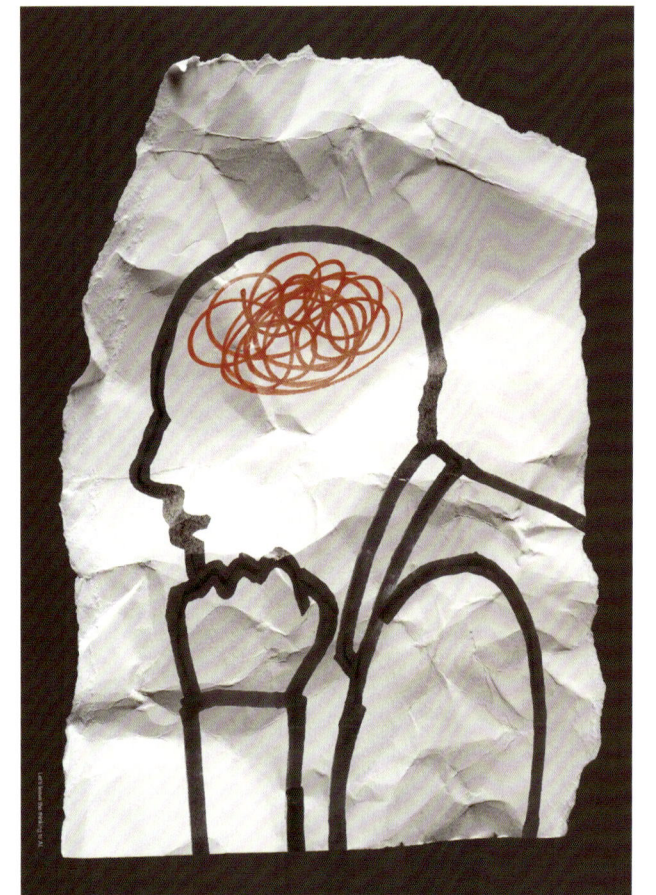

Title: Let's Leave the Thinking to AI.
Client: Self-initiated | **Design Firm:** PEACE Inc.

GUY VILLA JR.

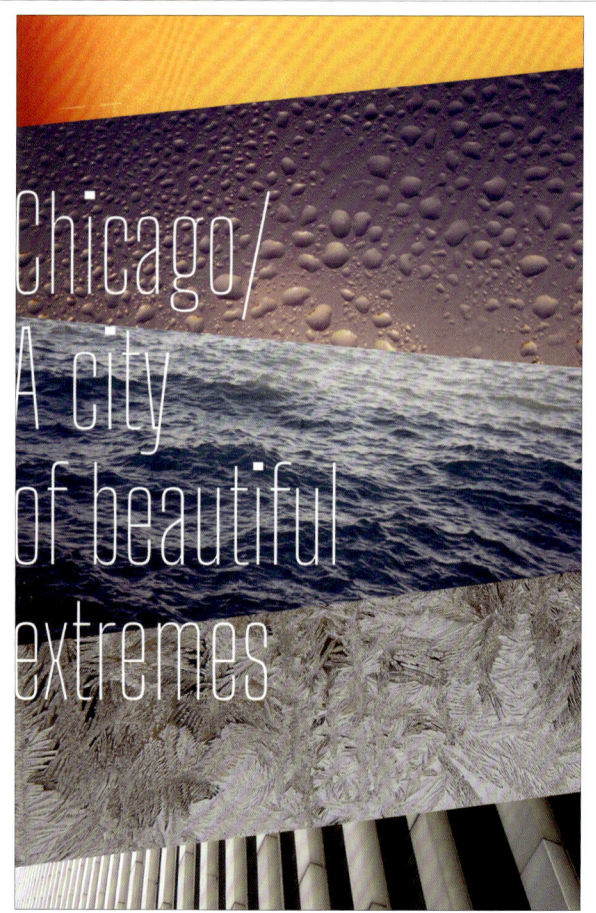

Title: What Does Chicago Mean to You?
Client: Chicago Graphic Design Club | **Design Firm:** Sharon and Guy

JOHN SPOSATO

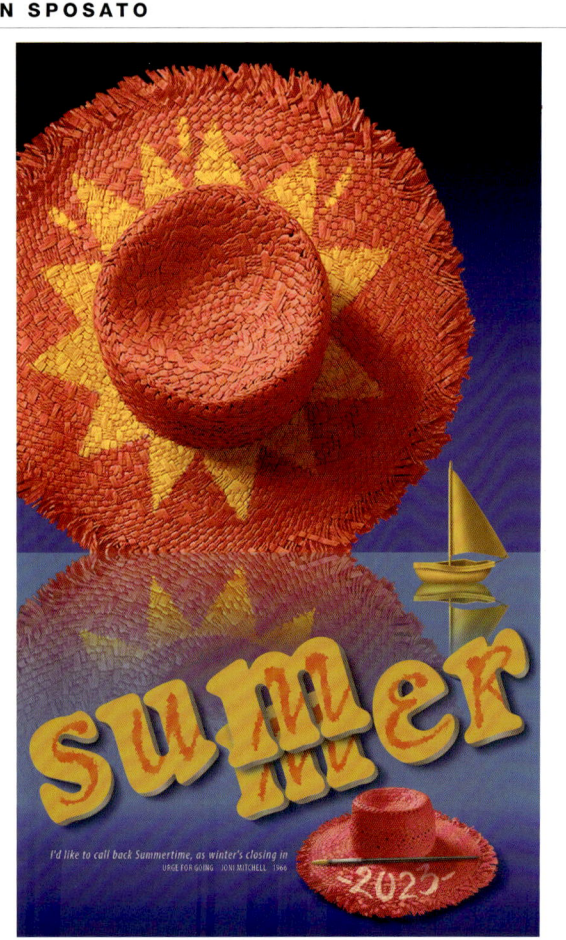

Title: Summer 2023 | **Client:** Self-initiated
Design Firm: John Sposato Design & Illustration

LISA WINSTANLEY

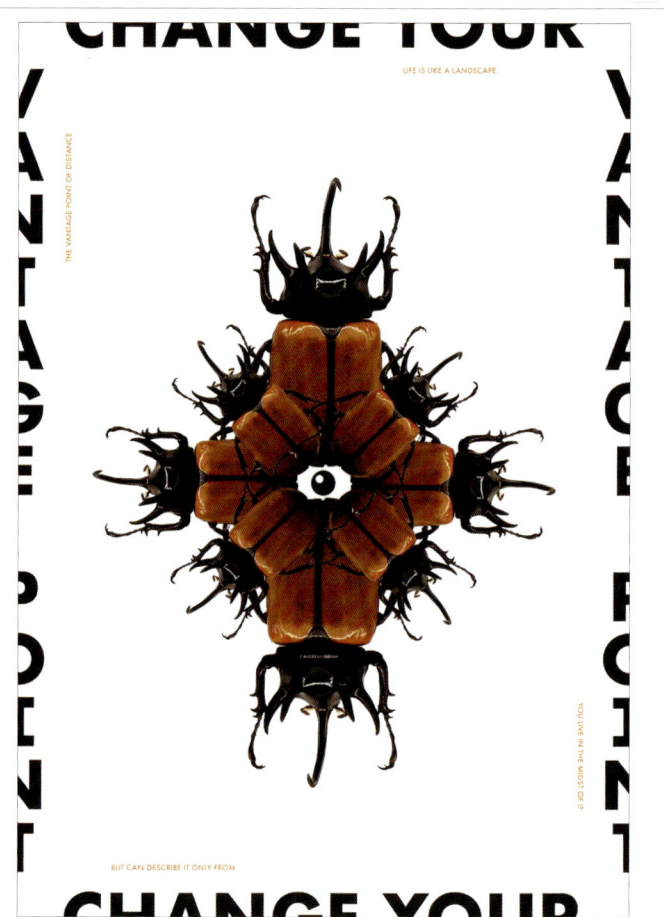

Title: Vantage Point | **Client:** Faculty Learning Community - NTU
Design Firm: Lisa Winstanley Design

193 SILVER PROMOTION

KEITA OTSUKA 🇯🇵

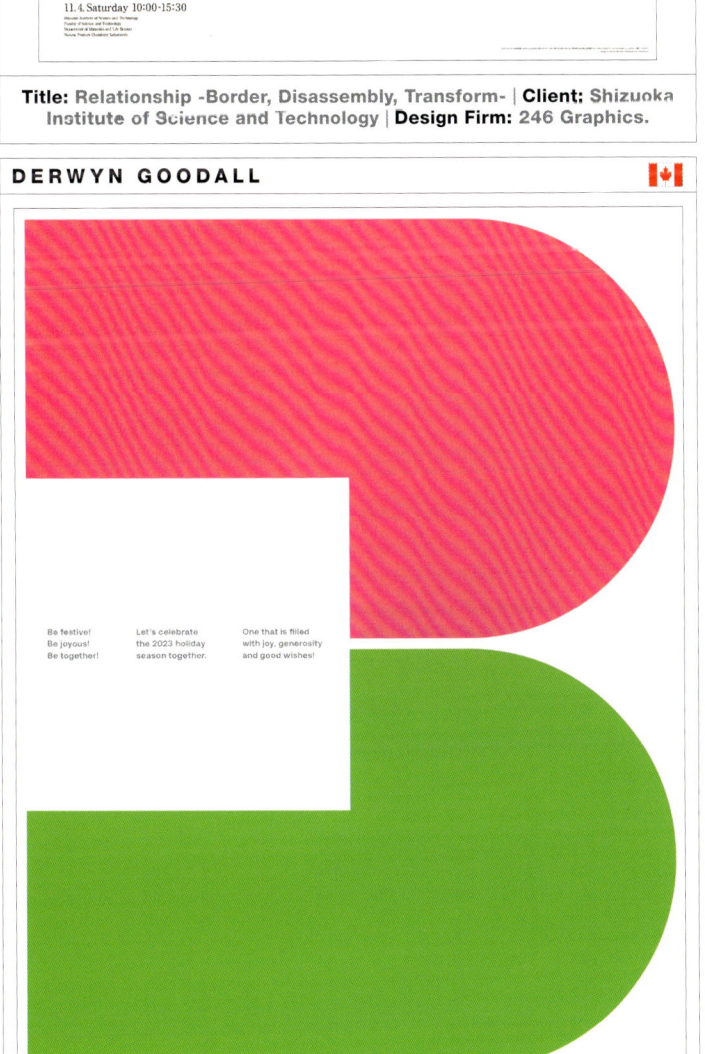

Title: Relationship -Border, Disassembly, Transform- | **Client:** Shizuoka Institute of Science and Technology | **Design Firm:** 246 Graphics.

LEGIS DESIGN 🇺🇸

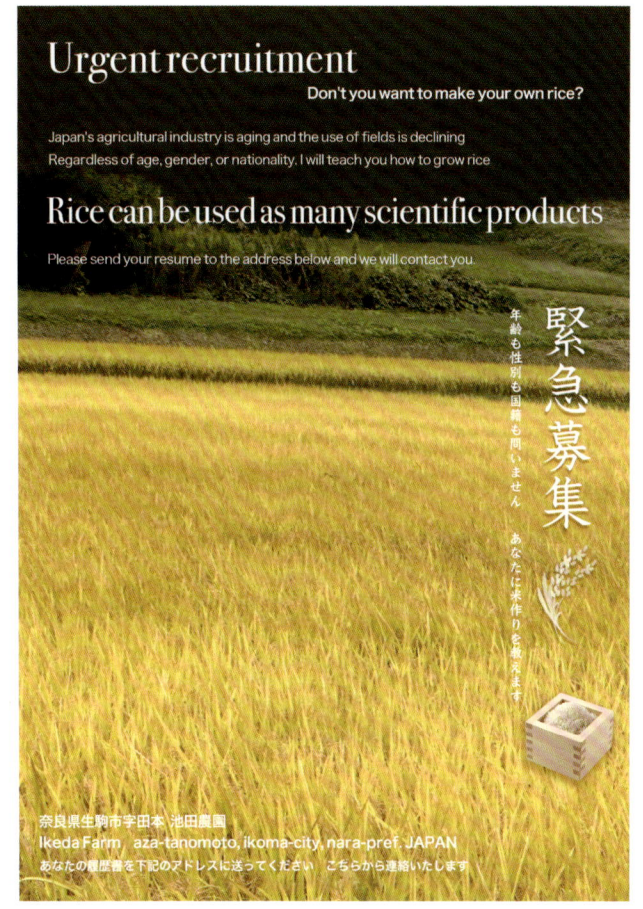

Title: Poster for Utilizing Rice Fields | **Client:** Ikeda Farm
Design Firm: Legis Design

DERWYN GOODALL 🇨🇦

Title: Be | **Client:** Self-initiated
Design Firm: Goodall Integrated Design

PARK SEOYUN, KIM JIEUN, JEON DAYOUNG (+2) 🇰🇷

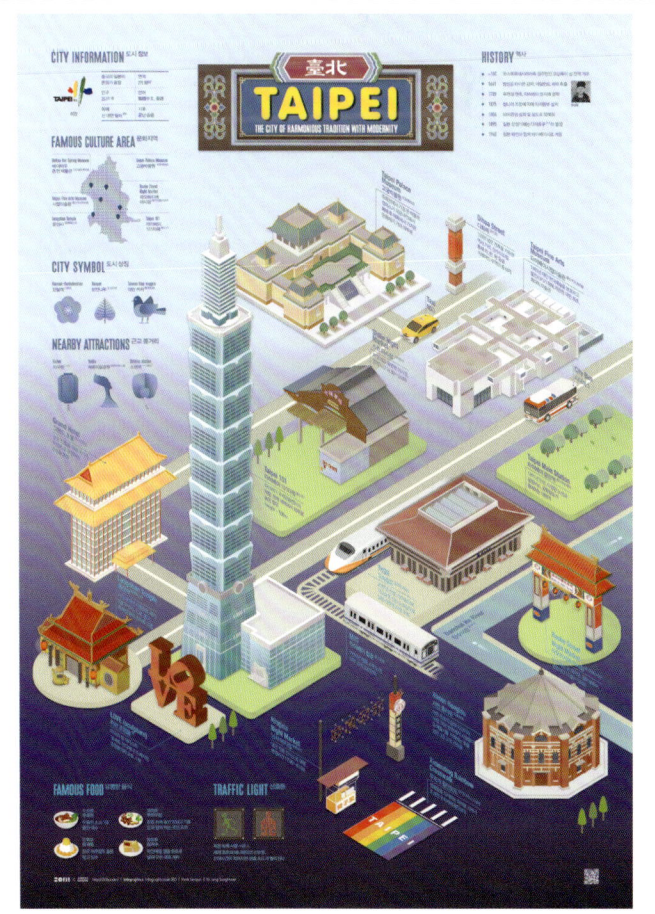

Title: 203_Story_Series | **Client:** Street H
Design Firm: 203 Infographic Lab

PROMOTION

ARIEL FREANER 🇺🇸
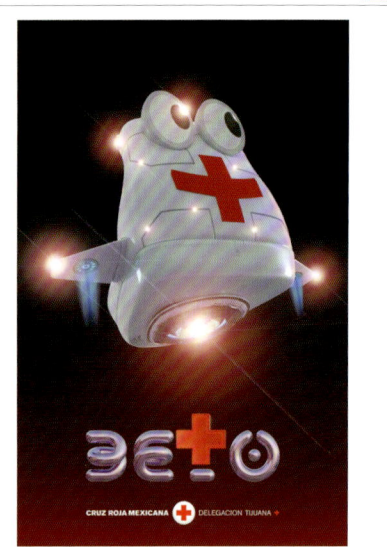
Title: Tijuana Red Cross Donation Beto Campaign
Clients: Red Cross of Tijuana, Jorge Astiazaran
Design Firm: Freaner Creative & Design

LISA MAIONE 🇺🇸
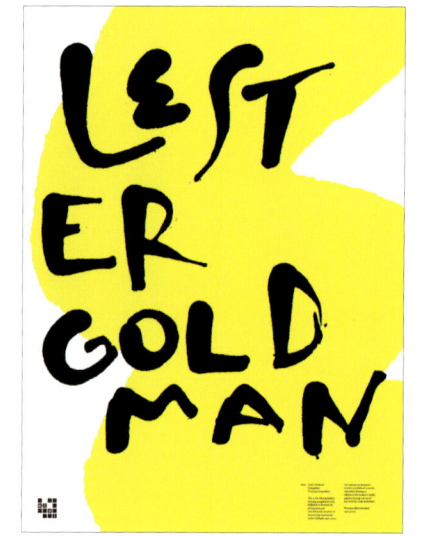
Title: Lester Goldman Drawing Competition
Client: Kansas City Art Institute
Design Firm: For Instance: A Design Practice

RAFAEL FERNANDES 🇧🇷
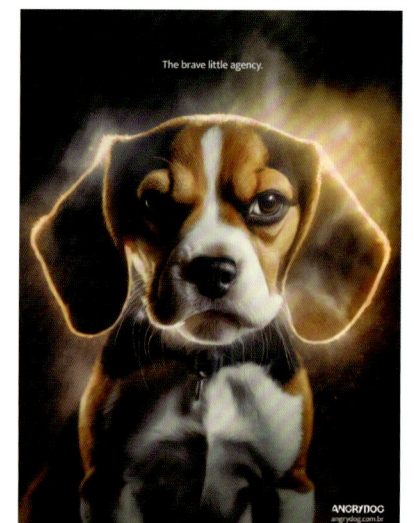
Title: The Brave Little Agency
Client: Self-initiated
Design Firm: Angry Dog

DERWYN GOODALL 🇨🇦
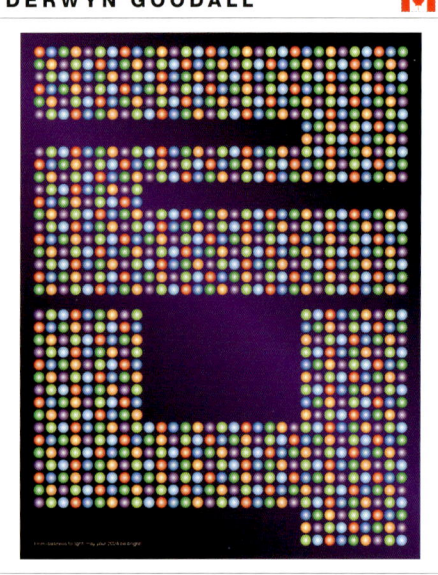
Title: 24
Client: Self-initiated
Design Firm: Goodall Integrated Design

ARIEL FREANER 🇺🇸
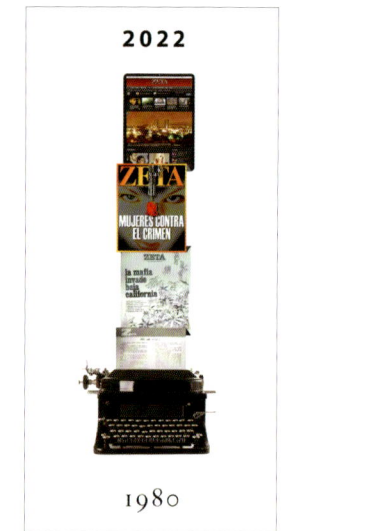
Title: ZETA 42 Years Anniversary Poster
Client: ZETA Weekly
Design Firm: Freaner Creative & Design

KEVIN HAGAN 🇺🇸
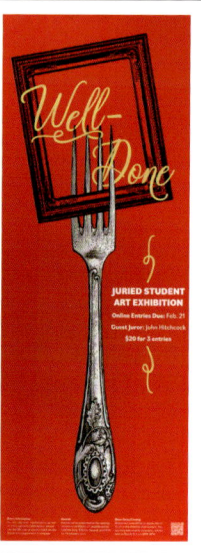
Title: Well Done | **Client:** University of Louisiana at Lafayette Department of Visual Arts
Design Firm: Hidden Impact

ARIEL FREANER 🇺🇸
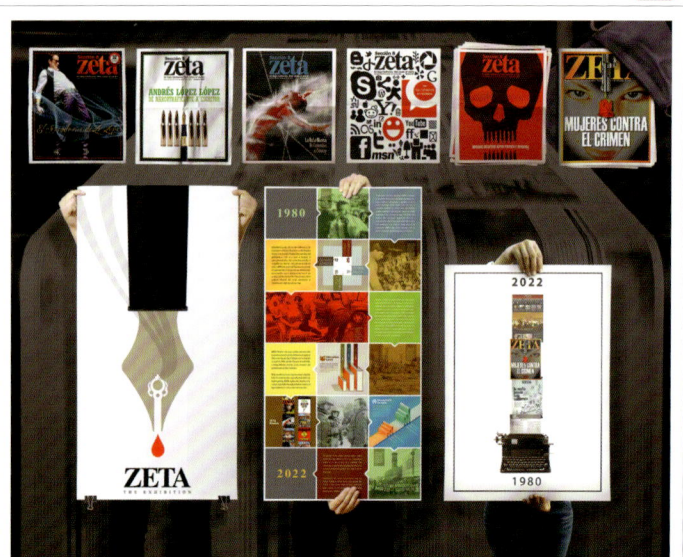
Title: ZETA Advertisers Poster | **Client:** ZETA Weekly
Design Firm: Freaner Creative & Design

JANG WON LEE 🇰🇷
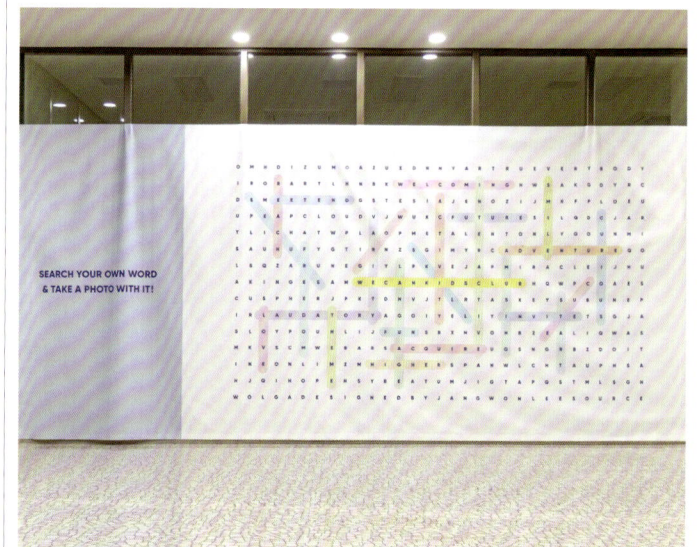
Title: The Giant Wecan Kids Club Signature Word Search Fabric Poster
Client: Wecan Kids Club | **Design Firm:** Whimsical Studio

SEITA ISHIKAWA

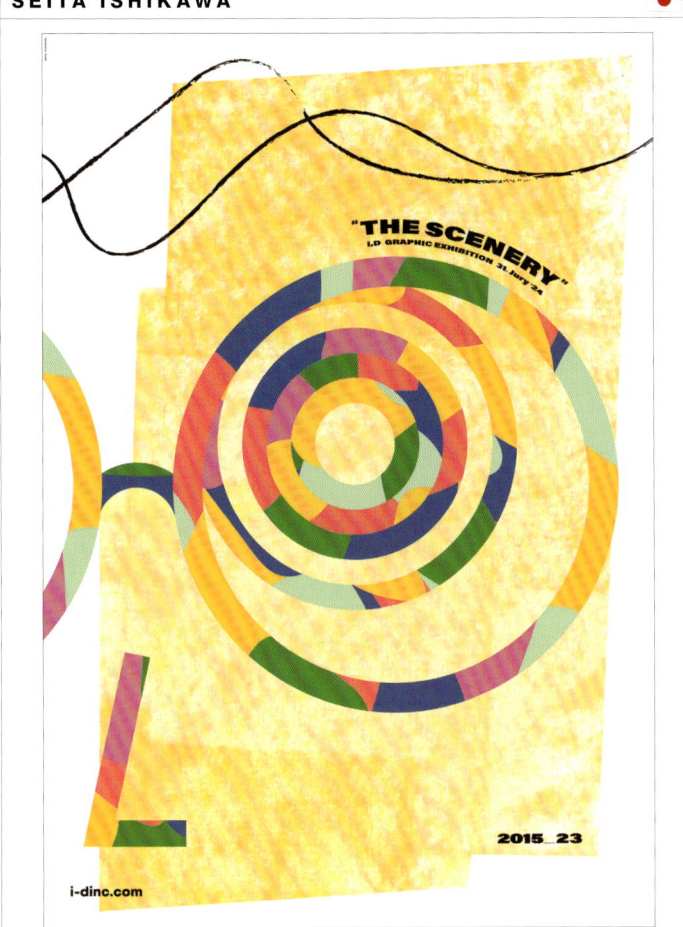

Title: THE SCENERY | **Client:** Self-initiated
Design Firm: i,D

SEAN FADEN

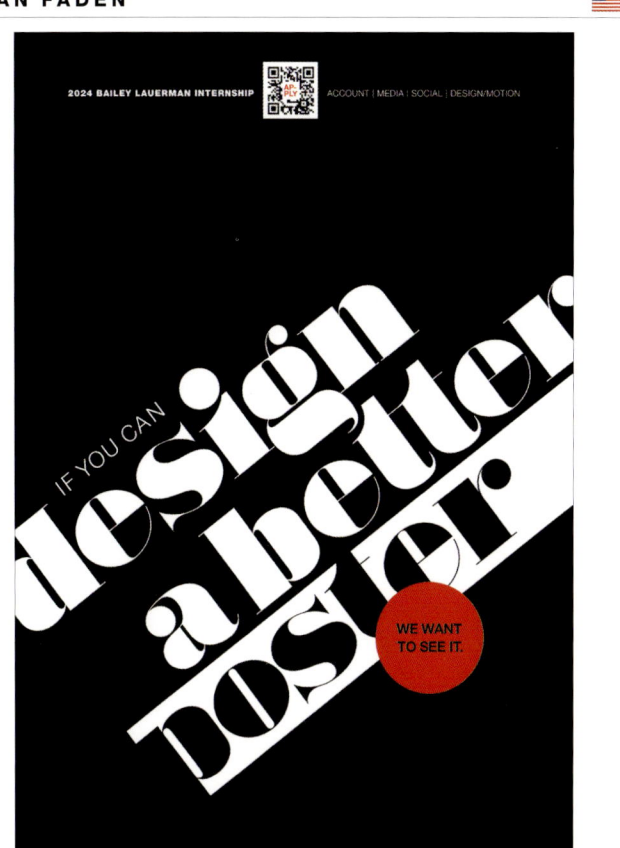

Title: Call to Interns | **Client:** Self-Initiated
Design Firm: Bailey Lauerman

DAEKI SHIM

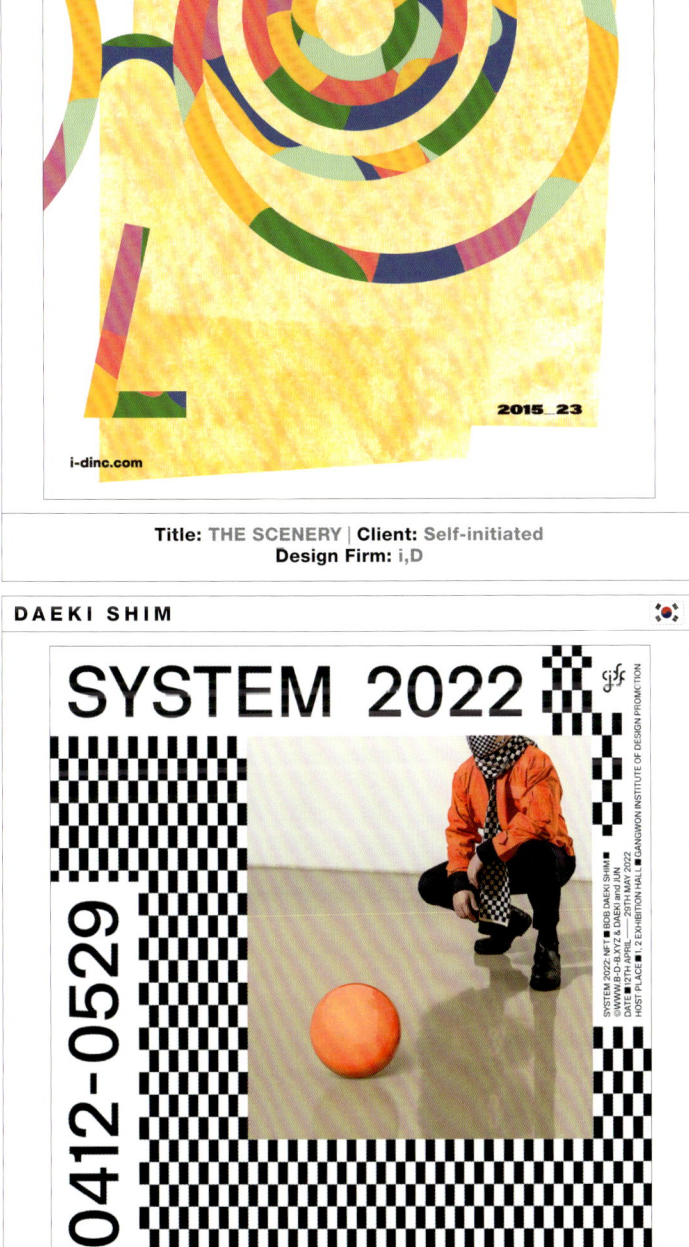

Title: SYSTEM 2022
Clients: Gangwon State, Gangwon Institute of Design Promotion (GIDP)
Design Firm: ©DAEKI and JUN

DAEKI SHIM, HYOJUN SHIM

Title: DDP dnA: Design & Art | **Clients:** Seoul Metropolitan Government, Dongdaemun Design Plaza (DDP), Seoul Design Foundation
Design Firm: ©DAEKI and JUN

196 SILVER PUBLIC & SOCIAL SERVICES

JOSHUA LOWE 🇺🇸

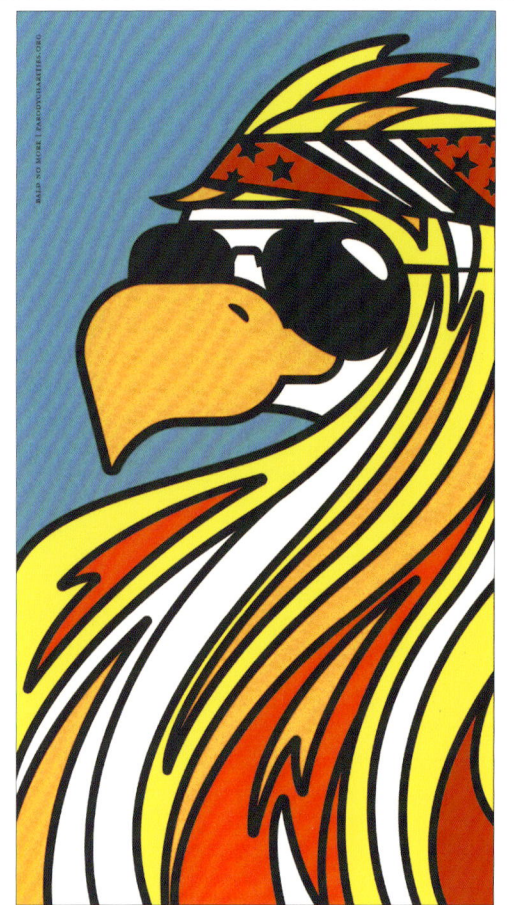

Title: Bald No More: Extensions for Eagles | **Client:** ParodyCharities.org
Design Firm: University of Nebraska

EUNJIN YU 🇰🇷

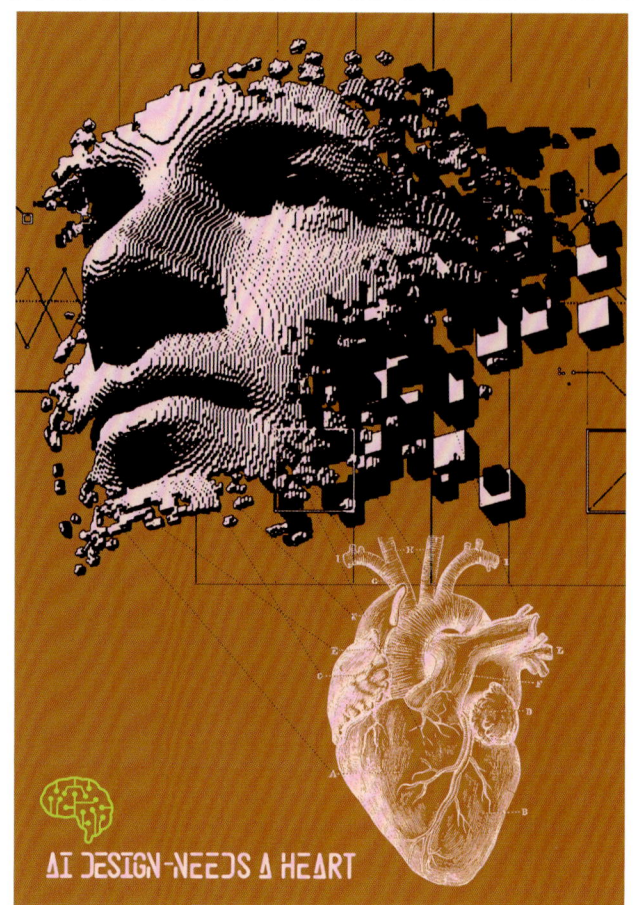

Title: AI-DESIGN NEEDS A HEART | **Client:** Information and Communication Technology Division | **Design Firm:** EJ Communication Studio

LI ZHANG 🇺🇸

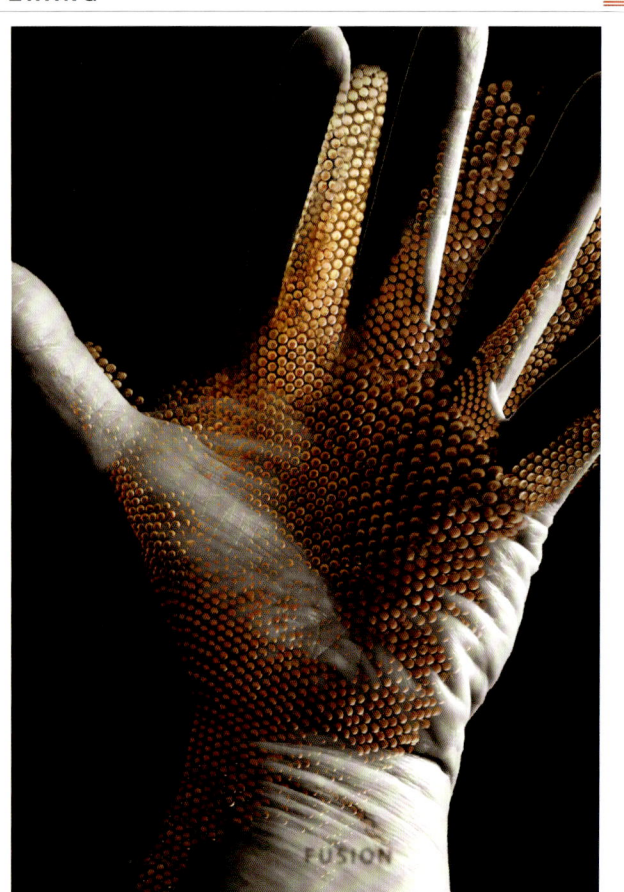

Title: Fusion
Client: Egypt Helwan University
Design Firm: Purdue University

ARIEL FREANER 🇺🇸

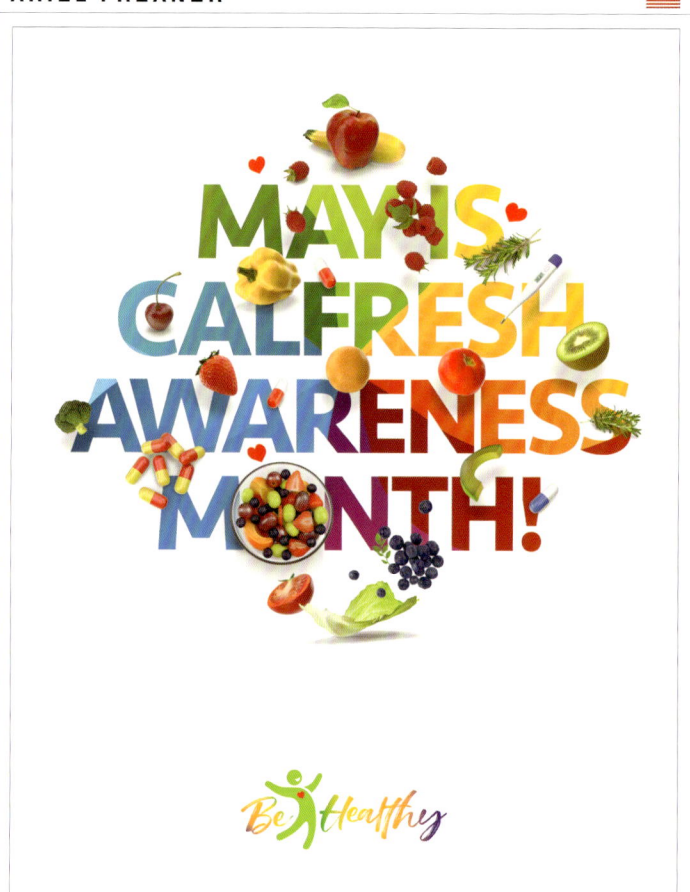

Title: Cal Fresh May Awareness Month 2023 | **Clients:** County of San Diego Cal Fresh HHSA Medicare, Ismael Lopez, Alberto Garcia
Design Firm: Freaner Creative & Design

197 SILVER — PUBLIC & SOCIAL SERVICES

MICHAEL SCHILLIG, ALAN SCHNELLER

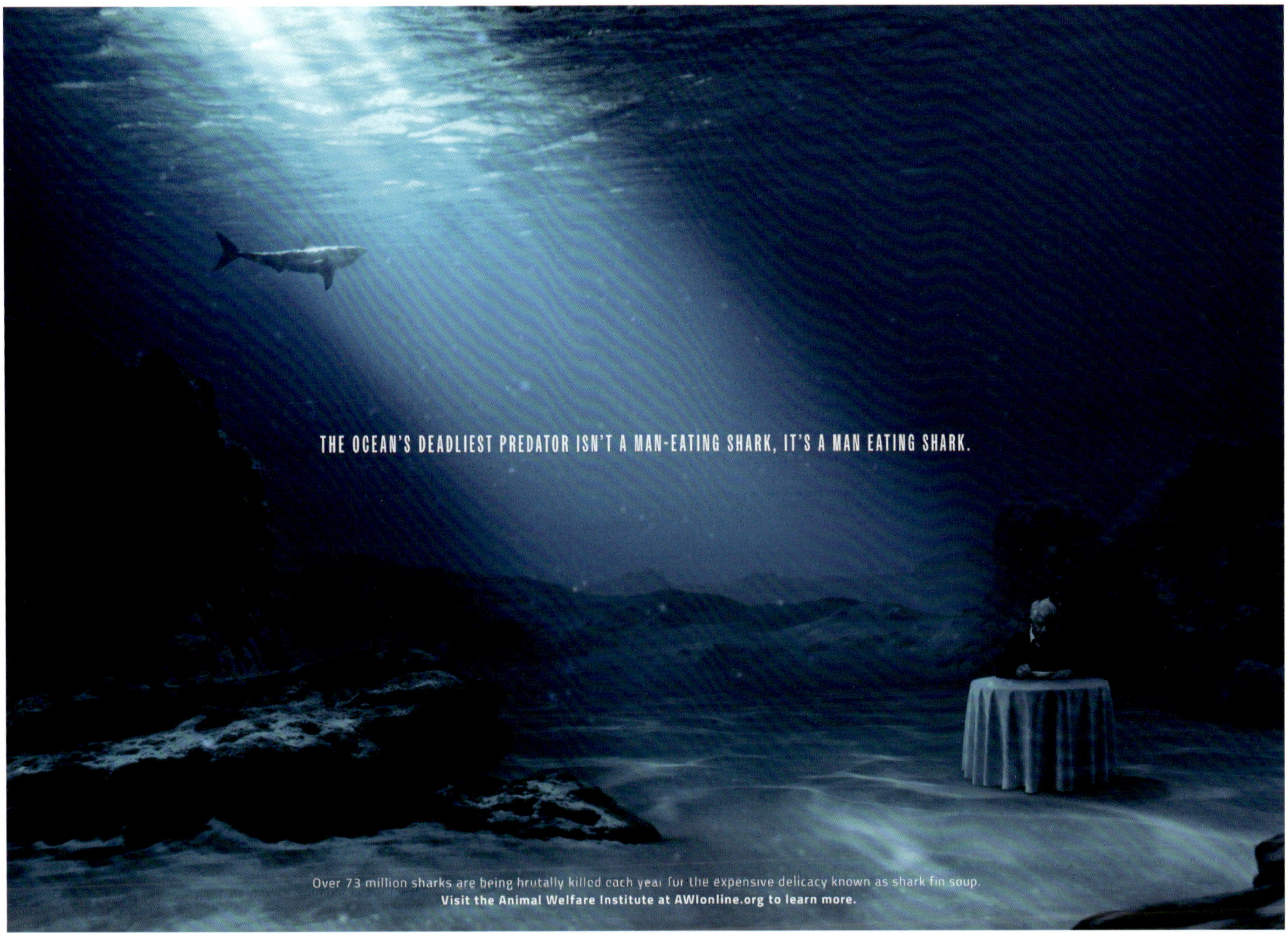

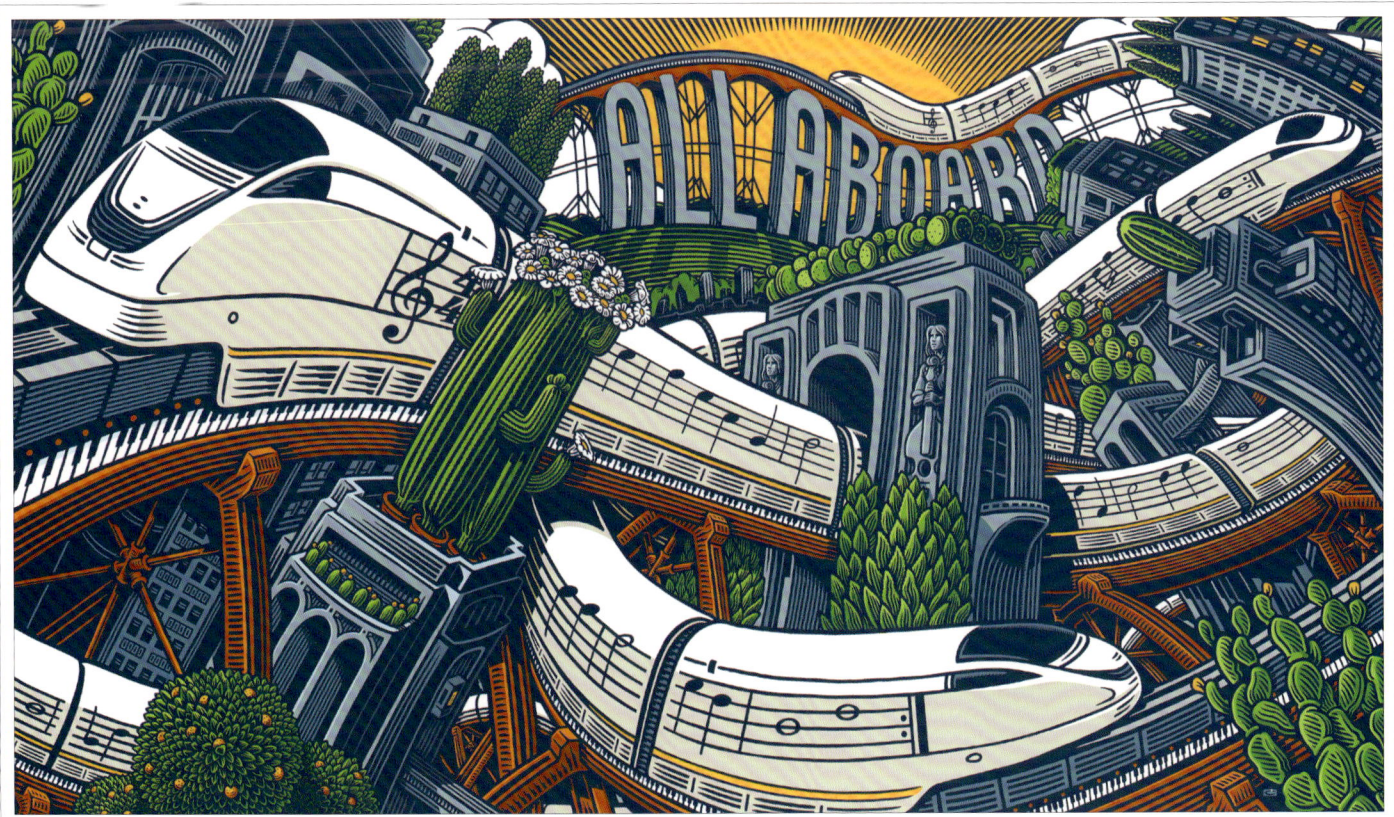

Title: Man Eating Shark | **Client:** Animal Welfare Institute (AWI) | **Design Firm:** PPK

TOM ORTEGA

Title: First Place Poster | **Client:** First Place Arizona | **Design Firm:** Bob Case Illustration

198 SILVER — PUBLIC & SOCIAL SERVICES, RETAIL

ROGIER ROSEMA

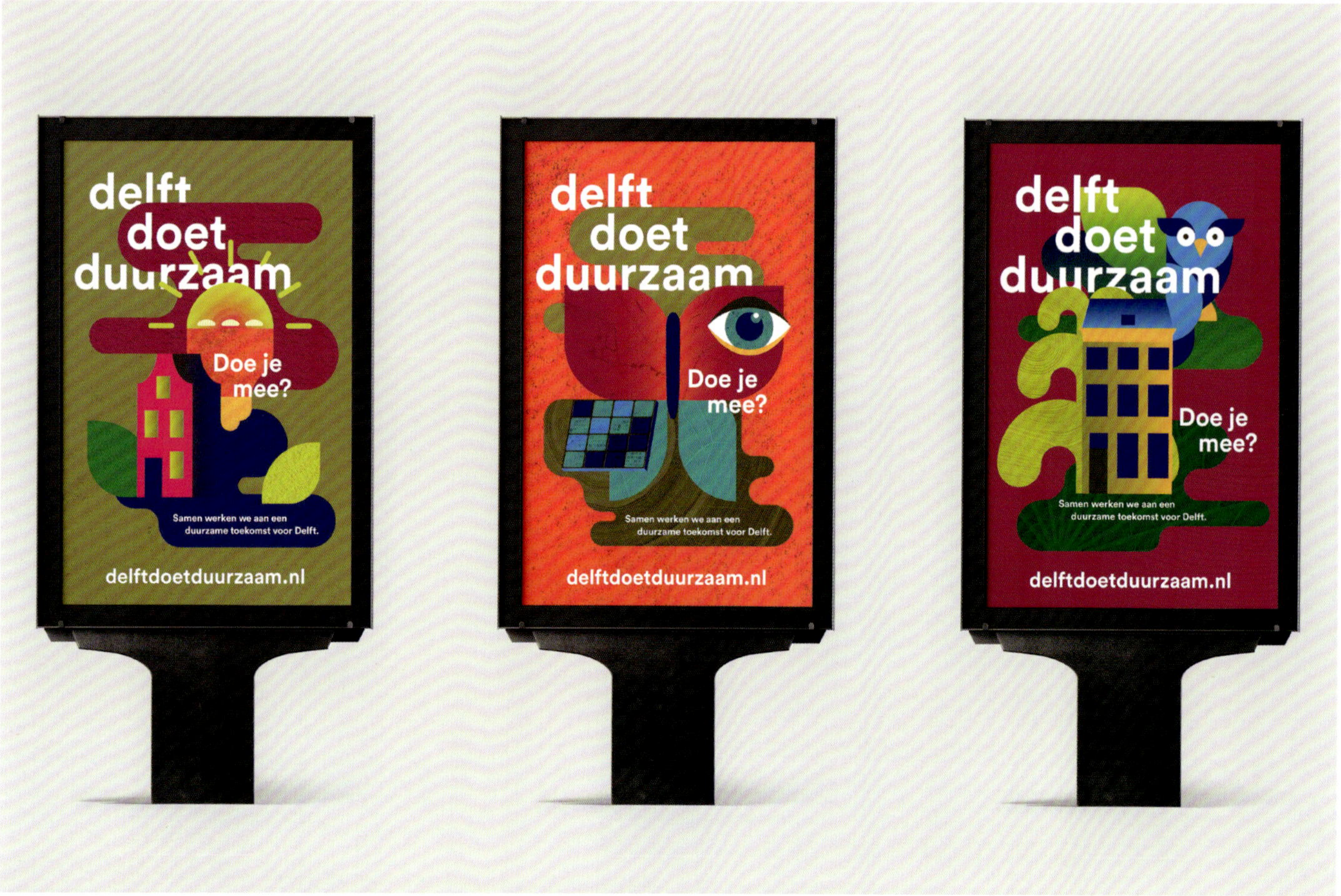

Title: Delft Doet Duurzaam | Client: Municipality of Delft | Design Firm: Things To Make and Do

DAVID SIEREN

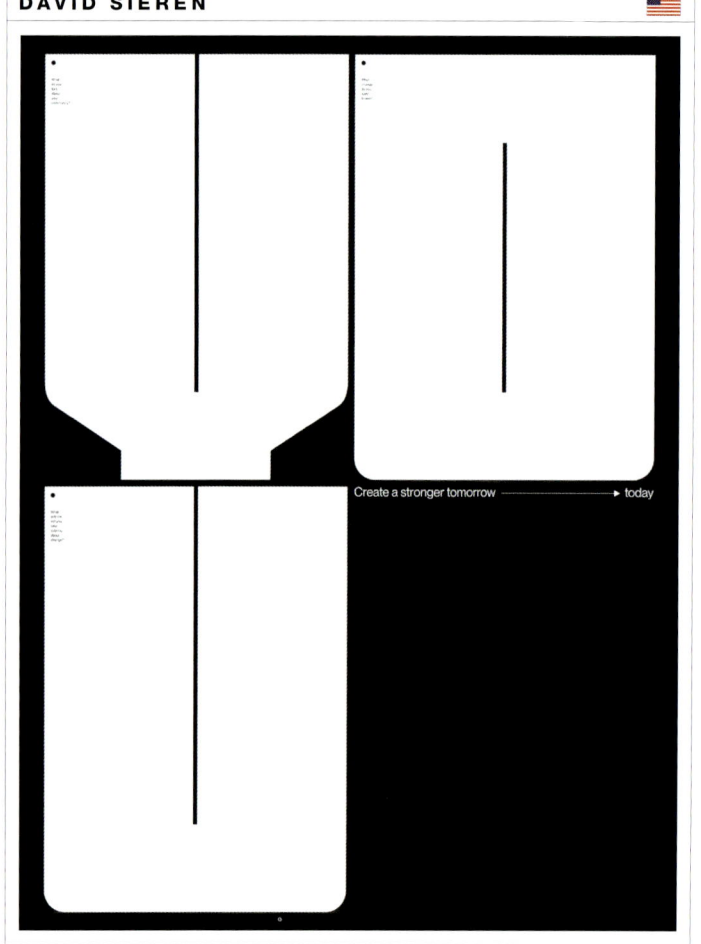

Title: You Create Tomorrow | Client: Self-initiated
Design Firm: One Design Company

RANDY CLARK

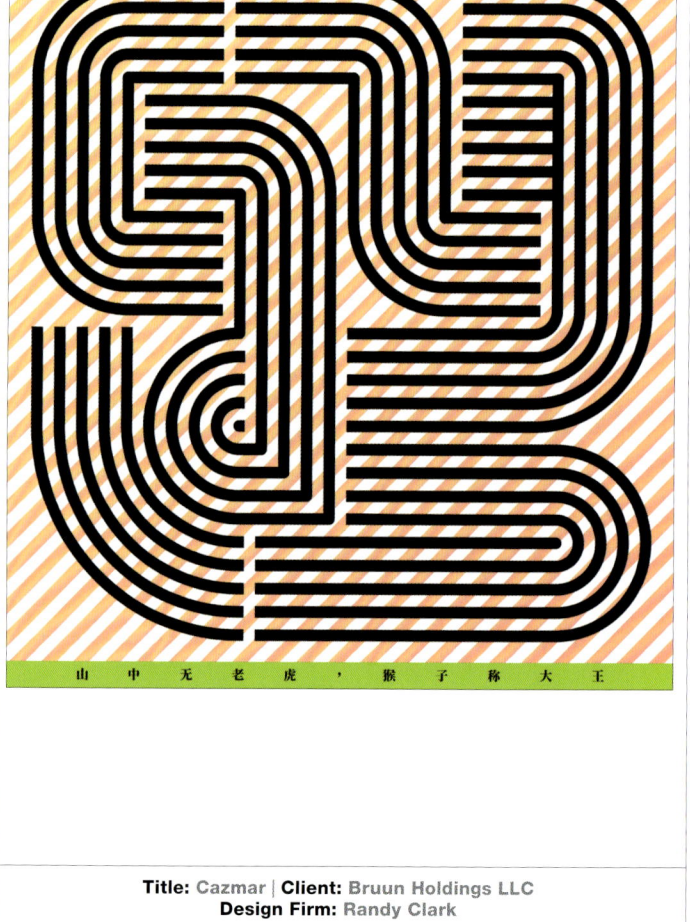

Title: Cazmar | Client: Bruun Holdings LLC
Design Firm: Randy Clark

RICH WALLACE

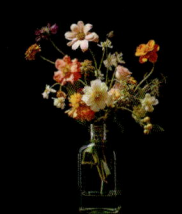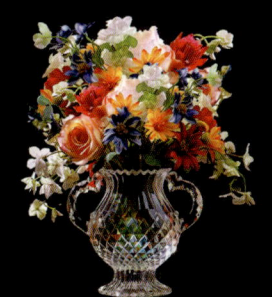

How amazing was last night?

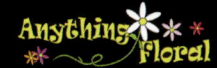

Express yourself with flowers.   **Anything Floral**

Title: Express Yourself with Flowers | Client: Anything Floral | Design Firm: Not William

RICH WALLACE

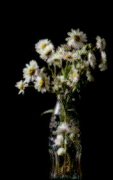 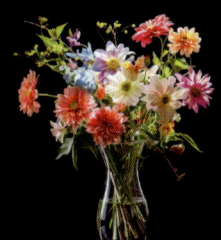 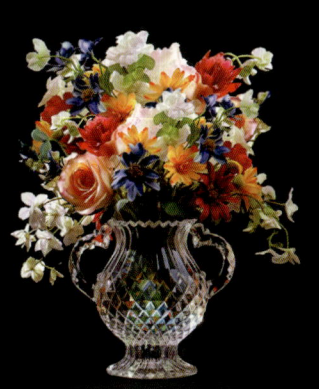

Pre Season   *Regular Season*   *Playoff Season*

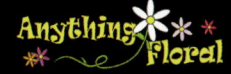

The perfect gift for any season.   **Anything Floral**

Title: Football Seasons | Client: Anything Floral | Design Firm: Not William

200 SILVER — SOCIAL & POLITICAL

BROOKS BRALEY 🇺🇸

Title: Peace Together | **Client:** International Poster Biennale for Peace: Nanjing, China | **Design Firm:** BraleyArts

RENE V. STEINER 🇨🇦

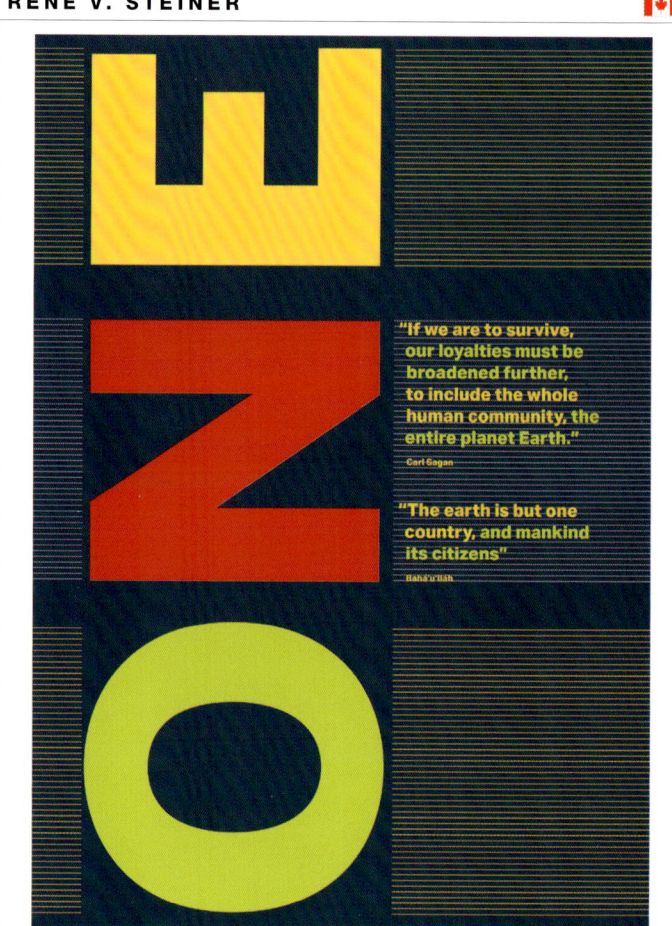

Title: One | **Client:** Self-initiated
Design Firm: Steiner Graphics

ARNAUD GHELFI 🇺🇸

Title: Drops (Cease Fire Now) | **Client:** Self-initiated
Design Firm: Atelier Starno

DERWYN GOODALL 🇨🇦

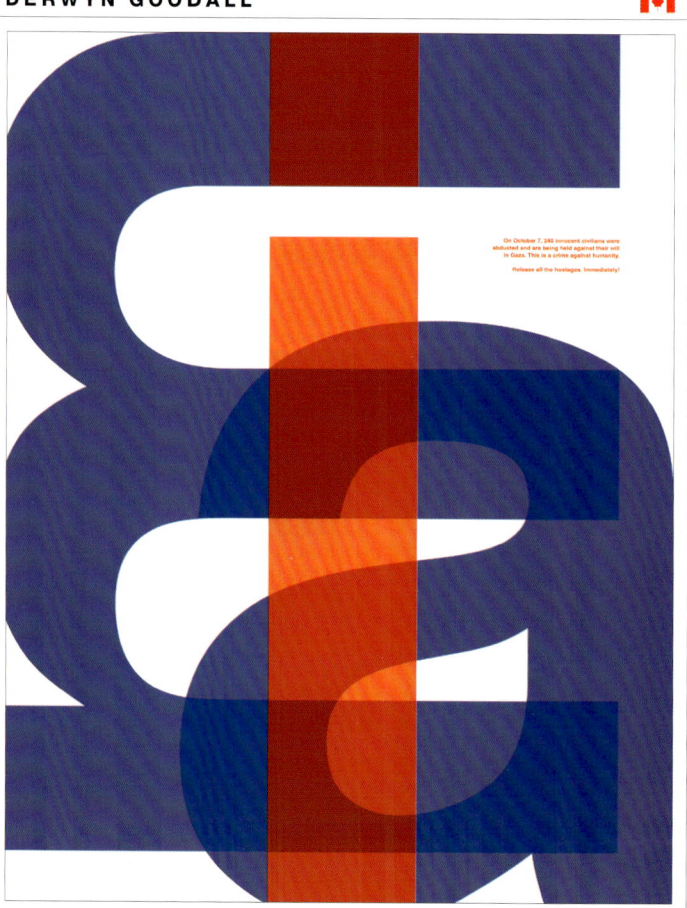

Title: M. I. A. | **Client:** Self-initiated
Design Firm: Goodall Integrated Design

201 SILVER — SOCIAL & POLITICAL

LISA WINSTANLEY

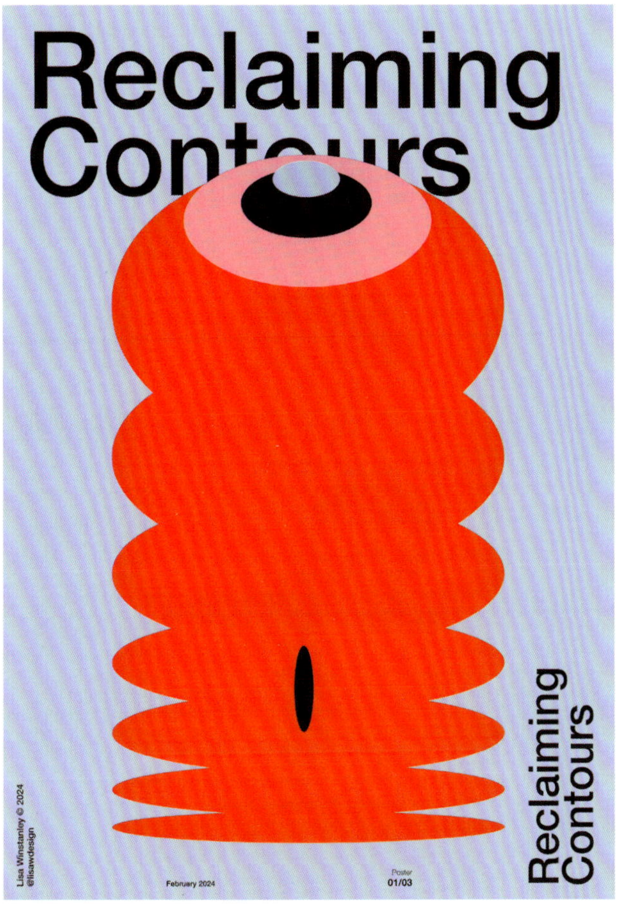

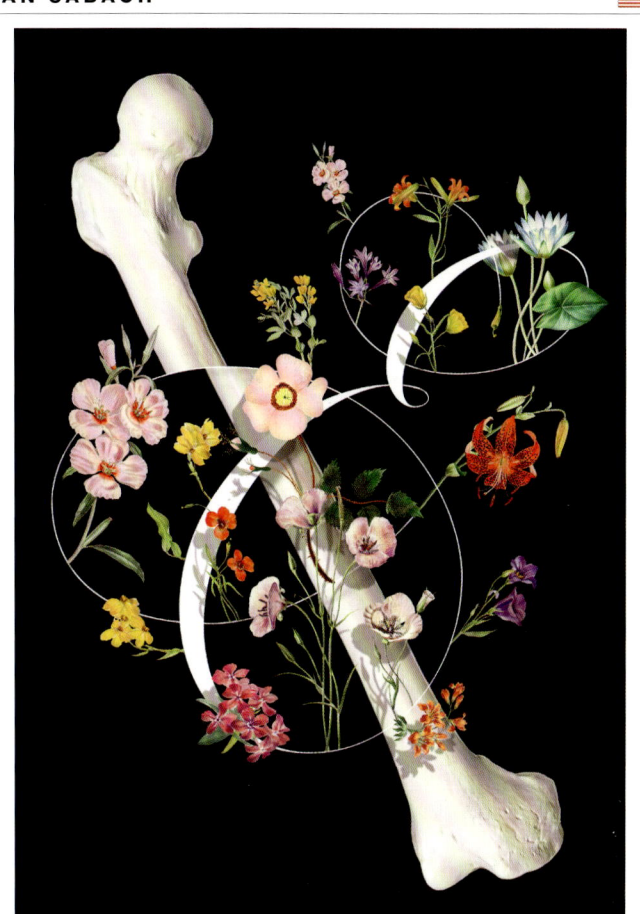

Title: Reclaiming Contours | **Client:** Nanyang Technological University School of Art, Design & Media | **Design Firm:** Lisa Winstanley Design

JAN ŠABACH

Title: Empathy | **Client:** Golden Bee Biennale
Design Firm: Code Switch

SHUICHI NOGAMI

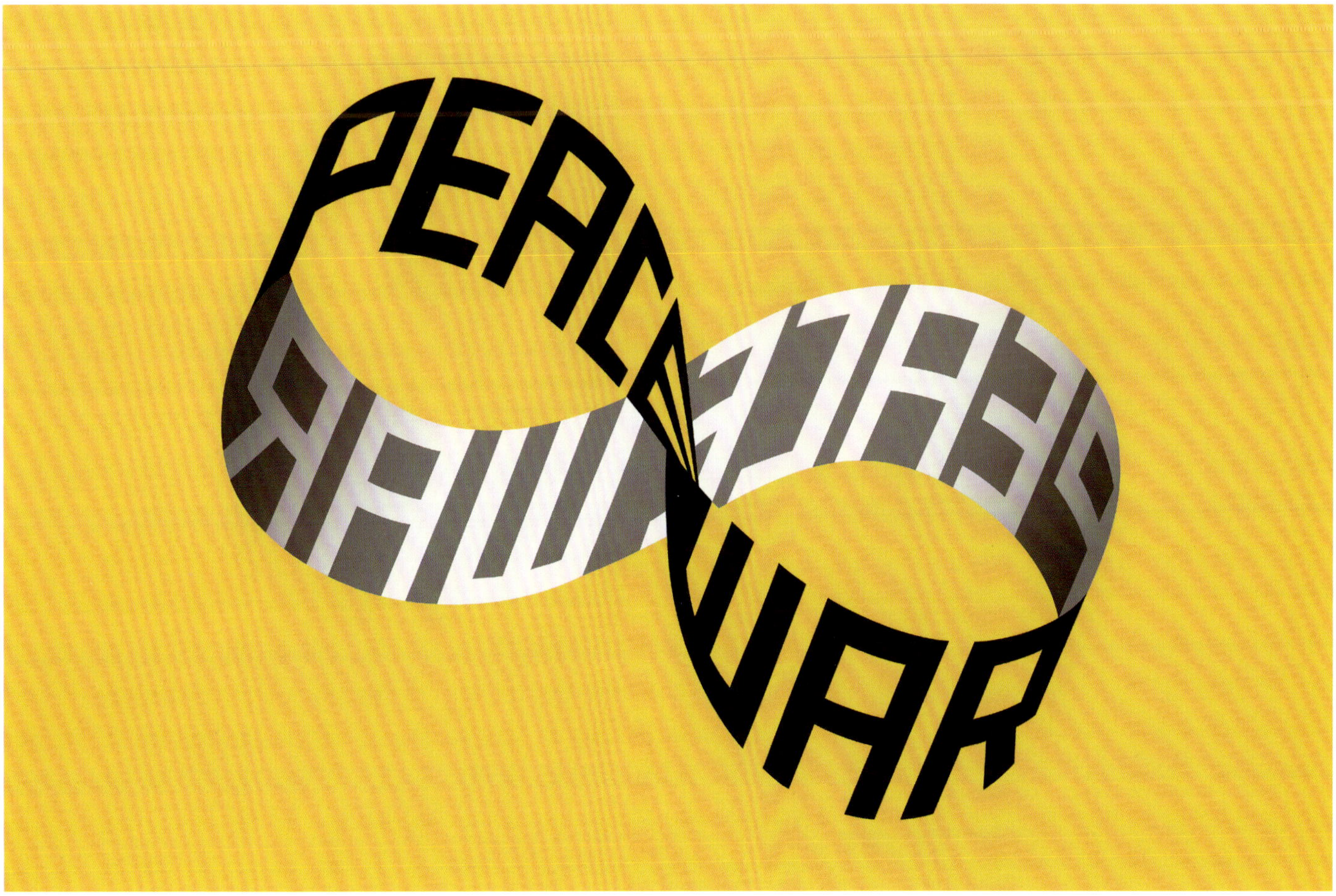

Title: War and Peace | **Client:** Self-initiated | **Design Firm:** Nogami Design Office

202 SILVER — SOCIAL & POLITICAL

DERWYN GOODALL 🇨🇦

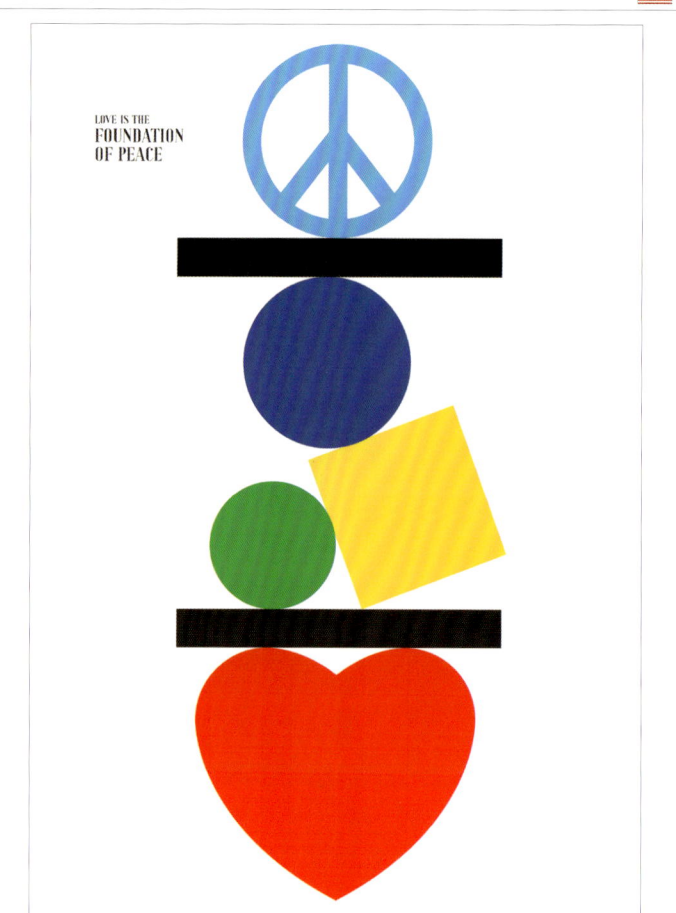

Title: Mariupol: 86 Days of Strength | **Client:** The 4th Block 12th International Triennial | **Design Firm:** Goodall Integrated Design

JOHN O'NEILL 🇺🇸

Title: Love is the Foundation of Peace | **Client:** Self-initiated
Design Firm: John O'Neill

STUDIO INTERNATIONAL 🇭🇷

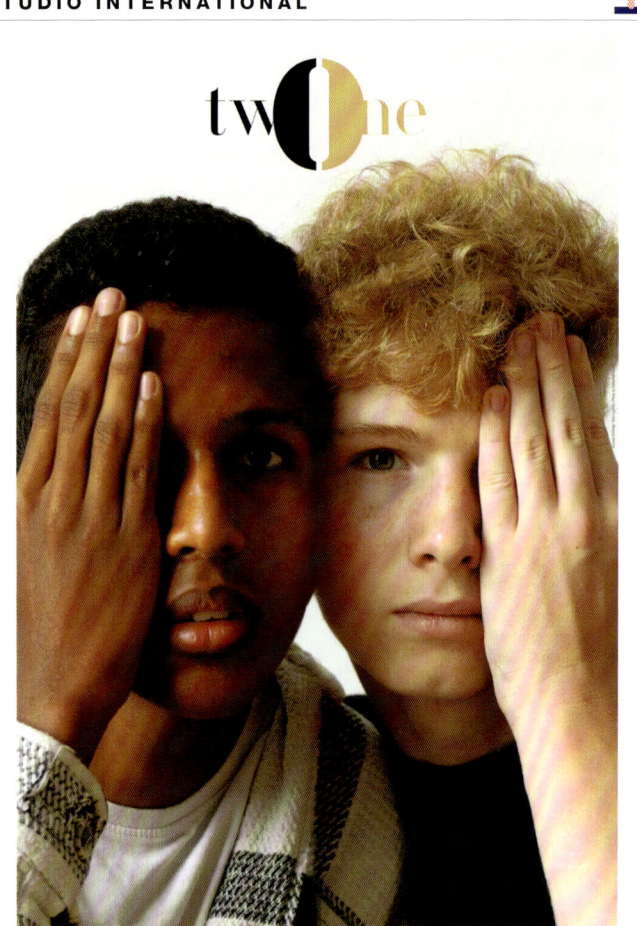

Title: TWO / ONE | **Client:** UNCHR Croatia
Design Firm: STUDIO INTERNATIONAL

COCO CERRELLA 🇦🇷

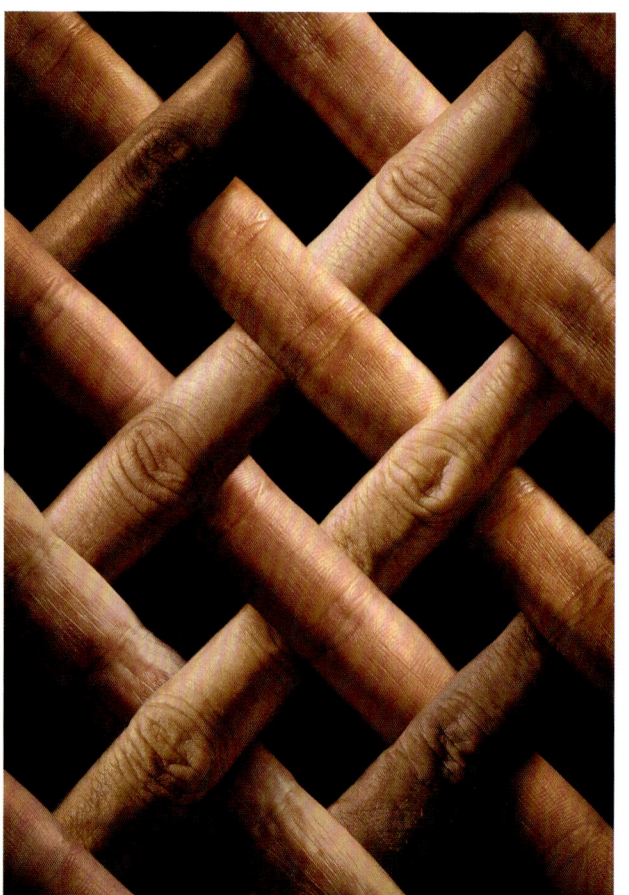

Title: Human Pastafrola (Civilitas) | **Client:** Posters Without Borders
Design Firm: Coco Cerrella

203 SILVER — SOCIAL & POLITICAL

TOYOTSUGU ITOH 🇯🇵

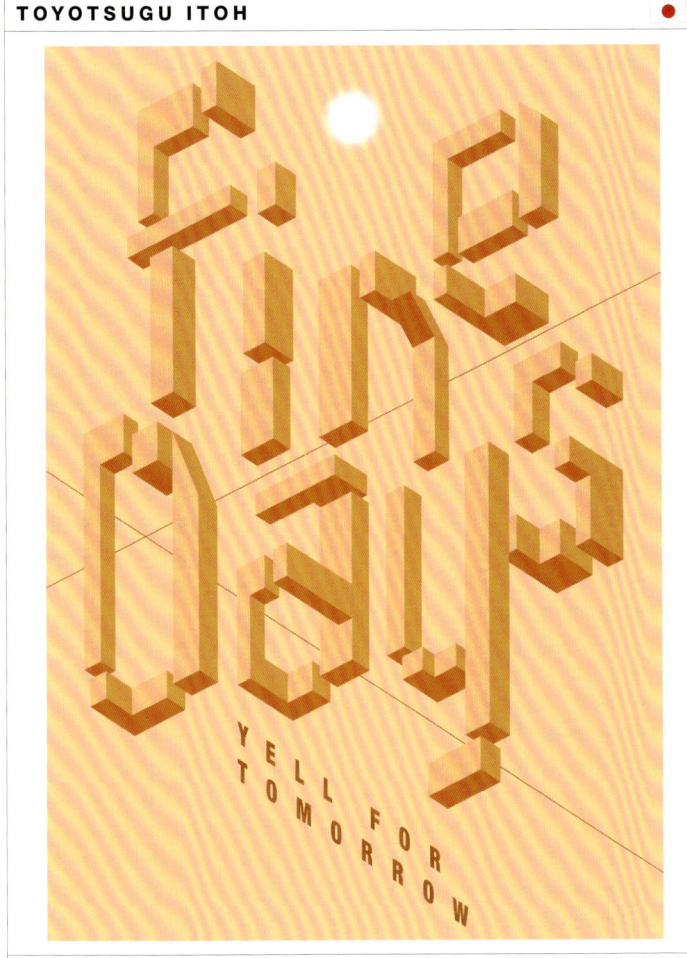

Title: Fine Days | **Client:** Japan Graphic Design Association Inc.
Design Firm: Toyotsugu Itoh Design Office

DERWYN GOODALL 🇨🇦

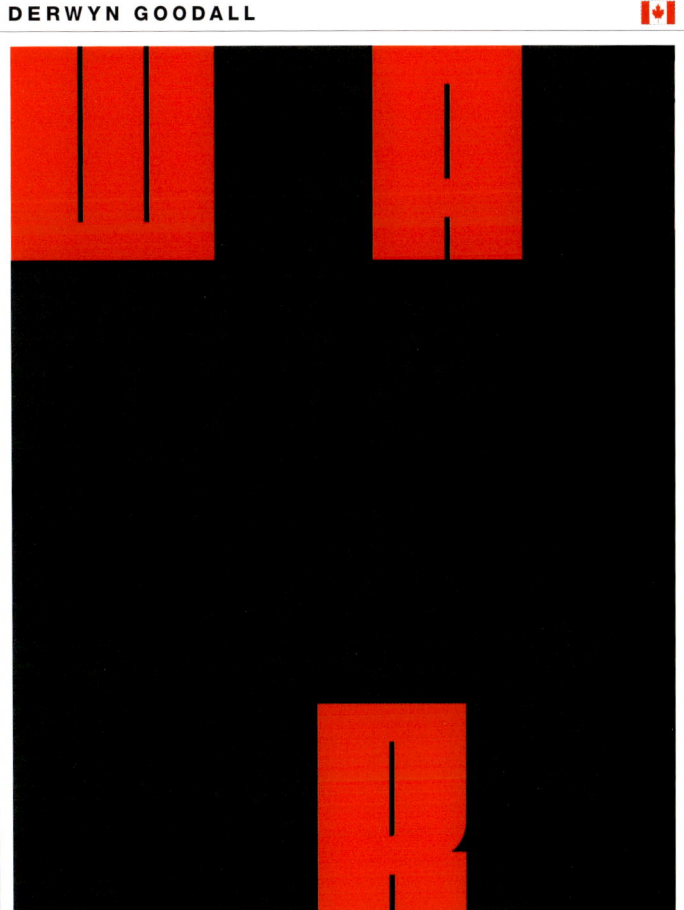

Title: War, What is It Good For? | **Client:** Self-initiated
Design Firm: Goodall Integrated Design

BROOKS BRALEY 🇺🇸

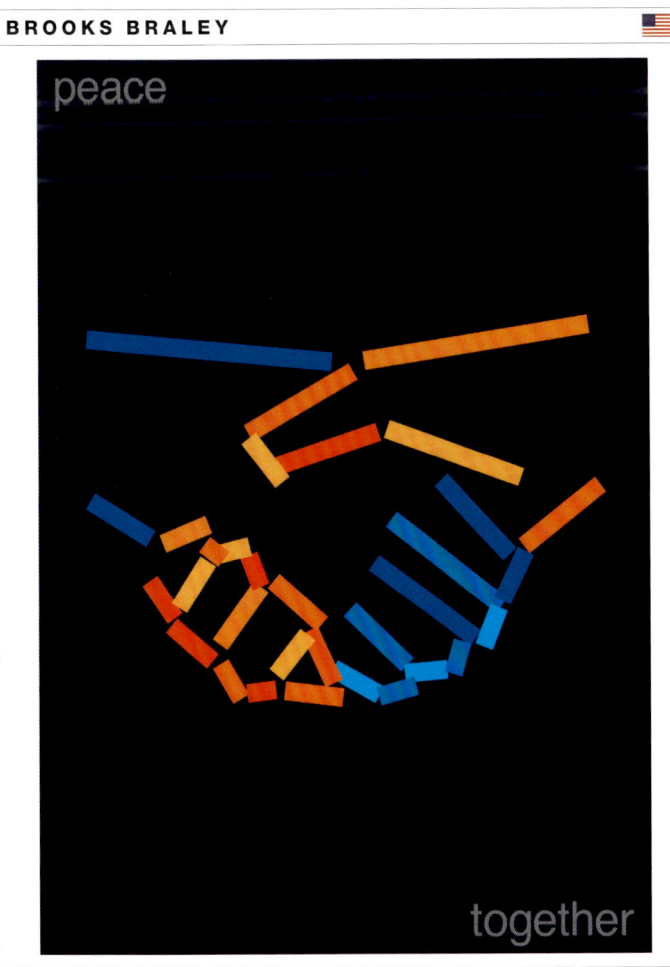

Title: Peace Hands | **Client:** International Poster Biennale for Peace: Nanjing, China | **Design Firm:** BraleyArts

WOLFGANG GAST 🇩🇪

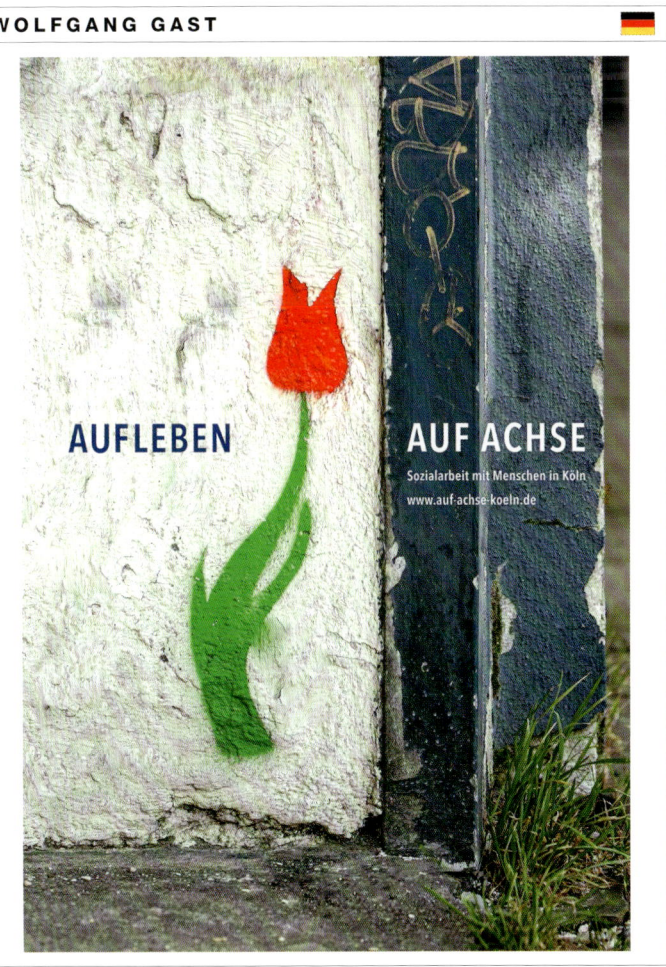

Title: AUFLEBEN | **Client:** AUF ACHSE/KJSH e.V.
Design Firm: Gastdesign

204 SILVER — SOCIAL & POLITICAL

R.P. BISSLAND

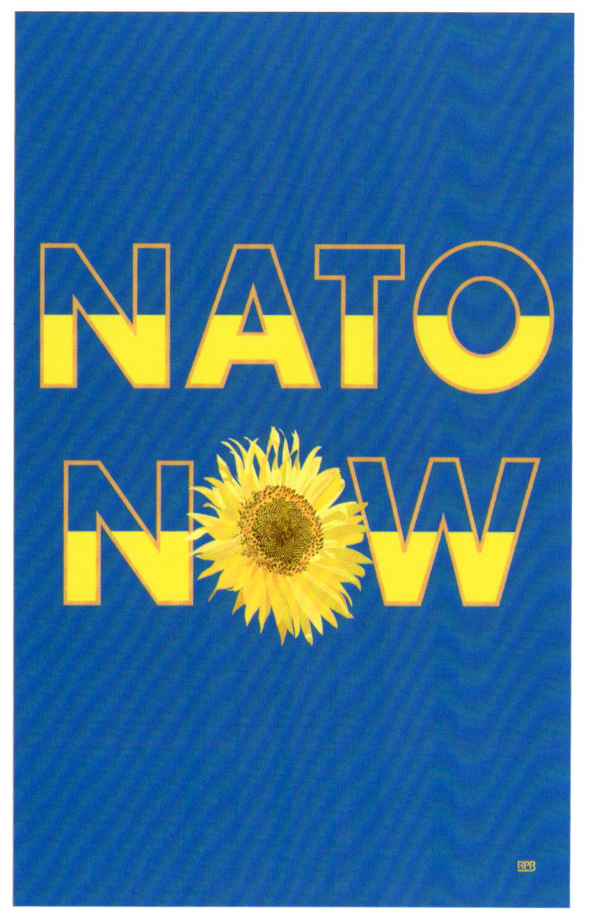

Title: Nato Now | **Client:** Self-initiated
Design Firm: Design SubTerra

CARMIT MAKLER HALLER, CARMIT DESIGN STUDIO

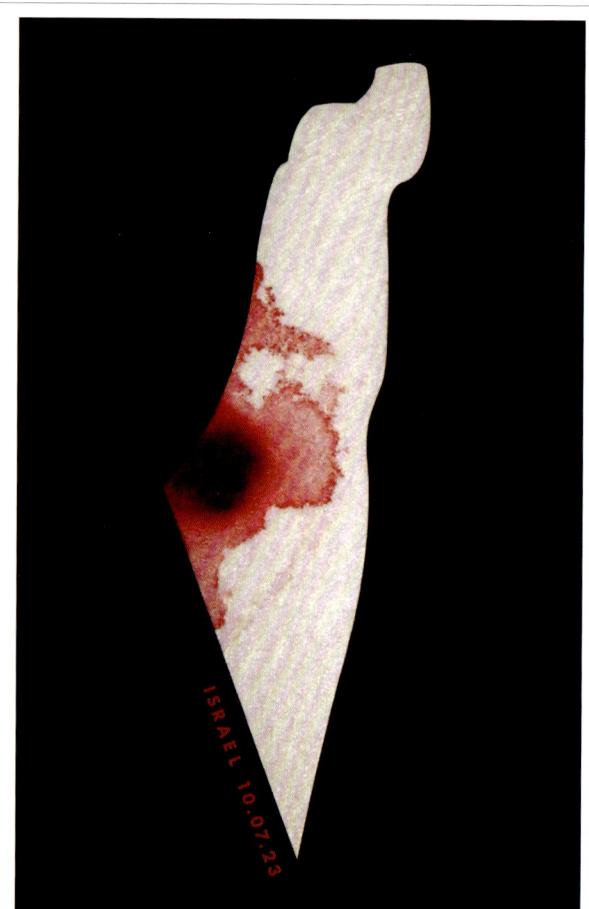

Title: Israel 10.7.2023 | **Client:** Stop War Poster Exhibition
Design Firm: Carmit Design Studio

MAI KATO

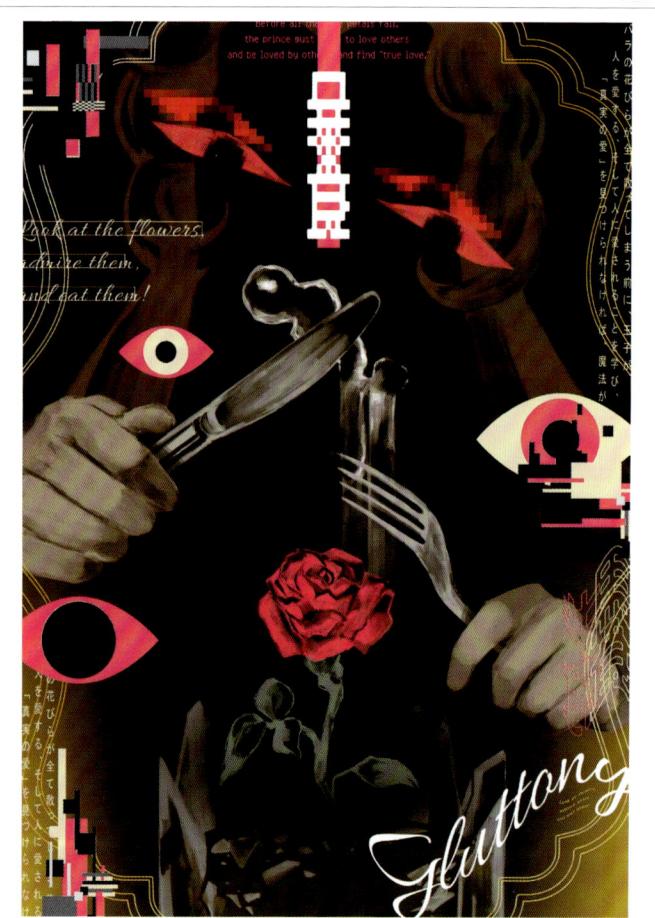

Title: Glutton | **Client:** Self-initiated
Design Firm: PEACE Inc.

YUQIN NI

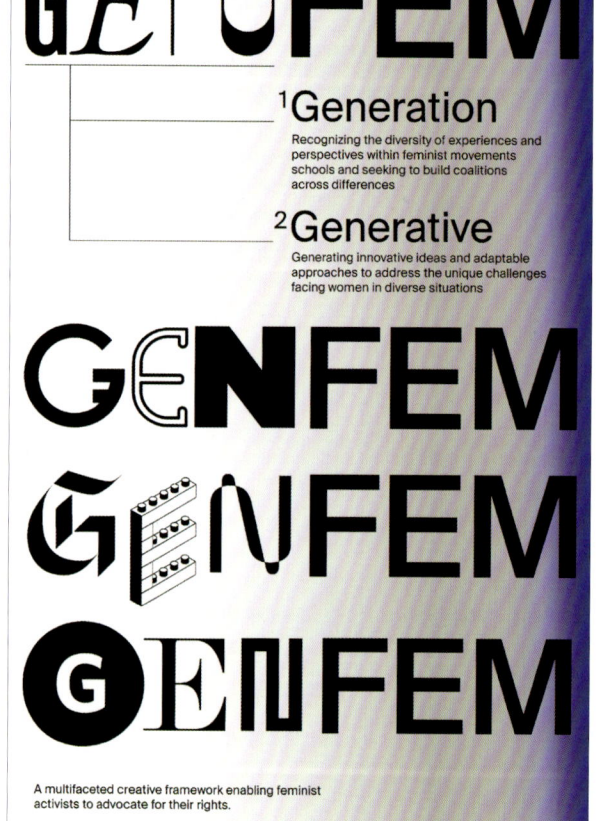

Title: GENFEM Campaign | **Client:** Bizarrely Basic
Design Firm: Studio XXY

CARMIT MAKLER HALLER, CARMIT DESIGN STUDIO

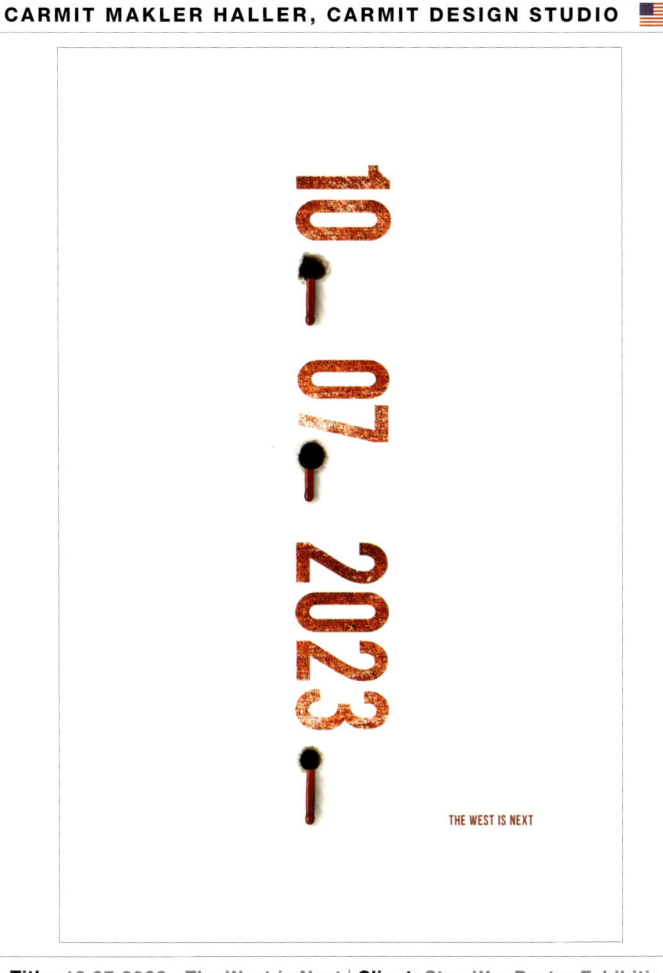

Title: 10.07.2023—The West is Next | **Client:** Stop War Poster Exhibition
Design Firm: Carmit Design Studio

MARLENA BUCZEK SMITH

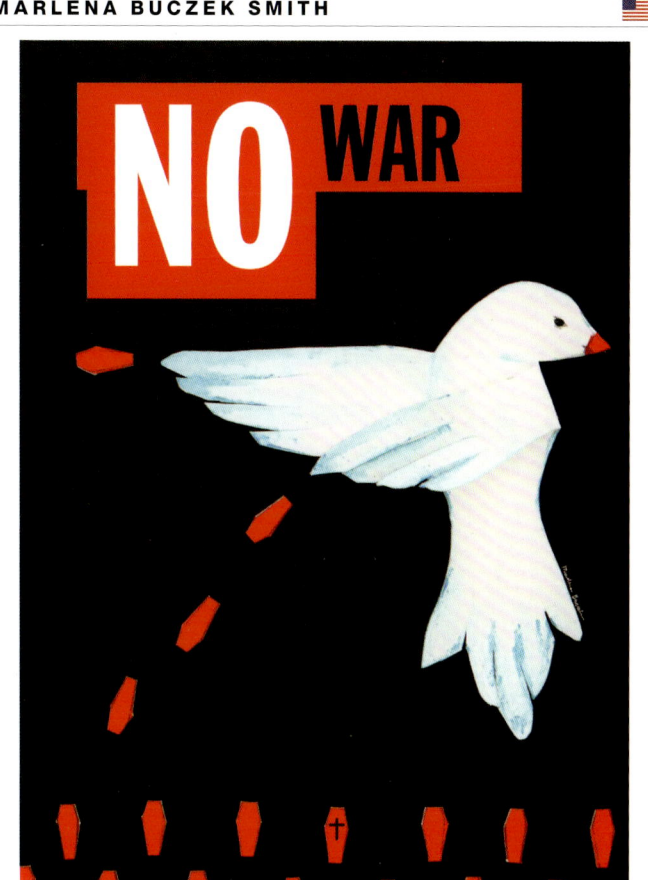

Title: No War | **Client:** Self-initiated
Design Firm: Marlena Buczek Smith

JACK HARRIS

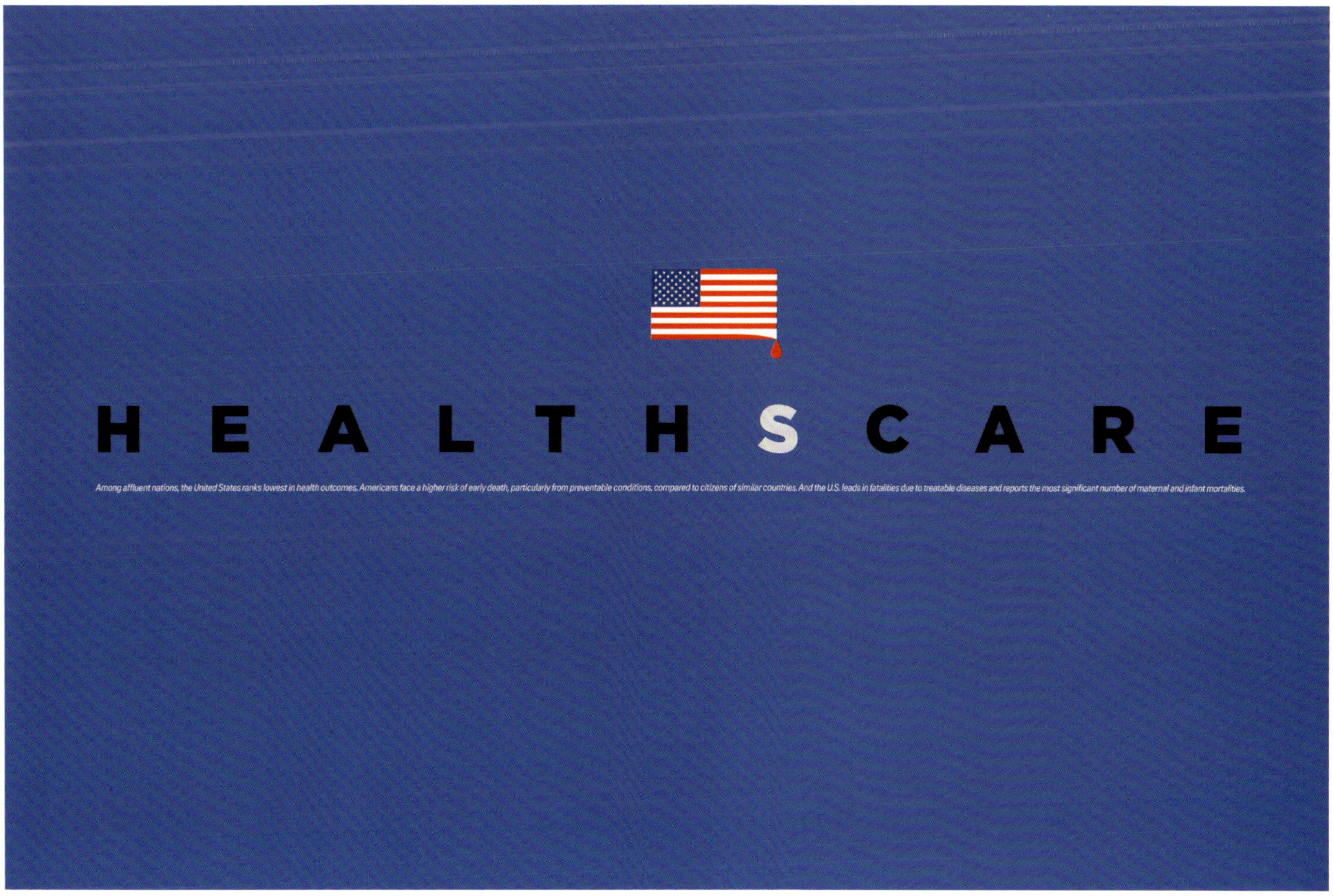

Title: Healthscare | **Client:** Self-initiated | **Design Firm:** Jack Harris

SOCIAL & POLITICAL

HENRY BECKER 🇺🇸
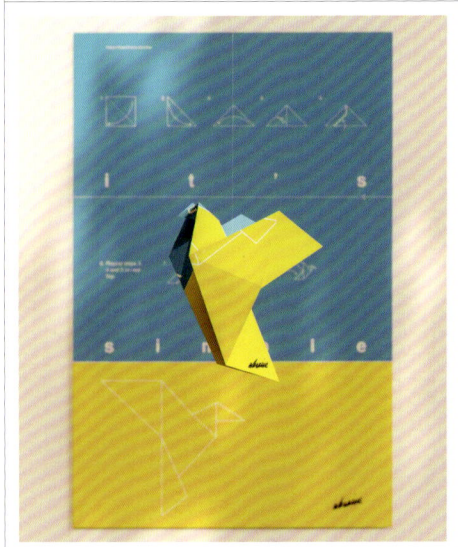
Title: Fold for Peace: Ukraine's One Simple Wish
Client: University of Utah
Design Firm: Becker Studio

CHRIS CORNEAL 🇺🇸
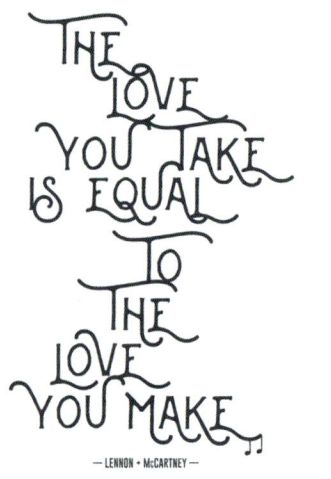
Title: The Love You Take/Make
Client: Self-initiated
Design Firm: Symbiotic Solutions

ROGER WONG 🇺🇸
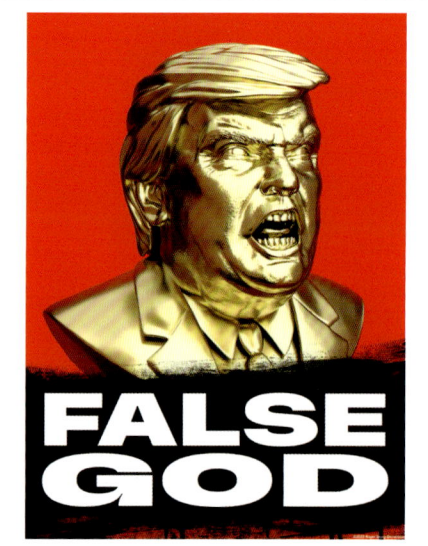
Title: Trump: False God
Client: Self-initiated
Design Firm: Wong.Digital

NORIYUKI KASAI 🇯🇵
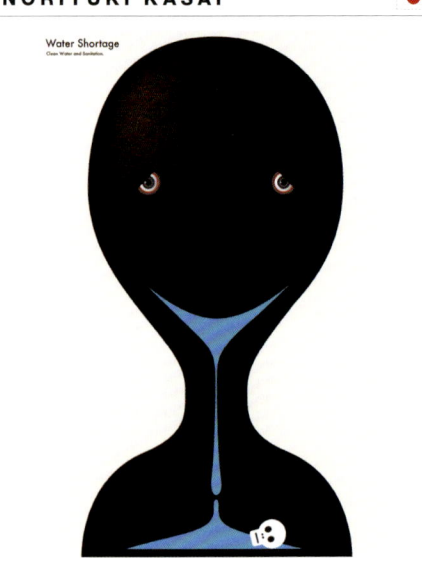
Title: Water Shortage
Client: Graphic Communication Laboratory
Design Firm: Noriyuki Kasai

RANDY CLARK 🇨🇳
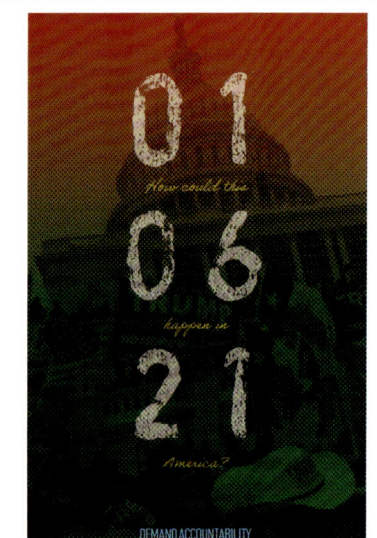
Title: Demand Accountability
Client: Self-initiated
Design Firm: Randy Clark

MEAGHAN A. DEE 🇺🇸
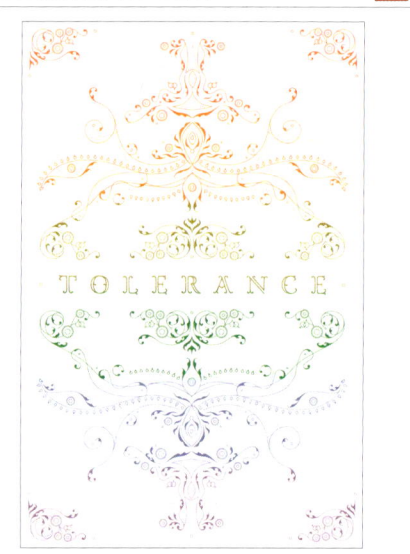
Title: Tolerance
Client: Mirko Ilic Corp.
Design Firm: Meaghan A. Dee

JACK HARRIS 🇺🇸
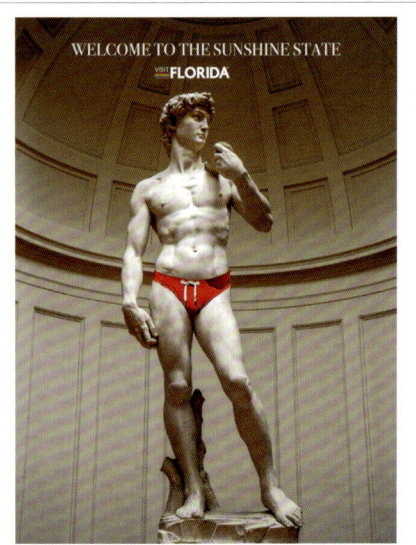
Title: Welcome to the Sunshine State
Client: Self-initiated
Design Firm: Jack Harris

ARNAUD GHELFI 🇺🇸
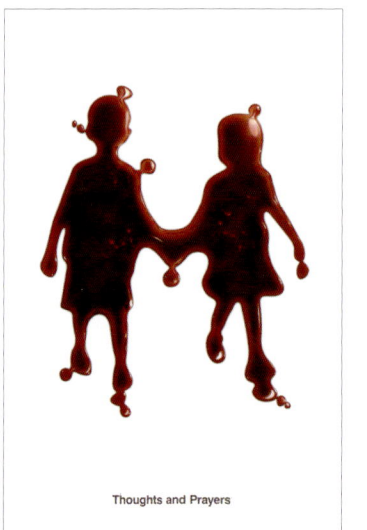
Title: Thoughts and Prayers
Client: Self-initiated
Design Firm: Atelier Starno

FERNANDO PALOMINO 🇺🇸
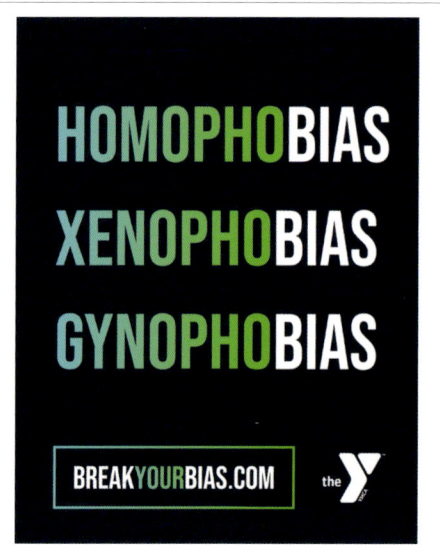
Title: Break Your Bias
Client: YMCA of the North
Design Firm: Preston Spire

207 SILVER — SOCIAL & POLITICAL

TOYOTSUGU ITOH

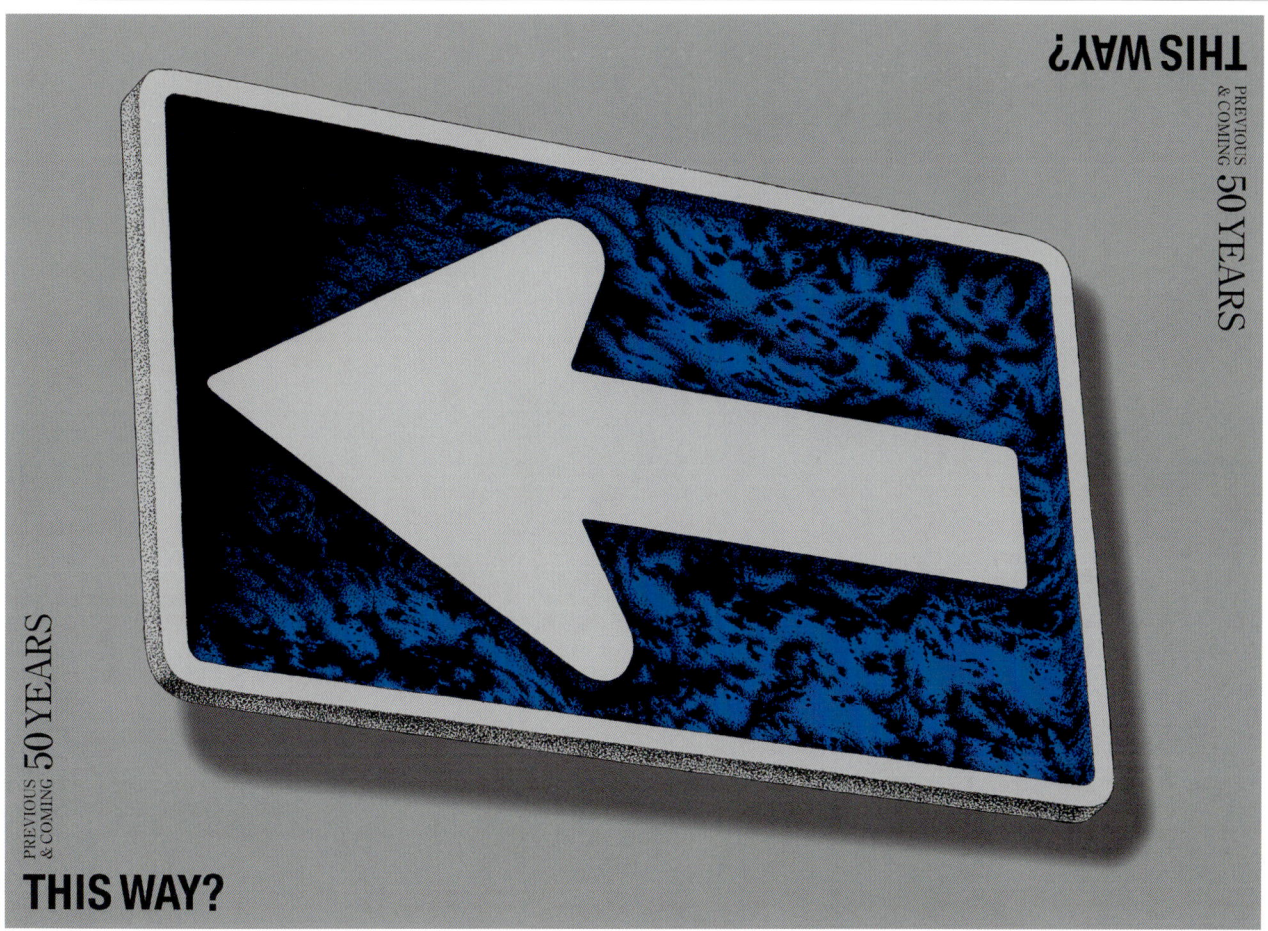

Title: THIS WAY? | Client: Chubu Creators Club | Design Firm: Toyotsugu Itoh Design Office

STEVE JAMES

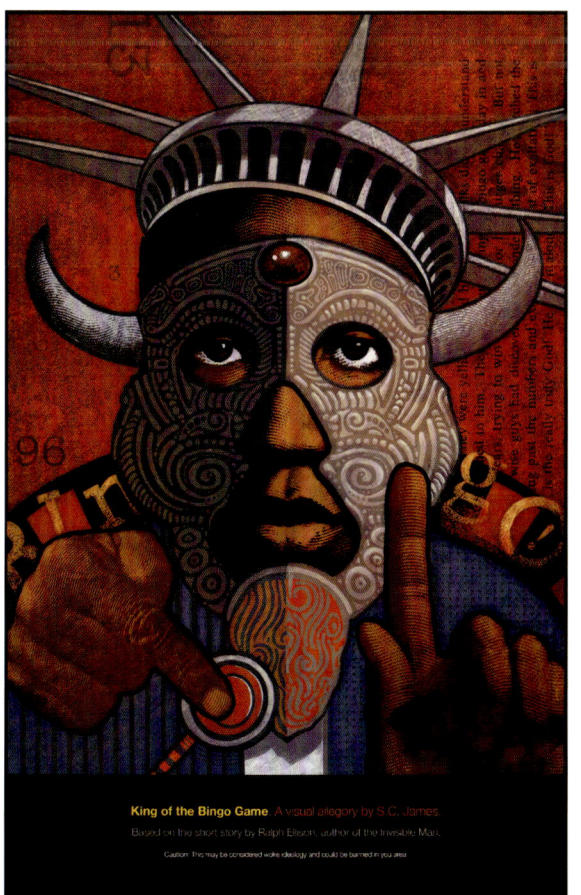

Title: King of the Bingo Game | Client: Self-initiated
Design Firm: The Union Design Company

JEFF GATES

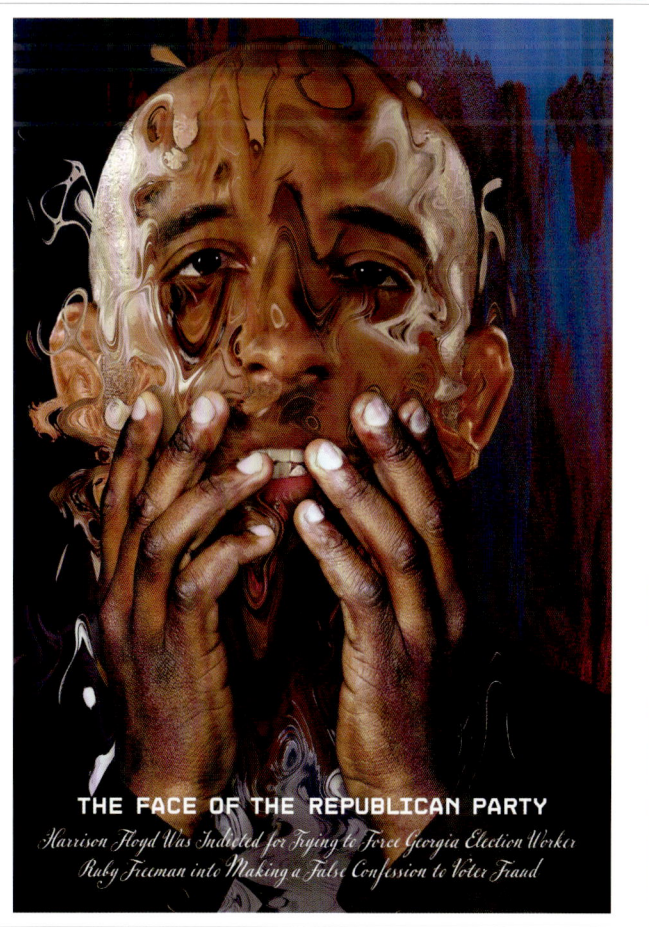

Title: Faces of the Republican Party | Client: Self-initiated
Design Firm: Chamomile Tea Party

ERIC BOELTS

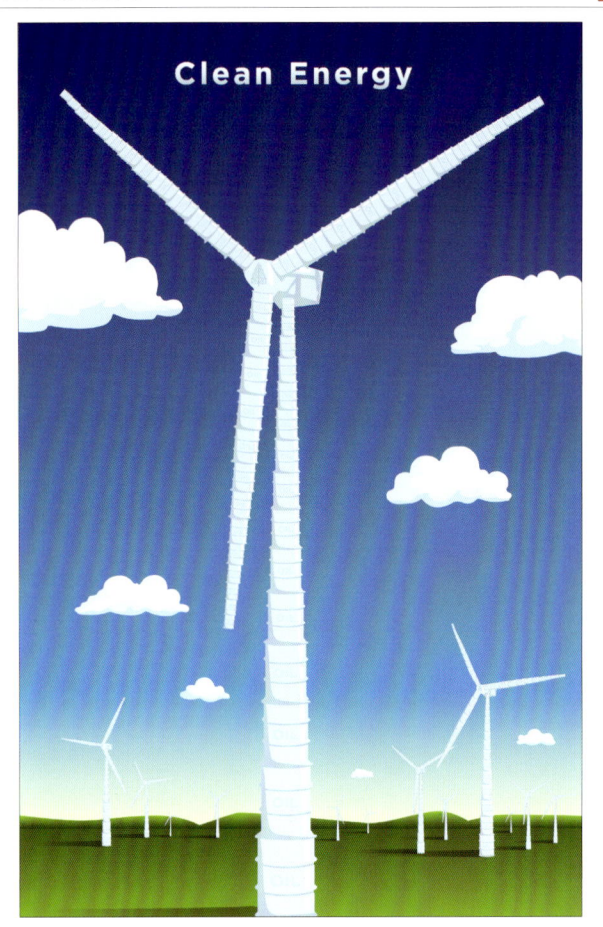

Title: Clean Energy | **Clients:** Seoul, Korea Design Association
Design Firm: Brain Bolts

MARLENA BUCZEK SMITH

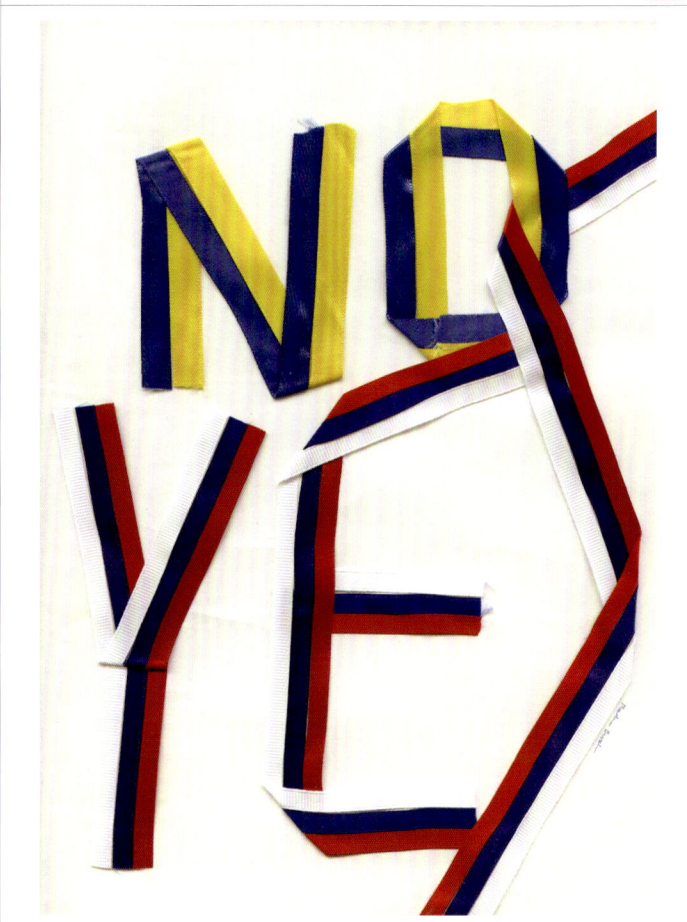

Title: No Yes | **Client:** Self-initiated
Design Firm: Marlena Buczek Smith

WESAM MAZHAR HADDAD

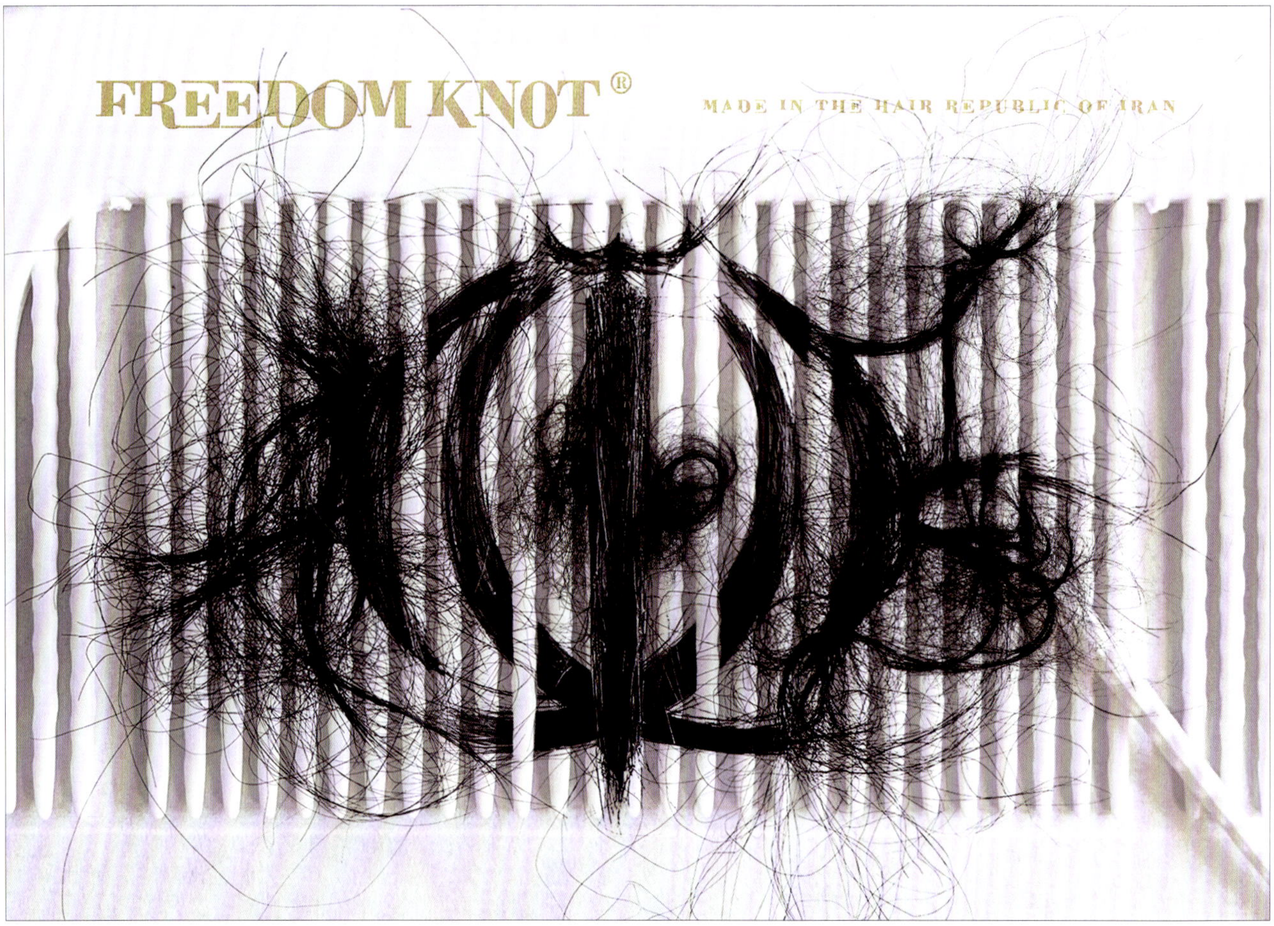

Title: Freedom Knot | **Client:** Woman, Life, Freedom | **Design Firm:** Wesam Mazhar Haddad

FERNANDO PALOMINO

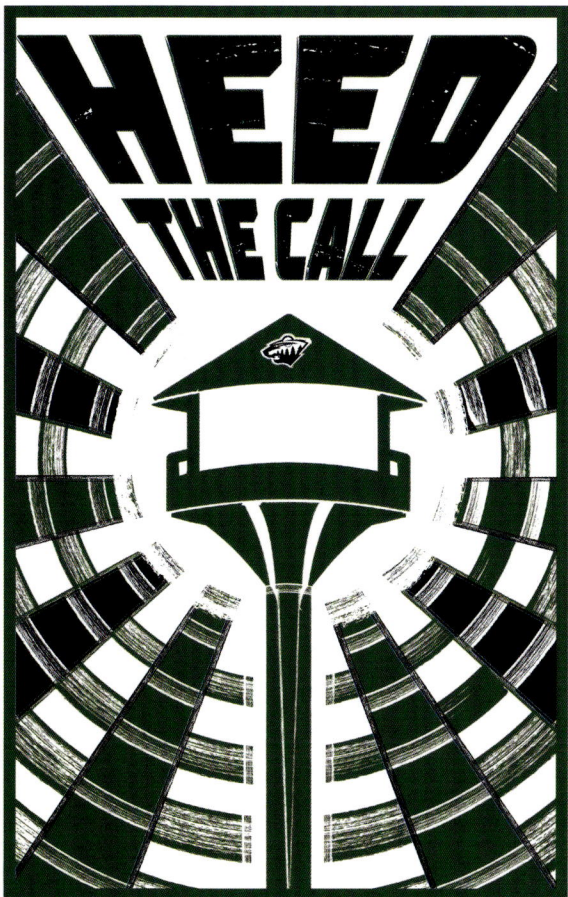

Title: Heed the Call | **Client:** Minnesota Wild
Design Firm: Preston Spire

SÉRGIO DUARTE

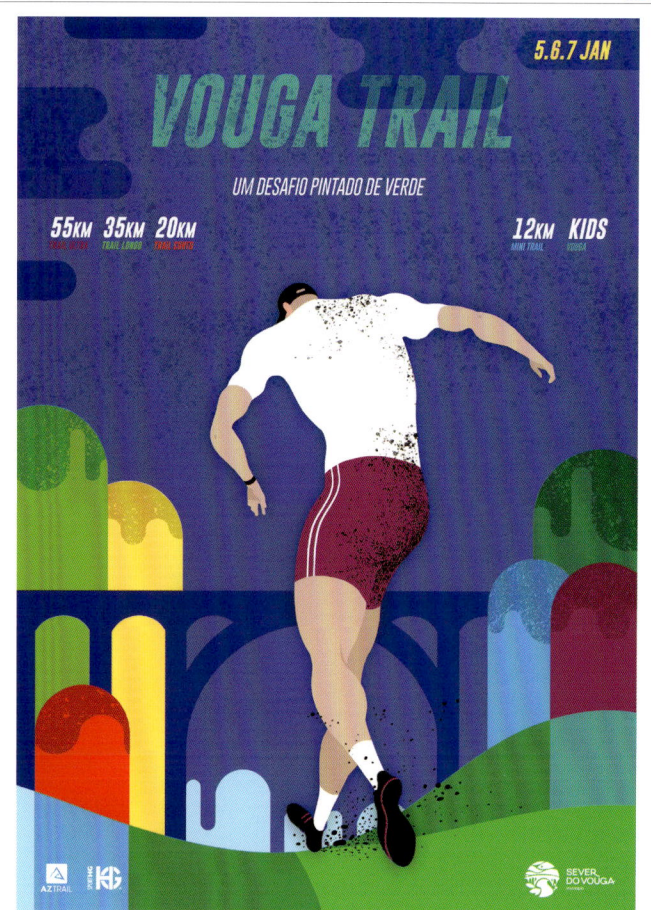

Title: Vouga Trail | **Client:** Câmara Municipal de Sever do Vouga
Design Firm: Duas Faces Design

RICH WALLACE

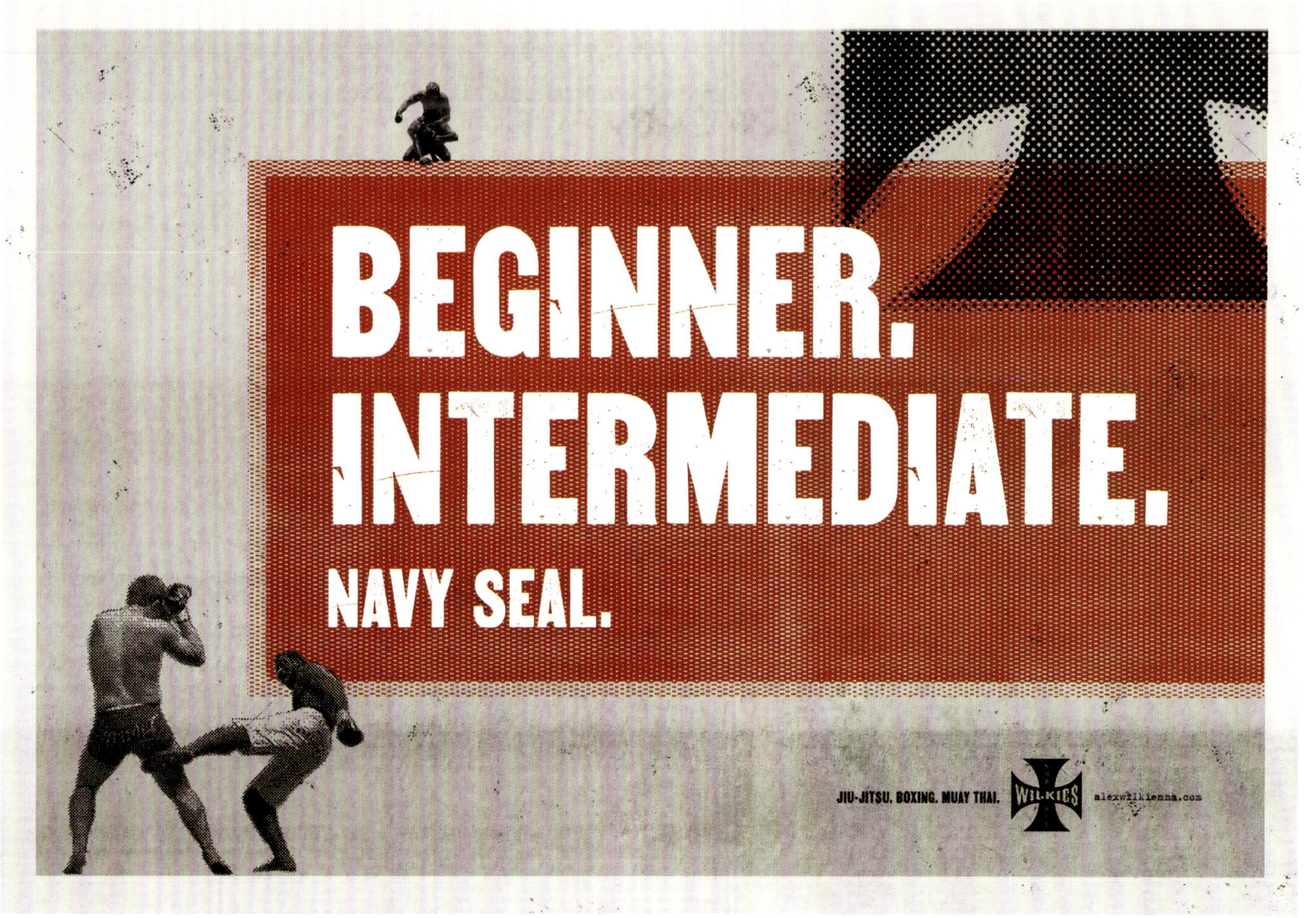

Title: Train Like Your Life Depends on It | **Client:** Wilkies Martial Arts | **Design Firm:** Not William

210 SILVER — **SPORTS**

GRANT GUNDERSON 🇺🇸

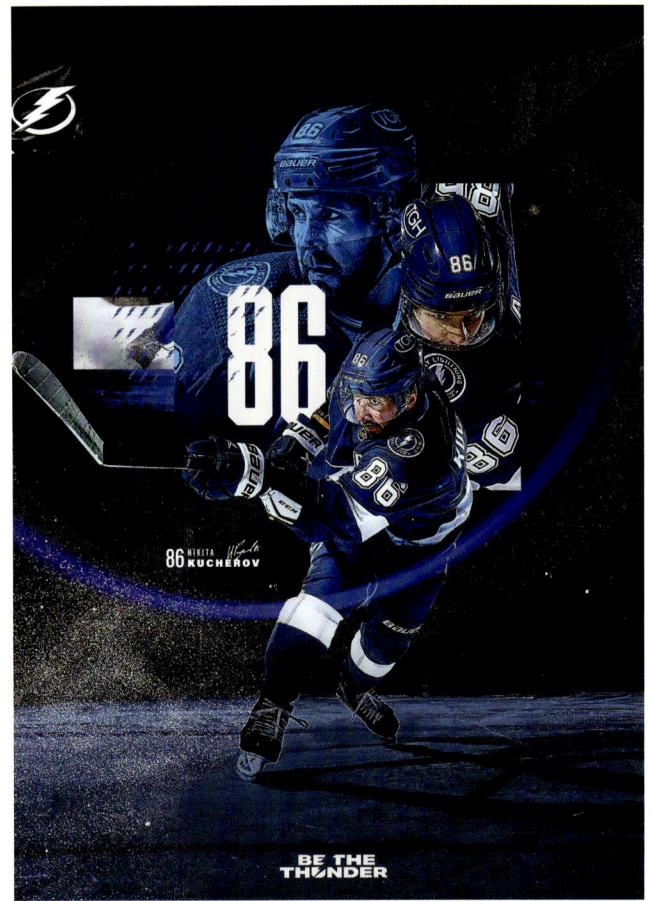

Title: 2023-24 Season Branding | **Client:** Tampa Bay Lightning
Design Firm: Dunn&Co.

CASEY STOKES 🇺🇸

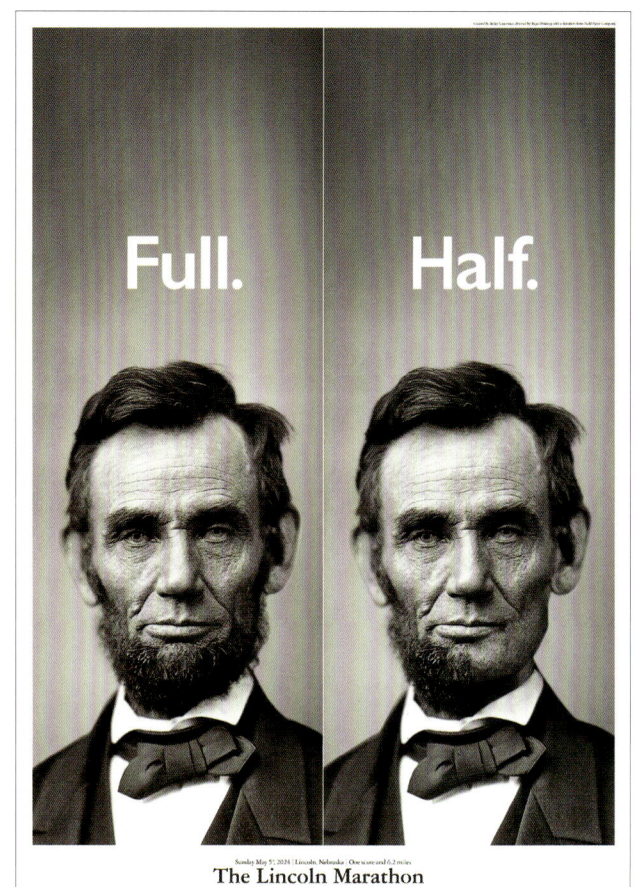

Title: Full. Half. | **Client:** Lincoln Track Club
Design Firm: Bailey Lauerman

JOVANEY HOLLINGSWORTH 🇺🇸

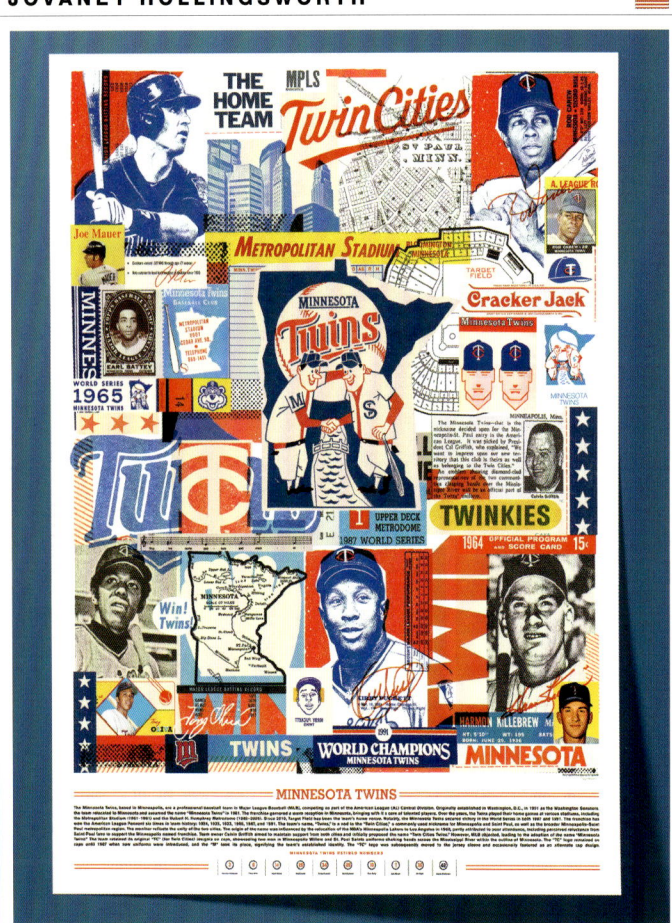

Title: Minnesota Twins History Poster | **Client:** Minnesota Twins
Design Firm: DLR Group

CRISTIANA RODRIGUES 🇵🇹

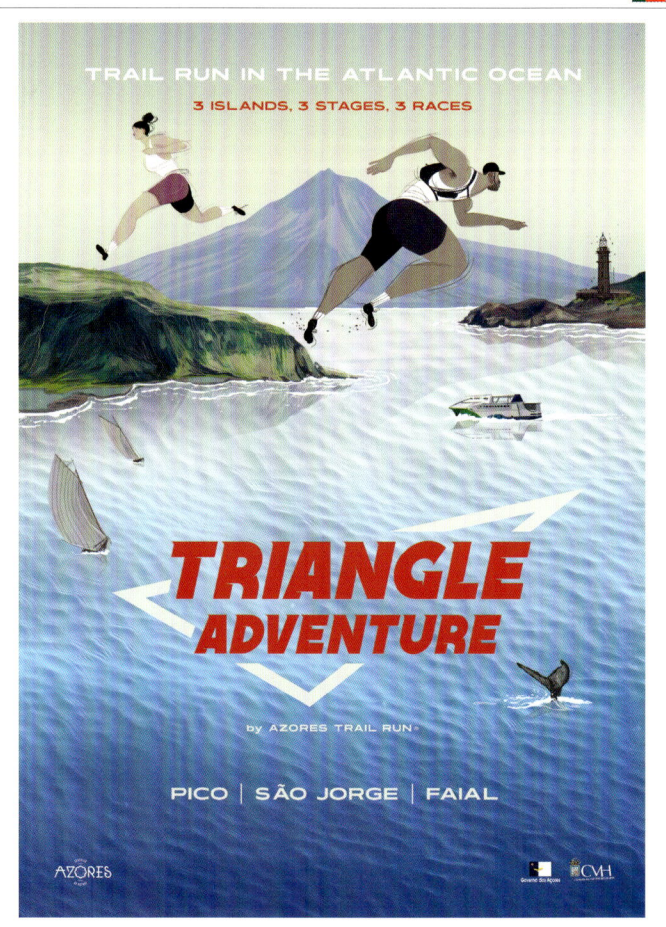

Title: Triangle Adventure | **Client:** Azores Trail Run
Design Firm: Duas Faces Design

211 SILVER　　　　　　　　　　　　　　　　　　　　　　　　　　　　　　　TELEVISION

LEROY & ROSE

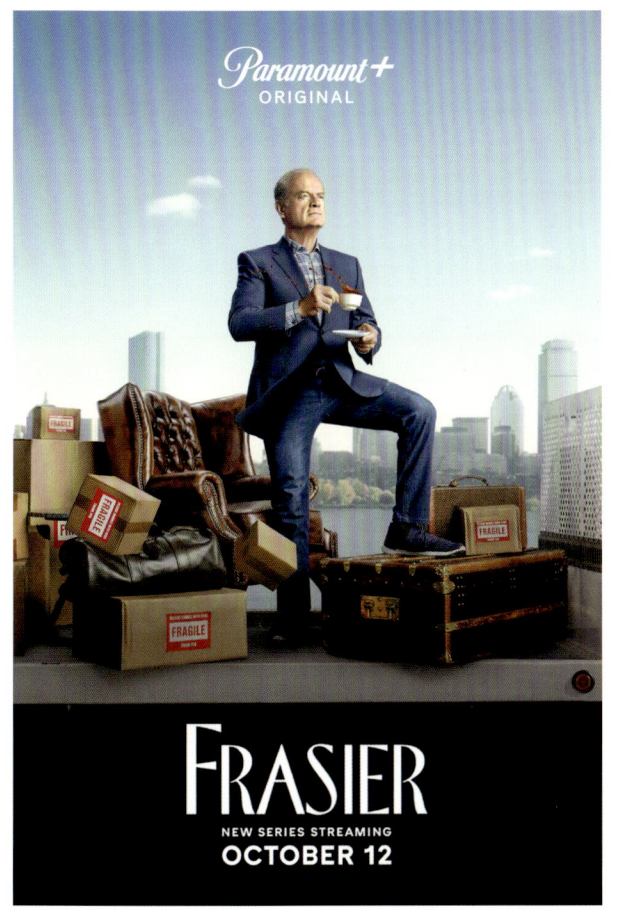

Title: Frasier: Moving Truck | Client: Paramount+
Design Firm: Leroy & Rose

LEROY & ROSE

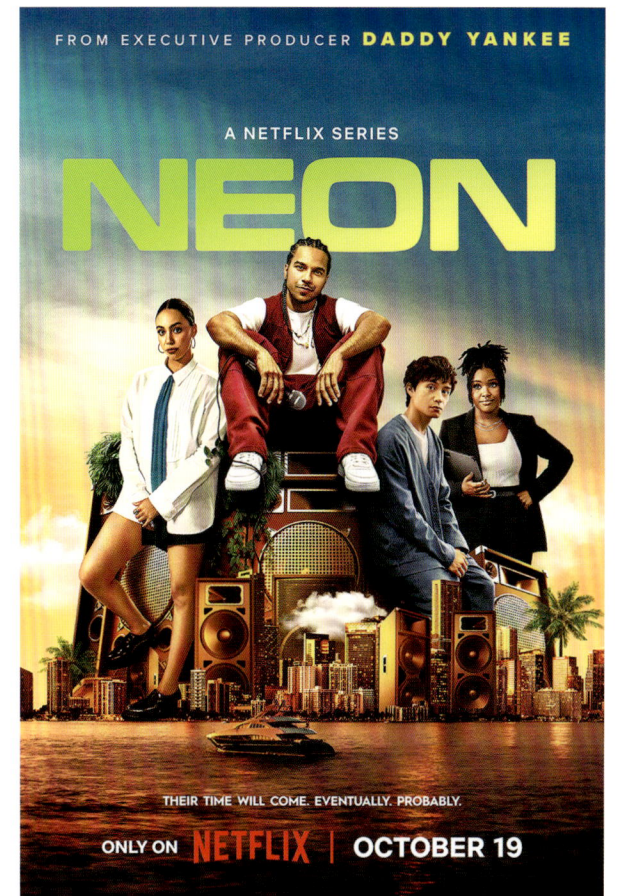

Title: Neon | Client: Netflix
Design Firm: Leroy & Rose

LEROY & ROSE

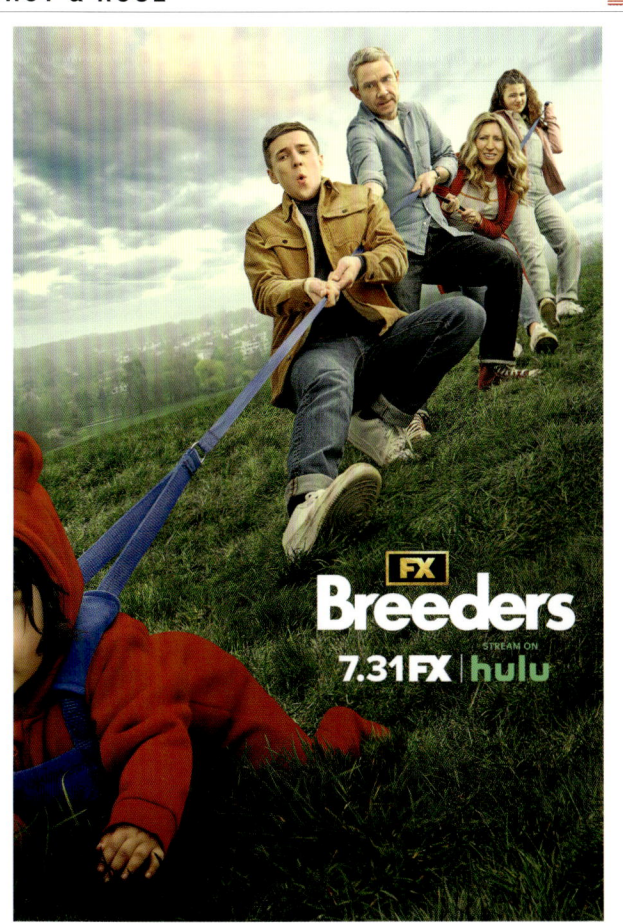

Title: Breeders: Season 4 | Client: FX
Design Firm: Leroy & Rose

LOUIS PERCIVAL

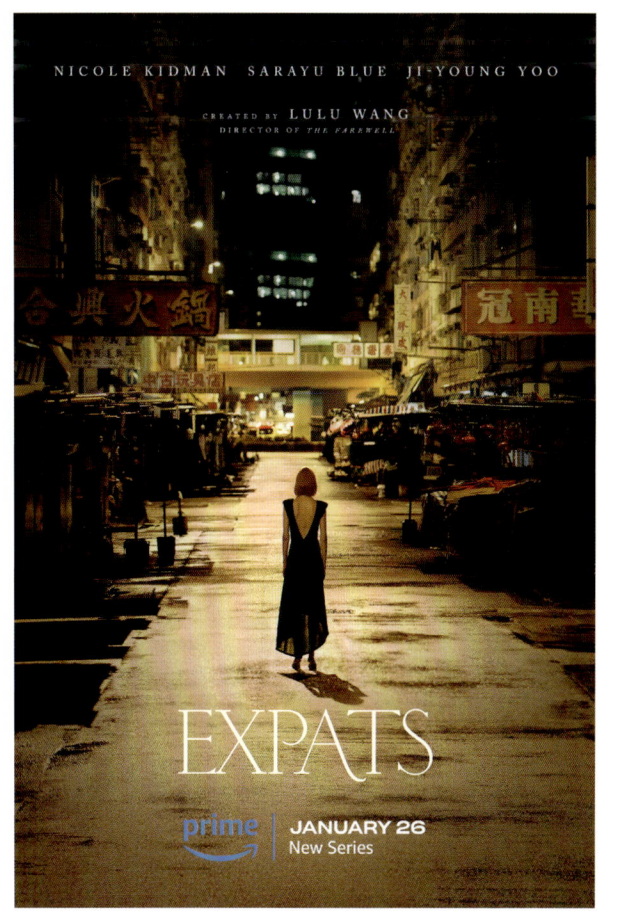

Title: Expats Teaser Poster | Client: Amazon Studios
Design Firm: MOCEAN

212 SILVER — TELEVISION

LEROY & ROSE 🇺🇸

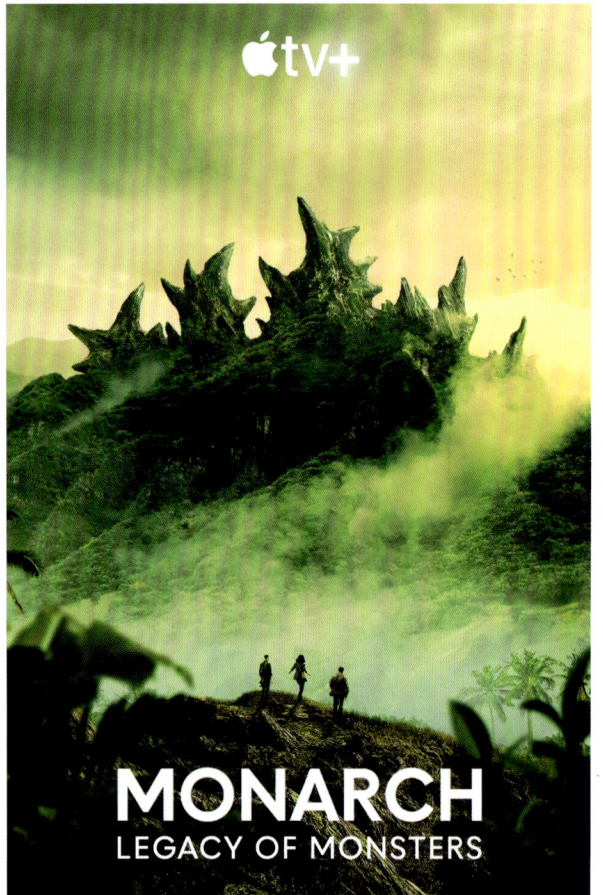

Title: Monarch: Legacy of Monsters | **Client:** Apple
Design Firm: Leroy & Rose

LEROY & ROSE 🇺🇸

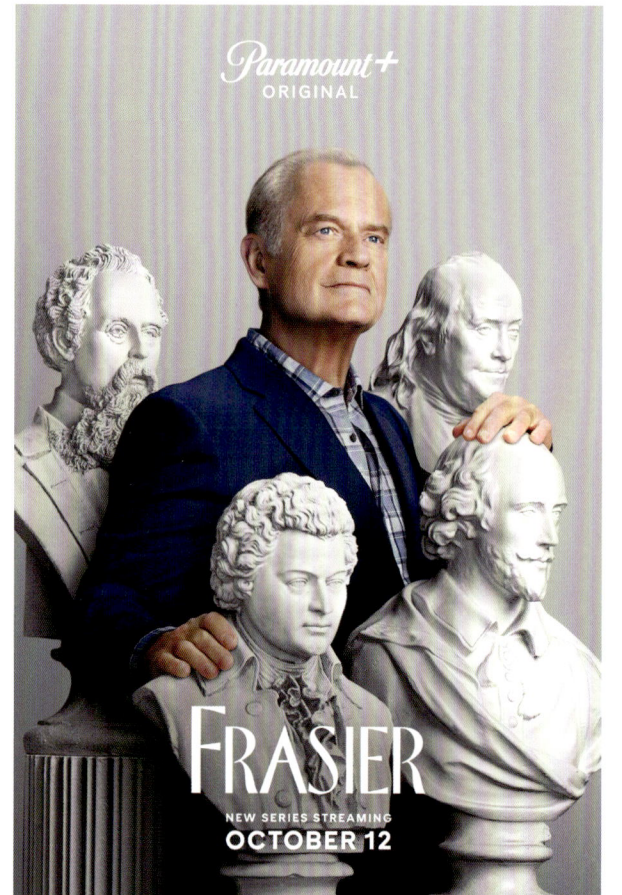

Title: Frasier: Busts | **Client:** Paramount+
Design Firm: Leroy & Rose

RHUBARB 🇺🇸

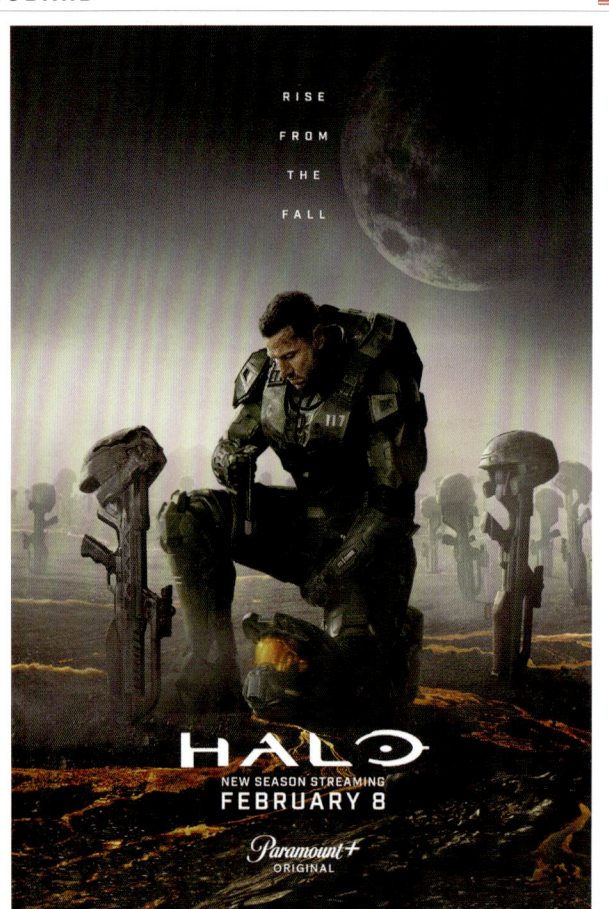

Title: Halo S2 Campaign Art | **Client:** Paramount+
Design Firm: Rhubarb

FX NETWORKS 🇺🇸

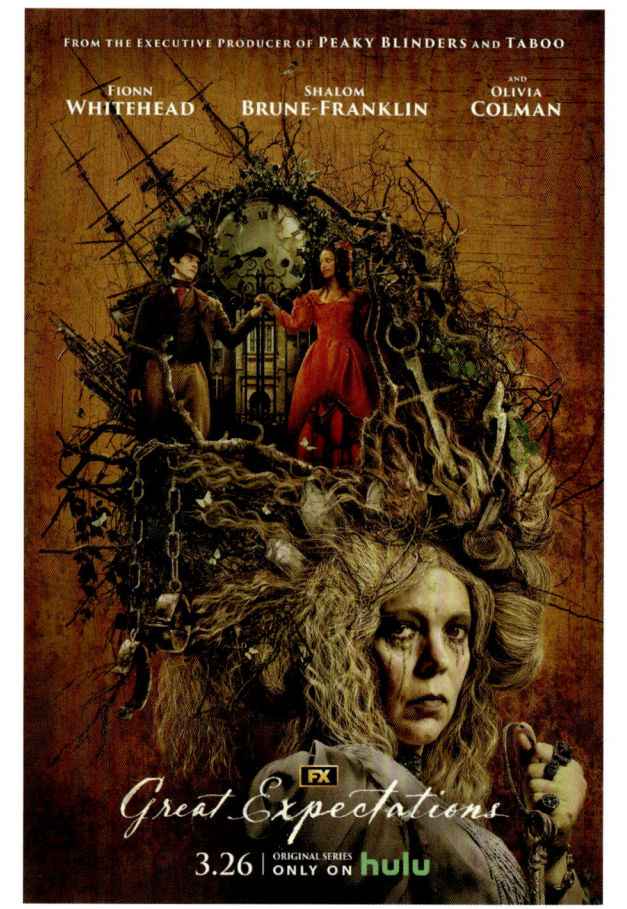

Title: Great Expectations - Headpiece Payoff | **Client:** FX Networks
Design Firm: AV Print

213 SILVER — TELEVISION

LOUIS PERCIVAL 🇺🇸

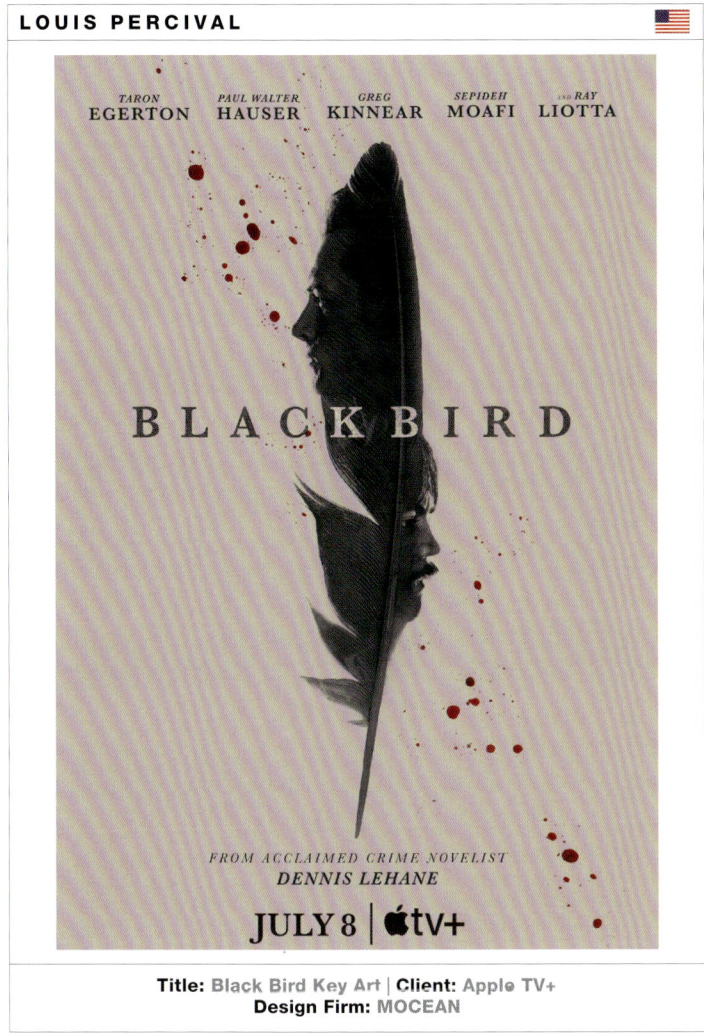

Title: Black Bird Key Art | **Client:** Apple TV+
Design Firm: MOCEAN

HBO 🇺🇸

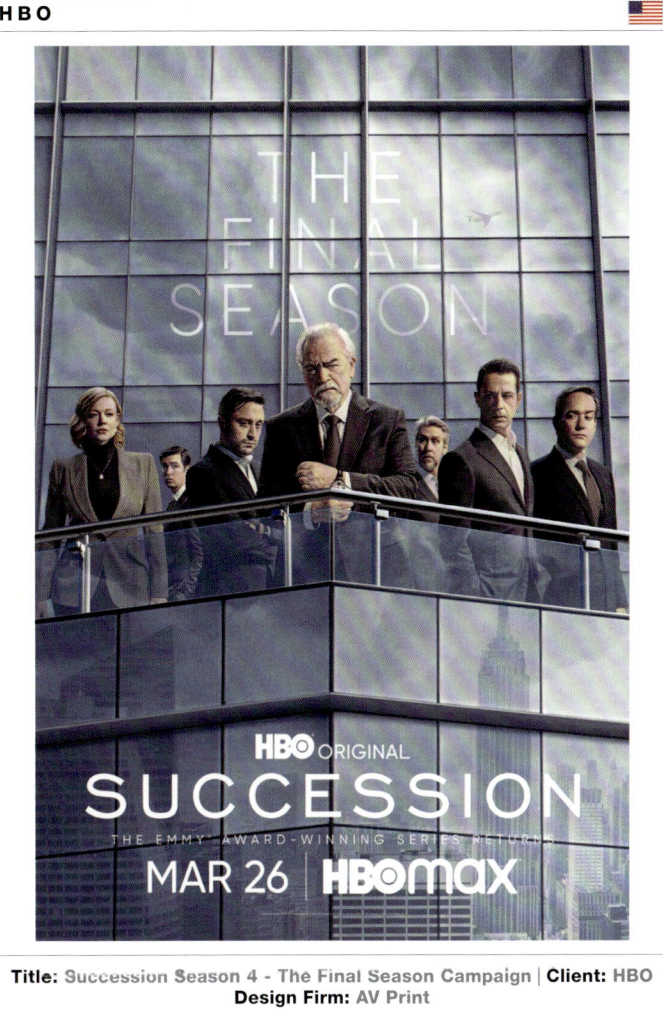

Title: Succession Season 4 - The Final Season Campaign | **Client:** HBO
Design Firm: AV Print

HBO 🇺🇸

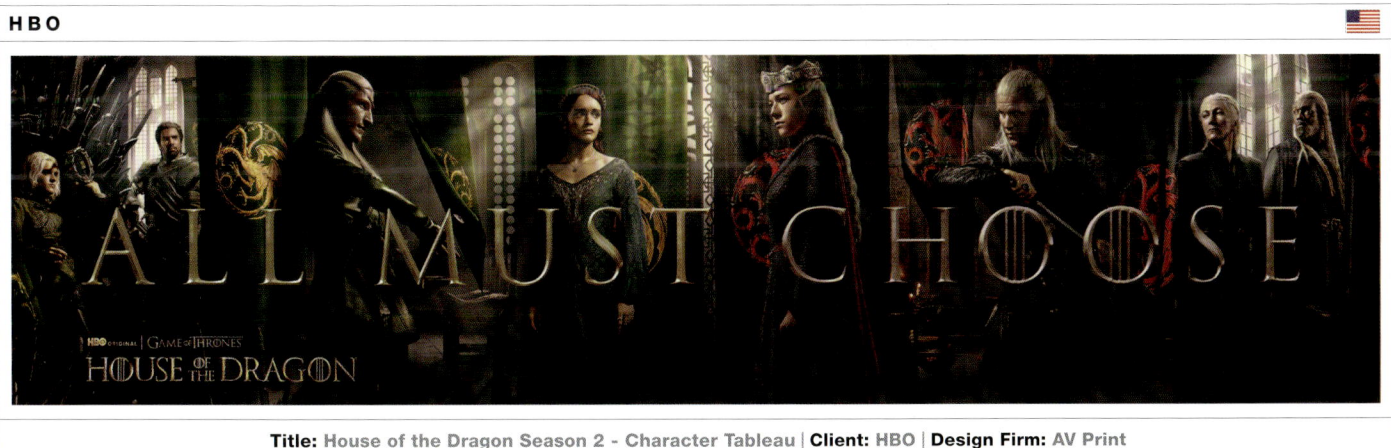

Title: House of the Dragon Season 2 - Character Tableau | **Client:** HBO | **Design Firm:** AV Print

---

This year's entries showcase a rich and diverse approach to poster design from all over the world.

Paul Garbett, *Co-founder & Designer, Studio Garbett*

What I find particularly striking about the Graphis Poster Competition is the excellent variety of posters and themes, such as movies, advertising, and free author posters.

Sven Lindhorst-Emme, *Founder & Designer, Studio Lindhorst-Emme+Hinrichs*

BERNARDO GARCIA VALENCIA

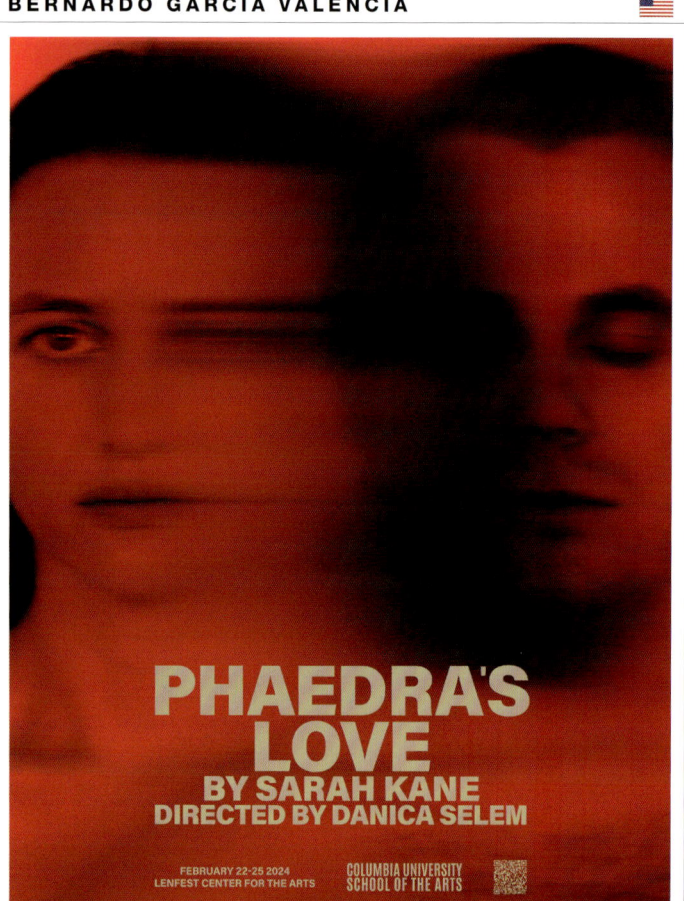

Title: Phaedra's Love | Client: Columbia University School of the Arts
Design Firm: Bernardo Garcia Valencia

STEPHAN BUNDI

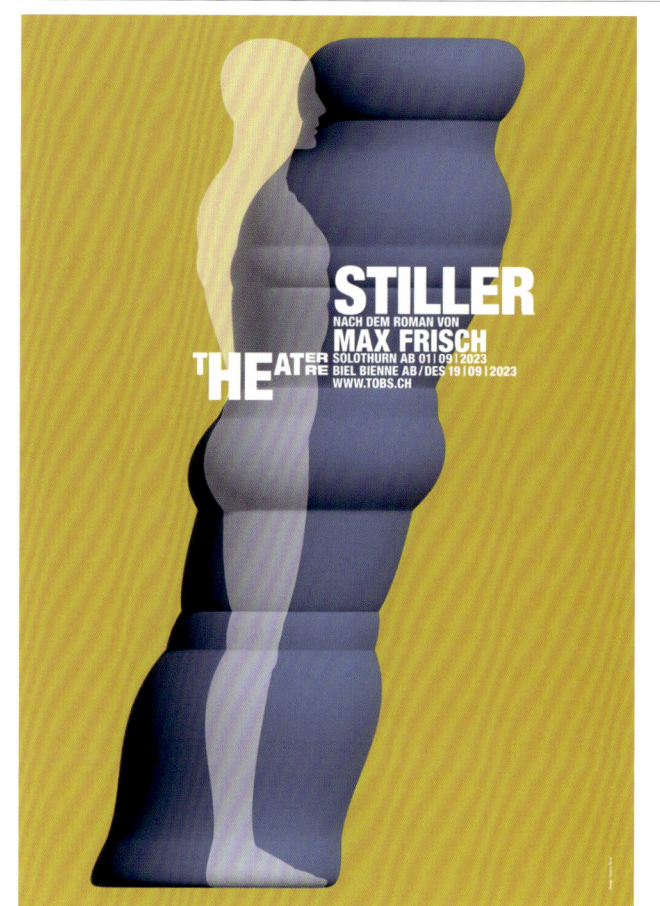

Title: Stiller | Client: Theater Orchester Biel Solothurn
Design Firm: Atelier Bundi AG

ÉMILIE CHEN

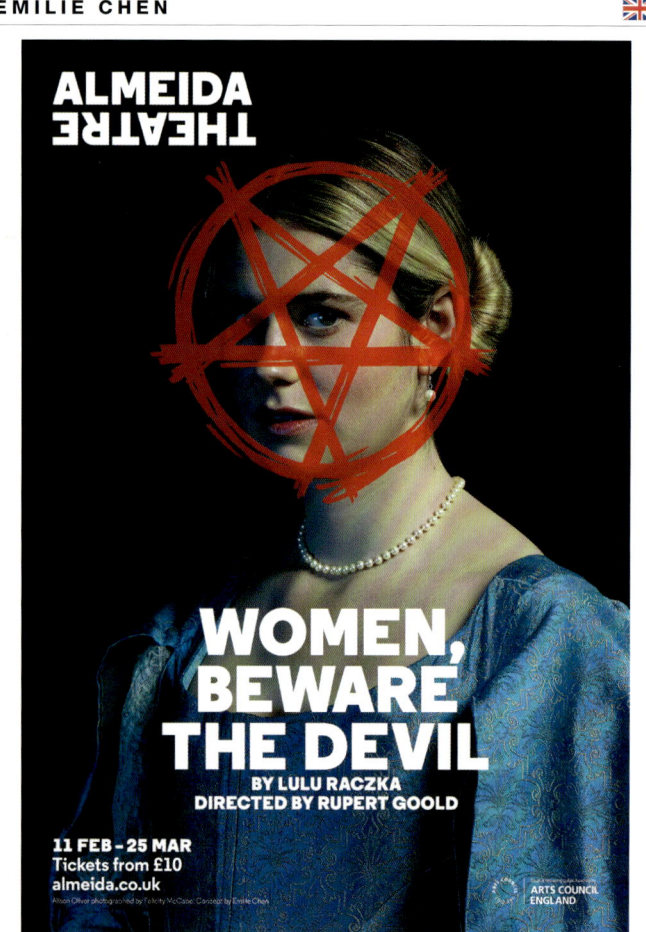

Title: Women, Beware the Devil | Client: Almeida Theatre
Design Firm: Émilie Chen LTD

OSBORNE SHIWAN

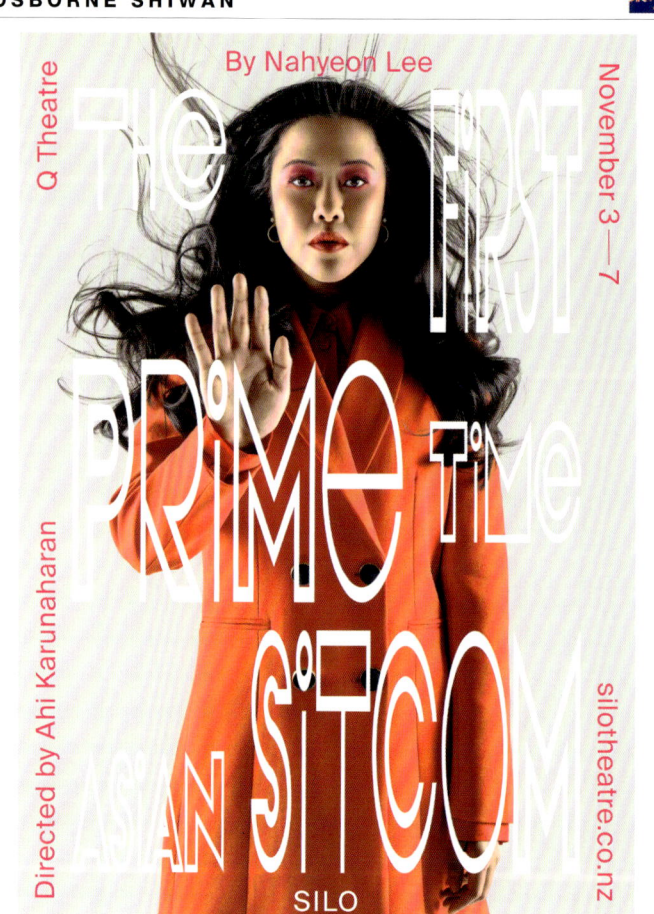

Title: The First Prime Time Asian Sitcom | Client: Silo Theatre
Design Firm: Osborne Shiwan

215 SILVER THEATER

MIRKO ILIC

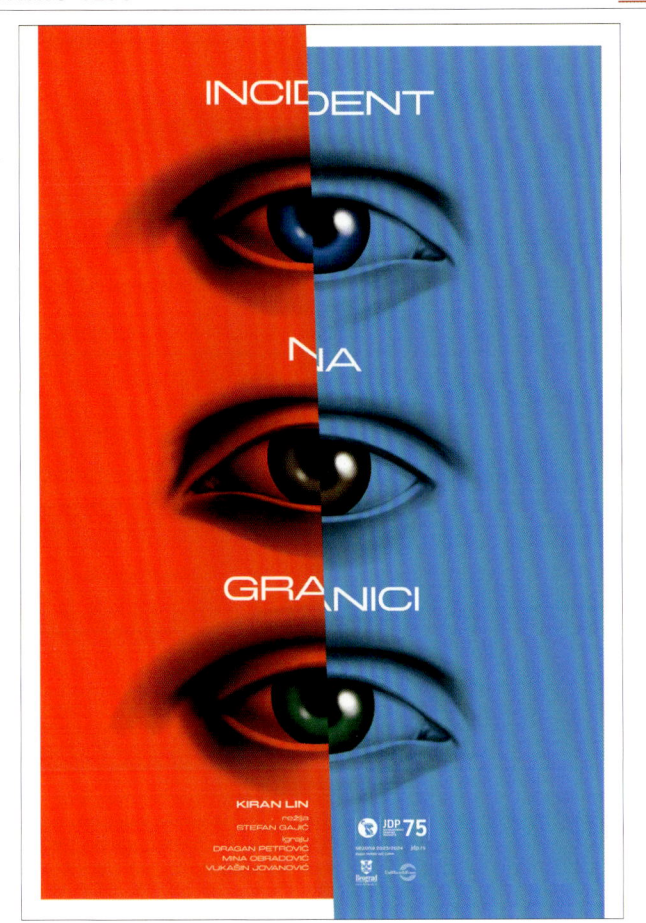

Title: An Incident at the Border | Client: JDP-Yugoslav Drama Theater in Belgrade, Serbia | Design Firm: Mirko Ilic Corp.

WIESŁAW GRZEGORCZYK

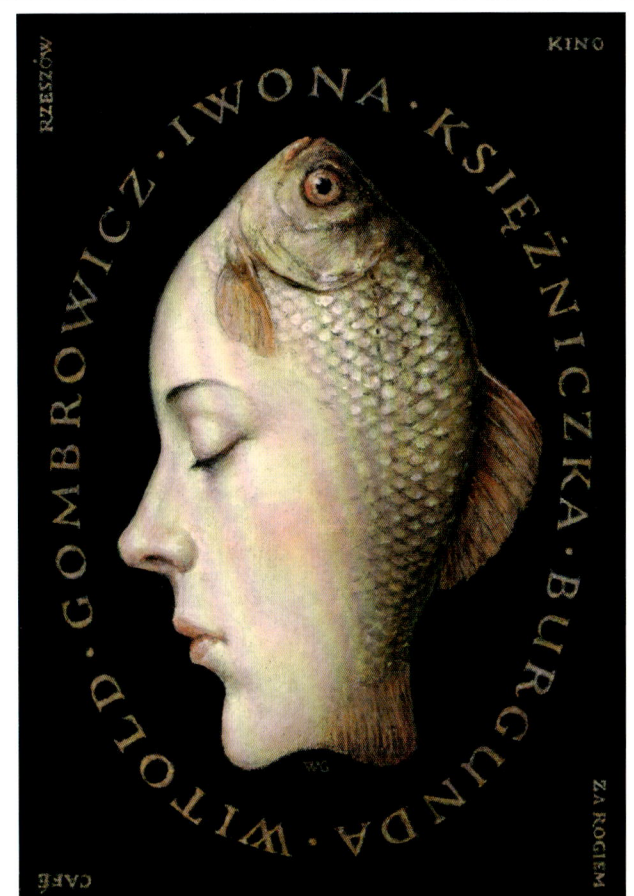

Title: Witold Gombrowicz – Ivona, Princess of Burgundia | Client: Kino za Rogiem Café Rzeszów | Design Firm: Wiesław Grzegorczyk

ANDREW SOBOL

Title: What You Will, or Twelfth Night | Client: Theatre at the Mill
Design Firm: Andrewsobol.com

MIRKO ILIC

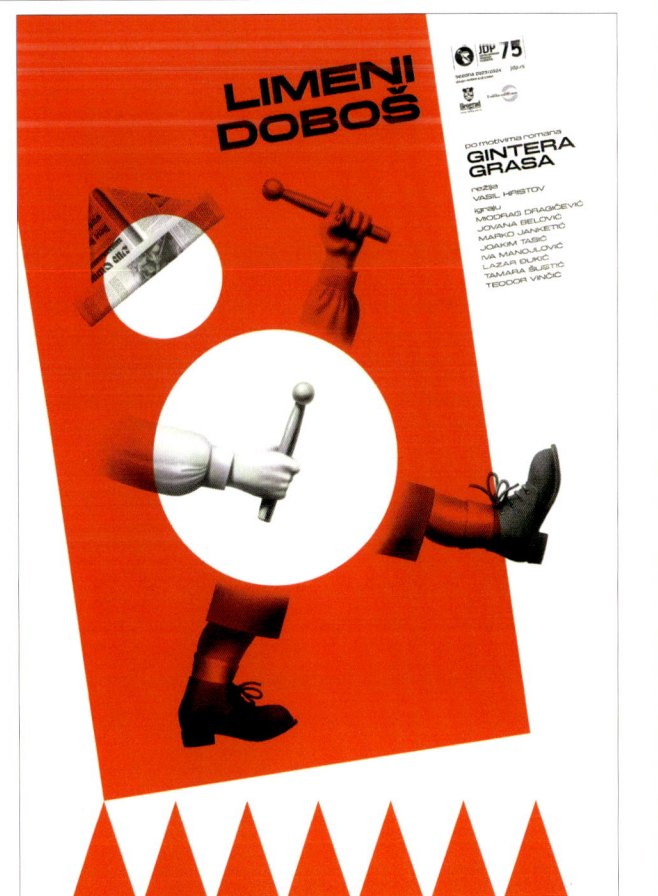

Title: The Tin Drum | Client: JDP-Yugoslav Drama Theater in Belgrade, Serbia | Design Firm: Mirko Ilic Corp.

216 SILVER   THEATER

PAM PATTERSON 🇺🇸

Title: Men Cry Too | **Client:** Barnsdall Gallery Theatre
Design Firm: 14-Forty

STEPHAN BUNDI 🇨🇭

Title: Auf Hoher See / Striptease
Client: Theater Orchester Biel Solothurn | **Design Firm:** Atelier Bundi AG

GÜRBÜZ DOĞAN EKŞIOĞLU 🇲🇰

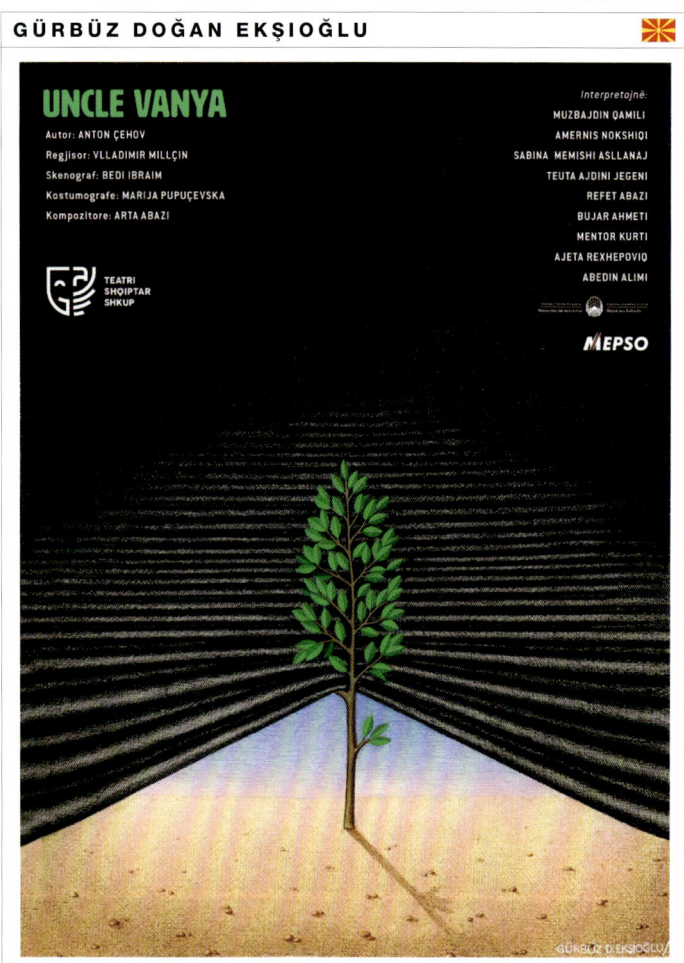

Title: Uncle Vanya | **Client:** The Albanian Theater Skopje
Design Firm: EGGRA

ANASTASIA TEMIRKHANOVA 🇨🇭

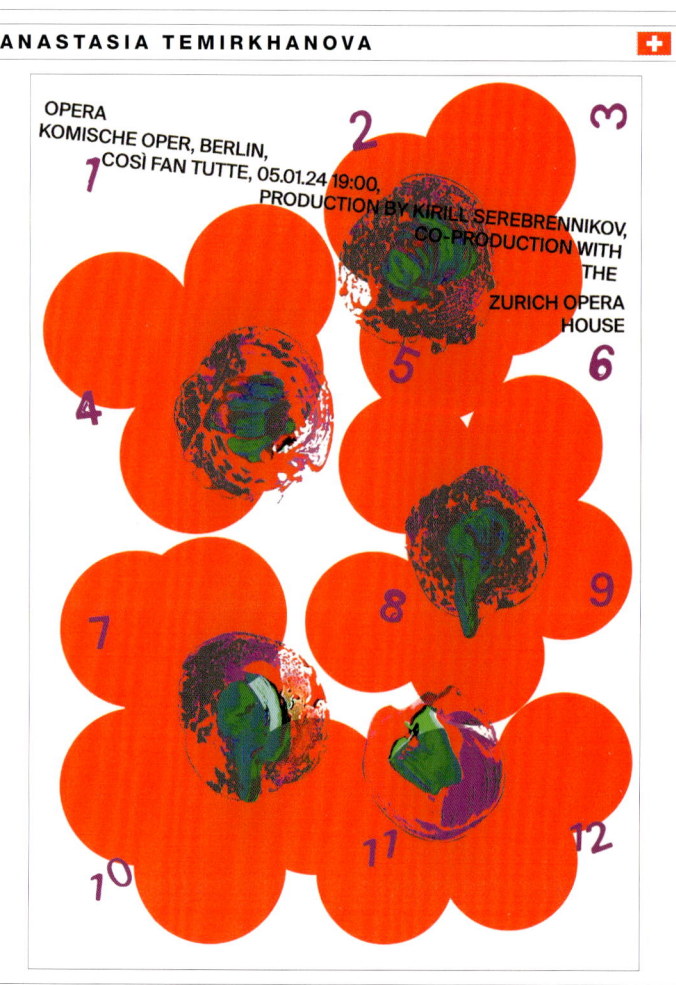

Title: Cosi Fan Tutte | **Client:** Komische Oper
Design Firm: Anastasia Temirkhanova

217 SILVER THEATER

ANDREW SOBOL 🇺🇸

Title: Lifespan of a Fact | **Client:** Theatre at the Mill
Design Firm: Andrewsobol.com

JAN ŠABACH 🇺🇸

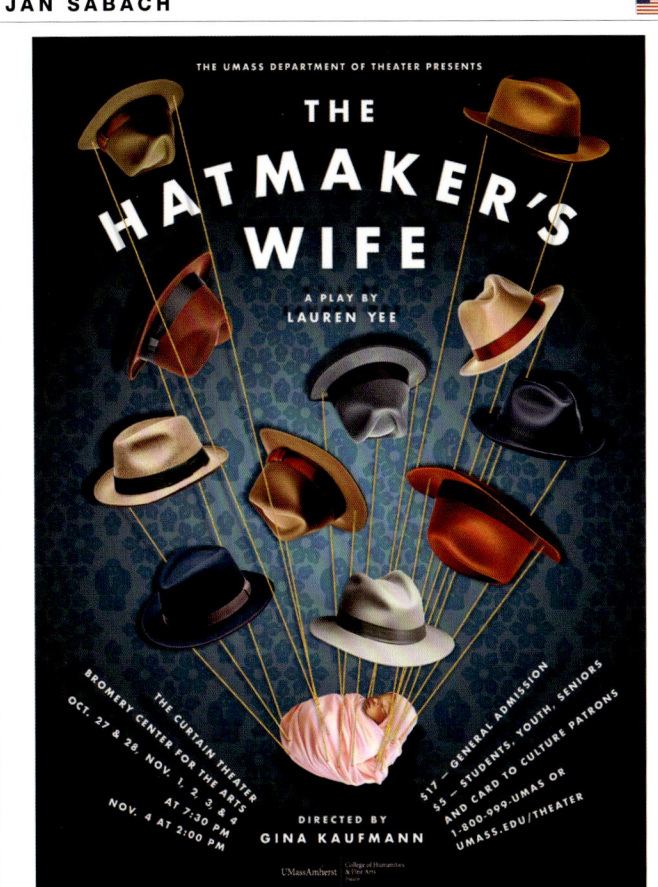

Title: The Hatmaker's Wife | **Client:** University of Massachusetts Amherst Theatre Department | **Design Firm:** Code Switch

MIRKO ILIC 🇺🇸

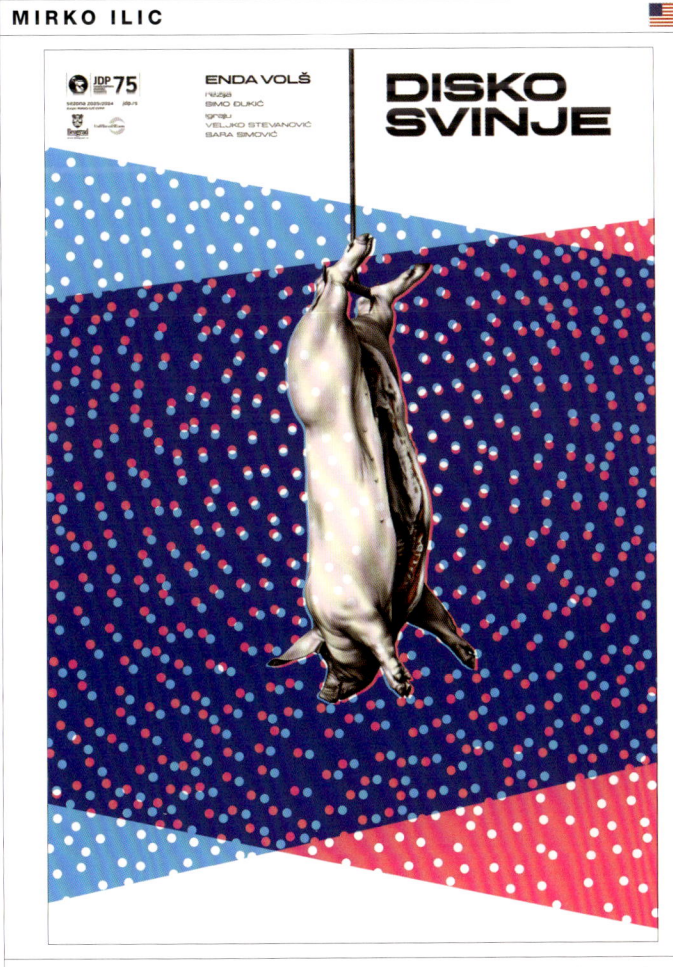

Title: Disco Pigs | **Client:** JDP-Yugoslav Drama Theater in Belgrade, Serbia | **Design Firm:** Mirko Ilic Corp.

STEPHAN BUNDI 🇨🇭

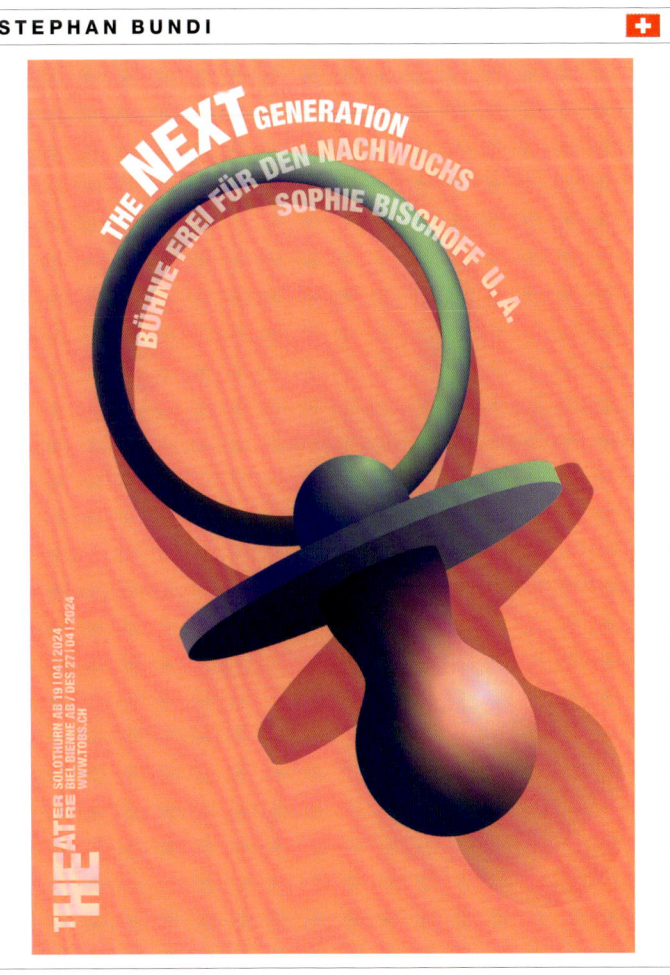

Title: Next Generation | **Client:** Theater Orchester Biel Solothurn
Design Firm: Atelier Bundi AG

THEATER

ÉMILIE CHEN 🇬🇧
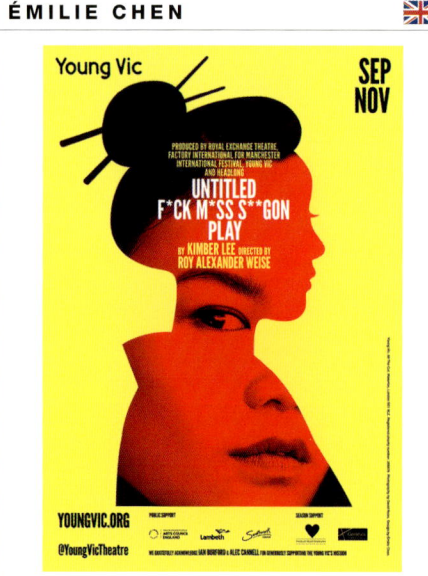
Title: Untitled F*ck M*ss S**gon Play Poster
Clients: Young Vic, Royal Theatre Exchange
Design Firm: Émilie Chen LTD

MIRKO ILIC 🇺🇸

Title: The Loser | **Client:** JDP-Yugoslav Drama Theater in Belgrade, Serbia
Design Firm: Mirko Ilic Corp.

ANDREW SOBOL 🇺🇸
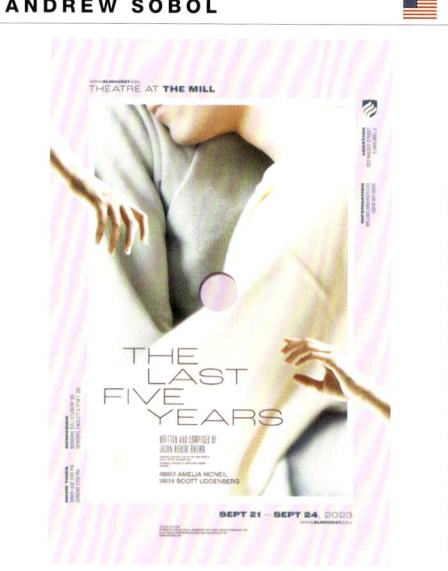
Title: The Last Five Years
Client: Theatre at the Mill
Design Firm: Andrewsobol.com

ANDREW SOBOL 🇺🇸
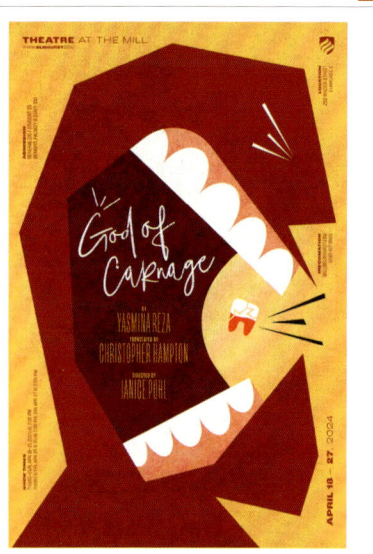
Title: God of Carnage
Client: Theatre at the Mill
Design Firm: Andrewsobol.com

ROGER W. DORMANN 🇺🇸
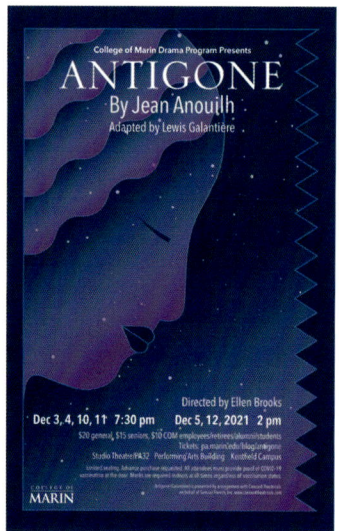
Title: Antigone
Client: College of Marin Drama Program
Design Firm: Roger W. Dormann

JULIANE PETRI 🇪🇸
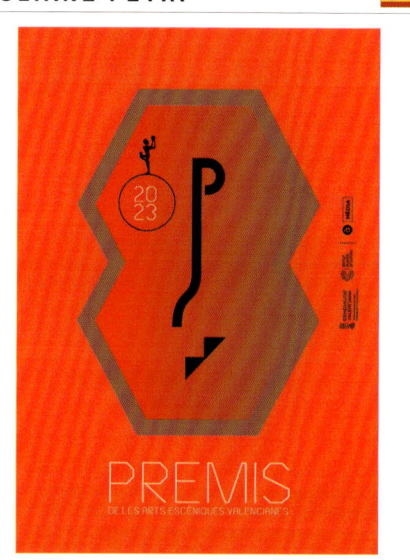
Title: Poster of the Valencian Performing Arts Awards Gala 2023 | **Clients:** Generalitat Valenciana, Institut Valencià de Cultura | **Design Firm:** Juliane Petri

OVIDIU HRIN 🇷🇴
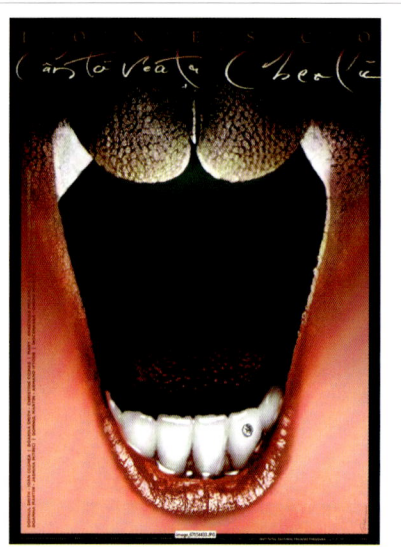
Title: The Bald Soprano
Client: Aualeu Theater Company
Design Firm: Synopsismedia

ÉMILIE CHEN 🇬🇧
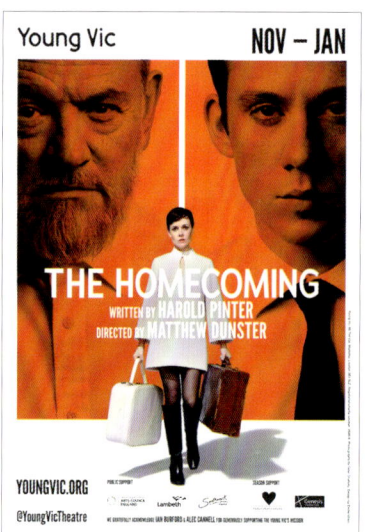
Title: The Homecoming Poster
Client: Young Vic
Design Firm: Émilie Chen LTD

BERNARDO GARCIA VALENCIA 🇺🇸
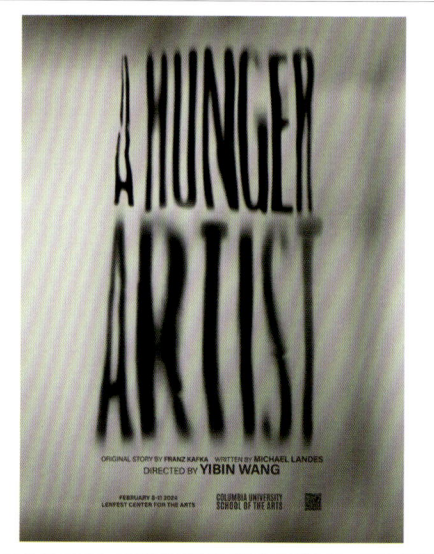
Title: A Hunger Artist
Client: Columbia University School of the Arts
Design Firm: Bernardo Garcia Valencia

219 SILVER — TOURISM

MICHAEL BRALEY 🇺🇸

Title: Krakow: Where History Meets Culture | **Client:** City of Krakow International Poster Competition | **Design Firm:** Braley Design

CLAIRE ZOU 🇺🇸

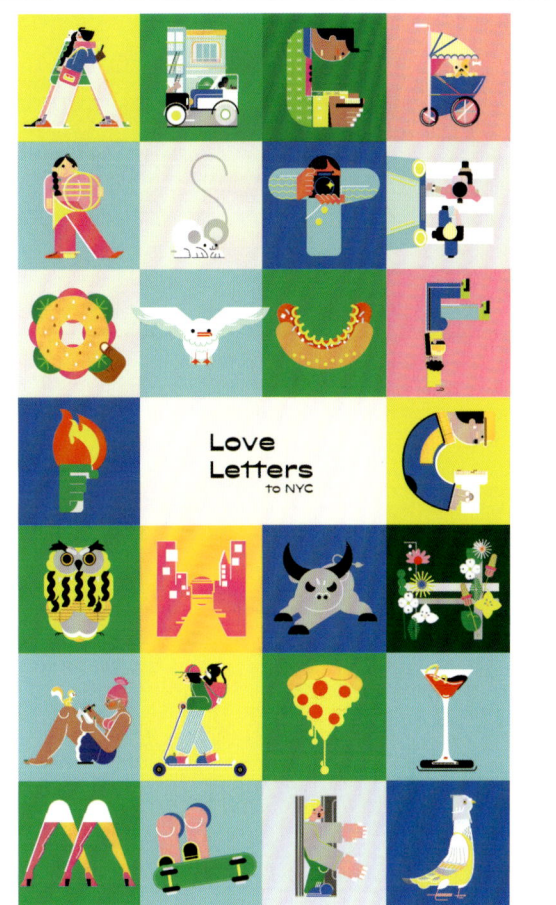

Title: Love Letters to NYC | **Client:** Self-Initiated
Design Firm: Claire Zou

MASAHITO TATSUTOMI 🇯🇵

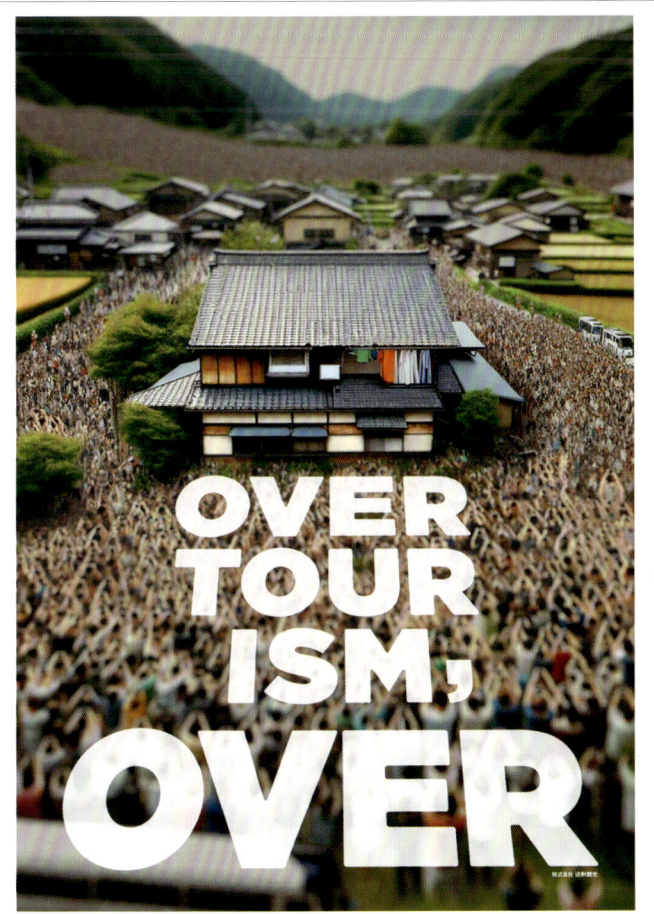

Title: OVER TOURISM, OVER | **Client:** Japan Overtourist Inc.
Design Firm: PEACE Inc.

DAISUKE KASHIWA 🇯🇵

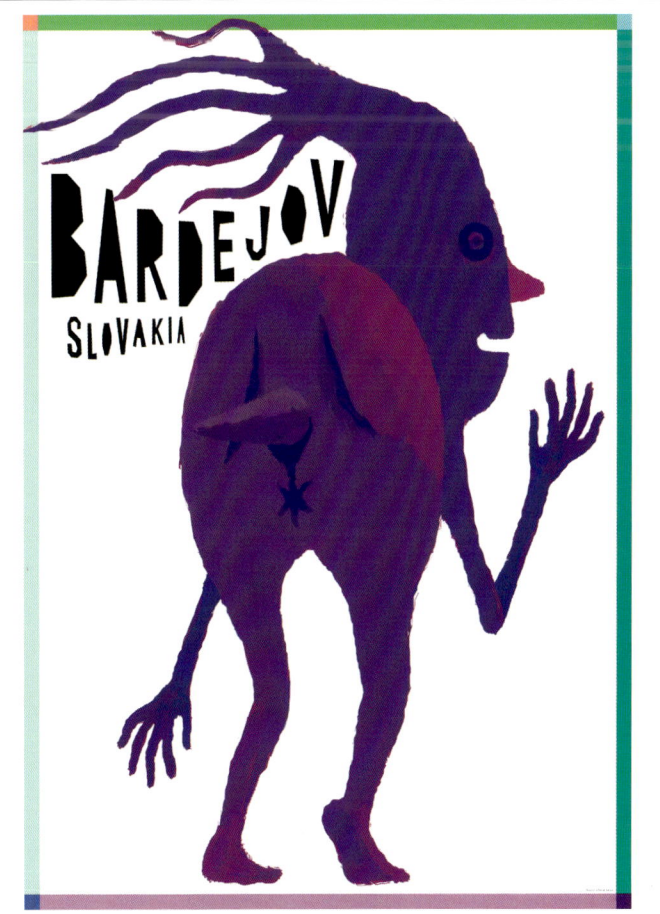

Title: Bardejov, Slovakia | **Client:** International Poster Exhibition City of Bardejov 2 | **Design Firm:** Daisuke Kashiwa

220 SILVER TYPOGRAPHY

KIMBERLY ELAM

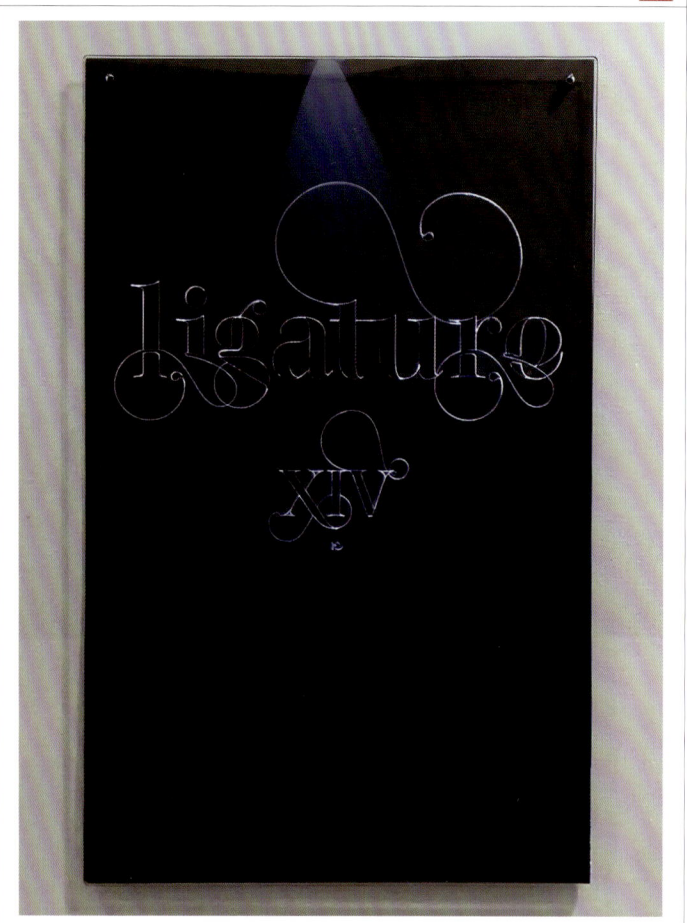

Title: Ligature XIV Typography Show Poster | Client: Ringling College Typography Club | Design Firm: Kimberly Elam Design

DOUGLAS MAY

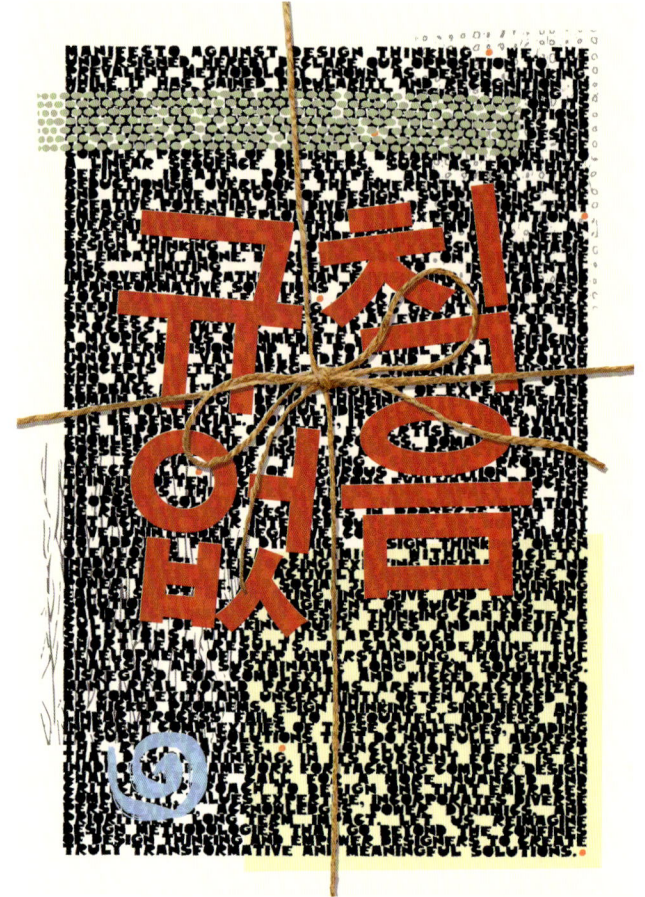

Title: No Rules | Client: Oesol International Typography Awards
Design Firm: May & Co.

EZEKIEL DUKE BOWER

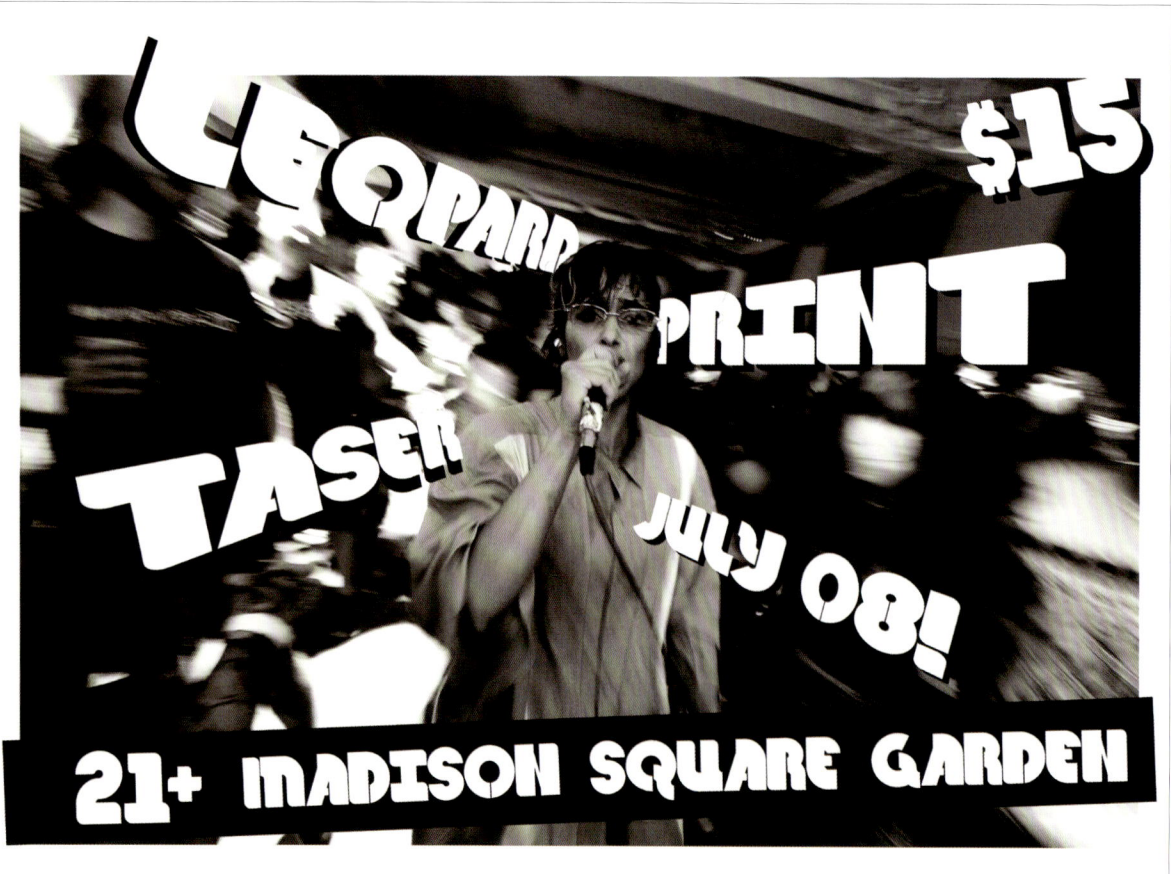

Title: Leopard Print Taser! Live at Madison Square Garden (Type Specimen) | Client: Self-initiated | Design Firm: Ezekiel Duke Bower

HOON-DONG CHUNG

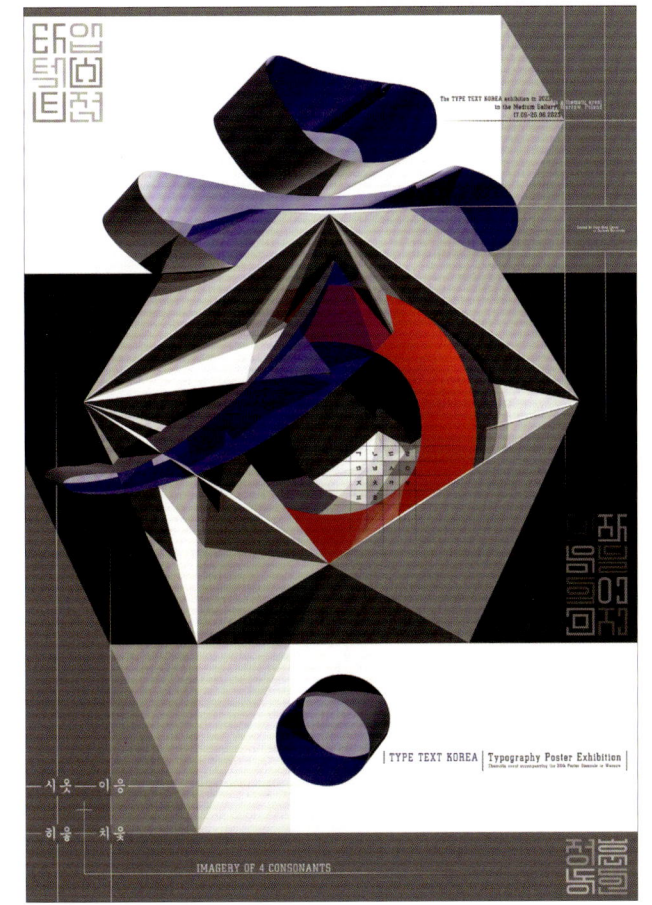

Title: Imagery of 4 Consonants | **Client:** 'TYPE TEXT KOREA' Typography Poster Exhibition | **Design Firm:** Dankook University

IVAN KASHLAKOV

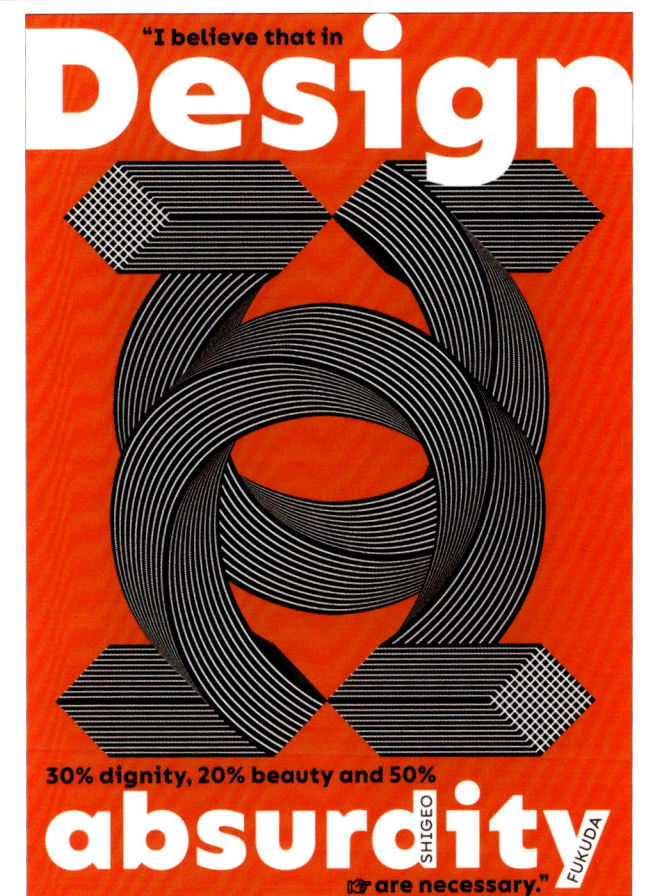

Title: Fukuda Wisdom | **Client:** TypeForward
Design Firm: Ivan Kashlakov

RIKKE HANSEN

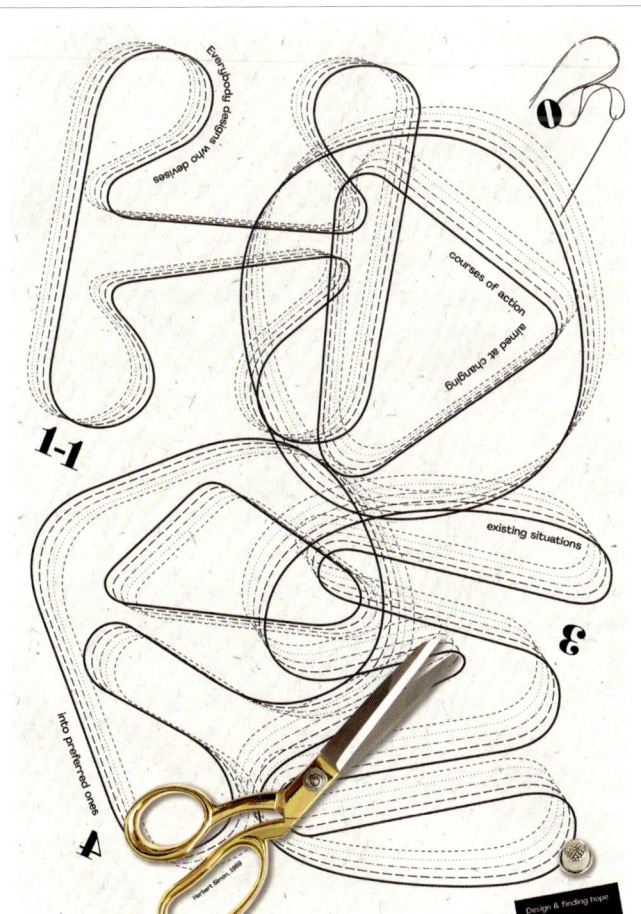

Title: Design and Finding Hope | **Client:** KICD
Design Firm: Rikke Hansen

ZHONGJUN YIN

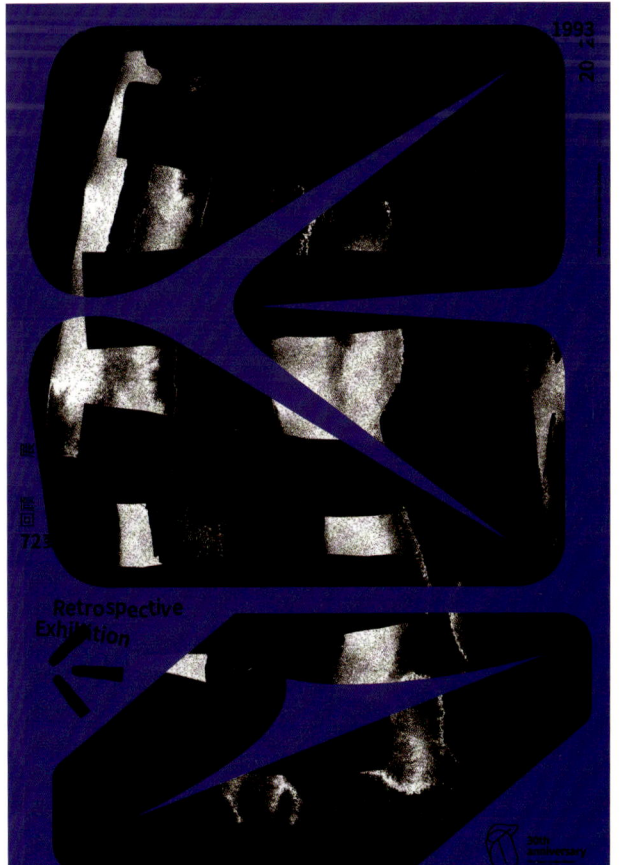

Title: 72 Changes Retrospective Exhibition #2 | **Client:** Self-initiated
Design Firm: Dalian RYCX Design

JA EUN KU

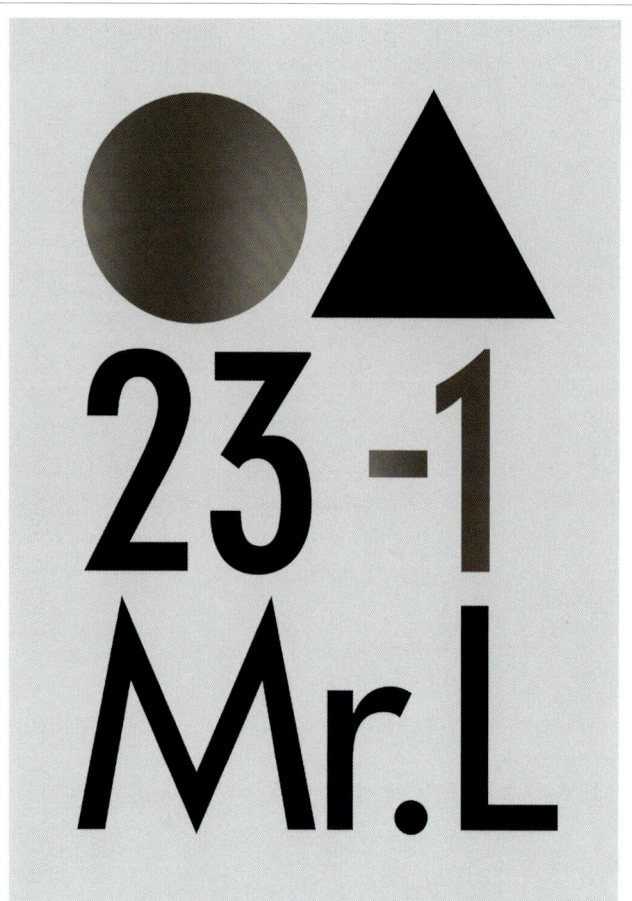

Title: Find the Hidden | **Client:** KST
Design Firm: Seoul Institution of the Arts

HUFAX ARTS

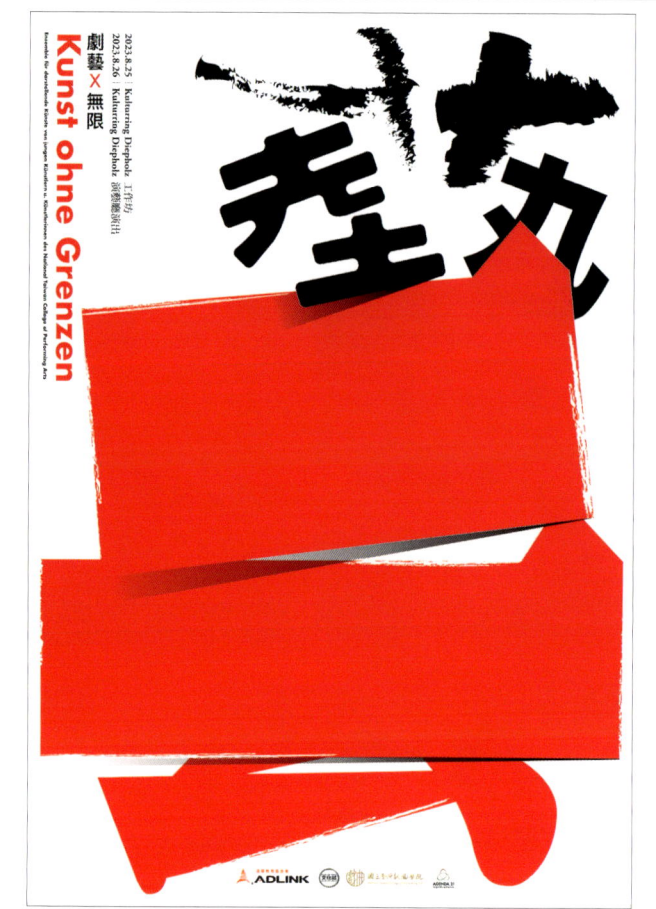

Title: Show Type | **Client:** The ADLink Education Foundation
Design Firm: Hufax Arts/FJCU

JOHN NORDYKE

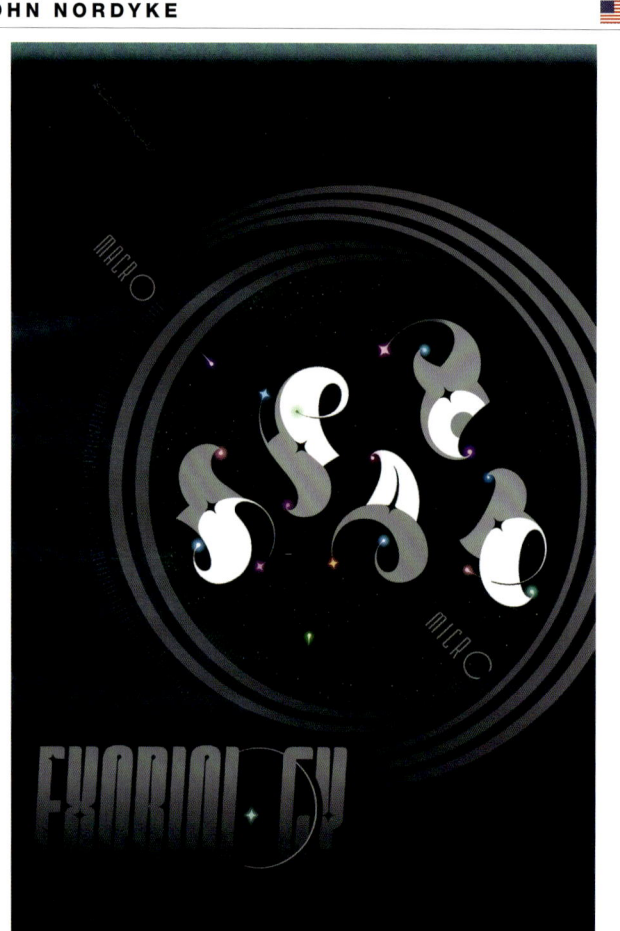

Title: Space: Exobiology | **Client:** Self-initiated
Design Firm: John Nordyke

CHIKAKO OGUMA

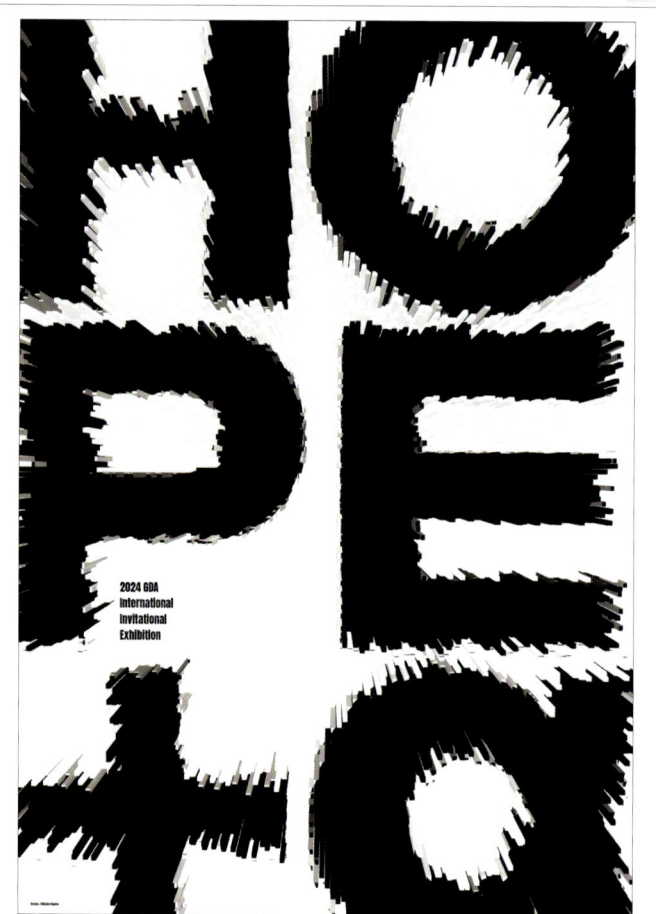

Title: HOPE +α | **Client:** Gyeonggi Design Association
Design Firm: Chikako Oguma

Graphis Honorable Mentions

224 HONORABLE MENTIONS

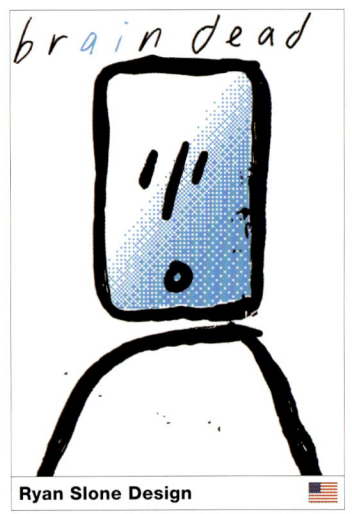
Ryan Slone Design

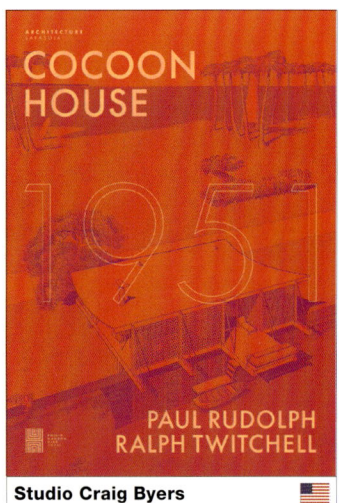
Studio Craig Byers

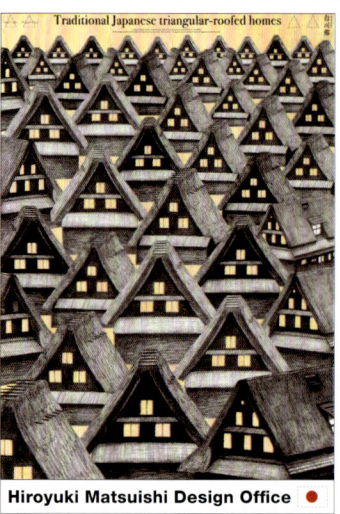
Hiroyuki Matsuishi Design Office

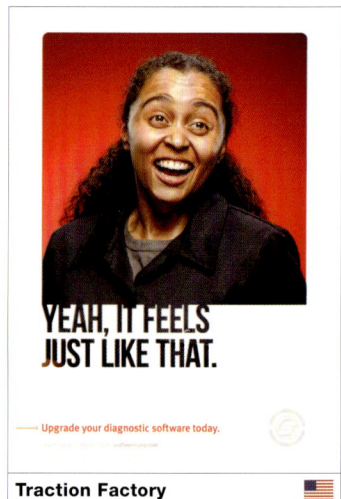
Traction Factory

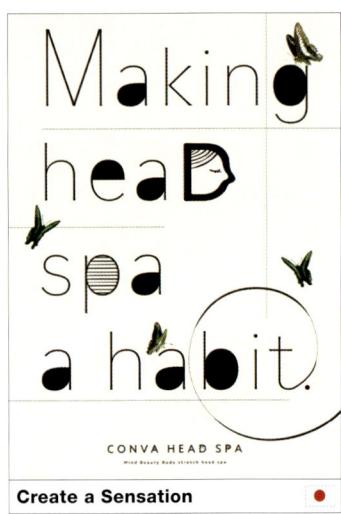
Create a Sensation

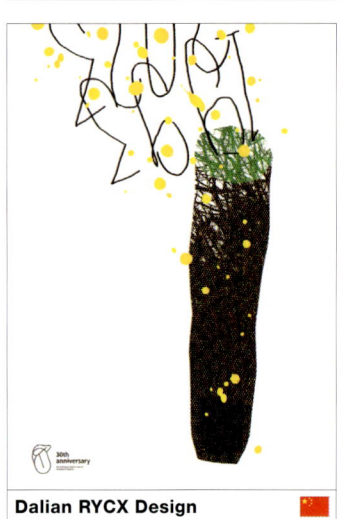
Dalian RYCX Design

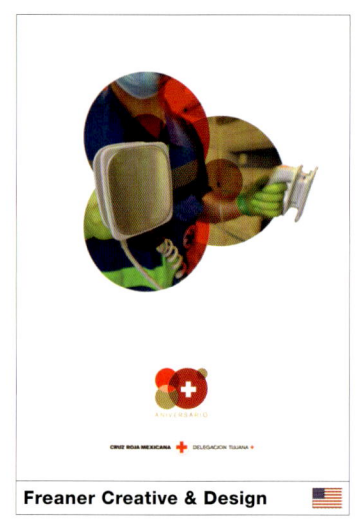
Freaner Creative & Design

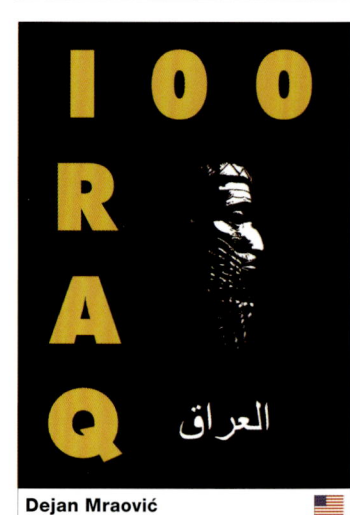
Dejan Mraović

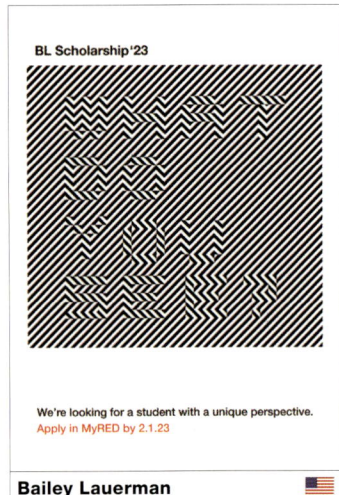
Bailey Lauerman

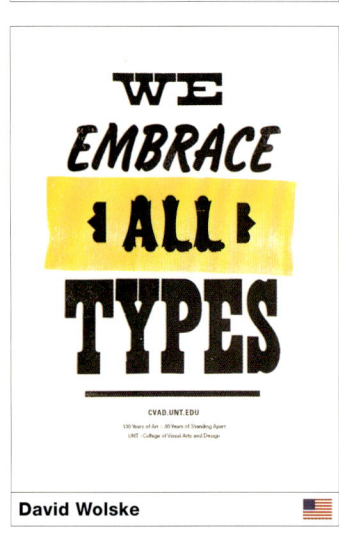
David Wolske

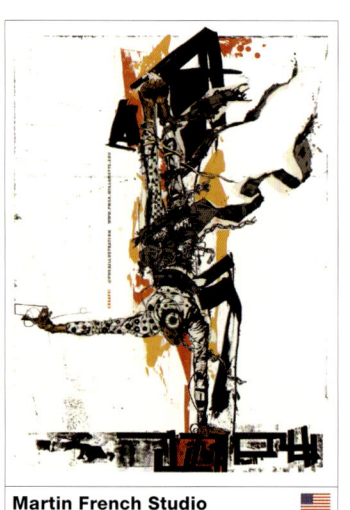
Martin French Studio

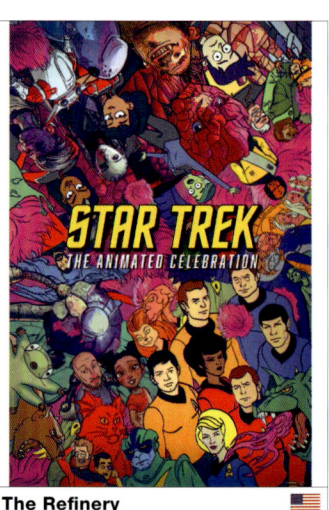
The Refinery

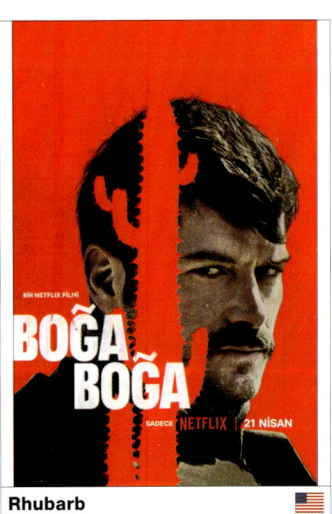
Rhubarb

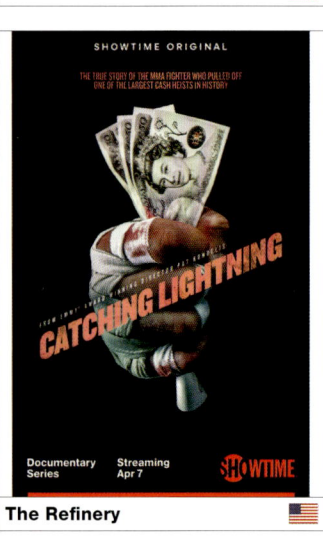
The Refinery

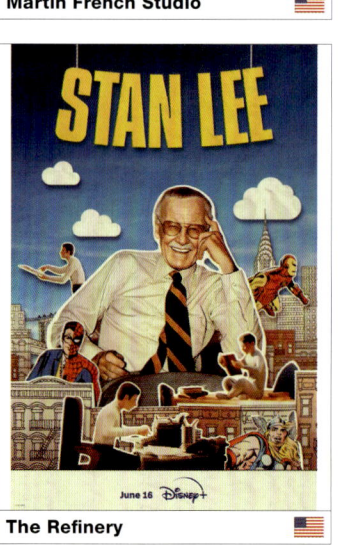
The Refinery

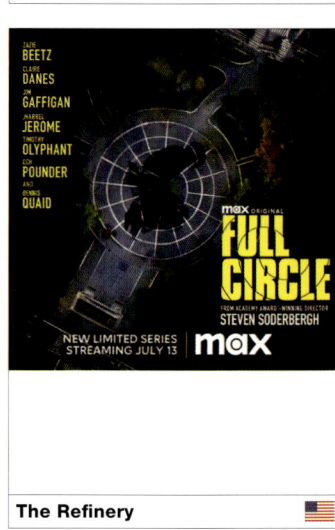
The Refinery

225 HONORABLE MENTIONS

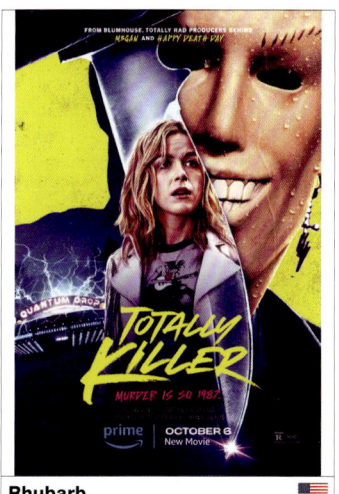
Rhubarb

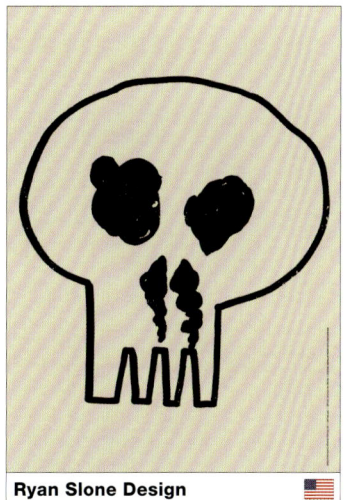
Ryan Slone Design

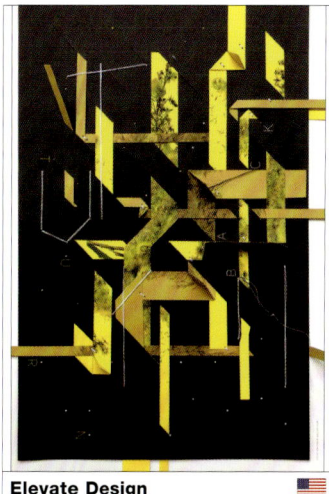
Elevate Design

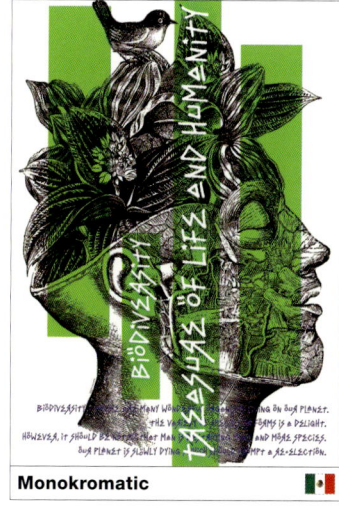
Monokromatic

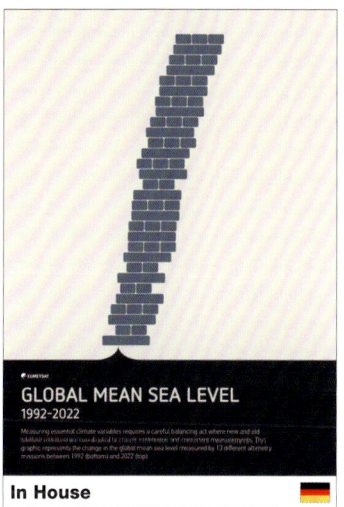
In House

Studio Eduard Cehovin

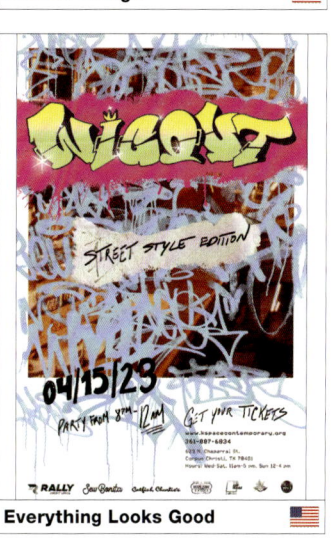
Everything Looks Good

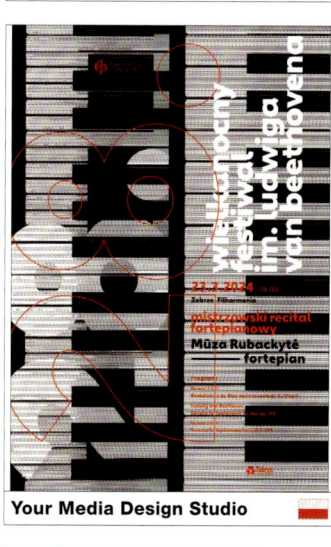
Your Media Design Studio

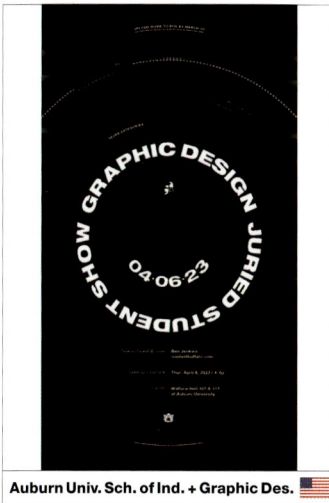
Auburn Univ. Sch. of Ind. + Graphic Des.

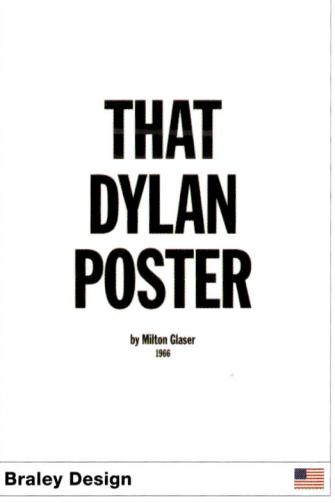
Braley Design

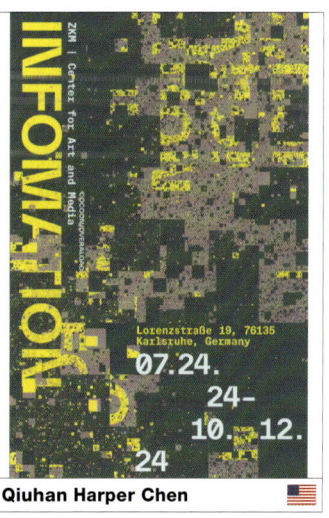
Qiuhan Harper Chen

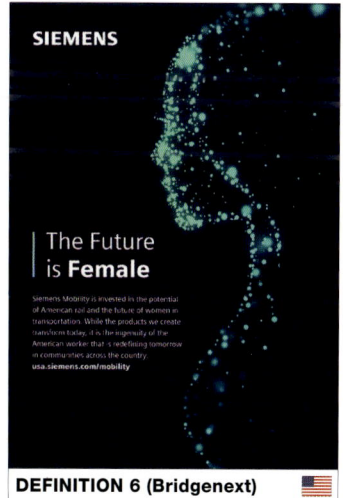
DEFINITION 6 (Bridgenext)

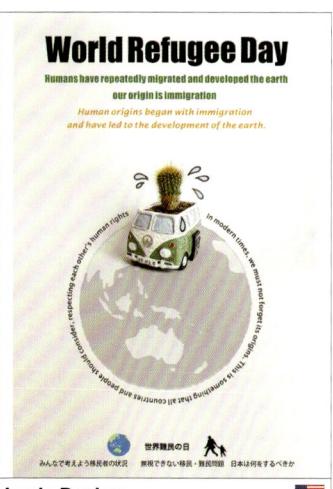
Legis Design

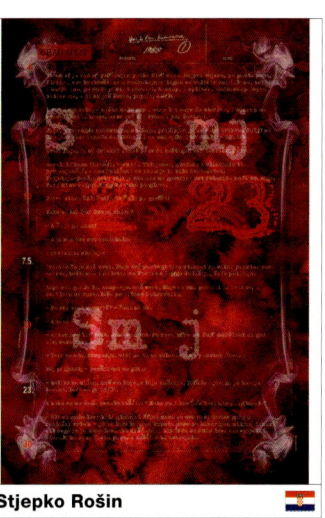
Stjepko Rošin

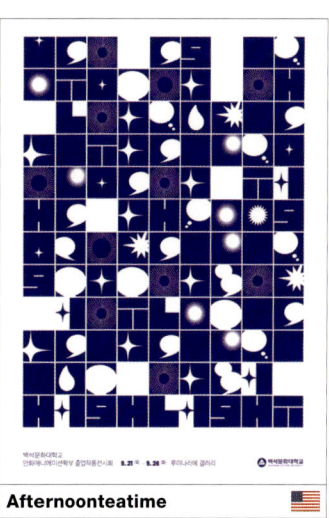
Afternoonteatime

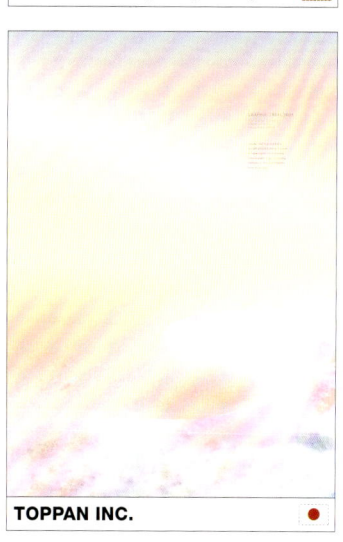
TOPPAN INC.

226 HONORABLE MENTIONS

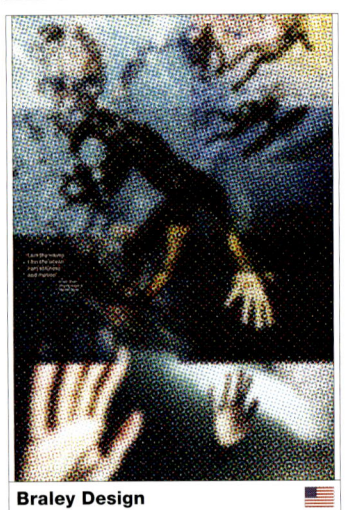
Braley Design

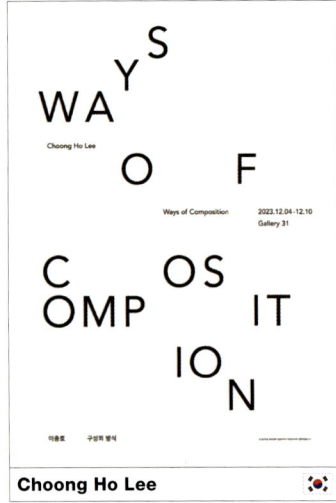
Choong Ho Lee

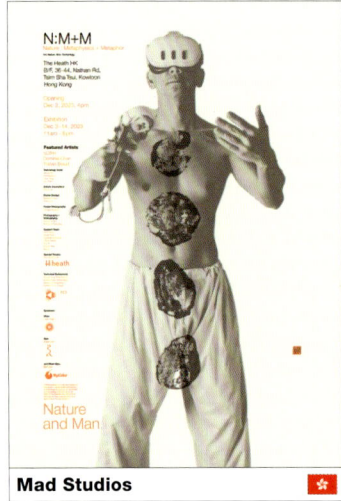
Mad Studios

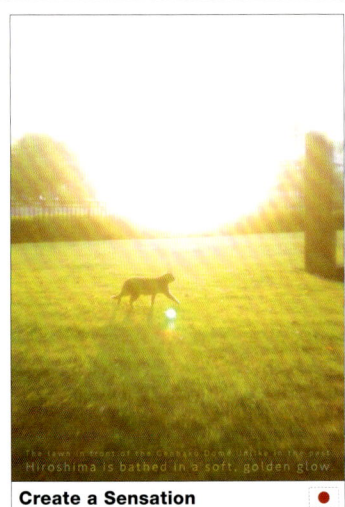
Create a Sensation

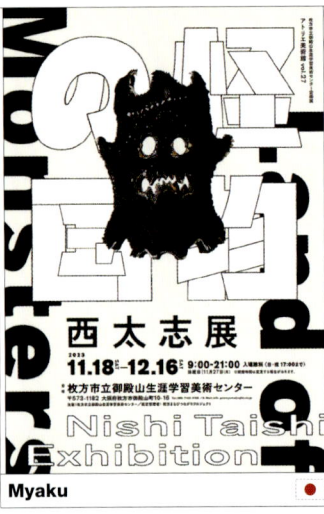
Myaku

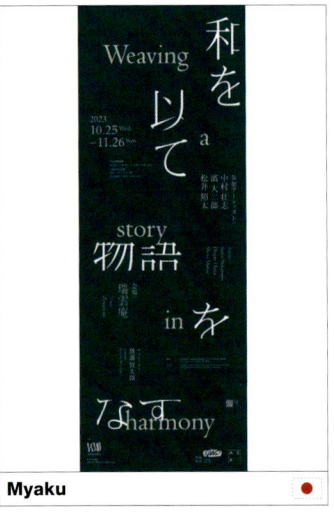
Myaku

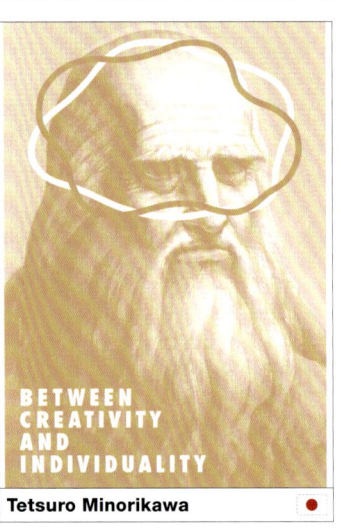
Tetsuro Minorikawa

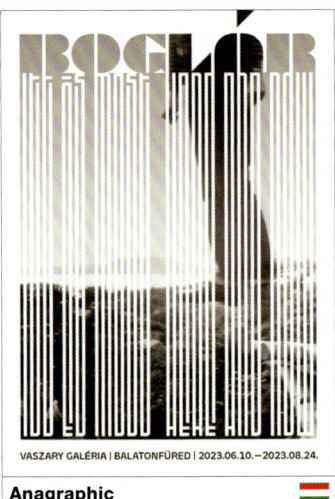
Anagraphic

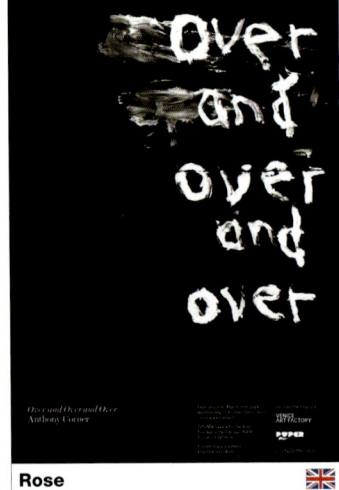
Rose

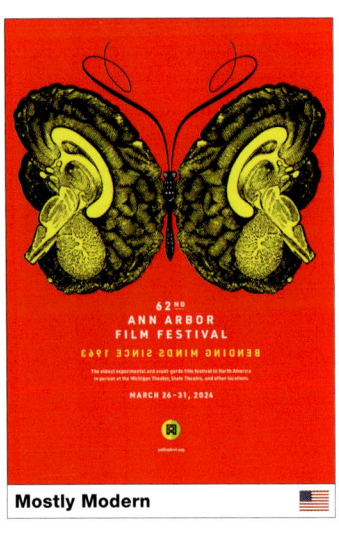
Mostly Modern

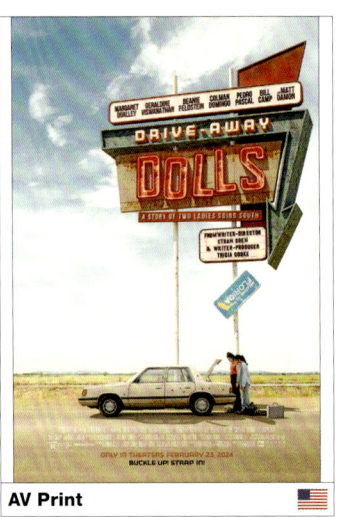
AV Print

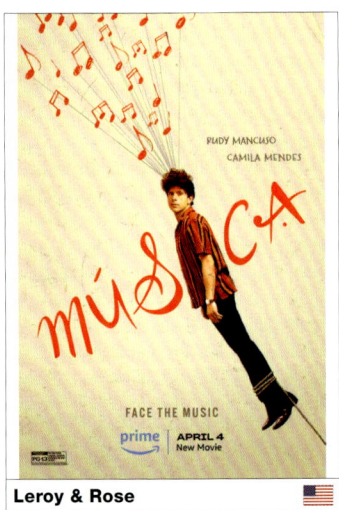
Leroy & Rose

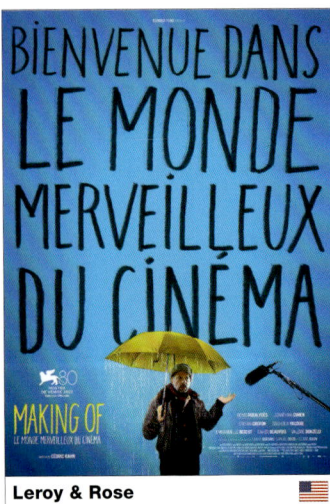
Leroy & Rose

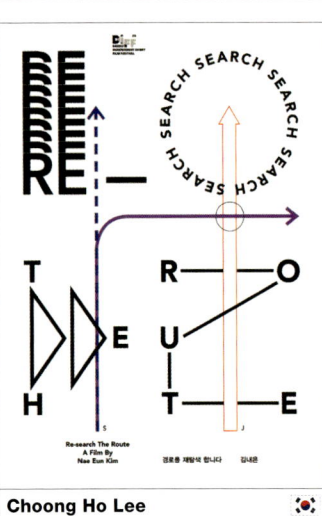
Choong Ho Lee

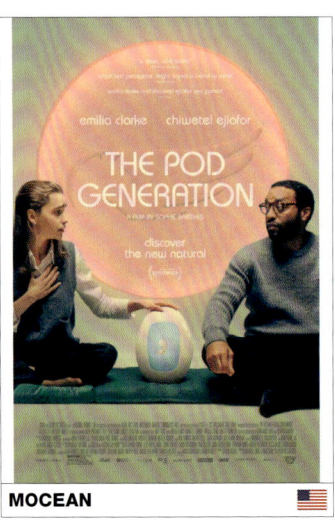
MOCEAN

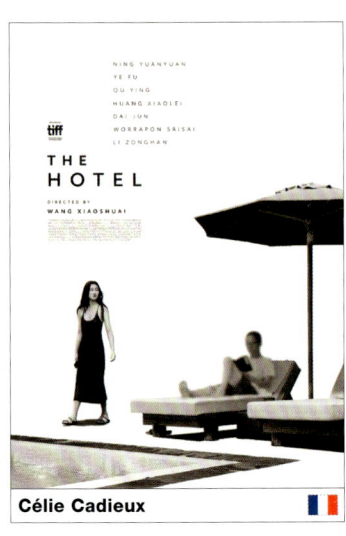
Célie Cadieux

227 HONORABLE MENTIONS

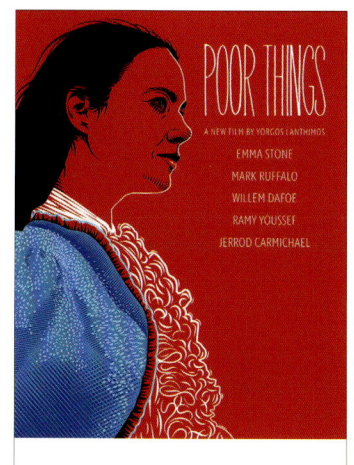
Only Child Art 🇺🇸

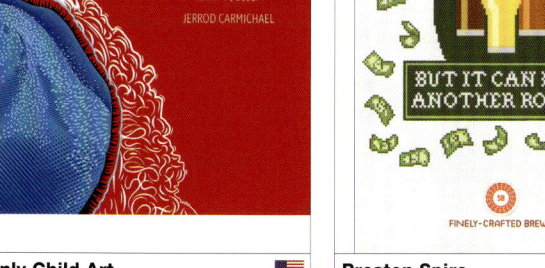
Preston Spire 🇺🇸

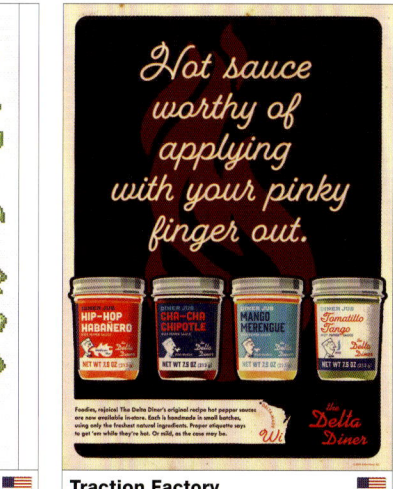
Traction Factory 🇺🇸

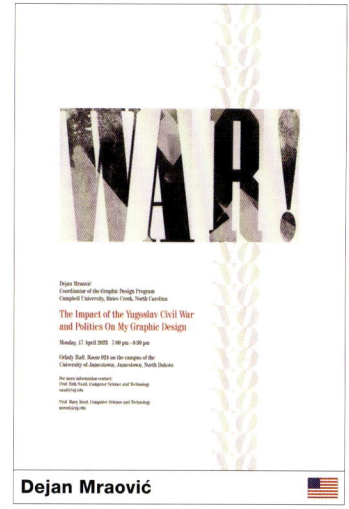
Dejan Mraović 🇺🇸

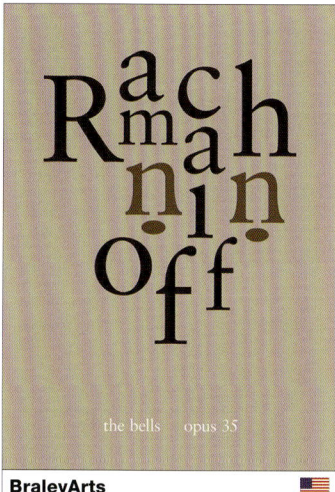
BraleyArts 🇺🇸

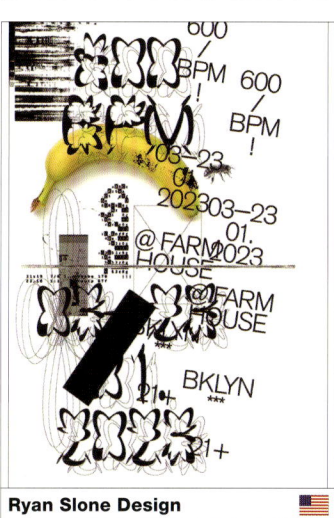
Ryan Slone Design 🇺🇸

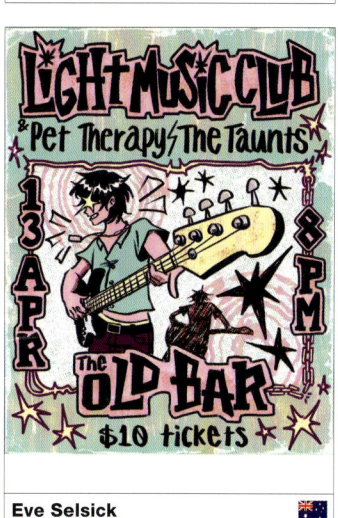
Eve Selsick 🇦🇺

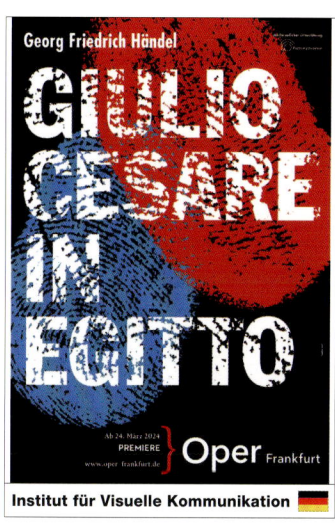
Institut für Visuelle Kommunikation 🇩🇪

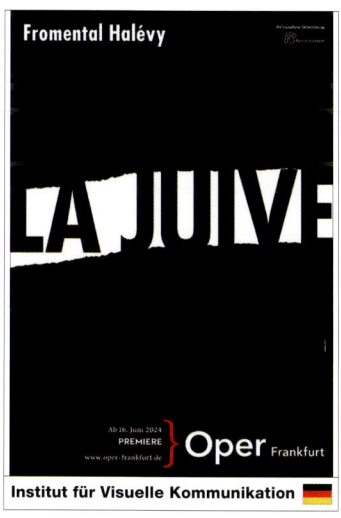
Institut für Visuelle Kommunikation 🇩🇪

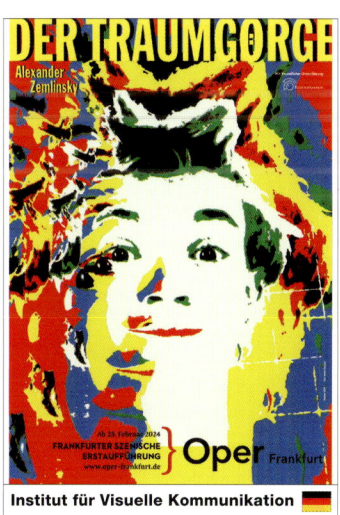
Institut für Visuelle Kommunikation 🇩🇪

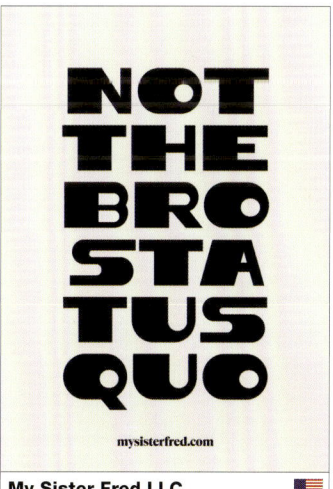
My Sister Fred LLC 🇺🇸

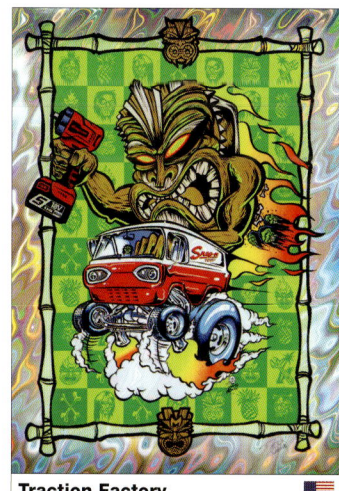
Traction Factory 🇺🇸

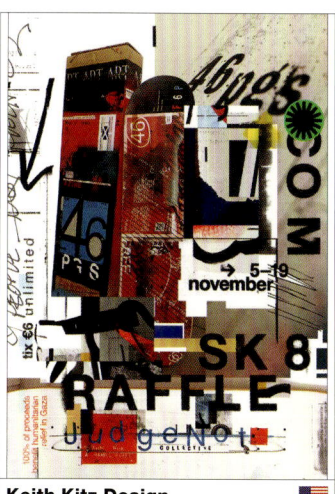
Keith Kitz Design 🇺🇸

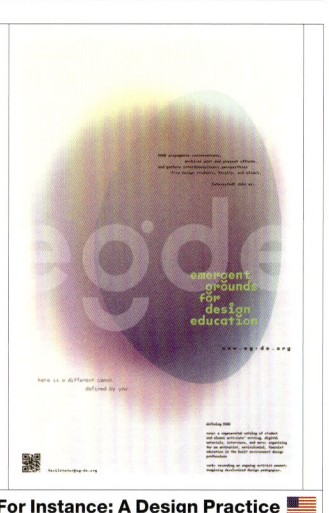
For Instance: A Design Practice 🇺🇸

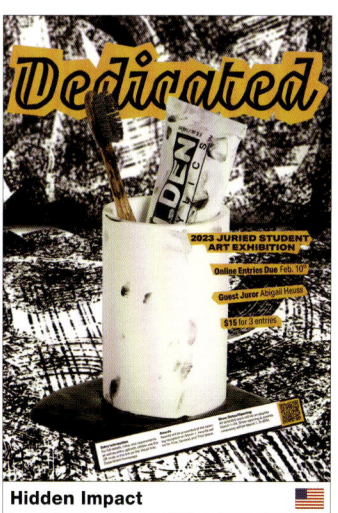
Hidden Impact 🇺🇸

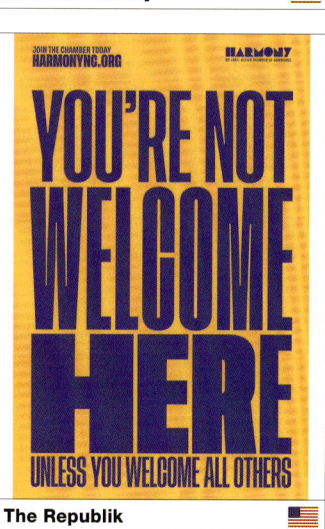
The Republik 🇺🇸

228 HONORABLE MENTIONS

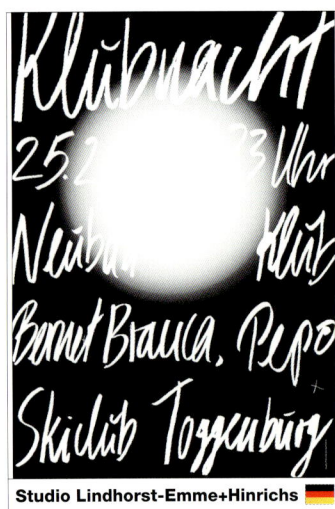
Studio Lindhorst-Emme+Hinrichs 🇩🇪

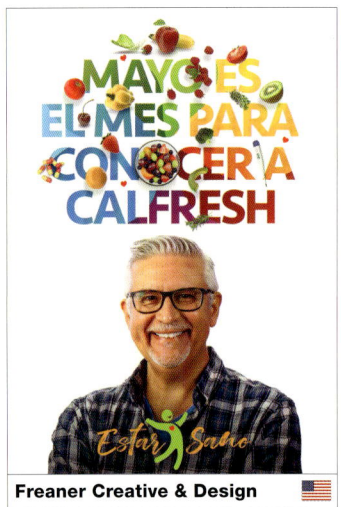
Freaner Creative & Design 🇺🇸

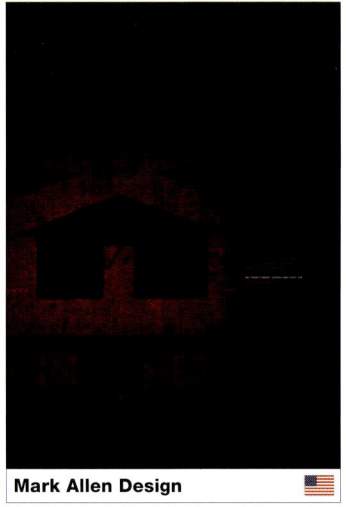
Mark Allen Design 🇺🇸

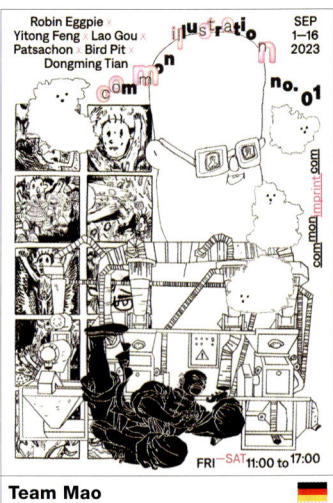
Team Mao 🇩🇪

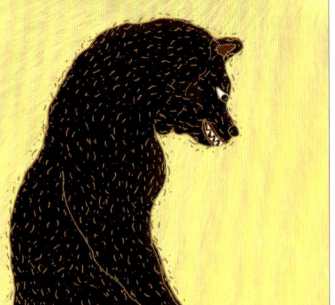
Brain Bolts 🇺🇸

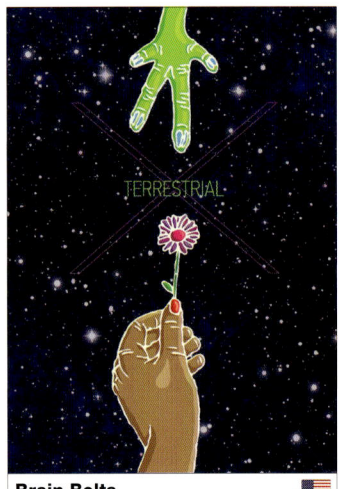
Brain Bolts 🇺🇸

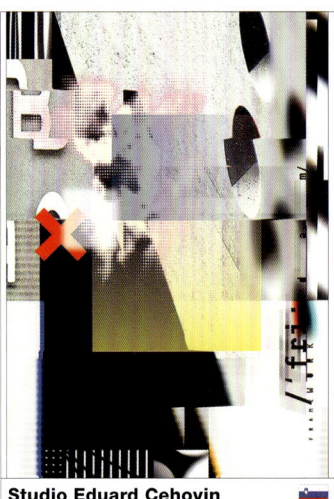
Studio Eduard Cehovin 🇸🇮

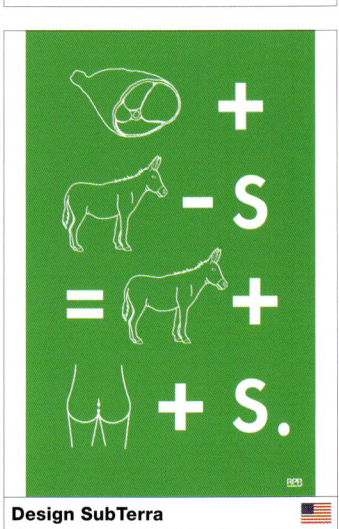
Design SubTerra 🇺🇸

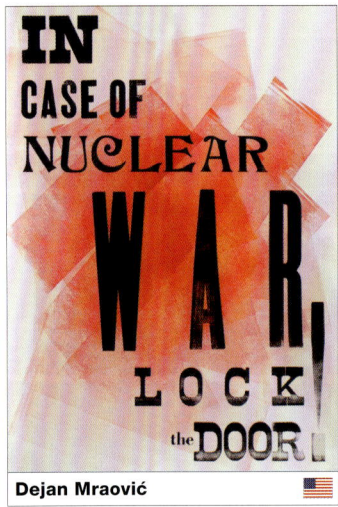
Dejan Mraović 🇺🇸

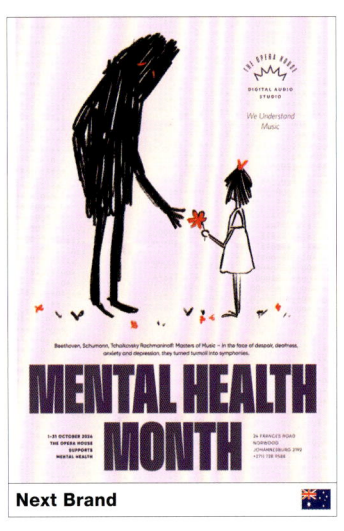
Next Brand 🇦🇺

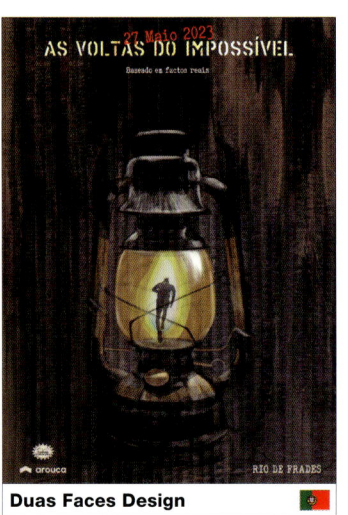
Duas Faces Design 🇵🇹

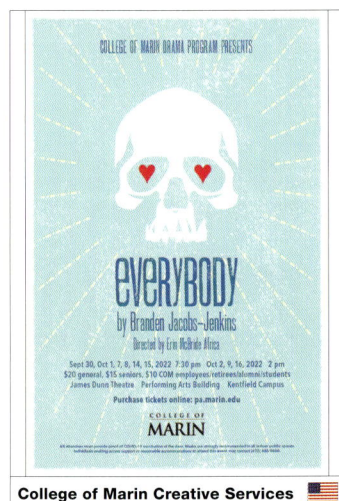
College of Marin Creative Services 🇺🇸

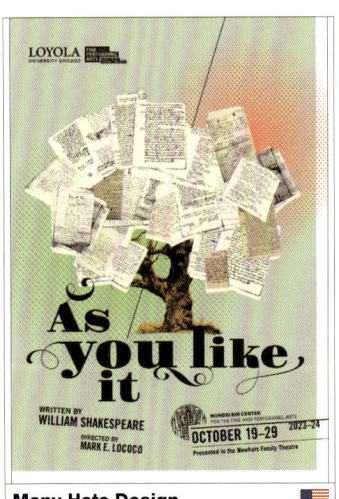
Many Hats Design 🇺🇸

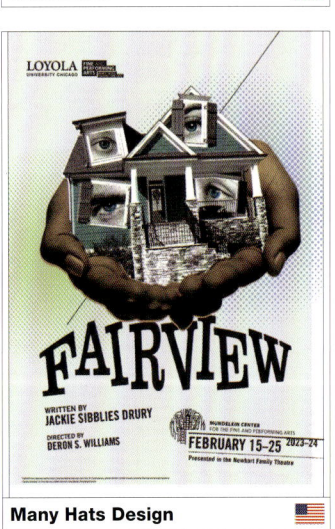
Many Hats Design 🇺🇸

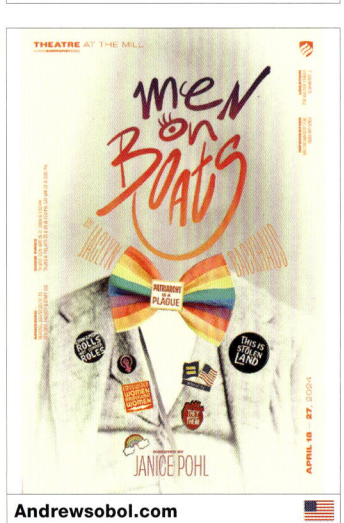
Andrewsobol.com 🇺🇸

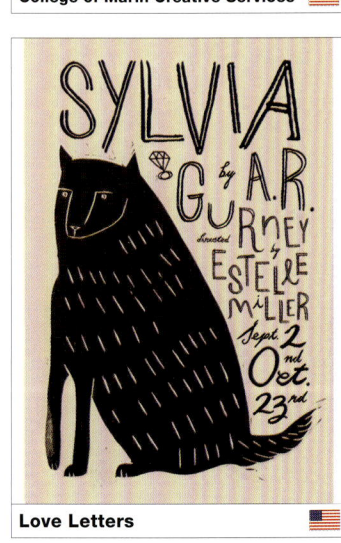
Love Letters 🇺🇸

229 HONORABLE MENTIONS

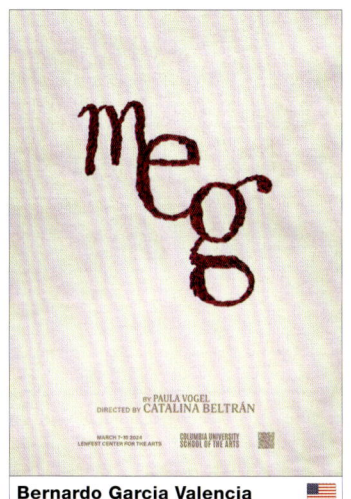
Bernardo Garcia Valencia

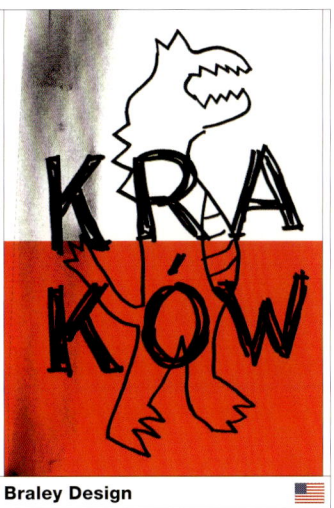
Braley Design

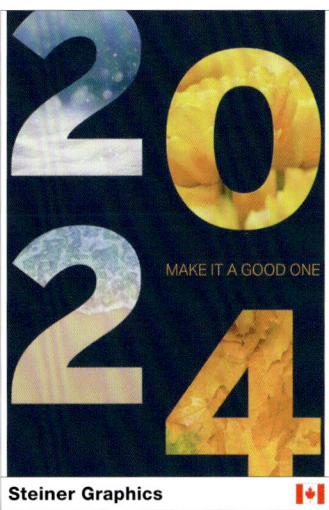
Steiner Graphics

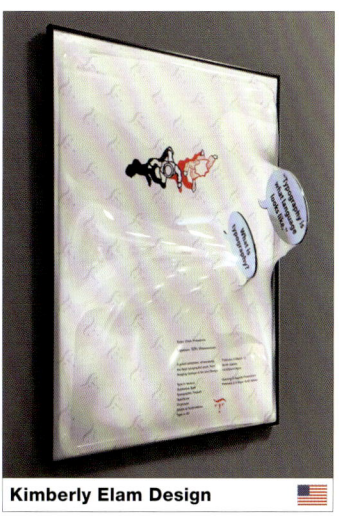
Kimberly Elam Design

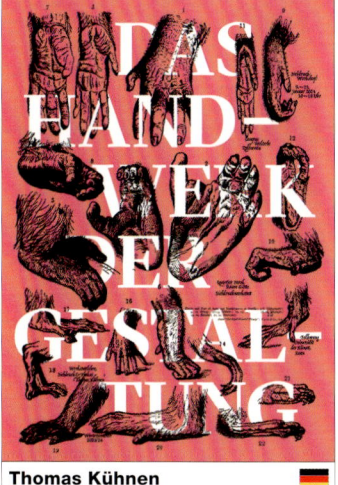
Thomas Kühnen

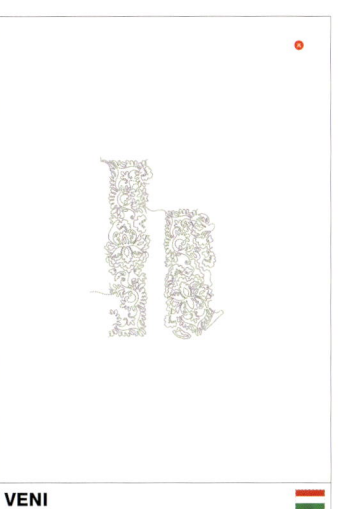
VENI

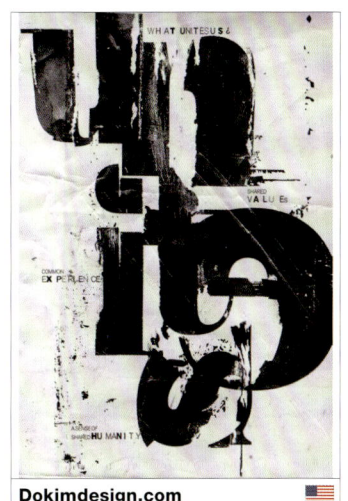
Dokimdesign.com

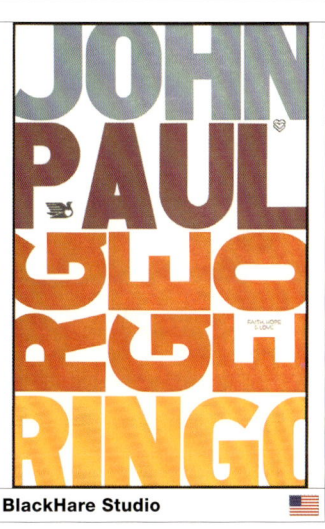
BlackHare Studio

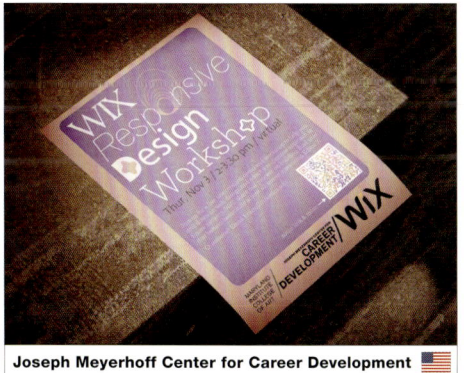
Joseph Meyerhoff Center for Career Development

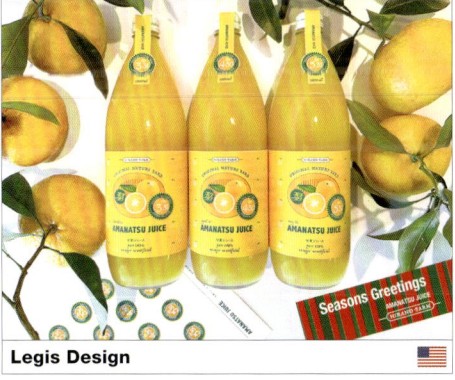
Legis Design

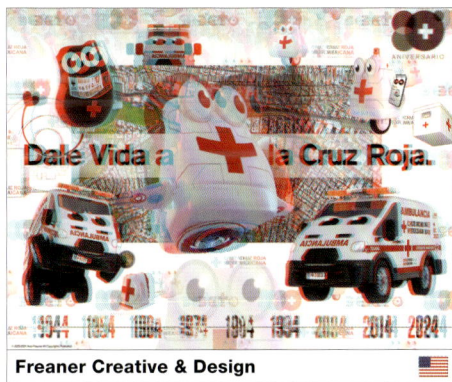
Freaner Creative & Design

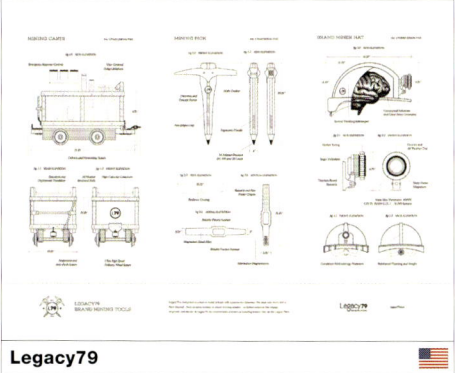
Legacy79

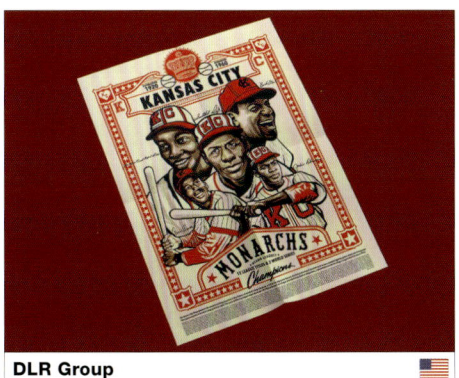
DLR Group

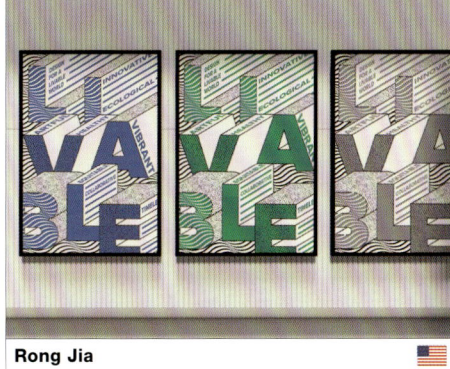
Rong Jia

The variety and immense creativity of the submissions made for an exciting and contemplative experience.

Liz English, *Senior Art Director, MOCEAN*

Credits&Commentary

PLATINUM WINNERS:

28 SHOE DESIGN | Design Firm: João Machado Design
Designer: João Machado | Client: Self-initiated | Main Contributor: João Machado
Assignment: This poster was not commissioned by any client. It was created for my sole pleasure, and, from my perspective, with some humor. Who knows? It is an image that may be 'open' to be used by some entity related to the footwear industry.
Approach: A imagem é de leitura imediata. Penso que o espetador é, neste caso, surpreendido com algum humor pelo óbvio, onde está expresso, através de um compasso de desenho 'muito sexy', o princípio do rigor do desenho.

29 TUSKEGEE AIRMEN | Design Firm: The Union Design Company
Designer: Steve James | Client: Self-initiated | Main Contributor: Steve James
Assignment: Vintage-style posters during WW2 did not always depict African Americans and other groups who saw combat. The goal was to revive that style of retro and add some historical context as the ideas of taking away American history is all too prevalent in certain parts of the country.
Approach: I researched all for of vintage war poster styles and historical accounts of these storied U.S. soldiers.
Results: The process resulted in a poster in which was welcomed by all Americans who celebrate our war heros including veterans and educators.

30 ZEITZEUGEN, SCHWEIZER PLAKATE IM WELTFORMAT, SWISS POSTER EXHIBITION, POSTERS FROM 1940 TILL TODAY | Design Firm: Melchior Imboden
Designer: Melchior Imboden | Client: Dreiländer Museum Lörrach, Germany
Art Director: Melchior Imboden | Main Contributor: Melchior Imboden
Assignment: I designed this poster for an exhibition at the Dreiländer Museum in Lörrach. The exhibition presents a selection of outstanding Swiss posters in Swiss sice, 90,5 x 128 cm, world format from 1940 to the present day.
Approach: To start, I created several lines of typography. Each line contains a word with the title of the exhibition and additional information. The lines are deliberately designed in different colors and with a color gradient to indicate the diverse spectrum of the various Swiss posters and the variety of creations.
Results: The management of the museum was extremely pleased with the result. The poster will also be sold at the museum shop.

31 SHARP DRESSED MAN | Design Firm: dGwaltneyArt
Designer: David H. Gwaltney | Client: Self-initiated
Digital Artist: David H. Gwaltney | Main Contributor: David H. Gwaltney
Assignment: Self promotion for The Artists Galley's 2023 January Show, "New". New work(s) that has not previously shown in the Gallery or to the general public.
Approach: As an exhibiting artist at the Artists Gallery in Virginia Beach, the "Sharp Dressed Man" poster was created to promote my series of signed limited edition prints of original digital paintings on canvas. Created on Apple iPad Pro using Procreate.
Results: Invitation to a month long one man show at the Virginia Beach Central Library and as an exhibitor to the Virginia Beach Boardwalk Art Show, Portsmouth Seawall Art Show and Arts In the Middle Show in Urbanna,VA.

32 CITY TREE FALL FESTIVAL 2023 | Design Firm: Freaner Creative & Design
Designer: Ariel Freaner | Client: City Tree Christina Schools | Main Contributor: Ariel Freaner
Assignment: City Tree Christina Schools needed a poster for their 2023 Fall Festival.
Approach: We developed a poster utilizing natural and festive fall elements. We use stylized typography for elegance and to provide a religious touch without utilizing religious elements to welcome all religions, families, and members of their community.
Results: Great turnout, increase in ticket sales, and on-site festival revenue.

33 SERIES OF EVENT POSTERS FOR THE RYMKIEWICZ FESTIVAL
Design Firm: Katarzyna Zapart | Designer: Katarzyna Zapart | Client: Fundacja Evviva L'arte
Assignment: Festival Rymkiewiczowski is a festival dedicated to Jarosław Rymkiewicz, a Polish poet. I had designed a whole visual identity, logo and posters for the venue. The festival's events were exhibitions, theatre plays, concerts, debates and conferences. The topic of the first edition was "Dziady, Upiory, Przodkowie", which means: "Dziady (old Slavic pagan ritual connected to "feeding" the souls of the dead), Ghosts, Ancestors".
Approach: My first idea was to use medieval Danse Macabre motifs. After many trials, I decided to stick to some human element from paintings or photos of people connected to the topic, and marbled paper as a background. The shape of the logo works as a x-ray or a scene of a surreal events: we can see skulls or bones of the depicted people, veins or colorful spots. I chose 2 fonts for the titles and mixed them: Museo Sans as a base and Digestive to give it a "ghosty" touch.
Results: The client was very open for the creative solutions so the cooperation was a success. The posters were used not only as an outdoor advertising, but also as a postcards to be taken by the participants. The client was content with the outcome of the collaboration.

34 ED SHEERAN | Design Firm: THERE IS STUDIO | Designers: Sean Freeman, Eve Steben
Client: Another Planet Entertainment | Main Contributors: Sean Freeman, Eve Steben
Assignment: We were commissioned to create an exclusive poster design for the one-night-only Ed Sheeran acoustic solo show at the Fox Theatre, in Oakland California.
Approach: We designed a super bold type-led poster using a mix of graphic contemporary fonts, with a smidge of funkiness and plenty of nice typographic moments. We elevated Ed's enjoyment of butterflies into a dimensional, alive and tactile composition using a variety of beautiful specimens covering the largest letters - with his name shining through the colourful wings and brightly peppered with some cute ladybugs.
Results: The poster was offered as a collectible merchandise item, printed in very limited edition exclusively for fans attending the event. A copy was offered on the night of the show as a special present to the artist, from the management team. A hero signed poster was also framed to feature in a music poster collection at the venue.

35 CARMEN | Design Firm: Atelier Bundi AG
Designer: Stephan Bundi | Client: Sommeroper Selzach | Art Director: Stephan Bundi
Illustrator: Stephan Bundi | Main Contributor: Stephan Bundi
Assignment: Opera by Georges Bizet. Carmen is stabbed to death out of jealousy.
Approach: By cutting across the poster (and across Carmen) I created a trompe l'oeil, a trick of the eye. The viewer is immediately irritated if the poster is damaged or is the damage part of the visual interpretation. When printing, it was particularly important that the light and shadows looked as real as possible on the slightly rolled paper.
Results: The poster motif was also used for the program booklet, advertisements and other advertising material.

36 LYCEUM COMPETITION CALL FOR ENTRIES | Design Firm: Skolos-Wedell
Designers: Nancy Skolos, Thomas Wedell | Client: Lyceum Fellowship Committee
Photographer: Thomas Wedell | Main Contributors: Nancy Skolos, Thomas Wedell
Assignment: The poster was the 2024 call for entries for the Lyceum Fellowship, an annual student architecture competition. The 2024 program asked students to design a Center For Regenerative Building that would explore the potential symbiosis between the environment and the inevitable growth of human settlement by creating a maker space to function as a component of a regional economic and ecological metabolism.
Approach: Create a regenerative image to reinforce the project prompt that regenerated optically in various ways as it passed through a series of plexiglass dowel rods.

37 TIN TOY TIMES | Design Firm: CollierGraphica | Designer: Steve Collier
Client: Self-initiated | Main Contributor: Steve Collier
Assignment: Promotional poster for tin toys.
Approach: Design and produce poster to bring about interest in tin toys.
Results: Successful.

38 WOMEN. LIFE. FREEDOM. | Design Firm: Gallery BI
Designer: Byoung-il Sun | Client: National Human Rights Commission of the Republic of Korea
Artist: Byoung-il Sun | Main Contributor: Byoung-il Sun
Assignment: This poster is about human rights issues. Especially women's rights are a big problem in some countries. This poster aims to convey the message of hope for freedom in the midst of much persecution and suffering.
Approach: The poster combines human images and butterflies for a strong approach to women's rights. The combination of a woman and a butterfly simultaneously reveals the beauty of a woman and the beauty of a butterfly, metaphorically expressing that basic human rights are human rights and that butterflies are also the basis of all ecosystems, and that everything should be a human right without basic freedom and discrimination.
Results: The project poster attracted a lot of eyes and attention with its beauty and focus on women's rights. At the very least, it was judged to be a new and creative approach to the idea and composition that generated interest and empathy for the issue.

39 TOLERANCE | Design Firm: Dankook University | Designer: Hoon-Dong Chung
Client: Self-initiated | Main Contributor: Hoon-Dong Chung
Assignment: Tolerance is to embrace difference to be together. This work symbolizes the starting point of 'tolerance' and the ending point of 'conflict' in a integrated form.
Approach: Contrast and harmony.
Results: The latest work.

GOLD WINNERS:

41 ORCAS ISLAND FILM FESTIVAL 2023 POSTER | Design Firm: Huber Design Werks
Designer: Paul Huber | Client: Orcas Island Film Festival | Art Director: Paul Huber
Creative Directors: Paul Huber, Donna Laslo, Carl Spence | Main Contributor: Paul Huber
Assignment: Orcas Island, WA, is a quiet and pristine festival environment where film lovers can wander, reflect and digest films as well as enjoy the quaint village of Eastsound. During our annual mid-October festival, we screen over 30 incredible films over the course of five days. Our goals? Effectively market this unique festival to both enhance the overall experience and drive ticket sales and attendance.
Approach: The OIFF takes place in the San Juan Islands. The 6,000 year-round residents are collectively intelligent, creative, literate, self-entertaining, and empathetic. Those qualities make for a fascinating community that chooses to live on this less-than-accessible island. Our hope was that we could convey that quirky sense of place and spirit best through Midjourney's AI capability. The creative result was a poster featuring a mysterious projector of sorts deep in one of the island's dense fir forest.
Results: As the ninth annual Orcas Island Film Festival, it was the most successful in both attendance and revenues. And this quirky poster was embraced thoroughly by both locals and off-island attendees.

42 41ST ANNIVERSARY OF THE COLEGIO DE SONORA: TRIBUTE TO THE PAINTER HELGA KREBS | Design Firm: Ivette Valenzuela Design | Designer: Ivette Valenzuela
Client: Colson | Main Contributor: Ivette Valenzuela
Assignment: To design a poster to commemorate the 41st anniversary of El Colegio de Sonora (Colson), a leading institution in research and higher education in Social Sciences and Humanities. It is a tribute to the outstanding Chilean painter Helga Kreps, an internationally renowned visual artist and symbol of creativity and cultural diversity.
Approach: The tribute transcends the boundaries of art to become a reflection on themes such as migration, exile, solidarity, and the infinite creativity expressed through images and words. The poster design was inspired by her pictorial work, using a collage that fuses her different styles and themes. The artist's face was recreated with vector strokes, while the filler was made up of representative fragments of her vast artistic production.
Results: This symbolic image was present throughout the year in various manifestations. Even the educational campus was dressed in these graphics throughout the year, celebrating the legacy of this extraordinary artist and her impact on society.

43 TE WHEKE / THE OCTOPUS | Design Firm: Osborne Shiwan
Designers: Lloyd Osborne, Shabnam Shiwan | Client: Atamira Dance Company
Creative Directors: Lloyd Osborne, Shabnam Shiwan | Photographers: Toaki Okano, Petra Leary
Main Contributor: Osborne Shiwan
Assignment: Atamira Dance Company is Aotearoa New Zealand's leading Māori contemporary dance theatre creator. Te Wheke is a collaborative new work, bringing together Aotearoa's leading names in dance. Eight choreographers and dancers are symbolised by the eight tentacles of Te Wheke, The Octopus, a guardian on this journey from past into future. Our key communication audience were Māori and those wanting to experience contemporary Māori culture.
Approach: Our campaigns built on the brand platform 'mythologies woven in movement'. Custom lettering, typography and portraiture combine with dance expressions to create a sense of rhythm and movement. We worked closely with the client to identify key figurative movements within the practice. This was photographed by drone. Portraiture is sliced through, in eight parts, to create a graphic watery distortion. A full graphic typeface

was created, based on the Māori art of tukutuku panelling. Typographic forms fade in and out, interweaving with figures, like seaweed, creating a sense of rhythm and movement. When used as a series, the typography links the posters together as it overlaps the edges.
Results: The campaign uses Te Reo Māori and English to reflect changes within Aotearoa, as more people learn the Māori language. The Te Wheke campaign ran nationwide in Aotearoa and was highly successful, including two sell-out Tamakai Makaurau, Auckland shows. Atamira has recently toured North America with Te Wheke.

44 THE HEARTBEAT OF MEXICO | Design Firm: Legacy79 | Designer: Genaro Solis Rivero
Client: Baylor University Department of Modern Languages and Cultures
Main Contributor: Genaro Solis Rivero
Assignment: The project aimed to design a poster to promote a Mariachi Masterclass and performance for the Department of Modern Languages and Cultures at Baylor University.
Approach: This proposed solution combined the heart's shape with a guitar. The guitar illustration was rendered by folklore birds interlacing the guitar strings, forming an intricate pattern and shapes. These birds and styles of illustration are homages to folklore and handcraft artists in Mexico. At the same time, the strings form a visual rhythm while metaphorically discovering the heartbeat of Mexico, the music.
Results: The poster communicates the folklore and music of Mexican culture very effectively. It plays on the metaphor of flying birds forming the guitar—constructing the melodies and the guitar, an iconic Mexican instrument.

45 DESIGN FOR TOMORROW | Design Firm: National Kaohsiung University of Science & Technology (NKUST) | Designer: Chong-Wen Chen
Client: NKUST College of Innovation & Design | Main Contributor: Chong-Wen Chen
Assignment: This poster promotes the newly launched College of Innovation and Design at NKUST, which is dedicated to integrating sustainability with design education from a global perspective. The poster illustrates this by incorporating the UN's 17 Sustainable Development Goals (SDGs) into design thinking. It emphasizes that today's design practices should consider tomorrow's outcomes to create a better future.
Approach: The poster shows creativity by extracting a single letter from each SDG to present the vertically composed phrase: "Design for Tomorrow." Pencils marked with the numbers and themes of the 17 SDGs are used not only as symbols of the designer's tools but also as representations of the college's commitment to nurturing sustainable design thinking and skills among students.
Results: This poster will be distributed to international academic and non-profit institutions to promote the College of Innovation and Design at NKUST, aiming to foster potential collaborations in research and design practices.

46 NATIONAL MARINE MAMMAL FOUNDATION: RESEARCH. INNOVATION. DISCOVERY. | Design Firm: Freaner Creative & Design | Designer: Ariel Freaner
Client: National Marine Mammal Foundation | Digital Artist: Ariel Freaner
Main Contributor: Ariel Freaner
Assignment: The National Marine Mammal Foundation needed a poster for education forums and promotions.
Approach: We develop a poster that encompasses knowledge of marine life in a visually enlightening as a leader in marine mammal science, medicine, and conservation.
Results: Increase in awareness and brand position.

47 CREATIVE ENCOUNTERS | Design Firm: Auburn University School of Industrial + Graphic Design | Designers: Mario F. Bocanegra Martinez, Courtney Windham
Client: MACAA (Mid-America College Art Association)
Main Contributors: Mario F. Bocanegra Martinez, Courtney Windham
Assignment: Mario F. Bocanegra Martinez and Courtney Windham teamed up to create a compelling series of promotional materials for their panel session, 'Creative Encounters: Exploring the Art of "Thinking Through Making"', at the MACAA Satellite Conference. This creative venture not only highlights the designers' skills but also encourages participation and engagement within the design community.
Approach: Mario and Courtney define 'creative encounter' as a pivotal moment in design where unexpected connections are made, often in overlooked situations. Illustrating this concept, Mario and Courtney orchestrated two experimental sessions. In the first, Mario presented an array of photographic remnants from his "Alphabetum" series while Courtney contributed various typographic sources and custom AI-generated images. Together, they crafted a series of collages. The next session saw Mario bringing 10-12 layouts, exploring grid systems, scale, contrast, and hierarchy. These layouts served as creative springboards for each to develop collaged poster designs. Subsequently, each designer digitally enhanced their collaged posters, culminating in the creation of four distinct posters and an animated version.
Results: An animated version of the poster series was developed and posted to Linkedin and Instagram to reach potential participants. Ultimately, the promotional campaign for the panel session's call for submissions garnered twelve submissions from diverse regions of the United States, with the campaign culminating in selecting eight outstanding proposals. These will be showcased at the conference in March 2024. Mario and Courtney are set to host two engaging sessions, dedicated to exploring the unique creative encounters experienced by fellow designers, educators, and students.

48 SVA BLOOD DRIVE | Design Firm: Viktor Koen | Designer: Viktor Koen
Client: School of Visual Arts | Main Contributor: Viktor Koen
Assignment: Poster promoting the first School of Visual Arts Blood Drive during Halloween 2023. The campaign also promoted the need and benefits of blood donation, awareness to blood shortages, and fostering community among students and faculty.
Approach: Halloween spirit provided the mood and creative approach to a challenging subject such as blood donation to students. The character of Count Orlok from F. W. Murnau's 1922 silent masterpiece, Nosferatu, also served as inspirational.
Results: A striking visual attracting attention through bold composition and character to promote the desperate need for blood donation but also a meaningful opportunity to strengthen school ties and contribute to our community at large.

49 THE YELLOW WALLPAPER | Design Firm: Viktor Koen | Designer: Viktor Koen
Client: School of Visual Arts | Main Contributor: Viktor Koen
Assignment: Poster for School of Visual Arts MFA Illustration department exhibition based on the short story The Yellow Wallpaper, by Charlotte Perkins Gilman.
Approach: A ghostly house, a haunted wallpaper and the color yellow inspired this cryptic composition where everything happens underneath.
Results: A mysterious poster that attracts with its stark composition and atmospheric depth while inviting the discovery of hidden clues layer after layer. This is to mirror the gradual succession of events to the narrative's eerie conclusion. The show was exhibited at SVA's Chelsey Gallery in May 2023.

50 SVA SUMMER ILLUSTRATION RESIDENCY | Design Firm: Viktor Koen
Designer: Viktor Koen | Client: School of Visual Arts | Main Contributor: Viktor Koen
Assignment: Promotional poster for School of Visual Arts Summer Illustration Residency program at the 2023 MoCCA Comics festival in NY.
Approach: The aquatic theme of a diver provided the mood and approach to promoting this Summer-in-the-City intensive illustration program at SVA.
Results: Splashing into work through June and July in NYC is no easy sell but the diagonal composition of a diver morphing into colors, art supplies and energy proved an effective way to promote summer as the perfect time to learn and transform.

51 "ART THINKING & DESIGN THINKING" IN THE GRAPHIC ART COURSE
Design Firm: Kiyoung An Graphic Art Course Laboratory | Designer: Kiyoung An
Client: KINDAI University Department of Arts | Art Director: Kiyoung An
Main Contributor: Kiyoung An
Assignment: This is a poster for the new semester's course selection and assignment briefings. It is also one of the materials for understanding the creative images in this course.

52 FATAL ATTRACTION | Design Firm: Canyon | Designers: Paramount+, Canyon
Client: Paramount+ | Art Directors: Chris Hawkins (Paramount+), Sabrina Nguyen-Tran (Paramount+) | Creative Directors: Chad Rachild (Canyon), Senior Creative Director of Key Art: Steve Chan (Paramount+) | Vice Presidents: Photography: Christine Ramage (Paramount+), Creative Director: Stacey Batzer | Senior Vice Presidents: Creative Director: Becca Schader (Paramount+), Design Lead: Matt Hernandez (Paramount+), Accounts: Courtney Olsen (Canyon) Account Director: Matt D'Auria (Canyon) | Marketing Manager: Sr Manager Creative Production, Operations, Management: Tara Marin (Paramount+) | Photographer: Zoey Grossman
Project Manager: Dagny McCartney (Canyon) | Main Contributors: Paramount+, Canyon
Assignment: This new Paramount+ series is "a reimagining of the film that explores the themes of marriage and infidelity through the lens of modern attitudes toward strong women, personality disorders, and coercive control." The assignment was to focus on the story of Dan and Alex in a new light and towing the line of not going to sexual and overt.
Approach: We began with a sketch phase, then moved to the photoshoot with photographer Zoey Grossman. The build explore resulted in a striking campaign. The first phase of the campaign hit the streets with the red and black tease campaign with iconic type "I won't be ignored, Dan", the campaign evolved weeks later with the character teases with, "I won't be ignored", over the two characters faces. The Key art reveal weeks later with the voyeruistic, "Elevator" Key Art that gave a glimpse into the character's world and the "Embrace" Key Art art for the accolades.
Results: The project was a success with shedding new light on an iconic story.

53 THE CHANGELING, KEY ART | Design Firm: The Refinery
Designer: The Refinery | Client: Apple TV+ | Main Contributor: The Refinery
Assignment: In The Changeling, a fairy tale becomes a nightmare. To help sell this dark and twisted fable, our client tasked us with a few considerations: ideate on the folklore, the symbolism, and how to place Easter eggs in the art. We were also asked to keep both Apollo and Emma's story in mind as we ideated.
Approach: Who do you become when you stop trusting the world you live in? Someone you don't recognize. This unsettling and uncanny feeling is a key component of The Changeling and the guiding theme behind our Key Art. We used a specific scene from the series to serve as a representation of this weird, twisted world. This moment is significant for both of our leads: it's the exact instance that the world as they know it falls apart.
Results: Our art created a sense of danger and curiosity, provoking viewers to keep watching and asking questions. Our clients were pleased with this solve and its ability to hit the important points they outlined during the initial phase of this project.

54 STING | Design Firm: The Refinery | Designer: The Refinery
Client: Well Go USA Entertainment | Main Contributor: The Refinery
Assignment: Create a teaser to build anticipation for a cosmic horror flick.
Approach: A memorable visual that features the creature as a focal point and creates a gleeful if squeamish feeling of dread.
Results: A spider, lit by moonlight, crawls across old floorboards. The blue and silver color palette casts a quiet chill, placing us in the dead of night. The spider itself is small and familiar, but the shadow it casts suggests something otherworldly. Is this shadow a trick of the light? Or is it a warning, signaling this particular spider's predatory potential? Everything in this image suggests the latter.

55 LAWMEN BASS REEVES KEY ART CAMPAIGN | Design Firm: Paramount+
Designer: Paramount+ | Client: Self-initiated | Photographer: Kwaku Alston
Main Contributor: Paramount+
Assignment: Establish the series as the next can't-miss, action-packed Taylor Sheridan drama from Paramount+ and introduce audiences to the historical figure known as Bass Reeves in a series unmatched in scale by any previous adaptation of his life story.
Approach: For the Pursuit art, we crafted an action-packed visual narrative for "Lawmen Bass Reeves," spotlighting the titular character's vitality through a striking pose on a white horse amid a dust-stirred backdrop. The poster's design merges Western grit with epic storytelling to spark viewers' imaginations and anticipation for the series. On the character art, dramatically backlit, desaturated action shots of talent, emerging from smoke, enhancing each character's personality, determination and commitment to justice.
Results: The campaign was met with great enthusiasm, evidenced by strong social media engagement and increased subscription predictions for Paramount+. The poster's blend of historical reverence and cinematic excitement effectively amplified viewer anticipation and series premiere success.

56 PAIN HUSTLERS CHARACTER ART | Design Firm: Rhubarb | Designer: Rhubarb
Client: Netflix | Executive Creative Director: Ryan Jones | Creative Director: Adrianne Deluna
Chief Creative Officer: Andrew Irving | Account Director: Geysel Junne
Marketing: Sway Benns (Netflix) | Main Contributor: Rhubarb

233 CREDITS&COMMENTARY

Assignment: Create a poster series to create intrigue and interest for "Pain Hustlers", a film that explores the darker side of the pharmaceutical industry in a unique way.
Approach: Instead of making a dark and moody poster, we leaned into an ironically bright palette and feeling, inspired by the Florida location of the film. The characters' faces were cropped off to give a sense of shame, that they have something to hide.
Results: The posters were plastered all over Los Angeles and New York and were used in social media promotions as well.

57 FARGO | Design Firm: ARSONAL | Designer: ARSONAL | Client: FX Networks
Others: Stephanie Gibbons, Creative Director/President, Creative, Strategy & Digital Marketing Michael Brittain, Creative Director / SVP Print Design Rob Wilson, VP Print Design Sarin Markarian, Director Print Design Laura Handy, Project Director, Print Design Lisa Lejeune, Production Director, Print Design | Main Contributors: ARSONAL, FX Networks
Assignment: For the 5th season, Fargo revisits Joel and Ethan Coen's original 1996 movie and focus on wife of the car salesman. The goal for season 5's key art campaign was to highlight how extreme and bizarre the characters are as well as to showcase the contrast of qualities that exists within their personalities.
Approach: It was important to be iconic and to keep consistency with the past campaigns of this series. To achieve this we pulled iconography from the story that symbolizes and communicates the tone of this season which is a contrast between crime drama with high stakes and comedy with humorous undertones.
Results: The art successfully exhibits the quirkiness of the characters with an underlying sense of drama. The figurine art in particular was a bit hit, receiving a lot of buzz and excited fans before the premiere.

58 HOARDERS | Design Firm: SJI Associates | Designers: John Lyness, Chad Hornberger
Clients: A+E Networks, Jacqui Bussey-Sr. Creative Director, Matt Ehmann-Creative Director, Wes Bent-Production Manager | President: Suzy Jurist | Art Director: David O'Hanlon
Project Manager: Hannah Holdsworth | Main Contributor: SJI Associates
Assignment: Draw viewers into the real-life stories of people struggling with hoarding, highlighting the overwhelming obstacles those dedicated to helping them can face.
Approach: Stacks of old books, boxes, and electronics help to recreate the claustrophobic, often tragic living situations depicted in the show.
Results: This key art drove interest and awareness for the new season, and was repurposed for social, digital, and on-air graphics, driving tune-in and streaming views.

59 ALL THE LIGHT WE CANNOT SEE CHARACTER POSTERS | Design Firm: Rhubarb
Designer: Rhubarb | Client: Netflix | Executive Creative Director: Ryan Jones
Creative Director: Adrianne Deluna | Chief Creative Officer: Andrew Irving
Photographer: Atsushi Nishijima | Marketing: Erin Mumy | Account Director: Geysel Junne
Main Contributor: Rhubarb
Assignment: The story behind All The Light We Cannot See takes place in the final days of WWII, when the paths of a blind French girl and a German soldier collide. Our task was to create a character campaign that created an emotional impact on the viewer and revealed each character's personality and role.
Approach: Using the photography shot on set, we strategically chose images that had a visceral quality, and had the right elements in the frame to be able to tell a story.
Results: The images were used as wild posting in the out-of-home media campaign.

60 THE BOYS IN THE BOAT | Design Firm: The Refinery
Designer: The Refinery | Client: Amazon Studios | Main Contributor: The Refinery
Assignment: To deliver a classic-yet-modern and emotionally evocative campaign for the film adaptation about the 1936 Berlin Olympic US rowing team.
Approach: A restrained yet impactful campaign that relied on an emotionally charged and beautiful image—the kind that linger in a viewer's mind and heart.
Results: In one image, the team stands in silhouette, backs to the viewer. The tall oars in their hands evoke spears, promising a challenge ahead. The murky sky suggests the future is unknown—but the tinge of gold hints at victory. In the second image, the team sits inside their boat, gazing upward at their coach, who stands on the dock. In contrast to their athletic gear, the coach wears a suit and hat. Once again, a murky sky tinged with gold gently hints at victory—but not without unforeseen trials. The oars laid across the dock evoke a ladder of sorts, which in combination with the gilded light may strike the viewer as almost spiritual. Certainly forces of Good versus Evil collide in 1936—a global reality this otherwise intimate image quietly acknowledges.

61 CODE 8 PART II TEASER POSTER | Design Firm: Rhubarb | Designer: Rhubarb
Client: Netflix | Marketing: Robin Dybevik, Netflix | Chief Creative Officer: Andrew Irving
Executive Creative Director: Ryan Jones | Creative Director: Adrianne Deluna
Art Director: Simone Ferraro | Account Director: Geysel Junne | Main Contributor: Rhubarb
Assignment: The goal was set to create excitement around the sequel to Code 8, and elevate anticipation for the forthcoming film.
Approach: Fans of the original film saw the two protagonists part ways. Our approach was to show the audience that they were back together, and despite their differences, they were fighting a common enemy.
Results: The movie poster was an effective teaser for the film, creating a buzz online and on social media. The art was featured on both actor's Instagram accounts.

62 UPLOAD S3 KEY ART | Design Firm: Rhubarb | Designer: Rhubarb
Client: Amazon Studios | Photographer: Pamela Littky | Executive Creative Director: Ryan Jones
Creative Director: Adrianne Deluna | Chief Creative Officer: Andrew Irving
Account Director: Geysel Junne | Main Contributor: Rhubarb
Assignment: Create a poster for the third season of the popular Amazon Prime series "Upload", a futuristic satirical comedy series that pokes fun at our modern digital culture and imagines what life and death will be like in 2033.
Approach: Characters bounce back and forth between real life and a virtual afterlife, causing delightful chaos and confusion. We created an updated homage to Magritte's "The Blank Signature" that featured characters in various stages of digital appearance.
Results: This season was a huge hit, and so was the key art. Posters were featured in out of home applications, as well as digital and social media advertising.

63 SECRETS OF THE OCTOPUS | Design Firm: SJI Associates | Designer: David O'Hanlon
Clients: National Geographic, EVP Creative - Chris Spencer, VP Design - Brian Everett, Design Director - Mariano Barreiro, Project Manager - Leah Wojda | President: Suzy Jurist
Art Director: David O'Hanlon | Production Artist: Michael Stampone
Project Manager: Hannah Holdsworth | Main Contributor: SJI Associates
Assignment: Explore the mesmerizing, mysterious world of one of the earth's most surprising creatures: the octopus.
Approach: This key art depicted an octopus interacting with its own type treatment.
Results: This key art drove interest and awareness for the series, and was showcased in social, digital, OOH, and on-air graphics, driving tune-in and streaming views.

64 NAPOLEON | Design Firm: The Refinery | Designer: The Refinery
Clients: Apple TV+, Sony Pictures Entertainment | Main Contributor: The Refinery
Assignment: Napoleon's greatest challenge was the protagonist himself. How do we harness history? How do we convey the scale, grandiosity, and complexity of this conqueror? And how do we deliver a polished, modern finish to invite a younger generation to delve deep into the past? We aimed to answer all these questions with our teaser.
Approach: In order to introduce fans to Joaquin Phoenix's Napoleon, we opted for a tight crop, featuring the signature hat of Napoleon slightly shading the unmistakable face of our lead. The stoic, unwavering stare of an era's most ruthless conqueror is not obscured by a dusty historic lens. He's in sharp focus, forcing us to reckon with him: the man who came from nothing, who managed to conquer everything.
Results: Our clients were pleased with this powerful teaser. The singular focus on the titular character piqued the interest of audiences and promised an inventive, unique look into the life of the historical figure.

65 NAPOLEON | Design Firm: The Refinery | Designer: The Refinery
Clients: Apple TV+, Sony Pictures Entertainment | Main Contributor: The Refinery
Assignment: For this Key Art, we were tasked with re-creating a portrait of Napoleon.
Approach: To imitate the portrait, we chose a shot of our titular character sitting alone in a room. Napoleon slings his arm over a plush chair, his gaze focused and cast downward, as if he's plotting his next move. The pose, along with the polished, photographic execution, reads like the painting has come to life.
Results: We successfully recreated the portrait of Napoleon, creating a compelling piece of Key Art for the film.

66 HOT Design Firm: Marlena Buczek Smith | Designer: Marlena Buczek Smith
Client: Self-initiated | Main Contributor: Marlena Buczek Smith
Assignment: More frequent and more extreme weather changes will have an impact on our future, most of all on our children.
Results: If we are not conscious of our environment, than we are lost.

67 FOR LIVES & CHILDREN | Design Firm: National Kaohsiung University of Science & Technology (NKUST) | Designer: Chong-Wen Chen
Client: NKUST College of Innovation & Design | Main Contributor: Chong-Wen Chen
Assignment: This poster supports the global initiative to create a sustainable environment, guided by the UN's 17 Sustainable Development Goals (SDGs). These goals highlight the necessity of empathy and foresight for all inhabitants of our planet, a theme encapsulated in the poster's title. The College of Innovation and Design embraces this ethos as its core principle, striving to foster design thinking that not only enhances students' aesthetic sensibilities but also nurtures their compassion for all life and the environment.
Approach: Demonstrating inventive creativity, this poster constructs the phrase "For Lives & Children" by vertically aligning a single letter from each SDG. The design features wooden road signs inscribed with the numbers and themes of the 17 SDGs amidst a flourish of flowers. Menelaus blue morpho butterflies are depicted fluttering among the flowers. Their presence serves as a hopeful symbol that the successful implementation of the SDGs will allow such beautiful creatures to thrive once more.
Results: This newly launched poster will be distributed to international academic and non-profit institutions to promote the College of Innovation and Design at NKUST, aiming to foster potential collaborations in research and design practices.

68 "MORE IS MORE" PRESENTATION POSTER | Design Firm: Studio Hinrichs
Designer: Kit Hinrichs | Client: ArtCenter College of Design
Main Contributor: Kit Hinrichs
Assignment: To inform design students and enthusiasts of the upcoming presentation and book signing and to entice them to attend.
Approach: The poster builds off Rich Silverstein's testimonial that despite being taught that "less is more," "in Kit's case, the more the merrier." Featuring quotes offered by other designers and artists, the poster was meant to spark the curiosity of potential attendees.
Results: The event was filled beyond capacity and the available books sold out.

69 ANET 30TH ANNIVERSARY EXHIBITION | Design Firm: Toyotsugu Itoh Design Office
Designer: Toyotsugu Itoh | Client: Aichi Art and Culture Network (ANET)
Photographer: Isao Takahashi | Main Contributor: Toyotsugu Itoh
Assignment: Poster for 30th anniversary exhibition of Aichi Art and Culture Network (ANET), the organization of artists and designers in Aichi Prefecture, Japan.
Approach: I expressed a window with forms connecting to 4 letters of this organization's contracted name "ANET". I designed the will of this organization to open and put a message to society in opportunity of 30th anniversary.
Results: Through promotion of this exhibition, I obtained some favorable feedback.

70 SHIPYARD OPEN STUDIOS SPRING 2024 | Design Firm: Craig-Teerlink Design
Designer: Jean Craig-Teerlink | Clients: Shipyard Trust for the Arts, Barbara Ockel
Creative Director: Jean Craig-Teerlink | Illustrator: Jean Craig-Teerlink
Main Contributor: Jean Craig-Teerlink
Assignment: I designed a new 40th Anniversary identity for Hunters Point Shipyard Artists, the largest artist community in the US. Each Spring, the Artists open their studios to the public for Open Studios weekend. I created imagery celebrating their iconic location on the San Francisco Bay facing the largest Gantry Crane in the world.
Approach: The identity was conceived to appeal to both the artists and their patrons. The identity features a dramatic rendering of the view overlooking Shipyard buildings toward the San Franicsco Bay and the narrow pier upon which sits the massive Gantry Crane. The typeface DIN, reflecting the industrial land environment, is paired with original letterforms that capture the Bay in organic, swirling forms.
Results: Those receiving the image responded: 'The graphic you sent is gorgeous!' and 'These are absolutely stunning—thank you!'. Shipyard Trust for the Arts President, Bar-

bara Ockel, reports, "Ticket sales are up 20% and all the artists really love the image and are using it in their own promotional efforts, which helps everyone."

71 FOLHA DE SALA | Design Firm: 1/4 Studio | Designers: Ana Mota, Jorge Araújo
Clients: Galeria Ocupa!, Sput&nik the Window | Creative Directors: Ana Mota, Jorge Araújo
Main Contributor: 1/4 Studio
Assignment: Commissioned by Galeria Ocupa! and Sput&nik the Window, for the exhibit "Folha de Sala" by Rui Mota. The exhibition is made up of what the artist called "extroverted objects" that can expand the concept of Sculpture beyond their limits by using their surroundings as plastic material. The brief was: to create an image that, like the exhibition, could expand the concept of itself beyond its limits.
Approach: The communication created tried to match this self-awareness and intentional redundancy. We used the room sheet as the "image" for the poster and layered it onto itself, creating an "optical spatial" composition. Taking the title into consideration, we came up with the core idea of "a room sheet about a room sheet about a room sheet about a room sheet." This conveyed several aspects of the exhibition. The applications are endless as this solution can, in theory, grow infinitely.
Results: The result was approved by the client and produced as part of the communication for the exhibition.

72 THE GENEALOGY OF JAPANESE GRAPHIC DESIGN | Design Firm: Leo Lin Design
Designer: Leo Lin | Client: National Taiwan Normal University Department of Design
Main Contributor: Leo Lin
Assignment: A document and poster exhibition introducing the development and influence of Japanese modern graphic design.
Approach: The Chinese character "日" in Japan is combined with the Japanese national flag "Hinomaru" image, gradually expanding from the inside to the outside, which symbolizes the development and inheritance of Japanese graphic design.

73 JOÃO MACHADO DESIGN | Design Firm: João Machado Design
Designer: João Machado | Client: Self-initiated | Main Contributor: João Machado
Assignment: This poster was created as part of a retrospective exhibition of my work that will take place this year in Lisbon.
Approach: I decided to 'give my portrait' to the poster that will promote my retrospective exhibition, this year, of 50 years of work as a graphic designer. As always, a work marked by an explosion of color.

74 DYNAMIC | Design Firm: Carmit Design Studio | Designer: Carmit Makler Haller
Client: CEIDA (Chinese Europe International Design Culture Association)
Main Contributors: Carmit Makler Haller, Carmit Design Studio
Assignment: CEIDA—(Chinese Europe International Design Culture Association) invitation for "International Dynamic Poster Exhibition," Digital Hefei, China, Summer 2023.
Approach: Showcasing each letter from top to bottom, creating a movement to the word. The black gradient adds both depth and speed.
Results: Displayed at the International Dynamic Poster Exhibition at Digital Hefei, China.

75 FUTURE | Design Firm: Tsushima Design | Designer: Hajime Tsushima
Client: Osaka Poster Fest | Main Contributor: Hajime Tsushima
Assignment: This is a poster for a virtual and a real exhibition. The real exhibition was held at the Osaka University of Arts Gallery from November 27th to December 1st, 2023. The theme is the future.
Approach: In the future, the latest technologies such as space exploration, artificial intelligence, and virtual reality will become crucial elements. Reflecting diversity and inclusivity, the design imagines various cultures, races, genders, abilities, and more.
Results: The real exhibition was visited by many people. The virtual version of the exhibition is also currently being held.

76 WATER | Design Firm: João Machado Design | Designer: João Machado
Client: Ogaki Poster Museum | Main Contributor: João Machado
Assignment: At the invitation of the Ogaki Poster Museum, this poster was requested to be part of the exhibition entitled 'Water' that will take place in autumn 2024, within the context of the Gifu National Cultural Festival in Japan.
Approach: The composition of the image is structured based on a triangle, giving it great solidity. It results from a framework and a reading that I hope will not be immediate, but that will challenge the viewer to discover 3 images = 3 fish in their natural habitat.

77 ARTIFICIAL. INTELLIGENT? | Design Firm: Elevate Design
Designer: Kelly Salchow MacArthur | Client: 27th BDAK International Exhibition
Main Contributor: Kelly Salchow MacArthur
Assignment: The 27th Brand Design Association of Korea's International Invitational Exhibition prompted poster designs to address the theme of artificial intelligence.
Approach: While AI may be very helpful in some cases, I recognize it to be an unharnessed liability at this time. It threatens life as we know it, as humanity's space for roles, ideas, and creativity will be replaced. Overlayed photos of neon-lit fluorescent plexiglass create an unnatural image and palette. Formal considerations are intentionally a bit off, as if devoid of human oversight.
Results: The poster was included in the exhibition—its critical view of AI in contrast to some other entries.

78 THINGS YOU AND I MET | Design Firm: TopLeft LLC
Designers: Jin Kwang Kim, Dho Yee Chung | Client: Self-initiated
Artists: Jin Kwang Kim, Dho Yee Chung | Main Contributors: Jin Kwang Kim, Dho Yee Chung
Assignment: This poster was exhibited at the CICA Museum International Exhibition "NEWBODIES/NOBODIES" at Cafritz Foundation Arts Center, Montgomery College, MD, in March 2024. Our conception is to speculate mundane objects in the autonomous mode of cultural and social output. Objects that were once desired now become active participants in the network that can share stories as communication passes on through time and space. Our encounter with things entails a collision with their previous or past experience, twisted grotesquely into endless desire for commodity.
Approach: Our projects invite things to an ethereal and immaterial sphere of digital culture. Our digital images took a process of collapsing and disembodying material structure through the manipulation of digitalized objects. They were digitally cut, morphed, and rendered with the incorporation of 3D modeling and virtual reality technologies. The aesthetic of extreme artificiality and virtuality signifies our resistance against object's status as capitalist commodity. If a digital image is another form of thing, our work is an immortal site that sentience beings ceaselessly infuse with immaterialization.
Results: A 10-minute experimental video combining real footage taken in charity shops with 3D animation was exhibited together with a series of posters. We hope this project invites the audience to contemplate everyday commodities that are taken for granted.

79 FUTURE? | Design Firm: Carmit Design Studio | Designer: Carmit Makler Haller
Client: Osaka Poster Fest | Main Contributor: Carmit Makler Haller
Assignment: I got an invitation to take part in the 2023 Osaka Poster Fest. I decided to focus on Artificial Intelligence. No doubt it is a potent tool. Will it fix humanity's problems? Will it end peoples' suffering? Or will it conjure new dilemmas—such as bias data, ethics, transparency, regulations and accuracy? I can't help but wonder who is at the helm. Only time, or Future, will tell.
Approach: The enclosed poster is displaying the AI environment by using algorithms as textures, AI functions and current platforms (ChatGPT, Midjourney, Open AI) along with a textured nervous system, generated by AI, inside the typeface. The layout suggests a chart overloaded with data, implying a sense of overwhelm within a chaotic order. The general color palette is of a warm and optimistic future yet the question mark on the last letter suggests a doubtful one.
Results: Displayed for a week at the Osaka Poster Fest, 2023: Future exhibition.

80 TRACE OF VIOLENCE, IRAQ 2003–2023 | Design Firm: Tetsuro Minorikawa
Designer: Tetsuro Minorikawa | Client: Tomayouz Excellence Award
Main Contributor: Tetsuro Minorikawa
Assignment: This poster is created for invitation poster exhibition themed "Iraq 2003: 20 Years Later." This is related to US forces entering the heart of the Iraqi capital, Baghdad, on the 9th of April, 2003.
Approach: This poster shows the trace of violence in Iraq. This hand is a trace of violence. And this is a tombstone. This tombstone has sadness. My condolences to all those who died in this war.
Results: I was able to symbolically visualize the traces of violence and sadness.

81 100 BEST POSTER 22 (MAIN EXHIBITION 2023)
Design Firm: Studio Lindhorst-Emme+Hinrichs
Designers: Lea Hinrichs, Sven Lindhorst-Emme | Client: 100 Beste Plakate Verein
Main Contributors: Lea Hinrichs, Sven Lindhorst-Emme, Erkin Karamemet, Sophia Richter
Assignment: Design a poster for the 100 Best Poster Germany, Austria, Switzerland Competition in 2023. The CI including Poster, Wallpaper, Flyer, The exhibition Design, Social Media, Screen, Invitations and the Certificates and the Anual-Book.
Approach: We decided to have the "100" as our Main Keyvisual combined with 10 colors. As Font we choose the Modena Variable Font by Erkin Karamemet (Dinamo-Type).
Results: The combinations of the many different "100" in slim, bold, black, extended or condensed and the 10 colors results in very colorful and differnet media.

82, 83 CITY TREE ANNUAL FESTIVAL CAKE RUN POSTER | Design Firm: Freaner Creative & Design | Designer: Ariel Freaner | Client: City Tree Christina Schools
Illustrator: Ariel Freaner | Main Contributor: Ariel Freaner
Assignment: City Tree Christina Schools celebrated their 2023 Fall Festival and needed a poster to promote their "Cake Race," a race where contestants eat cake. :)
Approach: We developed a poster for City Tree Christina Schools that resembles a simple race car made of pieces of cake. The digital illustration and design are colorful and fun for family and friends.
Results: Great turnout and increment in participants in the "Cake Race."

84 73. BERLINALE – KEY VISUAL AND POSTERS | Design Firm: Claudia Schramke
Designer: Claudia Schramke | Client: International Film Festival Berlin – Berlinale
Main Contributor: Claudia Schramke
Assignment: I was commissioned to design the visual identity for the 73rd International Film Festival Berlin. The Berlinale is a highlight in Berlin's cultural program with international appeal and is also a significant economic factor for the city. Regarding the design of the key visual, the clients wished for a visual connection between the festival and the city of Berlin. In addition to creating the Main Festival Poster Series, the primary goal was to develop a strong and flexible Key Visual System.
Approach: As a Berliner, I know my city and understand that its unique identity arises from the diversity of people living here. This concept forms the core of my design, showcasing the Berlin audience of the film festival and visually uniting the city and the festival as a cinematic experience. The posters and Key Visual focus on those who make the Berlinale a lively, stimulating, and joyful event. In designing the poster motifs, I opted for an abstract representation based on geometric shapes. The 15 different figures symbolize the diversity and distinctiveness of all people. The design as a Key Visual not only works as a poster but also allows for significant creative flexibility. With the bold red cinema seats, it becomes a versatile branding element that can be applied to all required formats of festival graphics.
Results: The posters for the International Berlin Film Festival portray the characteristic and rich diversity of individuals in Berlin, presenting the Berlinale as a truly inclusive and welcoming event. In the face of the challenging times, the image of a filled cinema hall stands out as a powerful symbol, celebrating freedom, cultural vibrancy, cinema, and togetherness. The design communicated effectively and convinced the festival leadership, as well as the public of Berlin and the festival attendees.

85 CINANIMA 24 | Design Firm: João Machado Design
Designer: João Machado | Clients: Organização Nascente - Cooperativa de Acção Cultural, CRL, Câmara Municipal de Espinho | Main Contributor: João Machado
Assignment: Cooperativa Nascente de Acção Cultural, CRL. Cinanima is an international animation film festival organised by NASCENTE - Cooperative Society and Espinho's City Hall every year, during the month of November. Since its first edition in 1977, I've been doing all the posters for this Festival.
Approach: It is an image that encompasses elements of the process of creating the illustration itself. This year's image is represented by a type of insect, whose body and wings simulate the tools (the central body represents the pencil, the wings represent the film reels) that give rise to the illustration.

86 WHICH HUMAN RIGHTS? FILM FESTIVAL | Design Firm: Fol | Designer: Volkan Ölmez
Client: Documentarist | Creative Director: Volkan Ölmez | Main Contributor: Volkan Ölmez
Assignment: Which Human Rights? Film Festival is an event organised every year in Istanbul where documentary films based on human rights are screened. This year's theme of the festival was Women's Rights.
Approach: The image used in the production of the poster was produced to represent the headscarf and basic human rights of Iranian women.
Results: The hair covering the entire poster represents all the basic problems experienced by women through their hair. The bead on the hair is a traditional jewellery used especially by local women in the east and used as a hair ornament. By making this jewellery the focal point of the poster, we talked about women who want to show their hair and jewellery freely. In all the streets we decorated the walls with women's hair.

87 TIRANA INTERNATIONAL FILM FESTIVAL 2022 | Design Firm: EGGRA
Designer: Igor Nastevski | Client: Tirana Film Institute | Design Director: Ngadhnjim Mehmeti
Main Contributor: Igor Nastevski
Assignment: Tirana Film Institute is an Albanian creative industry whose main focus is based on promoting the creative industry products in Albania and cooperating with European organizations in order to share common audiovisual products. Tirana Film Institute carries out its activities in organising artistic, cultural and cinematographic film weeks, national and international festivals. TFI is also engaged with film and audiovisual production, design of publicity campaigns, various marketing activities, promotion and film distribution. TFI has started a new successful experience as a film distributor getting support from the Media Program of Creative Europe.
Approach: This was the change of the very first slogan of TIFF 2003 (Think Different, Watch Alike) on the occasion of the 20th anniversary of Tirana International Film Festival. 20 years ago, when this festival was established, Albanians in general but also filmmakers in particular found it impossible to travel to Europe without a visa to follow the latest developments and new cinematographic trends in the world. As a matter of course, the verb WATCH of the slogan was the original goal of TIFF's establishment. Since then, about 40,000 films were entered during these years from 120 countries. There are thousands of filmmakers around the world, well-known producers and distributors, who spare no effort to be part of the Official Selection. The key visual should communicate 20 years anniversary of the festival.
Results: 3d illustration of the film camera dolly slider within typographic image of the number 2 and 0 was the solution to reflect the anniversary of the Tirana International Film Festival. We used vivid colours to catch the Tirana's mediterranean spirit.

88 THE CREATOR - TEASER POSTER | Design Firm: AV Print | Designer: AV Print
Clients: 20th Century Studios, Jordan Stallings - Director, Creative Advertising - 20th Century Studios, Arnaldo D'Alfonso - Global EVP & Creative Director - 20th Century Studios, Joe Tamusaitis - VP, Creative Advertising - 20th Century Studios | Main Contributor: AV Print
Assignment: Getting to work on this highly-anticipated film from the director of Rogue One was an incredible opportunity as well as an awesome creative challenge. Our clients at 20th Century Studios encouraged us to think about this science fiction film beyond the usual framework the genre imposes and dig into the deeper themes.
Approach: This film provided us with so many unique examples of juxtaposition that it became clear the art should highlight that dichotomy. We wanted to mix the fantastical science fiction world this film created with a grounded view of a lush, green Earth. The robot in the foreground stands in tall grass, spectating over a field against a gorgeous pink sunset. It feels like home, but there are so many details and elements that tell you it's not.
Results: With this teaser we've presented audiences with a very old world tableau and infused it with imaginative futuristic elements to relay the depth and wonder this world and film have to offer. It encourages viewers to see how humanity evolves and endures in an uncertain future.

89 THE ROOSTER TEASER KEY ART | Design Firm: Barlow.Agency
Designer: Barlow.Agency | Client: Thousand Mile Productions | Main Contributor: Barlow.Agency
Assignment: In our endeavor to promote the forthcoming feature film 'The Rooster,' our objective was to craft a captivating and enigmatic image that alludes to a recurring motif in the storyline—the ping pong ball.
Approach: Utilizing on-set unit photography of 'The Rooster,' we skillfully manipulated the image to feature the film's recurring motif—a ping pong ball held by the rooster's head. This deliberate alteration imbues the picture with an unsettling yet intriguing tease for the forthcoming feature film.
Results: Emerging as a client favorite during our presentation, this project is now being internally rolled out in preparation for the wide release of the film.

90 MISSION: IMPOSSIBLE - DEAD RECKONING PART 1, DOLBY EXCLUSIVE POSTER
Design Firm: AV Print | Designer: AV Print | Clients: Paramount Pictures, Brian Pianko, EVP Head of Creative Advertising - Paramount Pictures, Charlie Ward – Senior Manager Creative Advertising - Paramount Pictures Main Contributor: AV Print
Assignment: Working on one of the most well known action franchises ever provided us with an awesome opportunity and creative challenge. After some initial rounds, our focus became centered on specialty release posters. One driving force of the recent campaigns has been to showcase the set-piece stunts elevated by Tom Cruise doing said stunts himself. This leads to some incredible photography to pull and work from.
Approach: While the main art and supporting creative pieces became photoreal executions of these stunts and the creation of ensemble montages - this limited release poster let us play with more stylized representations. This particular stunt was one of our favorites and we sought several ways to sell the tension and stomach dropping perspective in a graphic manner. This led us down a path of bold color and non-traditional type.
Results: The client emphasized a desire to have a piece that played with the iconic M:I which helps the overall franchise sell to stand out among what became a rather long film title. Skewing those letters and having the train smash through the space felt irresistible visually. Putting the whole lock-up on such an explosive red and adding the falling debris helped the action read even quicker. Audiences can feel the urgency of this moment through the poster - a moment sure to bring them back for Part 2.

91 JOHN WICK: CHAPTER 4 - THEATRICAL CAMPAIGN | Design Firm: AV Print
Designer: AV Print | Clients: Lionsgate, Keri Moore, Co-President of Marketing - Lionsgate, Jack Teed, SVP, Global Creative Advertising - Lionsgate, John Cunha, Director, Global Creative Advertising - Lionsgate | Other: Phantom City Creative | Main Contributor: AV Print
Assignment: Working on the campaign with Lionsgate was absolutely stunning. The depth and range of the sets, locations, photography and costuming all were an overwhelming embarrassment of riches. With so much source material to work with we were able to explore a wide range of approaches. One thing the client wanted to convey with this campaign was John's journey - the lighting over his pieces tell the story of a sunrise to sunset of a single day, what audiences may recognize as his final day.
Approach: With the central tone and sunset color palette set by those Keanu forward pieces we were then able to showcase the breadth of color and vibrancy the film has to offer with the other supporting character and international pieces.
Results: Through the full character suite and outdoor campaign we sold the story of a world-wide action extravaganza. Exactly the kind of film people have come to expect from the John Wick franchise.

92 DISARMED SHORT FILM KEY ART | Design Firm: Barlow.Agency
Designer: Barlow.Agency | Client: Last One Standing Productions
Main Contributor: Barlow.Agency
Assignment: We aimed to distill a short film's essence, portraying a woman grappling with PTSD from gun violence and self-sabotaging mental health stemming from a robbery, while subtly hinting at the climactic twist.
Approach: Constrained by budget, we crafted a compelling image using stock photography, skilfully manipulating elements like reversing elements of the gun and hands. We ended with a captivating image that encapsulates the narrative of self-sabotage and becoming one's own worst enemy in the context of gun violence, our mission was to distill these complex themes into a singular, evocative image.
Results: The artwork debuted on social media, significantly boosting promotion for the film and contributing to its acceptance into various short film festivals worldwide.

93 HMS BELFAST | Design Firm: Rose | Designer: Rose | Client: Imperial War Museum
Photographer: Julian Calverley | Main Contributor: Rose
Assignment: Create a marketing campaign for HMS Belfast – a historic warship and museum, and one of London's most iconic landmarks. With nine decks exploring stories of life on board during conflict and peace, the Imperial War Museums wanted to position HMS Belfast as a must see attraction for families and history lovers alike.
Approach: Previous campaigns focused on and depicted the vast array of stories and experiences audiences can encounter, resulting in complex visuals and narratives. We chose a simpler, bolder approach, conveying the majestic, iconic nature of the war-ship, elevating it to an almost Hollywood-esque status, whilst paying homage to A M Cassandre's classic Normandie poster from the 1930s. We also added a subtitle referencing its many epic stories, in a bid to appeal to broader audiences.
Results: The campaign launched in April 2023 and has enjoyed widespread success in attracting new audiences, with revenue increasing by 17% in the first 6 months.

94 20 YEARS POSTER MUSEUM | Design Firm: Fons Hickmann m23
Designer: Fons Hickmann | Client: Plakatmuseum Emmerich | Main Contributor: Fons Hickmann
Assignment: A poster celebrating the anniversary of the PAN Museum in Emmerich. The words »20 Years of Poster Museum« are creatively fused in a tongue-in-cheek manner with chocolate analogies, paying homage to the museum's unique location in a repurposed chocolate factory. These two posters reference each other, as they promote two different events, prompting the question, »Do you prefer white or dark chocolate?«

95 «WAU ANIMALS AS ART» | Design Firm: Dreamis GmbH | Designer: Marc Philip Seidel
Client: Eduard Spörri Art Museum | Main Contributor: Marc Philip Seidel
Assignment: The order included the design of the key visual for marketing and communication measures for the new special exhibition "WAU! Animals as Art" in the Eduard Spörri Art Museum. The design needed to be rich in colors, shapes and styles intended to trigger a "WOW!" effect. The animal should be used in several roles: as an artistic construct, as a symbolically charged object and as a decorative element. The design solution is intended to inspire young and old and invite them to the exhibition.
Approach: The analysis of the various works of art revealed an enormous range of approaches to the "animal" motif. The research has included posters from outstanding Swiss advertising designers such as Hans Erni, Claude Kuhn and Herbert Leupin. The exhibition features a porcelain figure with a chrome steel mirror glaze, which inspired the choice of this metallic effect for the poster paper and the geometric dog with a silver line being placed in the center. An exhibited bone by the artist Garda Alexander also adopts this silver metallic color. The dog was a constant companion in the life of the artist Eduard Spörri. This ensures a connection to the museum's namesake.
Results: The opening was a great success and the client as well as guests young and old were enthusiastic about the poster and the exhibition "WAU!". There was already a lot of enthusiastic feedback in advance about the invitation flyer that was sent out. The balancing act between old tradition (origami) and contemporary art (3D model of the dog) has been successful. The poster design was highly praised by the printing company and displayed as a highlight in the customer area.

96 RACHMANINOFF 150 | Design Firm: Chase Design | Designer: Zhizheng Xie
Client: Golden Bee Biennale | Art Director: Shangrong Tsai
Creative Director: Kuo-Hsun Wen | Main Contributor: Zhizheng Xie
Assignment: The poster commemorates the 150th anniversary of Rachmaninoff's birth.
Approach: Rachmaninov's music is rigorous and orderly, and I use black and white color blocks to make isomorphism with his characters in the picture.
Results: The poster was selected to be included in The Golden Bee Biennale.

97 ORQUESTA FILARMÓNICA DE SONORA. SEASON 2024
Design Firm: Ivette Valenzuela Design | Designer: Ivette Valenzuela
Client: Instituto Sonorense de Cultura | Main Contributor: Ivette Valenzuela
Assignment: The objective was to create a vivid image for the new Sonora Philharmonic Orchestra's 2024 season, to mark the entrance of a young conductor to the orchestra.
Approach: This is the first poster of a series that will be deployed throughout the year, maintaining a consistent color palette with a colorless background, but differing musical instruments. The iridescent and metallic tones of the wind instruments intertwine together, offering a unique visual experience.
Results: The poster's impact succeeded in communicating and attracting enthusiasts and professionals to an event like no other. The public's reception in the state of Sonora

has been extraordinary, spreading the image throughout the year on various platforms, including social networks and media. The greatest achievement lies in the ability of the lineup to fill the venues with an audience eager to enjoy the music.

98 RAISE YOUR LIGHTERS | Design Firm: PPK | Designer: Alan Schneller
Client: Smokin' Havanas | Executive Creative Director: Paul Prato
Creative Director: Michael Schillig | Art Director: Alan Schneller | Copywriter: Michael Schillig
Main Contributors: Michael Schillig, Alan Schneller
Assignment: Promote a popular rock & roll band from called the Smokin' Havanas who have come out with an exciting new album and are going on tour.
Approach: We wanted to feature their name and fiery performances in a visually powerful and memorable way. So, we used a lighter to create their name out of fire and, in the process, even brought back that old concert tradition where fans would salute musicians by raising their lighters. The posters were designed to be hung at venues where the band was playing to generate some added buzz, excitement and anticipation.
Results: The band thought the poster was hot and helped "spark" the attention and curiosity of new fans while continuing to excite their ultra-passionate current fan base.

99 LEWIS CAPALDI | Design Firm: THERE IS STUDIO
Designers: Sean Freeman, Eve Steben | Client: Another Planet Entertainment
Main Contributors: Sean Freeman, Eve Steben
Assignment: We were commissioned to create an exclusive poster design for the one-night-only Lewis Capaldi performance at the Greek Theatre, in Berkeley California.
Approach: Inspired by the visuals of his "Broken by Desire to Be Heavenly Sent" album and live show tour visuals, we created this swirling minimalist composition, with bold romantic soft pink type. Printed with lush spot gloss for extra shiny blacks.
Results: The poster was offered as a collectible merchandise item, printed in very limited edition exclusively for fans attending the event. A copy was offered on the night of the show as a special present to the artist, from the management team. A hero signed poster was also framed to feature in a music poster collection.

100 YOUNG THE GIANT — LIVE IN OREGON | Design Firm: The Studio of Mikey Lavi
Designer: Mikey Lavi | Client: Young the Giant | Print Producer: Homemade Merchandise LLC
Client Support: Activist Artist Management | Main Contributor: Mikey Lavi
Assignment: Design a commemorative screen print poster for Young the Giant's performance at McMenamins Edgefield in Troutdale, Oregon on August 12th, 2023.
Approach: The band wanted a vibrant, modern and psychedelic feeling poster to celebrate their performance in Oregon.
Results: They loved it!

101 THE NATIONAL — LIVE AT OSHEAGA | Design Firm: The Studio of Mikey Lavi
Designer: Mikey Lavi | Client: The National | Print Producer: The Cardboardbox Project
Main Contributor: Mikey Lavi
Assignment: Design a poster to commemorate The National's performance at the Osheaga Music & Arts Festival in Montreal, Québec.
Approach: Sometimes a gig poster doesn't need a deep, clever, specific meaning. We simply wanted to create an expressive piece that captures the energy of the festival, The National's performance and felt like a modern painting. The design appeals to The National's design tastes as well as celebrating the "Arts" aspect of the Osheaga festival.
Results: Client loved it. It sold out and we printed a 2nd edition in an alternate colorway available exclusively to their fan club.

102 SOME SPRING SWING | Design Firm: Chemi Montes Design | Designer: Chemi Montes
Client: American University Department of Performing Arts Jazz Ensemble
Main Contributor: Chemi Montes

103 JAZZ & CLARINET | Design Firm: ALVARO MONTANHA Design
Designer: ALVARO MONTANHA Design | Client: Matosinhos City Councel
Main Contributor: ALVARO MONTANHA Design
Assignment: Matosinhos em Jazz is one of the most popular jazz festivals in Portugal. A gateway to the memory of jazz in Portugal, this festival has been transformed into a perfect symbiosis between tradition and the trends and creative expressions typical of this movement. This years theme was "The Clarinet".
Approach: Based on a high contrasts illustration with 8 shades of black, we developed a sober poster, based on a creative and powerful hand-drawn design, reflecting the good ageing of the festival and its organization.
Results: The poster continued the success of the previous festivals and triggered positive reactions from the organization, the musicians and the public.

104 LE NOZZE DI FIGARO | Design Firm: Institut für Visuelle Kommunikation
Designer: Gunter Rambow | Client: Oper Frankfurt | Main Contributor: Gunter Rambow
Assignment: Opera by Wolfgang Amadeus Mozart
Approach: This production is brilliant and colorful. On the field: players from four generations and different social classes who represent different models of love and life.
Results: Poster for advertisement and poster pillars

105 TANNHAUSER | Design Firm: Institut für Visuelle Kommunikation
Designer: Gunter Rambow | Client: Oper Frankfurt | Main Contributor: Gunter Rambow
Assignment: Opera by Richard Wagner
Approach: After Tannhauser was able to live out his erotic desires uninhibited with the love goddess Venus, he was forced back into the morally strict Wartburg society.
Results: Poster for advertisement and poster pillars

106 CARNIVAL AT THE OPERA | Design Firm: Sun Design Production
Designers: Xian Liyun, Liang Gang | Client: Cultural Terminal Goclaw
Main Contributor: Xian Liyun
Assignment: To organize a carnival about a famous opera and make it known to a large number of people so that during this carnival the audience will attend the performance.
Approach: The idea strategy was to create an exciting image and interest in the opera, and to imagine symbols and stories. A colorful and excited motif to evoke the opera, including singing, acting, costumes, and staging.
Results: The poster design announced the opera festival and gathered audiences to share the inspiration of famous opera composers such as Mozart, Bizet, and Verdi.

107 THE RAKE'S PROGRESS | Design Firm: Atelier Bundi AG | Designer: Stephan Bundi
Client: Theater Orchester Biel Solothurn | Main Contributor: Stephan Bundi
Assignment: Opera by Igor Stravinsky based on William Hogarth's work. The path that leads from debauchery to an asylum, as depicted by Hogarth, is shown on the poster as a staircase leading down to hellfire - or up to heaven.
Approach: A reduction of numerous sinful acts to a staircase that leads in two directions.
Results: Visual for the poster, advertisements, and program title.

108 MUSICAL KOPERNIK (COPERNICUS) | Design Firm: Katarzyna Zapart
Designer: Katarzyna Zapart | Client: Opera Krakowska
Assignment: The goal of the Musical was to celebrate 550th anniversary of the birth of Mikołaj Kopernik, Polish astronomer, author of "De revolutionibus orbium coelestium" and scientific proof of the heliocentric theory.
Approach: I had a bit limited space for my creativity because the client was convinced that the poster should be quite literal and show a face of the hero himself. After many attempts I decided to try to show the movement. As we say, he "stopped the Sun and moved the Earth" - this phrase became my main inspiration. A golden circle behind Copernicus is the Sun, and his hair is moved with the wind caused by the movement of the Earth.
Results: The poster was visible in Cracow and the musical was very popular.

109 SUCCESS | Design Firm: ALVARO MONTANHA Design
Designer: ALVARO MONTANHA Design | Client: Self-initiated
Main Contributor: ALVARO MONTANHA Design
Assignment: Create a poster that was more representative of the industry, to show our creativity and presence in areas that we have always been involved in, despite being better known in the worlds of music and culture.
Approach: Inspired by the constant growth of Portuguese entrepreneurs, this design portrays them with dynamic colors and tones of strength and perseverance. The "industry" theme is conveyed through the simplified illustration of the sides of two factory buildings, forming two upward arrows. In the background, a new day - bright and positive - is rising, bringing optimism to industrial entrepreneurs.
Results: Positive feedback from industrial entrepreneurs, reminding them that industry is important to us, and that we value it: "Your Success is Our Own."

110, 111 TODD HIDO: THE END SENDS ADVANCE WARNING
Design Firm: Aufuldish & Warinner | Designer: Bob Aufuldish | Client: Nazraeli Press
Photographer: Todd Hido | Main Contributor: Bob Aufuldish
Assignment: Design a limited edition poster to promote the photographer Todd Hido's monograph The End Sends Advance Warning.
Approach: Apply typography quietly to the strongest photograph available.
Results: The poster has sold out.

112 CRAIG CUTLER PROMO | Design Firm: Craig Frazier Studio
Designer: Craig Frazier | Client: Self-initiated | Creative Director: Craig Frazier
Executive Producer: Fela Cortes | Main Contributor: Craig Cutler
Assignment: A new promotional series of posters.
Approach: A sculpture study using ceramics that play with color, shape and balance. Craig Frazier designed the type.
Results: Series of promotional posters.

113 AWAKENING OF AI | Design Firm: Dalian RYCX Design | Designer: Zhongjun Yin
Client: Self-initiated | Creative Director: Zhongjun Yin | Main Contributor: Zhongjun Yin
Assignment: At present, the era of artificial intelligence revolution is becoming a hot spot that attracts global attention. However, the resulting unknown risks to humans have become the focus of widespread debate in the international community.
Approach: The continuous iteration and rapid evolution of AI-derived ChatGPT are constantly breaking the limits of human cognition. Cutting-edge AI scientists predict that the future development of artificial general intelligence (AGI) may pose a threat to human survival, and some uncertain turning point may become a hidden danger for human civilization. Computer scientist Geoffrey Hinton once said that if humans are not careful, artificial intelligence "could take over everything."
Results: How to keep artificial intelligence in a cage controllable by humans has become a new challenge facing the international community in the future.

114, 115 SPECIAL RETIREMENT GIFT | Design Firm: PPK
Designer: Javier Quintana | Client: Big Cat Rescue | Executive Creative Director: Paul Prato
Creative Directors: Michael Schillig, Javier Quintana | Copywriter: Michael Schillig
Art Director: Javier Quintana | Main Contributors: Michael Schillig, Javier Quintana
Assignment: Big Cat Rescue is one of the world's largest sanctuaries for exotic cats and has provided homes for over 100 abandoned, abused and orphaned big cats. Their mission is to stop the abuse and killing of big cats and keep them where they belong – in the wild. Our assignment was to come up with a way to make people aware of how big cats who become too old to perform in circuses often end up facing a not so happy retirement.
Approach: We created this poster to help Big Cat Rescue educate people on the truth of what can happen to big cats once they lose their value and become a financial burden on some circuses. Unfortunately, there is no tracking how many ultimately end up being killed and sold for their valuable fur, bones and other parts on the black market.
Results: This poster was meant to shock people and stimulate further discussion regarding this issue. We hoped to entice people to visit BigCatRescue.org to learn more and find out ways they can help support big cats and alleviate their suffering and death.

116 GLOBAL COMMITMENTS | Design Firm: National Kaohsiung University of Science & Technology (NKUST) | Designer: Chong-Wen Chen
Client: NKUST College of Innovation & Design | Main Contributor: Chong-Wen Chen
Assignment: This poster design calls for collective global actions toward a brighter future through the UN's 17 Sustainable Development Goals (SDGs). The College of Innovation and Design at NKUST draws inspiration from this poster to promote related research, aiming to collaborate and share its findings with universities, governments, and non-profit organizations internationally.
Approach: The poster applies a creative method by extracting a single letter from each SDG to present the phrase: "Global Commitments." Fountain pens marked with the numbers and themes of the 17 SDGs represent the act of signing agreements, highlighting the collective effort required to achieve a sustainable future.

Results: This poster will be distributed to international academic and non-profit institutions to promote the College of Innovation and Design at NKUST, aiming to foster potential collaborations in research and design practices.

117 WISH PEACE DAY! | Design Firm: Purdue University | Designer: Do Gyun Kim
Client: Self-initiated | Main Contributor: Do Gyun Kim
Assignment: The longer the war persists, the sooner we all anticipate its conclusion. In this work, a candle transforms into a dove, a symbol of peace, to convey hope. Additionally, their reality is metaphorically represented in accordance with the colors of Ukraine.
Approach: Typography is also synchronized with colours to express well-wishes for peace, akin to a joyful birthday. This symbolic transformation of the candle into a dove signifies the power of hope in the face of adversity. The typography displayed on the image of the dove symbolizes the collective desire for peace in various languages.
Results: This poster has been reimagined as a motion poster to captivate audiences with the dynamic movement of typography on the screen, reinforcing the idea that peace is not passive but an active, evolving process.

118 LOVE IS ART IS LOVE | Design Firm: Studio A N D | Designer: Jean-Benoit Levy
Client: Slanted Magazine | Main Contributor: Jean-Benoit Levy
Assignment: As the peaceful light of a glowing heart expands toward the darkness, uncolored edges are exposed to colors and are transformed toward a more positive state. The poster's borders are straight and dark, representing the limited world of ignorance and fear. The light in the center is the universal energy that we all have inside of us.
Approach: How to merge a rounded center with straight edges? This is the challenge that triggered me to transform a round shape into a straight rectangle. The darkness of the exterior world is on the edges while the light is in the center, step by step merging into each other, both sides are influencing each other.
Results: The German magazine Slanted published this poster in their book ART for LOVE. This poster was part of a fundraiser by Slanted to help two non-profit organizations, MSF – Medecins-Sans-Frontières, as well as ARTHELPS. This poster also won gold at the competition "Poster for : Happy" in China.

119 LAPINLAHTI, OPENNESS, COMMUNALITY, AND PARTICIPATION
Design Firm: Antonio Castro Design | Designer: Antonio Castro H.
Client: Save Lapinlahti with a Poster | Main Contributor: Antonio Castro H.
Assignment: I made this poster for the Save Lapinlahti with a Poster event organized by Pekka Loiri and Klaus Welp. The poster competition was about the future of the Lapinlahti Community that is under threat from an international real estate corporation. The Lapinlahti Community is located in a former psychiatric hospital in Lapinlahti, Helsinki, now a vibrant urban center of art, culture, and mental well-being.
Approach: I decided to use emblematic symbols from Finland, their national flower, the Lily of the Valley to represent art, culture, etc. and one of Finland's most important architects, Alvar Aalto's famous flower vase, to represent conservation.
Results: The chosen posters were exhibited in the Lapinlahti Park in Helsinki in July, 2023. Unfortunately my poster was not chosen, but I had a blast working on it.

120 BEWARE THE AGE OF AI SINGULARITY | Design Firm: Carmit Design Studio
Designer: Carmit Makler Haller | Client: Borderless Graphic Designers Group: Graphic Design & Artificial Intelligence International Poster Competition Call
Main Contributor: Carmit Makler Haller
Assignment: An entry for Graphic design & Artificial intelligence International Poster Competition Call. The topic is Artificial Intelligence and graphic design: is it good or bad? I present the dangerous outcomes of AI once it reaches singularity. In other words: AI intelligence extends over the point of no return. Computers and AI have limitless power and control over mankind. Who's at the helm now?
Approach: The poster showcases a flow chart, presenting the dangerous sequences / scenarios once AI reaches singularity. The words "beware" and "the end" typed in as a code—suggest the harsh implications of AI intelligence.
Results: The entry was selected as a finalist at the competition.

121 ISRAEL, PALESTINA | Design Firm: Studio Pekka Loiri
Designer: Pekka Loiri | Client: Mankind
Assignment: Is the situation in Israel and Gaza eternal and unending?
Approach: Designing a poster is the job of the poster artist, an effort to make an impact. I try to appeal to all those who have the opportunity to influence Israel and Palestine.
Results: The power of posters has widely been used when starting wars and perpetuate enmity throughout the ages. One poster won't improve the situation, but as above; I have to do my job because I feel sick thinking about that huge tragedy.

122 HUMAN SHADOW ETCHED IN STONE | Design Firm: Tsushima Design
Designer: Hajime Tsushima | Client: Japan Graphic Designers Association Hiroshima
Main Contributor: Hajime Tsushima
Assignment: This is a poster for the Peace Poster Exhibition held every year in Hiroshima.
Approach: This is a poster for peace poster exhibition. The human shadow etched in stone symbolizes the devastating impact of the atomic bombs on Hiroshima and Nagasaki. These shadows serve as a lasting testament to the suffering and sacrifice of the survivors. The horrors of the atomic bomb emphasize the urgency of nuclear disarmament and the importance of abolishing nuclear weapons.
Results: Many people visited this peace poster exhibition.

123 OCTOBER 7TH, 2023—HEART SERIES | Design Firm: Carmit Design Studio
Designer: Carmit Makler Haller | Client: Stop War Poster Exhibition
Photographer: Carmit Makler Haller | Digital Artists: Jorge Gamboa, Mal De Ojo
Main Contributors: Carmit Makler Haller, Carmit Design Studio
Assignment: On October 7th, 2023, Hamas attacked the Israeli towns and Kibutz near the Gaza stripe. For eight hours Hamas slaughtered, killed, raped and beheaded 1,400 people. 240 were kidnapped and held as hostages. These pieces describe the way many of us have been feeling ever since that massacre, especially in Israel.
Approach: The series displays the heart in different stages, since October 7th and on. The first scene showcases a heart—or one's life—wounded by a bullet, causing it to bleed. It conveys the massacre killings by the Hamas terrorists, and the emotional shock Israel went through. In the second piece—the wound staged into a huge hole, alluding the nation's broken spirit, as if in a state of Trauma. The last piece presents an anemone inside the broken heart, implying growth and change, between despair and hope. The anemone is Israel's national flower, sprouting during the springtime in Southern Israel, where the massacre took place.
Results: An entry for "Stop War" Poster Exhibition.

124 INTERACTION | Design Firm: Purdue University | Designer: Li Zhang
Client: The Korean Society of Science and Art | Main Contributor: Li Zhang
Assignment: I was invited to design for The Korean Society of Science and Art on the topic of a new era.
Approach: My work shows the relationship between A.I. and humans and the concepts of interaction in the era of the technological revolution. The word "Interaction", artificial colors, and elements are carved in the symbolic forms of humans while the human form/hand shape and gesture are embedded in digital dotted/AI form.
Results: It has been successfully exhibited in Korea, Turkey, China, and Egypt.

125 HATE CORRODES | Design Firm: Steiner Graphics | Designer: Rene V. Steiner
Client: Self-initiated | Main Contributor: Rene V. Steiner
Assignment: The rise in hate crimes against minorities worldwide is indicative of a deeper malaise spurred on by the relentless and frenzied expressions of outrage fanned by social media. Hate, said Maya Angelou, "has caused a lot of problems in the world, but has not solved one yet." The countervailing forces of love and empathy must prevail if we are to navigate the rough seas humankind faces in the coming years.
Approach: The recent convulsions taking place in the Middle East brought to mind the corrosive effect of rust on metal. Rust has the cabability to degrade what on the surface seems impenetrable — so too is hatred's effect on the human heart.
Results: The poster resonated well with target audiences.

126 PEACE. NOT WAR. | Design Firm: Kim Wild Designs | Designer: Kim Wild
Client: Self-initiated | Main Contributor: Kim Wild
Assignment: The goal was to bring awareness to all the innocent civilians who have lost their lives in the Israel, Palestine conflict, particularly those who lost their lives in the October 7, 2023, attack with the killing of hundreds of innocent people.
Approach: The flower used in the poster design is inspired by Israel's state flower, which is the red Anemone Coronaria flower.
Results: The poster brings awareness to the killing of innocents that comes with war.

127 TERRORISM | Design Firm: Goodall Integrated Design | Designer: Derwyn Goodall
Client: Self-initiated | Main Contributor: Derwyn Goodall
Assignment: To create a memorable poster on the topic of terrorism.
Approach: The horror of terrorism is unlike anything else. Dark, forboding and ominous, arising out of the abyss.
Results: Strong results from all walks of life.

128 MADE FOR THE COLD | Design Firm: Bailey Lauerman
Designer: Sarah Northcutt | Client: Special Olympics Nebraska | Creative Director: Carter Weitz
Motion Designer: Casey Stokes | Copywriter: Sophia Messineo | Retoucher: Gayle Adams
Illustrators: Sarah Northcutt, Firefly AI | Account Director: Emma Gallagher
Main Contributor: Sarah Northcutt
Assignment: Participants of the Polar Plunge are a special breed. As the temp drops their pulse rises. You could say that they are Made for the Cold.
Approach: The conceptual solution is centered around visualizing the extremes of joy and trepidation that comes with plunging in Nebraska winters.
Results: This year, the Special Olympics Nebraska registered 1300+ plungers for the event and raised over $380,000.

129 THE ENFIELD POLTERGEIST | Design Firm: Leroy & Rose
Designer: Leroy & Rose | Client: Apple

130 MANHUNT | Design Firm: Leroy & Rose | Designer: Leroy & Rose | Client: Apple

131 BETTER ANGELS: THE GOSPEL ACCORDING TO TAMMY FAYE
Design Firm: Célie Cadieux | Designer: Célie Cadieux
Client: Vice Studios | Main Contributor: Célie Cadieux
Assignment: This poster was commissioned by Vice Studios for the release of Better Angels: The Gospel According To Tammy Faye at the 2024 Sundance Film Festival. The series retells the story of American icon Tammy Faye Messner. The goal was to produce a poster that remained faithful to the unconventional story while breaking away from clichés and previous films about her.
Approach: My poster is a portrait of Tammy Faye Messner created with more than 375 shots from the series. It offers a fresh perspective on her story. It is representative of the way she gathered people, of her multifaceted personality, but also of the way she was put in a box. While distanced it may seem like we see the whole picture, life is often more complex, and what appears to be reality could just well be a TV screen.
Results: The poster successfully distinguished the film from previous productions about the same topic. It was displayed during the 2024 Sundance Film Festival and on social media where it gained attention.

132 THE BEAR: SEASON 2 | Design Firm: Leroy & Rose | Designer: Leroy & Rose | Client: FX
Assignment: The goal for The Bear season 2 key art was to continue the excitement and energy set in place from the hit first season. Since we also designed the key art for season 1, we wanted to distinctively differentiate the two pieces of art while maintaining an eclectic style and tone. For Season 2, our goal was to thread themes of chaos and tension that mimic the stress Carmy is battling throughout the show's plotline.
Approach: For the Season 2 artwork, we aimed to allude to any tension within the previous season's theme. The clock plate indicates the sense of urgency and pressure the characters face and the smaller scene was used to indicate the transition the restaurant experiences and how each character has their part to play. The more intricate composite helps display each character and uses them as devices to further express character dynamics and relations as the show has progressed. Further, the season 2 art is intended to show each character's journey from the first to the current.
Results: The Bear continually elevates itself as a top award winning television masterpiece. The Bear's second season has received 13 Emmy nominations, 10 Emmy wins, 5 SAG Award nominations, 1 SAG Award win and 2 People's Choice nominations while continuing to wow audiences worldwide. We're so thrilled to be a part of this show.

238 CREDITS&COMMENTARY

133 THE CHANGELING TEASER KEY ART | Design Firm: MOCEAN
Designer: Kishan Muthucumaru | Client: Apple TV+ | Creative Director: Nathaniel Wheeler
Associate Creative Director: Robert Dunbar | Production Artist: Kevin Crothers
Production: Kae Singhaseni | Account Executive: Samuel Pak
Main Contributor: Kishan Muthucumaru

134 PAINS OF YOUTH | Design Firm: Mirko Ilic Corp. | Designer: Mirko Ilic
Client: JDP-Yugoslav Drama Theater in Belgrade, Serbia | Illustrator: Mirko Ilic
Main Contributor: Mirko Ilic
Assignment: Pains of Youth is a shocking, erotically charged play by the Austrian writer Ferdinand Bruckner that depicts the moral corruption and cynicism of a group of medical students in 1923 Vienna. For these young people, youth itself is a fatal disease, and the idea of death by suicide is always present in their minds. A discontented post-war generation diagnose youth to be their sickness and do their best to destroy it.

135 THE DEVELOPMENT PATH OF BORA ŠNAJDER | Design Firm: Mirko Ilic Corp.
Designer: Mirko Ilic | Client: JDP-Yugoslav Drama Theater in Belgrade, Serbia
Illustrator: Mirko Ilic | Main Contributor: Mirko Ilic
Assignment: Aleksandar Popović's play The Development Path of Bora Šnajder follows several connections, the most important of which are: the socialist social milieu in which incompetent and unprepared careerists rise, the conflict between social and private work, and the meeting of an anonymous person with ideology and its laws.

136 URINETOWN: THE MUSICAL | Design Firm: Chemi Montes Design
Designer: Chemi Montes | Client: American University Department of Performing Arts
Photographers: Wall background image by Pixabay, for Stockvault. Digitally edited by Chemi Montes | Main Contributor: Chemi Montes

137 SWITZERLAND | Design Firm: Atelier Bundi AG | Designer: Stephan Bundi
Client: Theater Orchester Biel Solothurn | Art Director: Stephan Bundi
Illustrator: Stephan Bundi | Main Contributor: Stephan Bundi
Assignment: Play by Joanna Murray-Smith about Patricia Highsmith in Switzerland. Highsmith collected weapons, particularly knives. The oppressive atmosphere during her meeting with the young publisher is depicted with a shark fin.
Approach: The knife takes on a dual meaning.
Results: Visual for the poster, advertisements, and program title.

138 DAS KURZE LEBEN DER FAKTEN (THE LIFESPAN OF A FACT)
Design Firm: Atelier Bundi AG | Designer: Stephan Bundi
Client: Theater Orchester Biel Solothurn | Main Contributor: Stephan Bundi
Assignment: (The Lifespan of a Fact) Play by Jeremy Kareken, David Murrell, and Gordon Farrell. Explores the difference between facts and their literary interpretation.
Approach: Precision (facts) and its embellishment.
Results: Visual for the poster, advertisements, and program title.

139 CYRANO | Design Firm: Atelier Bundi AG | Designer: Stephan Bundi
Client: Theater Orchester Biel Solothurn | Art Director: Stephan Bundi
Illustrator: Stephan Bundi | Main Contributor: Stephan Bundi
Assignment: Poster for the tragicomedy "Cyrano" by Edmond de Rostand.
Approach: Cyrano of Bergerac is mocked because of his big nose. His poems, on the other hand, are touching; he leaves them to his rival. A game with "masks" and deception.
Results: The poster has won several awards.

140 LOVE LAHAINA MAUI | Design Firm: Atelier Starno | Designer: Arnaud Ghelfi
Client: Self-initiated | Main Contributor: Arnaud Ghelfi
Assignment: In the aftermath of the devastating fire on the island of Maui, Hawaii, I created this poster to show my love to the people affected by that catastrophic event.
Approach: Created a heart shape visual made of native Hawaiian flowers on a white background. A splash of colors and joy as a memory of what Lahaina once was and what it will become again one day soon.
Results: Sold as fundraising for the aid organizations working on the ground of Maui.

141 STOP WAR! – POSTER | Design Firm: Barbara Galinska | Designer: Barbara Galinska
Client: Self-initiated | Main Contributor: Barbara Galinska
Assignment: "STOP WAR!," originated from an international calligraphy challenge in November 2023. My reaction to the topic was to move away from a typical calligraphic rendition towards an impactful piece addressing the global issue of war. Thus my main goals were to find a new original solution and turn it into a powerful symbol for peace.
Approach: The prevailing emotions around the phrase "Stop war!" are hopelessness, desperation, fear, anger, and rage. My way to achieve this intensity is to choose strong contrasting colours, as well as use the background of one word as the space where to write another word. The red letters of "STOP" bound the black "WAR!," creating an anxiety-inducing maze. Following the red duct of STOP one is able to move to the exit of the maze and find oneself outside WAR and the whole graphic altogether.
Results: The artwork gained global recognition, the first notable success being its appearance as a mural in Brooklyn and Tel Aviv. The design was projected on the big wall of a local cultural centre to mark the second anniversary of the Russian invasion of Ukraine. The posters have been widely used in demonstrations against the Israeli-Palestine conflict. The children from the Padua Children International Summer Villages are all going to wear T-shits with "Stop war!" in 2024 to manifest their commitment to a more peaceful world. My "Stop war!" graphic was also drawn on Bridlington South Beach by beach art activist Fred Brown. I've also been approached by Brave Poets, the organizers of a big charity event in London, namely a concert called "Artists for Humanity", who ordered a project for the event, which I have already delivered.

142 POSTER OF EXHIBITION ON FIFTY YEARS OF DESIGN EXCHANGE BETWEEN TAIWAN AND SOUTH KOREA | Design Firm: Leo Lin Design | Designer: Leo Lin
Client: National Taiwan Normal University Department of Design | Main Contributor: Leo Lin
Assignment: Create a poster for the exhibition on Fifty Years of Design Exchange between Taiwan and South Korea.
Approach: The use of fonts combined with the national colors of Taiwan and South Korea presents an image of mutual exchange and integration, and expresses the long-term cultural exchanges and understanding between designers from the two countries.

143 SAVING ANIMALS FROM EXTINCTION (SAFE PROGRAM)
Design Firm: Fallano Faulkner & Associates | Designer: Frank Fallano
Client: Associations of Zoos & Aquariums | Photographers: CROCODILE: Design/Photo/Illustration: Frank Fallano • Reference Photos: Greg Lepera, St. Aug. Alligator Farm, FLAMINGO: Design/Photo/Illustration: Frank Fallano • Reference Photos: Reid Park Zoo • Daniel Hilliard, Ph.D. (ZCOG), HORNBILL: Design/Photo/Illustration: Frank Fallano • Reference Photos: Roger Sweeney, JAGUAR: Design/Photo/Illustration: Frank Fallano • Reference Photos: Palm Beach Zoo, MONARCH: Design/Photo/Illustration: Frank Fallano • Reference Photos: Thom Benson • Jennifer D., Candice Rennels, OKC Zoo, SONGBIRD: Design/Photo/Illustration: Frank Fallano • Reference Photos: Roshan Patel, Smithsonian • Matt Igleski, Lincoln Park Zoo, MEXICAN WOLF: Design/Photo/Illustration: Frank Fallano • Reference Photos: Michelle Steinmeyer
Main Contributor: Frank Fallano
Assignment: Create a series of posters featuring animals in the association's SAFE program (Saving Animals From Extinction). The client's creative requirements included: The additional capability of member institutions to brand the posters with their logo and offer it for their own sales and promotional efforts. The client suggested a style inspired by vintage travel posters of the 1930s-40s.
Approach: We (FF&A) created posters, one for each endangered species selected. The client provided some reference photography and we used some of our own existing images as well as images shot specifically for the project. Each image was created using a number of techniques– photography, photo compositing, as well as digital drawing and conventional ink on paper drawing. In addition, the series was tied together with some common elements–distant horizon lines with changing angles of view, breaking the frame boundary with elements to enliven the composition, and treating a few items as flat graphic shapes to evoke the vintage posters mentioned in the client's brief.
Results: This group of posters is new and research data has not yet been compiled.

SILVER WINNERS:
145 PHILIP HANSON HISS AWARD CELEBRATION POSTER
Design Firm: Studio Craig Byers | Designer: Craig Byers
Client: Architecture Sarasota | Main Contributor: Studio Craig Byers

145 ARCHITECTURE SARASOTA MODERNS THAT MATTER: SARASOTA 100 EXHIBITION POSTER | Design Firm: Studio Craig Byers | Designer: Craig Byers
Client: Architecture Sarasota | Main Contributor: Studio Craig Byers

145 QUESTIONS CONQUERED | Design Firm: Traction Factory | Designer: Mike Basse
Client: Snap-on Diagnostics | Creative Director: David Brown | Art Director: Mike Basse
Copywriter: S.J. Barlament | Retoucher: Hac Job | Project Manager: Pam Sallis
Account Director: Shannon Egan | Main Contributor: Mike Basse

146 STILA, THE PERFECT LINE | Design Firm: Stila (In-House) | Designer: Mina Kim
Client: Self-initiated | Main Contributor: Mina Kim

146 SIXTY YEARS OF DESIGN IN CRYSTAL | Design Firm: Andrea Ruggiero Design
Designer: Andrea Ruggiero | Client: Arnolfo di Cambio | Main Contributor: Andrea Ruggiero

146 ST. FRANCIS OF THE MOUNTAINS | Design Firm: Alan Rellaford Design
Designer: Alan Rellaford | Client: Episcopal Diocese of Northern California
Photographer: Ruth Rich | Main Contributor: Alan Rellaford

146 RACHMANINOFF 150 | Design Firm: Braley Design | Designer: Michael Braley
Clients: Golden Bee Biennale, Self-initiated | Illustrator: Kate Davis
Main Contributor: Michael Braley

147 RACHMANINOFF 150 | Design Firm: Braley Design | Designer: Michael Braley
Clients: Golden Bee Biennale, Self-initiated | Main Contributor: Michael Braley

147 60 YEARS OF ARS PROGRAM - RTV NATIONAL PUBLIC BROADCASTER SLOVENIA | Design Firm: Bojana Fajmut | Designer: Bojana Fajmut
Clients: RTV Slovenija, Radio Slovenia Third Channel - ARS Program
Client Support: Ingrid Kovač Brus | Main Contributor: Bojana Fajmut

147 HOMAGE TO PELE POSTER | Design Firm: Ray Visual Communications
Designer: Scott Ray | Client: Self-initiated | Main Contributor: Scott Ray

147 MILTON LOVE | Design Firm: Coco Cerrella | Designer: Coco Cerrella
Client: Designers for Milton Glaser | Main Contributor: Coco Cerrella

148 YEAR OF THE DRAGON | Design Firm: Gravdahl Design | Designer: John Gravdahl
Client: Self-initiated | Main Contributor: John Gravdahl

148 COUNTY OF SAN DIEGO CROP STATISTICS & ANNUAL REPORT
Design Firm: Freaner Creative & Design | Designer: Ariel Freaner
Client: County of San Diego Agriculture, Weights and Measures | Digital Artist: Ariel Freaner
Main Contributor: Ariel Freaner

148 MAKE THIS YEAR THE GREATEST. | Design Firm: Nikkeisha, Inc.
Designer: Ayaka Kawamata | Client: Self-initiated | Creative Director: Hiroyuki Nakamura
Art Director: Hiroyuki Nakamura | Copywriter: Keika Katsumata
Illustrator: Ayaka Kawamata | Main Contributor: Nikkeisha, Inc.

149 LUEG BUDGET EXHIBIT POSTERS | Design Firm: Freaner Creative & Design
Designer: Ariel Freaner | Clients: County of San Diego Land Use & Environment, Donna Durckel
Digital Artist: Ariel Freaner | Main Contributor: Ariel Freaner

149 RED CROSS CORPORATE POSTER SERIES | Design Firm: Freaner Creative & Design
Designer: Ariel Freaner | Clients: Red Cross of Tijuana, Jorge Astiazaran
Digital Artist: Ariel Freaner | Main Contributor: Ariel Freaner

149 RED CROSS ALWAYS HERE FOR YOU POSTERS CAMPAIGN
Design Firm: Freaner Creative & Design | Designer: Ariel Freaner
Clients: Red Cross of Tijuana, Jorge Astiazaran | Main Contributor: Ariel Freaner

150 WINTER DANCE WORKS 2023 | Design Firm: Hyungjookim Designlab
Designer: Hyungjoo A. Kim | Client: Purdue Contemporary Dance Company
Photographer: Melodie Yvonne | Main Contributor: Hyungjoo A. Kim

239 CREDITS & COMMENTARY

150 SPRING DANCE WORKS 2024 | Design Firm: Hyungjookim Designlab
Designer: Hyungjoo A. Kim | Client: Purdue Contemporary Dance Company
Photographer: Greta Bell | Main Contributor: Hyungjoo A. Kim

150 SWAN LAKE – 2023/2024 SEASON PERFORMANCE | Design Firm: Mythic
Designer: Alex-Marie Ablan | Client: Charlotte Ballet | Chief Creative Officer: Lee James
Executive Creative Director: David Olsen | Art Director: Alejandro Cerudo
Copywriter: Alexandra Frazier | Photographer: Quinn Wharton
Production Artist: Jeff Buchbinder | Account Manager: Emilie Boone
Account Supervisor: Riley McLeod | Project Managers: Deanna Shuford, Madison Racel
\Main Contributor: Alex-Marie Ablan

150 NEED A LITTLE PICK ME UP? | Design Firm: DEFINITION 6 (Bridgenext)
Designer: YiJun Jiang | Client: Saia LTL Freight | Advertising Agency: DEFINITION 6 (Bridgenext)
Main Contributor: YiJun Jiang

151 PROFESS LESS / LISTEN MORE | Design Firm: Aufuldish & Warinner
Designer: Bob Aufuldish | Client: I Profess: The Graphic Design Manifesto 20th Anniversary
Exhibition | Main Contributor: Bob Aufuldish

151 UCLA EXTENSION FALL_QUARTER 2023 | Design Firm: Braley Design
Designer: Michael Braley | Client: UCLA Extension | Main Contributor: Michael Braley

151 BAUHAUS & KINDAI GRAPHIC ART COURSE
Design Firm: Kiyoung An Graphic Art Course Laboratory | Designer: Kiyoung An
Client: KINDAI University Department of Arts | Art Director: Kiyoung An
Main Contributor: Kiyoung An

151 BEIJING OPERA CULTURE | Design Firm: Tainan University of Technology
Designer: Chia-Hui Lien | Client: Self-initated | Main Contributor: Chia-Hui Lien

152 JESSUP 2024: THE CASE CONCERNING THE STERREN FORTY
Design Firm: White & Case LLP | Designer: Donna Manahan
Client: International Law Students Association | Project Manager: Paul McMillan
Art Director: Karolina Pietrynczak | Main Contributor: Donna Manahan

152 THE ART OF THE POSTER: ARTCENTER LECTURE | Design Firm: Braley Design
Designer: Michael Braley | Clients: Self-initiated, ArtCenter College of Design
Main Contributor: Michael Braley

152 DON'T CUT MY FUTURE | Design Firm: CCC + JC. Jacinta & Carlos
Designers: Carlos Casimiro Costa, Jacinta Costa [Costas] | Client: IPB Community
Main Contributors: Carlos Casimiro Costa, Jacinta Costa [Costas]

152 COHABITATIONS: FALL/SPRING 2023-2024 EVENT SERIES
Design Firm: Pratt Institute Communications and Marketing
Designer: Pratt Institute Creative Services | Client: Pratt Institute School of Architecture
Creative Director: David Frisco | Senior Designer: Robert McConnell
Project Manager: Stephanie Greenberg | Vice President of Marketing: James Kempster
Print Producer: Christopher Keating | Main Contributor: Pratt Institute Creative Services

153 MB: TYPOGRAPHIC POSTER WORKSHOP | Design Firm: Braley Design
Designer: Michael Braley | Clients: Self-initiated, Iowa State University
Main Contributor: Michael Braley

153 NO NOW | Design Firm: Goodall Integrated Design | Designer: Derwyn Goodall
Client: Self-initiated | Main Contributor: Derwyn Goodall

153 FAYETTEVILLE STATE UNIVERSITY-POSTER CAMPAIGN | Design Firm: The Republik
Designers: Brad Magner, Dallas West | Client: Fayettevile State University
Creative Group Head: Robert Shaw West | Creative Directors: Brad Magner, Matt Shapiro
Art Directors: Brad Magner, Matt Shapiro, Dallas West, Robert Shaw West
Copywriter: Dwayne Fry | Account Executives: Kirk deViere, Vanessa Nguyen
Main Contributor: Robert Shaw West

154 STUDY ABROAD WITH CSU! | Design Firm: Gravdahl Design | Designer: John Gravdahl
Client: Colorado State University International Programs | Main Contributor: John Gravdahl

154 PUBLIC ART, CALL FOR PROPOSALS | Design Firm: Jack Harris
Designer: Jack Harris | Client: Farmingdale State College | Illustrator: Adobe Stock
Main Contributor: Jack Harris

154 KIDS ARE SPONGES | Design Firm: Serve Marketing | Designer: Katrina Moenning
Client: Office of Early Childhood Initiative | Creative Director: Gary Mueller
Art Director: Katrina Moenning | Retoucher: Anthony Giacomino | Copywriter: Seth Gordon
Account Director: Lauren Sutter | Main Contributors: Gary Mueller, Katrina Moenning,
Anthony Giacomino, Seth Gordon, Lauren Sutter

154 SOCRATES | Design Firm: Randy Clark | Designer: Randy Clark
Client: Self-initiated | Main Contributor: Randy Clark

154 AMERICAN NIGHTMARE | Design Firm: Territory Studio | Designer: Territory Studio
Client: Netflix | Main Contributor: Territory Studio

154 THE AMERICAN BUFFALO | Design Firm: SJI Associates | Designer: David O'Hanlon
Clients: PBS Creative Services: Ira Rubenstein–Chief Digital and Marketing Officer,
Stacey Librecht–Vice President/Creative Services, John Ruppenthal–Creative Director,
Jared Traver– Sr. Director of Production, Claire Quin–Sr. Print & Digital Producer
Illustrator: John Isaiah Pepion | President: Suzy Jurist | Art Director: David O'Hanlon
Main Contributor: SJI Associates

154 LIL NAS X - LONG LIVE MONTERO TOUR POSTER | Design Firm: Saad Moosajee
Designer: Minkwan Kim | Client: Lil Nas X | Creative Director: Saad Moosajee
Design Lead: Minkwan Kim | Art Director: Minkwan Kim | Main Contributor: Minkwan Kim

154 IRENE SOLÀ | Design Firm: Anagraphic | Designer: Anna Farkas
Client: Magvető | Main Contributor: Anna Farkas

154 FLY WITH ME | Design Firm: SJI Associates | Designer: Christian Luis
Clients: Chika Offurum, American Experience Films | President: Suzy Jurist
Art Director: David O'Hanlon | Copywriter: David O'Hanlon
Project Manager: Hannah Holdsworth | Main Contributor: SJI Associates

155 THE RIOT REPORT | Design Firm: SJI Associates | Designer: Christian Luis
Clients: Chika Offurum, American Experience Films | President: Suzy Jurist
Art Director: David O'Hanlon | Project Manager: Hannah Holdsworth
Production Artist: Michael Stampone | Main Contributor: SJI Associates

155 HISTORY 365 (FAST CHANNEL BRAND IDENTITY) | Design Firm: SJI Associates
Designers: Andrew Zimmerman, Adam Selbst, Rick Gerwitz | Client: A+E Networks
President: Suzy Jurist | Art Director: David O'Hanlon | Project Manager: Hannah Holdsworth
Production Artist: Michael Stampone | Main Contributor: SJI Associates

155 FROM S2, KEY ART | Design Firm: The Refinery | Designer: The Refinery
Client: MGM+ | Main Contributor: The Refinery

155 NAPOLEON, KEY ART | Design Firm: The Refinery | Designer: The Refinery
Clients: Apple TV+, Sony Pictures Entertainment | Main Contributor: The Refinery

156 SEXY BEAST CAMPAIGN ART | Design Firm: Rhubarb
Designer: Rhubarb | Client: Paramount+ | Executive Creative Director: Ryan Jones
Creative Directors: Adrianne Deluna, Steve Chan, Paramount+ | Art Director: Bruce Ventanilla
Chief Creative Officer: Andrew Irving | Photographer: Alan Clarke | Marketing: Kevin Bjelajac,
Paramount+ | Others: Matt Hernanadez, SVP Head of Design at Paramount+, Vanessa Brandon,
Supervising Producer, Paramount+, Tara Marin, Sr. Manager, Paramount+, Christine Ramage,
VP of Photography, Paramount+, Courtney Smith, Sr. Director, Paramount+
Account Director: Geysel Junne | Marketing Manager: Devin Rome | Main Contributor: Rhubarb

156 FARGO | Design Firm: ARSONAL | Designer: ARSONAL | Client: FX Networks
Art Director: ARSONAL | Others: Stephanie Gibbons, Creative Director/President, Creative,
Strategy & Digital Marketing Michael Brittain, Creative Director / SVP Print Design Rob Wilson,
VP Print Design Sarin Markarian, Director Print Design Laura Handy, Project Director,
Print Design Lisa Lejeune, Production Director, Print Design
Main Contributors: ARSONAL, FX Networks

156 YOUR LUCKY DAY | Design Firm: The Refinery | Designer: The Refinery
Client: Well Go USA Entertainment | Main Contributor: The Refinery

156 THE GREAT S3 | Design Firm: The Refinery | Designer: The Refinery
Client: Hulu | Main Contributor: The Refinery

157 PERCY JACKSON AND THE OLYMPIANS | Design Firm: The Refinery
Designer: The Refinery | Client: Disney Entertainment Television | Main Contributor: The Refinery

157 NAZI TOWN, USA | Design Firm: SJI Associates | Designer: Christian Luis
Clients: Chika Offurum, American Experience Films | President: Suzy Jurist
Art Director: David O'Hanlon | Copywriter: David O'Hanlon
Project Manager: Hannah Holdsworth | Production Artist: Michael Stampone
Main Contributor: SJI Associates

157 THE BUSING BATTLEGROUND | Design Firm: SJI Associates | Designer: David O'Hanlon
Clients: Chika Offurum, American Experience Films | President: Suzy Jurist
Art Director: David O'Hanlon | Copywriter: Katrina Day | Project Manager: Hannah Holdsworth
Production Artist: Michael Stampone | Main Contributor: SJI Associates

157 BLACK MAFIA FAMILY S3, KEY ART | Design Firm: The Refinery
Designer: The Refinery | Client: STARZ | Main Contributor: The Refinery

158 GENIUS: MLKX, KEY ART | Design Firm: The Refinery | Designer: The Refinery
Client: National Geographic | Main Contributor: The Refinery

158 THE GIRLS ON THE BUS | Design Firm: The Refinery | Designer: The Refinery
Client: Max | Main Contributor: The Refinery

158 CASA SUSANNA | Design Firm: SJI Associates | Designer: David O'Hanlon
Clients: Chika Offurum, American Experience Films | President: Suzy Jurist
Art Director: David O'Hanlon | Main Contributor: SJI Associates

158 INTERVENTION (FAST CHANNEL BRAND IDENTITY) | Design Firm: SJI Associates
Designer: Chad Hornberger | Client: A+E Networks | President: Suzy Jurist
Art Director: David O'Hanlon | Project Manager: Hannah Holdsworth
Main Contributor: SJI Associates

159 LOS (CASÍ) ÍDOLOS DE BAHÍA COLORADA KEY ART | Design Firm: Rhubarb
Designer: Rhubarb | Client: Netflix | Executive Creative Director: Ryan Jones
Creative Director: Adrianne Deluna | Chief Creative Officer: Andrew Irving
Illustrator: Liza Shumskaya | Title: Giovanni Bautista
Marketing: Rodrigo García-Robles, Netflix | Account Director: Geysel Junne
Main Contributor: Rhubarb

159 ANTHEM | Design Firm: The Refinery | Designer: The Refinery
Client: Hulu | Main Contributor: The Refinery

159 RAISING KANAN | Design Firm: ARSONAL | Designer: ARSONAL
Client: STARZ | Others: Whitney Abeel – SVP, Originals and Digital Marketing Roxana Munoz
– (Former) Director, Originals Marketing Sherelle Penalosa – Manager, Originals Marketing
Main Contributors: ARSONAL, STARZ

159 THE GREATEST HITS | Design Firm: The Refinery | Designer: The Refinery
Client: Searchlight Pictures | Main Contributor: The Refinery

160 POISONED GROUND: THE TRAGEDY AT LOVE CANAL | Design Firm: SJI Associates
Designer: Chad Hornberger | Clients: Chika Offurum, American Experience Films
Art Director: David O'Hanlon | Copywriter: Katrina Day | President: Suzy Jurist
Project Manager: Hannah Holdsworth | Production Artist: Michael Stampone
Main Contributor: SJI Associates

240 CREDITS & COMMENTARY

160 BLACK CAKE KEY ART | Design Firm: Rhubarb | Designer: Rhubarb
Client: Hulu | Executive Creative Director: Ryan Jones
Creative Group Head: Angela Gervasio-Hewett | Creative Director: Adrianne Deluna
Chief Creative Officer: Andrew Irving | Account Director: Geysel Junne
Photographer: Matt Sayles | Main Contributor: Rhubarb

160 THE END OF SEX | Design Firm: The Refinery | Designer: The Refinery
Client: Blue Fox Entertainment | Main Contributor: The Refinery

160 JUSTIFIED: CITY PRIMEVAL, KEY ART | Design Firm: The Refinery
Designer: The Refinery | Client: FX Networks | Main Contributor: The Refinery

161 THE CROWDED ROOM, KEY ART | Design Firm: The Refinery
Designer: The Refinery | Client: Apple TV+ | Main Contributor: The Refinery

161 MINX S2, KEY ART | Design Firm: The Refinery | Designer: The Refinery
Client: STARZ | Main Contributor: The Refinery

161 FLOAT KEY ART | Design Firm: Rhubarb | Designers: Rhubarb, Jean Pierre Llanos Garcia
Client: Lionsgate | Executive Creative Director: Ryan Jones | Creative Director: Adrianne Deluna
Chief Creative Officer: Andrew Irving | Account Director: Geysel Junne
Main Contributor: Rhubarb

161 NAPOLEON, INTERNATIONAL WILDPOSTS | Design Firm: The Refinery
Designer: The Refinery | Clients: Apple TV+, Sony Pictures Entertainment
Main Contributor: The Refinery

162 DON'T CREATE GARBAGE | Design Firm: Tainan University of Technology
Designer: Chia-Hui Lien | Client: Self-initiated | Main Contributor: Chia-Hui Lien

162 BALLOONS ARE MONSTERS | Design Firm: Arcana Academy | Designer: Lee Walters
Client: Balloon Brigade | Executive Creative Directors: Shane Hutton, Lee Walters
Producer: Jessica Darke Lightfoot | Main Contributor: Lee Walters

162 SAVE WATER, SAVE LIFE, NO WATER, NO LIFE | Design Firm: Namseoul University
Designer: Mi-Jung Lee | Client: Ministry of Environment | Professor: Mi-Jung Lee
Main Contributor: Mi-Jung Lee

162 NATURE: HANDLE WITH CARE | Design Firm: Goodall Integrated Design
Designer: Derwyn Goodall | Clients: 2nd Yangmingshan Art Festival, 22th Tianmu Waterway Festival | Main Contributor: Derwyn Goodall

163 COP28 | Design Firm: Tsushima Design | Designer: Hajime Tsushima
Client: Emirates International Poster Festival | Main Contributor: Hajime Tsushima

163 WATER FOR LIFE | Design Firm: João Machado Design | Designer: João Machado
Client: UnknownDesign | Main Contributor: João Machado

163 CELEBRATE EL PASO: CASTNER RANGE NATIONAL MONUMENT
Design Firm: Anne M. Giangiulio | Designer: Anne M. Giangiulio
Client: Self-initiated | Main Contributor: Anne M. Giangiulio

163 PURE NATURE | Design Firm: May & Co. | Designer: Douglas May
Client: 2023 CDAK International Special Exhibition | Main Contributor: Douglas May

164 I IMAGINE... PEACE AND TRANQUILITY | Design Firm: Braley Design
Designer: Michael Braley | Client: Self-initiated | Main Contributor: Michael Braley

164 BIO | Design Firm: João Machado Design | Designer: João Machado
Client: UnknownDesign | Main Contributor: João Machado

164 FINDING HOPE, FINDING FUTURE | Design Firm: Hyungjookim Designlab
Designer: Hyungjoo A. Kim | Client: Emirates International Poster Festival
Main Contributor: Hyungjoo A. Kim

164 PAPA JOHNS POSTERS | Design Firm: Addison | Designer: JG Debray
Client: Papa Johns | Creative Director: Kevin Barclay | Writers: Kevin Barclay, JG Debray
Managing Director: Judy Sandford | Account Director: Russ Kuhner
Strategy: Russ Kuhner | Naming: Russ Kuhner | Main Contributor: JG Debray

165 ORANGE FOREST | Design Firm: Wesam Mazhar Haddad
Designer: Wesam Mazhar Haddad | Client: Self-initiated
Main Contributor: Wesam Mazhar Haddad

165 SAVE ME | Design Firm: João Machado Design | Designer: João Machado
Client: UnknownDesign | Main Contributor: João Machado

165 "CLEAN WATER" U40 POSTER DESIGN COMPETITION
Design Firm: Toyotsugu Itoh Design Office | Designer: Toyotsugu Itoh
Client: Ogaki Poster Museum | Main Contributor: Toyotsugu Itoh

165 FINAL FOOTPRINT | Design Firm: National Kaohsiung University of Science and Technology (NKUST) | Designer: Chong-Wen Chen | Client: Self-initiated
Main Contributor: Chong-Wen Chen

166 HERBERT BAYER HOMAGE | Design Firm: Braley Design | Designer: Michael Braley
Client: United States International Poster Biennial (USIPB) | Main Contributor: Michael Braley

166 CMTG 2023 | Design Firm: Peace Inc. | Designer: Lee Giltae
Client: Self-initiated | Art Director: Lee Giltae

166 OMAHA CHESS CITY CHAMPIONSHIPS | Design Firm: University of Nebraska
Designer: Joshua Lowe | Client: Nebraska State Chess Association
Main Contributor: Joshua Lowe

166 COMEDY LOCALIZED POSTER | Design Firm: David Habben Illustration
Designer: David Habben | Client: SLUG Magazine
Creative Director: Grace White | Main Contributor: David Habben

167 J IS FOR JAZZ | Design Firm: Braley Design | Designer: Michael Braley
Client: We Want Jazz 2023 | Main Contributor: Michael Braley

167 TOKAS OPEN STUDIO | Design Firm: Chikako Oguma
Designer: Chikako Oguma | Client: TOKAS (Tokyo Arts and Space)
Art Director: Chikako Oguma | Main Contributor: Chikako Oguma

167 WHAT NEW CHOICES FOR THE FUTURE? | Design Firm: AYA KAWABATA DESIGN
Designer: Aya Kawabata | Client: Design Event Shibuya 2023
Main Contributor: Design Event at Shibuya Tokyo

167 SOLAR CITIES | Design Firm: Fons Hickmann m23 | Designer: Fons Hickmann
Client: Daegu Korea | Main Contributor: Fons Hickmann

168 IMAGINE PEACE | Design Firm: Braley Design | Designer: Michael Braley
Client: Nanjing International Biennial of Poster for Peace 2023 | Main Contributor: Michael Braley

168 IOWA STATE UNIVERSITY LECTURE POSTER | Design Firm: Braley Design
Designer: Michael Braley | Clients: Self-initiated, Iowa State University
Main Contributor: Michael Braley

168 MILTON GLASER | Design Firm: Synopsismedia | Designer: Ovidiu Hrin
Client: Typopassage TM Poster Museum | Main Contributor: Ovidiu Hrin

168 THIS IS A POSTER FOR PEACE | Design Firm: Braley Design
Designer: Michael Braley | Client: Nanjing International Biennial of Poster for Peace 2023
Main Contributor: Michael Braley

169 SAN FRANCISCO ANTIQUARIAN BOOK & PAPER FAIR
Design Firm: Studio Hinrichs | Designer: Kit Hinrichs
Client: Nancy Johnson Events Management | Main Contributor: Kit Hinrichs

169 LESTER BEALL HOMAGE | Design Firm: Braley Design
Designer: Michael Braley | Client: United States International Poster Biennial (USIPB)
Main Contributor: Michael Braley

169 WIGOUT AT THE DISCO | Design Firm: Everything Looks Good
Designer: Alexandria Canchola | Client: K Space Contemporary
Main Contributor: Alexandria Canchola

169 2023 GARDENERS' MARKET POSTER | Design Firm: Design SubTerra
Designer: R.P. Bissland | Client: Cahe Valley Gardeners' Market Association
Main Contributor: R.P. Bissland

170 HUMARI KAHANI POSTERS | Design Firm: Shantanu Suman
Designer: Shantanu Suman | Clients: Tawoos Initiative, Virasat
Main Contributor: Shantanu Suman

170 SUBARU TARGA FLORIO POSTER | Design Firm: Automotive Events
Designer: Greg Oznowich | Clients: Dominick Infante, Subaru of America
Creative Director: Greg Oznowich | Account Manager: Iain Dobson
Project Manager: Brittany Mannella | Project Coordinator: Emma Layshock
Main Contributor: Automotive Events

170 RACHMANINOFF | Design Firm: Carmit Design Studio
Designer: Carmit Makler Haller | Client: Golden Bee Biennale
Main Contributors: Carmit Makler Haller, Carmit Design Studio

170 AGI SPECIAL PROJECT 2023: ONE/UNO | Design Firm: Studio Hinrichs
Designer: Kit Hinrichs | Client: Alliance Graphique Internationale (AGI)
Main Contributor: Kit Hinrichs

170 2024 WILLIAM H. ELY ILLUSTRATION THESIS EXHIBITION
Design Firm: University of the Arts | Designer: Ari Santiago | Client: Self-initiated
Art Director: Daniel Fishel | Illustrator: Ari Santiago | Main Contributor: Ari Santiago

170 PLANNED OBSOLESCENCE | Design Firm: Braley Design
Designer: Michael Braley | Client: SIPSM: Salón Internacional del Póster San Mateo
Main Contributor: Michael Braley

170 ILLUSTRATION WEST 62 | Design Firm: Martin French Studio
Designer: Martin French | Client: Society of Illustrators Los Angeles
Main Contributor: Martin French

170 JURIED STUDENT EXHIBITION POSTER (NORTHWEST MISSOURI STATE UNIVERSITY) | Design Firm: Feixue Mei | Designer: Feixue Mei
Client: Northwest Missouri State University | Main Contributor: Feixue Mei

170 IN DIALOGUE — ERNST LUDWIG KIRCHNER AND LINHAN YU
Design Firm: Team Mao | Designer: Siyu Mao | Client: Gallery Nadan

171 THE 69TH NEW YORK TDC EXHIBITION AT OSAKA
Design Firm: TOMOKUSA DESIGN | Designer: Yuta Tomokusa
Client: Japan Typography Association | Main Contributor: Yuta Tomokusa

171 ETERNAL | Design Firm: Human Paradise Studio | Designer: Brad Tzou
Client: Self-initiated | Main Contributor: Brad Tzou

171 BORDERLESS | Design Firm: Andrea Szabó | Designer: Andrea Szabó
Client: Association of Hungarian Fine and Applied Artists | Main Contributor: Andrea Szabó

171 TRANSITION. ZURICH DESIGN WEEKS 2023
Design Firm: Res Eichenberger Design | Designer: Res Eichenberger
Client: Zurich Design Weeks | Main Contributor: Res Eichenberger Design

172 SENSORIAL SYSTEM- DECODING INTIMACY THROUGH MULTI-SENSORY INFORMATION DESIGN | Design Firm: Chloe Zhang | Designer: Chloe Zhang
Client: Self-initiated | Main Contributor: Chloe Zhang

241 CREDITS & COMMENTARY

172 DIE WILDE JAGD [THE WILD HUNT] | Design Firm: Studio +Fronczek
Designer: Sascha Fronczek | Client: Deutsches Fleischermuseum
Exhibition Designer: Verena Stella Gompf | Junior Designer: Jana Renger
Main Contributor: Sascha Fronczek

172 CREATIVE ENERGY / KREATIVE ENERGIE | Design Firm: Braley Design
Designer: Michael Braley | Client: Anfachen Awards VI | Main Contributor: Michael Braley

172 XU LI SCHOOL OF DESIGN EXHIBITION POSTERS | Design Firm: Underline Studio
Designer: Fidel Peña | Client: George Brown College School of Design
Art Directors: Claire Dawson, Fidel Peña | Main Contributor: Underline Studio

173 FLIGHT OF GOOD FORTUNE | Design Firm: Lisa Winstanley Design
Designer: Lisa Winstanley | Client: KWVD International Invitational Design Exhibition
Main Contributor: Lisa Winstanley

173 STARTING FROM ZERO | Design Firm: Design Studio FLORALIEN Inc.
Designer: Miyoko Kawamura | Client: New Art ZERO Association
Main Contributor: Miyoko Kawamura

173 UNITED STATES INTERNATIONAL POSTER BIENNIAL 2023
Design Firm: Braley Design | Designer: Michael Braley
Client: United States International Poster Biennial (USIPB) | Main Contributor: Michael Braley

173 MEET DESIGN | Design Firm: Gon.C Studio | Designer: Choe Gon
Client: Gwangju Design Biennale 2023 | Main Contributor: Choe Gon

174 2024 POLYPHONE FESTIVAL: A FESTIVAL OF NEW AND EMERGING MUSICALS
Design Firm: University of the Arts | Designer: Kevin Mercer | Client: Self-initiated
Art Director: Daniel Fishel | Illustrator: Katelyn Harris | Main Contributor: Katelyn Harris

174 FREE YOUR MIND | Design Firm: Studio Eduard Cehovin | Designer: Eduard Cehovin
Client: 2023 First Contemporary Local Youth Art Festival, China
Creative Director: Eduard Cehovin | Main Contributor: Eduard Cehovin

174 FESTIVAL FILMAR EN AMÉRICA LATINA 22 | Design Firm: WePlayDesign
Designers: Sophie Rubin, Cédric Rossel | Client: Filmar en América Latina
Main Contributor: WePlayDesign

174 WOMEN TEXAS FILM FESTIVAL POSTER 2023
Design Firm: Ray Visual Communications | Designer: Scott Ray
Client: Women Texas Film Festival | Main Contributor: Scott Ray

175 LA DESIGN FESTIVAL 2023: DESIGN FOR THE PEOPLE | Design Firm: Braley Design
Designer: Michael Braley | Client: LA Design Festival 2023 | Illustrator: Kate Davis
Main Contributor: Michael Braley

175 FAR° – FESTIVAL DES ARTS VIVANTS | Design Firm: WePlayDesign
Designers: Sophie Rubin, Cédric Rossel | Client: Far° | Main Contributor: WePlayDesign

175 SCULPTURE FESTIVAL | Design Firm: Team Mao
Designer: Siyu Mao | Client: DRK Kliniken Berlin Westend

175 FADE POSTER BY ECHO FILM FESTIVAL | Design Firm: CAO Design
Designer: Yvonne Cao | Client: ECHO Film Festival | Main Contributor: Yvonne Cao

176 INFINITY POOL - MASKS TEASER POSTER | Design Firm: AV Print
Designer: AV Print | Client: NEON | Main Contributor: AV Print

176 UNTITLED | Design Firm: VIEW - Visual Impact East West
Designer: Fong 'Captain' Huang | Client: Alexander Pitcher
Main Contributor: Fong 'Captain' Huang

176 THE BIKERIDERS TEASER POSTER | Design Firm: MOCEAN
Designer: Jeff Wadley | Clients: 20th Century Fox, Focus Features
Executive Creative Director: Kishan Muthucumaru | Creative Director: Jason Low
Associate Creative Director: Charlie Le | Account Executive: Samuel Pak
Vice President: Flora Gallego | Production Artist: Kevin Crothers
Production: Kae Singhaseni | Main Contributor: Jeff Wadley

176 THE OUTSIDER | Design Firm: Célie Cadieux | Designer: Célie Cadieux
Client: The Magician's Niece | Main Contributor: Célie Cadieux

177 CIVIL WAR - LIBERTY TEASER POSTER | Design Firm: AV Print
Designer: AV Print | Client: A24 | Main Contributor: AV Print

177 I.S.S. PAYOFF POSTER | Design Firm: MOCEAN | Designers: Jeff Wadley, Robert Dunbar
Client: Bleecker Street Media | Executive Creative Director: Kishan Muthucumaru
Account Executive: Tanya Mekhtikhanyan | Production Artist: Kevin Crothers
Production: Kae Singhaseni | Main Contributors: Jeff Wadley, Robert Dunbar

177 VISIONS | Design Firm: Leroy & Rose | Designer: Leroy & Rose | Client: SND

177 BIRTH/REBIRTH PAYOFF POSTER | Design Firm: MOCEAN
Designer: Bob Delgado | Client: IFC Films | Executive Creative Director: Kishan Muthucumaru
Creative Director: Nathaniel Wheeler | Associate Creative Director: Robert Dunbar
Production Artist: Kevin Crothers | Production: Kae Singhaseni | Main Contributor: Bob Delgado

178 MALUM TEASER AND DIGITAL POSTERS | Design Firm: MOCEAN
Designers: Robert Dunbar, Kishan Muthucumaru, Bob Delgado
Client: Welcome Villain | Creative Director: Nathaniel Wheeler
Production Artist: Kevin Crothers | Production: Kae Singhaseni
Main Contributors: Robert Dunbar, Kishan Muthucumaru, Bob Delgado

178 LAST SUMMER OF NATHAN LEE | Design Firm: VIEW - Visual Impact East West
Designer: Fong 'Captain' Huang | Client: Quentin Lee | Main Contributor: Fong 'Captain' Huang

178 UN HOMME EN FUITE | Design Firm: Leroy & Rose
Designer: Leroy & Rose | Client: Tandem Films

178 AS AVES | Design Firm: Duas Faces Design | Designer: Sérgio Duarte | Client: Pixbee
Creative Director: Sérgio Duarte | Design Associate: Daniel de Sousa | Director: Pedro Magano
Illustrator: Cristiana Rodrigues | Typeface Designer: Sérgio Duarte | Photographer: Jorge Costa
Producer: Pedro Sá | Main Contributor: Cristiana Rodrigues

179 THE TASTE OF THINGS PAYOFF POSTER | Design Firm: MOCEAN
Designer: Charlie Le | Client: IFC Films | Executive Creative Director: Kishan Muthucumaru
Creative Director: Jason Low | Account Executive: Tanya Mekhtikhanyan
Production Artist: Kevin Crothers | Production: Kae Singhaseni | Main Contributor: Charlie Le

179 BIG RIVER | Design Firm: Evb Creative, Inc. | Designer: Eric van den Brulle
Client: Atsushi Funahashi | Photographer: Eric van den Brulle
Main Contributor: Eric van den Brulle

179 WHEN EVIL LURKS PAYOFF AND DIGITAL POSTER | Design Firm: MOCEAN
Designer: Jeff Wadley | Client: IFC Films | Executive Creative Director: Kishan Muthucumaru
Creative Director: Nathaniel Wheeler | Associate Creative Director: Robert Dunbar
Production Artist: Kevin Crothers | Production: Kae Singhaseni | Main Contributor: Jeff Wadley

179 UNE VIE | Design Firm: Leroy & Rose | Designer: Leroy & Rose | Client: SND

180 OPPENHEIMER | Design Firm: Owen Gildersleeve Ltd. | Designer: Owen Gildersleeve
Client: Self-initiated | Main Contributor: Owen Gildersleeve

180 THE HOLDOVERS - PAYOFF POSTER | Design Firm: AV Print | Designer: AV Print
Client: Focus Features | SVP Creative Advertising: Blair Green | Vice President: Marcus Kaye
Project Coordinator: Deanna Shiverick | Assistant: Evie Kennedy | Main Contributor: AV Print

180 POLITE SOCIETY - PAYOFF POSTER | Design Firm: AV Print | Designer: AV Print
Client: Focus Features | SVP Creative Advertising: Blair Green | Vice President: Marcus Kaye
Project Coordinator: Deanna Shiverick | Assistant: Evie Kennedy | Main Contributor: AV Print

180 BACK TO BLACK - BLACK TEASER | Design Firm: AV Print | Designer: AV Print
Client: Focus Features | SVP Creative Advertising: Blair Green | Vice President: Marcus Kaye
Project Coordinator: Deanna Shiverick | Assistant: Evie Kennedy | Main Contributor: AV Print

180 ATOMIC STUDIOS PRESENTS | Design Firm: Stephanie Scott Designs
Designer: Stephanie Scott | Client: Atomic | Main Contributor: Stephanie Scott

180 SEARCHING FOR JUSTICE | Design Firm: Articoolisan
Designer: Edin Beslic | Client: Admon Film

180 THE LOST DAUGHTER FILM POSTER SERIES | Design Firm: Maida Studio
Designer: Adam Maida | Clients: Netflix, Mondo | Artist: Adam Maida
Main Contributor: Adam Maida

180 TALK TO ME TEASER POSTER | Design Firm: MOCEAN | Designer: Robert Dunbar
Client: A24 | Executive Creative Director: Kishan Muthucumaru
Creative Director: Nathaniel Wheeler | Production Artist: Kevin Crothers
Production: Kae Singhaseni | Main Contributor: Robert Dunbar

180 POSTERS FOR THE SHORT FILM "THE LONG WAY HOME"
Design Firm: Tangram Strategic Design | Designers: Enrico Sempi, Pamela Cino
Client: Chloë De Carvalho | Ad Agency: Enrico Sempi | Main Contributor: AFI Conservatory

181 THE SWEET EAST | Design Firm: Célie Cadieux | Designer: Célie Cadieux
Client: The Match Factory | Font Designer: Lenny Vigden | Main Contributor: Célie Cadieux

181 FINGERNAILS TEASER AND PAYOFF POSTERS | Design Firm: MOCEAN
Designers: Scotti Everhart, Nathaniel Wheeler | Client: Apple TV+
Executive Creative Director: Kishan Muthucumaru | Associate Creative Director: Charlie Le
Vice President: Flora Gallego | Production Artist: Kevin Crothers | Production: Kae Singhaseni
Main Contributors: Scotti Everhart, Nathaniel Wheeler

181 KEY THE BOYS SHORT FILM KEY ART | Design Firm: Barlow.Agency
Designer: Barlow.Agency | Client: Stefan Hunt Films | Photographer: Leo Harunah
Main Contributor: Barlow.Agency

181 MUSICA ("CITY") | Design Firm: Leroy & Rose | Designer: Leroy & Rose | Client: Amazon

182 DILWORTH COFFEE POSTER CAMPAIGN
Design Firm: The Republik | Designer: Matt Shapiro | Client: Dilworth Coffee
Creative Directors: Robert Shaw West, Matt Shapiro | Art Directors: Robert Shaw West,
Matt Shapiro | Copywriters: Neil Hinson, Dwayne Fry | Main Contributor: Robert Shaw West

182 AMANATSU JUICE CAMPAIGN POSTER | Design Firm: Legis Design
Designer: Mayumi Kato | Client: Hirano Farm | Photographer: Mayumi Kato
Main Contributor: Legis Design

182 GLORIOUS WING TREE | Design Firm: PPK | Designer: Gabby Cotilla
Client: Glory Days Grill | Executive Creative Director: Paul Prato
Creative Director: Michael Schillig | Art Director: Gabby Cotilla | Copywriter: Michael Schillig
Graphic Designer: Melanie Mosquera | Account Executive: Logan Haley
Account Director: Courtney Babic | Main Contributors: Michael Schillig, Gabby Cotilla

183 DUMOL 2023 COLLECTOR'S POSTER | Design Firm: Craig Frazier Studio
Designer: Craig Frazier | Client: DuMOL Winery | Main Contributor: Craig Frazier

183 DUMOL POSTERS | Design Firm: Craig Frazier Studio | Designer: Craig Frazier
Client: DuMOL Winery | Executive Producer: Fela Cortés | Photographer: Craig Cutler
Main Contributor: Craig Cutler

183 SOAK IT ALL IN | Design Firm: Rob Fiocca | Designer: Rob Fiocca
Client: D'Italiano | Main Contributor: Rob Fiocca

242 CREDITS & COMMENTARY

183 GLAM BON | Design Firm: Shell Royster | Designer: Shell Royster
Client: Cinnabon | Social Media Manager: Hannah Gregus | Food Stylist: Katelyn H. Hudson
Main Contributor: Shell Royster

184 CALL OF DUTY: MODERN WARFARE III X WARZONE - KEY ART POSTER SERIES
Design Firm: PETROL Advertising | Designer: PETROL Advertising
Clients: Activision, Infinity Ward, Raven Software
Main Contributors: Activision, PETROL Advertising

184 WARCRAFT RUMBLE - CAMPAIGN KEY ART POSTERS
Design Firm: PETROL Advertising | Designer: PETROL Advertising
Client: Blizzard Entertainment | Main Contributors: Blizzard Entertainment, PETROL Advertising

184 LIES OF P - CAMPAIGN KEY ART POSTER SERIES
Design Firm: PETROL Advertising | Designer: PETROL Advertising | Client: Neowiz
Main Contributors: Neowiz, PETROL Advertising

184 LORDS OF THE FALLEN - WIDE WORLD ART
Design Firm: PETROL Advertising | Designer: PETROL Advertising | Client: CI Games
Main Contributors: CI Games, PETROL Advertising

184 LORDS OF THE FALLEN - EDGE COVER
Design Firm: PETROL Advertising | Designer: PETROL Advertising
Clients: CI Games, Hexworks | Main Contributors: CI Games, PETROL Advertising

185 STAR WARS OUTLAWS - PRIMARY KEY ART POSTER
Design Firm: PETROL Advertising | Designer: PETROL Advertising
Clients: Ubisoft, Massive Entertainment | Main Contributors: Ubisoft, PETROL Advertising

185 JBL - DARE TO DIVE IN CAMPAIGN POSTER SERIES
Design Firm: PETROL Advertising | Designer: PETROL Advertising | Client: JBL Quantum
Main Contributors: JBL Quantum, PETROL Advertising

186 CALL OF DUTY: MODERN WARFARE III - KEY ART POSTER SERIES
Design Firm: PETROL Advertising | Designer: PETROL Advertising
Clients: Activision, Infinity Ward | Main Contributors: Activision, PETROL Advertising

186 HIDEAWAY ISLAND POSTER | Design Firm: Justin Kunz Illustration
Designer: Justin Kunz | Client: Quest Posse | Main Contributor: Justin Kunz

186 RADIOLOGIA AO CENTRO | Design Firm: Duas Faces Design
Designer: Sérgio Duarte | Client: Associação Hemisfério Disciplinado
Web Designer: Tiago Araújo | Motion Designer: Tiago Cardoso
Copywriter: Carla Solano | Main Contributor: Beatriz Antunes

186 LIKE SUMMER FLOWERS | Design Firm: Team Mao
Designer: Siyu Mao | Client: Museum Wehrmuehle

187 MOMŰ | Design Firm: Anagraphic | Designer: Anna Farkas
Client: Balatonfüred Modern Art Center | Main Contributor: Anna Farkas

187 SAGENZAUBER | Design Firm: Dreamis GmbH
Designer: Marc Philip Seidel | Client: Museum Burghalde Lenzburg
Main Contributor: Marc Philip Seidel

187 TWO IS NOT A NUMBER | Design Firm: Fons Hickmann m23
Designer: Fons Hickmann | Client: Fantastic Twins | Main Contributor: Fons Hickmann

187 RACHMANINOFF 150 | Design Firm: Code Switch | Designer: Jan Šabach
Client: Golden Bee Biennale | Main Contributor: Jan Šabach

188 POMERIGGI MUSICALI 2023-2024 | Design Firm: Venti Caratteruzzi
Designer: Carlo Fiore | Client: Fondazione I Pomeriggi Musicali - Milano
Photographers: Dean Drobot, Antonio Guillem, SB Arts Media, Ljubaphoto, Lorenza Daverio
Art Director: Carlo Fiore

188 UNFINISHED SYMPHONY | Design Firm: Ron Taft Brand Innovation & Media Arts
Designer: Ron Taft | Client: Orchestra Moderne NYC | Main Contributor: Ron Taft

188 JAZZ KICKS BAND HALLOWEEN CONCERT | Design Firm: Design SubTerra
Designer: R.P. Bissland | Client: Jazz Kicks Band | Main Contributor: R.P. Bissland

188 BALTIMORE BOOM BAP SOCIETY PERFORMANCE POSTER SERIES
Design Firm: Isaac Jung | Designer: Seunghun Jung | Client: Baltimore Boom Bap Society
Print Producer: Huiting Lian | Main Contributors: Erik Spangler, Wendel Patrick

189 AMBROSIUS: ALBUM RELEASE CONCERT POSTER | Design Firm: Braley Design
Designer: Michael Braley | Client: Ambrosius | Main Contributor: Michael Braley

189 RACHMANINOFF 150 | Design Firm: Ivan Kashlakov | Designer: Ivan Kashlakov
Client: Golden Bee Biennale | Main Contributor: Ivan Kashlakov

189 WES 100 | Design Firm: Martin French Studio | Designer: Martin French
Client: 33Third | Main Contributor: Martin French

189 MIMA SMISLA - BALANS (POSTER) | Design Firm: Primoz Zorko
Designer: Primoz Zorko | Client: Balans | Photographer: Marijo Zupanov
Main Contributor: Primoz Zorko

190 DIE BANDITEN - THE BANDITS | Design Firm: Institut für Visuelle Kommunikation
Designer: Gunter Rambow | Client: Oper Frankfurt | Main Contributor: Gunter Rambow

190 AIDA | Design Firm: Institut für Visuelle Kommunikation | Designer: Gunter Rambow
Client: Oper Frankfurt | Main Contributor: Gunter Rambow

190 MACERATA OPERA FESTIVAL 2023 | Design Firm: Venti Caratteruzzi
Designer: Carlo Fiore | Client: Associazione Arena Sferisterio

190 LOKC SEASON POSTERS 2023 | Design Firm: Bailey Lauerman
Designer: Madison Sinclair | Client: Lyric Opera of Kansas City
Creative Director: David Thornhill | Copywriter: Sophia Messineo
Account Director: Liz Urbaniak | Main Contributor: Sarah Northcutt

191 PETER GRIMES | Design Firm: Rose | Designer: Rose | Client: English National Opera
Copywriter: Andy Rigden | Photographer: Geert De Taeye | Main Contributor: Rose

191 JENŮFA | Design Firm: Rose | Designer: Rose | Client: English National Opera
Photographer: Slevin Aaron | Retoucher: Nick Nedeljkovic | Main Contributor: Rose

191 THE BARBER OF SEVILLE | Design Firm: Rose | Designer: Rose
Client: English National Opera | Copywriter: Andy Rigden
Photographer: Lauren Stowell | Main Contributor: Rose

191 LA TRAVIATA | Design Firm: Rose | Designer: Rose | Client: English National Opera
Copywriter: Andy Rigden | Illustrator: Domagoj Šokčević | Main Contributor: Rose

192 LET'S LEAVE THE THINKING TO AI. | Design Firm: PEACE Inc. | Designer: Kanta Abe
Client: Self-initiated | Main Contributor: Kanta Abe

192 WHAT DOES CHICAGO MEAN TO YOU? | Design Firm: Sharon and Guy
Designers: Guy Villa Jr., Sharon Oiga | Client: Chicago Graphic Design Club
Photographer: Guy Villa Jr. | Main Contributor: Guy Villa Jr.

192 SUMMER 2023 | Design Firm: John Sposato Design & Illustration
Designer: John Sposato | Client: Self-initiated | Photographer: John Sposato
Illustrator: John Sposato | Main Contributor: John Sposato

192 VANTAGE POINT | Design Firm: Lisa Winstanley Design
Designer: Lisa Winstanley | Client: Faculty Learning Community - NTU
Main Contributor: Lisa Winstanley

193 RELATIONSHIP -BORDER, DISASSEMBLY, TRANSFORM-
Design Firm: 246 Graphics. | Designer: Takashi Matsuda
Client: Shizuoka Institute of Science and Technology | Chief Creative Director: Takashi Matsuda
Art Director: Takashi Matsuda | Main Contributor: Keita Otsuka

193 POSTER FOR UTILIZING RICE FIELDS | Design Firm: Legis Design
Designer: Mayumi Kato | Client: Ikeda Farm | Photographer: Mayumi Kato
Main Contributor: Legis Design

193 BE | Design Firm: Goodall Integrated Design | Designer: Derwyn Goodall
Client: Self-initiated | Main Contributor: Derwyn Goodall

193 203_STORY_SERIES | Design Firm: 203 Infographic Lab
Designer: 203 | Client: Street H | Design Director: Jang Sunghwan
Main Contributors: Park Seoyun, Kim Jieun, Jeon Dayoung, Na Yegeol, Seo Jungwoo

194 TIJUANA RED CROSS DONATION BETO CAMPAIGN
Design Firm: Freaner Creative & Design | Designer: Ariel Freaner
Clients: Red Cross of Tijuana, Jorge Astiazaran | Digital Artist: Ariel Freaner
Illustrator: Ariel Freaner | Main Contributor: Ariel Freaner

194 LESTER GOLDMAN DRAWING COMPETITION
Design Firm: For Instance: A Design Practice | Designer: Lisa Maione
Client: Kansas City Art Institute | Main Contributor: Lisa Maione

194 THE BRAVE LITTLE AGENCY | Design Firm: Angry Dog | Designer: Rafael Fernandes
Client: Self-initiated | Main Contributor: Rafael Fernandes

194 24 | Design Firm: Goodall Integrated Design | Designer: Derwyn Goodall
Client: Self-initiated | Main Contributor: Derwyn Goodall

194 ZETA 42 YEARS ANNIVERSARY POSTER | Design Firm: Freaner Creative & Design
Designer: Ariel Freaner | Client: ZETA Weekly | Digital Artist: Ariel Freaner
Main Contributor: Ariel Freaner

194 WELL DONE | Design Firm: Hidden Impact | Designer: Kevin Hagan
Client: University of Louisiana at Lafayette Department of Visual Arts
Main Contributor: Kevin Hagan

194 ZETA ADVERTISERS POSTER | Design Firm: Freaner Creative & Design
Designer: Ariel Freaner | Client: ZETA Weekly | Digital Artist: Ariel Freaner
Main Contributor: Ariel Freaner

194 THE GIANT WECAN KIDS CLUB SIGNATURE WORD SEARCH FABRIC POSTER
Design Firm: Whimsical Studio | Designer: Jang Won Lee | Client: Wecan Kids Club
Main Contributor: Jang Won Lee

195 THE SCENERY | Design Firm: i,D | Designer: Seita Ishikawa
Client: Self-initiated | Main Contributor: Seita Ishikawa

195 CALL TO INTERNS | Design Firm: Bailey Lauerman | Designer: Sean Faden
Client: Self-initiated | Copywriter: Joey Googe | Design Director: Jim Ma
Account Supervisor: Zoe Matheson | Production Manager: Gayle Adams
Printer: Regal Printing | Main Contributor: Sean Faden

195 SYSTEM 2022 | Design Firm: ©DAEKI and JUN | Designer: DaeKi Shim
Clients: Gangwon State, Gangwon Institute of Design Promotion (GIDP)
Creative Director: DaeKi Shim | Photographer: Jinsol Kim (JSK Studio)
Main Contributor: DaeKi Shim

195 DDP DNA: DESIGN & ART | Design Firm: ©DAEKI and JUN
Designers: DaeKi Shim, HyoJun Shim | Clients: Seoul Metropolitan Government,
Dongdaemun Design Plaza (DDP), Seoul Design Foundation
Creative Directors: DaeKi Shim, HyoJun Shim | Main Contributors: DaeKi Shim, HyoJun Shim

243 CREDITS & COMMENTARY

196 BALD NO MORE: EXTENSIONS FOR EAGLES | Design Firm: University of Nebraska
Designer: Joshua Lowe | Client: ParodyCharities.org | Main Contributor: Joshua Lowe

196 AI-DESIGN NEEDS A HEART | Design Firm: EJ Communication Studio
Designer: Eunjin Yu | Client: Information and Communication Technology Division
Main Contributor: Eunjin Yu

196 FUSION | Design Firm: Purdue University | Designer: Li Zhang
Client: Egypt Helwan University | Main Contributor: Li Zhang

196 CAL FRESH MAY AWARENESS MONTH 2023
Design Firm: Freaner Creative & Design | Designer: Ariel Freaner
Clients: County of San Diego Cal Fresh HHSA Medicare, Ismael Lopez, Alberto Garcia
Main Contributor: Ariel Freaner

197 MAN EATING SHARK | Design Firm: PPK | Designer: Alan Schneller
Client: Animal Welfare Institute (AWI) | Executive Creative Director: Paul Prato
Creative Director: Michael Schillig | Copywriter: Michael Schillig
Art Director: Alan Schneller | Main Contributors: Michael Schillig, Alan Schneller

197 FIRST PLACE POSTER | Design Firm: Bob Case Illustration | Designer: Bob Case
Client: First Place Arizona | Illustrator: Bob Case | Main Contributor: Tom Ortega

198 DELFT DOET DUURZAAM | Design Firm: Things To Make and Do
Designer: Cindy van der Meijden | Client: Municipality of Delft
Account Director: Lennaert van der Hoeven | Main Contributor: Rogier Rosema

198 YOU CREATE TOMORROW | Design Firm: One Design Company
Designer: David Sieren | Client: Self-initiated | Main Contributor: David Sieren

198 CAZMAR | Design Firm: Randy Clark | Designer: Randy Clark
Client: Bruun Holdings LLC | Main Contributor: Randy Clark

199 EXPRESS YOURSELF WITH FLOWERS | Design Firm: Not William
Designer: Rich Wallace | Client: Anything Floral | Writer: Debbie Kasher
Photographer: Rich Wallace | Creative Directors: Rich Wallace, Debbie Kasher
Art Director: Rich Wallace | Main Contributor: Rich Wallace

199 FOOTBALL SEASONS | Design Firm: Not William | Designer: Rich Wallace
Client: Anything Floral | Photographer: Layla | Creative Director: Rich Wallace
Copywriter: Rich Wallace | Art Director: Rich Wallace | Main Contributor: Rich Wallace

200 PEACE TOGETHER | Design Firm: BraleyArts | Designer: Brooks Braley
Client: International Poster Biennale for Peace: Nanjing, China | Main Contributor: Brooks Braley

200 ONE | Design Firm: Steiner Graphics | Designer: Rene V. Steiner
Client: Self-initiated | Main Contributor: Rene V. Steiner

200 DROPS (CEASE FIRE NOW) | Design Firm: Atelier Starno
Designer: Arnaud Ghelfi | Client: Self-initiated | Main Contributor: Arnaud Ghelfi

200 M. I. A. | Design Firm: Goodall Integrated Design | Designer: Derwyn Goodall
Client: Self-initiated | Main Contributor: Derwyn Goodall

201 RECLAIMING CONTOURS | Design Firm: Lisa Winstanley Design
Designer: Lisa Winstanley | Client: Nanyang Technological University School of Art, Design & Media | Main Contributor: Lisa Winstanley

201 EMPATHY | Design Firm: Code Switch | Designer: Jan Šabach
Client: Golden Bee Biennale | Main Contributor: Jan Šabach

201 WAR AND PEACE | Design Firm: Nogami Design Office
Designer: Shuichi Nogami | Client: Self-initiated

202 MARIUPOL: 86 DAYS OF STRENGTH | Design Firm: Goodall Integrated Design
Designer: Derwyn Goodall | Client: The 4th Block 12th International Triennial
Main Contributor: Derwyn Goodall

202 LOVE IS THE FOUNDATION OF PEACE | Design Firm: John O'Neill
Designer: John O'Neill | Client: Self-initiated

202 TWO / ONE | Design Firm: STUDIO INTERNATIONAL | Designer: Boris Ljubicic
Client: UNCHR Croatia | Art Director: Boris Ljubicic | Artist: Boris Ljubicic
Photographer: Darko Bavoljak | Main Contributor: STUDIO INTERNATIONAL

202 HUMAN PASTAFROLA (CIVILITAS) | Design Firm: Coco Cerrella
Designer: Coco Cerrella | Client: Posters Without Borders
Photographer: Fernando Lendoiro | Main Contributor: Coco Cerrella

203 FINE DAYS | Design Firm: Toyotsugu Itoh Design Office | Designer: Toyotsugu Itoh
Client: Japan Graphic Design Association Inc. | Main Contributor: Toyotsugu Itoh

203 WAR, WHAT IS IT GOOD FOR? | Design Firm: Goodall Integrated Design
Designer: Derwyn Goodall | Client: Self-initiated | Main Contributor: Derwyn Goodall

203 PEACE HANDS | Design Firm: BraleyArts | Designer: Brooks Braley
Client: International Poster Biennale for Peace: Nanjing, China | Main Contributor: Brooks Braley

203 AUFLEBEN | Design Firm: Gastdesign | Designer: Wolfgang Gast
Client: AUF ACHSE/KJSH e.V. | Main Contributor: Wolfgang Gast

204 NATO NOW | Design Firm: Design SubTerra | Designer: R.P. Bissland
Client: Self-initiated | Main Contributor: R.P. Bissland

204 ISRAEL 10.7.2023 | Design Firm: Carmit Design Studio
Designer: Carmit Makler Haller | Client: Stop War Poster Exhibition
Main Contributors: Carmit Makler Haller, Carmit Design Studio

204 GLUTTON | Design Firm: PEACE Inc. | Designer: Mai Kato
Client: Self-initiated | Main Contributor: Mai Kato

204 GENFEM CAMPAIGN | Design Firm: Studio XXY | Designer: Yuqin Ni
Client: Bizarrely Basic | Main Contributor: Yuqin Ni

205 10.07.2023—THE WEST IS NEXT | Design Firm: Carmit Design Studio
Designer: Carmit Makler Haller | Client: Stop War Poster Exhibition
Main Contributors: Carmit Makler Haller, Carmit Design Studio

205 NO WAR | Design Firm: Marlena Buczek Smith
Designer: Marlena Buczek Smith | Client: Self-initiated

205 HEALTHSCARE | Design Firm: Jack Harris | Designer: Jack Harris
Client: Self-initiated | Main Contributor: Jack Harris

206 FOLD FOR PEACE: UKRAINE'S ONE SIMPLE WISH | Design Firm: Becker Studio
Designer: Henry Becker | Client: University of Utah | CGI: Kevin Tomas
Main Contributor: Henry Becker

206 THE LOVE YOU TAKE/MAKE | Design Firm: Symbiotic Solutions
Designer: Chris Corneal | Client: Self-initiated | Main Contributor: Chris Corneal

206 TRUMP: FALSE GOD | Design Firm: Wong.Digital | Designer: Roger Wong
Client: Self-initiated | Illustrator: Roberto Vescovi

206 WATER SHORTAGE | Design Firm: Noriyuki Kasai | Designer: Noriyuki Kasai
Client: Graphic Communication Laboratory | Art Director: Noriyuki Kasai
Main Contributor: Noriyuki Kasai

206 DEMAND ACCOUNTABILITY | Design Firm: Randy Clark | Designer: Randy Clark
Client: Self-initiated | Photographer: Tyler Merbler | Main Contributor: Randy Clark

206 TOLERANCE | Design Firm: Meaghan A. Dee | Designer: Meaghan A. Dee
Client: Mirko Ilic Corp. | Main Contributor: Meaghan A. Dee

206 WELCOME TO THE SUNSHINE STATE | Design Firm: Jack Harris
Designer: Jack Harris | Client: Self-initiated | Photographer: Jörg Bittner Unna
Main Contributor: Jack Harris

206 THOUGHTS AND PRAYERS | Design Firm: Atelier Starno
Designer: Arnaud Ghelfi | Client: Self-initiated | Illustrators: Kenn Brown, Chris Wren
Main Contributor: Arnaud Ghelfi

206 BREAK YOUR BIAS | Design Firm: Preston Spire | Designer: Fernando Palomino
Client: YMCA of the North | Chief Creative Officer: Chris Preston | Copywriter: Aylä Larsen
Production Manager: Beth Elmore | Account Director: Erin Burk
Main Contributor: Fernando Palomino

207 THIS WAY? | Design Firm: Toyotsugu Itoh Design Office | Designer: Toyotsugu Itoh
Client: Chubu Creators Club | Main Contributor: Toyotsugu Itoh

207 KING OF THE BINGO GAME | Design Firm: The Union Design Company
Designer: Steve James | Client: Self-initiated | Main Contributor: Steve James

207 FACES OF THE REPUBLICAN PARTY | Design Firm: Chamomile Tea Party
Designer: Jeff Gates | Client: Self-initiated | Main Contributor: Jeff Gates

208 CLEAN ENERGY | Design Firm: Brain Bolts | Designer: Eric Boelts
Clients: Seoul, Korea Design Association | Main Contributor: Eric Boelts

208 NO YES | Design Firm: Marlena Buczek Smith | Designer: Marlena Buczek Smith
Client: Self-initiated | Main Contributor: Marlena Buczek Smith

208 FREEDOM KNOT | Design Firm: Wesam Mazhar Haddad
Designer: Wesam Mazhar Haddad | Client: Woman, Life, Freedom
Main Contributor: Wesam Mazhar Haddad

209 HEED THE CALL | Design Firm: Preston Spire | Designer: Fernando Palomino
Client: Minnesota Wild | Chief Creative Officer: Chris Preston | Art Director: Brett Essman
Copywriter: Charlie Tournat | Production Artist: Mike Fritz | Account Director: Ron Hall
Project Manager: Kelsey Winter | Main Contributor: Fernando Palomino

209 VOUGA TRAIL | Design Firm: Duas Faces Design | Designer: Sérgio Duarte
Client: Câmara Municipal de Sever do Vouga | Creative Director: Sérgio Duarte
Illustrator: Cristiana Rodrigues | Copywriter: Beatriz Antunes
Motion Designer: Tiago Cardoso | Main Contributor: Sérgio Duarte

209 TRAIN LIKE YOUR LIFE DEPENDS ON IT | Design Firm: Not William
Designer: Rich Wallace | Client: Wilkies Martial Arts | Writer: Richard Ryan
Creative Directors: Rich Wallace, Richard Ryan | Art Director: Rich Wallace

210 2023-24 SEASON BRANDING | Design Firm: Dunn&Co. | Designer: Grant Gunderson
Client: Tampa Bay Lightning | Creative Directors: Max Dempster, Stephanie Morrison
Chief Creative Officer: Troy Dunn | Senior Account Executive: Jessica Hall
Main Contributor: Grant Gunderson

210 FULL. HALF. | Design Firm: Bailey Lauerman | Designer: Gayle Adams
Client: Lincoln Track Club | Chief Creative Officer: Carter Weitz
Creative Director: Casey Stokes | Copywriter: Joey Googe
Account Supervisor: Emma Gallagher | Printer: Regal Printing
Production Manager: Gayle Adams | Main Contributor: Casey Stokes

210 MINNESOTA TWINS HISTORY POSTER | Design Firm: DLR Group
Designer: Jovaney Hollingsworth | Client: Minnesota Twins
Main Contributor: Jovaney Hollingsworth

244 CREDITS&COMMENTARY

210 TRIANGLE ADVENTURE | Design Firm: Duas Faces Design
Designer: Sérgio Duarte | Client: Azores Trail Run | Creative Director: Sérgio Duarte
Executive Director: Mário Leal | Illustrator: Cristiana Rodrigues | Copywriter: Beatriz Antunes
Main Contributor: Cristiana Rodrigues

211 FRASIER: MOVING TRUCK | Design Firm: Leroy & Rose
Designer: Leroy & Rose | Client: Paramount+

211 NEON | Design Firm: Leroy & Rose | Designer: Leroy & Rose | Client: Netflix

211 BREEDERS: SEASON 4 | Design Firm: Leroy & Rose | Designer: Leroy & Rose | Client: FX

211 EXPATS TEASER POSTER | Design Firm: MOCEAN | Designer: Louis Percival
Client: Amazon Studios | Executive Creative Director: Kishan Muthucumaru
Creative Director: Nathaniel Wheeler | Associate Creative Director: Robert Dunbar
Vice President: Flora Gallego | Production Artist: Kevin Crothers | Production: Kae Singhaseni
Account Executive: Samuel Pak | Main Contributor: Louis Percival

212 MONARCH: LEGACY OF MONSTERS | Design Firm: Leroy & Rose
Designer: Leroy & Rose | Client: Apple

212 FRASIER: BUSTS | Design Firm: Leroy & Rose
Designer: Leroy & Rose | Client: Paramount+

212 HALO S2 CAMPAIGN ART | Design Firm: Rhubarb
Designer: Rhubarb | Client: Paramount+ | Chief Creative Officer: Andrew Irving
Executive Creative Director: Ryan Jones | Creative Directors: Adrianne Deluna, Steve Chan
Art Director: Edwin Alvarenga | Photographer: James Minchin | Marketing: Kevin Bjelajac
Digital Artists: Alexis Goodwin, Serhil Klosov | Account Director: Geysel Junne
Senior Manager: Tara Marin | Marketing Manager: Devin Rome | Other: Rech
Main Contributor: Rhubarb

212 GREAT EXPECTATIONS - HEADPIECE PAYOFF | Design Firm: AV Print
Designer: AV Print | Clients: FX Networks, Stephanie Gibbons, FX Networks, Creative Director/
President, Creative, Strategy & Digital, Multi- Platform Marketing, Michael Brittain,
FX Networks, Creative Director/SVP Print Design, Rob Wilson, FX Networks, VP Print Design,
Lisa Lejeune, FX Networks, Production Director, Print Design, Julia Panchenko, FX Networks,
Project Manager Print Design, Claudia Traina, FX Networks, Jr Project Manager, Print Design
Main Contributor: FX Networks

213 BLACK BIRD KEY ART | Design Firm: MOCEAN | Designer: Louis Percival
Client: Apple TV+ | Executive Creative Director: Kishan Muthucumaru
Creative Director: Nathaniel Wheeler | Associate Creative Director: Robert Dunbar
Production Artist: Kevin Crothers | Production: Kae Singhaseni
Main Contributor: Louis Percival

213 SUCCESSION SEASON 4 - THE FINAL SEASON CAMPAIGN
Design Firm: AV Print | Designer: AV Print | Client: HBO | Main Contributor: HBO

213 HOUSE OF THE DRAGON SEASON 2 - CHARACTER TABLEAU
Design Firm: AV Print | Designer: AV Print | Client: HBO | Main Contributor: HBO

214 PHAEDRA'S LOVE | Design Firm: Bernardo Garcia Valencia
Designer: Bernardo Garcia Valencia | Client: Columbia University School of the Arts
Creative Directors: Bernardo Garcia Valencia, Danica Selem
Photographer: Bernardo Garcia Valencia

214 STILLER | Design Firm: Atelier Bundi AG | Designer: Stephan Bundi
Client: Theater Orchester Biel Solothurn | Main Contributor: Stephan Bundi

214 WOMEN, BEWARE THE DEVIL | Design Firm: Émilie Chen LTD | Designer: Émilie Chen
Client: Almeida Theatre | Photographer: Felicity McCabe | Main Contributor: Émilie Chen

214 THE FIRST PRIME TIME ASIAN SITCOM | Design Firm: Osborne Shiwan
Designers: Lloyd Osborne, Shabnam Shiwan | Client: Silo Theatre
Creative Directors: Lloyd Osborne, Shabnam Shiwan | Photographer: Toaki Okano
Main Contributor: Osborne Shiwan

215 AN INCIDENT AT THE BORDER | Design Firm: Mirko Ilic Corp. | Designer: Mirko Ilic
Client: JDP-Yugoslav Drama Theater in Belgrade, Serbia | Illustrator: Mirko Ilic
Main Contributor: Mirko Ilic

215 WITOLD GOMBROWICZ – IVONA, PRINCESS OF BURGUNDIA
Design Firm: Wiesław Grzegorczyk | Designer: Wiesław Grzegorczyk
Client: Kino za Rogiem Café Rzeszów

215 WHAT YOU WILL, OR TWELFTH NIGHT | Design Firm: Andrewsobol.com
Designer: Andrew Sobol | Client: Theatre at the Mill | Main Contributor: Andrew Sobol

215 THE TIN DRUM | Design Firm: Mirko Ilic Corp | Designer: Mirko Ilic
Client: JDP-Yugoslav Drama Theater in Belgrade, Serbia | Illustrator: Mirko Ilic
Main Contributor: Mirko Ilic

216 MEN CRY TOO | Design Firm: 14-Forty | Designer: Benjamin Nicolas
Client: Barnsdall Gallery Theatre | Creative Director: Pam Patterson
Main Contributor: Pam Patterson

216 AUF HOHER SEE / STRIPTEASE | Design Firm: Atelier Bundi AG
Designer: Stephan Bundi | Client: Theater Orchester Biel Solothurn
Art Director: Stephan Bundi | Illustrator: Stephan Bundi | Main Contributor: Stephan Bundi

216 UNCLE VANYA | Design Firm: EGGRA | Designer: Ngadhnjim Mehmeti
Client: The Albanian Theater Skopje | Illustrator: Gürbüz Doğan Ekşioğlu
Main Contributor: Gürbüz Doğan Ekşioğlu

216 COSI FAN TUTTE | Design Firm: Anastasia Temirkhanova
Designer: Anastasia Temirkhanova | Client: Komische Oper
Main Contributor: Anastasia Temirkhanova

217 LIFESPAN OF A FACT | Design Firm: Andrewsobol.com | Designer: Andrew Sobol
Client: Theatre at the Mill | Main Contributor: Andrew Sobol

217 THE HATMAKER'S WIFE | Design Firm: Code Switch | Designer: Jan Šabach
Client: University of Massachusetts Amherst Theatre Department
Main Contributor: Jan Šabach

217 DISCO PIGS | Design Firm: Mirko Ilic Corp. | Designer: Mirko Ilic
Client: JDP-Yugoslav Drama Theater in Belgrade, Serbia | Illustrator: Mirko Ilic
Main Contributor: Mirko Ilic

217 NEXT GENERATION | Design Firm: Atelier Bundi AG
Designer: Stephan Bundi | Client: Theater Orchester Biel Solothurn
Art Director: Stephan Bundi | Illustrator: Stephan Bundi
Main Contributor: Stephan Bundi

218 UNTITLED F*CK M*SS SGON PLAY POSTER** | Design Firm: Émilie Chen LTD
Designer: Émilie Chen | Clients: Young Vic, Royal Theatre Exchange
Photographer: David Reiss | Main Contributor: Émilie Chen

218 THE LOSER | Design Firm: Mirko Ilic Corp. | Designer: Mirko Ilic
Client: JDP-Yugoslav Drama Theater in Belgrade, Serbia | Illustrator: Mirko Ilic
Main Contributor: Mirko Ilic

218 THE LAST FIVE YEARS | Design Firm: Andrewsobol.com | Designer: Andrew Sobol
Client: Theatre at the Mill | Main Contributor: Andrew Sobol

218 GOD OF CARNAGE | Design Firm: Andrewsobol.com | Designer: Andrew Sobol
Client: Theatre at the Mill | Main Contributor: Andrew Sobol

218 ANTIGONE | Design Firm: Roger W. Dormann | Designer: Roger W. Dormann
Client: College of Marin Drama Program | Illustrator: Roger W. Dormann
Main Contributor: Roger W. Dormann

218 POSTER OF THE VALENCIAN PERFORMING ARTS AWARDS GALA 2023
Design Firm: Juliane Petri | Designer: Juliane Petri
Clients: Generalitat Valenciana, Institut Valencià de Cultura | Main Contributor: Juliane Petri

218 THE BALD SOPRANO | Design Firm: Synopsismedia | Designer: Ovidiu Hrin
Client: Aualeu Theater Company | Main Contributor: Ovidiu Hrin

218 THE HOMECOMING POSTER | Design Firm: Émilie Chen LTD
Designer: Émilie Chen | Client: Young Vic | Photographer: Dean Chalkley
Retoucher: Darkroom Digital | Main Contributor: Émilie Chen

218 A HUNGER ARTIST | Design Firm: Bernardo Garcia Valencia
Designer: Bernardo Garcia Valencia | Client: Columbia University School of the Arts

219 KRAKOW: WHERE HISTORY MEETS CULTURE | Design Firm: Braley Design
Designer: Michael Braley | Client: City of Krakow International Poster Competition
Main Contributor: Michael Braley

219 LOVE LETTERS TO NYC | Design Firm: Claire Zou
Designer: Claire Zou | Client: Self-initiated | Main Contributor: Claire Zou

219 OVER TOURISM, OVER | Design Firm: PEACE Inc. | Designer: Masahito Tatsutomi
Client: Japan Overtourist Inc. | Main Contributor: Masahito Tatsutomi

219 BARDEJOV, SLOVAKIA | Design Firm: Daisuke Kashiwa | Designer: Daisuke Kashiwa
Client: International Poster Exhibition City of Bardejov 2 | Main Contributor: Daisuke Kashiwa

220 LIGATURE XIV TYPOGRAPHY SHOW POSTER | Design Firm: Kimberly Elam Design
Designer: Kimberly Elam | Client: Ringling College Typography Club
Main Contributor: Kimberly Elam

220 NO RULES | Design Firm: May & Co. | Designer: Douglas May
Client: Oesol International Typography Awards | Main Contributor: Douglas May

220 LEOPARD PRINT TASER! LIVE AT MADISON SQUARE GARDEN (TYPE SPECIMEN)
Design Firm: Ezekiel Duke Bower | Designer: Ezekiel Duke Bower | Client: Self-initiated
Main Contributor: Ezekiel Duke Bower

221 IMAGERY OF 4 CONSONANTS | Design Firm: Dankook University
Designer: Hoon-Dong Chung | Client: 'TYPE TEXT KOREA' Typography Poster Exhibition
Main Contributor: Hoon-Dong Chung

221 FUKUDA WISDOM | Design Firm: Ivan Kashlakov | Designer: Ivan Kashlakov
Client: TypeForward | Main Contributor: Ivan Kashlakov

221 DESIGN AND FINDING HOPE | Design Firm: Rikke Hansen
Designer: Rikke Hansen | Client: KICD | Main Contributor: Rikke Hansen

221 72 CHANGES RETROSPECTIVE EXHIBITION #2 | Design Firm: Dalian RYCX Design
Designer: Zhongjun Yin | Client: Self-initiated | Creative Director: Zhongjun Yin
Main Contributor: Zhongjun Yin

222 FIND THE HIDDEN | Design Firm: Seoul Institution of the Arts
Designer: Ja Eun Ku | Client: KST | Main Contributor: Ja Eun Ku

222 SHOW TYPE | Design Firm: Hufax Arts/FJCU | Designer: Fa-Hsiang Hu
Client: The ADLink Education Foundation | Main Contributor: Hufax Arts

222 SPACE: EXOBIOLOGY | Design Firm: John Nordyke | Designer: John Nordyke
Client: Self-initiated | Main Contributor: John Nordyke

222 HOPE +A | Design Firm: Chikako Oguma | Designer: Chikako Oguma
Client: Gyeonggi Design Association | Art Director: Chikako Oguma
Main Contributor: Chikako Oguma

Index

246 INDEX

DESIGN FIRMS

1/4 Studio 71
14-Forty 216
203 Infographic Lab 193
246 Graphics. 193
Addison 164
Alan Rellaford Design 146
ALVARO MONTANHA Design 103, 109
Anagraphic 154, 187
Anastasia Temirkhanova 216
Andrea Ruggiero Design 146
Andrewsobol.com 215, 217, 218
Angry Dog 194
Anne M. Giangiulio 163
Antonio Castro Design 119
Arcana Academy 162
ARSONAL 57, 156, 159
Articoolisan 180
Atelier Bundi AG 35, 107, 137-139, 214, 216, 217
Atelier Starno 140, 200, 206
Auburn University School of Industrial + Graphic Design 47
Aufuldish & Warinner 110, 111, 151
Automotive Events 170
AV Print 88, 90, 91, 176, 177, 180, 212, 213
AYA KAWABATA DESIGN 167
Bailey Lauerman 128, 190, 195, 210
Barbara Galinska 141
Barlow.Agency 89, 92, 181
Becker Studio 206
Bernardo Garcia Valencia 214, 218
Bob Case Illustration 197
Bojana Fajmut 147
Brain Bolts 208
Braley Design 146, 147, 151-153, 164, 166-170, 172, 173, 175, 189, 219
BraleyArts 200, 203
Canyon 52
CAO Design 175
Carmit Design Studio 74, 79, 120, 123, 170, 204, 205
CCC + JC. Jacinta & Carlos 152
Célie Cadieux 131, 176, 181
Chamomile Tea Party 207
Chase Design 96
Chemi Montes Design 102, 136
Chikako Oguma 167, 222
Chloe Zhang 172
Claire Zou 219
Claudia Schramke 84
Coco Cerrella 147, 202
Code Switch 187, 201, 217
CollierGraphica 37
Craig Frazier Studio 112, 183
Craig-Teerlink Design 70
©DAEKI and JUN 195
Daisuke Kashiwa 219
Dalian RYCX Design 113, 221
Dankook University 39, 221
David Habben Illustration 166
DEFINITION 6 (Bridgenext) 150
Design Studio FLORALIEN Inc. 173
Design SubTerra 169, 188, 204
dGwaltneyArt 31
DLR Group 210
Dreamis GmbH 95, 187
Duas Faces Design 178, 186, 209, 210
Dunn&Co. 210
EJ Communication Studio 196
Elevate Design 77
Émilie Chen LTD 214, 218
Evb Creative, Inc. 179
Everything Looks Good 169
Ezekiel Duke Bower 220
Fallano Faulkner & Associates 143
Feixue Mei 170
Fol 86
Fons Hickmann m23 94, 167, 187
For Instance: A Design Practice 194
Freaner Creative & Design 32, 46, 82, 83, 148, 149, 194, 196
Gallery BI 38
Gastdesign 203
Gon.C Studio 173
Goodall Integrated Design 127, 153, 162, 193, 194, 200, 202, 203
Gravdahl Design 148, 154
Hidden Impact 194
Huber Design Werks 41
Hufax Arts/FJCU 222
Human Paradise Studio 171
Hyungjookim Designlab 150, 164
i,D 195
Institut für Visuelle Kommunikation 104, 105, 190
Isaac Jung 188
Ivan Kashlakov 189, 221
Ivette Valenzuela Design 42, 97
Jack Harris 154, 205, 206
John Nordyke 222
John O'Neill 202
John Sposato Design & Illustration 192
João Machado Design 28, 73, 76, 85, 163-165
Juliane Petri 218
Justin Kunz Illustration 186
Katarzyna Zapart 33, 108
Kim Wild Designs 126
Kimberly Elam Design 220
Kiyoung An Graphic Art Course Laboratory 51, 151
Legacy79 44
Legis Design 182, 193
Leo Lin Design 72, 142
Leroy & Rose 129, 130, 132, 177-179, 181, 211, 212
Lisa Winstanley Design 173, 192, 201
Maida Studio 180
Marlena Buczek Smith 66, 205, 208
Martin French Studio 170, 189
May & Co. 163, 220
Meaghan A. Dee 206
Melchior Imboden 30
Mirko Ilic Corp. 134, 135, 215, 217, 218
MOCEAN 133, 176-181, 211, 213
Mythic 150
Namseoul University 162
National Kaohsiung University of Science and Technology (NKUST) 45, 67, 116, 165
Nikkeisha, Inc. 148
Nogami Design Office 201
Noriyuki Kasai 206
Not William 199, 209
One Design Company 198
Osborne Shiwan 43, 214
Owen Gildersleeve Ltd. 180
Paramount+ 55
PEACE Inc. 166, 192, 204, 219
PETROL Advertising 184-186
PPK 98, 114, 115, 182, 197
Pratt Institute Communications & Marketing 152
Preston Spire 206, 209
Primoz Zorko 189
Purdue University 117, 124, 196
Randy Clark 154, 198, 206
Ray Visual Communications 147, 174
Res Eichenberger Design 171
Rhubarb 56, 59, 61, 62, 156, 159-161, 212
Rikke Hansen 221
Rob Fiocca 183
Roger W. Dormann 218
Ron Taft Brand Innovation & Media Arts 188
Rose 93, 191
Saad Moosajee 154
Seoul Institution of the Arts 222
Serve Marketing 154
Shantanu Suman 170
Sharon and Guy 192
Shell Royster 183
SJI Associates 58, 63, 154, 155, 157, 158, 160
Skolos-Wedell 36
Steiner Graphics 125, 200
Stephanie Scott Designs 180
Stila (In-House) 146
Studio +Fronczek 172
Studio A N D 118
Studio Craig Byers 145
Studio Eduard Cehovin 174
Studio Hinrichs 68, 169, 170
STUDIO INTERNATIONAL 202
Studio Lindhorst-Emme+Hinrichs 81
Studio Pekka Loiri 121
Studio XXY 204
Sun Design Production 106
Symbiotic Solutions 206
Synopsismedia 168, 218
Tainan University of Technology 151, 162
Tangram Strategic Design 180
Team Mao 170, 175, 186
Territory Studio 154
Tetsuro Minorikawa 80
The Refinery 53, 54, 60, 64, 65, 155-161
The Republik 153, 182
The Studio of Mikey Lavi 100, 101
The Union Design Company 29, 207
THERE IS STUDIO 34, 99
Things To Make & Do 198
TOMOKUSA DESIGN 171
TopLeft LLC 78
Toyotsugu Itoh Design Office 69, 165, 203, 207
Traction Factory 145
Tsushima Design 75, 122, 163
Underline Studio 172
The Union Design Company 29, 207
University of Nebraska 166, 196
University of the Arts 170, 174
Venti Caratteruzzi 188, 190
VIEW - Visual Impact East West 176, 178
Viktor Koen 48-50
WePlayDesign 174, 175
Wesam Mazhar Haddad 165, 208
Whimsical Studio 194
White & Case LLP 152
Wiesław Grzegorczyk 215
Wong.Digital 206

CLIENTS/CLIENT SUPPORT

100 Beste Plakate Verein 81
2023 CDAK International Special Exhibition 163
2023 First Contemporary Local Youth Art Festival, China 174
20th Century Fox 176
20th Century Studios 88
22th Tianmu Waterway Festival 162
27th BDAK International Exhibition 77
2nd Yangmingshan Art Festival 162
33Third 189
A+E Networks 58, 155, 158
A24 177, 180
Activision 184, 186
Admon Film 180
Aichi Art and Culture Network (ANET) 69
Alliance Graphique Internationale (AGI) 170
Almeida Theatre 214
Amazon Studios 60, 62, 211
Amazon 181
Ambrosius 189
American Experience Films 154, 155, 157, 158, 160
American University Department of Performing Arts 136
American University Department of Performing Arts Jazz Ensemble 102
Anfachen Awards VI 172
Animal Welfare Institute (AWI) 197
Another Planet Entertainment 34, 99
Anything Floral 199
Apple TV+ 53, 64, 65, 133, 155, 161, 181, 213
Apple 129, 130, 212
Architecture Sarasota 145
ArtCenter College of Design 68, 152
Association of Hungarian Fine and Applied Artists 171
Associação Hemisfério Disciplinado 186
Associations of Zoos & Aquariums 143
Associazione Arena Sferisterio 190
Astiazaran, Jorge 149, 194
Atamira Dance Company 43
Atomic 180
Aualeu Theater Company 218
AUF ACHSE/KJSH e.V. 203
Azores Trail Run 210
Balans 189
Balatonfüred Modern Art Center 187
Balloon Brigade 162
Baltimore Boom Bap Society 188
Barnsdall Gallery Theatre 216
Barreiro, Mariano 63
Baylor University Department of Modern Languages and Cultures 44
Bent, Wes 58
Big Cat Rescue 114, 115
Bizarrely Basic 204
Bleecker Street Media 177
Blizzard Entertainment 184
Blue Fox Entertainment 160
Borderless Graphic Designers Group: Graphic Design & Artificial Intelligence International Poster Competition Call 120
Brittain, Michael 212
Bruun Holdings LLC 198
Bussey, Jacqui 58
Cahe Valley Gardeners' Market Association 169
Câmara Municipal de Espinho 85
Câmara Municipal de Sever do Vouga 209
CEIDA (Chinese Europe International Design Culture Association) 74
Charlotte Ballet 150
Chicago Graphic Design Club 192
Chubu Creators Club 207
CI Games 184
Cinnabon 183
City of Krakow International Poster Competition 219
City Tree Christina Schools 32, 82, 83
College of Marin Drama Program 218
Colorado State University International Programs 154
Colson 42
Columbia University School of the Arts 214, 218
County of San Diego Agriculture, Weights and Measures 148
County of San Diego Cal Fresh HHSA Medicare 196
County of San Diego Land Use & Environment 149
Cultural Terminal Goclaw 106
Cunha, John 91
D'Alfonso, Arnaldo 88
D'Italiano 183
Daegu Korea 167
De Carvalho, Chloë 180
Design Event Shibuya 2023 167
Designers for Milton Glaser 147
Deutsches Fleischermuseum 172
di Cambio, Arnolfo 146
Dilworth Coffee 182
Disney Entertainment Television 157
Documentarist 86
Dongdaemun Design Plaza (DDP) 195
Dreiländer Museum Lörrach, Germany 30
DRK Kliniken Berlin Westend 175
DuMOL Winery 183
Durckel, Donna 149
ECHO Film Festival 175
Eduard Spörri Art Museum 95
Egypt Helwan University 196
Ehmann, Matt 58
Emirates International Poster Festival 163, 164
English National Opera 191
Episcopal Diocese of Northern California 146
Everett, Brian 63
Faculty Learning Community - NTU 192
Fantastic Twins 187
Farmingdale State College 154
Far° 175
Fayettevile State University 153
Filmar en América Latina 174
First Place Arizona 197
Focus Features 176, 180
Fondazione I Pomeriggi Musicali - Milano 188
Funahashi, Atsushi 179
Fundacja Evviva L'arte 33
FX Networks 57, 156, 160, 212
FX 132, 211
Galeria Ocupa! 71
Gallery Nadan 170
Gangwon Institute of Design Promotion (GIDP) 195
Gangwon State 195
Garcia, Alberto 196
Generalitat Valenciana 218
George Brown College School of Design 172
Gibbons, Stephanie 212
Glory Days Grill 182
Golden Bee Biennale 96, 146, 147, 170, 187, 189, 201
Graphic Communication Laboratory 206
Gwangju Design Biennale 2023 173
Gyeonggi Design Association 222
HBO 213

247 INDEX

Hexworks	184
Hirano Farm	182
Hulu	156, 159, 160
I Profess: The Graphic Design Manifesto 20th Anniversary Exhibition	151
IFC Films	177, 179
Ikeda Farm	193
Imperial War Museum	93
Infante, Dominick	170
Infinity Ward	184, 186
Information and Communication Technology Division	196
Institut Valencià de Cultura	218
Instituto Sonorense de Cultura	97
International Film Festival Berlin – Berlinale	84
International Law Students Association	152
International Poster Biennale for Peace: Nanjing, China	200, 203
International Poster Exhibition City of Bardejov 2	219
Iowa State University	153, 168
IPB Community	152
Japan Graphic Design Association Inc.	203
Japan Graphic Designers Association Hiroshima	122
Japan Overtourist Inc.	219
Japan Typography Association	171
Jazz Kicks Band	188
JBL Quantum	185
JDP-Yugoslav Drama Theater in Belgrade, Serbia	134, 135, 215, 217, 218
K Space Contemporary	169
Kansas City Art Institute	194
KICD	221
KINDAI University Department of Arts	51, 151
Kino za Rogiem Caf. Rzesz.w	215
Komische Oper	216
Korea Design Association	208
KST	222
KWVD International Invitational Design Exhibition	173
LA Design Festival 2023	175
Last One Standing Productions	92
Lee, Quentin	178
Lejeune, Lisa	212
Libbrecht, Stacey	154
Lil Nas X	154
Lincoln Track Club	210
Lionsgate	91, 161
Lopez, Ismael	196
Lyceum Fellowship Committee	36
Lyric Opera of Kansas City	190
MACAA (Mid-America College Art Association)	47
Magvető	154
Mankind	121
Massive Entertainment	185
Matosinhos City Councel	103
Max	158
MGM+	155
Ministry of Environment	162
Minnesota Twins	210
Minnesota Wild	209
Mirko Ilic Corp.	206
Mondo	180
Moore, Keri	91
Municipality of Delft	198
Museum Burghalde Lenzburg	187
Museum Wehrmuehle	186
Nancy Johnson Events Management	169
Nanjing International Biennial of Poster for Peace 2023	168
Nanyang Technological University School of Art, Design & Media	201
National Geographic	63, 158
National Human Rights Commission of the Republic of Korea	38
National Marine Mammal Foundation	46
National Taiwan Normal University Department of Design	72, 142
Nazraeli Press	110, 111
Nebraska State Chess Association	166
NEON	176
Neowiz	184
Netflix	56, 59, 61, 154, 159, 180, 211
New Art ZERO Association	173
NKUST College of Innovation & Design	45, 67, 116
Northwest Missouri State University	170
Ockel, Barbara	70
Oesol International Typography Awards	220
Office of Early Childhood Initiative	154
Offurum, Chika	154, 155, 157, 158, 160
Ogaki Poster Museum	76, 165
Oper Frankfurt	104, 105, 190
Opera Krakowska	108
Orcas Island Film Festival	41
Orchestra Moderne NYC	188
Organização Nascente - Cooperativa de Acção Cultural CRL	85
Osaka Poster Fest	75, 79
Panchenko, Julia	212
Papa Johns	104
Paramount Pictures	90
Paramount+	52, 156, 211, 212
ParodyCharities.org	196
PBS Creative Services	154
Pianko, Brian	90
Pitcher, Alexander	176
Pixbee	178
Plakatmuseum Emmerich	94
Posters Without Borders	202
Pratt Institute School of Architecture	152
Purdue Contemporary Dance Company	150
Quest Posse	186
Quin, Claire	154
Radio Slovenia Third Channel - ARS Program	147
Raven Software	184
Red Cross of Tijuana	149, 194
Ringling College Typography Club	220
Royal Theatre Exchange	218
RTV Slovenija	147
Rubenstein, Ira	154
Ruppenthal, John	154
Saia LTL Freight	150
Save Lapinlahti with a Poster	119
School of Visual Arts	48-50
Searchlight Pictures	159
Seoul Design Foundation	195
Seoul Metropolitan Government	195
Seoul	208
Shipyard Trust for the Arts	70
Shizuoka Institute of Science and Technology	193
Silo Theatre	214
SIPSM: Salón Internacional del Póster San Mateo	170
Slanted Magazine	118
SLUG Magazine	166
Smokin' Havanas	98
Snap-on Diagnostics	145
SND	177, 179
Society of Illustrators Los Angeles	170
Sommeroper Selzach	35
Sony Pictures Entertainment	64, 65, 155, 161
Special Olympics Nebraska	128
Spencer, Chris	63
Sput&nik the Window	71
Stallings, Jordan	88
STARZ	157, 159, 161
Stefan Hunt Films	181
Stop War Poster Exhibition	123, 204, 205
Street H	193
Subaru of America	170
Tampa Bay Lightning	210
Tamusaitis, Joe	88
Tandem Films	178
Tawoos Initiative	170
Teed, Jack	91
The 4th Block 12th International Triennial	202
The ADLink Education Foundation	222
The Albanian Theater Skopje	216
The Korean Society of Science and Art	124
The Magician's Niece	176
The Match Factory	181
The National	101
Theater Orchester Biel Solothurn	107, 137-139, 214, 216, 217
Theatre at the Mill	215, 217, 218
Thousand Mile Productions	89
Tirana Film Institute	87
TOKAS (Tokyo Arts and Space)	167
Tomayouz Excellence Award	80
Traina, Claudia	212
Traver, Jared	154
'TYPE TEXT KOREA' Typography Poster Exhibition	221
TypeForward	221
Typopassage TM Poster Museum	168
Ubisoft	185
UCLA Extension	151
UNCHR Croatia	202
United States International Poster Biennial (USIPB)	166, 169, 173
University of Louisiana at Lafayette Department of Visual Arts	194
University of Massachusetts Amherst Theatre Department	217
University of Utah	206
UnknownDesign	163-165
Vice Studios	131
Virasat	170
Ward, Charlie	90
We Want Jazz 2023	167
Wecan Kids Club	194
Welcome Villain	178
Well Go USA Entertainment	54, 156
Wilkies Martial Arts	209
Wilson, Rob	212
Wojda, Leah	63
Woman, Life, Freedom	208
Women Texas Film Festival	174
YMCA of the North	206
Young the Giant	100
Young Vic	218
ZETA Weekly	194
Zürich Design Weeks	171

GRAPHIC, SENIOR, JUNIOR, TYPE., SET, ASSISTANT, LOGO DESIGNERS/CREATIVE TEAMS/DESIGN ASSOCIATES, DIRECTORS

203	193
Abe, Kanta	192
Ablan, Alex-Marie	150
Adams, Gayle	210
ALVARO MONTANHA Design	103, 109
An, Kiyoung	51, 151
Araújo, Jorge	71
ARSONAL	57, 156, 159
Aufuldish, Bob	110, 111, 151
AV Print	88, 90, 91, 176, 177, 180, 212, 213
Barlow.Agency	89, 92, 181
Basse, Mike	145
Becker, Henry	206
Beslic, Edin	180
Bissland, R.P.	169, 188, 204
Boelts, Eric	208
Bower, Ezekiel Duke	220
Braley, Brooks	200, 203
Braley, Michael	146, 147, 151-153, 164, 166-170, 172, 173, 175, 189, 219
Bundi, Stephan	35, 107, 137-139, 214, 216, 217
Byers, Craig	145
Cadieux, Célie	131, 176, 181
Canchola, Alexandria	169
Canyon	52
Cao, Yvonne	175
Case, Bob	197
Cehovin, Eduard	174
Cerrella, Coco	147, 202
Chen, Chong-Wen	45, 67, 116, 165
Chen, Émilie	214, 218
Chung, Dho Yee	78
Chung, Hoon-Dong	39, 221
Cino, Pamela	180
Clark, Randy	154, 198, 206
Collier, Steve	37
Corneal, Chris	206
Costa, Carlos Casimiro	152
Costa, Jacinta	152
Cotilla, Gabby	182
Craig-Teerlink, Jean	70
Debray, JG	164
Dee, Meaghan A.	206
Delgado, Bob	177, 178
Dormann, Roger W.	218
Duarte, Sérgio	178, 186, 209, 210
Dunbar, Robert	177, 178, 180
Eichenberger, Res	171
Elam, Kimberly	220
Everhart, Scotti	181
Faden, Sean	195
Fajmut, Bojana	147
Fallano, Frank	143
Farkas, Anna	154, 187
Fernandes, Rafael	194
Fiocca, Rob	183
Fiore, Carlo	188, 190
Frazier, Craig	112, 183
Freaner, Ariel	32, 46, 82, 83, 148, 149, 194, 196
Freeman, Sean	34, 99
French, Martin	170, 189
Fronczek, Sascha	172
Galinska, Barbara	141
Gang, Liang	106
Garcia, Jean Pierre Llanos	161
Gast, Wolfgang	203
Gates, Jeff	207
Gerwitz, Rick	155
Ghelfi, Arnaud	140, 200, 206
Giangiulio, Anne M.	163
Gildersleeve, Owen	180
Giltae, Lee	166
Gon, Choe	173
Goodall, Derwyn	127, 153, 162, 193, 194, 200, 201, 203
Gravdahl, John	148, 154
Grzegorczyk, Wiesław	215
Gunderson, Grant	210
Gwaltney, David H.	31
H., Antonio Castro	119
Habben, David	166
Haddad, Wesam Mazhar	165, 208
Hagan, Kevin	194
Haller, Carmit Makler	74, 79, 120, 123, 170, 204, 205
Hansen, Rikke	221
Harris, Jack	154, 205, 206
Hickmann, Fons	94, 167, 187
Hinrichs, Kit	68, 169, 170
Hinrichs, Lea	81
Hollingsworth, Jovaney	210
Hornberger, Chad	58, 158, 160
Hrin, Ovidiu	168, 218
Hu, Fa-Hsiang	222
Huang, Fong 'Captain'	176, 178
Huber, Paul	41
Ilic, Mirko	134, 135, 215, 217, 218
Imboden, Melchior	30
Ishikawa, Seita	195
Itoh, Toyotsugu	69, 165, 203, 207
James, Steve	29, 207
Jiang, YiJun	150
Jung, Seunghun	188
Kasai, Noriyuki	206
Kashiwa, Daisuke	219
Kashlakov, Ivan	189, 221
Kato, Mai	204
Kato, Mayumi	182, 193
Kawabata, Aya	167
Kawamata, Ayaka	148
Kawamura, Miyoko	173
Kim, Do Gyun	117
Kim, Hyungjoo A.	150, 164
Kim, Jin Kwang	78
Kim, Mina	146
Kim, Minkwan	154
Koen, Viktor	48-50
Ku, Ja Eun	222
Kunz, Justin	186
Lavi, Mikey	100, 101
Le, Charlie	179
Lee, Jang Won	194
Lee, Mi-Jung	162
Leroy & Rose	129, 130, 132, 177-179, 181, 211, 212
Levy, Jean-Benoit	118
Lien, Chia-Hui	151, 162
Lin, Leo	72, 142
Lindhorst-Emme, Sven	81
Liyun, Xian	106
Ljubicic, Boris	202
Loiri, Pekka	121
Lowe, Joshua	166, 196
Luis, Christian	154, 155, 157
Lyness, John	58
MacArthur, Kelly Salchow	77
Machado, João	28, 73, 76, 85, 163-165
Magner, Brad	153
Maida, Adam	180
Maione, Lisa	194
Manahan, Donna	152
Mao, Siyu	170, 175, 186
Martinez, Mario F. Bocanegra	47
Matsuda, Takashi	193
May, Douglas	163, 220
McConnell, Robert	152
Mehmeti, Ngadhnjim	216
Mei, Feixue	170
Mercer, Kevin	174
Minorikawa, Tetsuro	80
Moenning, Katrina	154
Montes, Chemi	102, 136
Mosquera, Melanie	182
Mota, Ana	71
Muthucumaru, Kishan	133, 178
Nastevski, Igor	87

248 INDEX

Ni, Yuqin	204
Nicolas, Benjamin	216
Nogami, Shuichi	201
Nordyke, John	222
Northcutt, Sarah	128
O'Hanlon, David	63, 154, 157, 158
Ölmez, Volkan	86
O'Neill, John	202
Oguma, Chikako	167, 222
Oiga, Sharon	192
Osborne, Lloyd	43, 214
Oznowich, Greg	170
Palomino, Fernando	206, 209
Paramount+	52, 55
Percival, Louis	211, 213
Petri, Juliane	218
PETROL Advertising	184-186
Peña, Fidel	172
Pratt Institute Creative Services	152
Quintana, Javier	114, 115
Rambow, Gunter	104, 105, 190
Ray, Scott	147, 174
Rellaford, Alan	146
Renger, Jana	172
Rhubarb	56, 59, 61, 62, 156, 159-161, 212
Rivero, Genaro Solis	44
Rose	93, 191
Rossel, Cédric	174, 175
Royster, Shell	183
Rubin, Sophie	174, 175
Ruggiero, Andrea	146
Šabach, Jan	187, 201, 217
Santiago, Ari	170
Schneller, Alan	98, 197
Schramke, Claudia	84
Scott, Stephanie	180
Seidel, Marc Philip	95, 187
Selbst, Adam	155
Sempi, Enrico	180
Shapiro, Matt	182
Shim, DaeKi	195
Shim, HyoJun	195
Shiwan, Shabnam	43, 214
Sieren, David	198
Sinclair, Madison	190
Skolos, Nancy	36
Smith, Marlena Buczek	66, 205, 208
Sobol, Andrew	215, 217, 218
Sposato, John	192
Steben, Eve	34, 99
Steiner, Rene V.	125, 200
Suman, Shantanu	170
Sun, Byoung-il	38
Taft, Ron	188
Tatsutomi, Masahito	219
Temirkhanova, Anastasia	216
Territory Studio	154
The Refinery	53, 54, 60, 64, 65, 155-161
Tomokusa, Yuta	171
Tsushima, Hajime	75, 122, 163
Tzou, Brad	171
Valencia, Bernardo Garcia	214, 218
Valenzuela, Ivette	42, 97
van den Brulle, Eric	179
van der Meijden, Cindy	198
Villa Jr., Guy	192
Wadley, Jeff	176, 177, 179
Wallace, Rich	199, 209
Walters, Lee	162
Wedell, Thomas	36
West, Dallas	153
Wheeler, Nathaniel	181
Wild, Kim	126
Windham, Courtney	47
Winstanley, Lisa	173, 192, 201
Wong, Roger	206
Xie, Zhizheng	96
Yin, Zhongjun	113, 221
Yu, Eunjin	196
Zapart, Katarzyna	33, 108
Zhang, Chloe	172
Zhang, Li	124, 196
Zimmerman, Andrew	155
Zorko, Primoz	189
Zou, Claire	219

CREATIVE DIRECTORS/CHIEF CREATIVE DIRECTORS, OFFICERS/ASSOCIATE, EXECUTIVE CREATIVE DIRECTORS/CREATIVE GROUP HEADS

Araújo, Jorge	71
Barclay, Kevin	164
Brown, David	145
Cehovin, Eduard	174
Chan, Steve	52, 156, 212
Craig-Teerlink, Jean	70
Deluna, Adrianne	56, 59, 61, 62, 156, 159-161, 212
Dempster, Max	210
Duarte, Sérgio	178, 209, 210
Dunbar, Robert	133, 177, 179, 211, 213
Dunn, Troy	210
Frazier, Craig	112
Frisco, David	152
Gervasio-Hewett, Angela	160
Huber, Paul	41
Hutton, Shane	162
Irving, Andrew	56, 59, 61, 62, 156, 159-161, 212
James, Lee	150
Jones, Ryan	56, 59, 61, 62, 156, 159-161, 212
Kasher, Debbie	199
Laslo, Donna	41
Le, Charlie	176, 181
Low, Jason	176, 179
Magner, Brad	153
Matsuda, Takashi	193
Moosajee, Saad	154
Morrison, Stephanie	210
Mota, Ana	71
Mueller, Gary	154
Muthucumaru, Kishan	176, 177, 179-181, 211, 213
Nakamura, Hiroyuki	148
Ölmez, Volkan	86
Olsen, David	150
Osborne, Lloyd	43, 214
Oznowich, Greg	170
Patterson, Pam	216
Prato, Paul	98, 114, 115, 182, 197
Preston, Chris	206, 209
Quintana, Javier	114, 115
Rachild, Chad	52
Ryan, Richard	209
Schillig, Michael	98, 114, 115, 182, 197
Selem, Danica	214
Shapiro, Matt	153, 182
Shim, DaeKi	195
Shim, HyoJun	195
Shiwan, Shabnam	43, 214
Spence, Carl	41
Stokes, Casey	210
Thornhill, David	190
Valencia, Bernardo Garcia	214
Wallace, Rich	199, 209
Walters, Lee	162
Weitz, Carter	128, 210
Wen, Kuo-Hsun	96
West, Robert Shaw	153, 182
Wheeler, Nathaniel	133, 177-180, 211, 213
White, Grace	166
Yin, Zhongjun	113, 221

DESIGN DIRECTORS, ASSOCIATES, LEADS/DIRECTORS/EXECUTIVE, ART DIRECTORS

Alvarenga, Edwin	212
An, Kiyoung	51, 151
ARSONAL	156
Basse, Mike	145
Bundi, Stephan	35, 137, 139, 216, 217
Cerudo, Alejandro	150
Cotilla, Gabby	182
Dawson, Claire	172
de Sousa, Daniel	178
Essman, Brett	209
Ferraro, Simone	61
Fiore, Carlo	188
Fishel, Daniel	170, 174
Hawkins, Chris	52
Huber, Paul	41
Imboden, Melchior	30
Kasai, Noriyuki	206
Kim, Minkwan	154
Leal, Mário	210
Ljubicic, Boris	202
Ma, Jim	195
Magano, Pedro	178
Magner, Brad	153
Matsuda, Takashi	193
Mehmeti, Ngadhnjim	87
Moenning, Katrina	154
Nakamura, Hiroyuki	148
Nguyen-Tran, Sabrina	52
O'Hanlon, David	58, 63, 154, 155, 157, 158, 160
Oguma, Chikako	167, 222
Peña, Fidel	172
Pietrynczak, Karolina	152
Quintana, Javier	114, 115
Schneller, Alan	98, 197
Shapiro, Matt	153, 182
Sunghwan, Jang	193
Tsai, Shangrong	96
Ventanilla, Bruce	156
Wallace, Rich	199, 209
West, Dallas	153
West, Robert Shaw	153, 182

ILLUSTRATORS

Adobe Stock	154
Brown, Kenn	206
Bundi, Stephan	35, 137, 139, 216, 217
Case, Bob	197
Craig-Teerlink, Jean	70
Davis, Kate	146, 175
Dormann, Roger W.	218
Ekşioğlu, Gürbüz Doğan	216
Firefly AI	128
Freaner, Ariel	82, 83, 194
Harris, Katelyn	174
Ilic, Mirko	134, 135, 215, 217, 218
Kawamata, Ayaka	148
Northcutt, Sarah	128
Pepion, John Isaiah	154
Rodrigues, Cristiana	178, 209, 210
Santiago, Ari	170
Shumskaya, Liza	159
Šokčević, Domagoj	191
Sposato, John	192
Wren, Chris	206

ARTISTS/DIGITAL ARTISTS/EXHIBITION, FONT, MOTION, TYPEFACE, WEB DESIGNERS

Araújo, Tiago	186
Cardoso, Tiago	186, 209
De Ojo, Mal	123
Duarte, Sérgio	178
Freaner, Ariel	46, 148, 149, 194
Gamboa, Jorge	123
Gompf, Verena Stella	172
Goodwin, Alexis	212
Gwaltney, David H.	31
Klosov, Serhil	212
Ljubicic, Boris	202
Maida, Adam	180
Stokes, Casey	128
Sun, Byoung-il	38
Vigden, Lenny	181

PHOTOGRAPHERS/RETOUCHERS

Aaron, Slevin	191
Adams, Gayle	128
Alston, Kwaku	55
Bavoljak, Darko	202
Bell, Greta	150
Benson, Thom	143
Calverley, Julian	93
Chalkley, Dean	218
Clarke, Alan	156
Costa, Jorge	178
Cutler, Craig	183
Darkroom Digital	218
Daverio, Lorenza	188
De Taeye, Geert	191
Drobot, Dean	188
Fallano, Frank	143
Giacomino, Anthony	154
Grossman, Zoey	52
Guillem, Antonio	188
Hac Job	145
Haller, Carmit Makler	123
Harunah, Leo	181
Hido, Todd	110, 111
Kato, Mayumi	182, 193
Kim, Jinsol	195
Layla	199
Leary, Petra	43
Lendoiro, Fernando	202
Lepera, Greg	143
Littky, Pamela	62
Ljubaphoto	188
McCabe, Felicity	214
Merbler, Tyler	206
Minchin, James	212
Nedeljkovic, Nick	191
Nishijima, Atsushi	59
Okano, Toaki	43, 214
Patel, Roshan	143
Pixabay	136
Reiss, David	218
Rich, Ruth	146
Sayles, Matt	160
SB Arts Media	188
Sposato, John	192
Steinmeyer, Michelle	143
Stowell, Lauren	191
Sweeney, Roger	143
Takahashi, Isao	69
Unna, Jörg Bittner	206
Valencia, Bernardo Garcia	214
van den Brulle, Eric	179
Villa Jr., Guy	192
Wallace, Rich	199
Wedell, Thomas	36
Wharton, Quinn	150
Yvonne, Melodie	150
Zupanov, Marijo	189

WRITERS/COPYWRITERS

Antunes, Beatriz	209, 210
Barclay, Kevin	164
Barlament, S.J.	145
Day, Katrina	157, 160
Debray, JG	164
Frazier, Alexandra	150
Fry, Dwayne	153, 182
Googe, Joey	195, 210
Gordon, Seth	154
Hinson, Neil	182
Kasher, Debbie	199
Katsumata, Keika	148
Larsen, Aylâ	206
Messineo, Sophia	128, 190
O'Hanlon, David	154, 157
Rigden, Andy	191
Ryan, Richard	209
Schillig, Michael	98, 114, 115, 182, 197
Solano, Carla	186
Tournat, Charlie	209
Wallace, Rich	199

249 WINNERS DIRECTORY

PLATINUM

Atelier Bundi AG
www.atelierbundi.ch
Schlossstrasse 78
Boll Berne CH-3067
Switzerland
Tel +41 79 479 36 94
bundi@atelierbundi.ch

CollierGraphica
www.colliergraphica.com
2715 Chenevert St.
Houston, TX 77004
United States
Tel +1 713 894 0061
scollier44@gmail.com

Dankook University
www.dankook.ac.kr/web/international
College of Arts, 126, Jukjeon Suji Yongin Gyeonggi 448-701
South Korea
Tel +82 31 8005 3106
finvox3@naver.com

dGwaltneyArt
www.dgwaltneyart.com
5437 Branchwood Way
Virginia Beach, VA 23464
United States
Tel +1 757 581 1701
dgwaltneyart@gmail.com

Freaner Creative & Design
www.freaner.com
113 W. G St., No. 650
San Diego, CA 92101
United States
Tel +1 619 870 4699
arielfreaner@freaner.com

Gallery BI
www.gallerybi.com
#215, 216, 686, Cheonggyesan-ro, Sujeong-gu Seongnam-si, Gyeonggi-do 13105, Cheonansi Choongnam 31020
South Korea
Tel +82 105 276 5312
sunbi155@naver.com

João Machado Design
www.joaomachado.com
Rua Padre Xavier Coutinho, 125
Porto 4150-751
Portugal
Tel +351 934 835 598
geral@joaomachado.com

Katarzyna Zapart
www.zapart.co
Krakow
Poland
zapart1988@gmail.com

Melchior Imboden
www.melchiorimboden.ch
Eggertsbühl
CH-6374 Buochs
Switzerland
Tel +41 79 402 38 92
mail@melchiorimboden.ch

Skolos-Wedell
www.skolos-wedell.com
177 Everett Ave.
Providence, RI 02906
United States
Tel +1 617 291 8888
nancy@skolos-wedell.com

The Union Design Company
www.uniondesigncompany.com
1301 E. Debbie Lane,
Suite 102 #1536
Mansfield, TX 76063
United States
Tel +1 469 712 7545
sjames@uniondesigncompany.com

THERE IS STUDIO
www.sean-eve.com
London
United Kingdom
Tel +44 7572 460707
hello@thereis.co.uk

GOLD

1/4 Studio
www.quarterstudio.pt
Estrada da Circunvalação, 12115 Cave
Rua das Molares nº130 1ºEsq,
Porto 4250-155
Portugal
Tel +351 914 656 769
hello@quarterstudio.pt

ALVARO MONTANHA Design
www.alvaromontanha.com
R. Gonçalves Zarco, 1880
Leça da Palmeira 4450-324
Portugal
Tel +351 918 207 976
joana@alvaromontanha.com

Antonio Castro Design
www.acastrodesign.net
6148 Loma de Cristo Dr.
El Paso, TX 79912
United States
Tel +1 915 356 0775
antcastro@utep.edu

ARSONAL
www.arsonal.com
3524 Hayden Ave.
Culver City, CA 90232
United States
Tel +1 310 815 8824
info@arsonal.com

Atelier Bundi AG
www.atelierbundi.ch
Schlossstrasse 78
Boll Berne CH-3067
Switzerland
Tel +41 79 479 36 94
bundi@atelierbundi.ch

Atelier Starno
www.starno.com
9 Endeavor Cove
Corte Madera, CA 94925
United States
Tel +1 415 279 7301
ag@starno.com

Auburn University School of Industrial + Graphic Design
www.cadc.auburn.edu/design
210 S. Donahue Drive
Auburn, AL 36849
United States
Tel +1 334 844 2364
courtney.windham@auburn.edu

Aufuldish & Warinner
www.aufwar.com
183 The Alameda
San Anselmo, CA 94960
United States
Tel +1 415 721 7921
bob@aufwar.com

AV Print
www.avsquad.com
101 S. La Brea Ave., 2nd Floor
Los Angeles, CA 90036
United States
Tel +1 323 790 8888
PrintAccountTeam@avsquad.com

Bailey Lauerman
www.baileylauerman.com
1299 Farnam St., 9th Floor
Omaha, NE 68102
United States
Tel +1 402 514 9400
sfaden@baileylauerman.com

Barbara Galinska
www.facebook.com/baga.kaligrafia
Warsaw
Poland
Tel +48 603 794 561
barbara.art@post.pl

Barlow.Agency
www.barlow.agency
1-5 Woodburn St., Studio A3a
Redfern, NSW 2016
Australia
hello@barlow.agency

Canyon
www.canyondesigngroup.com
4929 Wilshire Blvd., #500
Los Angeles, CA 90010
United States
Tel +1 323 933 2203
awards@canyondesigngroup.com

Carmit Design Studio
www.carmitdesign.com
2208 Bettina Ave.
Belmont, CA 94002
United States
Tel +1 650 283 1308
carmit@carmitdesign.com

Célie Cadieux
www.celiecadieux.com
124 Rue de Tolbiac
Paris 75013
France
hello@celiecadieux.com

Chase Design
www.facebook.com/profile.php?id=100091409145451&mibextid=LQQJ4d
No. 69, Xuefu South Road
Minhou County, Fuzhou, Fujian,
福建 / 福建 350118
China
Tel +86 189 6526 9956
455913710@qq.com

Chemi Montes Design
www.american.edu/cas/faculty/cmontes.cfm
4400 Massachusetts Ave., NW
Washington, DC 20016
United States
Tel +1 202 885 1697
cmontes@american.edu

Claudia Schramke
www.claudiaschramke.de
Germany
ahoi@claudiaschramke.de

Craig Frazier Studio
www.craigfrazier.com
157 Throckmorton Ave., #D
Mill Valley, CA 94941
United States
Tel +1 415 389 1475
studio@craigfrazier.com

Craig-Teerlink Design
www.craigteerlink.com
422 Day St.
San Francisco, CA
United States
Tel +1 415 572 6488
jean@craigteerlink.com

Dalian RYCX Design
China
rycxcn@163.com

Dreamis GmbH
www.dreamis.ch
Affolternstrasse 101
8050 Zürich
Switzerland
Tel +41 435 359 906
seidel@dreamis.ch

EGGRA
www.eggra.com
Bul. Kliment Ohridski 11/4 MK
Blvd. Saint Clement of Ohrid 11/4, Skopje 1000
Macedonia
Tel +389 2 323 3395
eggra.pars@gmail.com

Elevate Design
www.elevatedesign.org
2600 Roseland Drive
Ann Arbor, MI 48103
United States
Tel +1 734 827 4242
salchow@msu.edu

Fallano Faulkner & Associates
www.fallano.com
19 S. Stricker St.
Baltimore, MD 21223
United States
Tel +1 410 945 2092
ffallano@fallano.com

Fol
www.volkanolmez.com
Süleyman Seba Cd. No. 79
Besiktas Istanbul
Turkey
Tel +90 54 2294 9493
volkan@volkanolmez.com

Fons Hickmann m23
www.fonshickmann.com
Gartenhaus,
Wilhelm-Busch-Straße 18a
12043 Berlin
Germany
Tel +49 30 6951 8501
fons@m23.de

Freaner Creative & Design
www.freaner.com
113 W. G St., No. 650
San Diego, CA 92101
United States
Tel +1 619 870 4699
arielfreaner@freaner.com

Goodall Integrated Design
www.goodallintegrated.com
35 Tyrrel Ave.
Toronto, ON M6G 2G1
Canada
Tel +1 416 435 3653
derwyn@goodallintegrated.com

Huber Design Werks
www.huberdesignwerks.com
239 Bromley Drive
Eastsound, WA 98245
United States
Tel +1 415 412 8690
paulhuber26@gmail.com

Institut für Visuelle Kommunikation
www.hbksaar.de/hochschule/institut-fuer-visuelle-kommunikation
Keplerstraße 3-5
66117 Saarbrücken
Germany
Tel +49 0 3843 686 503
GunterRambow@web.de

Ivette Valenzuela Design
www.ivettevalenzueladesign.com/posters
940 Edgecliff Drive
Reno, NV 89523
United States
Tel +1 775 742 6498
ivettevv@gmail.com

João Machado Design
www.joaomachado.com
Rua Padre Xavier Coutinho, 125
Porto 4150-751
Portugal
Tel +351 934 835 598
geral@joaomachado.com

Katarzyna Zapart
www.zapart.co
Krakow
Poland
zapart1988@gmail.com

Kim Wild Designs
www.kimwilddesigns.com
70 Leslie Lane
Smithtown, NY 11787
United States
Tel +1 516 287 5566
kimswild@gmail.com

Kiyoung An Graphic Art Course Laboratory
3 Chome-4-1 Kowakae
Osaka, Higashiosaka City, 0
Japan
aky6815@hotmail.com

Legacy79
www.legacy79.com
816 Camaron St.
San Antonio, TX 78212
United States
Tel +1 210 508 0225
genaro@legacy79.com

Leo Lin Design
New Taipei City
Taiwan
leoposter@yahoo.com.tw

Leroy & Rose
www.leroyandrose.com
1522F Cloverfield Blvd.
Santa Monica, CA 90404
United States
Tel +1 310 310 8679
adriana@leroyandrose.com

Marlena Buczek Smith
www.marlenabuczek.com
New York
United States
marlenabuczeksmith@gmail.com

Mirko Ilic Corp.
www.mirkoilic.com
41 Union Square W., Room 824
New York, NY 10003
United States
Tel +1 212 481 9737
studio@mirkoilic.com

MOCEAN
www.moceanla.com
2440 S. Sepulveda Blvd.,
Suite 150
Los Angeles, CA 90064
United States
Tel +1 310 481 0808
moceanawards@moceanla.com

250 WINNERS DIRECTORY

National Kaohsiung University of Science & Technology (NKUST)
www.nkust.edu.tw
No.1, University Road,
Yanchao Dist.
Kaohsiung City 824005
Taiwan
Tel +886 7 361 7141
cwc2022@nkust.edu.tw

Osborne Shiwan
www.osborneshiwan.com
New Zealand
Tel +64 21 274 0556
lloyd@osborneshiwan.com

Paramount+
www.paramount.com
Los Angeles, CA
United States
steve.chan@paramount.com

PPK
www.uniteppk.com
1102 N. Florida Ave.
Tampa, FL
United States
Tel +1 813 496 7000
kgoucher@uniteppk.com

Purdue University
www.purdue.edu
610 Purdue Mall
West Lafayette, IN 47907
United States
Tel +1 765 494 4600
kim4124@purdue.edu

Rhubarb
www.rhubarbagency.com
Los Angeles, CA
United States
Tel +1 818 720 0503
geysel@rhubarbagency.com

Rose
www.rosedesign.co.uk
70 Saint Marychurch St.
London SE16 4HZ
United Kingdom
Tel +44 020 7394 2800
hello@rosedesign.co.uk

SJI Associates
www.sjiassociates.com
127 W. 24 St., 2nd Floor
New York City, NY 10011
United States
Tel +1 212 391 4140
david@sjiassociates.com

Steiner Graphics
www.renesteiner.com
155 Dalhousie St., Suite 1062
Toronto, ON M5B 2P7
Canada
Tel +1 647 285 1658
rene@steinergraphics.com

Studio A N D
www.and.ch
2278 15th St., #4
San Francisco, CA 94114
United States
Tel +1 415 252 0506
usa@and.ch

Studio Hinrichs
www.studio-hinrichs.com
2064 Powell St.
San Francisco, CA 94133
United States
Tel +1 415 543 1776
reception@studio-hinrichs.com

Studio Lindhorst-Emme+Hinrichs
www.lindhorst-emme-hinrichs.de
Wilhelm-Busch-Str. 18a
Gartenhaus Berlin 12043
Germany
Tel +49 030 71 30 19 30
mail@lindhorst-emme-hinrichs.de

Studio Pekka Loiri
www.posterswithoutborders.com/Pekka-Loiri
Messitytonkatu 1C 43
Helsinki 00180
Finland
Tel +358 503 512104
loiripekka3@gmail.com

Sun Design Production
China
1023484137@qq.com

Tetsuro Minorikawa
www.minorikawa.net
Japan
info@minorikawa.net

The Refinery
www.therefinerycreative.com
Sherman Oaks Galleria
15301 Ventura Blvd., Bldg. D, Suite 300
Sherman Oaks, CA 91403
United States
Tel +1 818 843 0004
claire.delouraille@therefinerycreative.com

The Studio of Mikey Lavi
www.mikeylavi.com
Montreal, QC
Canada
hello@mikeylavi.com

THERE IS STUDIO
www.sean-eve.com
London
United Kingdom
eve@thereis.co.uk

TopLeft LLC
Michigan
United States
doy526@gmail.com

Toyotsugu Itoh Design Office
www.facebook.com/toyotsuguoffice
402 Royal Villa Tsurumai
4-17-8 Tsurumai, Showa-ku
Nagoya,
Aichi Prefecture 466-0064
Japan
Tel +81 52 731 9747
toyo-ito@ya2.so-net.ne.jp

Tsushima Design
www.tsushima-design.com
1-17-204, 1-17, Matsukawa-cho,
Minami-ku
Hiroshima 7320826
Japan
Tel +81 08 2567 5586
info@tsushima-design.com

Viktor Koen
www.viktorkoen.com
New York, NY
United States
Tel +1 212 592 2000
viktor@viktorkoen.com

SILVER

14-Forty
www.14-forty.com
2335 Hyperion Ave.
Los Angeles, CA 90027
United States
Tel +1 323 662 1440
info@14-forty.com

203 Infographic Lab
www.203x.co.kr
92-3, 3rd Floor
Dongmak-ro, Mapo-gu,
Seoul 04075
South Korea
Tel +82 10 4211 7715
pigcky@gmail.com

246 Graphics.
www.246.jp
Japan
matsuda@246.jp

Addison
www.addison.com
48 Wall St., 9th Floor
New York, NY 10005
United States
Tel +1 617 335 5522
acrosson@addison.com

Alan Rellaford Design
Chico, CA
United States
arellaford@gmail.com

Anagraphic
www.anagraphic.hu
Hungary
Tel +36 1 202 0555
anagraphic@anagraphic.hu

Anastasia Temirkhanova
www.atemirkhan.com
6900 Paradiso
Switzerland
Tel +41 76 496 47 02
th.a.tmrk@gmail.com

Andrea Ruggiero Design
www.andrearuggiero.design
195 Chrystie St., 502B
New York, NY 10012
United States
Tel +1 646 490 5531
studio@andrearuggiero.design

Andrea Szabó
Hungary
szaboandreaetel@gmail.com

Andrewsobol.com
www.andrewsobol.com
Chicago, IL
United States
andrew.sobol@elmhurst.edu

Angry Dog
www.angrydog.com.br
Rua Teodoro Sampaio, 352,
No. 171, Pinheiros
São Paulo, SP 05406-000
Brazil
ola@angrydog.com.br

Anne M. Giangiulio
www.annegiangiulio.com
500 W. University Ave.
El Paso, TX 79968
United States
Tel +1 915 222 1134
annegiangiulio@gmail.com

Arcana Academy
www.arcanaacademy.com
13323 W. Washington Blvd.
Los Angeles, CA
United States
Tel +1 310 279 5024
kensy.reissig@arcanaacademy.com

ARSONAL
www.arsonal.com
3524 Hayden Ave.
Culver City, CA 90232
United States
Tel +1 310 815 8824
info@arsonal.com

Articoolisan
www.articoolisan.com
Stupska Bb C2
Sarajevo, Sarajevo 71000
Bosnia and Herzegovina
Tel +387 0 63 393 416
edin.beslic@articoolisan.com

Atelier Bundi AG
www.atelierbundi.ch
Schlossstrasse 78
Boll Berne CH-3067
Switzerland
Tel +41 79 479 36 94
bundi@atelierbundi.ch

Atelier Starno
www.starno.com
9 Endeavor Cove
Corte Madera, CA 94925
United States
Tel +1 415 279 7301
ag@starno.com

Aufuldish & Warinner
www.aufwar.com
183 The Alameda
San Anselmo, CA 94960
United States
Tel +1 415 721 7921
bob@aufwar.com

Automotive Events
www.automotive-events.com
801 Canterbury Road, Suite C
Cleveland, OH, 44145
United States
Tel +1 440 356 1383
hq@aemoves.com

AV Print
www.avsquad.com
101 S. La Brea Ave., 2nd Floor
Los Angeles, CA 90036
United States
Tel +1 323 790 8888
PrintAccountTeam@avsquad.com

AYA KAWABATA DESIGN
www.ayakawabata.com
Tokyo
Japan
hello@ayakawabata.com

Bailey Lauerman
www.baileylauerman.com
1299 Farnam St., 9th Floor
Omaha, NE 68102
United States
Tel +1 402 514 9400
sfaden@baileylauerman.com

Barlow.Agency
www.barlow.agency
1-5 Woodburn St., Studio A3a
Redfern, NSW 2016
Australia
hello@barlow.agency

Becker Studio
www.instagram.com/henryjbecker
377 E. Westminster Ave.
Salt Lake City, UT 84115
United States
Tel +1 570 994 5417
henry.becker@utah.edu

Bernardo Garcia Valencia
www.bernardoemmanuel.com
New York City, NY
United States
hello@bernardoemmanuel.com

Bob Case Illustration
www.bobcasework.com
Phoenix, AZ
United States
bobcasework@gmail.com

Bojana Fajmut
www.bojanafajmut.eu
Tugomerjeva 2
Ljubljana 1000
Slovenia
Tel +386 41 213 468
info@bojanafajmut.eu

Brain Bolts
www.brainbolts.com
3760 Britting Ave.
Boulder, CO 80305
United States
Tel +1 303 543 7521
eric@brainbolts.com

Braley Design
www.braleydesign.com
3469 Lannette Lane
Lexington, KY 40503
United States
Tel +1 415 706 2700
braley@braleydesign.com

BraleyArts
United States
bdbraley@icloud.com

CAO Design
United States
yvecao@gmail.com

Carmit Design Studio
www.carmitdesign.com
2208 Bettina Ave.
Belmont, CA 94002
United States
Tel +1 650 283 1308
carmit@carmitdesign.com

CCC + JC. Jacinta & Carlos
www.carlosjacinta.myportfolio.com
Rua Do Pomar N°1, Gondesende
Parque Natural de Montesinho
Bragança 5300-561
Portugal
Tel +91 470 9378
carlos.costa@ipb.pt

Célie Cadieux
www.celiecadieux.com
124 Rue de Tolbiac
Paris 75013
France
hello@celiecadieux.com

Chamomile Tea Party
www.chamomileteaparty.com
United States
info@chamomileteaparty.com

Chikako Oguma
www.chikako-oguma.com
1-10-22-1403 Nakameguro
Meguro-ku
Tokyo 153-0061
Japan
Tel +81 90 6045 2037
koguma75@gmail.com

Chloe Zhang
United States
chloezrn0528@gmail.com

Claire Zou
www.clairezou.art
4427 Purves St., 12E
Queens, NY 11101
United States
Tel +1 917 843 6822
clairezoudesign@gmail.com

251 WINNERS DIRECTORY

Coco Cerrella
www.coco.com.ar
3368 Inclan
Buenos Aires 1258
Argentina
Tel +54 9 11 6569 6337
info@coco.com.ar

Code Switch
www.codeswitchdesign.com
262 Crescent St.
Northampton, MA 01060
United States
Tel +1 718 310 8966
jansabach@mac.com

Craig Frazier Studio
www.craigfrazier.com
157 Throckmorton Ave., #D
Mill Valley, CA 94941
United States
Tel +1 415 389 1475
studio@craigfrazier.com

©DAEKI and JUN
www.DAEKI-and-JUN.com
Hannam-dong
Seoul 04418
South Korea
Tel +82 10 8650 3465
win.daekiandjun@gmail.com

Daisuke Kashiwa
www.kashiwadaisuke.net
#401 Kozawa Bldg., 43 Furusawa
Asao-ku Kawasaki City,
Kanagawa 2150026
Japan
Tel +81 80 3556 4640
info@kashiwadaisuke.net

Dalian RYCX Design
China
rycxcn@163.com

Dankook University
www.dankook.ac.kr/web/international
College of Arts, 126, Jukjeon
Suji Yongin, Gyeonggi 448-701
South Korea
Tel +82 31 8005 3106
finvox3@naver.com

David Habben Illustration
www.habbenink.com
United States
hello@habbenink.com

DEFINITION 6 (Bridgenext)
www.bridgenext.com
420 Plasters Ave.
Atlanta, GA 30324
United States
Tel +1 404 870 0323
jiangyjamber@gmail.com

Design Studio FLORALIEN Inc.
Japan
kazuosansan@icloud.com

Design SubTerra
www.designsubterra.com
1590 Canyon Road
Providence, UT 84332
United States
Tel +1 435 792 3101
rain9@xmission.com

DLR Group
www.dlrgroup.com
United States
awells@dlrgroup.com

Dreamis GmbH
www.dreamis.ch
Affolternstrasse 101
8050 Zürich
Switzerland
Tel +41 435 359 906
seidel@dreamis.ch

Duas Faces Design
www.duasfaces.net
Rua Escultor Barata Feyo,
140 - 2°, Escritório 2.5
Porto 4250-076
Portugal
Tel +351 912 452 123
sergio@duasfaces.net

Dunn&Co.
www.dunn-co.com
202 S. 22nd St.
Tampa, FL 33605
United States
Tel +1 813 350 7990
julia@dunn-co.com

EGGRA
www.eggra.com
Bldg. Kliment Ohridski 11/4 MK
Blvd. Saint Clement of Ohrid
11/4, Skopje 1000
Macedonia
Tel +389 2 323 3395
eggra.pars@gmail.com

EJ Communication Studio
www.gallerybi.com
105-902, 15 Geumho-ro
Seongdong-gu, Seoul 04740
South Korea
Tel +82 10 3842 4238
eunjiniker@naver.com

Émilie Chen LTD
www.emiliechen.com
London
United Kingdom
hello@emiliechen.com

Evb Creative, Inc.
www.evbcreative.com
242 Baltic St., Suite 14
Brooklyn, NY 11201
United States
Tel +1 317 431 5097
vandenbrulle@yahoo.com

Everything Looks Good
United States
alexandria.canchola@tamucc.edu

Ezekiel Duke Dower
www.ebower1.myportfolio.com
1661 Market St., Apt. 538
Denver, CO 80202
United States
Tel +1 720 428 0504
knowblemusic@gmail.com

Feixue Mei
www.feixuemei.info
1213 Fox Road, Apt. 2
Maryville, MO 64468
United States
Tel +1 804 869 3685
feixuefeixuemei@gmail.com

Fons Hickmann m23
www.fonshickmann.com
Gartenhaus,
Wilhelm-Busch-Straße 18a
12043 Berlin
Germany
Tel +49 30 6951 8501
fons@m23.de

For Instance: A Design Practice
www.work.forinstance.org
4109 Holmes St.
Kansas City, MO 64110
United State
Tel +1 713 818 0261
lisamaione@icloud.com

Freaner Creative & Design
www.freaner.com
113 W. G St., No. 650
San Diego, CA 92101
United States
Tel +1 619 870 4699
arielfreaner@freaner.com

Gastdesign
www.gastdesign.de
Peter-Loer-St. 20
Neuss 41462
Germany
Tel +49 1577 28 71 899
info@gastdesign.de

Gon.C Studio
www.instagram.com/choe_gon
101-505, Seoha-ro 184
Buk-gu, Gwangju 61119
South Korea
Tel +82 10 7433 1674
gon.choe@gmail.com

Goodall Integrated Design
www.goodallintegrated.com
35 Tyrrel Ave.
Toronto, ON M6G 2G1
Canada
Tel +1 416 435 3653
derwyn@goodallintegrated.com

Gravdahl Design
www.gravdahldesign.com
406 E. Lake St.
Fort Collins, CO 80524
United States
Tel +1 970 482 8807
john@gravdahldesign.com

Hidden Impact
www.visualarts.louisiana.edu/node/164
312 Upland Drive
Lafayette, LA 70506
United States
Tel +1 337 371 1855
kevin.hagan@lusfiber.net

Hufax Arts/FJCU
www.facebook.com/HufaxArts
13F., No. 17, Lane 47, Section 1
Baofu Road, Yonghe Dist.,
New Taipei City 23444
Taiwan
Tel +88 693 399 1520
hufa@ms12.hinet.net

Human Paradise Studio
www.humanparadise.com
Taipei
Taiwan
humanparadise@mac.com

Hyungjookim Designlab
www.cla.purdue.edu/academic/rueffschool/ad/vcd/Faculty.html
552 W. Wood St.
West Lafayette, IN 47907
United States
Tel +1 765 409 1039
hakim@purdue.edu

i,D
www.i-dinc.com
3316-4, Odo
Higashiibaraki-gun,
Ibaraki 3113114
Japan
Tel +81 90 4203 0731
seitartype3@gmail.com

Institut für Visuelle Kommunikation
www.hbksaar.de/hochschule/institut-fuer-visuelle-kommunikation
Keplerstraße 3-5
66117 Saarbrücken
Germany
Tel +49 0 3843 686 503
GunterRambow@web.de

Isaac Jung
www.isaacjung.design
5916 Woodside Ave.
Woodside, NY 11377
United States
Tel +1 312 340 9652
isaacjung.design@gmail.com

Ivan Kashlakov
www.linktr.ee/kashlak.art
Sofia
Bulgaria
kashlak.art@gmail.com

Jack Harris
www.jackharris.com
25 Frank Ave.
South Farmingdale, NY 11735
United States
Tel +1 302 290 0225
jackharris@me.com

João Machado Design
www.joaomachado.com
Rua Padre Xavier Coutinho, 125
Porto 4150-751
Portugal
Tel +351 934 835 598
geral@joaomachado.com

John Nordyke
www.johnnordyke.com
West Hartford, CT
United States
nordyke@hartford.edu

John O'Neill
www.johnloneilldesign.com
Cloquet, MN
United States
jloneill@d.umn.edu

John Sposato Design & Illustration
www.johnsposato.carbonmade.com
New York
United States
Tel +1 845 365 1940
johnsposatodesign@gmail.com

Juliane Petri
www.julianepetri.com
Calle Almudín, 16 Bajo
Valencia 46003
Spain
Tel +34 610 262 359
studio@julianepetri.com

Justin Kunz Illustration
www.justinkunz.com
Lindon, UT
United States
jk@justinkunz.com

Kimberly Elam Design
www.behance.net/kelam
2700 N. Tamiami Trail
Sarasota, FL 34234
United States
Tel +1 941 387 4955
kelam@c.ringling.edu

Kiyoung An Graphic Art Course Laboratory
3 Chome-4-1 Kowakae
Osaka, Higashiosaka City, 0
Japan
aky6815@hotmail.com

Legis Design
273 Ramona Ave.
Sierra Madre, CA 91024
United States
legis@pa2.so-net.ne.jp

Leroy & Rose
www.leroyandrose.com
1522F Cloverfield Blvd.
Santa Monica, CA 90404
United States
Tel +1 310 310 8679
adriana@leroyandrose.com

Lisa Winstanley Design
www.lisawinstanley.com
52J Nanyang View
02-17 Singapore 639668
Singapore
Tel +65 8343 7608
lwinstanley@ntu.edu.sg

Maida Studio
www.adammaida.com
50 Quebec Ave.
Toronto, ON M6P 4B4
Canada
Tel +1 416 884 1003
adammaida@me.com

Marlena Buczek Smith
www.marlenabuczek.com
New York
United States
marlenabuczeksmith@gmail.com

Martin French Studio
www.martinfrench.com
511 NW. Broadway
Portland, OR 97209
United States
Tel +1 503 926 2809
studio@martinfrench.com

May & Co.
www.mayandco.com
6316 Berwyn Lane
Dallas, TX 75214
United States
Tel +1 214 536 0599
dougm@mayandco.com

Meaghan A. Dee
www.meaghand.com
Blacksburg, VA
United States
meaghand@vt.edu

Mirko Ilic Corp.
www.mirkoilic.com
41 Union Square W., Room 824
New York, NY 10003
United States
Tel +1 212 481 9737
studio@mirkoilic.com

MOCEAN
www.moceanla.com
2440 S. Sepulveda Blvd.,
Suite 150
Los Angeles, CA 90064
United States
Tel +1 310 481 0808
moceanawards@moceanla.com

Mythic
www.mythic.us
6201 Fairview Road, Suite 200
Charlotte, NC 28210
United States
Tel +1 980 500 0828
dshuford@mythic.us

Namseoul University
www.sunbi.kr
91 Daehak-ro, Seonghwan-eup,
Seobuk-gu
Cheonan-si, Chungcheongnam-do
South Korea
Tel +82 105 276 5312
sunbi155@naver.com

National Kaohsiung University of Science & Technology (NKUST)
www.nkust.edu.tw
No. 1, University Road,
Yanchao Dist.
Kaohsiung City 824005
Taiwan
Tel +886 7 361 7141
cwc2022@nkust.edu.tw

Nikkeisha, Inc.
www.nks.co.jp
11th Floor, Akasaka K-Tower,
1-2-7 Motoakasaka
Minato-Ku, Tokyo 107-0051
Japan
nakamu02@gmail.com

Nogami Design Office
www.nogamidesignoffice.com
4-17-9-716 Kikawahigashi
Yodogawa-ku
Osaka 532-0012
Japan
Tel +81 90 3033 9317
ndo@kf6.so-net.ne.jp

252 WINNERS DIRECTORY

Noriyuki Kasai
2-42-1 Asahigaoka Nerima-ku
Tokyo 176-8525
Japan
Tel +81 3 5995 8691
kasai.noriyuki@nihon-u.ac.jp

Not William
Berkeley Heights, NJ
United States
Tel +1 718 207 3285
wallacerich1@gmail.com

One Design Company
www.onedesigncompany.com
230 W. Superior St.
Chicago, IL 60654
United States
Tel +1 312 602 3335
billing@onedesigncompany.com

Osborne Shiwan
www.osborneshiwan.com
New Zealand
Tel +64 21 274 0556
lloyd@osborneshiwan.com

Owen Gildersleeve Ltd.
www.owengildersleeve.com
7 Orange Row
Brighton SXE BN1 1UQ
United Kingdom
Tel +44 79 3233 1841
hello@owengildersleeve.com

PEACE Inc.
www.4peace.co.jp
Japan
k.ueda@4peace.co.jp

PETROL Advertising
www.petrolad.com
443 N. Varney St.
Burbank, CA 91502
United States
bnessan@petrolad.com

PPK
www.uniteppk.com
1102 N. Florida Ave.
Tampa, FL
United States
Tel +1 813 496 7000
kgoucher@uniteppk.com

Pratt Institute Communications & Marketing
www.pratt.edu/administrative-departments/communications-and-marketing
536 Myrtle Ave., Third Floor E.
Brooklyn, New York 11205
United States
creativeservices@pratt.edu

Preston Spire
www.prestonspire.com
105 S. 5th Ave., Suite 200
Minneapolis, MN 55401
United States
Tel +1 612 843 4000
invoices@prestonspire.com

Primoz Zorko
www.primozzorko.com
Puhova 1
1000 Ljubljana
Slovenia
Tel +386 40 291 173
hello@primozzorko.com

Purdue University
www.purdue.edu
610 Purdue Mall
West Lafayette, IN 47907
United States
Tel +1 765 494 4600
kim4124@purdue.edu

Randy Clark
www.randyclark.myportfolio.com
88 Daxue Road, Ouhai District
Wenzhou, Zhejiang
China
Tel +86 5775 5870 000
randyclarkmfa@icloud.com

Ray Visual Communications
United States
scott@peterson.com

Res Eichenberger Design
www.reseichenberger.ch
Neptunstrasse 25
Zurich 8032
Switzerland
Tel +414 3499 8336
studio@reseichenberger.ch

Rhubarb
www.rhubarbagency.com
Los Angeles, CA
United States
Tel +1 818 720 0503
geysel@rhubarbagency.com

Rikke Hansen
www.wheelsandwaves.dk
Klovtoftvej 32
Roedding 6630
Denmark
Tel +452 331 3560
rh@wheelsandwaves.dk

Rob Fiocca
www.fioccastudio.com
69 Pelham Ave.
Toronto, ON M6N 1A5
Canada
Tel +1 416 516 0034
production@fioccastudio.com

Roger W. Dormann
www.rdormanndesign.com
Lagunitas, CA
United States
roger@rdormanndesign.com

Ron Taft Brand Innovation & Media Arts
www.rontaft.com
2934 Beverly Glen Circle, #372
Los Angeles, CA 90077
United States
Tel +1 310 339 2442
ron@rontaft.com

Rose
www.rosedesign.co.uk
70 Saint Marychurch St.
London, SE16 4HZ
United Kingdom
Tel +44 020 7394 2800
hello@rosedesign.co.uk

Saad Moosajee
www.moosajee.co
119 Ingraham St., 4th Floor
Brooklyn, NY 11237
United States
studio@moosajee.co

Seoul Institution of the Arts
Seoul
South Korea
jku528@gmail.com

Serve Marketing
www.servemarketing.org
250 W. Coventry Court, Suite 300
Milwaukee, WI 53217
United States
Tel +1 262 515 5544
lauren.sutter@bvk.com

Shantanu Suman
www.shantanusuman.com
Muncie, IN
United States
sumansantanu@gmail.com

Sharon and Guy
www.sharonandguy.com
Chicago, IL
United States
guyvilla@gmail.com

Shell Royster
www.shellroyster.com
United States
sbr2pro@gmail.com

SJI Associates
www.sjiassociates.com
127 W. 24 St., 2nd Floor
New York City, NY 10011
United States
Tel +1 212 391 4140
david@sjiassociates.com

Steiner Graphics
www.renesteiner.com
155 Dalhousie St., Suite 1062
Toronto, ON M5B 2P7
Canada
Tel +1 647 285 1658
rene@steinergraphics.com

Stephanie Scott Designs
www.stephaniescott.design
18 Barrel Yards Blvd., Unit 4
Waterloo, ON N2L 0G1
Canada
Tel +1 519 589 9612
info@stephaniescott.design

Stila (In-House)
www.stilacosmetics.com
Glendale, CA
United States
minakim0128@gmail.com

Studio +Fronczek
www.saschafronczek.de
Karlsruhe, BW
Germany
hello@saschafronczek.de

Studio Craig Byers
www.studiocraigbyers.com
4609 Del Sol Blvd.
Sarasota, FL 34243
United States
Tel +1 917 597 4388
byers.craig@gmail.com

Studio Eduard Cehovin
www.designresearch.si
Ulica Milana Majcna 35
Ljubljana SI-1000
Slovenia
Tel +386 40 458 657
eduard.cehovin@siol.net

Studio Hinrichs
www.studio-hinrichs.com
2064 Powell St.
San Francisco, CA 94133
United States
Tel +1 415 543 1776
reception@studio-hinrichs.com

STUDIO INTERNATIONAL
www.studio-international.com
Bucojiceva 43 Bucojiceva 43/III
Zagreb HR-10 000
Croatia
Tel +385 13 760 171
boris@studio-international.com

Studio XXY
www.xxystudio.com
California
United States
hello@xxystudio.com

Symbiotic Solutions
United States
corneal@msu.edu

Synopsismedia
www.synopsismedia.com
St. Evlyia Celebi 5
Timișoara, Timis 300226
Romania
Tel +40 723 152 138
ovidiu@synopsismedia.com

Tainan University of Technology
www.tut.edu.tw
No. 529, Zhongzheng Road
Yongkang District, Tainan City 710302
Taiwan
Tel +09 29360129
superpolly0217@gmail.com

Tangram Strategic Design
www.tangramsd.it
Viale Buonarroti 10/C
Novara, NO 28100
Italy
Tel +39 032 135 662
esempi@tangramsd.it

Team Mao
www.siyumao.com
Mittenwalder St. 38
Berlin 10961
Germany
Tel +49 176 7880 5578
hi@siyumao.com

Territory Studio
www.territorystudio.com
132 Goswell Road
London EC1V 7DY
United Kingdom
Tel +44 020 3141 9430
adam.cole@territorystudio.com

The Refinery
www.therefinerycreative.com
Sherman Oaks Galleria
15301 Ventura Blvd., Bldg. D, Suite 300
Sherman Oaks, CA 91403
United States
Tel +1 818 843 0004
claire.delouraille@therefinerycreative.com

The Republik
www.therepublik.com
North Carolina
United States
Tel +1 919 956 9400
hello@therepublik.com

The Union Design Company
www.uniondesigncompany.com
1301 E. Debbie Lane, Suite 102 #1536
Mansfield, TX 76063
United States
Tel +1 469 712 7545
sjames@uniondesigncompany.com

Things To Make and Do
www.thingstomakeanddo.nl
Adelheidstraat 74
2595 EE The Hague
The Netherlands
Tel +31 070 73 70 554
info@thingstomakeanddo.nl

TOMOKUSA DESIGN
www.tomokusa.com
25-47, Hiejima-cho
Kadoma City, Osaka, 5710037
Japan
Tel +81 906 919 2710
info@tomokusa.com

Toyotsugu Itoh Design Office
www.facebook.com/toyotsuguoffice
402 Royal Villa Tsurumai
4-17-8 Tsurumai, Showa-ku
Nagoya,
Aichi Prefecture 466-0064
Japan
Tel +81 52 731 9747
toyo-ito@ya2.so-net.ne.jp

Traction Factory
www.tractionfactory.com
247 S. Water St.
Milwaukee, WI 53204
United States
Tel +1 414 944 0900
tf_awards@tractionfactory.com

Tsushima Design
www.tsushima-design.com
1-17-204, 1-17, Matsukawa-cho, Minami-ku
Hiroshima 7320826
Japan
Tel +81 08 2567 5586
info@tsushima-design.com

Underline Studio
www.underlinestudio.com
247 Wallace Ave., 2nd Floor
Toronto, ON M6H 1V5
Canada
Tel +1 416 341 0475
studiomanager@underlinestudio.com

University of Nebraska
www.unl.edu
1400 R. St.
Lincoln, NE 68588
United States
joshua.lowe@unl.edu

University of the Arts
www.uartsillustration.com
333 S. Broad St.
Philadelphia, PA 19107
United States
Tel +1 215 717 6241
fisheld@uarts.edu

Venti Caratteruzzi
www.venticaratteruzzi.com
Via Principe di Villafranca 83
Palermo, PA 90141
Italy
Tel +39 328 462 2494
carlo@venticaratteruzzi.com

VIEW - Visual Impact East West
www.visualimpacteastwest.com
Burbank, CA
United States
hello@visualimpacteastwest.com

WePlayDesign
www.weplaydesign.ch
Chemin de l'Ancienne-Pension 2
Grandvaux, Vaud 1091
Switzerland
Tel +41 79 474 65 38
hello@weplaydesign.ch

Wesam Mazhar Haddad
www.wesamhaddad.com
Fairfield, NJ 07004
United States
haddadwesam@hotmail.com

Whimsical Studio
www.thewhimsicalstudio.co
A/247 Moolthedu Manandhavady
Valery Post 670645
South Korea
Tel +91 95266 65443
info@thewhimsicalstudio.co

White & Case LLP
www.whitecase.com
1221 Ave. of the Americas
New York, NY 10020
United States
Tel +44 20 7532 2852
aureen.gaba@whitecase.com

Wieslaw Grzegorczyk
www.ur.edu.pl/en/home
Ulica Jagiellońska 32/6
Rzeszów 35-025
Poland
Tel +48 60 337 30 85
wieslaw@grzegorczyk.eu

Wong.Digital
www.wong.digital
440 N. Barranca Ave., Suite 2822
Covina, CA 91723
United States
Tel +1 415 309 0790
roger@wong.digital

253 WINNERS BY COUNTRY

Visit Graphis.com to view the work within each country, state, or province.

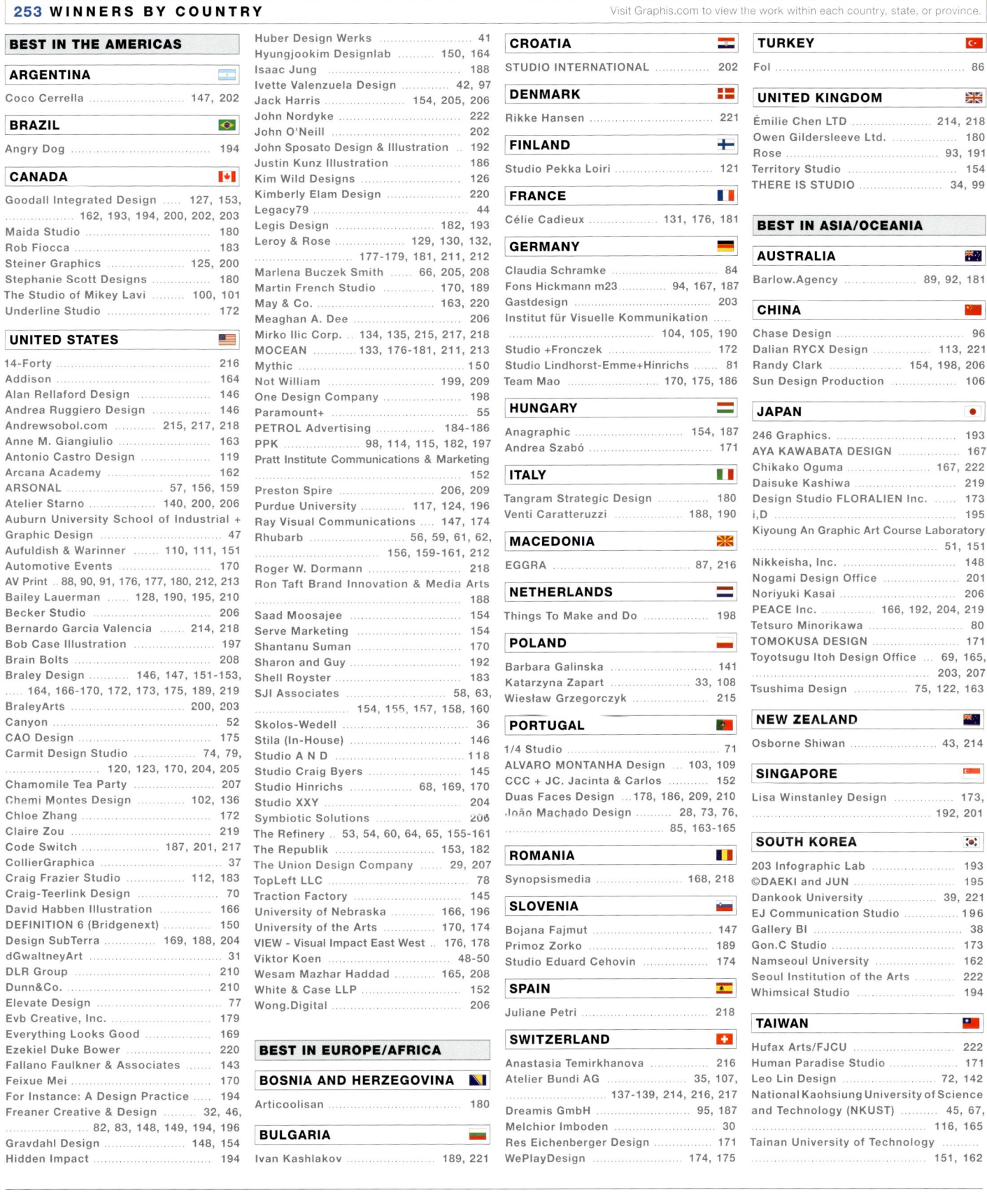

BEST IN THE AMERICAS

ARGENTINA
Coco Cerrella 147, 202

BRAZIL
Angry Dog 194

CANADA
Goodall Integrated Design 127, 153,
.... 162, 193, 194, 200, 202, 203
Maida Studio 180
Rob Fiocca 183
Steiner Graphics 125, 340
Stephanie Scott Designs 180
The Studio of Mikey Lavi 100, 101
Underline Studio 172

UNITED STATES
14-Forty 216
Addison 164
Alan Rellaford Design 146
Andrea Ruggiero Design 146
Andrewsobol.com 215, 217, 218
Anne M. Giangiulio 163
Antonio Castro Design 119
Arcana Academy 162
ARSONAL 57, 156, 159
Atelier Starno 140, 200, 206
Auburn University School of Industrial +
Graphic Design 47
Aufdlish & Warriner 110, 111, 151
Automotive Events 170
AV Print .. 88, 90, 91, 176, 177, 180, 212, 213
Bailey Lauerman 128, 190, 195, 210
Becker Studio 206
Bernardo Garcia Valencia 214, 218
Bob Case Illustration 197
Brain Bolts 208
Braley Design 146, 147, 151-153,
..... 164, 166-170, 172, 173, 175, 189, 219
BraleyArts 200, 203
Canyon 52
CAO Design 175
Carmit Design Studio 74, 79,
.... 120, 123, 170, 204, 205
Chamomile Tea Party 207
Chemi Montes Design 102, 136
Chloe Zhang 172
Claire Zou 219
Code Switch 187, 201, 217
CollierGraphica 37
Craig Frazier Studio 112, 183
Craig-Teerlink Design 70
David Habben Illustration 166
DEFINITION 6 (Bridgenext) 150
Design SubTerra 169, 188, 204
dGwaltneyArt 31
DLR Group 210
Dunn&Co. 210
Elevate Design 77
Evb Creative, Inc. 179
Everything Looks Good 169
Ezekiel Duke Bower 220
Fallano Faulkner & Associates 143
Feixue Mei 170
For Instance: A Design Practice 194
Freaner Creative & Design 32, 46,
.... 82, 83, 148, 149, 194, 196
Gravdahl Design 148, 154
Hidden Impact 194

Huber Design Werks 41
Hyungjookim Designlab 150, 164
Isaac Jung 188
Ivette Valenzuela Design 42, 97
Jack Harris 154, 205, 206
John Nordyke 222
John O'Neill 202
John Sposato Design & Illustration ... 192
Justin Kunz Illustration 186
Kim Wild Designs 126
Kimberly Elam Design 220
Legacy79 44
Legis Design 182, 193
Leroy & Rose 129, 130, 132,
.... 177-179, 181, 211, 212
Marlena Buczek Smith 184-186
Martin French Studio 170, 189
May & Co. 163, 220
Meaghan A. Dee 206
Mirko Ilic Corp. .. 134, 135, 215, 217, 218
MOCEAN 133, 176-181, 211, 213
Mythic 150
Not William 199, 209
One Design Company 198
Paramount+ 55
PETROL Advertising 184-186
PPK 98, 114, 115, 182, 197
Pratt Institute Communications & Marketing
.... 152
Preston Spire 206, 209
Purdue University 117, 124, 196
Ray Visual Communications 147, 174
Rhubarb 56, 59, 61, 62,
.... 156, 159-161, 212
Roger W. Dormann 218
Ron Taft Brand Innovation & Media Arts
.... 188
Saad Moosajee 154
Serve Marketing 154
Shantanu Suman 170
Sharon and Guy 192
Shell Royster 183
SJI Associates 58, 63,
.... 154, 155, 157, 158, 160
Skolos-Wedell 36
Stila (In-House) 146
Studio A N D 118
Studio Craig Byers 145
Studio Hinrichs 68, 169, 170
Studio XXY 204
Symbiotic Solutions 206
The Refinery .. 53, 54, 60, 64, 65, 155-161
The Republik 153, 182
The Union Design Company 29, 207
TopLeft LLC 78
Traction Factory 145
University of Nebraska 166, 196
University of the Arts 170, 174
VIEW - Visual Impact East West .. 176, 178
Viktor Koen 48-50
Wesam Mazhar Haddad 165, 208
White & Case LLP 152
Wong.Digital 206

BEST IN EUROPE/AFRICA

BOSNIA AND HERZEGOVINA
Articoolisan 180

BULGARIA
Ivan Kashlakov 189, 221

CROATIA
STUDIO INTERNATIONAL 202

DENMARK
Rikke Hansen 221

FINLAND
Studio Pekka Loiri 121

FRANCE
Célie Cadieux 131, 176, 181

GERMANY
Claudia Schramke 84
Fons Hickmann m23 .... 94, 167, 187
Gastdesign 203
Institut für Visuelle Kommunikation
.... 104, 105, 190
Studio +Fronczek 172
Studio Lindhorst-Emme+Hinrichs ... 81
Team Mao 170, 175, 186

HUNGARY
Anagraphic 154, 187
Andrea Szabó 171

ITALY
Tangram Strategic Design 180
Venti Caratteruzzi 188, 190

MACEDONIA
EGGRA 87, 216

NETHERLANDS
Things To Make and Do 198

POLAND
Barbara Galinska 141
Katarzyna Zapart 33, 108
Wiesław Grzegorczyk 215

PORTUGAL
1/4 Studio 71
ALVARO MONTANHA Design .. 103, 109
CCC + JC. Jacinta & Carlos 152
Duas Faces Design ... 178, 186, 209, 210
João Machado Design 28, 73, 76,
.... 85, 163-165

ROMANIA
Synopsismedia 168, 218

SLOVENIA
Bojana Fajmut 147
Primoz Zorko 189
Studio Eduard Cehovin 174

SPAIN
Juliane Petri 218

SWITZERLAND
Anastasia Temirkhanova 216
Atelier Bundi AG 35, 107,
.... 137-139, 214, 216, 217
Dreamis GmbH 95, 187
Melchior Imboden 30
Res Eichenberger Design 171
WePlayDesign 174, 175

TURKEY
Fol 86

UNITED KINGDOM
Émilie Chen LTD 214, 218
Owen Gildersleeve Ltd. 180
Rose 93, 191
Territory Studio 154
THERE IS STUDIO 34, 99

BEST IN ASIA/OCEANIA

AUSTRALIA
Barlow.Agency 89, 92, 181

CHINA
Chase Design 96
Dalian RYCX Design 113, 221
Randy Clark 154, 198, 206
Sun Design Production 106

JAPAN
246 Graphics. 193
AYA KAWABATA DESIGN 167
Chikako Oguma 167, 222
Daisuke Kashiwa 219
Design Studio FLORALIEN Inc. ... 173
i,D 195
Kiyoung An Graphic Art Course Laboratory
.... 51, 151
Nikkeisha, Inc. 148
Nogami Design Office 201
Noriyuki Kasai 206
PEACE Inc. 166, 192, 204, 219
Tetsuro Minorikawa 80
TOMOKUSA DESIGN 171
Toyotsugu Itoh Design Office ... 69, 165,
.... 203, 207
Tsushima Design 75, 122, 163

NEW ZEALAND
Osborne Shiwan 43, 214

SINGAPORE
Lisa Winstanley Design 173,
.... 192, 201

SOUTH KOREA
203 Infographic Lab 193
©DAEKI and JUN 195
Dankook University 39, 221
EJ Communication Studio 196
Gallery BI 38
Gon.C Studio 173
Namseoul University 162
Seoul Institution of the Arts 222
Whimsical Studio 194

TAIWAN
Hufax Arts/FJCU 222
Human Paradise Studio 171
Leo Lin Design 72, 142
National Kaohsiung University of Science
and Technology (NKUST) 45, 67,
.... 116, 165
Tainan University of Technology
.... 151, 162

I applaud all those who took such care, talent, and craftsmanship in their work; every one of you deserves the praise and acknowledgment contained within the pages of this annual. Bravo to you all.

Brad Hochberg, *Co-founder & Creative Director, The Refinery*

Graphis Titles

New Talent Annual 2024

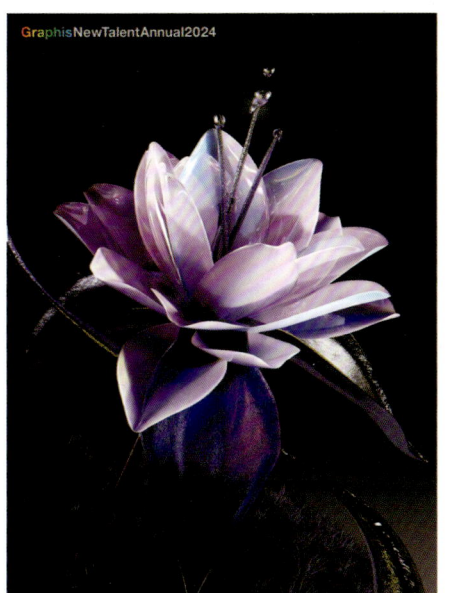

2024
Hardcover: 256 pages
200-plus color illustrations
Trim: 8.5 x 11.75"
ISBN: 978-1-954632-29-5
US $75

Awards: Graphis presents 13 Platinum, 132 Gold, 587 Silver, and 858 Honorable Mentions.
Platinum-winning Instructors: Rob Clayton, Simon Johnston, Stephen Serrato, Ming Tai, David Tillinghast, HyoJun Shim, Peter Bergman, Nathan Savage, Billy Magbua, Justin Colt, Natasha Jen, Richard Mehl, William Meek
Content: The New Talent 2024 Annual presents award-winning work submitted by teachers and students of prominent schools, who are dedicated to shaping the next generation of graphic designers. Platinum winners share their creative process, providing valuable insights and inspiration for aspiring creatives. A special section that revisits the Platinum-winning works from the past decade, offering a unique lens on the evolution of creative excellence.

Photography Annual 2024

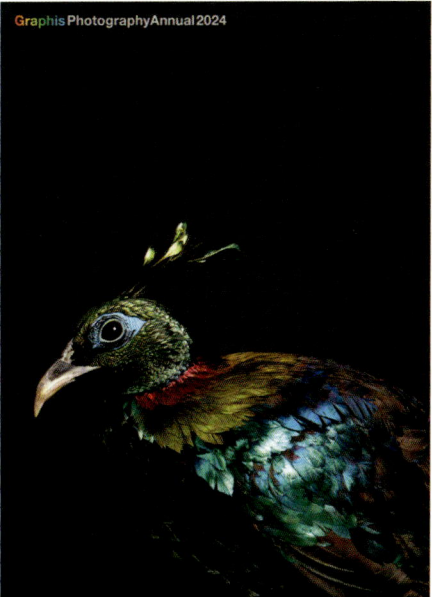

2024
Hardcover: 256 pages
200-plus color illustrations
Trim: 8.5 x 11.75"
ISBN: 978-1-954632-28-8
US $75

Awards: Graphis presents 12 Platinum, 102 Gold, and 216 Silver awards, along with 54 Honorable Mentions.
Platinum Winners: Craig Cutler, Lindsey Drennan, Jonathan Knowles, James Minchin, Artem Nazarov, Peter Samuels, Howard Schatz, John Surace, and Paco Macias Velasco.
Content: This book is full of exceptional work by our masterful judges, our Platinum, Gold, and Silver award winners, and our Honorable Mentions. It also includes a retrospective on our Platinum 2014 Photography winners, a list of international photography museums and galleries, and an In Memoriam list of photographers who have passed away this past year. The digital copy has an extra 52 pages of additional content for you to peruse.

Advertising Annual 2024

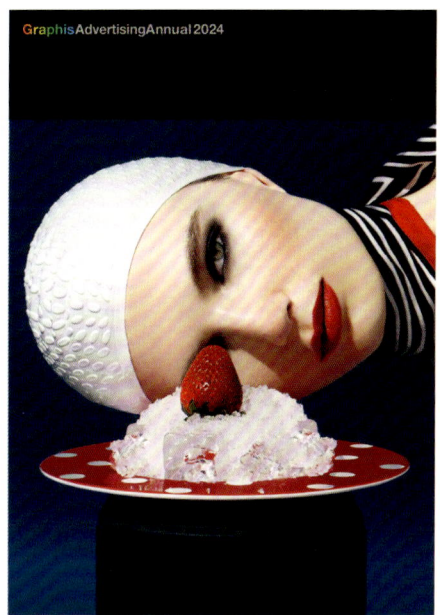

2024
Hardcover: 224 pages
200-plus color illustrations
Trim: 8.5 x 11.75"
ISBN: 978-1-954632-25-7
US $75

Awards: Graphis presents 15 Platinum, 61 Gold, and 99 Silver awards, along with 14 Honorable Mentions.
Platinum Winners: ARSONAL, Brunner, Célie Cadieux, Extra Credit Projects, Freaner Creative & Design, PangHao Art Studio, Partners + Napier, PETROL Advertising, ReThink, Rhubarb, SJI Associates, Sukle Advertising, and SUPERFY.
Content: This Annual includes amazing Platinum, Gold, and Silver Award-winning print and video advertisements from well-established firms and agencies. Honorable Mentions are also presented. Also featured in the annual is a selection of award-winning work from the competition judges and our yearly In Memoriam list of the advertising talent we've lost over the last year.

Design Annual 2024

2023
Hardcover: 272 pages
200-plus color illustrations
Trim: 8.5 x 11.75"
ISBN: 978-1-954632-22-4
US $75

Awards: Graphis presents 12 Platinum, 108 Gold, and 436 Silver awards, along with 182 Honorable Mentions.
Platinum Winners: Presenting AV Print, The Balbusso Twins, Carmit Design Studio, Journey Group, Michael Pantuso Design, Namseoul University, Omdesign, PepsiCo Design & Innovation, Studio Eduardo Aires, Sun Design Production, Underline Studio, and Wonderlust Industries, Inc.
Content: This book includes award-winning work from the judges, as well as Platinum, Gold, and Silver-winning work from internationally renowned designers and design firms. Honorable Mentions are presented, and a list of designers that we have lost this past year and a directory of design museums are also included.

Packaging 10

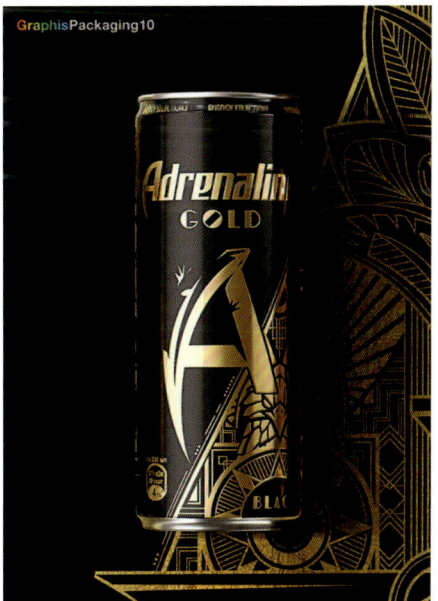

2022
Hardcover: 240 pages
200-plus color illustrations
Trim: 8.5 x 11.75"
ISBN: 978-1-954632-12-7
US $75

Awards: Graphis presents 12 Platinum, 100 Gold, 204 Silver, and 249 Honorable Mentions for innovative work in product packaging.
Platinum Winners: Michele Gomes Bush (Next), Chad Roberts (Chad Roberts Design Ltd.), XiongBo Deng (Shenzhen Lingyun Creative Packaging Design Co., Ltd.) and Lu Chen (Xiaomi), Vishal Vora (Sol Benito), Mattia Conconi (Gottschalk+Ash Int'l), and Frank Anselmo (New York Mets), Ivan Bell (Stranger & Stranger), Brian Steele (SLATE), and the team at PepsiCo Design & Innovation.
Content: This book contains award-winning packaging from the judges, as well as international Platinum, Gold, and Silver-winning packaging designs from designers and design firms from around the world. Honorable Mentions are presented, and a feature of award-winning work from our Packaging 9 Annual is also included.

Narrative Design: Kit Hinrichs

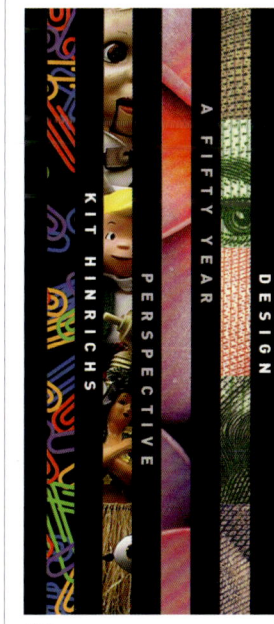

2023
Hardcover: 248 pages
200-plus color illustrations
Trim: 9 x 12"
ISBN: 978-1-954632-03-5
US $65

Narrative Design: A Fifty-Year Perspective is a collection of over 50 years of work from the obsessive graphic designer Kit Hinrichs. To the legendary AIGA medalist, author, teacher, and collector, design is the business of telling a story. It's not just about communicating a product or a corporate ethos—it's about contributing to the collective culture of storytelling. Presented in the book are not individual case studies but rather categories of work and graphic approaches to assignments that have wowed clients and dazzled viewers. The work is arranged to communicate Hinrichs' creative thinking, which always leads to a unique and effective solution to any design conundrum.

Books are available at graphis.com/publications

www.**Graphis**.com